Outcomes for Children and Youth with Emotional and Behavioral Disorders and Their Families

Outcomes for Children and Youth with Emotional and Behavioral Disorders and Their Families

Programs and Evaluation Best Practices

Edited by
Michael H. Epstein,
Krista Kutash,
and
Albert Duchnowski

pro·ed
An International Publisher

8700 Shoal Creek Boulevard
Austin, Texas 78757-6897

This book is designed in Italia and New Century Schoolbook.

Production Director: Alan Grimes
Production Coordinator: Karen Swain
Managing Editor: Chris Olson
Staff Copyeditor: Suzi Hunn
Art Director: Thomas Barkley
Designer: Lee Anne Landry
Reprints Buyer: Alicia Woods
Preproduction Coordinator: Chris Anne Worsham
Project Editor: Martin Hanft
Production Assistant: Dolly Fisk Jackson
Production Assistant: Claudette Landry

Printed in the United States of America

2   3   4   5   6   7   8   9   10   02 01 00 99

Contents

IV. Applied Research 483

V. Conclusion 657

Preface

In the field of children's mental health, *Unclaimed Children* (Knitzer, 1982) is often referenced as a seminal work that serves as a baseline from which progress in the field may be measured. When the report was published in 1982, children who had emotional and behavioral disorders were described as a critically underserved group. In addition, support for their families was virtually nonexistent. Focusing on the public sector, Knitzer identified gaps in all the major child-serving agencies, including education, mental health, child welfare, and juvenile justice. For example, only a fraction of the estimated number of children in need of special education programs were identified for placement by the school system. Those children who were identified and served by the mental health system typically were offered outpatient therapy, and, if symptoms progressed, residential treatment usually was the only alternative available. The child welfare system in most states required parents to give up custody of their children before mental health services would be supported by public funding. While a few promising, innovative, community-based programs were identified and described by Knitzer, lack of leadership and lack of collaboration at the federal, state, and local levels were identified as barriers to the widespread adoption of programs that might lead to systemic change and improved outcomes for children and families.

Since 1982, there has been an explosion of activity in the field of children's mental health in terms of increased advocacy, federal and private support, the generation of new information, and, more recently, an increase in research. At the federal level, several initiatives have been funded by a variety of agencies aimed at improving services for children and youth who have emotional and behavioral disorders and for their families. In 1984, the National Institute for Mental Health (NIMH) funded the Child and Adolescent Service System Program (CASSP), which has served as a catalyst and focal point for much of the development in the service system for children who have emotional and behavioral disorders and their families. That same year the NIMH cofunded, along with the National Institute for Disability and Rehabilitation Research, two Research and Training centers focused on these children and their families. The Office of Special Education Programs (OSEP) initiated a research program for Children and Youth Who Have Serious Emotional Disturbance, supporting the development of collaborative service-system models. Congress approved a funding level of $60 million for fiscal 1995 for the Comprehensive Children's Mental Health Services Program, through which the Center for

Mental Health Services (CMHS) is currently administering a services demonstration project in 22 sites across the country. In the private sector, the Robert Wood Johnson Foundation and the Annie E. Casey Foundation have funded children's initiatives totaling over $30 million.

Progress in the field, however, has not always been smooth, or guided by a comprehensive strategic plan. This is probably inevitable in a complex, multifaceted endeavor such as improving services for children with serious emotional or behavioral disorders. With the rapid increase in demonstration projects across the country, there is a concern about the lack of fully trained professionals who can effectively implement service models that are intensive but delivered in the community, that are respectful of families rather than critical of them, and that are congruent with the families' cultural backgrounds. University curricula need to incorporate training derived from promising models in the field for a new generation of professionals in the child-serving disciplines. Although many types of program models are being implemented in the field, the empirical support for these models is scarce but critical in this era of accountability. And perhaps the most significant challenge is developing research-and-evaluation strategies that are meaningful to the program staff and consumers, that provide information to the profession, and that are comprehensive in assessing both the implementation of the services and the outcomes of the services.

This book has been published to address these challenges and to contribute to the growing knowledge base in the field. Some of the current best practices in services for children and their families, as well as in the research and evaluation of these services, have been presented. We hope that these models will serve as a foundation for the establishment of standards of practice and standards of research and evaluation that ultimately improve outcomes for children and their families. For example, the field has reached a point where the demonstration of integrity in the implementation of intervention models is essential. The service interventions in this field are multifaceted and complex, especially those that use the wraparound approach. Practitioners and researchers need to develop quality control methods to ensure that the planned interventions are actually being implemented as they were intended. Otherwise, we will not be confident of the meaning of program outcomes and research results. In the chapters that follow, we have assembled a series of papers that cover several aspects of the services field, written by a group of authors who are representative of the multiple disciplines and roles that are moving the field forward. The author list includes researchers, practitioners, federal- and state-level policymakers, advocates, and family members. Some names will be recognized as those of pioneers in the field of children's mental health services, and all of the authors have become authorities in their topic area.

Part 1 of the text presents an authoritative perspective on systems-of-care programs and the characteristics of children and youth with serious emotional disorders and families who receive services. Part 2 provides comprehensive descriptions of several innovative programs for children and youth and their families and reports the outcomes of these programs. Part 3 presents detailed descriptions of methods and procedures used in researching and evaluating services and programs. Part 4 includes program descriptions and the outcomes of several experimental studies supported by the NIMH, OSEP, and the CMHS.

Our goal has been to make available a book that would be useful to the many audiences that are associated with this comprehensive field. The mix of program description and research is deliberate, because we feel that this newly developing field will progress most effectively if researchers, practitioners, families, and advocates work as partners in all aspects of its development. The work of this talented group of authors convinces us that this is the right approach. Finally, we hope that the book will be used by academicians who are responsible for training professionals in the various disciplines involving children and their families. There are some new approaches that are producing positive outcomes, and newly trained professionals need to gain the skills necessary to implement the most effective treatments available.

Michael H. Epstein
Krista Kutash
Albert Duchnowski

References

Knitzer, J. (1982). *Unclaimed children: The failure of public responsibility to children and adolescents in need of mental health services.* Washington, DC: Children's Defense Fund.

Contributors

Jeffrey A. Anderson, MA
University of South Florida
Florida Mental Health Institute
Child & Family Studies
13301 Bruce B. Downs Boulevard
Tampa, FL 33612-3899

Mary I. Armstrong, MSW, MBA
University of South Florida
Florida Mental Health Institute
Child & Family Studies
13301 Bruce B. Downs Boulevard
Tampa, FL 33612-3899

Charles M. Borduin, PhD
University of Missouri–Columbia
Department of Psychology
McAlester Hall
Columbia, MO 65211

L. Adlai Boyd, PhD
University of South Florida
Florida Mental Health Institute
Child & Family Studies
13301 Bruce B. Downs Boulevard
Tampa, FL 33612-3899

Ana Maria Brannan, PhD
Center for Mental Health Policy
Vanderbilt University
1207 18th Avenue South
Nashville, TN 37212

Eric C. Brown, MS
University of South Florida
Florida Mental Health Institute
Child & Family Studies
13301 Bruce B. Downs Boulevard
Tampa, FL 33612-3899

Eric J. Bruns, PhD
University of Vermont
Department of Psychology
John Dewey Hall
Burlington, VT 05405

John D. Burchard, PhD
University of Vermont
Department of Psychology
John Dewey Hall
Burlington, VT 05405

Barbara J. Burns, PhD
Duke University Medical Center
Department of Psychiatry
Box 3454
Durham, NC 27710

Michael O. Calloway, PhD
University of North Carolina
*   at Chapel Hill*
Cecil G. Steps Center for Health
*   Services Research*
725 Airport Road
Chapel Hill, NC 27599-7590

Mary Lynn Cantrell
Positive Education Program
3100 Euclid Avenue
Cleveland, OH 44115

Robert P. Cantrell
Positive Education Program
3100 Euclid Avenue
Cleveland, OH 44115

Thomas Catron, PhD
Vanderbilt University
Department of Psychiatry
1500 21st Avenue S, Suite 2200
Nashville, TN 37212

Ana Mari Cauce, PhD
University of Washington
Department of Psychology
Box 351525
Seattle, WA 98195

Hewitt B. "Rusty" Clark, PhD
University of South Florida
Florida Mental Health Institute
Child & Family Studies
13301 Bruce B. Downs Boulevard
Tampa, FL 33612-3899

Robert F. Dedrick, PhD
University of South Florida
Department of Measurement
  & Research
4202 East Fowler Avenue
Tampa, FL 33612

Albert J. Duchnowski, PhD
University of South Florida
Florida Mental Health Institute
Research & Training Center
13301 Bruce B. Downs Boulevard
Tampa, FL 33612-3899

Debra J. Elliott, PhD
Portland State University
Regional Research Institute
P.O. Box 751
Portland, OR 97207-0751

Lara Embry
University of Washington
Department of Psychology
Box 351525
Seattle, WA 98195

Michael H. Epstein, EdD
Northern Illinois University
Department of Educational Psychology
  Counseling & Special Education
Dekalb, IL 60115-2854

Mary E. Evans, PhD
University of South Florida
College of Nursing
12901 Bruce B. Downs Blvd.
Tampa, FL 33612

Randall Feltman, MSW
Chief Administrative Office
County of Ventura
800 South Victoria Avenue
Ventura, CA 93009

Robert M. Friedman, PhD
University of South Florida
Florida Health Institute
Child & Family Studies
13301 Bruce B. Downs Boulevard
Tampa, FL 33612-3899

Barbara J. Friesen, PhD
Portland State University
Regional Research Institute
Research and Training Center on Family
  Support and Children's Mental
  Health
P.O. Box 751
Portland, OR 97207-0751

Paul E. Greenbaum, PhD
University of South Florida
Florida Mental Health Institute
Child & Family Studies
13301 Bruce B. Downs Boulevard
Tampa, FL 33612-3899

Kimberly Swisher Hall, MA
University of South Florida
Florida Mental Health Institute
Child & Family Studies
13301 Bruce B. Downs Boulevard
Tampa, FL 33612-3899

Vicki S. Harris, PhD
Vanderbilt University
Vanderbilt Institute for Public Policy
  Studies
GPC Box 163
Nashville, TN 37203

Craig Anne Heflinger, PhD
Vanderbilt University
Center for Mental Health Policy
1207 18th Avenue South
Nashville, TN 37212

Jennifer Heger
Seattle Mental Health Institute
1600 East Olive
Seattle, WA 98122

Scott W. Henggeler, PhD
Medical University of South Carolina
Department of Psychiatry & Behavioral
  Sciences
171 Ashley Avenue–Annex III
Charleston, SC 29425-0742

Kimberly Hoagwood, PhD
National Institute of Mental Health
5600 Fishers Lane
Rockville, MD 20857

Steven Huz, MPA
New York State Office of Mental Health
Bureau of Children & Families
44 Holland Avenue
Albany, NY 12229

Craig K. Ichinose, PhD
Ventura County Public Social
  Services Agency
Evaluation and Research
505 Poli Street
Ventura, CA 93001-2632

Robert J. Illback
REACH of Louisville, Inc.
101 E. Kentucky Street
Louisville, KY 40203

Matthew C. Johnsen, PhD
Row Sciences Inc.
1700 Research Blvd.
Suite 400
Rockville, MD 20850-3142

Kelly J. Kelleher, MD, MPH
University of Pittsburgh
School of Medicine
Child Services Research
  & Development
3510 Fifth Avenue, Suite 1
Pittsburgh, PA 15213

Donald W. Kingdon, PhD
Ventura County Mental Health
Administration Building
300 North Hillmont Avenue
Ventura, CA 93003-1699

Paul E. Koren, PhD
Portland State University
Regional Research Institute
P.O. Box 751
Portland, OR 97207-0751

Nancy M. Koroloff, PhD
Portland State University
Regional Research Institute
P.O. Box 751
Portland, OR 97207-0751

Anne D. Kuppinger, MEd
New York State Office of Mental Health
Bureau of Children & Families
44 Holland Avenue
Albany, NY 12229

Krista Kutash, PhD
University of South Florida
Florida Mental Health Institute
Child & Family Studies
13301 Bruce B. Downs Boulevard
Tampa, FL 33612-3899

Sharon P. Lardieri
University of South Florida
Florida Mental Health Institute
Child & Family Studies
13301 Bruce B. Downs Boulevard
Tampa, FL 33612-3899

Barbara Lee, PhD
University of South Florida
Florida Mental Health Institute
Child & Family Studies
13301 Bruce B. Downs Boulevard
Tampa, FL 33612-3899

Yvette Lohr
Youth Care, Inc.
190 Queen Anne Avenue North
Suite 333
Seattle, WA 98109

Ira S. Lourie, MD
Human Services Collaborative
2262 Hall Place, NW
Suite 204
Washington, DC 20007

Linda T. Maultsby, BS
Duke University Medical Center
Department of Psychiatry
Box 3454
Durham, NC 27710

Beth Barrett McDonald, MA
University of South Florida
Florida Mental Health Institute
Child & Family Studies
13301 Bruce B. Downs Boulevard
Tampa, FL 33612-3899

Thomas L. McNulty, PhD
University of Georgia
Department of Sociology
Athens, GA 30602

Charles J. Morgan
Youth Care, Inc.
190 Queen Anne Avenue North
Suite 333
Seattle, WA 98109

Joseph P. Morrissey, PhD
University of North Carolina at
  Chapel Hill
Cecil G. Steps Center for Health Services
  Research
725 Airport Road
Chapel Hill, NC 27599-7590

C. Michael Nelson, EdD
University of Kentucky
Department of Special Education
229 Taylor Education Building
Lexington, KY 40601

Denine A. Northrup
Vanderbilt University
Center for Mental Health Policy
1207 18th Avenue South
Nashville, TN 37212

Matthew Paradise
University of Washington
Department of Psychology
Box 351525
Seattle, WA 98195

Mark E. Prange, PhD
University of South Florida
Florida Mental Health Institute
Child & Family Studies
13301 Bruce B. Downs Boulevard
Tampa, FL 33612-3899

Amy M. Pugh, MS
University of South Florida
Florida Mental Health Institute
Child & Family Studies
13301 Bruce B. Downs Boulevard
Tampa, FL 33612-3899

Kevin P. Quinn, EdD
State University of New York—Albany
ED 230
Albany, NY 12222

Vestena Robbins Rivera, MA
University of South Florida
Florida Mental Health Institute
Child & Family Studies
13301 Bruce B. Downs Boulevard
Tampa, FL 33612-3899

Abram Rosenblatt, PhD
University of California, San Francisco
Department of Psychiatry
44 Montgomery Street
Suite 1450
San Francisco, CA 94104

Daniel Sanders, PhD
REACH of Louisville, Inc.
101 E. Kentucky St.
Louisville, KY 40203

Suzanne Santarcangelo, PhD
Vermont Consultation Network
P.O. Box 112
Waterbury, VT 05767

Sonja K. Schoenwald, PhD
Medical University of South Carolina
Department of Psychiatry & Behavioral
   Sciences
171 Ashley Avenue–Annex III
Charleston, SC 29425-0742

Sarah Hudson Scholle,PhD
University of Pittsburgh Medical Center
3501 Forbes Avenue, Suite 718
Pittsburgh, PA 15213

Nirbhay N. Singh, PhD
Virginia Commonwealth University
Department of Psychiatry
Medical College of Virginia
P.O. Box 980489
Richmond, VA 23298

Douglas A. Smith
Positive Education Program
3100 Euclid Avenue
Cleveland, OH 44115

Susan E. Sonnichsen, MS
Vanderbilt University
Center for Mental Health Policy
1207 18th Avenue South
Nashville, TN 37212

Beverly Stephens, BA
Portland State University
Regional Research Institute
Research and Training Center on Family
   Support and Children's Mental
   Health
P.O. Box 751
Portland, OR 97207-0751

Elizabeth Steinhardt Stewart, MA
University of South Florida
Florida Mental Health Institute
Child & Family Studies
13301 Bruce B. Downs Boulevard
Tampa, FL 33612-3899

Beth A. Stroul, MEd
Management & Training Innovations
6725 Curran Street
McLean, VA 22101

James Theofelis
Youth Care, Inc.
190 Queen Anne Avenue North
Suite 333
Seattle, WA 98109

Victoria Wagner
100 W. Harrison, Suite 100
South Tower
Seattle, WA 98119

Bahr Weiss
Vanderbilt University
Department of Psychology & Human
    Development
GPC Box 512
Nashville, TN 37203

Nancy Wolff, PhD
Rutgers University
Institute for Health, Health Care,
    & Aging Research
30 College Avenue
P.O. Box 5070
New Brunswick, NJ 08903-5070

James T. Yoe, PhD
Maine Department of Mental Health
40 State House Station
Augusta, ME 04330

Introduction

Community-Based Systems of Care: From Advocacy to Outcomes

1

Ira S. Lourie, Beth A. Stroul,
and Robert M. Friedman

The emergence of the concepts and philosophy of a system of care for children and adolescents with serious emotional disturbance has been an evolutionary process. The roots of this philosophy can be traced to the report of the Joint Commission on the Mental Health of Children (1969), commissioned by Congress in 1965. The Joint Commission found that many children and adolescents with serious emotional disturbance were not receiving needed services or were served inappropriately in excessively restrictive settings. The Joint Commission called for a nationwide system of child advocacy aimed at meeting the full range of needs of those children. A major contribution of the Joint Commission was its observation that many children have multiple needs and require services provided under the aegis of a number of major public agencies, such as those providing services in mental health, child welfare, juvenile justice, or special education. Although entering one of these systems allowed for the provision of some specific services, it often made it difficult to obtain necessary services from the other agencies. Services were delivered in a fragmented and often contradictory manner; there was little or no coordination among the various child-serving agencies and no systematic approach to the planning and implementation of services.

The findings of the Joint Commission were confirmed by numerous subsequent studies, task forces, commissions, and reports, such as the President's Commission on Mental Health (1978) and the report of the U.S. Congress Office of Technology Assessment (1986). A study published by the Children's Defense Fund, entitled *Unclaimed Children* (Knitzer, 1982), documented that of the 3 million children with serious emotional disturbance in this country, two thirds were not receiving the services they needed and many more were receiving inappropriate care. These children were characterized as "unclaimed," essentially abandoned by the agencies responsible for helping them. All of these reports concurred that coordinated systems of care providing a range of services are required in order to serve these youngsters and their families effectively, and they called for concerted action to develop systems of care nationwide.

In 1982, Knitzer referred to the federal role in children's mental health as the "unfulfilled promise," saying that federal leadership in the area was largely missing. The few federal programs that were undertaken were either poorly funded or short-lived. As a result of a great deal of advocacy from a coalition of individuals and groups, Congress appropriated funds for a federal initiative in the area of child mental health, and in 1984 the National Institute of Mental Health (NIMH) launched the Child and Adolescent Service System Program (CASSP). The target population for this initiative was defined as children and adolescents with severe emotional disturbance and their families, and the goal was to assist states and communities to develop systems of care for this group. With the assistance of federal grants, states were asked to create an interagency process that would: (a) ensure multiagency planning and system development for the care of children and adolescents with severe emotional disturbance, (b) increase the ability of mental health agencies to be equal partners in this process, (c) include families in the system development, and (d) ensure that the special needs of cultural and ethnic minorities were addressed. Before its 10th anniversary, CASSP had already involved all 50 states and a number of territories and had stimulated a great deal of progress toward improved service systems for children and adolescents with serious emotional disturbance and their families (Davis, Yelton, Katz-Leavy, & Lourie, 1995).

One of the activities of CASSP was to articulate and further define the system-of-care concept. A project was initiated to clarify what the system should encompass, how it might be organized, what components should compose such a system, and what principles should guide service delivery. The effort resulted in the publication of a monograph entitled *A System of Care for Children and Adolescents with Severe Emotional Disturbances* (Stroul & Friedman, 1986). This document, which was revised and updated in 1994, has set the tone and philosophy for understanding the needs of this population and has created the conceptual framework for planning and developing the service system required to meet these needs. This concept and philosophy have remained the basis for many of the children's-system reform efforts over the last decade.

CASSP is currently under the auspices of the Center for Mental Health Services (CMHS) of the Substance Abuse and Mental Health Services Administration (SAMHSA), U.S. Department of Health and Human Services. CASSP has been renamed the Planning and Systems Development Program and is one of a number of activities of the Child, Adolescent, and Family Branch of the

CMHS. In addition to providing funds to states, the branch has funded local service demonstrations, research demonstrations, and family organizations. A significant addition to federal children's mental health activities is the CMHS Child, Adolescent, and Family Mental Health Services Program. Established in 1992, this program provides grants to states and communities to develop a broad array of community-based services. This program has grown rapidly; by fiscal year 1996 the appropriation had neared $70 million, and 22 sites across the nation were receiving funds with which to build their systems of care. These sites are furthering the evolutionary development and refinement of the system-of-care concept and philosophy by implementing their systems of care using a variety of organizational and service-delivery approaches.

In addition to these grant programs, a variety of technical assistance activities are supported by the Child, Adolescent, and Family Branch, including the funding of the National Technical Assistance Center for Children's Mental Health at Georgetown University, the Research and Training Center for Children's Mental Health at the University of South Florida, the Research and Training Center on Family Support and Children's Mental Health at Portland State University, and the National Resource Network for Child and Family Mental Health Services at the Washington Business Group on Health. These centers have conducted a wide range of research, evaluation, and technical assistance activities that have further elucidated the system-of-care concept and its implementation.

The evolution of the system-of-care concept also has been furthered by a number of demonstrations. One of the first examples of a comprehensive community-based system of care was developed in Ventura County, California. This system development initiative was funded by the California legislature as a demonstration, and it is now being replicated in other areas in California (Hernandez & Goldman, 1996; Stroul, Lourie, Goldman, & Katz-Leavy, 1992).

While many communities were struggling to find the resources with which to build systems of care, in 1988 the Robert Wood Johnson Foundation launched a $20 million initiative that has provided such funds to eight communities. These communities demonstrated promising new ways of organizing and financing service systems (Cole, 1996; Cole & Poe, 1993). Another demonstration, at Fort Bragg in North Carolina, was funded by the Civilian Health and Medical Program of the Uniformed Services (CHAMPUS). Fort Bragg built a rich array of services, and it can teach a great deal about how to organize and operate a system of care (Pires, 1997). The Annie E. Casey Foundation also launched an initiative to develop systems of care. This initiative has focused on urban neighborhoods, with the goal of bringing together all agencies and resources needed to improve outcomes for disadvantaged children (King & Meyers, 1996). All of these demonstrations, as well as many noteworthy state and local initiatives, have used the system-of-care concept and philosophy to guide their system development efforts.

The System-of-Care Philosophy

A system of care has been defined as "a comprehensive spectrum of mental health and other necessary services which are organized into a coordinated network to meet the multiple and changing needs of children and adolescents with severe emotional disturbances and their families" (Stroul & Friedman, 1986, p. iv). One of the most basic features of the system-of-care concept is that it does not represent a prescribed structure for assembling a network of services and agencies. Rather, it represents a philosophy about the way in which services should be delivered to children and their families. Within this philosophical framework, all community systems should be based on a set of basic values and operational principles, regardless of variations in specific services or organizational configurations. The unifying nature of this philosophy has brought diverse states and communities together in a national effort to change the way in which children and their families are served. These values and principles can be and have been used to define and guide service systems for many populations of children and adolescents who are at risk and their families.

The national effort to define the system of care sought input and consultation from policymakers, parents, administrators, researchers, advocates, and other stakeholders. A consensus emerged as to the values and principles that should be included in the system-of-care philosophy. Through this process, three core values and a set of 10 principles were developed to provide a philosophical framework for the system-of-care model (see Figure 1.1). (For a complete discussion of these core values and principles, see Stroul & Friedman, 1996.) The system-of-care framework was conceptualized with the child and family at the focus of service delivery (i.e., child centered and family focused), and with needed services surrounding them. This is graphically represented in Figure 1.2; the services that may be included in the array surrounding the child and family are displayed in Figure 1.3.

Principles for the Development
of Local Systems of Care

It is important to understand that conceptualizing a system of care represents only a preliminary step in the service system improvement process. Development of a system-of-care model is a planning task that must be followed by implementation activities.

In the decade since the original elucidation of the principles of the system of care, there have been numerous attempts at creating such local systems in communities across the country. The shift from a traditional service-delivery process to a true system of care was found to be a difficult transition. Lourie (1994) studied this process and discovered that local system development

Core Values

1. The system of care should be child-centered and family focused, with the needs of the child and family dictating the types and mix of services provided.

2. The system of care should be community based, with the locus of services as well as management and decision making responsibility resting at the community level.

3. The system of care should be culturally competent, with agencies, programs, and services that are responsive to the cultural, racial, and ethnic differences of the populations they serve.

Guiding Principles

1. Children with emotional disturbances should have access to a comprehensive array of services that address the child's physical, emotional, social, and educational needs.

2. Children with emotional disturbances should receive individualized services in accordance with the unique needs and potentials of each child and guided by an individualized service plan.

3. Children with emotional disturbances should receive services within the least restrictive, most normative environment that is clinically appropriate.

4. The families and surrogate families of children with emotional disturbances should be full participants in all aspects of the planning and delivery of services.

5. Children with emotional disturbances should receive services that are integrated, with linkages between child-serving agencies and programs and mechanisms for planning, developing, and coordinating services.

6. Children with emotional disturbances should be provided with case management or similar mechanisms to ensure that multiple services are delivered in a coordinated and therapeutic manner and that they can move through the system of services in accordance with their changing needs.

7. Early identification and intervention for children with emotional disturbances should be promoted by the system of care in order to enhance the likelihood of positive outcomes.

(continues)

Figure 1.1. Core values and principles for the system of care. From *A System of Care for Children and Adolescents With Severe Emotional Disturbances* (p. xxiv), by B. Stroul and R. M. Friedman, 1986 (Rev. ed.), Washington, DC: Georgetown University Child Development Center, National Technical Assistance Center for Children's Mental Health. Copyright 1986 by B. Stroul and R. M. Friedman. Reprinted by permission.

> 8. Children with emotional disturbances should be ensured smooth transitions to the adult service system as they reach maturity.
>
> 9. The rights of children with emotional disturbances should be protected, and effective advocacy efforts for children and youth with emotional disturbances should be promoted.
>
> 10. Children with emotional disturbances should receive services without regard to race, religion, national origin, sex, physical disability, or other characteristics, and services should be sensitive and responsive to cultural differences and special needs.

Figure 1.1. Continued.

requires that a number of core elements be present if it is to move ahead. Eleven such elements were identified (see Figure 1.4). Four of these are considered critical, and are discussed below.

Shared Vision and the Development of a Core Group

Successful local systems of care typically have a core group of individuals who share a vision of the problems in the current system, the need for change, the desired outcomes, and the strategies that should be used to effect change. This group consists of individuals who are committed to making the system work better and are positioned so that they can have an impact on the development of local services. What they have in common is a vision of an "ideal" system of care for troubled children and a growing frustration with the barriers that exist to building such a system. The energy for local system change and service integration emanates from this group as the members come to a consensus on the goals necessary to build a new, integrated system of care. System change is a difficult process, but a strong core group with a shared vision can overcome the inertia of traditional systems.

Leadership

The second core element is leadership, which can take hold of the local vision and maneuver it into the formation of a system change movement. This leadership may come from one individual or from several individuals in the core group. The role of leadership is to act as a catalyst and to help the core group develop strategies with which to implement the vision. Thus, leadership may facilitate, explicate, and motivate the initiative. While leadership alone will not drive system change, its role in every case is undeniable. Without this essential element,

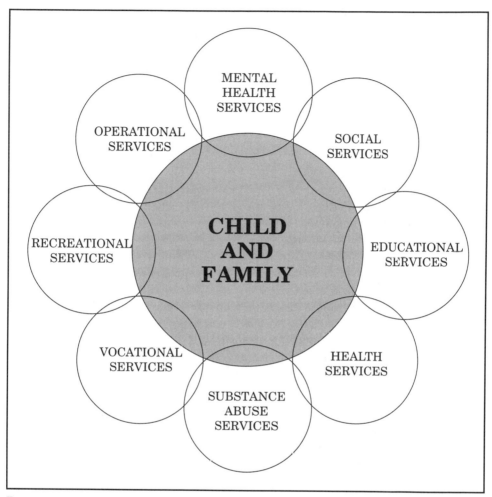

Figure 1.2. The system-of-care framework. From *A System of Care for Children and Adolescents With Severe Emotional Disturbances* (p. xxvi), by B. Stroul and R. M. Friedman, 1986 (Rev. ed.), Washington, DC: Georgetown University Child Development Center, National Technical Assistance Center for Children's Mental Health. Copyright 1986 by B. Stroul and R. M. Friedman. Reprinted by permission.

a core group will become frustrated and wither as it struggles with problems, unable to envision or implement solutions.

Trigger Mechanism and Incremental Opportunism

Most system change efforts are triggered by some event that the leaders use to move the system-building agenda forward. Stockdill (1991) discussed the

I. Mental Health Services	V. Substance Abuse Services
Nonresidential Services:	*Nonresidential Services:*
Prevention	Prevention
Early Identification & Intervention	Early Intervention
Assessment	Assessment
Outpatient Treatment	Outpatient Services
Home-Based Services	Day Treatment
Day Treatment	Ambulatory Detoxification
Emergency Services	Relapse Prevention
Residential Services:	*Residential Services:*
Therapeutic Foster Care	Residential Detoxification
Therapeutic Group Care	Community Residential
Therapeutic Camp Services	Treatment & Recovery
Independent Living Services	Services
Residential Treatment Services	Inpatient Hospitalization
Crisis Residential Services	
Inpatient Hospitalization	VI. Vocational Services
	Career Education
II. Social Services	Vocational Assessment
Protective Services	Job Survival Skills Training
Financial Assistance	Vocational Skills Training
Home Aid Services	Work Experiences
Respite Care	Job Finding, Placement,
Shelter Services	& Retention Services
Foster Care	Supported Employment
Adoption	VII. Recreational Services
III. Educational Services	Relationships with Significant
Assessment & Planning	Others
Resource Rooms	After-School Programs
Self-Contained Special Education	Summer Camps
Special Schools	Special Recreational Projects
Home-Bound Instruction	VIII. Operational Services
Residential Schools	Case Management
Alternative Programs	Juvenile Justice Services
IV. Health Services	Family Support & Self-Help
Health Education & Prevention	Groups
Screening & Assessment	Advocacy
Primary Care	Transportation
Acute Care	Legal Services
Long-Term Care	Volunteer Programs

Figure 1.3. Components of the system of care. From *A System of Care for Children and Adolescents With Severe Emotional Disturbances* (p. xxix), by B. Stroul and R. M. Friedman, 1986 (Rev. ed.), Washington, DC: Georgetown University Child Development Center, National Technical Assistance Center for Children's Mental Health. Copyright 1986 by B. Stroul and R. M. Friedman. Reprinted by permission.

- Shared Vision and the Development of a Core Group

- Leadership

- Use of a Trigger Mechanism and Incremental Opportunism

- State–Local Synergy

- Governance Growing Out of the Shared Vision and Supportive Leadership

- Needs-Based Assessment and Individualized Care Planning Approaches

- Minimizing Categorical Population Definitions

- Blurring of Professional and Agency Boundaries

- "Giving Away" (Sharing Resources and Power)

- Restructure of Finance and Creative Financing

- Time for Development

Figure 1.4. Core elements for the development of systems of care.

concept of "incremental opportunism," in which change agents use some event to leverage small advances toward system change. Examples of such events include programmatic changes, lawsuits, legislation, bureaucratic change, advocacy, and research findings. Trigger mechanisms become available to communities incrementally, and a series of such triggers can work together in an additive way. Most communities that have achieved success in system development have used more than one trigger in creating their systems.

State–Local Synergy

Local system development and system integration can develop only to a limited degree without state support or backing. Conversely, state system change cannot progress unless community change follows. However, recent local and state system-building processes have not always been in concert with each other, perhaps because the need for and the realities of system change are different at each level. State and local political and service-delivery issues are very different, and any system change effort must satisfy both government levels—a difficult task. Regardless of state and local differences, there must be congruence between the two levels on the directions in which the system needs to be changed.

Research and Evaluation on Systems of Care

There has been a great deal of attention spent on evaluating the success of the system-of-care concept. The first attempts to do so under CASSP were unidimensional, simply measuring whether state governments had done what they had set out to do. The focus was on broad goals, such as whether a state now had a child mental health unit, a full-time child mental health staff, or a discrete budget. In addition, the development of interagency planning processes aimed at the population of children and adolescents with severe emotional disturbance and their families was a major evaluation interest, as was the degree to which family involvement and cultural competence had improved. As the system-of-care concept matured over time, so did the attempts to evaluate and research the processes and outcomes of system-of-care efforts. Just as systems of care proved difficult to implement at both state and local levels, so evaluations of those systems of care proved equally difficult to conceptualize and implement. Several major issues that have emerged concerning the evaluation of systems of care are discussed below.

Before the process of researching and evaluating systems of care can be fully understood, it is important to recognize that the system-of-care approach does not represent a discrete program. Rather, the values and principles represent a framework within which services should be delivered to children and adolescents with serious emotional disturbance and their families. How this framework is applied, as a particular constellation and organization of services, varies from community to community. Similarly, the experience of each child within a system of care, even in the same community, is highly variable, depending on the child's strengths, needs, clinical status, level of functioning, and family situation. Thus, the "system-of-care approach" is not a unitary, neatly defined clinical intervention that simply can be measured to assess its efficacy.

It is noteworthy that Stroul and Friedman (1986) afforded research an important role in the development of their model of a comprehensive array of services organized into a system of care. This model was designed "to be a guide, based on the best available empirical data and clinical experience to date. It is offered as a starting point . . . as a baseline from which change can be made as additional research, experience, and innovation dictate" (p. 26). During the past 10 years, there has been a significant increase in activity across the country to improve services for children with severe emotional disturbance and their families. This movement has been supported by a coalition of policymakers, family members, practitioners, researchers, and other advocates. There is a developing research base in this field that is transforming knowledge into action by systematically describing the children and families and the services they receive, testing a complex array of factors influencing services for children and their families, and ultimately prescribing, within the context of a system, specific services that are effective under certain conditions for specific children and their families.

The initial research results from the first demonstrations, begun in the 1980s, serve as a foundation for this growing knowledge base. Some of these findings have been presented in special issues of the *Journal of Emotional and Behavioral Disorders* (Kutash, Duchnowski, & Sondheimer, 1994) and the *Journal of Child and Family Studies* (Clark & Clarke, 1996), as well as in a monograph by Stroul (1993). In addition, Rosenblatt (this volume) reviews the outcome results of 20 community-based system-of-care studies. While the results of these studies are only initial attempts to understand the system of care, they do suggest that the system of care can work to improve the outcomes for children and families.

What are the implications of this growing empirical foundation for future research and evaluation efforts? Researchers and evaluators attempting to investigate the system of care need to recognize the following: (a) the existence of multiple levels of outcome, (b) the need to define the intervention and assess the fidelity of the intervention, (c) the developmental nature of systems of care, (d) the existence of multiple perspectives, and (e) the need for both quantitative and qualitative approaches to research and evaluation. Each of these is discussed briefly.

Focusing on Multiple Outcome Levels

It is important to recognize that there are multiple domains under which to measure outcomes for systems of care that are designed to serve children with serious emotional disturbance and their parents. One recent model presents five outcome domains: symptoms, overall functioning, consumer perspectives, environmental contexts, and systems (Hoagwood, Jensen, Petti, & Burns, 1996). Other models, such as the evaluation of the CMIIS Child, Adolescent, and Family Mental Health Services Program, emphasize the system infrastructure, service delivery, and child and family outcome domains (Macro International, 1996).

All of these domains are important. However, what is most important, both from a system development and a system evaluation perspective, is to be clear about what the system improvement goals are and which domains should be the focus of measurement. A priority goal in one system, for example, may be to improve system-level outcomes (such as the number of children in out-of-home placements), while a priority goal in another system may be to reduce symptoms or improve the overall level of functioning of the children who are served. Clearly, these different goals would dictate different levels of focus for outcome measurement.

Specifying the priority goals for systems of care is essential because the interventions that are designed and implemented would presumably differ, depending on the goal. If the goal is to reduce out-of-home placements, there are clearly a number of organizational, policy, and fiscal interventions that can be used. These can include the development of new gatekeeping procedures before residential placements are approved, a change in fiscal incentives, or a new policy supporting in-home services. Such interventions, especially if targeted for the appropriate population, may very well be successful in achieving the desired systemic outcome of reducing the use of out-of-home care. In and of themselves, however, they may not be sufficient to achieve other goals, such as symptom reduction or improved functioning for the children who are served.

The manner in which the overall intervention is thought to be related to particular outcomes for a particular population is considered a "theory of change." The theory of change related to the system-of-care concept emphasizes system-level interventions (e.g., the development of interagency collaborations), program-level interventions (e.g., the development of new services), and a third level, at which the child and family interact with the service providers. The system-of-care model recognizes that, to produce positive changes at the level of child and family interacting with the providers, it is essential to modify actual treatment and intervention practices. As already indicated, the system-of-care model provides general guidance about changes in the interactions between program and child-and-family levels by promoting the application of interventions that are, for example, individualized, family-focused, culturally competent, and strength-based. However, these general principles remain to be translated into a theory of change at the level of practice. There have been several attempts to articulate such a theory of change at the practice level within a system-of-care framework (see Friedman, in press); these efforts are in their early stages.

An important point is that research and evaluation on systems of care for children with serious emotional disturbance and their families must begin with a clear statement of priority goals and a theory of change that links particular interventions with desired outcomes. If the priority goals are focused only at the system level, the interventions and measurement should focus only on the system level. However, if the priority goals are improvements at the level of the child and family, then the theory must be clear about the changes that need to be made at the practice level in order to achieve the desired outcomes.

It is also essential that the theory of change indicate the types of outcomes that particular interventions are intended to effect. It has been pointed out that one of the main challenges in the children's mental health field is describing the theorized linkages between system-level interventions and child-level outcomes, and finding ways to test the accuracy of these theorized linkages (Friedman, in press; Morrissey, Johnsen, & Calloway, 1995). What is the theory of change, for example, that links the introduction of flexible funding within a system of care or an interagency gatekeeping mechanism to changes at the child and family level? This is not to suggest that systemic level changes are worthwhile only if they lead to changes at the child and family level. Such changes are clearly worthwhile if they lead to priority goals that a community has identified, such as reductions in certain types of placements or cost savings, provided that they do not lead to worse child and family outcomes. From planning, research, and evaluation perspectives, however, it is important to be clear about the level at which goals, interventions, and, ultimately, measurement are focused.

Defining and Assessing the Intervention

Once a theory of change is articulated that offers interventions to produce the desired outcomes in the designated population, the next challenge that researchers and evaluators have is to determine if the intervention has been appropriately implemented. Such a determination can be made only if the intervention is operationally defined and described in adequate detail. It is not possible, for example, to determine if interventions are well coordinated, culturally competent, or family-focused unless an adequate description is provided of the practices that constitute adequate coordination, cultural competence, and family focus.

Once interventions are adequately described, regardless of the level or levels of focus, the next task is to assess the adequacy of implementation of the interventions (often called assessing the "fidelity" of the intervention). It may be, for example, that a planned intervention was not carried out because of a shortage of adequately trained staff or insufficient funding. There is much concern, in fact, in the children's mental health care field, not only with the need to have clearer theories of change and descriptions of intervention, but also with the difficulty in changing practice at the level of the child and family interacting with the system so that the intervention is applied as it has been proposed (McGrew, Bond, Dietzen, & Salyers, 1994).

It should be noted that the task of assessing the fidelity of implementation of the intervention becomes increasingly more difficult as the interventions become more complex. It is easier, for example, to assess if a manual for parent training is being followed by a practitioner than it is to assess if a comprehensive and individualized treatment plan is being developed and implemented by a family planning team. Despite the difficulty of assessing the fidelity of interventions, the task is essential and must be done in order to ensure that evaluation results are not the result of inadequate implementation.

In addition, it is essential that the theory be clear about the population to be served. This enables researchers to determine if the intended population, for whom the intervention was developed, is the population that actually has been served. Only if the intervention is affecting the intended population can the appropriateness of the theory of change and intervention be assessed for that particular population.

Considering the Developmental Nature of Systems of Care

It also should be recognized that the implementation of systems of care is inevitably a developmental process. Complex interventions are rarely static, and it therefore cannot be assumed that the system of care that is in place at point one will be the same 1 or 2 years later. Nor can it be assumed that, at a particular point in time, a system of care will have "matured" and, therefore, be ready for a rigorous outcome-based summative evaluation. If the outcomes of a system of care are evaluated prior to the adequate implementation of the intervention, the conclusions clearly cannot be interpreted as constituting a test of the theory of change. Rather, the results are a reflection of the level of implementation at a particular point in time.

Ideally, the evaluation of systems of care should be an ongoing process that describes the changes in implementation as they take place, provides useful progress data that are helpful in the identification and remediation of problems as they occur, and avoids reaching general conclusions about system effectiveness until implementation has advanced to an acceptable level. Unfortunately, however, funding policies often call for conclusions to be drawn relatively early in the process of system development, thereby running the risk of producing ambiguous, if not misleading, findings.

Incorporating Multiple Perspectives

In addition, any general conclusions that are reached by researchers should recognize the existence of multiple perspectives as well as multiple outcome domains. The system-of-care model, as presented here, emphasizes the importance of collaboration between parents and professionals, and between representatives of different agencies and systems. Given this emphasis, the conclusions of an evaluation should honor the importance of multiple perspectives. It may be, for example, that parents are more concerned about improvements in overall functioning than they are about symptom reduction, while clinicians are more concerned about reductions in symptoms. Results from an evaluation might presumably show that parents are more pleased than clinicians, or that improvements are greater in overall functioning than in symptom reduction. To average or aggregate results from different perspectives is to lose important information in an effort to reach a single conclusion. In emphasizing this point, Brown (1995) has called for "placing less emphasis on discovering the one, objective truth about a program's worth and [giving] more attention to the multiple perspectives that diverse interests bring to judgment and understanding" (p. 204). Such an approach is clearly consistent with a system-of-care model. Seeking out multiple perspectives, particularly in ways that are responsive to the cultural background of the participants, and giving voice to them in the findings, is an approach that provides for more culturally competent evaluations than approaches that either rely on only one or two perspectives or aggregate results to reach general conclusions.

Using Quantitative and Qualitative Approaches

Another issue in research and evaluation is the manner in which quantitative and qualitative approaches can complement each other in providing a more comprehensive analysis of a system of care than either approach can provide alone. Knapp (1995), in talking about the evaluation of comprehensive, collaborative services for children and families, emphasized the importance of both quantitative and qualitative data, particularly research and evaluation that "trace backward from the experiences, behavior, perceptions, and status of service recipients" (p. 12) as a means of determining how or if system-level changes impact at the level of the child and family. Friedman (in press) also discusses methods (e.g., in-depth case studies) of understanding the extent to which system-of-care principles are being implemented at the child and family level. The integration of qualitative and quantitative methodologies, and the use of approaches to study interventions in an in-depth manner, represent another one of the challenges for research and evaluation in systems of care.

Conclusion

The system-of-care model has already had a major impact on the children's mental health field; however, the full potential of this model to contribute to improving outcomes for children and their families is still to be realized. The advocacy efforts initiated in the early 1980s have resulted in an increased awareness of the need for a systemic response to the needs of children who have severe emotional disturbance and their families. Support from the federal and state level has assisted many local communities in progressing from only an awareness of the model to the actual implementation of a local system of care. The key agencies in these communities have shared the vision and the values articulated by Stroul and Friedman (1986), to develop a child-centered, family-focused system of care. In the mid-1990s, the concerns of policymakers who are responsible for mental health services have shifted from issues of accessibility and capacity to issues of effectiveness and accountability. To some degree this has been heightened by the advent of managed care and similar methods of funding mental health services.

There are several tasks that now face the proponents of the system-of-care approach in their work to continue to enhance its development, refinement, and effectiveness. We need to learn more about the strengths and weaknesses of this approach and the manner in which it operates. There needs to be a better articulation of who the children are who can best be served by this approach, as well as more specificity in describing the nature of the component interventions in the system. The complex challenges of interagency collaboration and methods of funding also need more examination.

In this chapter we have presented the basic concepts and philosophical framework for systems of care and described some of the implications of this framework for research and evaluation. The chapters in this text represent the current best practices in research and evaluation efforts to address these issues, and they represent the current status of the field in its journey from advocacy to outcomes.

References

Brown, P. (1995). The role of the evaluator in comprehensive community initiatives. In J. P. Connell, A. C. Kubisch, L. B. Schorr, & C. H. Weiss (Eds.), *New approaches to evaluating community initiatives* (pp. 201–225). Washington, DC: Aspen Institute.

Clark, H. B., & Clarke, R. T. (1996). Research on the wraparound process and individualized services for children with multi-system needs. *Journal of Child and Family Studies, 5*(1), 1–5.

Cole, R. (1996). The Robert Wood Johnson Foundation's mental health services program for youth. In B. Stroul (Ed.), *Children's mental health: Creating systems of care in a changing society* (pp. 235–248). Baltimore: Brookes.

Cole, R., & Poe, S. (1993). *Partnerships for care—systems of care for children with serious emotional disturbances and their families.* Washington, DC: Washington Business Group on Health, Robert Wood Johnson Foundation Mental Health Services Program for Youth.

Davis, M., Yelton, S., Katz-Leavy, J., & Lourie, I. S. (1995). Unclaimed children revisited: The status of state mental health service systems. *Journal of Mental Health Administration, 22*(2), 147–166.

Friedman, R. M. (in press). Services and service delivery systems for children with serious emotional disorders: Issues in assessing effectiveness. In C. T. Nixon & D. A. Northrup (Eds.), *Evaluating mental health services: How do programs for children "work" in the real world?* Thousand Oaks, CA: Sage.

Hernandez, M., & Goldman, S. (1996). A local approach to system development: Ventura County, California. In B. Stroul (Ed.), *Children's mental health: Creating systems of care in a changing society* (pp. 177–196). Baltimore: Brookes.

Hoagwood, K., Jensen, P. S., Petti, T., & Burns, B. J. (1996). Outcomes of mental health care for children and adolescents: I. A comprehensive conceptual model. *Journal of the American Academy of Child and Adolescent Psychiatry, 35,* 1055–1063.

Joint Commission on the Mental Health of Children. (1969). *Crisis in child mental health.* New York: Harper & Row.

King, B., & Meyers, J. (1996). The Annie E. Casey Foundation's mental health initiative for urban children. In B. Stroul (Ed.), *Children's mental health: Creating systems of care in a changing society* (pp. 249–261). Baltimore: Brookes.

Knapp, M. S. (1995). How shall we study comprehensive collaborative services for children and families? *Educational Researcher, 24,* 5–16.

Knitzer, J. (1982). *Unclaimed children: The failure of public responsibility to children and adolescents in need of mental health services.* Washington, DC: Children's Defense Fund.

Kutash, K., Duchnowski, A. J., & Sondheimer, D. L. (1994). Building the research base for children's mental health services. *Journal of Emotional and Behavioral Disorders, 2*(4), 194–197.

Lourie, I. (1994). *Principles of local system development for children and adolescents.* Chicago: Kaleidoscope.

Macro International. (1996). Annual report to Congress. Atlanta, GA: Author.

McGrew, J. H., Bond, G. R., Dietzen, L., & Salyers, M. (1994). Measuring the fidelity of implementation of a mental health program model. *Journal of Consulting and Clinical Psychology, 62*(4), 670–678.

Morrissey, J. P., Johnsen, M. C., & Calloway, M. O. (1995, November). *Evaluating performance and change in mental health systems serving children and youth: An interorganizational network approach.* Paper presented at the annual meeting of the American Public Health Association, Washington, DC.

Pires, S. A. (1997). Lessons learned from the Fort Bragg Demonstration: An overview. In S. A. Pires (Ed.), *Lessons learned from the Fort Bragg demonstration* (pp. 1–23). Tampa, FL: Research and Training Center for Children's Mental Health.

President's Commission on Mental Health. (1978). *Report of the sub-task panel on infants, children, and adolescents.* Washington, DC: U.S. Government Printing Office.

Stockdill, J. (1991). The NIMH in relation to state and local mental health administrators and policy makers: CASSP as a prototype. *Administration and Policy in Mental Health, 18*(6), 455–459.

Stroul, B. (1993). *Systems of care for children and adolescents with severe emotional disturbances: What are the results?* Washington, DC: Georgetown University Child Development Center, National Technical Assistance Center for Children's Mental Health.

Stroul, B., & Friedman, R. M. (1986). *A system of care for children and adolescents with severe emotional disturbances.* Washington, DC: Georgetown University Child Development Center, National Technical Assistance Center for Children's Mental Health.

Stroul, B., & Friedman, R. M. (1996). The system of care concept and philosophy. In B. Stroul (Ed.), *Children's mental health: Creating systems of care in a changing society* (pp. 3–22). Baltimore: Brookes.

Stroul, B., Lourie, I., Goldman, S., & Katz-Leavy, J. (1992). *Profiles of local systems of care for children and adolescents with severe emotional disturbances* (Rev. ed.). Washington, DC: Georgetown University Child Development Center, National Technical Assistance Center for Children's Mental Health.

U.S. Congress, Office of Technology Assessment. (1986). *Children's mental health: Problems and services—a background paper.* Washington, DC: Author.

National Adolescent and Child Treatment Study (NACTS): Outcomes for Children with Serious Emotional and Behavioral Disturbance

2

Paul E. Greenbaum, Robert F. Dedrick,
Robert M. Friedman, Krista Kutash,
Eric C. Brown, Sharon P. Lardieri,
and Amy M. Pugh

In the early 1980s, professionals in the children's mental health field began to make children with serious emotional disturbance (SED) and their families a top priority (Duchnowski & Friedman, 1990; Stroul & Friedman, 1986).[1] At the federal level, this policy decision was operationalized partially through the creation of the Child and Adolescent Service System Program (CASSP), which sought to promote the development of effective community-based systems of care specifically for children with the most severe problems and their families (Stroul & Friedman, 1986). The selection of this group of children as a target population was based largely on policy considerations; a "diagnosis" of SED did not exist (and still does not), and professionals had an incomplete understanding of who these children were, what their strengths and needs were, how such children develop over time, and how systems might best serve them.

At the same time as the National Institute of Mental Health (NIMH) was placing a priority on children with SED and their families, the National Institute on Disability and Rehabilitation Research (NIDRR) within the U.S. Department of Education also was increasing its attention to this group. As a result, a partnership between these two federal agencies was established that led to funding for two research and training centers. The goals for these centers were strengthening the knowledge base in the children's mental health field and increasing dissemination of information to researchers, policymakers, parents, advocates, and practitioners.

The call for proposals issued in 1984 by NIDRR and NIMH specifically requested that a study be designed and conducted that would describe these children with SED and their families, how they were being served, and their outcomes over time. In response to this call, the Florida Mental Health Institute (FMHI) of the University of South Florida established a Research and Training Center for Children's Mental Health. This article describes the National Adolescent and Child Treatment Study (NACTS), which was part of the center's activities.

There are two main approaches that can be taken to the type of descriptive study requested by NIDRR and NIMH. The first approach involves operationally defining serious emotional disturbance clinically or psychometrically, then assessing a large number of children and studying those who meet the operational definition. The second approach involves operationally defining serious emotional disturbance systemically by identifying children who are receiving intensive special services designed to serve children with serious emotional problems. Although both approaches have merit, the second approach was selected because of the lack of information about children with emotional disorders being served through public funding in mental health and education systems, and the need for the practitioners in the field to better understand how these systems were functioning.

For purposes of this study, the decision was made to operationally define children with SED as those who were (a) in a residential or inpatient mental health setting operated either fully or partially by public funds, or (b) in a special education program for children with serious emotional or behavioral disturbance. Given the large variation in how systems operate from state to state, and the interest in getting a broad picture of youngsters from many states, the decision was made to recruit participants from a geographically diverse group of states.

The Research and Training Center initially proposed a 4-year longitudinal study using a sequential cohort design. The decision to conduct such a study was based on the absence of longitudinal data for youngsters with serious problems served in mental health and education systems. Moreover, the longitudinal approach offers the best opportunity to assess change in functioning over time, and, in the absence of true experimental controls, provides a temporal basis for addressing causality, although such causal reasoning can not be offered without caveats.

Because funding from NIDRR and NIMH was to cover a 5-year period that would include an initial year to plan and coordinate data collection, the Research and Training Center proposed a four-wave design that would be as efficient as possible in providing not only longitudinal data, but also data about children at different ages. It was decided to conduct a four-wave study with three overlapping cohorts: children who were initially (a) 9–11 years, (b) 12–14 years, and (c) 15–17 years of age. Through this design, important information would be obtained about children in an age range of 9 to 21 years. This also would enable researchers to study younger children as they make the transition into adolescence, and older children as they move beyond the age at which they usually were served by children's systems.

During the fourth wave of NACTS, the Research and Training Center received additional funding to allow the study to continue through Wave 7. Thus, the results presented here are from a seven-wave study, designed to (a) provide a description along multiple domains and from multiple perspectives of children with SED who are served either in the mental health system or the special education system, and (b) understand their needs and strengths from professional, family, and their own perspectives.

The study was not designed to evaluate innovative or exemplary services. Rather, researchers sought children from a large number of mental health and education settings who would be representative not only of the children in the system, but also of the programs and services available. The specific purpose of the study was to compile descriptive data on children with SED, including (a) demographic and family characteristics, (b) level of psychological and adaptive functioning, (c) services received, and (d) outcomes, or how the children fared over time.

Method

Design

NACTS used a sequential cohort design of age cohorts ranging from 9 to 17 years (Schaie & Baltes, 1975; Stanger, Achenbach, & Verhulst, 1994). For purposes of this study, age cohorts were divided into three groups: 9–11 years, 12–14 years, and 15–17 years. Each cohort was followed once a year for 7 years. This data-collection plan, sometimes referred to as an accelerated longitudinal design, combines cross-sectional and longitudinal data; thus, in the present study, a developmental sequence spanning 15 years, from ages 9 to 23, could be examined. The design is efficient in terms of cost and time. However, these benefits can be realized only when a significant age-by-cohort interaction is absent. That is, data for different age cohorts from children of the same age, but collected at different times of measurement, should not be significantly different. For example, data from children in the oldest cohort, who were 15 years of age in 1985 (Wave 1 of the study), should not differ from data collected from children who were in the youngest cohort and 15 years of age in 1991 (Wave 6 of the study). If there were significant differences between data from these two groups of 15-year-olds, then combining the two sources into a single age group would be of questionable validity.

Participants

The target population for this study was children between the ages of 9 and 17 years during 1985 who had been identified with SED and who were being served in a publicly funded residential mental health treatment facility or community-based special education program. Six states (Alabama, Mississippi, Florida, Colorado, New Jersey, and Wisconsin) were selected as sites for sample selection to provide geographic diversity. Additional selection criteria for the states included demographic diversity and service availability. Obtaining cooperation from school and mental health authorities was a further requirement in state selection. Within each state, all children's mental health and special education programs that met criteria (e.g., ages 9–17 years, identified as SED by P.L. 94-142 criteria, or receiving mental health services from the public mental health system) were identified by the state directors of mental health and special education programs. One hundred and twenty-five sites were identified, and 121 sites (27 mental health and 94 special education) agreed to participate. Among the participating sites, the accessible population consisted of 1,393 eligible children. All the parents of these children in the accessible population were contacted and asked to allow their children to participate in the study. Of the eligible children, signed informed consent forms and interviews were completed for 812 (58.3%).

Sample Characteristics

The participants were ages 8 to 18 years (M = 13.89 years, SD = 2.35), had been identified as having SED, and were being served by either mental health (46%) or public school (54%) systems in accordance with P.L. 94-142. (It should be noted that 12 children were outside the target age range of 9–17 years: ages 8 years, n = 6; ages 18 years, n = 6. However, they were retained in the sample.) Research participants were predominately white (70% white, 22% African American, 5% Hispanic, and 3% other), and male (75%). The age distribution of the sample was 8 to 11 years (24.4%), 12 to 14 years (39.8%), and 15 to 18 years (35.8%). The majority (55%) of the children were from two-parent families; however, only 21% were from two-parent families composed of the biological parents. History of emotional, behavioral, substance use, or criminal problems for parents also was common, with 58.0% of the sample reporting having at least one parent with one or more of the aforementioned problems by the end of the study. All participants were paid volunteers.

Seventy-seven percent (n = 628) of the children interviewed during Wave 1 were successfully contacted and reinterviewed during Wave 7, resulting in an overall attrition rate of 23%. Among those participants not interviewed during Wave 7, 48% (n = 89) were unable to be contacted or their current whereabouts were unknown, 35% (n = 65) refused to be interviewed or missed their scheduled appointments, 11% (n = 20) were not interviewed because they were determined during earlier Waves to be untestable, and 5% (n = 10) were not interviewed because they had died during the study period. For parent respondents, 83% (n = 615) who completed Wave 1 interviews had corresponding parent interviews during the final wave of data collection.

Comparisons of selected variables between missing and nonmissing respondents were conducted for parent and child participants. These comparisons included analyses of demographic, educational, and clinical measures. For children, there was a significantly higher proportion of girls ($p < .01$) and New Jersey respondents ($p < .002$) among those who were no longer in the study. For parents, only minority status was associated with a significantly higher attrition rate ($p < .05$). None of the other variables was related to parent or child attrition. These variables included: gender, age cohort, math and reading grade level, *Diagnostic and Statistical Manual of Mental Disorders* (DSM-III; American Psychiatric Association, 1980) diagnoses (i.e., conduct disorder, anxiety disorder, depression disorder, attention-deficit disorder, and schizophrenic disorder); clinical status on any of the Child Behavior Checklist/4-18 (CBCL/4-18; Achenbach, 1991a) scales (eight syndrome scales, Externalizing, Internalizing, and Total Problems scales); and use of psychotropic medication.

Procedure

During the first year of the study (1985–1986), all children were administered a series of instruments in face-to-face interviews of approximately 2½ hours' duration by trained interviewers. During this time (Wave 1), parents or legal guardians of the children were administered a series of instruments over the telephone by trained interviewers. Mothers were the respondents of choice for the phone interviews. If the mother was not living in the home, the father or another parental figure (e.g., stepparent, foster parent) was interviewed. Children also were interviewed face to face during Waves 4 and 7, and parents or guardians were interviewed over the phone annually during Waves 2 through 6.

Instruments

Data were collected from several sources, including children, parents and caregivers, teachers, and clinical and educational records. These multiple sources provided information in four major areas: (a) demographic characteristics of children and their families (e.g., ethnicity, income, family composition), (b) psychological functioning (e.g., problem behaviors), (c) services (e.g., individual counseling), and (d) outcomes (e.g., academic achievement, contact with law enforcement). The instruments administered to children, parents and caregivers, and teachers, and records reviewed, are summarized in Table 2.1. These included widely used standardized instruments such as the Child Behavior Checklist/4-18 (CBCL/4-18; Achenbach, 1991a), Vineland Adaptive Behavior Scales (VABS; Sparrow, Balla, & Cicchetti, 1984), Wide Range Achievement Test—Arithmetic and Reading (WRAT; Jastak & Wilkinson, 1984), and Diagnostic Interview Schedule for Children—Child Version (DISC-C; Costello, Edelbrock, Dulcan, Kalas, & Klaric, 1984, revised June 1985). Because the

Table 2.1

Sources, Instruments, and Administration Schedule

				Wave			
Instruments	1	2	3	4	5	6	7
Children							
Structured Interview—Problems, services received	*			*			*
Slosson Intelligence Test (Slosson, 1983)	*						
Slosson Oral Reading Test (Slosson, 1983)	*						
Wide Range Achievement Test—Arithmetic (Jastak & Wilkinson, 1984)	*			*			*
Wide Range Achievement Test—Reading (Jastak & Wilkinson, 1984)	*			*			*
Family Adaptability & Cohesion Evaluation Scale III (FACES III; Olson et al., 1985)	*			*			
Rosenberg Self-Esteem Scale (Rosenberg, 1965)	*			*			*
Diagnostic Interview Schedule for Children (DISC-C; Costello et al., 1984)	*			*			*
Diagnostic Interview Schedule (DIS; Robins et al., 1982)							*
Vocational Decision-Making Inventory (Czerlinsky et al., 1982)	*						
Youth Self-Report (YSR; Achenbach, 1991c)				*			*
Alcohol Expectancy Questionnaire (AEQ-SF; Rather, 1990)				*			*
Social Skills Rating System—Child (Gresham & Elliott, 1990)				*			
Parent							
Structured Interview: Social, developmental, medical, service history, & service evaluation	*	*	*	*	*	*	
FACES-III	*			*		*	
Child Behavior Checklist (CBCL; Achenbach, 1991a)	*	*	*	*	*	*	
Vineland Adaptive Behavior Scales (Sparrow et al., 1984)	*			*		*	
Social Skills Rating System—Parent (Gresham & Elliott, 1990)				*			

(continues)

Table 2.1 *Continued*

Instruments	Wave						
	1	2	3	4	5	6	7
Teacher							
Behavior Problems Checklist (Quay & Peterson, 1987)	*			*			
Teacher Report Form (TRF; Achenbach, 1991b)	*			*			
Social Skills Rating System—Teacher (Gresham & Elliott, 1990)				*			
Clinical Record							
Records review	*						
Social-developmental-medical history	*						
Family composition	*						
Past history of services	*						
Educational information	*						

CBCL/4-18 and VABS were the primary instruments used to measure psychological functioning, these measures are described in more detail below.

CBCL/4-18

This instrument is a 118-item problem behavior scale that produces eight syndrome scales (i.e., Withdrawn, Somatic, Anxious-Depressed, Social, Thought, Attention, Delinquent, and Aggressive), two second-order factors (i.e., Externalizing and Internalizing), and a Total Problems score. This instrument was selected as one of the major measures of psychological functioning because it has been used widely and provides a convenient way to compare the sample from this study with samples from other studies. Additionally, the CBCL/4-18 has excellent psychometric properties. Reported reliabilities are high (Achenbach, 1991a) and construct validity is good (see Brown & Achenbach, 1993). Moreover, when we examined the CBCL/4-18 data specifically for the NACTS sample, measurement properties were strong. Internal consistency (i.e., Cronbach's alpha) was high and ranged from .72 to .94 for the CBCL syndrome scales. Convergent and discriminant validity also was present, as evidenced by a multitrait-multimethod study of parent, child, and teacher ratings of four selected clinical syndromes (Greenbaum, Dedrick, Prange, & Friedman, 1994). Tests of factor structure and invariance across gender and age also attested to the desirable measurement properties of the CBCL/4-18 (Dedrick, Greenbaum, Friedman, Wetherington, & Knoff, 1997; Greenbaum, Dedrick, & Friedman, 1994, 1995). Additionally, CBCL norms have been developed for a wide age range of children (4–18 years) and for both genders, thus making measurement of developmental continuity and change more amenable than scales that are discontinuous across developmental stages.

VABS, Interview Edition Survey Form

This instrument, a 297-item semistructured interview designed to measure social competence of children from birth to 19 years of age, was used as a second measure of functioning. Adaptive behavior is measured in four areas: (a) Communication, (b) Daily Living Skills, (c) Socialization, and (d) Motor Skills. The sum of scores in these areas yields a total, or composite, score. These scales have been normed on a representative national standardization sample of 4,800 individuals with and without disabilities. As with the CBCL/4-18, standard scores can be used to make comparisons with the general population. Standard scores have a mean equal to 100 (SD = 15). Lower scores indicate fewer adaptive skills.

Results

Selected results for children with SED are reported in four sections: (a) initial psychological and educational functioning, (b) level of psychological and adaptive functioning over time, (c) service utilization, and (d) overall functioning at the end of the study. The conducted analyses and the results are described in each section.

Initial Psychological and Educational Functioning

At the beginning of the study, the emotional and behavioral problems of the participants were extensive. The distribution of DSM-III disorders at or above a mild-moderate level as indicated by the DISC-C was as follows: conduct disorder, 66.9%; anxious disorder, 41.0%; depression disorder, 18.5%; attention-deficit disorder, 11.7%; and schizophrenic disorder, 4.7%. Multiple disorders were common, with 41.0% of the sample having two or more disorders. Among children with conduct disorder, the prevalence of an additional co-occurring disorder rose to 66.7%.

Children also were lagging in academic performance, with over 58% below grade level in reading and 93% below grade level in math. Measured intelligence levels were in the low-normal range with a mean IQ equal to 85.8 (SD = 17.1). Demographic and background characteristics of the children and their families at Wave 1 are summarized in Tables 2.2 and 2.3.

Table 2.2

Demographic and Background Characteristics of Children and Their Families at Entry Into NACTS

Characteristic	Percentage	Characteristic	Percentage
Gender (812)[a]		**State (812)[a]**	
Male	75.1	Alabama	12.3
Female	24.9	Colorado	22.2
		Florida	20.7
Age in years (812)[a]		Mississippi	5.8
8 to 11	24.4	New Jersey	14.5
12 to 14	39.8	Wisconsin	24.5
15 to 18	35.8		
		Family structure (740)[a]	
Reading achievement grade levels (764)[a]		Two-parent homes	54.1
2+ years below	46.7	Two biological	21.0
1 year below	12.2	Two adoptive	5.7
At grade level	31.2	One biological,	
1 year above	5.8	one stepparent	19.3
2+ years above	4.2	Other two parent	8.1
		One-parent homes	33.8
Math achievement grade levels (629)[a]		Homes with no parent	12.2
2+ years below	84.4	Other relative(s)	6.6
1 year below	9.2	Professional staff	5.5
At grade level	3.2		
1 year above	2.1	**Family History (740)[a]**	
2+ years above	1.1	Emotional/behavioral problems	
		Father	10.1
Ethnicity (812)[a]		Mother	18.5
Hispanic	4.7	Either parent	25.5
White	70.9	Both parents	3.1
African American	21.6		
Other (e.g., Native American, Asian American)	2.8		

(continues)

Table 2.2 *Continued*

Characteristic	Percentage	Characteristic	Percentage
Police involvement		DISC and DSM-III diagnoses at mild/moderate threshold (708)[a]	
Father	14.2		
Mother	5.4	Conduct disorder	66.9
Either parent	18.0	Depressive disorder	18.5
Both parents	1.6	Anxiety disorder	41.0
Alcohol/drug abuse		Attention-deficit disorder	11.7
Father	21.9	Schizophrenic disorder	4.7
Mother	12.2	Two or more disorders	41.0
Either parent	29.3		
Both parents	4.7	CBCL/4-18 scales (701)[a]	
Any of above problems		Pure internalizers	5.7
Father	30.3	Pure externalizers	20.5
Mother	25.4	Both internalizers and externalizers	54.5
Either parent	44.3	Neither internalizers nor externalizers	20.1
Both parents	11.4		

Note. DISC = Diagnostic Interview Schedule for Children (Costello et al., 1984); DSM = *Diagnostic and Statistical Manual,* 3rd ed., American Psychiatric Association, 1980; CBCL/4-18 = Child Behavior Checklist/4-18 (Achenbach, 1991).

[a]Numbers in parentheses indicate number of respondents.

Level of Psychological and Adaptive Functioning Over Time

Two important domains of children's mental health are psychological and adaptive functioning (Kazdin, 1993). Psychological functioning considers a child's emotional and behavioral problems and generally focuses on deviant behavior or dysfunctional symptoms. Adaptive functioning considers positive or effective interpersonal behavior and is considered strength-based. A major objective of NACTS was to examine psychological and adaptive functioning and how functioning changed over the 7-year time period.

The Total Problems score from the CBCL/4-18 was selected as the overall measure of psychological functioning (higher scores represented greater problems). Currently, there have been few prospective longitudinal studies that

Table 2.3

Descriptive Statistics for Selected Characteristics
of Children and Their Families at Entry into NACTS

Characteristic	M	SD	Range
Age at Wave 1 child interview (812)[a] 13.89		2.35	8.63–18.38
IQ (783)[a]	85.78	17.07	25–142
CBCL/4-18 scales (701)[ab]			
Total	69.55	9.68	39–92
Internalizing	64.79	10.51	31–87
Externalizing	68.86	10.28	37–96
Withdrawn	64.44	10.7	50–100
Somatic	56.64	8.27	50–95
Anxious	66.99	11.29	50–96
Social problems	67.61	11.37	50–100
Thought	64.95	11.08	50–100
Attention	69.68	10.97	50–98
Delinquent	67.76	10.35	50–98
Aggressive	69.38	12.07	50–100
VABS[c]			
Daily living skills (668)[a]	84.6	20.51	19–129
Communication skills (651)[a]	75.6	20.65	19–125
Socialization skills (665)[a]	75.5	22.48	19–143

Note. CBCL = Child Behavior Checklist (Achenbach, 1991a); VABS = Vineland Adaptive Behavior Scale (Sparrow et al., 1984).

[a]Numbers in parentheses indicate number of respondents.
[b]CBCL/4-18 scores are *T*-scores, with $M = 50$ and $SD = 10$ in the general population.
[c]Vineland scores are standardized, with $M = 100$ and $SD = 15$ in the general population.

examined the developmental course of psychological functioning among children with severe emotional disabilities. The few existing studies have used traditional two-wave designs in which data were collected at only two points in time. In recent years, such designs have been criticized as being inadequate for measuring change. Growth curve analysis (also known as random effects, variance component, and multilevel or hierarchical linear modeling) is a new technique designed to overcome many of the limitations of the earlier, more traditional approaches (Bryk & Raudenbush, 1992; Willett, 1988). In growth curve analysis, change is represented in a two-stage model encompassing both within- and between-subjects factors. In the first stage, each person's observed scores are modeled as a function of an individual growth function (i.e., within-subjects) plus random error. These growth functions may be linear or nonlinear, and the parameter estimates are outcomes to be explained in the second stage of analysis. At the second stage, parameter estimates from the first stage are tested for variation as a function of group differences (i.e., between-subjects factors such as gender, age, treatment facility).

The present study used a hierarchical linear modeling program (HLM/2L version 3.01; Bryk, Raudenbush, & Congdon, 1994) to conduct the growth curve analysis. Compared to ordinary least-squares (OLS) estimation, the two-stage weighted least-squares estimation procedure used in HLM provides improved measures of change. Other major benefits of HLM include allowing for unbalanced designs and missing data in the within-subject variables and the use of between-subject variables measured either continuously or discretely. Additionally, HLM does not require that the time intervals between data collection points be the same for each interval and for all subjects.

Specific research questions addressed were whether individuals had significant changes on the Total Problems scores of the CBCL/4-18 during the study period and whether these changes, if they occurred, differed between participants who at the beginning of the study were in community-based special education programs versus residential mental health treatment facilities. Other participant characteristics that were examined for differences in individual change rates included gender, age cohort, and race/ethnicity.

The participants used to address these questions were 580 children who had (a) a valid Wave 1 CBCL score, and (b) an IQ of greater than 69 or a math grade level score equal to or greater than the 6th grade level. This later criterion was used to eliminate any participants who may have had confounding organic problems. Characteristics of the 580 participants did not differ significantly from those of the total 812 participants in the NACTS sample (see Table 2.2 for a description of these sample characteristics). CBCL/4-18 data were collected once a year (from 1985 to 1991) from the parent (89.6%) or parent surrogate. During the sixth Wave of the study, data were collected only for participants who were 18 years of age or younger ($n = 203$).

The growth curve analysis proceeded in two stages. First, an individual growth model was fit to each participant's data. For example, a fitted individual growth curve for a selected participant from the sample is shown in Figure 2.1. For this participant, the growth model was given as

$$\hat{Y} = 71.60 - 3.22 \text{ (Time)}.$$

The value of 71.60 represents the predicted Total Problems T-score at the start of the study, and the value of -3.22 is the slope or rate of change per wave in T-score points for this individual. This equation accounted for 56.5% of the change over time. Based on preliminary analyses using ordinary least squares regression for each participant, a linear growth model was selected.

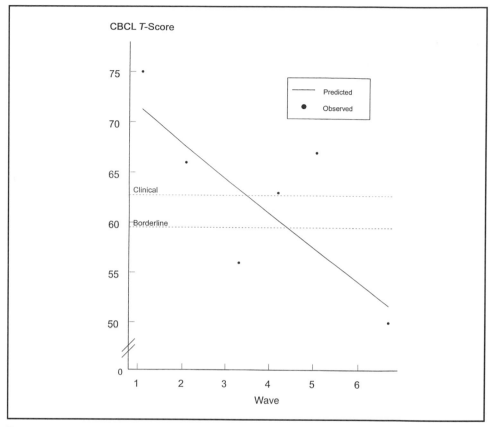

Figure 2.1. Predicted ordinary least squares (OLS) linear growth curve for a selected participant's Child Behavior Checklist (CBCL) Total Problems *T*-score.

The average equation for the sample of 580 participants without any predictors (i.e., unconditional model) was determined using HLM/2L version 3.01 (Bryk, Raudenbush, & Congdon, 1994) and was equal to

$$\hat{Y} = 69.63 - 1.84 \text{ (Time)}.$$

Results indicated that at entry into the study, mean *T*-scores were equal to 69.63 (*SD* = 9.50). These scores were in the clinical range (*T*-score > 63) as defined by Achenbach (1991a) and represented scores equal to the upper 97.5 percentile of the population. On average, Total Problems showed a significant decline of 1.84 *T*-score points per year (gamma* = −1.84, *t* = −15.57, *p* < .01).

In the second stage of the analysis, we examined if between-subjects factors (such as age cohort, gender, initial placement facility [special education/mental health residential], race/ethnicity, that is white/minority) and all two-way interactions between these factors, were related to the parameter estimates of the individual growth curves (i.e., intercept and slope). Examination of the effects of these factors on initial status (i.e., intercept) revealed a significant facility effect (gamma* = −3.68, t = −4.54, p < .001). Participants in mental health facilities had significantly more problem behaviors than participants in special education programs.

Examination of the effects of these same factors on the rate of change (i.e., slope) indicated a significant negative effect of cohort on the slope parameter (p < .001). This result meant that the older cohorts' Total Problems decreased more rapidly than the younger cohorts' (gamma* = −0.30, t = −5.80, p < .001). Figure 2.2 shows the predicted lines for the Total Problems scores for three age cohorts across the six waves of data collection. Additionally, a significant interaction between gender and race/ethnicity was found (gamma* = 1.67, t = 2.72, p < .01). Slope parameters for the four gender-by-race/ethnicity groups indi-

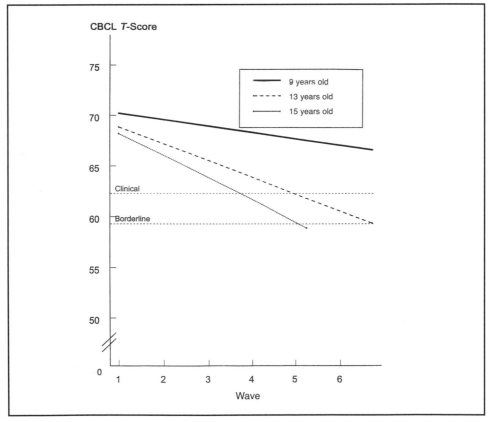

Figure 2.2. Three age cohorts predicted hierarchical (HLM) linear growth curves for the Child Behavior Checklist (CBCL) Total Problems T-score.

cated that for minority girls the decline was more rapid than for the other three groups (i.e., minority female slope = –2.51, minority male slope = –1.57, white female slope = –1.56, white male slope = –1.90, all $ps < .05$). The predicted lines for the four groups are shown in Figure 2.3. None of the other factors (i.e., gender, initial placement, or any two-way interaction) was a significant predictor of the rate of change. The summary for the between-subjects factors and their interactions as predictors of change for the CBCL/4-18 is given in Table 2.4.

VABS Adaptive functioning has been studied in developmentally delayed populations but has not been studied extensively among children with SED. Only a few studies have focused on change over time in social-adaptive behavior for children with SED. Using the CBCL/4-18 Total Problems and Competence behavior scales, Kazdin (1993) found that treatment of children with SED primarily focused on reducing emotional and behavioral problems and did not address prosocial training. Nevertheless, Kazdin found that children

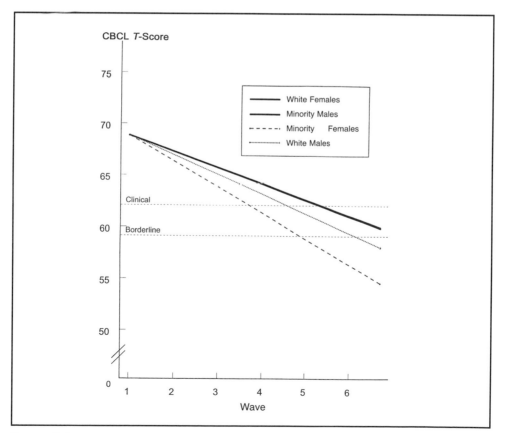

Figure 2.3. Predicted hierarchical (HLM) linear growth curves for the race/ethnicity by gender interaction on the Child Behavior Checklist (CBCL) Total Problems T-score.

Table 2.4

Summary of Growth Curve Analysis
for Factors Predicting Change
(Linear Slope) in CBCL/4–18 and VABS

Predictor	Gamma Coefficient	SE
CBCL/4-18[a]		
Gender (G)	−0.437	0.272
Facility (F)	−0.189	0.242
Age cohort (C)	−0.258***	0.053
Race/ethnicity (R)	0.182	0.267
G x F	0.082	0.577
G x C	−0.253	0.130
G X R	1.669**	0.615
F x C	0.088	0.106
F X R	0.220	0.569
C X R	−0.067	0.124
VABS[b]		
Gender (G)	0.408	0.382
Facility (F)	0.176	0.339
Age cohort (C)	0.378***	0.072
Race/ethnicity (R)	0.775*	0.360
G x F	−0.381	0.813
G x C	0.178	0.178
G X R	−1.310	0.814
F x C	−0.062	0.148
F X R	0.355	0.783
C X R	0.168	0.168

Note. CBCL/4-18 = Child Behavior Checklist. VABS =
Vineland Adaptive Behavior Scale.

[a]n = 580.
[b]n = 539.
*$p < .05$. **$p < .01$. ***$p < .001$.

receiving clinical treatment showed improvements in their emotional and behavioral problems as well as their social-adaptive skills.

A growth curve analysis, similar to that used for the CBCL/4-18, was used to measure change over time in adaptive functioning for children in NACTS. In this analysis, however, only three points in time (rather than six for the CBCL/4-18) were available, as VABS data were collected only during Waves 1, 4, and 6. Data from 539 participants who had IQ scores greater than 69 or WRAT math grade level scores greater than or equal to 6th grade level were used in a linear growth model to describe changes in adaptive behavior.

The average equation for the sample of 539 participants, without any predictors (i.e., unconditional model), was equal to

$$Y = 77.09 - 1.00 \text{ (Time)}.$$

Results indicated that average VABS Composite standard scores were equal to 77.09 ($SD = 11.74$) at entry into the study. These scores indicated that NACTS children, on average, were at the 6th percentile in adaptive behavior for the population when the study began. Overall, adaptive scores significantly declined by 1.00 point per year (i.e., gamma* $= -1.00$, $t = -6.27$, $p < .001$), so that the average predicted score was 72.09 at the end of the study. This score was equivalent to the 3rd percentile of the population.

In the second stage, we examined if four between-subjects factors (gender, initial placement facility, cohort, and race/ethnicity) and all two-way interactions between these factors were related to initial status (i.e., intercept). A significant cohort effect (gamma* $= -1.22$, $t = -3.50$, $p < .001$) was found for these initial scores, with the oldest cohort having lower VABS Composite standard scores at Wave 1 than the other two groups (e.g., 15 years, $M = 74.99$; 13 years, $M = 77.42$; 9 years, $M = 82.30$).

Examination of the effects of the same between-subjects factors and all two-way interactions on the rate of change (i.e., slope) revealed a significant positive effect of cohort on the slope parameter ($p < .001$). This result meant that the youngest cohort showed the greatest decline (e.g., 9 years, -2.70 points per wave), whereas the older cohorts showed the least decline (e.g., 15 years, -0.43 point per wave). The cohort effect on the rate of change is shown in Figure 2.4.

A significant main effect on the rate of change also was found for race/ethnicity (gamma* $= 0.78$, $t = 2.15$, $p < .05$), indicating that minority children's normative scores declined more rapidly than did those of their white peers (in fact, almost twice as fast). Slopes for minority and white children were -1.59 and -0.82, respectively, so that, at the end of the study, minority children's scores were 71.7 compared to 73.9 for white children (see Figure 2.5). None of the other between-subjects factors or their interactions were significantly related to the rate of change. The effects of the between-subjects factors on change in the VABS are summarized in Table 2.4.

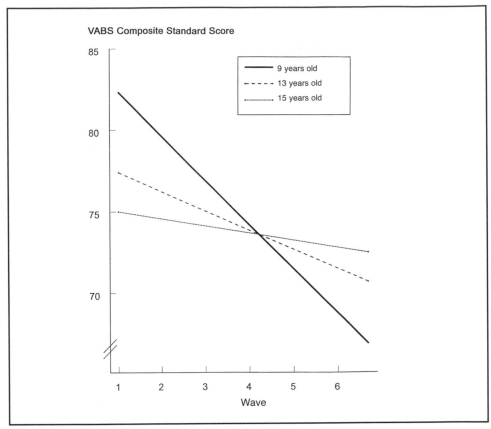

Figure 2.4. Three age cohorts predicted hierarchical (HLM) linear growth curves for the Vineland Adaptive Behavior (VABS) Composite standard score.

Results of the VABS growth curve analysis indicated a significant decline of the adaptive behavior of these children, relative to their normative peers. This decline was greatest for younger and minority children. It should be noted, however, that for all children, there was no loss in absolute level (i.e., raw score) of adaptive skills already acquired. Rather, the decline represents the inability to acquire new skills, particularly at a rate comparable to that of their peers without SED. This inability to maintain skills when measured at age-normed levels also was found for educational achievement (see "Educational Attainment").

Service Utilization

Another important purpose of NACTS was to examine children's utilization of 11 services during the course of the study. Of the 11 services, 6 formed a con-

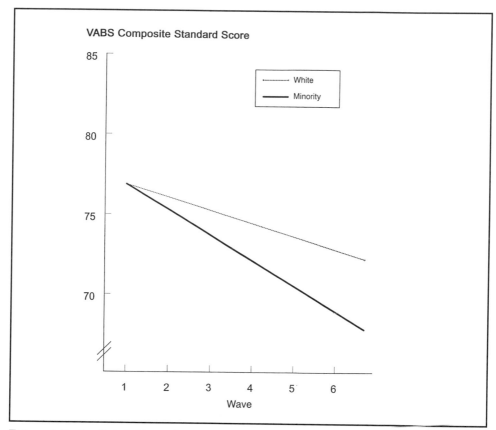

Figure 2.5. Predicted hierarchical (HLM) linear growth curves for the race/ethnicity main effect on the Vineland Adaptive Behavior (VABS) Composite standard score.

ceptually related cluster of mental health services: psychological testing, individual counseling, family counseling, group therapy, alcohol/drug counseling, and psychotropic medication. A Cronbach's alpha of .82 provided empirical support for the internal consistency of this service cluster. A second conceptual cluster of educational services was formed by special education classes and speech therapy. Cronbach's alpha for this cluster was .42, indicating weaker internal consistency. The remaining three services were conceptually distinct and consisted of vocational rehabilitation, child welfare, and nonroutine health care.

Overall rates of utilization were determined by assigning a value of 1 or 0 to a child for each Wave, representing whether or not a service was received. Service utilization was calculated for each child by summing across Waves the number of times a service was received and dividing by the total number of Waves. Data for three or more Waves were required for service utilization to be calculated.

Almost all children received a variety of services during the 7-year period of NACTS. Over one third (36.8%) utilized four of the following five service systems at least once during the course of the study: (a) mental health, (b) school-based special education, (c) child welfare, (d) juvenile justice, and (e) vocational rehabilitation. Only 5.8% used just one type of service system, whereas 14.9% and 39.7% received services from two and three systems, respectively. The most commonly utilized service system was mental health (93.1%), followed by juvenile justice (80.0%), school-based special education (70.9%), child welfare (68.9%), and vocational rehabilitation (11.6%).

Service utilization was examined in regard to the following children's characteristics: gender, age cohort, minority status, initial placement, and clinical status as measured by CBCL/4-18 Total Problem scores. The various service utilization rates for these characteristics are given in Tables 2.5 and 2.6. Significant differences ($p < .01$) in the utilization rates for the 11 services by demographic and clinical characteristics are demonstrated in Figures 2.6 and 2.7. For the mental health service cluster, there were significant differences by initial placement, with children in mental health placements receiving all of the six mental health services more often than children enrolled in special education programs (all $ps < .001$). Significant differences among these services also were found by clinical status (as measured by the CBCL/4-18 clinical cutoff level, T-score > 63). Children with more serious problem behavior received each of the six mental health services more often than did children who scored below clinical levels. Across age cohorts, there were significant differences ($p < .01$) for five mental health services, with the younger cohort (8–11 years) receiving more services than the 12–14 and 15–18 cohorts for four of the five services (psychological testing, individual counseling, family counseling, and group therapy). For alcohol/drug counseling, the pattern was reversed, with the youngest cohort receiving fewer services. There were no significant differences by cohort for receipt of psychotropic medication.

Within the second cluster of educational services, significant differences were found for receipt of special education classes by initial placement, gender, and age cohort (all $ps < .001$). Children who were initially in special education programs had higher utilization rates than those initially in mental health residential facilities; males had higher rates than females, and younger children received more special education classes than older children. No differences were found for either clinical status or race/ethnicity. The analysis of speech therapy indicated a significant ($p < .001$) age cohort difference, with the younger cohorts receiving more services. Additionally, there was a significant race/ethnicity difference ($p < .01$), with African Americans receiving more speech therapy than whites.

Among the three remaining services, significant differences were found for vocational rehabilitation by age cohort (older children received more services than younger children, $p < .01$); child welfare and nonroutine health care by initial placement (children in mental health residential facilities received more special education services, $ps < .001$), gender (females received more services

(text continues on page 45)

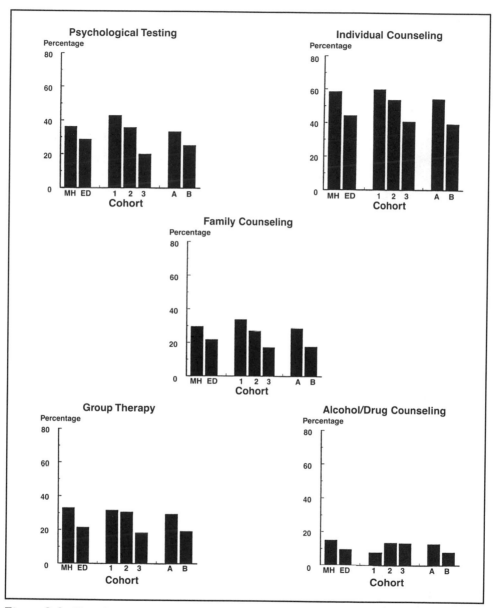

Figure 2.6. Significant mean differences between groups for mental health services at $p < .01$ by one-way ANOVA. Initial placement indicated by residential mental health (MH) and school (ED). Age at beginning of study indicated by cohorts 1, 2, and 3, aged 8–11, 12–14, and 15–18 years, respectively. Clinical status indicated by clinical level (C) and below clinical level (NC) on the Child Behavior Checklist.

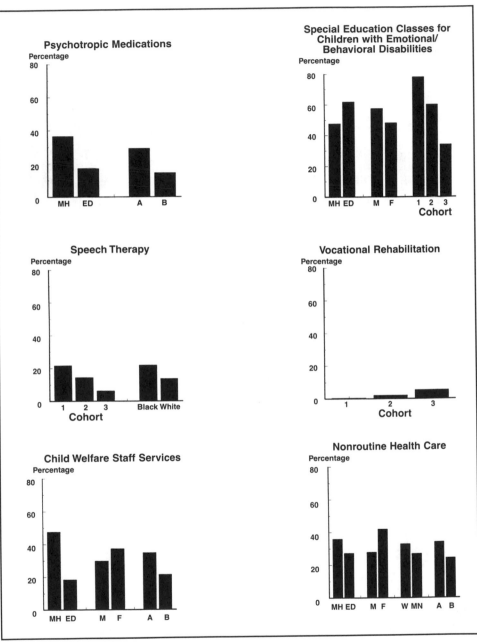

Figure 2.7. Significant mean differences between groups for mental health services at $p < .01$ by one-way ANOVA. Initial placement indicated by residential mental health (MH) and school (ED). Age at beginning of study indicated by cohorts 1, 2, and 3, aged 8–11, 12–14, and 15–18 years, respectively. Clinical status indicated by clinical level (C) and below clinical level (NC) on the Child Behavior Checklist. Gender indicated by Males (M) and Females (F). Race/ethnicity indicated by White (W) and Minority (MN).

Table 2.5

Mean Percentage Receiving Service for All Waves, Overall and by Group

Service	Overall	Initial Placement				Gender			
		MH	ED	df	F	Male	Female	df	F
Psychological testing	32.0	36.1	28.6	1,719	12.36**	33.2	27.9	1,719	ns
Individual counseling	50.4	58.3	43.6	1,739	47.44**	50.3	50.7	1,739	ns
Family counseling	25.1	29.4	21.6	1,739	18.32**	25.0	25.4	1,739	ns
Group therapy	26.7	32.9	21.4	1,718	32.13**	26.6	26.8	1,718	ns
Alcohol/drug counseling	11.9	14.9	9.4	1,733	16.31**	12.5	10.1	1,733	ns
Psychotropic medications	26.0	36.4	17.1	1,735	65.23**	25.3	28.3	1,735	ns
EB classes	55.1	47.5	61.7	1,768	48.82**	57.4	48.0	1,768	14.95**
Speech therapy	14.9	14.1	15.5	1,480	ns	14.0	18.6	1,480	ns
Vocational rehabilitation	2.7	3.4	2.1	1,734	ns	2.9	2.2	1,734	ns
Child welfare staff services	31.5	47.4	18.3	1,705	171.42**	29.6	37.1	1,705	6.80*
Nonroutine health care	31.1	35.7	27.1	1,737	22.49**	27.7	41.7	1,737	45.63**

Note. MH = residential mental health; ED = school; EB = special education classes for children with emotional/behavioral disabilities; ns = no significant difference, $p > .01$.

*$p < .01$. **$p < .001$.

Table 2.6

Mean Percentage Receiving Service for all Waves, by Age and Ethnicity

Service	Age Cohort in Years					Ethnicity				CBCL			
	8-11	12-14	15-18	df	F	W	M	df	F	A	B	df	F
Psychological testing	42.7	35.6	20.0	2,718	40.32**	32.1	31.6	1,719	ns	33.3	25.3	1,662	10.02*
Individual counseling	59.6	53.2	40.5	2,738	25.61**	51.5	47.3	1,739	ns	54.2	39.5	1,680	33.66**
Family counseling	33.6	26.9	17.1	2,738	26.18**	25.7	23.7	1,739	ns	28.4	17.6	1,680	24.55**
Group therapy	31.7	30.7	18.3	2,717	18.17**	27.2	25.3	1,718	ns	29.4	19.2	1,662	16.97**
Alcohol/drug counseling	7.7	13.4	13.2	2,732	6.34*	12.0	11.8	1,733	ns	12.7	7.8	1,677	10.04*
Psychotropic medications	32.3	23.1	25.0	2,734	ns	27.6	21.8	1,735	ns	29.0	14.3	1,678	26.74**
EB classes	78.1	60.0	33.9	2,767	211.72**	54.6	56.6	1,768	ns	55.6	52.8	1,688	ns
Speech therapy	21.5	14.2	6.1	2,479	10.35**	13.5	18.5	1,480	ns	14.4	17.2	1,448	ns
Vocational rehabilitation	0.4	2.0	5.2	2,733	20.64**	3.0	1.9	1,734	ns	2.9	2.6	1,677	ns
Child welfare staff services	27.4	34.9	30.7	2,704	ns	31.9	30.2	1,705	ns	34.6	21.3	1,666	21.57**
Nonroutine health care	28.8	31.4	32.4	2,736	ns	32.7	26.7	1,737	8.70*	33.7	24.0	1,680	20.49**

Note. W = white; M = minority; A, B = Children testing at or below, respectively, the clinical level on Total Problems Score of the Child Behavior Checklist (CBCL); EB = special education classes for children with emotional/behavioral disabilities; ns = no significant difference, $p > .01$.

*$p < .01$. **$p < .001$.

than males, $p < .01$); and clinical status (children in the clinical range received more services than children in the nonclinical range, $p < .001$). Whites also received significantly more nonroutine health care services than minority children ($p < .01$).

Overall Functioning at End of Study

A final purpose of NACTS was to examine outcomes for these children. Two types of outcomes were examined: (a) contact with law enforcement, and (b) educational attainment.

Contact With Law Enforcement

Based on a sample of 753 children with complete data on contact with law enforcement during Waves 4 through 6, approximately two thirds (66.5%) of the sample had at least one contact with police in which the child was believed to be the perpetrator of a crime. Further, 43.3% were arrested at least once, 49.3% were required to appear before a court or judge (these appearances included arrests and other court appearances), and 34.4% were adjudicated delinquent or convicted of a crime. Additional data, based on parent reports from Waves 2 through 6, indicated that most law violations were for property-related crimes (47.8%), followed by crimes against persons (30.5%), status offenses (29.4%), drug-related offenses (15.9%), and sex-related offenses (5.3)%. Adding data from children's self-reports of criminal activities unknown to law officials substantially increased the rates provided by parents: property-related crimes (62.3%), crimes against persons (38.3%), status offenses (35.0%), drug-related offenses (26.9%), and sex-related offenses (6.3%). Dispositions for these law violations consisted of the following: short-term stay in either a detention center or jail (50.8%), placement in probation or community control (47.6%), long-term stay in a training school (12.1%), jail (9.8%), home for delinquents, or halfway house (8.9%), and prison (6.9%; Lardieri, Newcomb, Greenbaum, & Brown, 1994).

Using survival analysis with 620 children who had complete data at Wave 1 and follow-up information on correctional placements during Waves 2 through 7, Prange, Greenbaum, and Friedman (1993) identified several demographic and behavioral variables as significant predictors of incarceration (i.e., placement in a detention center, jail, training school, home for delinquents, halfway house, or prison). Risk of having a juvenile justice or adult correctional placement was found to be greater for: (a) males, (b) minorities (i.e., African American, Hispanic, or other ethnic groups), (c) children initially residing in mental health facilities, and (d) children who were in midadolescence. CBCL/4-18 Externalizing scores and the number of conduct disorder symptoms also were found to be positively related to risk of incarceration. In contrast, number of phobic symptoms was associated negatively with this outcome.

In a series of competing-risks (i.e., correctional placement vs. residential mental health readmission) survival analyses of 184 children who had been successfully discharged from residential mental health facilities, Brown and Greenbaum (1995) found higher probabilities of subsequent incarceration for children who: (a) were male, (b) had higher levels of Externalizing behavior (CBCL/4-18), and (c) had a family history of contact with the police (all $ps < .05$). In contrast, subsequent readmission to a residential treatment center was more likely (all $ps < .05$) for children who: (a) were younger at time of discharge, (b) were nonwhite, (c) had families with less functional adaptability (Family Adaptability and Cohesion Scales; Olson, Portner, & Lavee, 1985), (d) had fewer communication skills (VABS), and (e) had higher levels of Internalizing behavior (CBCL/4-18). In total, 75% of these children were either readmitted to a residential mental health facility (45.1%) or a correctional facility (29.9%). Median length of time until reinstitutionalization was 10.5 months ($M = 16.1, SD = 14.7$) for readmission and 22.5 months ($M = 30.0, SD = 22.4$) for incarceration.

To assess whether these characteristics had a similar predictive relationship with frequency and duration of incarcerations, a series of multiple regression analyses were performed on (a) number of incarcerations, (b) average length of stay per incarceration, and (c) total length of time incarcerated over the study period (Lardieri et al., 1994). Over the course of NACTS, incarcerated children ($n = 211$) averaged two episodes (i.e., median = 2.0) with an average total duration of 320 days ($SD = 374.38$) in juvenile justice and correctional facilities. Average durations in the various placement types were as follows: (a) homes for delinquents and halfway houses, 150 days ($n = 66$), range = 1 to 546 days; (b) jails (Wave 4 through Wave 6 only), 180 days ($n = 103$), range = 1 to 929 days; (c) training schools, 335 days ($n = 73$), range = 7 to 2,080 days; and (d) prisons, 400 days ($n = 52$), range = 6 to 1,244 days. Results indicated that duration and frequency of incarcerations were significantly greater for males and older children, duration: $t (204) = 3.19$ and 2.10, frequency: $t (204) = 2.55$ and 2.28, respectively; all $ps < .05$. Additionally, duration was significantly greater for children with lower IQ scores, $t (204) = 2.55, p < .05$, and frequency was significantly greater for children from Colorodo, Wisconsin, and Alabama, $t (204) = 2.12, p < .05$.

Educational Attainment

Overall, educational outcomes were poor for the sample. Data on academic achievement in math and reading, as measured by the Wide Range Achievement Test (WRAT; Jastak & Wilkinson, 1984) demonstrated the extent to which these children lacked important academic skills.

For children who were 18 years of age or older and who had IQ scores equal to or greater than 70 ($n = 353$), 75.4% were below their appropriate reading grade levels. Comparable figures for math achievement were even lower, with 96.9% below appropriate grade levels. Among this group, only 25.1% had obtained a regular high school degree and 17.4% had received a General Educational Development (GED) degree. An additional 3.7% had completed at least one year of college. At the end of the study, 40.4% of those aged 18 years or older had not received a high school degree or GED and were not currently enrolled in an educational program. The remaining 13.4% reported still pursuing a high school degree, with 3.0% pursuing a GED, even though they were past the traditional age for high school students.

For children under age 18 who were still enrolled in school at the end of the study (n = 151), over half (53.6%) were in a classroom below their age-appropriate grade level, 35.1% were at their age-appropriate grade level, and 11.3% were in ungraded classroom settings. Scores in reading and mathematics from the WRAT showed similar patterns of underachievement. At the beginning of the study, 53.8% of the children under age 18 with IQ scores greater than or equal to 70 were reading below grade level, and 92.8% had below-grade math scores. By Wave 4, the comparable percentages had increased to 82.7% for reading and 96.8% for math. At the end of the study, 85.1% were below grade levels in reading and 94.3% were below grade levels in math.

In a sample of special education school-based children with IQ scores of 70 or above and complete parent interview data (n = 281), Brown, Foster-Johnson, Greenbaum, and Caso-Esposito (1995) found that, during the course of the study, 43.1% had dropped out of their school programs, 33.8% had been continuously enrolled, and only 23.1% graduated with either a high school degree (21.7%) or a GED (1.4%). Approximately one fourth of the dropouts ultimately returned to school to pursue their education. For children who dropped out of school (n = 121), parent and child interviews were reviewed to determine the reasons for leaving. Multiple reasons were noted. For the analysis, 15 distinct reasons were recorded and classified into three global categories: (a) behavioral, (b) programmatic, and (c) situational. Behavioral reasons included being bored, uninterested, unhappy, or frustrated with school (noted among 26.4% of all dropouts); being suspended, expelled, or chronically truant from school (16.4%); exhibiting alcohol- or drug-related behavior (4.1%); and running away from home (2.4%). Programmatic reasons for dropping out of school included being arrested or incarcerated (14.8%), entering a residential program (10.6%), and exiting a correctional or residential mental health program without returning to school (5.8%). Situational reasons included having to work (8.2%), aging out of a school program (8.1%), getting married or having a baby (4.9%), and moving away (3.3%). In 20.7% of the cases reviewed, the reason for dropping out of school could not be determined.

Using survival analysis, significant (p < .05) predictors of dropping out of school were analyzed as a function of the three types of global reasons for dropping out. Results are reported as unadjusted Odds Ratios (OR). An OR of 1.00 indicates no relationship (or independence of a predictor with dropping out), whereas ORs greater than 1.00 indicate a positive or direct association with dropping out. Characteristics of children dropping out because of behavioral reasons were (a) having a lower IQ score (OR = 1.02); (b) scoring in the clinical range on aggressive behavior (CBCL/4-18; OR = 2.97); (c) having a history of criminal offenses (i.e., property-related, person-related, or drug-related offenses; ORs = 2.18, 2.08, and 1.93, respectively); and (d) having a family history of school, emotional/behavioral, or alcohol/drug-related problem (ORs = 2.25, 2.24, and 3.20, respectively). Participants dropping out for programmatic reasons had (a) below the median socioeconomic status (OR = 2.31), (b) delinquent behavior scores in the clinical range (CBCL/4-18; OR = 2.70), and (c) a history of criminal offenses (i.e., status [truancy, curfew violations, running away from home], property-related, or person-related offenses; ORs = 2.40, 4.40, and 2.71, respectively). Participants dropping out for situational reasons were more likely to be (a) male (OR = 2.68), (b) older (OR = 1.27), (c) below the median on socioeconomic status (OR = 2.29), and (d) below average or failing on school competence measures of English, writing, math, and spelling achievement (CBCL/4-18; ORs = 2.29, 2.46, 2.30, and 5.08, respectively).

Discussion

NACTS was designed to increase our understanding of children with SED who are being served in the public mental health and educational service systems. Results indicate that, at entry into the study, the children already had serious problems in many domains and that those problems remained serious 7 years later, when the study was completed.

Findings at Wave 1

At Wave 1, 41% of the sample had two or more DSM-III disorders as determined by the DISC-C. The most prevalent disorder was conduct disorder (66.9% at the mild to moderate level), and 66.7% of those with a conduct disorder diagnosis also had at least one other co-occurring disorder. Rosenblatt and Attkisson (1993) also found that disruptive behavior disorders were the most common diagnostic category for children with SED receiving services in three California counties, and the high level of co-occurring disorders also is consistent with other studies of this population (Friedman, Kutash, & Duchnowski, 1996).

Another indication of significant difficulties in emotional and behavioral functioning can be found in the scores on the CBCL/4-18. The mean T-score on the Total Problems scale for children from the mental health sites was 71.9; for the educational sites, it was 67.8. Both scores are in the clinical range. Overall, 54.5% of the sample was initially in the clinical range both on Externalizing and Internalizing broadband scales, again indicating a high degree of co-occurrence of problems.

On the VABS, a measure of adaptive behavior, the mean Composite standardized scale score was 78.0, compared to a national norm of 100.0 ($SD = 15.0$). Scores were lower on the Communication and Socialization scales than they were on the scale that assessed activities of daily living. This Composite score of 78.0 contrasts with an average IQ of 85.8, indicating that although the children were about one standard deviation below average on IQ, they were even further behind on social and adaptive behaviors. Academically, sizable skill deficiencies also were present. Over 58.9% were below grade level in reading, and 93.6% were below grade level in math.

This constellation of problems in multiple domains including emotional and behavioral functioning, high prevalence of diagnosable disorders with frequent co-occurrence of disorders, and sizable deficiencies in social and adaptive behavior as well as academic skills is consistent with the results of other studies (e.g., Rosenblatt & Attkisson, 1993).

Functioning at Wave 7

Given this pattern of multiple problems and needs at Wave 1, a key concern is how emotional and behavioral functioning changes for children over time. The longitudinal design provided an excellent opportunity to make this assessment. An encouraging finding was that on the CBCL/4-18 the sample showed improvement that averaged out to 1.84 T-score points per year. This improvement was particularly large for the oldest cohort, who initially were between 15 and 17 years of age. In fact, this oldest group improved to the point that their mean T-score no longer was in the clinical range. Because of more modest improvement, the youngest cohort's mean T-score remained in the clinical range, whereas for the middle cohort, the final levels were in the borderline area.

This effect is an important finding that is worthy of further study. It may reflect (a) an instrument effect, with the CBCL/4-18 being less sensitive to problems at the older age range; (b) a cohort effect, with the youngest cohort encountering greater environmental stresses (Achenbach & Howell, 1993); or (c) an age effect, with children who enter the system prior to adolescence having problems that are either more resistant to change or that simply take longer to change. It should be noted, however, that although CBCL/4-18 scores improved overall, this improvement was slow, requiring at least 3 years before any group entered the normal range; it also was modest, with mean T-scores still in the borderline or clinical ranges for two of the age cohort groups at Wave 6.

Improvement was greatest for minority females, a finding that is difficult to interpret. For example, in a study of older children from the NACTS sample, Silver, Unger, and Friedman (1993), found that 38% of the young women in the 18–22 age range already had had one or more children, compared to 19% of the young men in the same age range. Although the sample size was too small to have been analyzed by race/ethnicity, there were some indications that CBCL/4-18 scores tended to decrease after parenting responsibilities began.

Thus, by itself, the finding of improvement on the CBCL/4-18 may be encouraging, but if the finding is associated with early parenthood, then the interpretation may not be as positive.

Similarly, Greenbaum, Prange, Friedman, and Silver (1991) found a high degree of co-morbidity between substance abuse disorders and emotional and behavioral disorders. They also pointed out that emotional and behavioral disorders are common antecedents to substance abuse disorders. Therefore, the improved scores on the CBCL/4-18 for the oldest age cohort in this study also might reflect the lack of sensitivity of that instrument to substance abuse problems in older adolescents and young adults.

The longitudinal findings with regard to social and adaptive behavior, academic skills, and school performance are not encouraging. However, the similar trends found for these measures of functional and academic domains support the construct validity of each of these separate measures. Overall, adaptive scores significantly declined by 1.00 point per year, so that at the end of the study the average score was 73.3, or almost 2 standard deviations below average. The greatest decline was shown by the youngest cohort, a finding that is consistent with the indication that the youngest cohort made the least progress on the CBCL/4-18. The scores of minority children declined more than did those of their white peers.

By the end of the study, 75.4% of the sample who were 18 years of age or older and who had IQ scores equal to or greater than 70 were below their appropriate grade level in reading, and 96.9% were below their appropriate grade level in math. It is not surprising, given these major academic skill deficiencies in combination with other problems, that 40.4% of this group did not have a high school diploma or a GED, and were not currently enrolled in school. About one quarter of the group did have a high school degree, 17.4% had received their GED, and 16.4% were still enrolled in some educational program. These findings are consistent with, and actually slightly higher than, national graduation data for students with emotional disturbance (36.1%; U.S. Department of Education, 1991). It is noteworthy as well that analyses of predictive factors for dropping out indicated that, in two of the three groups, those who had dropped out for situational reasons and those who had left school for other special programs or correctional settings were significantly below the median of the entire NACTS sample on income. Although the data do not give a full picture of the role of inadequate economic supports, they certainly suggest that income constitutes a risk factor in a population that has a variety of other problems. Consistent with this pattern was the finding by Silver et al. (1993) that only 60% of the 18–22-year-olds who were living in the community were working or looking for work. The median income for those who were working was only slightly above the minimum wage.

Additionally, a heavy involvement with the criminal justice system was found for the sample. During Waves 4 through 6, about two thirds of the children had at least one contact with law enforcement in which they were thought to be perpetrators of a crime. Almost half of the contacts were for crimes against property, and slightly more than one third were for crimes against people. At the same time, among youngsters discharged from a mental health placement, 75.0% were found to have been either readmitted to a mental health placement (45.1%) or incarcerated in a correctional setting (29.9%). Those youngsters most likely to be incarcerated in a correctional setting were male, scored higher on Externalizing problems on the CBCL/4-18, and came from families with a history of involvement with the justice system. In contrast, those most likely to be readmitted to a mental health placement were more likely to be minorities, to come from families that had more difficulty with adaptability, scored lower on the Communication scale of the VABS, and scored higher on the Internalizing scale of the CBCL/4-18.

The most striking implications of these results are the high degree of interrelatedness of the problems; their persistence over time; and the preponderance of negative outcomes in areas such as school, adaptive behavior, and criminal activity, and in subsequent re-placements in mental health settings or incarcerations. These data underscore the need for comprehensive and integrated services that must be provided for an extended period of time. This need presents a special challenge at a time when public systems move toward more managed care approaches. Although this study was not an evaluation of particular interventions, it seems apparent from the type and persistence of problems that short-term interventions with narrow foci are not likely to be successful with this population.

It also seems clear that, unless services can be provided effectively, not only will there be continuing difficulties for the individuals, but also great costs for society resulting from both the loss of productivity and the continued need for special services. The data suggest that this may be a multigenerational phenomenon because a high percentage of the NACTS sample become parents at early ages.

The findings from this study also raise issues about difference of age, gender, and race/ethnicity. More study concerning each of these areas is needed. One particular focus should be on the transition of youngsters from older adolescence to early adulthood, particularly among those children with SED who are receiving services at an early age, the youngest cohort in this study. Analysis of the results from NACTS indicates that it is these children who likely will have the most difficult transition to adulthood. The lack of educational and social preparedness and the absence of strong economic supports make this a particularly difficult transition. Researchers should continue to study this transition through the use of multiple measures and perspectives. It is difficult to interpret findings on a single measure, such as the CBCL/4-18, without knowing what is happening in other areas of functioning, and it is possible to come up with misleading conclusions unless functioning is studied in multiple areas.

The information from NACTS presents a rich and comprehensive set of descriptive and longitudinal findings about a large sample of children with

SED. These findings raise many clinical, service system, family, and methodological issues. More than anything else, however, they present a picture of a group of children on a long-time trajectory toward failure and despair who need a strong and consistent commitment to comprehensive and effective service.

Endnotes

* The asterisk indicates that empirical Bayes estimation was used in calculating the gamma coefficient.

1. For purposes of brevity, the term *children* is used in this article to include adolescents as well.

Authors' Note

Paul E. Greenbaum, Department of Child and Family Studies; Robert F. Dedrick, Department of Educational Measurement and Research; Robert M. Friedman, Department of Child and Family Studies; Krista Kutash, Department of Child and Family Studies; Eric C. Brown, Department of Child and Family Studies; Sharon P. Lardieri, Department of Child and Family Studies; Amy M. Pugh, Department of Child and Family Studies.

This research was supported by grants from the Center for Mental Health Services and the National Institute on Disability and Rehabilitation Research.

Correspondence concerning this article should be addressed to Paul E. Greenbaum, Department of Child and Family Studies, Florida Mental Health Institute, University of South Florida, 13301 Bruce B. Downs Boulevard, Tampa, FL 33612-3899. Telephone (813) 974-4553, Fax (813) 974-7563. Electronic mail may be sent to greenbau@hal.fmhi.usf.edu.

References

Achenbach, T. M. (1991a). *Manual for the child behavior checklist/4-18 and 1991 profile.* Burlington: University of Vermont, Department of Psychiatry.

Achenbach, T. M. (1991b). *Manual for the teacher's report form and 1991 profile.* Burlington: University of Vermont, Department of Psychiatry.

Achenbach, T. M. (1991c). *Manual for the youth self-report and 1991 profile.* Burlington: University of Vermont, Department of Psychiatry.

American Psychiatric Association. (1980). *Diagnostic and statistical manual of mental disorders* (3rd ed.). Washington, DC: Author.

Brown, E. C., Foster-Johnson, L., Greenbaum, P. E., & Caso-Esposito, R. (1995, April). *Characteristics related to school dropouts among students with severe emotional disabilities.* Poster session presented at the annual meeting of the American Educational Research Association, San Francisco.

Brown, E. C., & Greenbaum, P. E. (1995). Reinstitutionalization after discharge from residential mental health facilities: Competing-risks survival analyses. In C. Liberton, K. Kutash, & R. Friedman (Eds.), *The 7th annual research conference proceedings, a system of care for children's mental health: Expanding the research base* (pp. 271–276). Tampa: Florida Mental Health Institute.

Brown, J., & Achenbach, T. M. (1993). *Bibliography of published studies using the Child Behavior Checklist and related materials: 1993 edition.* Burlington: University of Vermont, Department of Psychiatry.

Bryk, A. S., & Raudenbush, S. W. (1992). *Hierarchical linear models: Applications and data analysis methods.* Newbury Park, CA: Sage.

Bryk, A. S., Raudenbush, S. W., & Congdon, R. T. (1994). *Hierarchical linear modeling with the HLM/2L and HLM/3L programs.* Chicago: Scientific Software International.

Costello, A., Edelbrock, C., Kalas, R., Kessler, M., & Klaric, S. (1984). *NIMH diagnostic interview schedule for children (DISC-C).* Rockville, MD: National Institute of Mental Health.

Dedrick, R. F., Greenbaum, P. E., Friedman, R. M., Wetherington, C. M., & Knoff, H. M. (in press). Testing the structure of the Child Behavior Checklist/4-18 using confirmatory factor analysis. *Educational and Psychological Measurement, 57,* 306–313.

Duchnowski, A. J., & Friedman, R. M. (1990). Children's mental health: Challenges for the nineties. *Journal of Mental Health Administration, 17,* 3–12.

Duchnowski, A. J., Johnson, M. K., Hall, K. S., Kutash, K., & Friedman, R. M. (1993). The alternatives to residential treatment study: Initial findings. *Journal of Emotional and Behavioral Disorders, 1,* 17–26.

Friedman, R. M., Kutash, K., & Duchnowski, A. J. (1996). The population of concern: Defining the issues. In B. A. Stroul (Ed.), *Systems of care for children and adolescents with severe emotional disturbances: Issues for the 1990's* (pp. 69–96). Baltimore: Brookes.

Greenbaum, P. E., Dedrick, R. F., & Friedman, R. M. (1994, August). *Exploring the structure of the Child Behavior Checklist/4-18: Second-order confirmatory factor analysis.* Poster session presented at the annual meeting of the American Psychological Association, Los Angeles.

Greenbaum, P. E., Dedrick, R. F., & Friedman, R. M. (1995, August). *Factorial invariance across age of the Child Behavior Checklist/4-18.* Poster session presented at the annual meeting of the American Psychological Association, New York.

Greenbaum, P. E., Dedrick, R. F., Prange, M. E., & Friedman, R. M. (1994). Parent, teacher, and child ratings of problem behaviors among youngsters with serious emotional disturbances: Evaluation of method effects using confirmatory factor analysis. *Psychological Assessment, 6,* 141–148.

Greenbaum, P. E., Prange, M. E., Friedman, R. M., & Silver, S. E. (1991). Substance abuse prevalence and comorbidity with other psychiatric disorders among adolescents with severe emotional disturbances. *Journal of the American Academy of Child and Adolescent Psychiatry, 30,* 575–583.

Jastak, S., & Wilkinson, G. S. (1984). *The Wide Range Achievement Test—Revised administration manual.* Wilmington, DE: Jastak Associates.

Kazdin, A. E. (1993). Changes in behavioral problems and prosocial functioning in child treatment. *Journal of Child and Family Studies, 2,* 5–22.

Lardieri, S., Newcomb, P., Greenbaum, P. E., & Brown, E. C. (1994, October). *Service system utilization among youth with serious emotional or behavioral problems: A conceptual framework update.* Paper presented at the fourth annual Virginia Beach Conference: Children and Adolescents with Emotional or Behavioral Disorders, Virginia Beach, VA.

Olson, D. H., Portner, J., & Lavee, Y. (1985). *FACES III: Family adaptability and cohesion evaluation scales.* St. Paul: University of Minnesota, Family Social Science.

Prange, M. E., Greenbaum, P. E., & Friedman, R. M. (1993, August). *Predicting correctional placements among adolescents with serious emotional disturbances.* Paper presented at the annual meeting of the American Psychological Association, Toronto, Ontario, Canada.

Rosenberg, M. (1965). *Society and the adolescent self-image.* Princeton, NJ: Princeton University Press.

Rosenblatt, A., & Attkisson, C. C. (1993). *The California AB377 evaluation: Three-year summary.* University of California, San Francisco.

Schaie, K. W., & Baltes, P. B. (1975). On sequential strategies in developmental research. *Human Development, 18,* 384–390.

Silver, S. E., Unger, K. V., & Friedman, R. M. (1993). Transition to young adulthood among youth with emotional disturbance. Unpublished manuscript, University of South Florida, Florida Mental Health Institute.

Slosson, R. L. (1983). *Slosson Intelligence Test (SIT) and Oral Reading Test (SORT) for children and adults.* East Aurora, NY: Slosson Education.

Sparrow, S. S., Balla, D. A., & Cicchetti, D. V. (1984). *Vineland adaptive behavior scales: Interview edition. Survey form manual.* Circle Pines, MN: American Guidance Service.

Stanger, C., Achenbach, T. M., & Verhulst, F. C. (1994). Accelerating longitudinal research on child psychopathology: A practical example. *Psychological Assessment, 6,* 102–107.

Stroul, B. A., & Friedman, R. M. (1986). *A system of care for severely emotionally disturbed children and youth.* Washington, DC: Georgetown University.

U. S. Department of Education. (1991). *To assure the free appropriate public education of all children with disabilities: Annual report to Congress on the implementation of the Individuals with Disabilities Act (13th edition).* Washington, DC.

Willett, J. B. (1988). Questions and answers in the measurement of change. In E. Rothkopf (Ed.), *Review of research in education (1988–89)* (pp. 345–422). Washington, DC: American Educational Research Association.

The Alternatives to Residential Treatment Study

3

Albert J. Duchnowski, Kimberly Swisher Hall,
Krista Kutash, and Robert M. Friedman

For almost 30 years, the children's mental health system has been described as being in need of reform. This conclusion has been reached by a variety of academic researchers, state and federal policymakers, and advocates based on the results of numerous studies, surveys, and reports. For example, in 1969 the Joint Commission on Mental Health (Ribicoff, 1970) concluded that mental health services for children were clearly inadequate and that only a fraction of children who were in need received help at the time that they were in need. The commission recommended extensive reforms that included the development of a continuum of care that would begin with preventive services and early intervention and include an expanded array of community-based treatment approaches. A dozen years later, Knitzer (1982) published the results of a study commissioned by the Children's Defense Fund. This report was titled *Unclaimed children: The failure of public responsibility to children and adolescents in need of mental health services;* it documented the failure of the public sector to meet the mental health needs of children effectively. In 1984, the National Institute of Mental Health (NIMH) launched the Child and Adolescent Service System Program (CASSP), an initiative that would eventually be implemented in all 50 states with the goal of improving services for children and their families through systemic reform that emphasized community-based services (Day & Roberts, 1991). However, reports issued by the U.S. Office of Technology Assessment (1986) and the Institute of Medicine (1989) continued to describe poor outcomes, fragmented services, and a gap between the knowledge base and practice in the children's mental health field (Saxe, Cross, & Silverman, 1988).

The need for reform and improvement in the system of care also has been supported by studies and reports generated by the education community. Each *Annual report to Congress on the implementation of the Education of Handicapped Children Act* (see, for example, U.S. Department of Education, 1995) has consistently documented the need to improve both the identification of and the services for children with serious emotional disturbances (SED). Similar to the findings of the Joint Commission Report in 1969, the annual reports revealed that less than a third of the children who are estimated to be in need are served in special education programs for children who have SED. Furthermore, the outcomes for these children have been described as worse than those for children served in programs for other disability groups (Wagner, D'Amico, Marder, Newman, & Blackorby, 1991).

Failure To Implement Proposed Policy

Within the past 10 years, researchers, policymakers, and advocates have become more focused on systemic issues that may contribute to poor outcomes. The CASSP framework of an integrated, comprehensive system of care had become part of virtually every state's Children's Mental Health Plan (Duchnowski & Friedman, 1990). However, surveys of programs across the country continued to reveal a fragmented system that underidentified and poorly served children in need (Knitzer, Steinberg, & Fleisch, 1990). CASSP had significantly influenced states to develop integrated systems of care that were community-based and composed of a continuum of services that offered varied levels of restrictiveness (Kahn & Kamerman, 1992), yet implementation was only sporadic and limited.

The reasons for this situation are certainly multiple and complex. Basic questions about the nature of the children themselves, the role of the family, and the appropriate mix of services and treatment modalities have yet to be fully answered (Burns & Friedman, 1990). However, some light has been shed on the problem through an analysis of the results of the few existing studies of children's mental health policy and service delivery. These studies indicate that there has been an overreliance on hospital and residential placement for the treatment of children with SED. While residential placement is viewed as a viable, albeit restrictive, component of the system of care, it is estimated that only a small number of children will need this level of care (Behar, Macbeth, & Holland, 1993; Friedman, 1987; Pires, 1990). In spite of the CASSP emphasis on in-home and community-based services, the 1980s and early 1990s have witnessed an increase in residential beds and a disproportionate amount of resources given to supporting these placements (Burns, 1991; Keisler & Morton, 1988; Weithorn, 1988). It is estimated that 70–75% of mental health funds are allocated to hospital and residential placements (Burns, 1991).

By the early 1990s, the conventional wisdom about treating children with serious emotional disabilities began to shift in terms of the desired location of treatment. Previously, it was assumed that intensive treatment could be delivered only in a hospital or institutional residential setting (Knitzer, 1993). This assumption was being challenged by an emerging collection of programs that attempted to keep the child in a community setting, preferably at home or in a homelike setting. The Kaleidoscope Program in the inner-city Chicago area emerged as a leader through many training activities for the CASSP community, and then through the adoption of its program principles by Alaska and Vermont for statewide program implementation. Another important influence at the time was the Ventura County Children's Demonstration Project in California. This program served as an example of cross-agency collaboration designed to implement an integrated service-delivery system with flexible funds and community-based programs. The Therapeutic Foster Care Program offered by the Pressley Ridge Youth Development Extension (PRYDE) was another influential program in terms of its training, research, and family preservation activities. Thus, a natural laboratory existed that made possible the examination of these emerging models of family-centered, child-focused treatment models, which served as alternatives to traditional institutional placement. Implicit in these programs was the shared value that care provided in community settings is a viable alternative to residential treatment and will lead to improved outcomes for children with SED and their families. However, just as community-based interventions are innovative and emerging, the methodologies for examining and evaluating them are also in a preliminary stage of development. Consequently, the data supporting this value is limited.

Need for Data

As the public sector becomes increasingly driven by the requirement to demonstrate accountability for its policies and programs, the children's mental health system will be required to support policy decisions with favorable outcomes. As Burns and Friedman (1990) have indicated, empirical data in the children's mental health field is sparse and methodologies are in a developmental stage. In this context of pressing need and evolving research strategy, the Alternatives to Residential Treatment Study (ARTS) was implemented. This study was designed to systematically describe five community-based programs across the country that serve children with SED and their families, in terms of the children and their families who were served, interventions employed, and outcomes for the children over time. While a randomized clinical trial might be the best approach for evaluating the efficacy of alternatives to residential treatment, we determined that available resources and current instrumentation could not adequately support such a study. Consequently, we designed a systematic, descriptive study that would provide important information to the field and contribute to the knowledge base.

Data for the ARTS were collected from five selected programs located in different regions of the United States. Although site selection was not random, the authors did develop a set of criteria for selecting the five sites (see Figure 3.1 for a description of these sites). Programs were chosen because they espoused the Child and Adolescent Service System Program (CASSP) values of being child and family centered, community based, collaborative, and alternatives to institutional or hospital placement (Florida Mental Health Institute, 1989). Selected programs were mature and stable. These sites were nominated and described as state-of-the-art programs in a study conducted by the CASSP Technical Assistance Center at Georgetown University (Goldman, 1988; Stroul, 1988), as well as being recommended by a national advisory board working with the authors. The programs also consented to participate in an extended, labor-intensive training and research process. Finally, the authors sought both geographic and cultural diversity in the population served by the sites.

ARTS was implemented to answer some important questions in the field. These questions were: What are the characteristics of the children served in these programs? What are their social-service histories? What services are delivered in these programs? What happens to children in these programs over time in terms of their symptoms, cognitive and emotional functioning, and the restrictiveness of their living conditions? Baseline results from an initial subsample of subjects in the study have been published in an earlier document (see Duchnowski, Johnson, Hall, Kutash, & Friedman, 1993). In the following sections of this chapter, we present a description of the methodology, results from data collection at program entry compared to one year later, and a discussion of the implications for policy development.

Method

Procedure

All youth entering the selected programs were eligible for study recruitment if they were between 6 and 18 years of age, if it was their first entry into the program, and if they and their caregivers agreed to participate in ARTS within the first month of program entry. Data on intellectual functioning (IQ scores), academic performance, and emotional, behavioral, and family functioning were collected at entry to the study (baseline) and at 12 months after entry to the program. Data reflecting services received and residential and educational placements following program admission were collected at 6- and 12-month intervals. The research protocols were administered as interviews; that is, all instruments were read to respondents to control for possible reading deficits. All youth entering these programs were targeted for inclusion in the study by

Alaska Youth Initiative (AYI)

AYI is a statewide program that provides highly individualized services for youth placed in residential facilities within the state. These youth are typically in need of intensive services during stabilization within the residential setting and after discharge and are at risk of out-of-state placement (Burchard & Clarke, 1990).

Kaleidoscope

The Kaleidoscope program provides services to youth with emotional disabilities and their families. To gain admittance to the program a youth must live in inner-city Chicago, be at risk of removal from home, or have fared poorly or failed in traditional treatment programs (Stroul, 1989).

Pressley Ridge Youth Development Extension (PRYDE)

PRYDE is an intensive therapeutic foster care program (Hawkins, Meadowcroft, Trout, & Luster, 1985) operated by the Pressley Ridge Schools in several locations including Pittsburgh, PA, Baltimore, MD, and West Virginia. This program represents one of the most individualized and intensive models of therapeutic foster care described in the literature (Stroul, 1989). Typically, children and adolescents in this program previously have had multiple out-of-home placements; are not able to live with their families for a variety of reasons, including abuse and neglect or the child's own treatment needs; and would otherwise require residential treatment services.

Ventura System of Care

Ventura is an interagency initiative among the four major child service systems (mental health, juvenile justice, child welfare, and education) of Ventura County, California, established to decrease the use of residential treatment for children who have emotional disabilities and to redirect these children to community- and family-based services (Jordan & Hernandez, 1990).

Vermont New Directions

Vermont's New Directions program is a statewide initiative that uses a combination of state and federal dollars from the mental health, education, and social service systems to provide highly individualized services to Vermont's most needy youngsters. The purpose of this initiative is to expand services for children and youth who are experiencing emotional difficulties and who are either at risk for or currently placed in residential or psychiatric facilities (Santarcangelo, Birkett, & McGrath, 1995).

Figure 3.1. Description of ARTS sites.

the program's admissions/referral person and received a flyer containing information about the study and informed consent forms (which ensured the completely voluntary nature of the study). Both parents and youth were able to ask questions at that time, and those who returned a signed informed consent were contacted for an interview.

Participants

Data sources included the parent or caregiver, the youth, local professionals, and case records. Initially, 163 youth and parents or caregivers were interviewed. This sample was nearly equally distributed among sites, with each site representing between 15 and 23% of the pool. The sample was 66% male, with an average age of 14.1 years (SD = 3.1 years), and were of diverse racial/ethnic backgrounds (65% Caucasian, 14% African American, 11% Native American or Alaskan Native, 9% Latino, and 1% Asian Pacific Islander). The average IQ for this sample of youth was 84.24 (SD = 16.67, n = 162), ranging from a low of 48 up to 138.

For the purposes of this chapter, data on the 144 youth/caregivers who completed the measures for both baseline and 12-month follow-up are presented. At point of entry into the program, these youth presented emotional, behavioral, and social problems that were severe and indicated extensive multisystem service histories (Cascardi, Kutash, & Duchnowski, 1994). A majority of the youth (67%) had received prior residential mental health services an average of four times, and 61% of the sample had prior involvement with law enforcement and juvenile justice systems, with an average of eight known contacts ranging from an informal disposition to jail time. Foster care placements also had been common for many of these youth, in addition to assistance from the welfare and social services system (69% had a prior history of abuse/neglect, with 55% having been removed from the home an average of 2.1 times, with the first incident occurring at 8.5 years of age on average.) Nearly 80% had received special education services prior to program entry. Average age at onset of emotional or behavioral problems was reported to be 6.8 years, while the average age of first help/intervention was 8.7 years.

The majority (61%) of the youth were referred to these alternatives to residential treatment programs from more restrictive, out-of-home residential settings, such as hospitals, residential treatment centers, and correctional facilities (37%), regular foster care and protective shelter placements (11%), or Professional Foster Treatment Families (12%). The remaining participants (39%) were in homes with at least one parent or other relative. Sixty-three youth (44%) had a treatment plan goal to return to or remain with their natural/adoptive family, and 30 (21%) were in or planning for independent living situations. Regardless of living setting, 92 (64%) of the natural/adoptive families reported that they were involved to some extent in the treatment planning or services of the program during the first year.

Measures

Demographic Information and Past Services History

Demographic information and past history of services received were assessed via semistructured interviews (Research and Training Center for Children's Mental Health, 1991). This protocol was first developed for the National Adolescent and Child Treatment Study (NACTS; see Chapter 4, this volume) and has served as a comprehensive interview for obtaining fact-based information, such as ethnicity, family composition, and service history. These interviews were conducted with parents/caregivers and youth themselves at program entry.

Intelligence Quotient and Academic Performance

Upon entry into the programs, the IQ of youth in the ARTS study was assessed using the Slosson Intelligence Test (SIT; Slosson, 1984). However, if youth had been administered a standardized IQ test (e.g., full scale WISC-R) within the previous 24 months, that score was recorded instead. Academic performance was measured by the Slosson Oral Reading Test (Slosson, 1963) for reading and the math subscale of the Revised Wide Range Achievement Test (Jastak & Wilkinson, 1984) for math. The Slosson Oral Reading Test (SORT) yields only a raw score and achieved grade level, while the Revised Wide Range Achievement Test (WRAT-R) yields a raw and a standard score, as well as achieved grade level. A youth's expected grade based upon age was used as a gross measure of baseline grade level. This sample's performance on math and reading skills tests at baseline indicated that the majority were performing below their expected grade level based on age (90% below in math, 80% below in reading).

Measures of Functioning

A variety of functional dimensions were assessed: emotional and behavioral functioning and level of impairment, functional impairment and social competence, and family characteristics and functioning.

In regard to the emotional and behavioral functioning and level of impairment, the Child Behavior Checklist (CBCL; Achenbach, 1991a), completed by the parent or caregiver, and the Youth Self Report (YSR; Achenbach, 1991b) are frequently cited measures used to assess the presence and severity of a variety of emotional and behavioral problems of childhood and adolescence. Parents and youth rate the problem behaviors using the following: 0 = no problem/not true, 1 = sometimes/somewhat true, 2 = often/frequently true. Summary responses yield total, internalizing, and externalizing behavior problem T-scores; a T-score above 63 is considered to be in the "clinical range." The parent/caregiver also rates this domain using the Revised Behavior Problem Checklist (RBPC; Quay & Peterson, 1987), which further explicates problem areas such as "conduct disorder" (see also Hagborg, 1990; Quay, 1983) and uses similar anchor points.

Rosenberg's (1989) Self-Esteem Scale, administered to the youth, is a brief 10-item youth report of general self-worth, using a 5-point Likert-type scale (strongly agree to strongly disagree). Scores range from 10–50, with low scores reflecting low self-esteem. It was developed as a brief, practical measure of global self-esteem emphasizing ease of administration and economy of time. Reliability and validity data have been reported by Crandall (1973; e.g., when scored as a 10-item scale, the Rosenburg Self-Esteem Scale correlated .60 with the Coopersmith Self-Esteem Inventory).

To assess functional impairment and social competence, the 1990 version of the Child and Adolescent Functional Assessment Scale (CAFAS; Hodges, 1991; Hodges, Bickman, & Kurtz, 1992) was completed by a trained local professional after completing detailed interviews with both the parent/caregiver and the youth. The CAFAS is a brief, multidimensional measure of impairment in youth functioning that yields a score at one of four levels of impairment (0 = no impairment, 10 = mild, 20 = moderate, and 30 = severe impairment in functioning). Five of the seven subscales on this measure were used: Role Performance, Thinking, Behavior Toward Self and Others, Moods/Emotions, and Substance Use.

Social competence was assessed using the Social Skills Rating System (SSRS; Gresham & Elliott, 1990). Ratings of youth social competence and overall adaptive functioning in the areas of cooperation, assertion, responsibility, and self-control were obtained from both the parent/caregiver and youth. Ratings range from 0–2, with 0 indicating that social skills in the identified area were "never" observed and 2 representing "very often" observed.

To determine family characteristics and functioning, the Family Adaptability and Cohesion Evaluation Scale III (FACES; Olson, Portner, & Lavee, 1985) and the Impact on Family Scale (IOF; Stein & Riessman, 1980) were used. These scales were not given to youth or parents if the child lived outside of the natural family setting for the majority of the year. The FACES was completed separately by both parent and child to reflect their perceived view of their own "family." It is a 20-item, self-report Likert-type scale, with 1 = almost never and 5 = almost always. It provides adaptability and cohesion scores, each ranging from a low of 10 to a high of 50.

The IOF scale was developed to measure the effect of a child's illness on the family system in the following areas: economic burden, social/familial impact, subjective distress/personal strain, and mastery. Wording on a few items was modified from "medical/hospital" to "service/treatment" and from "illness" to "problems" in order to better address the concerns of our sample. It is a 24-item Likert-type scale, with 1 = strongly agree and 4 = strongly disagree. Raw summary IOF scores (recoded in the direction of low score representing low impact) range from a low score of 24 to a high of 96, and can be used to describe any changes in impact ratings over time.

Because both of these scales were designed for more natural family settings and not to describe the often difficult challenges faced by professional staff caring for youth, our sample size for family rating scales was noticeably reduced. Only 56 youth (39%) were living in homes with natural or adoptive families, thus family functioning and impact data will be presented on the 47 parents who rated the IOF and 44 matched pairs of parent and youth who rated the FACES at baseline and 12 months.

Service Utilization

Information about the services youth received while in the programs was collected via our semistructured Follow-Up Parent/Caregiver Interview (Johnson, Duchnowski, Hall, & Wilson, 1992), completed at 6 and 12 months postentry to cover each 6-month time frame indicated. For the purposes of this chapter, responses were grouped to reflect service use by category across the full year. This interview contained a list of 47 community and residential services from 11 different service sectors (see Table 3.1). Caregivers responded "yes" or "no" to receipt of each service unit within the specified time frame (12 months from admission to program). Complete data for use of these services and placements were available for 144 youth across the full year.

Residential Environment

This topic comprises three areas: frequency of changes, level of restrictiveness, and change over time. Data were collected from caregivers for each living situation (type and duration) that the youth experienced over the first 12 months. These living settings varied from "at home with natural parent(s)" to "in a corrections setting" to "runaway."

Each change in living situation/placement was counted, resulting in the "number of changes" experienced by the youth. Running away was counted as a change in living situation unless the youth did not return to some placement or home, at which point it was scored as missing data.

Also of relevance to samples of this nature is the "level of restrictiveness" of residential placements. Over 25 placement types originally presented to the caregivers were recoded into 10 categories ranked by level of restrictiveness, from least restrictive, such as "lives independently," to most restrictive, such as "jail." These 10 ordinal categories are a revision of the Restrictiveness of Living Environment Scale (ROLES; Hawkins, Almeida, Fabry, and Reitz, 1992). The 10 categories of living environments, how the environments are listed in the ROLES, and the categories generated at baseline and at the 6- and 12-month data-collection intervals are presented in Table 3.2.

Frequencies of changes to more and less restrictive placements will be presented. Additionally, mean ratings for overall change in restrictiveness scores will be reported from first to last placement in the 12-month time frame. In a few cases, youth were reported to have run away for various lengths of time. For our purposes, if youth were still on runaway status at the end of 12 months ($n = 3$), they were not included in the analysis.

Table 3.1

Broad-Range Categories for Service Units Surveyed
on the 6- and 12-Month Caregiver Follow-Up

Category	Service Types
1. Mental Health Nonresidential Services in the Community	Psychiatric Evaluation for Medications Medication for Nerves, Behavior, etc. Psychiatric Evaluation for Possible Hospitalization Psychological Evaluation Speech Therapy Individual Therapy Family Therapy Group Therapy Out Patient Drug/Alcohol Treatment
2. In-Home Mental Health Services	In-Home Crisis Intervention Home-Based Services/Therapy
3. Support for Supervised Independent Living	Supervision in an Independent Living Setting
4. Mental Health Residential Care	Crisis Stabilization Center Alcohol/Drug Treatment Center General Hospital Psychiatric Unit Private Nonprofit Psychiatric Hospital Private Psychiatric Hospital State Hospital Residential Treatment Center Therapeutic Group Home
5. Paraprofessional Support	Self-Help/Support Group Guardian Ad Litem Big Brother/Big Sister Parent Training (for natural caregiver) Recreational Services Child Care
6. General Social Services	AFDC Food Stamps SSI Medicaid WIC Utility Assistance (gas, electric, etc.) Transportation (excluding school bus) Homeless Services Housing Assistance

(continues)

Table 3.1 *Continued*

Category	Service Types
7. General Health Services	Visiting Nurse Medical Hospital/ER (nonpsychiatric) Community Health Center Private Doctor
8. Child Welfare Supportive Services	Welfare Services (Proactive Family Services) Abuse Investigation
9. Child Welfare/Foster Care Residential	Regular Foster Care Therapeutic Foster Care
10. Juvenile Justice Probation Services	Probation
11. Juvenile Justice Residential Care	Corrections Halfway House Training School Jail, Juvenile Hall

Restrictiveness of Educational Setting

Information about educational settings was requested from the parent/caregiver at 6 and 12 months after admission. On a case-by-case basis, using guidelines of "least restrictive environment" principles in federal special education laws, the investigators determined whether a child moved from a more restrictive to a less restrictive setting over a period of one year. Students graduating high school or educational programs were considered to have moved to less restrictive settings, while students who dropped out were considered to have moved in a more restrictive direction.

Results

Analysis Plan

Within-subject Time Effects were tested using Repeated Measures ANOVA, and resulting F values are presented. Because of multiple comparisons, a more stringent p value of less than .01 was used as a critical level of significance testing. Analyses were conducted on scale responses over 1 year for four domains: academic performance; emotional behavioral functioning and levels of impairment; functional impairment and social competence; and family characteristics and functioning. Each is discussed separately. Additionally, services data and

Table 3.2

Various Codings for Category of Residential Restrictiveness

Revised Category Score	Scoring for the Restrictiveness of Living Environment Scale (ROLES; Hawkins et al., 1992)	Initial ARTS Categories of Living Environment Just Prior to Program Admission	ARTS 6-, 12-, 24-Month Follow-up Categories for Living Environments
1	Independent Living by Self (0.5) Independently Living with Friend (1.5)		Independent Living Alone (1) Independent Living with Friends (2)
2	Home of Natural Parents, for 18 Year Old (2) Home of Natural Parents, for a Child (2) School Dormitory (2.0) Home of Relative (2.5) Adoptive Home (2.5) Home of Family Friend (2.5)	Two-Parent Home (1, 2, 3, 4, 5) One-Parent Home (6, 7, 8, 9) Living with Relatives (10)	Home with Biological parent (more than 18 years old) (3) Home with Biological parent (less than 18 years old) (4) School Dormitory (5) Home of Relative (6) Adoptive Home (7) Home of Family Friend (8)
3	Supervised Independent Living (3.5)	Supervised Independent Living (15)	Supervised Independent Living (9)
4	Regular Foster Care (4) Specialized Foster Care (4.5)	Regular Foster Care (14)	Regular Foster Care (10)
5	Individual-home Emergency Shelter (5) Foster-family-based Treatment Home (5) Group Home (5.5) Residential Job Corps Center (5.5)	Individual Home Emergency Shelter (17) Professional Parenting Staff (11): Therapeutic Foster Care; Foster-family Based Treatment Home; Group Home	Individual-home Emergency Shelter (11) Foster-family-based Treatment Home/TFC (12) Residential Job Corps Center (14)
6	Group Emergency Shelter (6) Residential Treatment Center (6.5)	Group Emergency Shelter (18) Residential Treatment Center (16) Residential School (16)	Group Emergency Shelter (15) Residential School (16)
7	Wilderness Camp (24 hour, year-round) (7) Medical Hospital (inpatient) (7.5)		Wilderness/Therapeutic Camp (17) Inpatient Medical Hospital (18)
8	Drug-alcohol Rehab Center (inpatient) (8) Intensive Treatment Unit (8.5)	Psychiatric Hospital/Wing/Unit (19)	Psychiatric Hospital (13) Inpatient Drug/Alcohol Center (19) Intensive Treatment Unit (20)
9	State Mental Hospital (9) Youth Correction Center (9) County Detention Center (9)	Sex Offender Treatment House (21) Youth Corrections (21) Detention (21)	State Psychiatric Hospital (22) Youth "Correctional" Center (23) Detention Center (21)
10	Jail (10)	Jail (24)	Jail or Prison (24)

Note: ARTS interviews also provided categories for Homeless (25) and DK or Runaway (99).

restrictiveness of living and educational settings for the first year after admission to programs are presented.

Attrition

Sample sizes varied across measures because of missing data for each assessment and loss of respondents over time; therefore, separate t-test analyses were performed to test for attrition effects. No significant effects were found between respondents who remained in the study and those who dropped out based on sex, age, and baseline scores, except on prescores for the CBCL [Total Problems $t(1,157) = 2.11$, $p < .05$; Internalizing $t(1,157) = 2.39$, $p < .05$] and the Quay RBPC [Socialized Aggression $t(1,157) = -2.11$, $p < .05$; Anxiety-Withdrawal $t(1,157) = 2.07$, $p < .05$]. On the CBCL, youth with complete data had significantly higher Time 1 T-scores (greater behavioral problems) than those without complete data on CBCL Total and Internalizing scales, as well as on the RBPC Anxiety-Withdrawal subscale. Additionally, those with complete data had significantly lower RBPC Socialized Aggression Time 1 T-scores (less behavior problems) than those without complete data.

Academic Performance

Results for academic performance over the first year are presented in Table 3.3. Both math and reading raw scores revealed small but significant gains; reading showed improvement in number of words read after one year, $F(1,114) = 31.20$, $p < .001$, and math showed improvement in number of correctly completed problems, $F(1,109) = 11.46$, $p < .01$.

Table 3.3

Average Scores for Academic Performance Over 1 Year

Scale	n	Time 1 (Baseline)		Time 2 (12 months)		F Value
		Mean Score	SD	Mean Score	SD	
WRAT-R[1] (Math) Raw	110	23.77	6.71	25.35	7.08	11.46*
SORT[2] (Reading) Raw	115	125.05	60.83	136.01	56.98	31.20**

[1]Revised Wide Range Achievement Test (Jastak & Wilkinson, 1984).
[2]Slosson Oral Reading Test (Slosson, 1963).
*$p < .01$.
**$p < .001$.

Measures of Functioning

Emotional Behavioral Functioning and Levels of Impairment

Based on Achenbach's cutoff for "clinical range" scores (T-score above 63), 79% of youth revealed behavior problems in the clinical range at Time 1 on Externalizing, 63% on Internalizing, and 86% on Total Problem Scale. The average scores for Time 1 and Time 2 on three measures of youth's emotional and behavioral problems and functioning are presented in Table 3.4. On the CBCL, total T-scores, $F(1,126) = 16.16, p < .001$); Internalizing scale scores, $F(1,126) = 9.09$, $p < .01$; and Externalizing scale scores, $F(1,126) = 16.35, p < .001$ improved from Time 1 to Time 2, as did youths' self-report of problem behaviors over time. Additionally, the RBPC revealed a significant effect over time for youth in the area of Conduct Disorder, $F(1,127) = 7.70 \ p < .001$, which reveals a decrease in reported problems in this area.

Functional Impairment and Social Competence

The average total score on the Child and Adolescent Functional Assessment Scale (CAFAS) significantly improved from Time 1 to Time 2, $F(1,129) = 27.99$, $p < .001$, as did scores on all individual scales except Substance Use. There were no significant changes from Time 1 to Time 2 on the SSRS (see Table 3.5).

Family Characteristics and Functioning

None of the measures of family functioning or impact of the disability on the family revealed a significant time effect (see Table 3.6). Both parent and youth rate adaptability and cohesion are on the lower end of these scales, and this does not appear to change over time. Similarly, a moderate rating of "impact on the family" is given at both points in time.

Service Use and Stability of Living and Educational Environments

The longitudinal data collected from caregivers at 6 and 12 months post-program entry on services received once a youth entered a program can be summarized in the following ways: number and category of various types of services used, living situation and level of restrictiveness of placement, and changes in overall level of restrictiveness of educational services received.

Number and Category of Various Types of Services Used

For the 47 service types across the full year, an average of 14 ($SD = 5.0$) different service types were reported as received. The number of services used by youth/families ranged from 3 to 29.

Table 3.4

Average Scores for Emotional Behavioral Functioning Over 1 Year

Scale and Subscale	n	Time 1 (Baseline)		Time 2 (12 months)		F Value
		Mean T-Score	SD	Mean T-Score	SD	
Behavior Problems						
CBCL[1] Total	127	71.80	8.18	68.31	10.40	16.16**
Internalizing		67.69	9.24	64.87	10.00	9.09*
Externalizing		71.22	9.38	67.44	10.73	16.35**
YSR[2] Total	121	61.00	10.86	56.96	11.52	16.25**
Internalizing		58.11	10.33	54.83	11.66	11.16*
Externalizing		61.74	12.08	57.92	11.45	12.65*
RBPC[3] Attention Problem	128	55.68	9.93	54.51	9.62	1.76
Anxiety-withdrawn		55.49	9.55	54.07	9.63	2.85
Conduct Disorder		56.22	8.99	54.09	8.58	7.70**
Motor Excess		55.10	10.05	53.41	8.76	4.11
Psychotic Behavior		52.67	9.36	52.34	9.18	0.19
Socialized Aggression		56.34	8.39	55.34	8.10	1.99
Self Rating						
Self-Esteem[4] Raw Score	120	35.99	6.50	37.14	7.29	3.08

[1]Child Behavior Checklist (Achenbach, 1991a).
[2]Youth Self Report (Achenbach, 1991b).
[3]Revised Behavior Problem Checklist (Quay & Peterson, 1987).
[4]Self-Esteem Scale (Rosenberg, 1989).
*$p < .01$.
**$p < .001$.

Use of services summarized across 11 broad-range categories is shown in Table 3.7; these data reflect multiple responses. Case Management services is not included in the categories because all youth who participated in the study received this service. As illustrated in Table 3.7, an overwhelming majority (90%) of youth used services in Category 1, Mental Health Nonresidential Community Services. General Social Services, Category 6, also were highly utilized (85% of youth/families). The least frequently used services were Mental Health Residential (38%), which included RTCs, hospitals, and short-term

Table 3.5

Average Scores for Functional Impairment
and Social Competence Over 1 Year

Scale and Subscale	n	Time 1 (Baseline)		Time 2 (12 months)		F Value
		Mean Score	SD	Mean Score	SD	
Functional Impairment						
CAFAS[1] Average Total	130	14.34	6.71	10.85	7.16	27.99**
Role Performance		20.31	11.34	14.92	10.73	22.90**
Thinking		11.46	10.35	8.23	9.52	9.92*
Behavior Self/Other		19.54	10.26	15.15	10.29	6.97**
Emotional Health		16.92	9.47	12.00	9.27	21.79**
Substance Use		3.46	7.34	3.92	8.58	0.36
Social Competence						
SSRS[2] Parent Total	101	80.57	15.34	83.07	14.02	3.30
Student Total	107	99.96	20.35	97.80	18.39	1.28

[1]Child and Adolescent Functional Assessment Scale (Hodges, 1991; Hodges, Bickman, & Kurtz, 1992).

[2]Social Skills Rating System (Gresham & Elliott, 1990).

*$p < .01$

**$p < .001$

crisis stabilization; Juvenile Justice (22% Probation and 23% Residential); Child Welfare Supportive Services (18%); and Supervision for Independent Living (15%). It should be noted that most families used services from multiple categories. The frequency of use of services from more than one category is as follows: two categories of services were used by 3 youth (2.2%), three categories were used by 8 youth (6%), four categories were used by 24 youth (17.9%), five categories were used by 31 youth (23.1%), six categories were used by 28 youth (20.9%), seven categories were used by 24 youth (17.9%), eight categories were used by 11 youth (8.2%), and nine categories of services were used by 5 youth (3.7%). Over half of the youth used services in six to nine service categories.

Living Situation and Level of Restrictiveness of Placement

Three areas of living environment were analyzed: frequency of changes over a year, level of restrictiveness, and change over time.

Table 3.6

Average Scores for Family Functioning/Impact Over 1 Year

Scale and Subscale	n	Time 1 (Baseline)		Time 2 (12 months)		F Value
		Mean Score	SD	Mean Score	SD	
FACES Family Rating[1]						
Parent	44					
Adaptability Index		24.14	5.51	24.82	6.82	.31
Cohesion Index		35.71	6.38	35.71	6.80	.00
Youth	44					
Adaptability Index		23.93	7.69	24.85	8.09	1.13
Cohesion Index		32.05	9.65	29.93	10.57	2.56
Impact on Family Rating[2]						
Parent—Raw Scores	47	57.21	12.55	56.26	12.56	.31

[1]Family Adaptability and Cohesion Evaluation Scale III (Olson, Portner, & Lavee, 1985) scores range from a low of 20 to a high of 100.

[2]Impact on Family (Stein & Riessman, 1980) scores range from low impact = 24 to high impact = 96.

The average number of changes in living setting over the year for this sample ($n = 144$) was 3.2 ($SD = 5.4$), ranging from 0 to 48 changes. The majority of youth (61%) had either no changes in setting (32% of the youth remained in the same living setting), changed setting only once (17%), or had two changes in settings (12%).

The levels of restrictiveness for these placements prior to program entry, at the start of the program, and at the end of the first year, are shown in Table 3.8. Each youth's placement setting was recoded to scores ranging from 1 to 10. These categories ranged from a score of 1, least restrictive (e.g., lives independently) to 10, most restrictive (e.g., jail). Overall change in average ratings for the 139 youth with complete data reveal a slight nonsignificant decrease, $F = 2.33(1,138)$, ns, in level of restrictiveness scores from their placement immediately prior to program entry ($M = 4.66$, $SD = 2.5$, $n = 139$) to their last placement in the 12-month time frame ($M = 4.26$, $SD = 2.2$).

To determine if youth moved to a more, less, or equally restrictive placement setting during the 12-month time frame, the movement from their placement prior to entering the program compared to their last living setting was examined.

Table 3.7

Use of Services by Youth and/or Their Families
as Part of Treatment Within ARTS Programs ($n = 144$)

Category of Service	Number of Youth Who Used the Services Over 12 Months (Percentage)
Mental Health Nonresidential Services in the Community	130 (90%)
In-Home Mental Health Services	74 (51%)
Support for Supervised Independent Living	22 (15%)
Mental Health Residential Care	55 (38%)
Paraprofessional Support	110 (76%)
General Social Services	122 (85%)
General Health Services	118 (82%)
Child Welfare Supportive Services	26 (18%)
Child Welfare/Foster Care Residential	79 (55%)
Juvenile Justice Probation Services	32 (22%)
Juvenile Justice Residential Care	33 (23%)

The majority of the youth (72%) either remained at the same level of restrictiveness (32%) or moved to a less restrictive environment (40%), with only 28% of the youth moving to a more restrictive environment.

Changes in Overall Level of Restrictiveness of Educational Services Received

The overall categorical change in level of restrictiveness of educational placement setting was assessed. By the end of the first year, 44 youth (31%) were in a less restrictive educational setting than where they had begun that year. Eighty youth (56%) remained in an educational setting of the same level of restrictiveness, while 18 (13%) were in a more restrictive setting.

Conclusion and Implications

In this study, a multimethod, multisource data collection procedure was used to describe the children and adolescents served by five innovative programs

Table 3.8

Frequency and Percentages of Youth in Each Level of Residential Restrictiveness at Various Times ($n = 144$)

Rating	Number of Youth in Each Level of Restrictiveness of Living Setting (percentage)		
	Immediately Prior to Program Entry	First Setting After Program Entry	Living Setting at End of 12 Months
1 (independent living)	0	1 (1)	6 (4)
2	53 (37)	34 (24)	37 (25)
3	2 (1)	14 (9)	14 (9)
4	15 (10)	6 (4)	5 (3)
5	16 (11)	60 (42)	59 (41)
6	29 (20)	11 (7)	5 (3)
7	0	0	0
8	12 (8)	2 (1)	2 (1)
9	11 (7)	13 (9)	12 (8)
10 (jail)	4 (3)	2 (1)	1 (1)
runaway, don't know	2 (1)	1 (1)	3 (2)

and their outcomes after a year of treatment. A rich and systematic description has emerged that contributes to the growing knowledge base on comprehensive service systems for children who have emotional disabilities and their families. In addition, we are encouraged that, in several instances, the answers to the questions that guided this study are consistent with the findings from other related investigations.

Who Are the Children Served and What Are Their Service Histories?

These programs serve youths who have multiple problems that are of long duration and severe in intensity. With an average age of 14 years at admission, 61% of the youth had previous contact with the juvenile justice system on the average of eight times. They had an average of four placements in mental health residential treatment centers, and only 39% entered the current program from their home. The youth were predominantly male (66%), evidenced a below-average intelligence score (84.24), and demonstrated poor academic performance. As such, the ARTS sample is very similar to the children in the National Adolescent and Child Treatment Study (NACTS, see chapter 2). It is described in chapter 4. The similarities of the ARTS sample to those of the other two samples is important because without randomization in these studies, generalization of the findings is limited. By demonstrating similar characteristics in children who are identified as SED in different parts of the country, at different time periods, and by different agencies, we can feel more confident that the interventions that improved outcomes in the ARTS sites may have similar positive effects in other places, because the children are similar in terms of their needs and problems.

In addition, prior involvement with the child welfare system was common. Sixty-nine percent of the families had worked with a child protection worker because of a charge of abuse or neglect. Fifty-five percent of the children in the study had been placed out of their home because of a charge of abuse. Clearly, this is a group of youngsters that was well known to the major child-serving agencies prior to placement in the ARTS programs.

The average age of problem onset was reported to be 6.8 years, while the average age at the time of the first service was 8.7 years. On the average, almost five more years would elapse before the children were placed in the current program, a time during which there were multiple contacts with various agencies. It is noteworthy that the lag between age of onset and the age when the first service was initiated is identical to that reported in NACTS. The NACTS data were collected in 1985, while the ARTS data were collected six years later, suggesting that systems of care for these children were still not implementing aggressive early identification and intervention strategies.

There was an unexpectedly low number (36%) of children who were living with their family at the time of program entry. As each of these programs valued family preservation, we had anticipated that we would observe extensive work with families. However, the high percentage of children in state custody and in out-of-home placements indicates that many of the children already were estranged from their families before entering the programs under study. This may have contributed to the finding that only 34% of the children were in the custody of a family member after 12 months in the program. Many of the children had not been involved with their family for a long time.

These two findings, the long delay before the receipt of services and the high number of out-of-home placements, may be related, as there are indications that the problems of these children tend to get worse over time and without adequate interventions, out-of-home placement becomes the only viable option in view of the duration and severity of the problem. The average child in this study began to display the signs of emotional problems before age seven. In the years that followed, their problems grew in intensity and complexity. Their contacts with multiple service agencies increased and, ultimately, they became part of the foster care system. Their level of emotional and behavioral impairment was extreme, and two thirds of the youth no longer had a family to whom they could return for support and nurturing. Failure to provide effective early intervention resulted in the development of a group of youngsters who had severe problems in their early teenage years, had become wards of the child welfare system, and who would have a high probability of experiencing continued difficulties and costly service needs as they transitioned into adulthood (see chapter 2). The toll for failing to support families with young children who are at risk is high in terms of human suffering, as well as in the actual cost to the public sector. If the service system continues at its present level of functioning, policymakers and planners can expect to have continued and long-term involvement with these youth that will probably escalate in intensity.

What Happens to Children in These Programs Over Time in Terms of Their Cognitive and Emotional Functioning and Living Conditions?

The results from measures of emotional and behavioral functioning (CBCL and YSR) and functional impairment (CAFAS) are very encouraging. Scores at the 12-month interval were significantly lower than at program entry, indicating a reduction in emotional problems and functional impairment. Results from the RBPC indicated improvement on the conduct disorder subscale. It is noteworthy that while scores on the CBCL are significantly lower after 12 months of treatment, the average remained within the clinical range, illustrating the extreme level of emotional problems experienced by these children. The average for the YSR, however, was below the clinical range at posttest.

Scores on measures of academic performance taken at the 12-month point also are encouraging. While the average achievement level may still be below expected grade level, average scores for both reading and math were significantly higher after 12 months. As stated previously, this group of children consistently has demonstrated poor academic outcomes (Epstein, Kinder, & Bursuck, 1989). Results from testing in these programs, however, indicate that children with SED can improve academic performance and reverse the downward spiral of increasingly poorer test scores. These results are more positive than those found in NACTS (see chapter 2), in which academic performance continued to decrease over time.

These findings offer further support for the need to have comprehensive, integrated programs for children with SED. The programs studied by Epstein and his colleagues (1989) and the programs in the NACTS study were, for the most part, one dimensional. That is, they were either school-based programs that addressed only academic deficits or psychiatric treatment programs with a weak academic component. In the ARTS study, programs were comprehensive and simultaneously addressed academic, cognitive, emotional, and social domains. Programs for children with SED need to recognize the multiple-problem nature of the children and develop integrated treatment plans in order to achieve positive outcomes.

All of the other scales, such as self-esteem and the SSRS, yielded results that showed trends in a positive direction over the 12 months, but the differences were not statistically significant. Likewise, the measures of family functioning and impact on family yielded nonsignificant differences, though they showed a trend toward improved status. The results from the latter two measures may have been influenced by the small number of families available to complete the scales.

During the year that we observed these programs, we found evidence that the typical trend of more restrictiveness of placement setting for children with SED (Wagner, 1995) can be abated. After 12 months, 72% of the children lived in settings that were equally restrictive or less restrictive than those at program entry. Likewise, 87% of the children were being educated in settings that were equally restrictive or less restrictive than the setting at program entry. Like the findings for academic functioning, the literature describes the typical progress of these children as moving in a less positive direction as time goes on (Weithorn, 1988). It is encouraging to find evidence of children who have severe levels of impairment and are able to improve or at least hold their own during the course of a year.

What Services are Delivered in These Programs?

These programs promoted the value of supplying "whatever it takes" in developing individual treatment plans, and, in support of this, we found 47 different types of service that the children and their families received in these programs. There were, on average, 14 types of service received in the first 12 months of treatment, and all of the children received case management. When we combined these 47 services into 11 categories (see Table 1), we found that 80% of the children and their families received services in four to seven different categories, indicating a wide range of strategies in the treatment plans developed in these programs. While these programs are considered innovative, it is noteworthy that the most frequently used category of service was traditional outpatient mental health, with 90% of all participants receiving this service. This is of interest, since some researchers have questioned the efficacy of office-based psychotherapy in community clinics with this population of children (see, for example, Weisz & Weiss, 1989). On the other hand, 76% of the children and families received some type of service from a paraprofessional. While the design of the ARTS study does not lead to causal interpretation, there is an interesting comparison between these results and those of the Vanderbilt study of school-based services reported in chapter 22 of this volume. While children in all groups in their study exhibited improvement, they found no differences in improvement between children who were treated by professionals and those children who were in the control group and given academic tutoring by paraprofessionals. The question of how much each of the categories of service contributes to improved functioning of children in treatment is an important issue, especially with the emergence of managed care.

In summary, the results of this study must be viewed in the context of several limitations. Generalization is limited by the lack of randomization in subject assignment or site selection. In addition, comparison groups were not employed. On the other hand, there are several features of the study that make the findings useful to both policymakers and researchers. Knapp (1995) has pointed out that, given our limited knowledge base, the evaluation of comprehensive, collaborative services for children and families may "best be understood through studies that are strongly conceptualized, descriptive, comparative, . . . and collaborative" (p. 5). Our aim was to systematically describe several programs that were considered to be exemplars of the system of care framework (Stroul & Friedman, 1986), which values child-centered, family-focused treatment. We have demonstrated that there are such program models that serve children who have very serious problems and that employ a wide array of services. After 12 months of treatment, we found some evidence of improved levels of functioning for these children.

The complexity of the service array presents a challenge for future researchers in specifying more adequately the role of the various categories of service and their respective contributions to the overall improvement in functioning of the children. Policymakers are challenged to continue the implementation of such models of service in order to increase the base from which accountability and efficacy can be adequately evaluated.

While we are encouraged by many of the findings, there are several points of concern. Inasmuch as only 19 children were discharged during the first 12 months of treatment, the need for relatively long term programs must be considered. A very high number of children remained in state custody, and 28% were arrested during the first 12 months of service. We feel that the long delay in implementing comprehensive services for these children and their families may contribute to the exacerbation of their difficulties and the challenges faced by programs that serve children with such serious levels of impairment across several modalities of functioning. This is clearly a time for states and communities to invest in early identification and intervention, a strategy that has been supported empirically and replicated frequently (see, for example, Walker, Colvin, & Ramsey, 1995). In this era of an increased focus on public sector accountability, one of the important questions posed to policymakers and elected officials may be "Why are you waiting so long to support families?"

Authors' Note

The authors may be contacted at the
Research and Training Center for Children's
Mental Health, University of South Florida,
Florida Mental Health Institute, 13301
Bruce B. Downs Blvd., Tampa, FL 33612.

References

Achenbach, T. M. (1991a). *Manual for the Child Behavior Checklist/4-18 and 1991 profile.* Burlington: University of Vermont, Department of Psychiatry.

Achenbach, T. M. (1991b). *Manual for the Youth Self Report and 1991 profile.* Burlington: University of Vermont, Department of Psychiatry.

Behar, L. B., Macbeth, G., & Holland, J. M. (1993). Distribution and costs of mental health services within a system of care for children and adolescents. *Administration and Policy in Mental Health, 20,* 283–295.

Burchard, J. D., & Clarke, R. T. (1990). The role of individualized care in a service delivery system for children and adolescents with severely maladjusted behavior. *Journal of Mental Health Administration, 17,* 48–60.

Burns, B. J. (1991). Mental health service use by adolescents in the 1970s and 1980s. In A. Algarin & R. M. Friedman (Eds.), *Third annual research conference proceedings, A system of care for children's mental health: Building a research base* (pp. 3–19). Tampa: Research & Training Center for Children's Mental Health, Florida Mental Health Institute, University of South Florida.

Burns, B. J., & Friedman, R. M. (1990). Examining the research base for child mental health services and policy. *Journal of Mental Health Administration, 17*(1), 87–98.

Cascardi, M., Kutash, K., & Duchnowski, A. J. (1994, October). *Service utilization patterns in community-based programs for children and their families.* Paper presented at the 122nd annual convention of the American Public Health Association, Washington DC.

Crandall, R. (1973). The measurement of self-esteem and related concepts. In J. P. Robinson & P. R. Shaver (Eds.), *Measures of social psychological attitudes* (pp. 45–167). Ann Arbor: University of Michigan Press.

Day, C., & Roberts, M. (1991). Activities of the Child and Adolescent Service System Program for improving mental health services for children and families. *Journal of Clinical Child Psychology, 20,* 340–350.

Duchnowski, A. J., & Friedman, R. M. (1990). Children's mental health: Challenges for the 90s. *Journal of Mental Health Administration, 17,* 3–12.

Duchnowski, A. J., Johnson, M. K., Hall, K. S., Kutash, K., & Friedman, R. M. (1993). The alternatives to residential treatment study: Initial Findings. *Journal of Emotional and Behavioral Disorders, 1,* 17–26.

Epstein, M. H., Kinder, D., & Bursuck, B. (1989). The academic status of adolescents with behavioral disorders. *Behavioral Disorders, 14*(3), 157–165.

Florida Mental Health Institute. (1989). Child and Adolescent Service System Program (CASSP): A fifth anniversary. *Update, 5*(1), 16–19.

Friedman, R. M. (1987). *Service capacity in a balanced system of services for seriously emotionally disturbed children.* Tampa: Florida Mental Health Institute.

Goldman, S. K. (1988). *Community-based services for children and adolescents who are severely emotionally disturbed: Crisis services.* Washington, DC: Georgetown Child Development Center.

Gresham, F. M., & Elliott, S. N. (1990). *Social Skills Rating System manual.* Circle Pines, MN: American Guidance Service.

Hagborg, W. J. (1990). The Revised Behavior Problem Checklist and severely emotionally disturbed adolescents: Relationship to intelligence, academic achievement, and sociometric ratings. *Journal of Abnormal Child Psychology, 18,* 47–53.

Hawkins, R. P., Almeida, M. C., Fabry, B., & Reitz, A. L. (1992). A scale to measure restrictiveness of living environments for troubled children and youths. *Hospital and Community Psychiatry, 43,* 54–58.

Hawkins, R. P., Meadowcroft, P., Trout, B. A., & Luster, W. C. (1985). Foster family-based treatment. *Journal of Clinical Child Psychology, 14,* 220–228.

Hodges, K. (1991). *Manual for the Child and Adolescent Functional Assessment Scale.* Unpublished manuscript.

Hodges, K., Bickman, L., & Kurtz, S. (1992). A multidimensional measure of level of functioning for children and adolescents. In A. Algarin & R. M. Friedman (Eds.), *Proceedings of the fourth annual research conference, A system of care for children's mental health* (pp. 149–154). Tampa: University of South Florida.

Institute of Medicine. (1989). *Research on children and adolescents with mental, behavioral, and developmental disorders: Mobilizing a national initiative.* Washington, DC: National Academy.

Jastak, S., & Wilkinson, G. S. (1984). *The wide range achievement test—revised administration manual.* Wilmington, DE: Jastak.

Johnson, M. K., Duchnowski, A. J., Hall, K. S., & Wilson, D. Z. (1992). Follow-up parent/caregiver services interview. Unpublished assessment. Tampa, FL: Research and Training Center for Children's Mental Health.

Jordan, D. D., & Hernandez, M. (1990). The Ventura Planning Model: A proposal for mental health reform. *Journal of Mental Health Administration, 17,* 26–47.

Kahn, A. J., & Kamerman, S. B. (1992). *Integrating services integration: An overview of initiatives, issue, and possibilities.* New York: National Center for Children in Poverty, Columbia University.

Kiesler, C. A., & Morton, T. L. (1988). Prospective payment system for inpatient psychiatry: The advantages of controversy. *American Psychologist, 43,* 141–150.

Knapp, M. S. (1995). How should we study comprehensive services for children and families? *Educational Researcher, 24*(4), 5–16.

Knitzer, J. (1993). Children's mental health policy: Challenging the future. *Journal of Emotional and Behavioral Disorders, 1*(1), 8–16.

Knitzer, J. (1982). *Unclaimed children: The failure of public responsibility to children and adolescents in need of mental health services.* Washington, DC: Children's Defense Fund.

Knitzer, J., Steinberg, Z., & Fleisch, B. (1990). *At the schoolhouse door: An examination of programs and policies for children with behavioral and emotional problems.* New York: Bank Street College of Education.

Olson, D. H., Portner, J., & Lavee, Y. (1985). *FACES III.* St. Paul: University of Minnesota, Family Social Science.

Pires, S. (1990). *Sizing components of care.* Washington, DC: Georgetown University Child Development Center.

Quay, H. C. (1983). A dimensional approach to children's behavior disorders: The Revised Behavior Problem Checklist. *School Psychology Review, 12,* 244–249.

Quay, H. C., & Peterson, D. R. (1987). *Manual for the Revised Behavior Problem Checklist.* Coral Gables, FL: University of Miami.

Research and Training Center for Children's Mental Health. (1991). Parent and child interviews. Unpublished assessment. Tampa, FL: Author.

Ribicoff, A. (1970). Foreword. In Joint Commission on the Mental Health of Children (Ed.), *Crisis in child mental health: Challenge for the 1970s* (pp. xv–xvi). New York: Harper & Row.

Rosenberg, M. (1989). *Society and the adolescent self-image* (Rev. ed.). Middleton, CT: Wesleyan University Press.

Santarcangelo, S., Birkett, N., & McGrath, N. (1995). Therapeutic case management: Vermont's system of individualized care. In B. Frisen & J. Poertner (Eds.), *Building on family strengths: Case management for children and youth with emotional, behavioral, or mental disorders* (pp. 301–316). New York: Paul H. Brookes.

Saxe, L., Cross, T., & Silverman, N. (1988). Children's mental health: The gap between what we know and what we do. *American Psychologist, 43,* 800–807.

Slosson, R. L. (1963). *Slosson Oral Reading Test.* East Aurora, NY: Slosson Educational.

Slosson, R. L. (1984). *Slosson Intelligence Test.* East Aurora, NY: Slosson Educational.

Stein, R. E. K., & Riessman, C. K. (1980). The development of an Impact-on-Family Scale: Preliminary findings. *Medical Care, 18,* 465–472.

Stroul, B. A. (1988). *Series on community-based services for children and adolescents who are severely emotionally disturbed: Home-based services.* Washington, DC: Georgetown University Child Development Center.

Stroul, B. A. (1989). *Series on community-based services for children and adolescents who are severely emotionally disturbed: Therapeutic foster care.* Washington, DC: Georgetown University Child Development Center.

Stroul, B. A., & Friedman, R. M. (1986). *A system of care for severely emotionally disturbed children and youth* (Rev. ed.). Washington, DC: Georgetown University Child Development Center, CASSP Technical Assistance Center.

U.S. Department of Education. (1995). *Seventeenth annual report to Congress on the implementation of the Education of the Handicapped Act.* Washington, DC: Author.

U.S. Office of Technology Assessment. (1986). *Children's mental health: Problems and services—A background paper.* Washington, DC: U.S. Government Printing Office.

Wagner, M. (1995). Outcomes for youths with serious emotional disturbance in secondary schools and early adulthood. *The Future of Children: Critical Issues for Children and Youth, 5*(2), 90–112.

Wagner, M., D'Amico, R., Marder, C., Newman, L., & Blackorby, J. (1991). What happens next? Trends in postschool outcomes of youth with disabilities. *Second comprehensive report of the National Transitional Longitudinal Study of Special Education Students.* Menlo Park, CA: SRI International.

Walker, H., Colvin, G., & Ramsey, E. (1995). *Antisocial behavior in school: Strategies and best practices.* Pacific Grove, CA: Brooks/Cole.

Weisz, J. R., & Weiss, B. (1989). Assessing the effects of clinic-based psychotherapy with children and adolescents. *Journal of Consulting and Clinical Psychotherapy, 57*(6), 771–746.

Weithorn, L. A. (1988). Mental hospitalization of troublesome youth: An analysis of skyrocketing admission rates. *Stanford Law Review, 40,* 773–838.

Characteristics of Children, Youth, and Families Served by Local Interagency Systems of Care

4

Kevin P. Quinn
and Michael H. Epstein

C hildren and youth in the United States evince serious emotional disturbance (SED) at rates ranging between 11 and 26% (Bird et al., 1988;
Brandenberg, Friedman, & Silver, 1987; Costello et al., 1988) with
approximately 3–6% considered seriously emotionally disturbed (Kauffman,
1993). The problems these young people experience have detrimental personal,
social, and financial effects on the individuals themselves, their families, and
their communities. The dropout rate of students identified by their schools as
SED exceeds 50% (U.S. Department of Education, 1994). Upon leaving school,
30–40% of these students fail to engage in further education, vocational training, or employment, and those who work typically do so part-time for minimum
wage (Edgar, 1987; Wagner, Blackorby, Cameto, Heebeler, & Newman, 1993).
Young persons with SED account for a significantly disproportionate percentage
of placements outside the home and community. Although only 9% of all students eligible for special education are identified as SED, students with SED
constitute more than 50% of all special education pupils placed in residential
treatment programs (U.S. Department of Education, 1992). More than half of all
students identified as SED are arrested within three to five years of leaving
school (Wagner et al., 1993). As many as 72% of the 2.2 million young people
referred to protective services each year due to abuse or neglect (American Association for Protecting Children, 1988) may be experiencing severe emotional or
behavioral problems (Trupin, Tarico, Low, Jemelka, & McClellen, 1993). Finally,
young people experiencing emotional or behavioral problems are highly likely to
endure markedly problematic adjustment throughout adulthood (Kazdin, 1985;
Loeber, 1982; Wagner et al., 1993).

The extensive problems experienced by young people with SED and their families bring them into contact with a variety of human service providers (e.g., special education, mental health; Epstein, Cullinan, Quinn, & Cumbald, 1994; Trupin et al., 1993). The disconcerting status of children and youth with SED and their families has led to careful reconsideration of traditional conceptualizations and provisions of these human services (Knitzer, 1993). Reports from the Joint Commission on Mental Health (1969) and the President's Commission on Mental Health (1978) are frequently credited with initiating the current momentum for reconsidering our approaches to serving these individuals. Both reports, as well as others that followed (e.g., Knitzer, 1982; Office of Technology Assessment, 1986), cited a severe shortage of mental health care for children and youth as well as the inappropriately restrictive nature of the limited services that were available.

In response to the reported problems experienced by young persons with SED and the system responsible for serving them, Congress in 1984 established the Children and Adolescent Service System Program (CASSP) within the National Institute of Mental Health (Day & Roberts, 1991). In the CASSP model, a comprehensive array of community-based services are developed among all relevant public and private human service providers (Stroul & Friedman, 1986). Case management is provided to ensure that services are coordinated and also to provide children, youth, and families with a single point of entry into the system (Behar, 1985). The model also emphasizes a family-centered approach that focuses on strengths and needs, provides families with services in a culturally competent manner, and engages families as equal partners in the development of service plans. As the CASSP model has developed, its proponents have increasingly stressed the concept of "individualized care." Individualized care refers to specially tailored, flexible services that are not limited by eligibility criteria, funding patterns, or other regulatory constraints and are provided unconditionally, regardless of the seriousness or complexity of the presenting problems (Burchard & Clarke, 1990; Katz-Leavy, Lourie, Stroul, & Zeigler-Dendy, 1992).

The CASSP system of care model was, and is still, offered as a work in progress, a reference point for ongoing, empirically driven system improvement (Stroul & Friedman, 1986). The critical need for empirically identified causal factors, risk predictors, and intervention options that will allow us to better understand and alleviate the debilitating emotional or behavioral problems of young people is well documented (Institute of Medicine, 1989; National Advisory Mental Health Council, 1991; Office of Technology Assessment, 1986). Precisely defining target populations has been a widely recommended first step in empirically determining which services work for which individuals under which conditions (Burns & Friedman, 1990; Kutash, Duchnowski, & Sondheimer, 1994; Quinn, Epstein, Cumbald, & Holderness, in press; Saxe, Cross & Silverman, 1988). Who are these young people requiring highly individualized, carefully coordinated, comprehensively intensive interagency services? What is the range of types, severity, and duration of emotional or behavioral problems they experience? What family structures and dynamics, both positive and negative, are related to these problems? What has been their pattern of interactions with local human service providers? Given that the long-term prognosis for children and youth with SED is quite poor, posing serious ramifications for themselves, their families, and their communities, responses to these questions are particularly vital.

Recently, some progress has been made in responding to the above unanswered questions. In particular, considerable information is now available on children or youth who are identified by their schools as SED. Studies currently being conducted by SRI International (i.e., the National Longitudinal Transition Study of Special Education) have provided extensive data on individual and family characteristics, independent functioning, social experiences, school programs, characteristics and outcomes, employment characteristics, postsecondary participation, related service availability, and parental expectations (Marder, 1992; Valdes, Williamson, & Wagner, 1990).

Data on children, youth, and families served in other components of the system of care have only just begun to emerge in the professional literature. For example, Wells and Whittington (1993) reported the demographic characteristics, family functioning, and previous service use of a sample of children and youth treated in one private, not-for-profit residential mental health facility. Further, they compared the demographic and family characteristics of their sample to those of other clinical and nonclinical populations. Singh, Landrum, Donatelli, Hampton, and Ellis (1994) described the sociodemographic, treatment history, psychological, and educational characteristics of young people admitted to a public child and adolescent psychiatric hospital over a 1-year period. In a follow-up to that study, Landrum, Singh, Nemil, Ellis, and Best (1995) examined essentially the same characteristics in young people in five Virginia communities who were either at imminent risk of, or currently returning from, residential placement and so were targeted to receive coordinated, community-based, interagency services. Epstein et al. (1994) investigated the characteristics of young people served in five model community-based programs located throughout Illinois. Similarly, but with a national scope, the family characteristics and functioning, intellectual ability and academic achievement, and emotional and behavioral problems and competence of young people with SED being served in five state-of-the-art community-based programs were examined through the Alternatives to Residential Placement Study (ARTS) (Duchnowski, Johnson, Hall, Kutash, & Friedman, 1993). In California, Barber, Rosenblatt, Harris, and Attkisson (1992) analyzed the individual, familial, and social correlates of the emotional or behavioral problems experienced by children and youth served by a local mental health program, and Rosenblatt and Attkisson (1992) described children and youth served in coordinated systems of care in three different counties. Evans, Dollard, and McNulty (1992) identified characteristics that differentiated between youth with SED receiving intensive case management who abused alcohol or drugs and those who did not. Zeigler-Dendy (1989) surveyed key mental health personnel in each state about young people with emotional disturbance, obtaining information on more than 41,000 children and youth.

Taken together, these data make a valuable contribution to our understanding of the characteristics of children and youth specifically in need of local, interagency system-of-care services. Yet two facets of these studies also limit the confidence with which we can generalize their findings to all children and youth in need of system-of-care services. First, several of the studies examined the characteristics of young people served in a single component of the overall system, either education (e.g., Marder, 1992; Valdes et al., 1990) or mental health (Singh et al., 1994; Wells & Whittington, 1993). Whether or not their findings are indicative of young people served across other system components remains a question. Second, only four of the studies presented data collected on young people actually being served by local, interagency systems of care (i.e., Duchnowski et al., 1993; Epstein et al., 1994; Landrum et al., 1995; Rosenblatt & Attkisson, 1992). Caution must be taken in generalizing their findings to other communities.

By definition, young people in need of system-of-care services present the most intense, complex challenges. If local communities are to successfully provide highly individualized, carefully coordinated, interagency services, they will need to thoroughly understand the individuals to whom they are making this very serious, highly challenging commitment. The purposes of this chapter are (a) to detail procedures that stakeholders in local systems of care can follow to identify the pertinent characteristics of the children, youth, and families targeted for collaborative interagency services; (b) to review the findings of one community that implemented the procedures; (c) to review their findings in relationship to the characteristics identified in other communities; and (d) to discuss the implications these findings have for the system-of-care model and future research efforts.

Method

Setting

The data presented here were collected in a large suburban county outside of Chicago. Of the estimated 800,000 people living in the county, approximately 226,500 were 21 years old or younger, and 163,000 were school age (i.e., between the ages of 5 and 18). An estimated 8.5% of the total school-age population, or approximately 14,000 students, received special education services. Roughly 12.5% ($n = 1,750$) of all special education students were school-identified as seriously emotionally disturbed (SED). The county's population was predominantly white. Latinos (8.3%) and African-Americans (2.5%) constituted the largest minority groups. In 1990, county youth accounted for 311 separate psychiatric hospitalizations, and well over 100 children and youth entered long-term residential placement. Mental health, child welfare, and juvenile justice agencies and the school system all contributed to these placements.

Prior to data collection, an interagency group had been formed in the county to address the needs of children and youth with SED. The mission of this group was to bring together individuals and organizations to plan, develop, and provide services to county children and adolescents with SED and their families (see Cumbald, Petersen, Quinn, & Epstein, 1994). Membership included comprehensive representation from public and private providers, parents, and other concerned community groups. The group's composition, purposes, and principles of care were consistent with those of the CASSP system-of-care model.

The data reported here were collected as one component of a comprehensive needs assessment conducted by an interagency group in order to collectively evaluate their current practices and make informed system development decisions (see Epstein, Quinn, Cumbald, & Holderness, in press). One part of the needs assessment was an archival review of the case records of the young people currently being served by the various service providers composing the group. Identifying the specific characteristics of the individuals for whom system-of-care services were intended or provided was identified by the interagency group as a necessary first step to their gaining a thorough understanding of current system functioning. The archival review component of the needs assessment was designed to provide this information and resulted in the data reported here.

Participants

Identifying the general types of youngsters and families for whom the interagency group was interested in providing collaborative services was necessary prior to conducting the archival review. Not all the children, youth, and families in the system required intensive interagency collaboration and services. Thus, it was important to establish parameters for the children and families to be studied and ultimately served through the interagency program.

An interagency subcommittee drafted a target population definition. Target population definitions were obtained from nationally recognized system-of-care model programs and from each of the local agencies. The model program definitions provided a guide, and the local definitions ensured consideration of the local agencies' respective service populations. The target population definition the group eventually agreed upon identified the children and families targeted for interagency and system-of-care services, and also ensured that some individuals served by each agency met the delineated parameters (see Figure 4.1). Using the definition as a guide, representatives from the participating public agencies nominated 238 children and youth for inclusion in the archival review: 45 from child and family services, 65 from mental health, 89 from juvenile justice, 5 from alcohol and substance abuse, 8 from rehabilitation services, and 26 from the schools.

A child or adolescent referred to the Partnership for Family Preservation is at major risk for failing to develop the emotional, behavioral, academic, and vocational skills required by society to become an independent, self-sufficient adult and whose service needs are complex, requiring service coordination or interagency collaboration to foster growth. The child or adolescent is one who:

1. is a county resident;

2. is 21 years of age or younger and is currently being served by an agency represented by the Partnership for Family Preservation;

3. exhibits behaviors that:

    1. result in a serious diagnosis as measured by the current DSM III-R; or

    2. fall into one or more of the following categories:

        • severely impaired social, academic, and self-care functioning (grossly inappropriate and bizarre behavior or emotional reactions that are frequently inappropriate to the situation); or

        • serious, long-term management problems or conduct disorders, including extreme hyperactivity, impulsiveness, aggressiveness, or substance abuse; or

        • serious discomfort from anxiety, depression, irrational fears, and concerns including serious eating and sleeping disturbances, extreme sadness of suicidal proportion, maladaptive dependence on parents, persistent refusal to attend school or avoidance of nonfamilial social contact; or

        • seriously impaired contact with reality (e.g., confused thinking);

4. has impaired functioning that has the duration of at least 1 year or is of short duration and high intensity or danger.

5. is currently in a restrictive school, living, or treatment environment or is at risk of being separated from home or community because of:

    1. imminent placement in a more restrictive school living or treatment environment; or

    2. chronic family factors, such as the primary caretaker suffers from mental illness, the family is unable to meet the child's basic or emotional needs, the child is threatened or in danger of being harmed, or there has been documented child abuse or neglect;

6. has special-service needs that may

    1. include a history of multiple agency involvement over at least 1 year; or

    2. require the coordination of two or more service systems or agencies.

Figure 4.1. Children and adolescents network target population definition.

Data Collection

The archival review involved a systematic, retrospective analysis of the nominated individuals' case records. A three-tiered, multiple-gating system was used whereby the characteristics of fewer, more highly at-risk individuals were more closely scrutinized at each successive level. The three-tiered system is described in detail below.

Tier One: Demographic Information

On tier one, descriptive data were collected from the case records of the 238 nominated children and youth using the Population Demographics Overview (PDO) form. The data gathered on tier one were organized into three general categories: child and youth characteristics, family characteristics, and service utilization history. Descriptive data on child/youth characteristics included standard demographic information (e.g., age, sex, race) and each child's status with regard to the respective participating agencies. For example, information was gathered on activities provided by school (i.e., special education status, attendance, course failures, suspensions/expulsions), mental health (i.e., DSM III-R diagnosis, medication use), juvenile justice (i.e., adjudication history and status), child welfare (i.e., current guardianship), and alcohol and drug abuse (i.e., involvement with illicit substances). Descriptive family characteristics of interest included marital status, family configuration, employment status, public assistance eligibility, and familial history of mental illness, substance abuse, criminal activity, and family violence. Service utilization history involved documenting the various agencies these young people and families had contacted and recording the number and types (e.g., youth home, foster care, psychiatric hospital, residential facility) of placements and services.

Population demographic data were collected on the 238 nominated young people by three data collectors. A second reviewer independently collected reliability data for 33% of the examined files. Each time reliability data were collected, the two data collectors compared results to ensure that any systematic errors did not go uncorrected in future reviews. Collection of reliability data was evenly distributed over the course of data collection and reviewers. Item by item reliability percentages, calculated by dividing agreements by agreements plus disagreements and then multiplying by 100, ranged from a low of 75% for medication history to a high of 100% for demographic information. Reliability percentages for the remainder of the items fell between 86 and 98%.

Tier Two: Risk Factor Analysis

Each of the participating agencies nominated children and youth to be examined on tier two. Given the final archival review case list (i.e., those cases reviewed on tier one), each agency identified 15–20% of the children and youth with whom they worked, whose behaviors and circumstances they perceived to be the most complex, and who presented them with the greatest service challenges.

On tier two, quantitative data were gathered on the occurrence or non-occurrence of 21 specific behaviors (e.g., self-injury, fire-setting) that when evinced place children and youth at risk for placement outside their homes and communities (Burchard & Schaefer, 1992). Using the operational definitions Burchard and Schaefer (1992) developed for these behaviors, the case records targeted for review were assessed following these procedures: (a) determine whether or not the behavior in question was part of the presenting problem for this particular youngster, and (b) if so, determine the relative contribution of this behavior to the youngster's presenting problem or placement outside the home or community. The relative contribution of various behaviors to the youngster's overall presenting problem was estimated using a five-point Likert scale. Reliability data were independently collected on 50% of the reviewed records. Item by item interrater reliability percentages, calculated by dividing agreements by agreements plus disagreements and multiplying by 100, ranged from 83–100% with a mean of 91%.

Tier Three: Case Studies

From the list of individuals whose case records were reviewed on tier two, each agency identified one or two young people using the following criteria: (a) the child was or had recently been in residential placement, (b) at least one of the child's parents was willing to be interviewed regarding experiences with the local system of care, (c) the child was willing to be interviewed regarding experiences with the local system of care; and (d) the child and family were judged by the agency to be one of the most complex to whom they provided service. A total of eight young people were nominated.

The case studies consisted of another, more meticulous review of case records and in-depth separate interviews with the parents and child regarding their experiences with the local system of care. First, another more detailed archival data-collection instrument was designed that allowed data collectors to systematically gather case record data on the nominated children and youth, their families, and their respective interactions with the system of care. The instrument allowed for collection of information on demographics, presenting behaviors, significant life events, contacts with service providers, and the restrictiveness of residential and educational placements. The veracity of the information taken and recorded from the files for the case studies was enhanced by having both the case worker closest to the child or youth and family as well as the parents corroborate its accuracy. Second, semistructured individual interviews were conducted with seven of the eight nominated youth and at least one of their parents. A semistructured interview was used to ensure consistent data collection across interviewees and to provide for respondent elaboration (Lincoln & Guba, 1985; Miles & Huberman, 1994). The interviews consisted of a set of open-ended questions and in general focused on the individual principles on which the system of care paradigm is based.

Prior to conducting interviews, data collectors demonstrated proficiency with the audiotaping equipment, practiced their interviewing techniques on one another and with the principal researcher, conducted an interview with a volunteer parent not involved in the study, and carefully reviewed their experiences regarding these tasks with the principal researcher. A fidelity checklist of important interviewer behaviors and skills was developed, and mastery of each was required before interviewing for these case studies took place.

When completed, tier three provided a qualitative assessment of the pathways these children and youth had traveled to placement outside the local community. A series of longitudinal, multiaxial timelines were used to display a chronology of these individuals' presenting problems, significant life events, involvement with each source of care in the community, and the combined cost for the various configurations of services provided at a given time (Burchard & Schaefer, 1992). The resulting timelines were then used to provide the context for the separate child and family interviews. Together, these timelines and interviews provided detailed information on the patterns of service use characteristic of these young people and their families.

Results

Population Demographics Overview

Three categories of demographic information were collected for each individual in the sample: child and youth characteristics, family characteristics, and previous service use. Below, descriptive statistics are presented separately for each category of demographic information. In addition, patterns of placement history (correctional institution, psychiatric hospital, foster care, residential mental health, group home, relative/friend) among the participants were examined.

Child and Youth Characteristics

Descriptive statistics for children and youth ($N = 238$) characteristics are displayed in Table 4.1. The nominees' average age was approximately 15 years. Seventy-five percent were male, and just over 75% were white. Despite possessing average-range intelligence scores, a significant proportion of these young people had experienced difficulty in school, including course failures (27%) and grade retention (14%). Approximately 80% of the children were school-identified special education students, and the majority of these were identified as SED. Approximately one third of this sample had been prescribed medication as a result of their presenting problems. Mood disorder was the

(text continues on page 92)

Table 4.1
Characteristics of Nominated Children and Youth

Age (100%)[a]	**Mean** = 15.3 (**SD** = 2.9)

YEARS OLD

11 and younger	5.1%
12–13	13.8%
14–15	24.4%
16–17	40.4%
18–19	16.4%

Sex (100%)

Male	74.8%
Female	25.2%

Race (98.3%)

Caucasian	77.3%
African American	9.7%
Latino	8.4%
Asian	0.8%
Other	3.8%

IQ (WISC-R) (38.7%)

Full Scale, Mean = 93.9 (SD = 17.7)

Range	57–137

CATEGORICAL DISTRIBUTION

High (116 and above)	10.9%
Average (85–115)	53.0%
Low (84 and below)	35.9%

Failed Courses (100%)	Yes = 26.9%
Retained in Grade (100%)	Yes = 14.0%

Primary Educational Disability (43%)

Behavior Disordered/SED	91.2%
Mental Retardation	4.9%
Learning Disabilities	3.9%

Secondary Educational Disability (20%)

Learning Disabilities	72.3%
Behavior Disordered/SED	12.8%
Speech/Language Disorders	8.5%

(*continues*)

Table 4.1 *Continued*

Medication (100%)

Yes = 30.3%
No = 69.7%

DSM Diagnoses

AXIS I—CLINICAL SYNDROMES (62.6%)	PERCENTAGE
Depression	31.0%
ADHD	12.5%
Conduct Disorder	11.5%
Oppositional Defiant	6.1%
Posttraumatic Stress Syndrome	5.4%
Dysthymia	5.4%
Bipolar	2.1%
Other	25.7%

AXIS II—DEVELOPMENTAL DISORDERS, PERSONALITY DISORDERS (24.0%)

Personality Disorder	11.5%
Oppositional Defiant	10.1%
Developmental Disorders, Pervasive	7.8%
Borderline Personality	6.9%
Developmental Disorders, Specific	6.7%
Borderline Intellect	3.4%
Mental Retardation	3.4%

AXIS III—PHYSICAL CONDITIONS (15.0%)

Asthma and allergies	3.0%

AXIS IV—SEVERITY OF PSYCHOSOCIAL
STRESSORS (30.3%)

Mean = 3.6 (indicates moderate to severe stress)

AXIS V—GLOBAL FUNCTIONING (30.7%)

MEAN = 36.2 (INDICATES MAJOR IMPAIRMENTS IN
SEVERAL AREAS)

EVER ADJUDICATED (100%)

Yes = 68%
No = 32%

TOTAL ADJUDICATIONS (42%)	Mean = 2.0, Median = 1
	(continues)

Table 4.1 *Continued*

CURRENT ADJUDICATION STATUS (42%)	PERCENTAGE
Probation[b]	36.0%
Neglect[c]	13.0%
Supervision[b]	12.4%
Minor Requiring Authoritative Intervention[b,d]	10.6%
Intensive Probation[b]	9.3%
Abuse[c]	6.8%
Other[b,c]	11.8%

[a]Number in parentheses, percentage of $N = 238$ on which data were available on this variable.

[b]Juvenile justice agency.

[c]Child welfare agency.

[d]A less intrusive form of supervision for young people whose behavior patterns (e.g., running away from home, staying out past curfew, skipping school) indicate lack of control by their families but not necessarily specific acts of lawbreaking. In this status, detention by the court may result if further instances of the out-of-control behavior occur.

most prevalent diagnosis (40%) among those individuals who had been classified on Axis I of DSM-III-R, while disorders involving social conflicts (e.g., conduct disorder, oppositional defiance) were second most frequent (18%).

Either as a result of their own criminal conduct or their exposure to abuse or neglect, more than two thirds of these children and youth had been adjudicated in the juvenile courts. Almost half of these young people had been on some form of probation, whereas 20% had been adjudicated as neglected or abused. The average number of adjudications across all 238 individuals in the sample was 2.0 per person.

Family Characteristics

Descriptive statistics for family characteristics appear in Table 4.2. An intact nuclear family structure was characteristic of fewer than one third of the families in this sample, with divorce (46%) being the primary reason for families dissolving, Approximately half of these young people lived with one or both parents. Parental rights had been qualified in over 50% of these families due to contact with either the child welfare system (25%) or juvenile courts (32%). More than 60% of fathers and just less than 50% of mothers were employed full time, whereas just over 40% of these families received public assistance of some kind. A significant percentage of these families evidenced histories of mental illness, substance abuse, and criminal behavior that are widely believed to put children at risk for poor adjustment.

(text continues on page 94)

Table 4.2
Characteristics of Families of Nominated
Children and Youth

Parent Marital Status (94%)[a]	Percentage
Divorced	46.0%
Married	29.5%
Never married	12.5%
Separated	6.3%
Widowed	5.4%

With Whom Child Lives (94%)

Mother	23.8%
Both parents	21.3%
Residential	12.8%
Blended	11.9%
Foster	6.4%
Father	5.5%
Relative	5.5%
Adoptive	4.7%
Group Home	3.4%
Other	4.7%

Number of Siblings (100%)   Mean = 2.4, Range = 0–11

Conservatorship/Guardianship (93%)

County (juvenile justice)	31.5%
Both parents	25.2%
State (child welfare)	22.5%
Mother only	14.0%
Relative only	5.0%
Father only	1.8%

Receiving Public Assistance (100%)

Yes	41.6%
No	59.4%

Mother's Employment Status (87.8%)

Full-time	48.3%
Unemployed	19.6%
Homemaker	17.7%
Employed part time	6.7%
Other	6.7%

(continues)

Table 4.2 *Continued*

Father's Employment Status (79.0%)

Full-time	62.4%
Unemployed	10.1%
Other	27.5%

Family History (98%)

Mental illness	36.3%
Alcohol or drug abuse	61.5%
Criminal activity	26.1%
Family violence	58.9%

[a]Number in parentheses, percentage of $N = 238$ on which data were available on this variable.

Previous Service Use

In Table 4.3, descriptive statistics on the services previously used by these young people are presented. Special education services (79%), juvenile justice services (63%), and mental health services (57%) were all accessed by more than half the children and youth in this sample, and child welfare had served just over 45% of these children, youth, and families. Approximately 88% of these children and youth had been placed outside their homes at least once, and they averaged four separate placements in two distinct types of settings.

Patterns of Placement

Cluster analysis (Anderberg, 1973; SAS Institute, 1994) was applied to placement data (correctional institution, psychiatric hospital, foster care, residential mental health, group home, relative/friend) to discern whether an identifiable pattern of placements outside the home existed among the participants. Only children and youth aged 9–20 years were included in the analysis of placement patterns because they constituted 95% of the participants ($N = 226$). Because the distribution of black, Hispanic, Asian, and other participants by age and sex was extremely uneven, cluster analysis focused solely on white participants aged 9 to 20. Age group distribution for these 176 individuals (age in months, $M = 189.9, SD = 24.8$) was: 9–11 years, $n = 9$; 12–14 years, $n = 42$; 15–17 years, $n = 106$; and 18–20, $n = 19$. Females made up 26% ($n = 45$) of the group, and age groups did not differ significantly by sex.

Using the JMP hierarchical clustering procedure, participants were placed together according to the similarity of their placement histories. Initially, all of the 176 participants began as their own cluster, with the extent of their relationships to one another determined by their respective contacts with the six

Table 4.3

Services Utilized by Nominated Children and Youth

Kind of Service Ever Used (100%)[a]	Percentage
Special education	78.6%
Juvenile justice	63.0%
Mental health	57.1%
Child welfare	45.8%
Public aid	35.2%
Alcohol and substance abuse	17.2%
Other	59.7%

Out-of-Home Placements (100%)

Yes	87.8%
No	12.2%

Kind of Placement	Percentage of all placements	Percentage of youths placed[b]
Psychiatric hospital	34.0%	61.8%
Correctional institution	21.0%	36.6%
Foster care	17.5%	25.6%
Residential mental health	11.0%	27.7%
Group home	10.0%	20.2%
Family friend or relative	5.0%	13.0%
Independent living	0.5%	1.3%
Other	1.0%	1.7%

[a]Number in parentheses, percentage of $N = 238$, on which data were available on this variable.

[b]Percentages sum to more than 100% because of multiple placements.

placement variables. The two most closely related clusters were then combined into a new cluster, yielding 175 clusters. This step was repeated, resulting in one fewer cluster each step and eventually providing one final cluster.

The six steps leading up to the final cluster (i.e., cluster solutions two, three, four, five, six, and seven) were examined; the five-cluster solution (see Table 4.4) provided the most statistically significant, conceptually consistent interpretation. Few placements of any kind characterized Cluster 1. Cluster 2 placements were predominantly to a psychiatric hospital, and Cluster 3 placements were primarily to a correctional institution. To a moderate extent, participants composing Cluster 4 had a history of relative/friend and psychiatric hospital placements. Participants in Cluster 5 had a considerable history of foster care placements, and a moderate history of psychiatric hospital, group home, and residential mental health placements.

Table 4.4

Standardized Means and Standard Deviations of Prior Placement Frequency, by Cluster and by Six Placements

Cluster	n	Correctional Institution		Psychiatric Hospital		Residential Mental Health		Foster Care		Group Home		Relative/Friend	
		M	SD	M	SD	M	SD	M	SD	M	SD	M	SD
1	90	0.49	0.74	0.83	0.96	0.34	0.64	0.03	0.18	0.12	0.36	0.01	0.11
2	32	0.03	0.18	3.34	1.33	0.00	0.00	0.03	0.18	0.00	0.00	0.00	0.00
3	13	4.08	1.32	0.69	0.75	0.85	0.90	0.00	0.00	0.23	0.44	0.08	0.28
4	17	0.53	1.23	1.18	1.29	0.47	0.51	0.65	1.06	0.12	0.33	1.59	0.87
5	24	0.75	1.19	1.42	1.56	1.08	0.97	2.75	1.26	1.25	1.07	0.25	0.44

The participants composing these five clusters were then compared on the personal, family, and risk variables. Variables on which the clusters did not differ significantly included age group, DSM diagnostic grouping, IQ, parent marital status, maternal employment, mental illness risk, substance abuse risk, criminal convictions risk, within-family violence risk, or total risks. Variables on which the clusters differed significantly included gender, $\chi^2(4, N = 176) = 14.28, p < .006$; DSM status, $\chi^2(4, N = 176) = 22.89, p < .001$; medication, $\chi^2(4, N = 176) = 26.59, p < .001$; adjudications, $F(4,171) = 9.69, p < .001$; living arrangement, $\chi^2(12, N = 168) = 58.53, p < .001$; and public assistance, $\chi^2(4, N = 176) = 27.43, p < .001$.

Follow-up analyses identified which clusters differed on which variables. Female participants and those with a DSM diagnosis were overrepresented in Cluster 2 (psychiatric hospital placements). Participants on medication were disproportionately represented in Cluster 2 and underrepresented in Cluster 3 (correctional placements). Number of adjudications were significantly higher for participants in Cluster 3 than those in all other clusters. Also, adjudications for individuals in Cluster 1 (few placements) exceeded those for individuals in Cluster 2. Youth with a history of "least restrictive living arrangements" were significantly more likely to be in Cluster 2 and unlikely to be in Cluster 5 (multiple placement types). Histories of "somewhat restrictive living arrangements" appeared disproportionately in Cluster 4 (relative/friend, psychiatric hospital). A "restrictive living arrangement" history was also significantly characteristic of participants in Cluster 4. Histories of "most restrictive living arrangement" were disproportionately represented in Cluster 5 and disproportionately absent from Cluster 4. Participants with families on public assistance were especially likely to be in Cluster 1 and unlikely to be in Cluster 5.

Behavioral Characteristics

A complete list of the behaviors on which data were collected as well as mean scores (i.e., a measure of frequency and intensity) and standard deviations for each behavioral risk variable is presented in Table 4.5. Principal components factor analysis with varimax rotation was used to further analyze the data. Initial factor analysis indicated that 7 of the 21 behaviors (i.e., running away, sexual acting out, sexual abuse or assault, fire-setting, cruelty to animals, peer interactions) did not contribute to the factor structure (i.e., had factor loadings below .3). These items were dropped from subsequent analyses. The remaining items provided a statistically significant, conceptually relevant three-factor solution. Together, the three factors accounted for 59% of the variance. The first factor, labeled externalizing aggressive, accounted for 27% of the variance; the second factor, labeled externalizing nonaggressive, accounted for 17% of the variance; and the third factor, labeled intrapersonal, accounted for 15% of the variance. The items composing the factors and their respective factor item loadings are presented in Table 4.6.

Table 4.5

Means and Standard Deviation of Behaviors
That Predict At-Risk Status

	M	SD
Physical Aggression	3.67	0.95
Extreme Noncompliance	3.53	1.26
Peer Interactions	3.38	0.87
Extreme Verbal Abuse	3.29	1.27
Anxious	3.12	1.4
Sad	2.68	1.58
Life Threat	2.68	1.51
School Attendance	2.55	1.67
Property Damage	2.52	1.66
Strange Behaviors	2.38	1.73
Police Contacts	2.17	1.93
Self-Injury	1.82	1.64
Runaway	1.78	1.83
Theft	1.58	1.8
Sexual Acting Out	1.52	1.69
Suicide Attempt	1.27	1.71
Alcohol/Drug Use	1.2	1.68
Fire-Setting	0.88	1.55
Inappropriate Bowel Movements	0.8	1.42
Sexual Abuse or Assault	0.59	1.27
Cruelty to Animals	0.39	1.11

The items composing each factor along with their respective mean Likert scale scores is presented in Table 4.7. These scores indicate which underlying structures are most related to the at-risk status of these children and youth. Mean Likert scale ratings (i.e., a measure of frequency and intensity) for individual behaviors on the externalizing aggressive factor generally were high, suggesting that this factor is closely related to an at-risk status. Across all 66 subjects, the total mean for the five behavioral risk variables that loaded on the first factor was 15.68 out of a possible 20. Total factor and individual behavior Likert scale means indicated that the second factor, externalizing nonaggressive, contributed less to these individuals' presenting problems and out-of-community placements than did the first factor. The total factor mean was 9.1 of a possible 20, with only two items, school attendance and police contacts, averaging mod-

Table 4.6

Factor Scores for Reduced Three Factor Model of Risk Behaviors

Variable	Factor One Externalizing Aggressive	Factor Two Externalizing Nonaggressive	Factor Three Intrapersonal
Extreme Noncompliance	.81		
Physical Aggression	.80		
Extreme Verbal Abuse	.74		
Property Damage	.69		
Life Threat	.68		
Police Contacts		.79	
School Attendance		.73	
Alcohol/Drug Use		.68	
Strange Behavior		−.64	
Theft		.63	
Sad			.87
Suicide Attempt			.70
Anxious			.61
Self-Injury			.52

erate relationships to at-risk status. The remaining behaviors reflected only a mild relationship. The item reflecting strange behavior loaded negatively on this factor, indicating that presence of this risk variable was inversely related to the presence of the other behaviors. The average contribution to at-risk status made by the behavioral risk variables composing the third factor, intrapersonal, fell between those of the first two factors. The mean response was 8.89 out of a possible 16 points. In general, responses to the items indicated that these behaviors were mildly to moderately related to at-risk status.

Case Studies

Permanent products that resulted from the case study information gathering and reduction processes included: narrative case summaries, parent interview synopses, child interview synopses, multiaxial timelines, and cost matrices. The eight case studies were analyzed using pattern-matching (Yin, 1989) or pattern-coding (Miles & Huberman, 1994). Pattern-matching served three important functions in this study. First, it served to reduce each of the five data presentation formats (i.e., case study narrative, parent interview summary, child interview summary, multiaxial timelines, and costs matrix) into a smaller set of trends, themes, and constructs. Second, it allowed for the development of a

Table 4.7

Means of Behaviors That Predict At-Risk Status Organized by Factors

Variable	Factor One Externalizing Aggressive	Factor Two Externalizing Nonaggressive	Factor Three Intrapersonal
Extreme Noncompliance	3.53		
Physical Aggression	3.67		
Extreme Verbal Abuse	3.29		
Property Damage	2.52		
Life Threat	2.68		
Police Contacts		2.17	
School Attendance		2.55	
Alcohol/Drug Use		1.20	
Strange Behavior		2.38	
Theft		1.58	
Sad			2.68
Suicide Attempt			1.27
Anxious			3.12
Self-Injury			1.82

cognitive map for understanding the complex relationships among the variables being studied. Third, it laid the foundation for cross-case analysis by highlighting emerging trends, themes, and constructs within each case.

Across case studies, the data were analyzed inductively (Lincoln & Guba, 1985; Miles & Huberman, 1994). Inductive analysis involved the development of codes as data that were reduced to trends, themes, and constructs. Each data presentation technique was systematically transformed into naturally occurring units of information. These units of information then were placed into code categories (e.g., strong collaboration, weak case management) based on similar content and meaning using the constant comparison method (Lincoln & Guba, 1985). This simultaneous coding and analysis of data allowed for examination of similarities and differences in the cross-case data (Lincoln & Guba, 1985). The resulting categories served to integrate cross-case themes and trends in the data as they relate to the interactions between these young people with SED, their families, and the local system of care. The trustworthiness of these data was established using the following tactics for confirming findings: triangulation of data, checking for rival explanations, looking for negative evidence, and getting feedback from informants (Miles & Huberman, 1994).

Including complete versions of all five data presentation formats for all eight young people would exceed the scope of this chapter. Instead, general demographic information, descriptions of presenting problems, and the respective nominating agencies for each of the eight young people studied are provided in Table 4.8. These are then followed by 11 cross-case themes or trends that emerged from the data-reduction procedures.

Cross-Case Themes

A number of themes were consistently evident across the eight case studies:

1. Children and youth tended to enter the system of care at times of crisis; that is, they went directly from few or no services to very intensive services.

Table 4.8
Case Study Participant Information

Name	Age at Time of Study	Age at Service Entry	Years in System	Presenting Behaviors	Nominating Agency
Fred white/male	15	6	9	Physical aggression, property damage, fire-setting	Mental Health and Schools
Mark white/male	11	4	7	Fire-setting, sexual acting out, cruelty to animals, sexual assault	Mental Health and Schools
Jack white/male	17	10	7	Sexual assault, theft, breaking and entering, verbal aggression	Juvenile Justice and Schools
Mary white/female	16	10	6	Alcohol/drug abuse, suicide attempt, police contact, running away	Substance Abuse and Schools
Karen white/female	15	birth	15	Suicidal ideation, homicidal, fire-setting, physical aggression	Child Welfare and Schools
Juan Latino/male	14	12	2	Gang involvement, theft, suicide attempt, burglary, hallucinations, aggravated battery	Juvenile Justice and Schools
Jeff Latino/ Persian male	15	3	12	Drug dealing and abuse, physical aggression, running away, battery	Child Welfare, Substance Abuse, and Schools
Alan white/male	16	8	8	Defiance, physical aggression, battery, running away	Child Welfare and Schools

Prevention, early intervention, and midlevel services were rarely utilized by these children, youth, and families.

2. Relatedly, these young people frequently were first served by private providers (e.g., psychologists, psychiatrists) before entering the public system of care.

3. Among the eight case studies, there were a total of seven residential programs used and eight psychiatric hospitals. Many residential placements were outside the county and state.

4. Family services were only minimally involved while the children and youth were in residential care. Therefore, treatment gains, when they were made, failed to generalize when the child or youth returned home. Previous placement is a very strong predictor of future placement.

5. Six of the eight parents interviewed reported not being involved in planning for their child. The two parents who reported feeling involved both had successfully obtained residential placement for their child. At the suggestion of local service providers, they had refused to accept their child home upon discharge from the hospital, and were thus cited for neglect and had the local child protective service agency assume fiscal responsibility for their child's care.

6. These young people underwent an enormous number of psychological and psychiatric evaluations. For example, one youngster was evaluated 14 times over a 5-year period. Evaluations were often conducted as part of the process for placement by the referring agency and then were conducted almost immediately again as part of the admission process by the receiving agency. Diagnoses, medication types, and dosage levels often changed with each succeeding evaluation.

7. These young people invariably entered the system through one particular agency and over time "fanned out" to become involved with multiple agencies.

8. Lulls in the intensity of services (e.g., summer, expiration of time-limited services) often corresponded with behavioral regression.

9. These individuals were typically adolescents who had been involved with the local system of care for many years.

10. The vast majority of the expenses incurred serving these young people resulted from costs associated with hospitalization and residential placement.

11. Despite their ongoing contact with the system, at the time of this study these young people continued to exhibit significant emotional and behavioral problems.

Discussion

Existing studies on the characteristics of children and youth served by inter-agency systems of care provide the most pertinent context for discussing the present findings. As mentioned previously, Landrum et al. (1995), Rosen-blatt & Attkisson (1992), Epstein et al. (1994), and Duchnowski et al. (1993) reported on the characteristics of young people served by community-based programs in Virginia, Illinois, California, and nationwide, respectively. To a lesser extent, various studies on the individual service components composing the system of care also provide a basis for comparison.

Although young people ranging widely in age are currently being served in systems of care, it appears as though adolescents constitute the most representative age group. In the present study, 95% of the sample were age 12 or older; 16- and 17-year-olds constituted the largest percentage (40%), and the mean age was 15 years. Landrum et al. (1995) reported a slightly younger average age of 11.8. Approximately 75% of the Epstein et al. (1994) study fell between the ages of 12 and 16, over 70% of the Rosenblatt and Attkisson (1992) sample was age 12 or older, and the children and youth in the ARTS study (Duchnowski et al., 1993) averaged approximately 14 years old. These findings are consistent with those for young people served in a residential mental health program (Wells & Whittington, 1993) and identified by their schools as SED (Silver et al., 1992).

In the present study, the male prevalence of 75% closely matched the 77% and 80% male prevalence rate reported by Landrum et al. (1995) and Epstein et al. (1994), respectively. Additionally, these figures are consistent with national surveys of special education students identified as SED (Cullinan, Epstein, & Sabornie, 1992; Valdes et al., 1990). Male prevalence for the remaining two system-of-care studies were both slightly lower, with Rosenblatt and Attkisson (1992) reporting 64, 57, and 60% across their three target communities, and Duchnowski et al., (1993) reporting 64% for the ARTS sample. In contrast, the Wells and Whittington (1993) sample of young people referred to a residential mental health program was predominantly (i.e., 60%) female. We also found an overrepresentation of females in the psychiatric hospital cluster of our sample.

In the present study, more than 77% of the sample was white, a figure similar to the 71% reported by Duchnowski et al. (1993) and 66% reported by Epstein et al. (1994). Also, white individuals constituted the largest part of the sample in each of three California communities examined by Rosenblatt and Attkisson (1992): 63, 45, and 72%, respectively. Aggregated across sites, Latinos (22%) and African-Americans (12%) constituted the largest minority groups in the California study. However, the Landrum et al. (1995) Virginia sample was 54% African-American, a figure most closely matched by the 33% in Illinois reported by Epstein et al. (1994). Though small, the percentage of African American (9.7%) and Latino (8.4%) youth in our sample was approximately twice that found in the county's general population. Overrepresentation of minorities among young people with SED is a commonplace finding (Kauffman,

1993; U.S. Department of Education, 1994) and was also documented for African Americans in the California study, the only other community-based study for which the necessary general population data were reported. Presumably, differences in the racial makeup of these different groups of young people needing system-of-care services are related to geographic factors. That is, many communities in this country are predominantly homogenous with regard to racial and ethnic makeup, and that homogeneity is reflected in the study samples discussed here. In general, the findings of the present study are consistent with national surveys of special education students identified as SED in which the proportion of whites has ranged from about 67% (Chinn & Hughes, 1987; Valdes et al., 1990) to about 75% (Cullinan et al., 1992).

Findings across studies measuring intellectual functioning have been relatively consistent. It appears safe to conclude that, as was true in the current study, the majority of young people with SED being served by systems of care score within the normal to low-normal range on standardized measures of intelligence (Duchnowski et al., 1993; Epstein et al., 1994). The percentage of young people scoring more than 1 standard deviation above normal was 5% in the ARTS sample (Duchnowski et al., 1993), 15% in the Epstein et al. (1994) sample, and 10% in the present study. These findings are consistent with surveys of special education students identified as SED (Cullinan et al., 1992; Kauffman, 1993; Valdes et al., 1990).

The educational characteristics documented in the present study contribute to an emerging profile of young people with SED served by systems of care. In sum, the young people served in such systems typically experience significant academic deficits in most content areas, can be considered underachievers given their normal intelligence levels, are found by their schools to meet the eligibility requirements for special education as SED, are served in relatively restrictive educational settings (e.g., self-contained classrooms, alternative schools), and miss a significant amount of school because of truancy, suspension, or expulsion (Duchnowski et al., 1993; Epstein et al., 1994; Landrum et al., 1995). These educational characteristics are consonant with data from other studies of special education students (Cullinan et al., 1992; Epstein, Kinder, & Bursuck, 1989; Silver et al., 1992; Valdes et al., 1990). As mentioned previously, comorbidity of behavioral and academic problems frequently yields a very bleak prognosis (Kazdin, 1985; Loeber, 1982; Wagner et al., 1993). Based on the available data, the solution to the reciprocal interaction of learning and behavior problems in the classroom and school remains a critical but apparently elusive aspect of the total treatment effort.

Assessments of characteristic mental health functioning among young people served by systems of care have used psychiatric (e.g., the current version of the Diagnostic and Statistical Manual [DSM] l of Mental Disorders) and dimensional (e.g., the Child Behavior Checklist [CBCL]) classification systems. In both cases, what can accurately be characterized as behavioral excesses historically have been found to be most prevalent in this population. Using the DSM III-R classification system (American Psychiatric Association, 1987), Rosenblatt and Attkisson (1992) reported that more than 50% of their sample could be characterized as having significantly disruptive behaviors (37%) or adjustment disorders (20%). Mood disorders (22%), typically considered a behavioral deficit, were the only other diagnostic category that was characteristic of more than 10% of their sample. Under the CBCL classification system (Achenbach, 1985), 88% of the Duchnowski et al. (1993) sample fell within the extreme (81%) or borderline (7%) clinical range on the externalizing scales, and 79% fell within the extreme (63%) or borderline (16%) clinical range on the internalizing scales. However, only 9% of their sample exceeded the clinical cutoff for the internalizing scale alone, whereas 28% were externalizers only and 53% displayed both internalizing and externalizing disorders. Some evidence suggests that due to their covert, relatively nonaversive features, the actual prevalence of internalizing disorders is consistently underestimated in surveys of clinical populations (Kauffman, 1993). These reports on the mental health functioning of young people served by systems of care are consistent with previous surveys of clinical populations (Brandenberg, Friedman, & Silver, 1990).

In the present study, DSM disorders of the kind that can be considered internalizing were noted more than twice as frequently as those of an externalizing nature. This differentiates the present young people from those typically studied in mental health epidemiology research. The discrepancy in findings between the present study and the other research reports may be related to the target population definitions used, the nomination processes implemented, the geographical areas studied, or various clinical biases and systemic influences. Whatever the reasons, the present diagnostic data not only contradict other existing research, but also are inconsistent with the behavioral data collected on tier 2 of the archival review in this study.

The four individual behaviors most predictive of at-risk status for these young people were physical aggression, extreme noncompliance, peer interactions, and extreme verbal abuse; all are externalizing behaviors. Not until the fifth best predictor, anxious, was a behavior that can be characterized as internalizing identified. These findings are consistent with the types of behaviors displayed by young people served in Illinois systems of care (Epstein et al., 1994). In addition, this behavioral pattern is consistent with that found by Bruns, Burchard, and Yoe (1995) in their treatment efficacy evaluation of the Vermont System of Care. Baseline data on the occurrence of individual DAIC behaviors collected in the first month of their study indicated that physical aggression, property damage, self-injury, and life threat were the behaviors most frequently evinced by their sample. Finally, the present factor analysis of the DAIC items is consistent with two frequently used rating scales from which behavioral dimensions are extracted, specifically the Child Behavior Checklist (CBCL; Achenbach & Edelbrock, 1989) and the Revised Behavior Problem Checklist (RBPC; Quay & Peterson, 1987). For example, multivariate analyses of the CBCL provide two "broad-band" and numerous "narrow-band" classifications. The broad-band behavioral classifications are "overcontrolled" and "undercontrolled," and the most regularly reported narrow-band classifications are aggressive, hyperactive, delinquent, schizoid, depressed, and social-withdrawal. With regard to the broad-band classifications, overcontrolled generally approximates the intrapersonal factor identified in the current study, and undercontrolled approximates a combination of externalizing aggressive and externalizing nonaggressive. The current findings are similarly consistent with both the content and sequence of the CBCL's narrow-band classifications. Behavioral excesses occur more frequently and behavioral deficits occur less frequently.

Approximately 30% of the present sample was receiving prescribed drugs as an intervention. In their study of youth being served in community-based systems of care, Landrum et al. (1995) reported that 40% of their overall sample and 56% of their sample who were school-identified as SED were prescribed medication. Silver's (1989) investigation of students identified by their schools as SED and being served in residential treatment centers set the figure at 43%. The use of psychotropic medication by the general population of school-identified students with SED appears to be much lower—approximately 11% (Cullinan, Gadow, & Epstein, 1987; Cullinan et al., 1992). Given that young people with the most serious and complex problems constitute the target population of both local systems of care and residential treatment programs, it is not surprising that these individuals would be more likely to be prescribed medication. Nonetheless, psychotropic medication is a widely used intervention for children and adolescents with a variety of emotional and behavioral disorders. Given its potential for therapeutic and side effects, and the controversy that frequently surrounds its use, service providers need to be knowledgeable about medications in general, and to be skilled at monitoring the medications currently prescribed for treatment of the young people they serve (Epstein & Olinger, 1987). However, the cases reviewed in the present study typically yielded confusing information regarding current or past psychotropic medications of the nominees. Information available on this topic, if present in the case record, was usually vague or contradictory regarding precisely what medications were prescribed, the dosage, when the prescription began, how long the individual continued to take the medication, the reported effects, and reasons for its being discontinued.

Many young people with SED also come in contact with the juvenile or family court system due to their own illegal behavior or the abusive, neglectful behavior of their caretakers. In the present study, the proportion of children and adolescents on probation was about 50%. About 20% had histories of abuse or neglect. Thirty-five percent of the Landrum et al. (1995) sample had a history of legal charges arising from their own unlawful behavior. Fifty-six percent of the ARTS sample had been removed from their home due to abuse or neglect, and 59% had previous contact with the juvenile justice system. Silver's (1989) survey of special education students identified as SED and Zeigler-Dendy's (1989) survey of young people served in mental health programs found that about 33%

and 65%, respectively, had experienced abuse or neglect. Trupin et al. (1993) identified severe emotional or behavioral problems in 72% of their sample of young people referred to child protective services because of abuse or neglect.

Eighty-eight percent of the study population had been previously placed outside their homes at least once, and the average number of placements was four. About half of the Landrun et al. (1995) and Epstein et al. (1994) samples had been placed outside their homes. Duchnowski et al. (1993) reported previous out-of-home placements for 67% of their sample, with the average number of placements also being four. Hawkins, Almeida, and Samet (1989) noted the same average in their candidates for foster-family-based treatment. The relatively high rate of previous placement in the current study is consistent with Wells and Whittington's (1990) findings on 10–17-year-old youth (not psychotic and not mentally retarded) involved in their first referral to a large mental health group care program during a 1-year period. They found 93% of their sample had had at least one prior out-of-home placement. Regarding specific types of placements, a prior placement in corrections characterized 37% of our group and 24% of Silver's (1989); psychiatric hospital or residential treatment characterized 62% of our group and 30% of Silver's; and foster placement characterized 26% of our group and 25% of Silver's.

Family status has been assessed by several system-of-care investigators. Histories of mental illness (36%), alcohol or drug abuse (62%), criminal activity (26%), and family violence (59%) were significantly evident in the families composing our group. Though prevalence varied to some extent, Epstein et al. (1994) also found substantial evidence of these family stressors. Additionally, as was the case in the current study, intact nuclear families are a distinct minority among families served by systems of care (Duchnowski et al., 1993; Epstein et al., 1994; Landrum et al., 1995). Further, our study and the Landrum ct al. (1995) study document that parental custody has been qualified by the local or state government in a substantial portion of these families.

Without exception, and perhaps by definition, the children, youth, and families composing the system-of-care samples had contact with numerous service agencies. In our study, 79% of the sample had received special education services, 63% had been involved with the juvenile justice system, 57% had received mental health services, and 45% had been served by the local child welfare agency. Similar findings on multiagency contacts were reported in each of the three community-based systems of care studies that focused on this variable (Duchnowski et al., 1993; Epstein et al., 1994; Landrum et al., 1995).

Apparently, using case study methodology to examine the characteristics of children and youth served by systems of care has not been widely adopted. In addition to this study, Burchard and Burchard (1993) used case studies to evaluate the effectiveness of the Alaska Youth Initiative (AYI), one of the sites composing the ARTS sample. Although case study methods were used for needs assessment in the present study and for efficacy evaluation in the AYI study, they share numerous similarities. Specifically, the individuals studied in both instances for the most part were adolescents, exhibited externalizing behavior problems of a severe nature, had been involved with the service system for many years, had used and failed to benefit from most available service options, and had previously experienced repeated out-of-home placements.

Implications

Several implications for service provision can be inferred from these data. In general, the data support most, if not all, of the major principles on which systems of care are based (e.g. flexible, family focused, culturally competent, individualized, comprehensive, coordinated, community-based—see chapter 1 for full discussion). A few implications that we believe are most cogent are discussed in detail in the following paragraphs.

First, it appears as though significant numbers of youth who eventually require system-of-care services become known to the system at very young ages but do not receive intensive interventions until much later in their lives. Yet behavioral precursors to the onset of these problems have been identified, and systemic screening technologies have been developed that allow us to predict accurately which children are likely to develop the severe types of emotional or behavioral problems that eventually require intensive interagency interventions (Walker, Colvin, & Ramsey, 1995). Further, as seems evident among the children composing the present investigation, interventions developed specifically for the extremely challenging types of behavior typical of these individuals have proven less than successful (Zigler, Taussig, & Black, 1992). Interventions aimed at ameliorating the precursors of these extreme behaviors appear to be more promising (Hawkins, VonCleve, & Catalano, 1991). In short, evidence suggests that professionals can accurately identify and more successfully treat these individuals at younger ages, and should therefore focus on doing so.

Second, these and previous data document the long-term residential instability and, by implication, difficult family relationships these young people experience. Many have had numerous risk-producing family stressors, considerable family dissolution, government involvement in their custody, and one or more out-of-home placements. Nonetheless, family, in most cases, remains the single most important social institution in these young peoples' lives and therefore must be integrally involved in intervention. The challenge thus posed to service providers is to avoid viewing families solely in terms of these disconcerting characteristics and instead focus on a family's strengths and needs in order to increase the likelihood of their meaningful participation in treatment.

Third, as stated previously, these young people and their families almost invariably come into contact with numerous service agencies. Clearly, interagency coordination is needed. However, only one source of care is common to nearly every young person—school. In the present study, although each nominating source used identical criteria (i.e., the target population definition in Table 1), the schools were the only source whose names overlapped with another agency. That is, there was almost no duplication of nominations among mental health, child welfare, juvenile justice, alcohol and drug abuse, or rehabilitation services. Either through regular or special education, whether in a traditional or alternative curriculum, participation in school is the common denominator for almost all young people served in systems of care. Their presence is mandated by law and they spend, or should spend, a substantial part of their day there. Therefore the school setting may serve as a logical and natural host for interagency collaboration. Further, though we know educational performance is closely linked to postsecondary outcomes, serious concerns exist regarding the academic status and quality of instruction for students with SED (Knitzer, Steinberg, & Fleisch, 1990; Peacock Hill Working Group, 1991; Ruhl & Burlinghoff, 1992). These questions are particularly disturbing given the clear delineation over recent decades of empirically supported, effective instructional strategies for at-risk students (e.g., Algozzine, Ysseldyke, & Campbell, 1994; Christenson, Ysseldyke, & Thurlow, 1989). That is, the means to effectively remediate one of the characteristics that places students with SED at risk for a lifetime of difficulties is currently available but largely unused. If systems of care are to produce outcomes that not only allow children to remain in their homes and communities but also allow them to benefit fully and contribute while there, academic programming must be considered as carefully as behavioral or social programming.

Although useful, this study has limitations. First, although acceptable training standards were maintained, ensuring that data were collected in a reliable manner, we are assuming that the data in the files are accurate. The extent to which the files actually reflect the types of personal and family characteristics these children present and the community's response to these characteristics can not be assessed. This limitation is common to most archival review research. Second, the target population definition and nomination process were developed for use as part of a needs assessment for a single county. Given another target definition and nomination process, the results of the archival review might have been different. Finally, the sample was drawn from one county that is basically homogeneous in both ethnic (i.e., primarily Caucasian) and socioeconomic (i.e., middle-class) composition; thus, it would be difficult to generalize the findings to other communities, particularly those in urban or rural settings and those with a more culturally diverse population.

Identifying the characteristics of young people and families served by systems of care was identified as a needed first step in empirically investigating systems of care. Presumably, this was because identification of specific characteristics should have implications for interventions. Future research must put this presumption to an empirical test. Do detailed descriptions of children, youth, and families help predict the efficacy of discrete interventions? For example, do gender, age, or ethnicity differentiate service needs? Or do internalizers require different treatment than externalizers? Or are these and similar questions moot because generalizations of any kind are to be avoided and services entirely individualized? The present study and the other studies related to it have begun to fashion a response to the easiest-to-answer question of those posed in the introduction to this chapter: Who are the children and youth served by systems of care? Future research must address the more challenging question of which interventions work best with whom and under what conditions.

Authors' Note

Correspondence may be sent to Kevin P. Quinn, ED 230, State University of New York—Albany, Albany, NY 12222.

References

Achenbach, T. M. (1985). *Assessment and taxonomy of child and adolescent psychopathology.* Beverly Hills, CA: Sage.

Achenbach, T. M., & Edelbrock, C. S. (1989). Diagnostic, taxonomic and assessment issues. In T. H. Ollendick & M. Herson (Eds.), *Handbook of child psychopathology* (2nd ed.). New York: Plenum.

Algozzine, B., Ysseldyke, J. E., & Campbell, P. (1994). Strategies and tactics for effective instruction. *Teaching Exceptional Children, 26*(3), 34–36.

American Association for Protecting Children. (1988). *Highlights of official child abuse and neglect reporting.* Denver, CO: American Humane Association.

American Psychiatric Association. (1987). *Diagnostic and statistical manual of mental disorders—DSM-III-R* (3rd ed., rev.). Washington, DC: Author.

Anderberg, M. J. (1973). *Cluster analysis for applications.* New York: Academic.

Barber, C. C., Rosenblatt, A., Harris, L. M., & Attkisson, C. C. (1992). Use of mental health services among severely emotionally disturbed children and adolescents in San Francisco. *Journal of Child and Family Studies, 1,* 183–207.

Behar, L. (1985). Changing patterns of state responsibility: A case study of North Carolina. *Journal of Clinical Psychology, 14,* 188–195.

Bird, H., Canino, G., Rubio-Stipec, M., Gould, M. S., Ribera, J. C., Sesman, M., Woodberry, M., Heutos-Goldman, S., Pagan, A., Sanchez-Lakay, A., & Moscosco, M. (1988). Estimates of the prevalence of childhood maladjustment in a community survey in Puerto Rico. *Archives of General Psychiatry, 45,* 1120–1126.

Brandenberg, N. A., Friedman, R. M., & Silver, S. E. (1987). The epidemiology of childhood psychiatric disorders: Prevalence findings from recent studies. *Journal of the American Academy of Child and Adolescent Psychiatry, 29,* 76–83.

Bruns, E. J., Burchard, J. D., & Yoe, J. T. (1995). Evaluating the Vermont system of care: Outcomes associated with community-based wraparound services. *Journal of Child and Family Services, 4,* 321–340.

Burchard, J. D., & Burchard, S. N. (1993). *One kid at a time: Evaluative case studies and description of the Alaska Youth Initiative demonstration project.* Juneau, AK: State Division of Mental Health and Mental Retardation.

Burchard, J. D., & Clarke, R. T. (1990). The role of individualized care in a service delivery system for children and adolescents with severely maladjusted behavior. *Journal of Mental Health Administration, 17*(1), 48–54.

Burchard, J. D., & Schaefer, M. (1992). Improving accountability in a service delivery system in children's mental health. *Clinical Psychology Review, 12,* 867–882.

Burns, B. J., & Friedman, R. M. (1990). Examining the research base for children's mental health services and policy. *Journal of Mental Health Administration, 17,* 87–99.

Chinn, P. C., & Hughes, S. (1987). Representation of minority students in special education classes. *Remedial and Special Education, 8*(4), 41–46.

Christenson, S., Ysseldyke, J. E., & Thurlow, M. L. (1989). Critical instructional factors for students with mild handicaps: An integrative review. *Remedial and Special Education, 10,* 21–31.

Costello, E. J., Edelbrock, C. S., Costello, A. J., Dulcan, M. K., Burns, B., & Brent, D. (1988). Psychiatric disorders in pediatric primary care: The new hidden morbidity. *Pediatrics, 82,* 415–424.

Cullinan, D., Epstein, M. H., & Sabornie, E. J. (1992). Selected characteristics of a national sample of seriously emotionally disturbed adolescents. *Behavioral Disorders, 17,* 273–280.

Cullinan, D., Gadow, K. D., & Epstein, M. H. (1987). Psychotropic drug treatment among learning-disabled, educable mentally retarded, and seriously emotionally disturbed students. *Journal of Abnormal Child Psychology, 15,* 469–477.

Cumbald, C., Petersen, S., Quinn, K., & Epstein, M. H. (1994). Project CANDU: Children and adolescents network of DuPage county. *CASE in Point, 8,* 1–12.

Day, C., & Roberts, M. (1991). Activities of the child and adolescent service system program for improving mental health services for children and families. *Journal of Clinical Child Psychology, 20*(4), 340–350.

Duchnowski, A. J., Johnson, M. K., Hall, K. S., Kutash, K., & Friedman, R. M. (1993). The alternatives to residential treatment study: Initial findings. *Journal of Emotional and Behavioral Disorders, 1,* 17–25.

Edgar, E. (1987). Secondary programs in special education: Are many of them justifiable? *Exceptional Children, 53,* 555–561.

Epstein, M. H., Cullinan, D., Quinn, K. P., & Cumbald, C. (1994). Characteristics of children with emotional and behavioral disorders in community-based programs designed to prevent placement in residential facilities. *Journal of Emotional and Behavioral Disorders, 2,* 51–57.

Epstein, M. H., Kinder, D., & Bursuck, B. (1989). The academic status of adolescents with behavior disorders. *Behavioral Disorders, 14,* 157–165.

Epstein, M. H., & Olinger, E. (1987). Use of medication in school programs for behaviorally disordered pupils. *Behavioral Disorders, 12,* 138–145.

Epstein, M. H., Quinn, K., Cumbald, C., & Holderness, D. (in press). Needs assessment of community-based services for children and youth with emotional or behavioral disorders and their families: Part 1. A conceptual model. *Journal of Mental Health Administration.*

Evans, M. E., Dollard, N., & McNulty, T. L. (1992). Characteristics of seriously emotionally disturbed youth with and without substance abuse in intensive case management. *Journal of Child and Family Studies, 1,* 305–314.

Hawkins, J. D., VonCleve, E., & Catalano, R. F., Jr. (1991). Reducing early childhood aggression: Results of a primary prevention program. *Journal of the American Academy of Child and Adolescent Psychiatry, 30,* 208–217.

Hawkins, R. P., Almeida, C., & Samet, M. (1989). Comparative evaluation of foster-family-based treatment and five other placement choices: A preliminary report. In A. Algarin, R. M. Friedman, A. J. Duchnowski, K. M. Kutash, S. E. Silver, & M. K. Johnson (Eds.), *2nd annual conference proceedings of the Research and Training Center for Children's Mental Health: Building a research base* (pp. 98–119). Tampa: Florida Mental Health Institute.

Institute of Medicine. (1989). *Research on children and adolescents with mental, behavioral, and developmental disorders: Mobilizing a national initiative.* Washington, DC: National Academy.

Joint Commission on Mental Health of Children. (1969). *Crisis in child mental health: Challenge for the 1970s.* New York: Harper & Row.

Katz-Leavy, J. W., Lourie, I. S., Stroul, B. A., & Zeigler-Dendy, C. (1992). *Individualized services in a system of care.* Washington, DC: Georgetown University Child Development Center.

Kauffman, J. M. (1993). *Characteristics of behavior disorders of children and youth* (5th ed.). Columbus, OH: Merrill.

Kazdin, A. (1985). *Treatment of antisocial behavior in children and adolescents.* Homewood, IL: Dorsey.

Knitzer, J. (1982). *Unclaimed children.* Washington, DC: Children's Defense Fund.

Knitzer, J. (1993). Children's mental health policy: Challenging the future. *Journal of Emotional and Behavioral Disorders, 1,* 8–16.

Knitzer, J., Steinberg, Z., & Fleisch, B. (1990). *At the schoolhouse door: An examination of programs and policies for children with behavioral and emotional problems.* New York: Bank Street College of Education.

Kutash, K., Duchnowski, A. J., & Sondheimer, D. L. (1994). Building the research base for children's mental health services. *Journal of Emotional and Behavioral Disorders, 2,* 194–197.

Landrum, T. J., Singh, N. N., Nemil, M. S., Ellis, C. R., & Best, A. M. (1995). Characteristics of children and adolescents with serious emotional disturbance in systems of care. Part II: Community-based services. *Journal of Emotional and Behavior Disorders, 3,* 141–149.

Lincoln, Y. S., & Guba, E. G. (1985). *Naturalistic inquiry.* Beverly Hills, CA: Sage.

Loeber, R. (1982). The stability of antisocial and delinquent child behavior: A review. *Child Development, 53,* 1431–1446.

Marder, C. (1992). *Secondary school students classified as serious emotionally disturbed: How are they being served?* Menlo Park, CA: SRI International.

Miles, M. B., & Huberman, A. M. (1994). *Qualitative data analysis: A sourcebook of new methods.* Beverly Hills, CA: Sage.

National Advisory Mental Health Council. (1991). *National plan for research on child and adolescent mental disorders.* Rockville, MD: National Institute of Mental Health.

Office of Technology Assessment. (1986). *Children's mental health: Problems and services—A background paper* (OTA-BP-H-33). Washington, DC: U.S. Government Printing Office.

Peacock Hill Working Group. (1991). Problems and promises in special education and related services for children and youth with emotional and behavioral disorders. *Behavior Disorders, 16*(4), 139–146.

President's Commission on Mental Health. (1978). *Report of the subtask panel on infants, children, and adolescents.* Washington, DC: U.S. Government Printing Office.

Quay, H. C., & Peterson, D. R. (1987). *Manual for the Revised Behavior Problem Checklist.* Coral Gables, FL: Author.

Quinn, K., Epstein, M. H., Cumblad, C., & Holderness, D. (in press). Needs assessment of community-based services for children and youth with emotional or behavioral disorders and their families: Part 2. Implementation in a local system of care. *Journal of Mental Health Administration.*

Rosenblatt, A., & Attkisson, C. C. (1992). Integrating systems of care in California for youth with severe emotional disturbance. I: A descriptive overview of the California AB377 evaluation project. *Journal of Child and Family Studies, 1,* 93–113.

Ruhl, K. L., & Burlinghoff, D. H. (1992). Research on improving behaviorally disordered students' academic performance: A review of the literature. *Behavioral Disorders, 17,* 178–190.

SAS Institute. (1994). *JMP statistics and graphics guide.* Cary, NC: Author.

Saxe, L., Cross, T., & Silverman, N. (1988). Children's mental health: The gap between what we know and what we do. *American Psychologist, 43,* 800–807.

Silver, S. E. (1989). A comparison of children with serious emotional disturbances served in residential and school settings. In A. Algarin, R. M. Friedman, A. J. Duchnowski, K. M. Kutash, S. E. Silver, & M. K. Johnson (Eds.), *2nd Annual Conference Proceedings of the Research and Training Center for Children's Mental Health: Children's mental health services and policy: Building a research base* (pp. 249–277). Tampa: Florida Mental Health Institute.

Silver, S. E., Duchnowski, A. J., Kutash, K., Friedman, R. M., Eisen, M., Prange, M. E., Brandenburg, N. A., & Greenbaum, P. E. (1992). A comparison of children with serious emotional disturbances served in residential and school settings. *Journal of Child and Family Studies, 1,* 43–59.

Singh, N. N., Landrum, T. J., Donatelli, L., Hampton, C., & Ellis, C. R. (1994). Characteristics of children and adolescents with serious emotional disturbance in systems of care. Part I: Partial hospitalization and inpatient psychiatric services. *Journal of Emotional and Behavioral Disorders, 2,* 13–20.

Stroul, B. A., & Friedman, R. M. (1986). *A system of care for seriously emotionally disturbed children and youth.* Washington, DC: CASSP Technical Assistance Center.

Trupin, E. W., Tarico, V. S., Low, B. P., Jemelka, R., & McCellan, J. (1993). Children on child protective service caseloads: Prevalence and nature of serious emotional disturbance. *Child Abuse & Neglect, 17,* 345–355.

U.S. Department of Education. (1994). *Sixteenth annual report to Congress on the implementation of Individuals With Disabilities Education Act.* Washington, DC: U.S. Government Printing Office.

Valdes, K. A., Williamson, C. L., & Wagner, M. M. (1990). *The national longitudinal transition study of special education students: Statistical almanac. Vol. 3: Youth categorized as emotionally disturbed.* Menlo Park, CA: SRI International.

Wagner, M., Blackorby, J., Cameto, R., Hebbeler, K., & Newman, L. (1993). *The transition experiences of youth with disabilities: A summary of findings from the National Longitudinal Transition Study.* Palo Alto, CA: SRI.

Walker, H. M., Colvin, G., & Ramsey, E. (1995). *Antisocial behavior in school: Strategies and best practices.* Pacific Grove, CA: Brooks/Cole.

Wells, K., & Whittington, D. (1990). Prior services used by youths referred to mental health facilities: A closer look. In A. Algarin & R. Friedman (Eds.), *A system of care for children's mental health: Building a research base.* Tampa: Florida Mental Health Institute.

Wells, K., & Whittington, D. (1993). Characteristics of youths referred to residential treatment: Implications for program design. *Children and youth review, 15*(3), 195–217.

Yin, R. K. (1989). *Case study research: Design and methods.* Newbury Park, CA: Sage.

Zigler, E., Taussig, C., & Black, K. (1992). Early childhood intervention: A promising preventative for juvenile delinquency. *American Psychologist, 47*(8), 997–1006.

Zeigler-Dendy, C. A. (1989). The invisible children project: Methods and findings. In A. Algarin, R. M. Friedman, A. J. Duchnowski, K. M. Kutash, S. E. Silver, & M. K. Johnson (Eds.), *2nd annual conference proceedings of the Research and Training Center for Children's Mental Health: Children's mental health services and policy: Building a research base* (pp. 360–366). Tampa: Florida Mental Health Institute.

Program Descriptions: State, Local, and Families

New Directions: Evaluating Vermont's Statewide Model of Individualized Care

5

Suzanne Santarcangelo,
Eric J. Bruns, and James T. Yoe

The expansion of Vermont's system of care for children and adolescents experiencing severe emotional disturbance and their families required an evaluation approach that would provide information on client progress, program efficacy, and statewide systems change. In order to collect data in a manner that would not burden the youth, families, or service providers, indicators and measures that could be used in several levels of analysis were utilized. In this chapter we will describe service system expansion and its key components, the outcome measures utilized, outcomes of the expansion, and the future directions of Vermont's research efforts.

Vermont's Service System Expansion

In 1989, Vermont, like many other states, had no single service or agency providing the interagency linkages necessary to ensure a coordinated approach to service delivery for children experiencing severe emotional disturbance and their families. In addition, Vermont had twice the national average per capita of out-of-state placements for children and adolescents experiencing severe emotional disturbance. In response, policymakers and governmental agencies embarked on the development of a statewide model for delivery of coordinated and highly individualized community-based treatment options for children and adolescents and their families (Yoe, Santarcangelo, Atkins, & Burchard, 1996). Efforts at statewide development were closely linked with Vermont's interagency infrastructure, the foundation of which was built on the guiding principles of the Vermont Child and Adolescent Service System Program (see Appendix A for guiding principles).

Interagency case planning, review, and problem resolution processes were based on the assumption that children and adolescents should receive services within the least restrictive, most normalized environment that is clinically appropriate. These principles were codified into law through Vermont's Act 264. At the community level, 12 Local Interagency Teams (LITs) were mandated to include, at a minimum, the directors of Community Mental Health Children and Family Services, Child Welfare district offices, special education coordinators from each educational administration in the region, and a parent representative. Additionally, representatives from other child- and family-serving agencies are invited as members of the Local Interagency Team. This team is charged with providing multidisciplinary decision making in cases where a child and family's individual treatment team is unable to develop or implement a coordinated community-based plan for services.

At the state level, three groups are part of this mandate. First, the State Interagency Team (composed of the directors of Child Welfare, Mental Health, and Education and parent representatives) reviews cases when local interagency teams are unable to resolve issues. These case reviews allow policymakers and public sector managers to gain firsthand experience and insight into the challenges faced by children, families, and local providers. Second, the Case Review Sub-Committee of the State Interagency Team reviews all cases referred for intensive or restrictive residential placements. This subcommittee is composed of program staff from the three state departments. Third, a governor-appointed advisory board composed of parents, advocates, educators, legislators, and local providers provides direction for the development and maintenance of a statewide system-of-care plan for children and adolescents experiencing a severe emotional disturbance. This plan is updated and submitted to the Vermont State Legislature annually. The system-of-care plan outlines the full continuum of services necessary to provide comprehensive community-based treatment, and in addition the update highlights priorities for development and advocacy in the upcoming year.

Relying on the interagency structure of Act 264, the Vermont Department of Mental Health and Mental Retardation took a lead role in planning for the development of a comprehensive system of care for children and adolescents experiencing a severe emotional disturbance and their families. Each LIT region was asked to engage in a process of assessing the resources, strengths, and gaps in service delivery for their local area. These needs assessments were conducted and results reviewed with broad-based community input. This process culminated in the development of 3-year local implementation plans that outlined the services necessary in each region to achieve a continuum of services locally. In addition, each LIT region identified three priority areas and a subsequent proposal for service development. These plans were submitted to the State Interagency Team and created the blueprint for the Vermont statewide planning and development initiative.

From its inception, Vermont's model of statewide collaboration has been a community-wide effort. Interdisciplinary task forces with representatives from state and local public agencies, parents, advocates, and youth were established early in the process. These task forces reviewed state-of-the-art models in community-based service delivery in the areas of respite care, interagency case management, crisis stabilization services, intensive in-home services, and special education programming. Following these reviews, task force members customized models to fit Vermont's rural, philosophical, and economic character. At various stages of model development, feedback was solicited from children and adolescents directly involved in Vermont's public service system. Using this approach, Vermont has made considerable advances in developing a progressive system of care for children and families.

With a 1990 award of a Robert Wood Johnson Foundation grant for youth, Vermont was able to expand and enhance the community-based delivery system. This expansion, known as Vermont's "New Directions Initiative," was the direct result of the broad-based planning outlined above and took place over a 4-year period. Several service types were targeted for development, refinancing, or expansion. A brief description of New Directions programming is outlined below.

New Directions Initiative Program Types

Intensive Home-Based Services

These services are delivered in Vermont with the assumption that family integrity and unity should be preserved. Professional and paraprofessional staff are available for up to 20 hours a week to provide education, training, and support in the family home. Services are geared toward families whose children are at risk of removal to child welfare services or psychiatric hospitalization. Caseloads are low (three to four families at any given time), and services are delivered based on a 3-, 6-, or 12-month intervention model. Treatment techniques include solution-focused therapy, strength-based assessment, cognitive behavioral therapy, and psychoeducational approaches. All in-home services are closely coordinated with other child and family serving agencies. Treatment strategies, length of stay, and frequency of contact are based on the individual needs and strengths of each situation.

Respite Care

Respite care services (the number 1 priority in Vermont's system-of-care plan for three years), remain an integral part of the continuum. Respite services are designed as a planned break for youth and families. Respite services are custom designed for each child's interests and each family's situation. Each of Vermont's community mental health agencies has a designated respite coordinator (one quarter to one full-time equivalent) who recruits and trains respite workers and matches workers to a child and family. The matching process includes a review of child, worker, and family interests, hobbies and activities, age, sex, scheduling needs, and type of respite care requested (in home, out of home or overnight, or a combination). Respite services are generally available to families on an ongoing basis. However, financial considerations have led some programs to limit services to a 3-, 6-, or 12-month model per family. Additionally, some programs offer small group respite options whereby two or three children will be matched based on age, interests, and skills to participate in recreational activities together with one respite worker. The overall goal of respite service delivery is to decrease family stress and provide children with age-appropriate and enjoyable experiences in the community.

Specialized Education Programs

In Vermont, special education takes many forms. Two general models emerged as part of the New Directions Initiative: first, a "school within a school," and second, an alternative experiential community-based model of applied learning. The school-within-a-school model allows for resource rooms, structured study halls, and specialized tutorial areas to serve as a "home-base" for students needing more intensive emotional or behavioral supports. Specifically, students attend as many mainstreamed activities and classrooms as possible using the support, structure, and modified disciplinary procedures as their base. Adjunct mental health support is also available on site either through the presence of a school-based mental health team or through an identified support staff. The second model that emerged, "alternative education programs," provide all of the above components but add off-site community experiences to the educational services. Off-site experiences may emphasize vocational, community service, or applied learning (e.g., completing a math section by working with board feet at a local lumber yard) depending on the needs of the individual learner.

Crisis Stabilization Services

Each of Vermont's 10 community mental health centers operates a 24-hour emergency response service. These programs provide an immediate clinical response for emergency screening of individuals experiencing a severe emotional reaction that could result in suicide or homicide. Traditionally, these programs are geared toward adults. The New Directions Initiative provided funding and training to enhance the ability of target programs in effectively responding to families whose youth and children were experiencing severe emotional disturbance.

Parent Support Networks

The Vermont chapter of the Federation of Families for Children's Mental Health partnered with the New Directions Initiative to increase the availability of parent support groups across the state. The purpose of this network is to provide support, information, advocacy, and referral for parents coping with a child who is difficult to care for.

Therapeutic Case Management Services

The underlying philosophies of Vermont's system of care (e.g., unconditional care, flexible funding, child- and family-centered treatment, and interagency collaboration) provided the framework for therapeutic case-management services. The goal of these services is to coordinate and deliver all elements of a child and family treatment plan in a manner that is responsive to their unique situations. Therapeutic case-management services emerged as the glue that holds the system together. Therapeutic case managers create an individualized treatment team for each child and family they serve. Teams include all persons involved in the youth's treatment as well as natural helpers identified by the youth or family. These treatment teams develop individualized treatment services that are responsive to the unique strengths, needs, and potentials of the child, family, and community. Treatment planning and decision making is determined by treatment team consensus. Additionally, therapeutic case managers routinely identify and communicate to state agencies on policy, and process barriers to providing individualized services for children, youth, and families.

The development of therapeutic case-management services occurred in Vermont based on a target population phase-in plan. Specifically, it was recognized that such services should be available to all children who were experiencing a severe emotional disturbance. However, due to limited resources, target groups were prioritized in the following manner: (a) those youth referred to or currently placed in out-of-state residential facilities; (b) youth at risk of out-of-county or out-of-home placements; (c) youth requiring multiple services, referred to LIT teams; and (d) all children experiencing a severe emotional disturbance requiring multiple services. In order to accomplish the reintegration or diversion of youth from residential facilities, initial caseload size was set at no more that five youths in the initial stage of reintegration, and no more than 12 youths at any given time. It has been Vermont's experience that these children and families receive an average of 7 to 10 hours of mental health intervention per week. Subsequently, most caseloads fall in the range of four to seven youths at any given time.

Therapeutic case-management services in Vermont embody what has come to be known as "Wraparound Care" (Burchard & Clarke, 1990). As such, the tensions between the development of a continuum-of-care services and truly customizing every treatment option to a child's and family's needs were inherent in the New Directions Initiative. Most notable was the tension between categorical funding strategies, which emphasized funding service types, and wraparound care efforts, which emphasized funding based on the family's and child's needs. However, the underlying goal of the therapeutic case-management model is to bring the best of each system and service together in a creative and individualized way on behalf of the child and family. This tension was viewed as a healthy and positive influence in Vermont's efforts to develop a comprehensive, integrated, yet flexible system of care. In order to nurture this effort, state and local program managers recognized the need to support case managers with outcome-based data to inform decision making related to resource allocation, service utilization, cost, and effectiveness. The staff, youth, and families involved in therapeutic case-management services served as the participants for the pilot of Vermont's statewide evaluation system.

At the end of the 4-year New Directions Initiative, 1,501 youth had been referred to new or expanding programs. Of these youth, 904 were reported to have been enrolled in services. A point-in-time summary of 310 active cases indicated 130 youth living with their biological family, 108 in foster care, 12 in temporary respite homes, 10 living independently, 48 in community-based residential (group) homes, and 2 in local psychiatric inpatient facilities. Of the youth involved in therapeutic case-management programs, 62% were male; ages ranged from 7–20 years, with a mean of 16 years; 78% of the youth were in the state's custody. At time of referral to services, 41% of the youth were residing in psychiatric or residential treatment centers. All youth involved were considered to be the most behavioral challenging in Vermont's system of care.

Vermont's Statewide Evaluation Efforts

The development of Vermont's statewide model of evaluation paralleled that of its service-delivery system. It was recognized that a multilevel approach was necessary to fully evaluate the impact of the New Directions Initiative. Service-system measures had to include systemic indicators (e.g., statewide outcomes), program information (e.g., efficacy of treatment model), and client-level variables (e.g., youth satisfaction and behavioral adjustment). Along these lines, an effort had to be made to operationalize variables and create measures that did not require an inordinate amount of additional paperwork for providers and families. Variables and subsequent measures were designed to be useful across client, program, and system levels of analysis. Examples of multipurpose data elements included behavioral adjustment, youth satisfaction, perceived levels of unconditional care, service cost, and level of restrictiveness in the living environment.

Behavioral Adjustment Indicators

In collaboration with researchers at the University of Vermont, state planning and evaluation staff conceptualized a behavioral checklist composed of those behaviors most indicative of a child's risk of removal into a more restrictive setting. This instrument, the Daily Adjustment Indicator Checklist (DAIC), became the cornerstone of the Vermont System for Tracking Client Progress (Schaefer et al., 1991). The DAIC is composed of 18 negative behaviors (e.g., physical aggression, property destruction, self-injury) and 6 positive behaviors (e.g., compliance, school attendance). The occurrence of the 24 behaviors are rated by the child's caretaker on a daily basis. This checklist allows caretakers to track a child's progress over time. In order to use the same information in evaluating the effectiveness of the system, the Quarterly Adjustment Indicator Checklist was adapted. The Quarterly Adjustment Indicator Checklist (QAIC) is composed of 22 of the indicators included on the DAIC and is completed on a quarterly basis by the youth's case manager. Using this scale, the occurrence of each behavior is rated over a 3-month period, indicating the number of days each behavior occurred on a 0–5 scale (e.g., 0 = never, 1 = 1 day, 2 = 2 days, 3 = 3–9 days, 4 = 10–30 days, 5 = 31–90 days). A principle component analysis was performed on the 22 QAIC behavior indicators. This analysis, based on a sample of 138 youth, revealed four distinct factors. Based on these factors, four behavioral subscales were developed for use in subsequent analyses, and two items (fire-setting and inappropriate bowel movements) were dropped from the analysis (see Table 5.1 for QAIC factors). A reliability analysis on all 22 behaviors yielded a Cronbach Alpha coefficient of .82, indicting a high level of internal consistency among items. In additional analysis performed on the four scales, alpha coefficients ranged from .61 for the internalizing scale to .77 for the externalizing scale.

The QAIC has been found to have excellent overall internal consistency, and the internal consistency of the four subscales ranged from adequate to excellent. Subsequent studies on this instrument showed a high degree of correspondence in behavioral ratings between DAICs completed by the primary caregiver and QAICs completed by the case manager (Yoe, Bruns, Santarcangelo, Tighe, & Burchard, 1993). Similarly, scores on the QAIC were well associated with caregiver scores on the parent version of the Child Behavior Checklist (CBCL; Achenbach & Edelbrock, 1991). Finally, case managers' scores on the QAIC have been found to have excellent 2-week test-retest reliability.

Restrictiveness of Living Environment Scale

The restrictiveness of residential placements was measured using the Restrictiveness of Living Environment Scale (ROLES) developed by Hawkins, Almeida, Fabry, & Reitz (1992). This instrument is used to rate residential settings on a scale ranging from 0.5 to 10, where 0.5 = least restrictive placement (independent

Table 5.1
QAIC Factors, Items and Variance Explained

Externalizing (21.3%)

Property damage
Extreme verbal abuse
Noncompliance
Physical aggression
Poor peer relations
Theft

Public Externalizing (7.7%)

Police contact
Alcohol-Drug Use
Truancy
Suicide attempt

Abuse Related (9.2%)

Sexual acting out
Sexual abuse/assault
Self-injury
Life threat
Strange behavior
Cruelty to animals
Running away

Internalizing (7.5%)

Anxious
Sad
Low self-confidence

living) and 10 = most restrictive placement (adult corrections). Residential placement information is obtained from the youth's case manager at referral and updated quarterly.

Youth Satisfaction Survey

The Youth Satisfaction Survey developed as part of Vermont's evaluation system has two sections. The first section asks youth to identify the services they are receiving and indicate how much contact they have had with service providers (e.g., therapists, case managers) over the past month. They are then asked to rate on a 5-point scale how satisfied they were with each service they received.

The second section of the survey assesses their perceptions of involvement and unconditional care. A reliability analysis on the current data yielded Cronbach Alpha coefficients of .75 and .46 for involvement ($N = 34$) and unconditional care ($N = 33$), respectively. It should be noted that the unconditional care scale was composed of only two items, which may account for lower reliability obtained in the scale analysis.

Financial Tracking and Demographics

Information on cost, client demographics, and service types is routinely collected by the various state departments. However, no single department had attempted to capture the full range of services and subsequent cost associated with serving these youth. The New Directions Initiative spurred the development of an individualized services data base. Therapeutic case managers and other service-system staff funded through the New Directions Initiative serve as key informants. Utilizing referral checklist and individualized budget analysis forms, descriptive, financial, service type, and behavioral information is gathered at referral (i.e., immediately before entry into New Directions programming) and updated every quarter that the youth is enrolled in services.

Expansion of the New Directions Initiative was based on the premise that the return of children from costly out-of-state residential care would provide additional funds for in-state program expansion. It was anticipated that financial restructuring would allow for more flexible, family-based services, as well as containing service costs. Outcome studies have attempted to document pertinent system-level changes such as cost containment, adherence to interagency principles, maintenance of those children labeled as the most challenging in community settings, and a strengthening of the interagency system of collaboration. However, in order to be more informative, system-level outcomes must be accompanied by evaluation of overall program effectiveness (e.g., reductions in problem behaviors) and assessment of consumer-level outcomes such as satisfaction with services and progress. By integrating data of multiple outcomes into each family's care plan, not only can the success of the system be measured, but each child's individualized treatment goals can also be assessed, and client service plans adjusted accordingly. Further examination of client-level outcomes also affords an opportunity to assess which services lead to the most positive outcomes for children and families. A summary of the three levels of outcomes (system, program, and consumer) can be found in Table 5.2.

Vermont's System-Level Outcomes

In 1989, Vermont's rate of out-of-state residential placement of children and adolescents per capita was over twice the national average. By August 1992,

Table 5.2

Evaluation Framework Used in Vermont's New Directions Initiative

Level of Evaluation	Outcome Indicators	Measurement Instrument
System	Cost Containment	Financial tracking of individual youth budgets
	Cost Reduction	Financial tracking of individual youth budgets
	Financial restructuring	Financial tracking of diverted out-of-state funds
	Residential Restrictiveness	Restrictiveness of Living Environment Scale
	Mainstreamed educational experiences	Referral checklist and quarterly update
	Maintenance of youth in the community	Daily Adjustment Indicator Checklist Quarterly Adjustment Indicator Checklist
	Provider collaboration	LIT team surveys and interviews
Program efficacy	Behavioral adjustment	Daily Adjustment Indicator Checklist Quarterly Adjustment Indicator Checklist
	Interagency collaboration	Financial tracking of blended service dollars
	Flexibility in funding	Financial tracking of service types and trends
	Residential Restrictiveness	Restrictiveness of Living Environment Scale
Client progress	Satisfaction with services	Parent satisfaction surveys Youth satisfaction surveys
	Satisfaction with Life	Children's Perceived Life Satisfaction Scale
	Behavioral adjustment	Daily Adjustment Indicator Checklist Quarterly Adjustment Indicator Checklist
	Unconditional Care	Youth Satisfaction Survey
	Involvement in treatment	Youth Satisfaction Survey

$1.2 million in state funds for out-of-state residential care was reallocated to the development of intensive community-based options for these youth in Vermont. The number of out-of-state placements had been reduced from 54 to 17 (Vermont Agency of Human Services, 1993). Several questions were posed. First, could intensive community-based services for the most challenging children and adolescents be maintained at or below initial out-of-state spending limits? Second, could children and adolescents experiencing the most problematic behavioral maladjustment be maintained in the community? Third, were interagency teams evidencing better collaboration and thus problem resolution locally?

Service Costs

Several Vermont studies have documented that lower overall costs result from serving children via community-based services. Tighe and Brooks (1994) matched 26 children in Vermont individualized care programs with 26 children referred to out-of-state facilities by Vermont's child welfare organization. The average total cost of serving these children in out-of-state residential treatment facilities was $4,893 per month, or about $58,718 per year. The average cost for a child served by community-based individualized services was less, $4,036 per month, or $48,427 per year. Annual costs have been found to be fairly consistent across outcome studies. For a different sample of youths, Bruns, Burchard, and Yoe (1995) found that the mean cost of individualized services per year was $43,440.

Maintenance of Challenging Children in the Community

The question of whether Vermont's system of individualized care can maintain children with challenging behavior in the community over time was addressed in two studies. Yoe, Santarcangelo, Atkins, and Burchard (1996) assessed 40 youths at referral to community-based care and again 12 months later. The results demonstrated a positive shift from residential care to less restrictive options (see Table 5.3). At time of referral, 63% of these youths were in restrictive residential

Table 5.3
Living Arrangements at Referral to Vermont
Community-Based Care and 12 Months Post-Referral
for 40 Children and Adolescents

Living Arrangements	At Referral	12 Months
Independent Living	2%	17%
With Family Member/Relative	17%	23%
Non–treatment oriented Foster Care	23%	8%
Therapeutic Case Management	16%	40%
Residential Treatment Facility	40%	10%
Other (Community-Care Home)	2%	2%

Note. From Bruns, Burchard, & Yoe (1995).

placements. One year later, 80% of the youths were residing with their families, in treatment-based foster care, or in independent living settings, and only 18% were residing in residential treatment or traditional foster care. (The additional 2% were residing in other community-based settings.) These findings were consistent with those of Bruns, Burchard, and Yoe (1995), who found that among 27 youths referred to community-based care, 70% of whom had previously been served in institutional settings, only 11% were placed out of the community 1 year after referral to wraparound services.

Similarly, Yoe, Santarcangelo, Atkins, and Burchard (1996) found that 1 year after entering individualized care, 70% of the 40 youths in their sample were being served in public school settings, with an additional 8% graduating from high school. Of the 28 youths maintained in public school, 26 required some form of special education support (i.e., classroom aide or resource room). Such results suggest that integration into more mainstreamed settings is an attainable goal for children and adolescents experiencing severe emotional disturbance.

The ability of providers to maintain children experiencing SED in community-based residential settings is especially encouraging when one considers that risk of reinstitutionalization is greatest within the 1st year of integration into the community. Such risk was illustrated by Brown and Greenbaum's (1994) national study of 184 youths "successfully" discharged from residential treatment. In this report, 32% of the children discharged from residential treatment were found to be reinstitutionalized within 1 year, a rate nearly three times that of the samples followed in studies of the Vermont system of individualized care. These results are particularly encouraging given the fact that the youth involved remain some of Vermont's most challenging.

Local Interagency Collaboration and Problem Resolution

Another systemic question to be addressed by the evaluation was one of "interagency process." That is, do local service providers report that the interagency processes set forth in Act 264 were used, that they were helpful and led to collaboration and problem resolution? In order to obtain information, participants ($N = 157$) on each of Vermont's 12 interagency teams were asked to fill out a questionnaire related to their perceptions of the interagency process. Maynard and Pandiani (1991) reported that 83% of respondents indicated that local agencies usually or always collaborate on case reviews, as compared to 27% who reported collaboration prior to the creation of Local Interagency Teams. Additionally, 67% of the respondents indicated that collaboration also occurs around improvement of local services, as compared to 20% prior to the creation of local interagency teams. These results suggest that Vermont's statewide system development was adhering to the principles set forth in Act 264. Similarly, referrals to Local Interagency Teams for problem resolution decreased by 65% after the passage of Act 264. While it is difficult to infer causality, it would appear that collaboration and problem resolution have increased as a result of

Vermont's system development, and that such local agency collaboration has reduced the need for formal problem resolution.

Program Efficacy Outcomes

The evaluation provided evidence that several of the overarching goals of developing a community-based service array were being met. The rate of out-of-state placement was reduced, individualized care was found to be cost-effective, children referred to community-based care were able to be maintained in the community, and local interagency teams experienced an increased level of self-reported collaboration. Further study was needed to assess whether the New Directions Initiative was providing quality services for children and families. Based on the principles of the model, it was believed that service quality could be inferred from (a) a reduction in behaviors that create a risk of more restrictive placement; (b) funding patterns that reflect more flexible utilization of agencies' monies; and (c) high levels of self-reported client satisfaction. In the current section, we will detail evaluation efforts that investigated whether community-based services for children and families resulted in better behavioral adjustment for children and the ability of agencies to provide more flexible funding for families. Though levels of child and parent satisfaction also provide evidence for program efficacy, these evaluation results will be described in the section on client-level outcomes.

Incidence of Negative and Positive Behaviors Among Youths

In addition to allowing for the production of reports of an individual child's adjustment across negative behaviors (Bruns & Woodworth, 1994), aggregated behavioral data from the DAIC allowed evaluators to investigate whether behavioral adjustment of youths enrolled in New Directions programs changed over time. Using a cohort of 27 youths in Vermont individualized services, the rate of severe negative behaviors (with 10 DAIC behaviors rated as the most serious by care providers) was found to be reduced significantly over the course of the 1st year of care. An average of 6.6 days on which a severe negative behavior occurred were reported during the first month after referral, compared to an average of 1.9 days in the 13th month of services (Bruns et al., 1995). See Table 5.4.

In addition to the decline in at-risk behaviors, the rate of DAIC positive behaviors increased during the first year of service. For example, the percentage of days per month on which a child was rated as compliant increased from 79% in the 1st month of services to 85% in the 13th month. Finally, convergent evidence for improvement in behavioral adjustment emerged from data collected

Table 5.4

Number of Times DAIC Individual Negative
Behaviors Were Exhibited in Month 1 and 1 Year
Postreferral for 27 Children and Adolescents

Individual Behavior	Month 1	Month 13
Physical Aggression	60	25
Property Damage	28	9
Theft	11	4
Running Away	9	3
Life Threat	23	1
Sexual Abuse/Assault	2	6
Suicide Attempt	0	0
Self-Injury	27	4
Fire-Setting	7	0
Police Contact	10	0
Total Negative Behaviors	177	52
Compliance Percentage	79%	85%

Note. Scores reflect incidence of each behavior for entire cohort
of 27 over 4-week periods at baseline and 1-year follow up. From
Bruns, Burchard, & Yoe (1995).

via the Child Behavior Checklist (Achenbach & Edelbrock, 1991). Nineteen
youths were tracked simultaneously with the CBCL. Results showed a significant reduction in mean Total Problem Behaviors, Externalizing Behaviors, and
Internalizing Behaviors *T*-scores. Of the 19, 17 were in the borderline or clinical
range for Total Problem Behaviors at entry into services. This number decreased
to 12 clients, 1 year postreferral. Results suggest that children and adolescents
with challenging behavior were not only capable of being maintained in the community, but that they also could show improvements in overall behavioral
adjustment, including a decrease in the rates of negative behaviors that might
jeopardize community-based service plans and disrupt the lives of other persons
in the community.

A comparison group was used to investigate whether such decreases in negative behaviors were a result of receiving individualized services or the result of
other service or measurement artifacts (Yoe, Bruns, and Burchard, 1995). Thirty
children enrolled in community-based services were matched by age, gender,
and behavioral adjustment at referral to 30 children referred to specialized educational programming for behaviorally challenging youths. Results showed that,
over time, clients enrolled in community-based individualized care experienced
significantly greater reduction in Total Negative Behaviors, as well as improving on two of four empirically derived subscales of the QAIC (Externalizing

Behaviors and Abuse Related Behaviors). Although children were not randomly assigned to the two groups, the results provided evidence that behavioral improvement of participants in community-based care was not a spontaneous or artifactual effect. In addition, the results suggest to service providers and policy-makers in Vermont that the most rapid, robust improvements in youths with severe emotional disturbance might ensue through providing individualized services to children in the community.

Funding Individualized Services

Tighe and Brooks (1994) attempted to evaluate the extent to which Vermont's goal of interagency collaboration was being met by analyzing the funding of services for 40 children and adolescents in individualized care. Financial collaboration was evidenced by the nontraditional use of traditional payer sources. For example, state and local education administrations paid for 34% of the individualized services, even though traditional education services accounted for only 27% of total costs. Costs of services have also been used to investigate the flexibility of individualized services, by associating costs of case management over time with service outcomes (e.g., behavioral adjustment; Bruns et al., 1995). Results indicated a significant correlation between changes in behavioral adjustment and changes in costs of case management. In other words, as behavioral challenges decrease, so do case-management services. Such findings demonstrated that plans of community-based care changed with the needs of the clients, suggesting that the system of care was indeed "individualized."

Studies investigating funding patterns of children's individualized plans of care have found small to negligible changes in total service costs over time (Bruns et al., 1995; Tighe & Brooks, 1994). However, case-management costs tend to decline over time, especially after the first 6 months. Furthermore, levels of severe negative behaviors and noncompliance expressed by children at the time of referral correlate significantly with future case-management costs. Age, however, does not relate to the amount of costs for services, or to the pattern of service costs over time. Such findings have significant implications for conducting needs assessments or anticipating future service demands. Total service costs may go down slightly over time, but hours spent on case-management duties are likely to vary depending on how developed the individualized system of care is, and the extent to which challenging behaviors are being expressed. Treatment team goals addressing problematic behaviors, though difficult to establish, may go far to reducing the time and money spent on implementation of each child's plan.

Behavioral maladjustment is not associated only with more billed case-management hours. Yoe et al. (1993) also found that the future restrictiveness of a child's residential placement, as assessed by the ROLES, was predicted by negative behaviors assessed by the QAIC and the DAIC in the 1st month of referral. Such a relationship suggests that assessing the rate of negative behaviors can be a useful way to anticipate the future residential needs of a child, and can be a good way to prepare a treatment team for the challenge a child will present.

Client-Level Outcomes

In developing and implementing a system of care, especially one representing a paradigm shift in service provision, it is critical to demonstrate impact on outcomes, such as reduced out-of-state placements, lower costs, and improved behavioral adjustment. However, an evaluation system must also use information to continuously refine and improve program operation. The research results presented in the following section provide program developers with client-level data that can help service providers know what factors influence positive outcomes in client satisfaction with life and services. In addition, client-level data can help predict what outcomes might result from particular service approaches. Determining how outcomes such as child behavior, costs, and satisfaction interact is a critical step in improving services for children and families.

Satisfaction with Life and Services

Tenets of community-based wraparound care promote a client-centered, involved, and unconditional approach to service delivery. Results reported by Santarcangelo (1994), as well as Rosen, Heckman, Carro, & Burchard (1994), attest to the overall satisfaction reported by participants in individualized services. Specifically, satisfaction surveys quantified on a 5-point scale (1 = not satisfied, 5 = very satisfied) demonstrated that children and adolescents consistently rated their overall service satisfaction and satisfaction with their treatment teams in the good to excellent range (means = 4.34 and 4.13, respectively). Furthermore, youths rated their satisfaction with therapeutic case managers (mean = 4.37) higher than that of any other provider. This was an especially encouraging result inasmuch as the New Directions Initiative emphasized therapeutic case managers as prominent influences in the children's lives. Survey questions also inquired whether youths felt involved with services (e.g., "How often do members of your treatment team ask for your ideas and opinions?") and whether youths felt services were unconditional (e.g., "Do you feel members of your treatment team will stick with you no matter what?"). Results showed that participants gave relatively high ratings on these two scale dimensions (means = 4.20 and 3.80, respectively), suggesting that they felt they had control over their services, were listened to, and perceived their care was unconditional.

In a study by Donnelly, Burchard, and Yoe (1994), 20 individualized-care participants were matched on age and sex to 20 youths receiving traditional residentially based services in the child welfare system. Researchers hoped to determine if youths in community-based individualized-care plans experienced higher service and life satisfaction than participants in more traditional residential delivery systems. Individualized-care participants reported significantly more ($p < .05$) satisfaction with services overall, felt more involved with planning, felt more strongly that their care was unconditional, felt more as though they had someone to talk to, and had a greater degree of general life satisfaction as measured by the Perceived Life Satisfaction Scale (Adelman, Taylor, & Nelson 1989).

These findings are particularly meaningful when involvement and perceptions of unconditional care are correlated to behavioral adjustment. Rosen et al. (1994) and Santarcangelo (1994) have demonstrated that greater feelings of involvement and unconditional care are associated with the expression of fewer negative behaviors as measured by the DAIC and QAIC. Similarly, general service satisfaction and life satisfaction revealed less robust yet nonetheless meaningful correlations to the expression of negative behaviors. Santarcangelo (1994) concluded that believing that caretakers will "stick with them no matter what" and feeling like a partner in treatment decisions may be more important to treatment outcomes than being satisfied with life or happy with services. Such findings suggest to providers that policies of "ejecting" children from residential placements or services may in fact maintain or exacerbate problem behaviors. Along these lines, providing youth with a voice in decision making may serve to help alleviate challenging behaviors.

Client-reported service satisfaction results become particularly useful for program developers when attempts are made to determine what factors lead to enhanced client satisfaction. Rosen et al. (1994) found that feelings of involvement in services are an important predictor of overall service satisfaction. Santarcangelo (1994) found that perceptions of both involvement and unconditional care were associated with increased life satisfaction, even more so than with general service satisfaction. The results of these studies suggest that the commitment of service providers to involving youths in treatment and to providing unconditional care may be important predictors of a child's well-being, over and above satisfaction with services. Finally, researchers have discerned that older children are more likely to be dissatisfied with services and with treatment teams than younger children (Donnelly et al., 1994; Santarcangelo 1994). Though older children did not express fewer feelings of involvement than younger clients, these findings, interpreted from a developmental perspective, may indicate that older youths wish to be less dependent on adults, and that dependence on adults in a treatment setting leads to lower satisfaction. Special efforts should be made to address older youths' sense of satisfaction with services.

Behavioral Adjustment as a Client-Level Outcome

Behavioral adjustment can be used at each level of evaluation (i.e., systemic, program, and client) as a measure of success. It is useful to examine the processes and patterns involved in containing or reducing the expression of negative behaviors and in enhancing and strengthening positive behaviors. Through such analyses, providers can be better informed as to what types of behavior to expect during the delivery of individualized services, as well as what aspects of care may need improvement.

Investigators have shown that clients referred to individualized services experience most dramatic reductions in problem behaviors within the first 6 months, followed by little change over the next 18 months (Bruns et al., 1995; Yoe et al., 1995). In addition, negative behaviors were reduced more rapidly and to a greater extent for clients of individualized services than for participants in less intensive school-based options. The types of behaviors most likely to exhibit immediate decreases include externalizing behaviors (e.g., physical aggression, extreme verbal abuse) and abuse-related behaviors (e.g., sexual acting out, running away). In contrast, internalizing behaviors, (e.g., sadness, anxiety) change more slowly. The QAIC subscale Community Externalizing Behaviors (e.g., truancy, substance abuse) shows little change over time, but was shown to be the only behavioral subscale on which children in individualized services exhibited fewer behaviors than a matched cohort of children receiving less intensive services.

These findings suggest that the intensity of individualized services may play a role in the observed rapid decline in the expression of "acting-out" behaviors, while mood problems and internalizing behaviors respond much more slowly. This may be because the formation of strong relationships with treatment providers is necessary for internalizing behaviors to decline. The ability of individualized care to keep the expression of "rebellious" or "delinquent" community externalizing behaviors at rates lower than that of other children (matched on overall negative behaviors) receiving fewer intensive services speaks to the possible importance of maintaining intensity in community-based individualized service plans. Maintaining intensity in client-centered services is especially important when one considers that negative behaviors are associated with higher cost and more restrictive living settings. Further study of the relationship between outcome variables such as behavioral adjustment and service composition and intensity will go far toward determining what components of care are most effective. Including reliable cost data in such analyses may shed light on a question of special relevance in this era of scarce funding: Which services, delivered in what ways and by whom, will reflect the most effective utilization of limited resources?

What services are related to satisfaction or behavioral adjustment? Unfortunately, research on the subject is scarce. Donnelly et al. (1994) found significant correlations between satisfaction with case-management services, respite services, and therapy, and a host of positive satisfaction outcomes, such as having someone to talk to, feeling as though progress is being made, and life satisfaction. It appears as though satisfaction with individual components of care is essential to feeling content with one's progress and one's life. Scant evidence at this time, however, links satisfaction with particular service types and outcomes such as behavioral adjustment. A notable exception is respite services. Santarcangelo (1994) found that youths who were happy with their respite care expressed fewer problem behaviors and felt better about themselves in general than those less satisfied with their respite care. This suggests that this relatively inexpensive service may play a critical role in the well-being and behavioral adjustment of children in care.

Conclusion

The New Directions Initiative allowed Vermont to expand and strengthen its community-based delivery options for children and families. Evaluation methodology has provided public sector managers and policymakers with rich information related to cost maintenance and reduction and adherence to a philosophy that indicates that the most challenging youth can be served in a community-based treatment system. Additionally it was shown that elements of involvement and the unconditional nature of care in service provision may be crucial to a child's success. Along these lines, providers should expect externalizing behaviors to be the most amenable to treatment in the first 6 months. Providers also should pay close attention to the delivery of respite care options for all children and families for several reasons. First, respite care has been found by previous researchers to be the most popular service component among parents caring for children experiencing developmental or behavioral problems (Cohen, 1982; Marcenko & Smith, 1991). Second, Vermont youths' satisfaction with respite services was correlated with the expression of fewer problem behaviors and with positive feelings about themselves (Santarcangelo, 1994). Finally, families caring for children experiencing SED who utilized Vermont's system of respite care were found to utilize out-of-home placement less often than families placed on waiting lists for respite services, and they perceived the need for future out-of-home placement to be less than that of wait-list families (Bruns & Sturtevant, 1996).

The multitiered strategy employed in the New Directions Initiative allowed evaluators to address the needs of various audiences with minimal changes in data collection. However, future designs must incorporate an immediate feedback loop. Results of various analyses need to be fed back to the end user at every level of decision making. That is, policymakers as well as consumers need to see the results of analyses much sooner in order to ensure both continued investment in the evaluation system and informed decision making related to policy, program, and treatment decisions. Similarly, data needs to presented in formats that are easily understood by the most novice of readers. Lastly, data collection needs to be flexible so that youths and families receiving less intensive services or diverted from entering the system with early intervention have an opportunity to respond to less intensive yet equally informative and meaningful surveys.

Appendix 5.A
Vermont's Guiding Principles
for a System of Care

on Behalf of Children and Adolescents
with a Severe Emotional Disturbance and Their Families

1. The system of care should provide a continuum of services to children and adolescents and their families that reflects a comprehensive approach (e.g., physical, psychological, educational/vocational, social services). Early identification and intervention should be included in the system of care in order to enhance the likelihood of positive outcomes.

2. Children and adolescents with a severe emotional disturbance should receive individualized services in accordance with the unique needs and potential of each child. These services should be guided by an individualized service plan.

3. Children and adolescents with a severe emotional disturbance should receive services in the least restrictive, most normal environment that is clinically appropriate.

4. The system of care should reflect an awareness of the child in the context of his/her family. Children and adolescents with a severe emotional disturbance and their families (and/or surrogate families) should participate in the development and implementation of services.

5. There should be optimal linkages between programs so that systems are integrated on several different levels, including planning, administrative, financial and service delivery,

6. Children and adolescents with a severe emotional disturbance should be ensured smooth transitions through the system of care, including transition to the adult service system. Services should be delivered in a coordinated and therapeutic manner in accordance with the changing needs of the children being served.

7. The rights of children and adolescents with a severe emotional disturbance should be protected. Effective advocacy efforts for children and adolescents with a severe emotional disturbance should be promoted. Children and adolescents with a severe emotional disturbance and their families should be assisted in becoming their own advocates.

8. Children and adolescents with a severe emotional disturbance should receive services without regard to race, religion, national origin, sex, physical disability, or socio-economic status. Services should be sensitive and responsive to cultural differences and special needs.

9. Programs within the system of care should be responsive to staff needs by providing:
   - adequate compensation
   - personal and professional support
   - opportunities for professional growth, and
   - ongoing training.

10. The process of system design and redesign will be based upon the latest research available in an ongoing evaluation process. Program evaluation will incorporate information from program recipients as well as service providers.

Authors' Notes

Suzanne Santarcangelo is owner at the Vermon Consultation Network: Promoting Positive Change.

Eric J. Bruns is a doctoral student at the University of Vermont, Department of Psychology.

James T. Yoe is director of quality improvement, Maine Department of Mental Health, Mental Retardation and Substance Abuse Services.

Correspondence may be addressed to Suzanne Santarcangelo, Vermont Consultation Network, P.O. Box 112, Waterbury, VT 05676.

References

Achenbach, T. M., & Edelbrock, C. (1991). Manual for the Child Behavior Checklist/4-18. Burlington: University of Vermont, Department of Psychiatry.

Adelman, H. S., Taylor, L., & Nelson, P. (1989). Minors' dissatisfaction with their life circumstances. *Child Psychiatry and Human Development, 20,* 35–147.

Brown, E. C., & Greenbaum, P. E. (1994, March). Reinstitutionalization after discharge from residential mental health facilities: An example of competing-risks survival analyses. Paper presented at the 7th annual Florida Mental Health Institute Research Conference, Tampa: A system of care for children's mental health: Expanding the research base.

Bruns, E. J., Burchard, J. D., & Yoe, J. T. (1995). Evaluating the Vermont system of care: Outcomes associated with community-based wraparound services. *Journal of Child and Family Studies, 4,* 321–339.

Bruns, E. J., & Sturtevant, J. (1996, April). Impact of respite care services on children experiencing emotional and behavioral problems and their families. Paper presented at the Building on Family Strengths conference, Portland, Oregon.

Bruns, E. J., & Woodworth, K. (1994). User's manual to the Vermont System for Tracking Client Progress Data Entry and Graphing Programs. Burlington: University of Vermont, Department of Psychology.

Burchard, J., & Clarke, R. (1990). The role of individualized care in a service delivery system for children and adolescents with severely maladjusted behavior. *Journal of Mental Health Administration, 17,* 48–60.

Cohen, S. (1982). Supporting families through respite care. *Rehabilitation Literature, 43,* 7–11.

Donnelly, J. W., Burchard, J. D., & Yoe, J. T. (1994, October). Satisfaction, involvement, and unconditional care: A comparison of youth receiving wraparound services with youth in group residential care. Paper presented at the 4th annual Virginia Beach Conference: Children and adolescents with emotional or behavioral disorders.

Hawkins, R. P., Almeida, B., Fabry, A. C., & Reitz, A. C. (1992). A scale to measure restrictiveness of living environments for troubled children and youth. *Hospital and Community Psychiatry, 43,* 54–59.

Marcenko, M. O., & Smith, L. K. (1991). Post adoption needs of families adopting children with developmental disabilities. *Children and Youth Services Review, 13,* 413–424.

Maynard A., & Pandiani J. (1991) Vermont state and local interagency team evaluation. Unpublished study, Vermont Department of Mental Health and Mental Retardation, Waterbury.

Rosen, L. D., Heckman, T., Carro, M. G., & Burchard, J. D. (1994). Satisfaction, involvement, and unconditional care: The perceptions of children and adolescents receiving wraparound services. *Journal of Child and Family Services, 3,* 55–67.

Santarcangelo, S. (1994). Consumer satisfaction: What children tell us about therapeutic case management and wraparound services. Unpublished doctoral dissertation, University of Vermont, Burlington.

Schaefer, M., Burchard, J., Harrington, N., Rogers, J., Tighe, T., & Welkowitz, J. (1991). A user's guide to the Daily Adjustment Indicator Checklist. Burlington: University of Vermont, Department of Psychology.

Tighe, T. A., & Brooks, T. (1994, March). Evaluating individualized services in Vermont: Intensity and patterns of services, costs, and financing. Paper presented at the 7th annual Florida Mental Health Institute Research Conference, Tampa: A system of care for children's mental health: Expanding the research base.

Vermont Agency of Human Services. (1993, January). 1993 Vermont System of Care Plan for children and adolescents experiencing a severe emotional disturbance and their families. Waterbury, VT: Agency of Human Services.

Yoe, J. T., Bruns, E. J., & Burchard, J. D. (1995, March). Evaluating Vermont's system of care for children and adolescents: A comparison of wraparound and school-based interventions. Paper presented at the 8th annual Florida Mental Health Institute Research Conference, Tampa, FL.

Yoe, J. T., Bruns, E. J., Santarcangelo, S., Tighe, T., & Burchard, J. D. (1993, March). A comparison of two behavioral assessment methods for children and adolescents. Paper presented at the 6th annual Florida Mental Health Institute Research Conference, Tampa, FL.

Yoe, J. T., Santarcangelo, S., Atkins, M., & Burchard, J. D. (1996). Wraparound care in Vermont: Program development, implementation, and evaluation of a statewide system of individualized services. *Journal of Child and Family Studies, 5,* 23–37.

Community-Based Services in Kentucky: Description and 5-Year Evaluation of Kentucky IMPACT

6

Robert J. Illback, C. Michael Nelson, and Daniel Sanders

W ith regard to the provision of appropriate services to its population of children with serious emotional disturbance (SED), Kentucky is typical of many states. A 1986 statewide survey revealed that 0.36% of the school-age population were identified and receiving special education services through their school districts.[1] Eighty-seven of 180 school districts reported that they identified and served no students in such programs (Kentucky Task Force on Over- and Underidentification, 1986). In comparison, authorities consider 3–6% to be a realistic estimate of the prevalence of schoolchildren who need special education and related services due to their emotional and behavioral disabilities (Institute of Medicine, 1989). In 1990, it was estimated that 51,000, or 5%, of children and youth in Kentucky potentially were eligible for human services assistance due to their severe emotional problems; 225,000 children and youth were "at risk" for the development of dysfunctional behavior. However, only about 500 children and youth were receiving community-based services. At the same time, dramatic increases occurred in psychiatric hospitalization and the use of Medicaid funds: from 74 beds in 3 facilities in 1980, at a cost of $4–5 million, to 500 beds in 13 facilities in 1989, at a cost of $36 million (Kentucky Cabinet for Human Resources, 1990). Guidance and collaboration at the state level was minimal; with minor exceptions, state regulations paralleled those at the federal level, and no procedures had been codified to operationalize existing policies.

Three events in the late 1980s established a climate conducive to change. First, the Department for Mental Health and Mental Retardation Services (DMHMRS), in response to national priorities (i.e., the Child and Adolescent

Service System Programs [CASSP] initiative), developed a call for coordinated, community-based services. Second, a grant from the Robert Wood Johnson Foundation facilitated the development and implementation of a service coordination model in the central Kentucky area, encompassing 17 counties and 23 school districts. This project, known as Bluegrass IMPACT, resulted in local, regional, and state interagency coordination and networking, as well as interagency agreements that led to uniform service nomination and consent forms, and interagency control over client acceptance, treatment planning, case review, and assignment of resources. It also provided funding for services that were otherwise difficult to obtain or were not available, including service coordination, flexible response teams, school support services, intensive in-home services, and therapeutic foster care. These additional resources enabled Bluegrass IMPACT to develop and test the feasibility of arrangements and services for the rest of the state.

The process of developing the Robert Wood Johnson grant proposal created legislative interest in the needs of Kentucky's children and youth with serious mental health problems. This interest led to the third critical event, passage of House Bill 838, which called for the development of a multiagency plan to meet the needs of children with mental health problems in the commonwealth. Specifically, HB 838 established a State Interagency Council (SIAC) and Regional Interagency Councils (RIACs) for services to children with emotional disturbance. This plan provided funding for additional services in the areas of intensive family-based support, intensive in-home services, family preservation programs, residential care, staffing for the 18 RIACs in the state, services for children with multiple problems, and for the development and support of a statewide SED evaluation plan. House Bill 838, which included the critical provision of a federal Medicaid match, targeted a total of $19.5 million for the biennium to this population.[2] State funds were allocated to the departments of Mental Health and Mental Retardation Services, Social Services, and Medicaid Services. House Bill 838 directed the agencies under these state departments to provide community-based services to children and their families.

Further impetus for change was provided by educational initiatives, which included the commission of a multidisciplinary task force to study and revise guidelines for identifying students with emotional and behavioral disorders (EBD) in Kentucky's schools,[3] as well as the Kentucky Educational Reform Act (KERA), also passed in 1990.[4] These events created a climate of shared responsibility for decision making regarding how to meet the needs of children and youth with, or at risk for, EBD.

These events (House Bill 838 in particular) resulted in a statewide comprehensive, community-based mental health initiative for children and youth with serious emotional disturbance (SED). Borrowing from the Bluegrass region's project, this initiative was named Kentucky IMPACT. In this chapter, we describe IMPACT, with specific focus on the results of the 5-year evaluation recently completed.

Implementation of Kentucky IMPACT

Target Population and Program Eligibility

The children and youth served by this project are considered to have severe emotional disabilities. They exhibit a wide range of problems in home, school, and community settings that interfere with their ability to adjust, learn, and live successfully with their families. Eligibility for Kentucky IMPACT services is based on the definition presented in Table 6.1. This definition is used as a guide; children and youth are accepted for IMPACT by a regional interagency committee. Therefore, not all participants strictly meet these eligibility criteria.

Table 6.1

Eligibility Definition for Kentucky IMPACT

"Severely emotionally disturbed child" means a child with a clinically significant disorder of thought, mood, perception, orientation, memory, or behavior that is listed in the current edition of the American Psychiatric Association's *Diagnostic and Statistical Manual of Mental Disorders* (DSM-IIIR) and that:

1. Presents substantial limitations that have persisted for at least 1 year or are judged by a mental health professional to be at high risk of continuing for 1 year without professional intervention in at least two of the following five areas:

    (a) "Self-care," defined as the ability to provide, sustain, and protect his or herself at a level appropriate to his or her age;

    (b) "Interpersonal relationships," defined as the ability to build and maintain satisfactory relationships with peers and adults;

    (c) "Family life," defined as the capacity to live in a family or family-type environment;

    (d) "Self-direction," defined as the child's ability to control his or her behavior and to make decisions in a manner appropriate to his or her age; and

    (e) "Education," defined as the ability to learn social and intellectual skills from teachers in available educational settings; or

2. Is a Kentucky resident and is receiving residential treatment for emotional disturbance through the interstate compact; or

3. Has been removed by the Department for Social Services from the home but has not been able to be maintained in a stable setting because of behavioral or emotional disturbance; or

4. Is a person under 21 years of age meeting the criteria of paragraph 1 of this subsection and who was receiving services prior to age 18 that must be continued for therapeutic benefit.

Program Goals and Validity Assumptions

A number of systems-level goals drive the Kentucky IMPACT program. Several are stated in the legislative intent, including: (a) increasing and improving available services, (b) coordinating services more effectively through interagency involvement and collaboration, (c) reducing dependency on psychiatric hospitalization, and (d) increasing the use of less restrictive community-based services. For children and families, a range of specific program goals include the following:

1. Children and youth will demonstrate improvement in social competence and concomitant decreases in behavioral and emotional difficulties, in home, school, and community settings.

2. Families will perceive increased social and professional support in their efforts to meet the needs of these challenging children and adolescents, and will perceive this support to be timely and responsive.

3. Children and youth will be placed in less restrictive treatment environments, and their placements will become more stable over time.

4. Professionals, parents, and the children themselves will perceive that they have made meaningful gains as a consequence of their involvement in the program.

Organizational Framework

Overall administration is provided by the State Interagency Council (SIAC), which is composed of state-level administrators and a parent; they develop interagency policies, coordinate the tracking of clients, and attend to any gaps in services in the regions. The SIAC also oversees 18 Regional Interagency Councils (RIACs) and provides them with technical assistance. RIACs are located in each of Kentucky's 18 area development districts. Each RIAC includes core representation from mental health, social services, education, and district courts, as well as parents. The Department of Social Services district manager or designee chairs RIAC meetings. Each RIAC provides a focus for interagency decisions regarding children and adolescents with severe emotional problems who need coordinated services from more than one agency, and who are at the greatest risk of hospitalization or residential placement. RIACs conduct regular interagency case reviews, approve the use of intensive family-based support services (IFBSS; i.e., wraparound services that are tailored to the needs of the child and family),[5] and provide consultation to the Medicaid hospital and residential use review teams regarding the availability of community-based services.

At least one full-time staff person (a local resources coordinator) in each RIAC coordinates the case review process, facilitates and evaluates referrals for review, and assigns cases to service coordinators, who are responsible for case management. The local resources coordinator also supervises service coordinators, makes recommendations concerning the use of IFBSS dollars, provides input to the Medicaid review team (with the advice of the SIAC), and monitors the status of children from the region being served in psychiatric hospitals and residential treatment facilities.

Service coordinators in each region are responsible for assisting the child and family in gaining access to needed social, medical, educational, vocational, residential, and other services. Their activities may include assessment, planning, linking, monitoring, accessing services, developing new services or programs, case coordination, individual advocacy, tracking and follow-up, enhancing natural support systems, and systems advocacy. The service coordination role is particularly important when children are at risk for hospital placement or when a child's plan for reentry back into the community is being developed and implemented.

Service Components

The services encompassed by IFBSS are designed to promote rehabilitation through the provision of care to children and adolescents with SED who are at greatest risk of relapse and rehospitalization or repeated use of emergency interventions. These services are tailored to meet specific, individual needs of the child or family that cannot be met through other means. These may include in-school or in-home support, respite care, therapeutic foster care, fees for specialized camps, and leisure or related activities. In essence, an individualized package of supportive resources are wrapped around the child and the family. Specially trained professionals coordinate, purchase, or provide those support services necessary to help children and youth live successfully at home and in the community. Examples of such services include crisis intervention and support, specialized evaluations, respite care, transportation, in-home attendants, specialized tutoring assistance with basic needs, and specialized skill development, such as behavior management. Trained part-time support staff frequently are matched with target families to provide many of these services. Although the level of intensity is carefully and regularly monitored, these services may be continued for as long as they are deemed necessary and are cost effective.

For children whose needs cannot be met through community-based services, psychiatric residential treatment facilities (PRTFs) provide an alternative to traditional psychiatric hospitalization. PRTFs are regionally based, small, homelike residential treatment facilities that are geared toward intensive, short-term therapeutic care. As of March 1995, a point-in-time survey of the five licensed facilities then operating revealed that there were 72 licensed beds (69 occupied), serving children in an age range of 10–17 (mean = 13.72). The average length of stay was 196.88 days, and 58 of the 69 placed children were in the custody of the Department of Social Services. Currently, six PRTFs have been established. Ultimately, each of the 18 area development districts will have at least one PRTF.

Evolutionary Program Changes

As Kentucky's systems change efforts have gained momentum, recognition of the need for services to children and families has grown. Fortunately, this heightened awareness has led to the development of formal mechanisms to promote local, regional, and state support. For example, local and state level parent groups (e.g., the Federation of Families for Children's Mental Health) have emerged. Multiagency parent conferences have been held, and professional groups have been formed around family issues (e.g., Kentucky Family-Based Services Association). Legislative subcommittees specifically devoted to the needs of children and families have been formed, and a Commission on Families and Children has been established to redesign services to children and their families. These organizations help maintain the attention of both the public and governmental bodies on the needs of children with EBD and their families, as well as setting an expectation for continued growth in the quantity and quality of available services.

With the passage of House Bill 838 came a commitment to systems change for children's mental health. Therefore, a human service delivery infrastructure had to be developed to support and maintain the professionals and families working in it. What began as a pool of shared resources and a desire to collaborate is evolving as a fundamental support structure for ever-changing service needs. In the 5 years since initial implementation, numerous changes have been made in Kentucky IMPACT to provide better training and technical assistance to professionals and families, and, ultimately, to improve services to children and their caregivers. These include the following:

Family Involvement

In addition to the development of parent advocacy groups mentioned earlier, other changes have been made to improve family involvement in Kentucky IMPACT. The original legislation was revised in 1992 to ensure a higher level of family involvement in the program. Parent representation became mandated on regional and state decision-making committees. A state advisory group made up of parent representatives also was formed. This group has played an extensive role in policy formulation. Increased family involvement also was fostered through a parent advocacy and self-help group aligned with the Kentucky Disabilities Coalition and through establishing a dedicated staff position within the Department of Mental Health (DMH). Finally, the Department has administered a CASSP service grant to promote family involvement. Models of innovative family involvement have been pilot tested and evaluated in a number of RIAC districts, including parent advocacy training, parent-designed resource development and allocation, parent networking through a computer-based bulletin board, and multicultural education.

Organizational Development

Organizational development at the regional level was promoted through another initiative. Based on the premise that organizational barriers or lack of capacity could impede the ability to implement the IMPACT program, regions were encouraged to submit proposals to DMH to request technical assistance on developmental issues or specific problems. A range of interventions has been funded, including treatment-oriented foster care, coordinating community responses to ADHD programming, "spinning off" a closely held nonprofit corporation for fundraising and community support, and a variety of training initiatives. Each of these projects was locally designed, then approved by a statewide screening committee. The majority of projects have made use of technical assistance provided by state- or national-level experts.

RIAC Review

Data from the evaluation system, in conjunction with other program data gathered by regions and the DMH, provided useful information for ongoing program planning. However, it was noted that the data were underused at the local level. Therefore, state planners initiated a process to promote periodic program analysis through RIAC reviews. The RIACs are asked to examine a report comparing certain data elements for their region to statewide data from the evaluation system and other sources. A site visit team, composed of persons with expertise in planning and implementing coordinated services, reviews their report, examines relevant data, reviews client records, observes some regional activities, and surveys families. This process results in a review document that provides comprehensive feedback and recommendations to the region. The focus of the document is continuous quality improvement. Areas in which the program is not in compliance with standards and regulations also are noted for correction. A statewide work group is developing a format and process to ensure that such efforts in quality improvement continue.

Psychiatric Residential Treatment Facilities

When the project began, one of the primary components envisioned was PRTFs, which, as noted previously, are small community-based programs designed as alternatives to large facilities and hospitals for longer-term care of children and youth with SED. These have been slow in developing (only six are in place) due to legislative requirements for certificates of need, zoning problems in some communities, and related financial and economic realities. A recent evaluation study details the scope, current functioning, effectiveness, and challenges surrounding these programs (Illback, Shelton, & Birkby, 1996). There remains a significant press for such placements, in light of drastically reduced hospitalization and the abundance of troubled adolescents in the IMPACT program.

Strategic Planning

Beginning early in 1993 and extending through spring 1995, an extensive strategic planning process was conducted, involving literally hundreds of IMPACT constituent group members. A strategic planning group identified five major domains needing attention. Strategic planning workgroups were formed across the state. Using a participatory planning process, each workgroup focused on one of the areas identified, as follows: (a) outcomes, (b) standards and best practices, (c) RIAC/ownership (interagency involvement), (d) human resources development, and, (e) financing (still to be completed). Extensive recommendations were made to the SIAC and adopted in April 1995, establishing the program agenda for the foreseeable future. The outcome workgroup made recommendations for the development of a more outcome oriented system with additional and more precise measures of system, child, and family variables.

Integrated Training

Each of the child-serving organizations in Kentucky provides extensive training opportunities for its providers, but much of this training is focused narrowly. In early 1996, the State Interagency Council commissioned a subcommittee (the Collaborative Training and Technical Assistance Group [CTTAG]) to assess the scope and focus of current provider training, develop strategies for integrating and coordinating initiatives, and formulate a plan to demonstrate coordination and integration of training in pilot regions. Through this ongoing project, tentative agreement has been reached on essential competencies that all organizations aspire to for their providers. A content analysis of current training in light of these goals has been accomplished; a set of principles for effective, integrated training has been delineated; a technology plan for the support of integrated training has been designed; and two regional pilot projects are in the early stages of implementation.

Evaluation of Kentucky IMPACT

A comprehensive evaluation plan is included in the legislative mandate. The DMH (which is responsible for leading program oversight and conducting the evaluation) uses these data for program development and improvement. The Kentucky legislature attaches particular importance to whether the program facilitates stable family life, productive school experiences, and positive relationships with friends and family members. The relative cost efficiency of the program, in contrast with alternative treatment approaches (e.g., hospitalization), also is of concern.

Program evaluation differs from the traditional research paradigm, in that evaluation is seen as a set of rigorous methods to make available technically adequate and relevant information about program processes and outcomes for program managers (e.g., funders, administrators, regional coordinators, and service providers). This information leads to more sound decision making at multiple levels as the program evolves. Therefore, program planning and evaluation are formative processes, contributing to ongoing program development and improvement, in addition to helping reach judgments about the worth of the program relative to its goals.

The evaluation plan addresses seven major program evaluation questions (Illback, 1991):

1. To what extent do children and youth who participate in the Kentucky IMPACT program move toward less restrictive and more stable placements?

2. To what extent do participants increase or improve their school/community adjustment and social skills or interpersonal relationships?

3. To what extent does behavior change occur in children in family living settings?

4. To what extent do families perceive that Kentucky IMPACT interventions are responsive, resulting in increased social support?

5. What is the nature and scope of programming and interagency collaboration for children served through the Kentucky IMPACT plan? How does the service array change over the course of treatment? What are the relationships between the extent and nature of interagency collaboration and child/family outcomes?

6. What factors predict a range of client outcomes in response to intensive, coordinated, community-based services? To what extent do persons close to the intervention perceive meaningful change in behavioral self-control, socialization, achievement, and overall family and school adjustment?

7. Relative to alternative treatment approaches, how cost efficient are services delivered through the Kentucky IMPACT plan?

Design and Measures

Data addressing the above questions are collected on children accepted into Kentucky IMPACT at specific time periods, including intake, every 3 months, every 6 months, every 12 months, and upon exit from the program. These data describe the status of children in the program and the services provided to them and their families. In addition, 12-month follow-up data are collected on each child who exits the program. The data collection schedule is described in Table 6.2.

Some of the instruments used by the evaluation were developed locally, while others are established and available commercially. A demographics and risk factor checklist was derived by an evaluation committee using common

Table 6.2
Kentucky IMPACT Evaluation System Data-Gathering Control Chart

Timeframe	Instrument	Person Responsible
Intake	Demographics	Service Coordinator
	Restrictiveness	
	Placement Stability	
	Child Behavior Checklist	Parent/caregiver
	Family Support	
	Family Empowerment	
	Classroom checklist	Teacher
Quarterly	Service Array/Service Intensity	Service Coordinator
6 months	ROLES/Placement Stability	Service Coordinator
	Progress evaluation	
	Progress evaluation	Teacher
	Child Behavior Checklist	Parent/caregiver
	Family Support	
	Progress evaluation	
	Progress evaluation	Child
12 months	ROLES/Placement Stability	Service Coordinator
	Progress evaluation	
	Progress evaluation	Teacher
	Child Behavior Checklist	Parent/caregiver
	Family Support	
	Progress evaluation	
	Progress evaluation	Child
	Classroom checklist	Teacher
Annually	ROLES/Placement Stability	Service Coordinator
	Progress evaluation	
	Progress evaluation	Teacher
	Child Behavior Checklist	Parent/caregiver
	Family Support	
	Progress evaluation	
	Progress evaluation	Child
	Classroom checklist	Teacher
Exit	Notice of Exit	Service Coordinator

variables such as gender, age, and child and family problem areas. These latter variables were derived from a literature review, and include overlapping dimensions such as poverty, family violence, divorce, abuse and neglect, school problems, and dangerousness (see Table 6.3).

The level of program restrictiveness is measured with an adaptation of an instrument developed by the Pressley Ridge Schools (Hawkins, Almeida, Fabry, & Reitz, 1992) called the Restrictiveness of Living Environments Scale (ROLES). This measure places a range of settings on an equal interval scale where 1 is least restrictive (e.g., independent living) and 10 is most restrictive (e.g., jail). The original Pressley Ridge Scale was validated through a consensual approach using a panel of experts. Adaptation to the range of placements available to children in Kentucky was accomplished through a similar panel approach. For each time interval (e.g., 6 months), the number of days the child spent in a particular setting is recorded, and the ratio of this number in relation to the total number of days (e.g., 182) is multiplied by the restrictiveness score for that setting (e.g., jail = 10.0). When all of the scores for that particular interval are summed, a total restrictiveness score for the interval is derived. On this form is also recorded the number of placements within the interval (1 represents no change in placements, 2 means that the child has lived in 2 settings during the interval). This allows for the creation of a placement stability variable.

The Child Behavior Checklist (CBCL; Achenbach & Edelbrock, 1991) is an established measure. It is administered to the parent (the teacher version was dropped due to noncompliance) at the end of each interval, and yields an overall domain score for both social competence and child psychopathology (problems). Additionally, it yields subscores such as activities, social, and school (competence) and internalizing and externalizing behavior (problems). There is an extensive literature documenting the technical adequacy of this scale and its broad applicability. Less well known is the Family Support Scale (Dunst, Trivette, & Jenkins, 1988), a 26-item social support measure that asks parents to rate the extent to which they receive helpful support in their ecology, including both informal (e.g., friends, neighbors, relatives), and formal (e.g., professional) support. This instrument is available in the public domain and has extensive validation data available.

Another locally developed set of instruments are the Perceptions of Child Progress Scales, which are designed to assess parent, service coordinator, teacher, and child perceptions of progress. Each is periodically asked to rate progress, using a 5-point Likert scale (running from much worse through much improved), in dimensions such as behavioral self-control, emotional adjustment, social skills/relationships, school achievement, school adjustment, and family adjustment. These data provide a degree of social validation for the more clinical and empirically derived measures.

Finally, each quarter, service coordinators fill out a service-delivery array checklist that specifies the services delivered within that time frame across

Table 6.3

Risk Factors by Gender

	Percent-age Female	Percent-age Male
Family/Setting Risks		
Family poverty	60.0	56.4
Parental divorce	52.9	58.3
Three or more siblings	34.0	32.4
Siblings in foster care	18.2	12.5
Family mental illness	39.5	37.1
Family violence	55.5	59.6
Family chemical dependence	50.9	52.4
Adopted	9.1	7.7
Family unavailable for aftercare	11.1	9.3
Parent in psychiatric hospital	15.1	14.7
Parent felony conviction	1.3	2.6
Siblings institutionalized	19.1	13.4
Negative peer influences	38.4	41.4
Child Risks		
Previously in psychiatric hospital	57.5	53.2
Physically abused	38.2	36.8
Sexually abused	56.4	24.2*
Chronic runaway	13.8	11.7
Chronic truant	24.0	22.3
Below grade level achievement	59.5	71.1*
Drug/alcohol abuse	8.7	7.3
Chronic suspension	20.0	37.2*
Other handicapping condition	14.9	16.6
Prior conviction	15.8	18.2
Chronic suicide	32.4	17.2*
Dangerousness		
Sexually abusive to others	6.5	6.1
Danger to others	43.1	62.9*
Danger to self	49.1	41.8
Fire-setting	5.3	21.5*

*10% discrepancy between genders noted.

domains such as case management, counseling/therapy, in-home services, support services, social services, education, therapeutic day services, crisis response, and residential services. Additionally, service coordinators are asked to rate service intensity (high, moderate, low) and agency involvement for each child-serving system (high, moderate, low).

The evaluation plan relies on a repeated-measures (quasi-experimental) design. Given that it was impractical to randomly assign eligible children to treatment and control groups, this design provides the greatest degree of experimental control and rigor possible (Cook & Campbell, 1979; Rossi & Freeman, 1993). A weakness of the design is that it does not provide for a direct contrast with an equivalent group of children who do not receive the treatment. Rather, the design relies on reviewing trends for a range of variables, over time, to assess the directionality of change in relation to program processes. The design also allows for exploratory analyses of relationships between process and outcome measures, and related hypothesis testing of the program's "logic model."

An automated management information system (MIS) has been designed and implemented at the Division of Mental Health to track and aggregate these data. In addition to providing relational databases for storage and retrieval of the information as it is received from local resource coordinators and service coordinators in each region, the MIS program has a flexible report generator that provides for statewide and regional summaries regarding important variables, reports due and past due reminders, and client profile summaries for the purposes of treatment planning and progress determination.

The first formal evaluation of Kentucky IMPACT took place in 1991 (Illback, 1991). At that time, data were available on 497 participants. An evaluation recently completed (Illback, Sanders, & Birkby, 1995) is based on a larger data set (approximately 2,000 participants) and a more fully developed program. Consequently, the most recent findings may be viewed with greater confidence and in a more summative fashion. A secondary reason for the 5-year evaluation was to consider modifications in evaluation procedures suggested by the data themselves, by program managers, and by strategic planners. In this section, four categories of evaluation questions will be addressed: (a) Who has been served by the Kentucky IMPACT program?, (b) What services have been provided to the participants?, (c) What changes have occurred in child and family functioning during involvement with the Kentucky IMPACT program?, and (d) What is the estimated per-child cost of the program compared with the cost of uncoordinated services?

Characteristics of Children and Youth Served

A description of the children and youth included in the evaluation sample is presented in Table 6.4.[6] Included in this sample are those who were accepted and served by the program as of June 1995 and for whom data were available (as of this writing, nearly 4,000 children have been accepted into the program, although not all have been served). The majority of program participants are boys. However, gender representation varies across age ranges as girls begin to pour into the system at adolescence. Early- to middle-year adolescents are overrepresented in the program to a substantial degree. This raises a number of challenging questions about program design and implementation. Although IMPACT is a statewide program, it is implemented by regional committees. Therefore, regional variables influence both which children are accepted and implementation priorities. One question raised by the data is whether young adolescents are the intended targets of the program, and whether relationships exist between age and outcome. It appears that in early to mid adolescence boys continue to predominate, but gradually the proportion of boys to girls becomes more balanced in late adolescence.

Children diagnosed ADHD with behavior disorders (e.g., oppositional defiant disorder) constitute the largest group served by Kentucky IMPACT. Children diagnosed with mood and anxiety disorders constitute the next largest subgroups. Small percentages of the children served have a primary diagnosis of

Table 6.4

Characteristics of the Children and Youth Served ($N = 1,971$)

Gender

Males	71.9%
Females	29.1%

Age Range

0–4	5–8	9–12	13–16	17–21
0.5%	10.4%	28.1%	42.3%	18.8%

Diagnosis	Percentage
Behavior (ADHD)	54.2
Mood	19.9
Anxiety	9.7
Development	1.9
Psychotic	2.6
Personality	0.5
Other	10.0

Program Duration Patterns

954 Exited, 33 Exited Twice
Average days in program = 423
Median days in program = 348
Maximum days in program = 1,359

developmental disorder, psychotic disorder, or personality disorder. A significant number of participants have been identified as having adjustment disorders.

At the time of acceptance into Kentucky IMPACT, data are collected by service coordinators regarding the presence of demographic, family, and child risk factors. An analysis of these risk factors by gender and age is presented in Tables 6.3 and 6.5. Gender differences in relation to risk factors are relatively few and predictable. Many of the differences that emerge across age ranges follow predictable developmental patterns. Most variables are relatively stable.

To identify patterns related to risk factors, a factor analysis was conducted (see Table 6.6). This analysis reveals a number of problem areas or underlying themes that cut across specific risks or problems experienced by participants. The specification of risks, conducted at intake, demonstrates that the needs of the population served are multiple and complex, yet they seem to fit some consistent patterns. Each of the factors should be viewed as a constellation of risks that "load" on a larger underlying variable (see factor labels). Whereas cluster analysis will show how "cases" cluster together around certain variables, factor analysis reveals the diversity of the population. Any individual may have multiple risk factor involvement; the factor analysis demonstrates patterns of group risks. Factors identified in Table 6.6 are listed in order of the variance for which they account. Not surprisingly, problems of conduct account for the greatest variance, closely followed by family abuse and violence. Overall, about 50% of the risk factor variance is shared by these underlying factors.

Service-Delivery Patterns

An analysis of the agencies serving children, by age range, at the time of their entry into Kentucky IMPACT is presented in Table 6.7. Agency involvement at intake is consistent with developmental expectations. The highest overall level of involvement is with the mental health system, followed by social services, both of which are reasonably consistent across ages. Juvenile court and special education involvement increase with age, as would be anticipated.

The services received by Kentucky IMPACT children are summarized in Table 6.8. Service coordination appears to be the most frequently occurring service area, with relatively high rates maintained in most RIAC districts. Little redirection in rates of service coordination are found over time, which raises questions concerning the degree to which the goal of reducing family dependence on IMPACT is being realized. The most extensively used support services are hourly respite, wraparound aides, and Big Brother programs. Relatively low rates are seen for the remaining support services. What seems most surprising is that almost half of program participants are served in regular education programs. This suggests that underidentification of children with EBD continues to be a problem in Kentucky. The remaining 50% are served in special education programs. A reduction in homebound instruction has occurred, although this may be partly due to a smaller number of participants, with more severely involved

Table 6.5

Risk Factors by Age Range

Risk Factors	Age Range (percentage)				
	0–4	5–8	9–12	13–16	17–21
Family/Setting Risks					
Family poverty	44.4	71.6	63.3	53.9	49.2
Parental divorce	55.6	53.4	54.4	59.7	55.7
Three or more siblings	11.1	27.9	34.5	32.6	34.2
Siblings in foster care	33.3	20.1	18.7	11.7	8.7
Family mental illness	44.4	37.3	38.9	38.5	34.5
Family violence	66.7	69.1	59.6	56.9	53.8
Family chemical dependence	66.7	52.9	52.9	52.3	48.9
Adopted	0.0	5.9	7.3	8.4	10.3
Family unavailable for aftercare	11.1	10.8	9.6	8.8	11.7
Siblings institutionalized	0.0	8.8	13.5	17.6	15.2
Parent in psychiatric hospital	22.2	12.3	14.4	6.6	12.8
Parent felony conviction	11.1	24.0	19.1	17.1	12.8
Child Risks					
Previous psychiatric hospitalization	0.0	31.4	44.4	60.5	69.8
Physically abused	33.3	47.5	40.2	35.2	31.5
Sexually abused	33.3	42.6	34.2	29.7	34.5
Chronic runaway	0.0	3.9	4.5	15.5	21.7
Chronic suicide	0.0	11.8	12.0	22.4	39.4
Chronic truant	0.0	2.9	10.2	27.6	42.4
Below grade level achievement	22.2	50.0	67.6	72.6	68.5
Drug/alcohol abuse	0.0	0.5	0.5	8.8	20.1
Chronic suspension	11.1	11.8	24.2	39.7	40.2
Other handicapping condition	22.2	16.7	16.9	14.4	18.5
Negative peer influences	22.2	19.6	29.5	46.9	54.9
Dangerousness Risks					
Sexually abusive to others	0.0	6.9	7.6	6.2	4.1
Prior felony conviction	0.0	0.0	1.1	2.5	4.6
Danger to others	77.8	63.7	60.0	56.8	50.5
Danger to self	55.6	43.1	41.6	43.0	49.2
Fire-setting	22.2	22.5	18.4	17.6	10.1

youth moving to residential care. A small percentage of participants receive overnight crisis care ("emergency/temporary shelter"), but a substantially higher percentage receive in-home crisis services. This is consistent with the program model, which emphasizes prevention of out-of-home placement. Slight increases in emergency psychiatric evaluation may be attributable to successful completers,

(text continues on page 159)

Table 6.6
Factor Analysis of Risks*

	Eigen-value	Cumulative variance
Factor 1 Conduct Problems, Juvenile Delinquency	**2.8824**	**10.3**
Chronic truancy .69670		
Chronic runaway .62106		
Negative peer influences .58884		
Drug/alcohol abuse .57030		
Chronic suspension .52044		
Prior felony conviction .36349		
Factor 2 Family Abuse, Violence, Disintegration	**2.1227**	**17.9**
Family violence .70345		
Physically abused .61862		
Family chemical dependency .57506		
Parent convicted of felony .46378		
Family unavailable for aftercare .44939		
Siblings in foster care .33387		
Sexually abused .31109		
Factor 3 Self-Injurious Behavior	**1.6794**	**23.9**
Chronic suicide .76430		
Danger to self .72126		
Previous psychiatric hospitalization .60191		
Factor 4 Dangerousness	**1.5094**	**29.3**
Fire-setting .64316		
Danger to others .62923		
Family unavailable for aftercare −.35373		
Chronic suspension .31057		
Factor 5 Family Distress	**1.3077**	**33.9**
Adopted −.70607		
Family poverty .60805		
Parental divorce .46640		

(continues)

Table 6.6 *Continued*

		Eigen-value	Cumulative variance
Factor 6 Family Disintegration		**1.2125**	**38.3**
Three or more siblings	.74565		
Siblings institutionalized	.65188		
Siblings in foster care	.49051		
Factor 7 Family Mental Illness		**1.1342**	**42.3**
Parent in psychiatric hospital	.79584		
Family mental illness	.72431		
Factor 8 Sexual Abuse		**1.0946**	**46.2**
Sexual abuse of others	.82622		
Sexually abused	.60945		

*Varimax rotated factor matrix.

Table 6.7

Agency Involvement by Age Range at Intake[a]

Age	Social Services	Mental Health	Juvenile Court	Special Education
0–4	77.8	100.0	11.1	44.4
5–8	64.7	87.7	3.4	55.9
9–12	61.6	86.5	10.7	62.9
13–16	62.6	85.6	31.6	63.3
17–21	68.2	82.1	39.1	61.4

[a]Figures are percentages.

Table 6.8

Services Received[a]

Services	3 Months	9 Months	2 Years
Service Coordination			
Assessment	77	47	43
Case coordination	95	90	81
Monitoring	85	87	81
Community resource development	43	36	35
Interagency treatment plan	80	71	67
Advocacy	47	43	38
Tracking/follow up	60	58	58
Referral to other agency/facility	46	39	39
Crisis intervention	28	26	24
Support Services			
In-home training	18	15	13
Other in-home intervention	12	11	10
Respite care-hourly	29	31	25
Overnight respite	7	8	9
Attendant/wraparound aide	25	31	23
Parent support/education group	11	9	11
Adult friend program (Big brother)	20	23	21
Tutor	8	8	4
Education Services			
Regular education	45	43	38
Special ed resource room	28	28	29
Special ed self-contained	22	22	24
Day treatment program	7	6	5
Homebound instruction	5	2	1
Individual counseling in school	15	13	11
Group counseling in school	8	10	9

[a]Figures are percentages.

having left the program by 2 years; those that remain may have more challenges and persistent needs.

Child and Family Outcomes

In this section, changes that appear to occur relative to major outcome variables are considered. Data portrayed in Table 6.9 for each of these dimensions

(*text continues on page 162*)

Table 6.9

Changes on Major Outcome Variables (Repeated Measures MANOVA)

		Mean Values			F-values for Changes During Period	
	N	start	6 months	1 year	1st 6 months	2nd 6 months
CBCL: Behavior Problems						
Total Problems	431	75.34	71.78	69.55	84.4***	93.2***
Internalizing	431	69.79	66.81	64.49	50.1***	84.4***
Externalizing	431	73.72	70.54	68.93	68.5***	54.2***
CBCL: Social Competence						
Total	208	30.37	32.00	33.46	10.9***	20.2***
Activities	382	40.91	41.70	41.98	2.6	2.4
School	260	30.45	31.39	32.65	3.5	16.7***
Social	345	31.08	33.57	34.74	20.0***	23.3***
Family Support						
Informal Kinship	509	2.122	2.162	2.174	0.7	0.6
Social Organization	509	1.399	1.377	1.385	0.2	0.0
Formal Kinship	509	1.781	1.748	1.698	0.6	3.5
Nuclear Family	509	1.995	1.924	1.940	1.7	0.2
Specialized Professional Services	509	1.587	1.926	1.947	86.0***	38.3***
Generic Professional Services	509	1.200	1.231	1.185	0.7	0.7

(continues)

Table 6.9 Continued

		Mean Values			F-values for Changes During Period	
	N	start	6 months	1 year	1st 6 months	2nd 6 months
Restrictiveness of Living Environment						
Psychiatric Hospital	953	0.6980	0.3251	0.3103	59.8***	27.1***
Residential Treatment	953	0.2986	0.2853	0.5424	0.1	30.5***
Foster Care	953	0.3715	0.4173	0.4497	2.7	5.2*
Family Home	953	1.263	1.363	1.290	19.2***	1.5

*Significant at .05 level. **Significant at .01 level. ***Significant at .001 level

are derived from two SPSS for Windows (version 7) operations: paired-samples T-tests and repeated measures MANOVA. The mean values are from T-tests using a listwise exclusion of cases so that the group of cases would be constant. F-values are from the repeated-measures MANOVA. Both procedures generate the number of cases and T-values (F-values are squared T-values); this overlap aids corroboration of the accuracy of result matching from the two sources.

The repeated measures MANOVA considers change in the second interval (between the time 2 measurement at 6 months and the time 3 measurement at 1 year) in the context of change during the first interval. It does this by considering the time 3 data relative to the mean of time 1 and time 2 data rather than relative to just the time 2 data from the beginning of the 2nd time interval. For example, the declining means on the "Psychiatric Hospital" line on the table show that during the first 6 months a person spends in the program, the number of days spent in psychiatric hospitals is reduced by roughly 50% from the number of days spent in such facilities during the 6 months prior to entry into the program. During the second 6 months, there is an additional reduction of about 5%. While a paired samples T-test would consider the slight reduction from .3251 to .3103 without regard to the initial .6980 level, the repeated measures MANOVA compares the .3103 to the mean of .3251 and .6980.

Using the repeated measures MANOVA in this situation can be thought of as a compromise between two simpler and more clear-cut ways of looking at improvement associated with a social program. One might assume that an improvement resulting from an intervention would behave like the kind of change seen in quantum physics. The intervention is associated with a permanent change to a new level, which becomes the new inertial situation; there is no tendency to return to the initial level, or to continue changing in the direction of the first change. If this assumption were appropriate in a real-world situation, one would want to use a simple paired-samples T-test comparing one time period with the preceding time period only. Alternatively, one could assume that an improvement associated with participation in a social program is likely to be temporary, and to completely dissipate. That is, inertial forces are pulling performance back to the preimprovement, initial level, and the prolongation of an improvement is a distinct achievement, rather than something to be taken for granted. Making this assumption, it would be appropriate to ignore intermediate data and use a simple paired-samples T-test to compare data for any period only with the initial level (e.g., compare .3103 with .6980, ignoring the intermediate level of .3251).

Using repeated-measures MANOVA to compare .3103 with the mean of .3251 and .6980 assumes that the portion of the prior improvement that can be expected to dissipate will be equal to the portion of the prior improvement that can be expected to remain permanent. Thus, the F value for the change during the second interval (27.1) is nearly half as big as the F value for the first interval (59.8), instead of being very small. (The F value for the paired-samples T-test for the reduction from .3251 to .3103 is only .13, which is not statistically significant at all.)

Behavior Problems

A central evaluation question is whether program participants make substantial behavior changes as a result of IMPACT services. Child Behavior Checklist (CBCL; Achenbach & Edelbrock, 1991) data are compared in Table 6.9. To a greater extent than for any other outcome measure, substantial positive gains are made by program participants in the area of behavior problems (decreased psychopathology). These changes appear to be sustained over time. While externalizing problems are more pronounced, the pattern and direction of change is similar for both internalizing and externalizing behavior. The evaluation design does not include a contrasting or comparison condition. Therefore, a functional relationship between program variables and the outcomes observed is not established. Nevertheless, it is heartening that gains of this magnitude are made and sustained by program participants (many, of course, remain in the clinical range).

Social Competence

Changes in CBCL ratings of social competence (a major program goal) over time also are presented in Table 6.9. In contrast with gains seen in the behavior problems area of the CBCL, social competence change is more modest at 1 year from program initiation. The finding of more limited change in social competence suggests that this area is more complicated and difficult to sustain and may take longer to occur. Informal focus group discussion with program staff also suggests that Kentucky IMPACT does not place a high priority on formal social skill intervention.

Family Support

Another evaluation question addresses the issue of changes in family perceptions of social support, as measured by the Family Support Satisfaction Scale (adapted from Dunst, Trivette, & Jenkins, 1988). Data shown in Table 8 represent mean domain scores and suggest that families perceive and are satisfied with the social and emotional support they receive from the Kentucky IMPACT program (Specialized Professional Services). This effect is sustained over time, and should be viewed as a positive indicator of program effectiveness. The question of greatest concern raised by these data is the extent to which participation in Kentucky IMPACT may unwittingly facilitate isolation by creating a dependency for support on a system that is, at best, intended to be transitory. The challenge, of course, is to formulate interventions that are helpful and supportive but at the same time promote self-sufficiency. This has become a greater focus for the program, and subsequent evaluative efforts will be geared toward more precise measurement of family competence and self-sufficiency.

Placement Restrictiveness

Data regarding the stability of residential placements for participants served by IMPACT are also presented in Table 6.9. This analysis addresses the question of whether program participants experience significant reductions over time in the restrictiveness of their placements (a key program goal), as measured by the Restrictiveness of Living Environments Scale (ROLES). The data reflect restrictiveness scores derived from this instrument (more restrictive settings yield higher scores). Patterns with respect to types of placement also were examined. The most dramatic gains are in reduction of psychiatric hospitalizations. At the same time, there is an increase in the use of residential treatment, possibly in reverse correlation to hospitalization patterns. On a more modest level, positive increases are seen in the use of foster care and family home living (initial 6 months).

These findings raise questions about the extent to which Kentucky IMPACT is fulfilling its stated goal of moving toward a community-based system of care. While there appear to be modest increases in such services, and dramatic reductions in hospitalizations, the extent to which residential treatment programming increases over time for many participants is of concern. In this context, the data raise a conceptual question relating to the value placed on various forms of treatment, and whether they are consistent with program intent. Certainly, it is far less expensive to serve these youngsters in residential programs than in psychiatric hospitals, but are the rates of community-based services adequate to infer that the program is meeting all of its goals? An alternative perspective might be that since the majority of participants are served and maintained in the community, IMPACT is fulfilling its mission. Consistent with this view, increases in residential treatment are not necessarily failures, but may represent the legitimate system function of helping "sort out" child and family needs and find the most appropriate level of care, which for the most challenging can include residential programs.

Placement Stability

The number of placements experienced by IMPACT participants in the year prior to their acceptance into the program was compared with the number of placements at 1 year and 2 years following admission. This analysis revealed that in the year prior to acceptance, children and youth experienced an average of 2.33 changes in placements, compared with an average of 1.53 placement changes after 1 year, and 1.67 placements 2 years after program entry. In all likelihood, stabilization of placement is a key to successes experienced within the program, given that it takes time and sustained effort to mobilize a community-based intervention.

Exiting Patterns

When participants leave the program, they are interviewed to determine their reasons for leaving. These data, presented in Table 6.10, also provide an indication of program outcome. A substantial portion of program participants (over a third), who leave Kentucky IMPACT are judged by service coordinators to have successfully completed the program. In light of the number and severity of participant needs and the complexity of the program, this figure seems relatively high. These data may provide one of the most effective measures of program success, in that clinical gains alone do not indicate that the individual has made sufficient progress to complete the program. On the other hand, it is worth noting that many individuals who are not judged to have successfully completed the program have probably nonetheless made substantial gains. Therefore, these data should not be interpreted to imply that two thirds are unsuccessful; the bulk of the data demonstrates just the opposite.

Participant Reactions

Another measure of program success is the perceptions of participants in Kentucky IMPACT regarding whether meaningful change has occurred in areas such as school achievement, emotional adjustment, family adjustment, relationship skills, school adjustment, and behavioral self-control. These data are evaluated

Table 6.10

Reason for Exiting

	Percentage
Program intervention complete	37.5
Child moved	21.1
Child/family chose to leave program	15.7
Child entered residential placement	8.2
Contact lost with child/family	2.0
Other reasons	14.9
Reasons unknown/not listed	0.7

after participants have spent a year in the program. The extent to which parents, teachers, service coordinators, and children agree on the degree to which change has occurred also was analyzed, using a short survey instrument (Likert scale). In general, it appears that parents, teachers, service coordinators, and children all perceive positive, meaningful change to have occurred after 1 year, but there are some interesting differences between the respondents. Approximately 75% of participating parents perceive some or much improvement on most variables (with the exception of school adjustment, which is lower). Teachers, on the other hand, give overall lower ratings of change (perhaps confirming parental judgments), with about 60% rating most variables as somewhat or much improved. Service coordinator ratings are consistent with parent ratings, in that about 70% rate somewhat or much improved on most variables (again, with the exception of school adjustment, which is lower). Finally, children rate most variables in the 75% range also, but they rate themselves lower on self-control and achievement.

These subtle differences between child and adult ratings may indicate that children perceive that they have not improved in self-control, even though adults perceive change in this area. Moreover, it appears that children are less likely to perceive that their school adjustment is problematic, even though adults view this as an area in which gains are not as evident. The overall impression left by these data is that Kentucky IMPACT is having a substantial effect on family-related, behavioral, and relationship-oriented functioning, but is not having as great an impact on school functioning. Clearly, schools play a vital role in the life of these youngsters, both in terms of learning and family support. A major challenge for the program is to enhance and improve school involvement and education-related outcomes.

Relationships Between Outcomes

To determine the independence of evaluation measures, an analysis was performed of the extent to which program outcomes are independent of one another. Correlations among gains in family support, social competence, and related behavior problems were computed to determine whether current instruments measure the same dimensions. Only one correlation between outcome measures was statistically significant (a modest inverse relationship between restrictiveness scores and successful completion). The higher the restrictiveness score, the lower the rate of successful completion. Low correlations between the remaining outcomes appear to indicate that they are relatively independent of one another, and can be evaluated in their own right. Thus, the instruments that are being used apparently do not overlap, which argues for their continuation. Conceptually, these findings support the use of multiple measures. On the other hand, judging "success" becomes more challenging, in that positive outcomes in one area will not necessarily be accompanied by similar outcomes in another. It is clear that this poses one of the most difficult questions for managers and evaluators: Who has been helped, how, and to what degree?

Cost-Efficiency

The average approximate cost saving to the "child-serving" system for these children is represented by the estimated cost of service delivery for the year prior to program entry, minus the estimated cost for the first year of IMPACT services. These data are based on estimates of program component costs multiplied by the number of days of service within specified time intervals. Both in the year prior to and in the first year of IMPACT participation, the total cost of programming for these youngsters is quite high and variable. Compared with the prior year, an approximate 36% reduction in estimated overall cost to the system is realized during the first year in the program ($13,898 estimated per-child cost for prior year; $8,886 for initial IMPACT year). An examination of the distribution of cost estimates reveals that extreme numbers (presumably highly expensive programs in residential/hospital settings) are drastically reduced in the first year of involvement, accounting for a significant portion of the overall cost reduction.

The savings generated by such reductions in overall cost are distributed across the child service system. While these projected savings do not appear in a specific budget or category, they allow more children to be served within the overall system. Extrapolating to the 1,971 children in the current study, a total potential savings of as much as $10 million can be projected, assuming that the costs would remain stable in the absence of the program. Thus, Kentucky IMPACT appears to be a cost-efficient intervention program.

Discussion

Current Status

The results just presented provide a descriptive analysis of what currently is known about a comprehensive, statewide system-of-care initiative for children with severe emotional and behavioral disabilities, Kentucky IMPACT. Begun in 1990, Kentucky IMPACT has evolved into a mature system. The evaluation data support the conclusion that Kentucky IMPACT has, in large measure, fulfilled its initial objectives. The program appears to be serving the population it was intended to serve. A comprehensive and individualized array of services has been developed. Substantial evidence of clinical gains exists in areas such as behavior problems, family support, placement stability, and consumer satisfaction. Drastic reductions in the psychiatric hospitalization of children are apparent, and these reductions appear to account for significant savings to the system as a whole.

One of the most important strengths of the program has been its openness to consider evaluation data, recognize potential problems, and make adjustments accordingly. Thus, certain themes and issues have been delineated over time as requiring additional focus and improvement. Some of the most promi nent issues raised by the most recent evaluation include: (a) differences across regions with respect to the number and characteristics of children served; (b) the relative contributions of schools to the system-of-care intervention and the need to promote greater involvement and ownership; (c) continued under-identification of children with EBD in schools, and less positive school-related outcomes; (d) limited use of home-based service approaches; (e) limited out-comes related to social competence, possibly attributable to lack of emphasis within the program; (f) concern about potential family isolation and depen-dence on the program; (g) increasing use of residential (out-of-home) pro-grams; (h) appropriateness of screening and eligibility determinations based on demographic, risk, or diagnostic variables; (i) criteria to determine who has been successful; and, (j) allocation of resources appropriately to maximize gains.

Future Directions

Future evaluation research will need to focus on discovering and more pre-cisely measuring process variables that are associated with outcomes, and structured analysis to better understand complex relationships among process and outcome variables. Toward this end, the Outcomes Workgroup's strategic planning recommendations seek to build on what has already been learned and to fill in some of the gaps.

One of the recommendations of the Outcomes Workgroup was to adopt a measure of family empowerment to be completed by parents at intake, 1 year, 2 years, and at exit. Another significant recommendation was to adopt an edu-cational status checklist used by Family Resource and Youth Services Centers, to be filled out by the teacher at intake or in October, and then each subsequent April (at the end of school year). This has a higher probability of involving teachers and procuring school-related data. The addition of family empower-ment and educational measures should increase the capacity of the evalua-tion to obtain relevant information. The family empowerment measure is espe-cially critical, given the need to better understand the role of the family in terms of involvement, skills and attitudes, and "engagement." It also is hoped that a more abbreviated teacher measure will yield an improved response rate, and perhaps more important, lead to increased interaction between teachers, service coordinators, and families. In addition to these changes to the evalua-tion design, a renewed effort will be made to enable families, program person-nel, legislators, and other concerned parties to use evaluation data in their decision making. Current software is being enhanced to generate more timely and readable reports for various purposes, and self-evaluation and program review formats are underway to ensure that program personnel routinely con-sider these data.

Conclusion

Although the results of Kentucky's systems change efforts have been heartening, the problems of effectively coordinating and delivering services to children and youth with SED are by no means solved. In the last biennium, Kentucky experienced major budgetary shortfalls that reduced the ability to fill key staff positions at the state level as well as in the RIACs. In addition, old attitudes and habitual patterns of service delivery have resulted in the continuation of barriers to providing integrated services in some regions. Notwithstanding these problems, the commitment to achieving the goal of integrated services for children with SED and their families remains firm at both state and local levels. The Kentucky Cabinet for Families and Children recently received a grant from the Center for Mental Health Services to strengthen current family support services through funding a family advocacy coordinator and a state parent council.

It would be presumptuous to claim that what we have presented is a total model for statewide services to these children and families. Indeed, a complete model does not exist. Although Kentucky IMPACT is a statewide program, direct administration and implementation occur at the local level. This means that local and regional variables have much influence on how the program is shaped to fit unique needs. Fortunately, the organizational structure of IMPACT permits and even encourages regional variation. Moreover, the variety of characteristics and needs from state to state preclude the adoption of a single model. While each state must develop programs that suit its unique characteristics and needs, certain components have general utility. These include organized political and public support, mechanisms for coordination and collaboration among agencies, strategies for pooling human and fiscal resources, and the elements of community-based service delivery.

Fortunately, the emergence of a number of integrated programs (Illback, 1994) allows program planners to study and potentially adopt components of programs that seem best suited to their needs. As more programs develop and information about their characteristics and benefits is disseminated, it will be possible for planners to use components of these programs as models.

While integrated community-based programming shows great promise for more effectively and efficiently meeting the needs of children and families, data regarding outcomes are not widely available. Although the evaluation just completed suggests that Kentucky IMPACT is an effective program, controlled studies are needed that document the results of integrated versus nonintegrated programming on the short- and long-term status of children and families, and on the allocation of public funds for education and human services. These studies should include comparisons of the effects of services that are integrated with those that are delivered without service coordination. Longitudinal studies should follow children and families through life and service events, detailing these events and their impact on both experimental and control groups. Given the dearth of systematic evaluations and of consistent research findings, reported outcomes should be regarded as "best practices" rather than as empirically proven techniques (E. Edgar, personal communication, July, 1991). We hope that, as the spate of new projects developed with the support of the Center for Mental Health Services, the Robert Wood Johnson Foundation, and the U.S. Office of Special Education and Rehabilitation Services develop, such data will be forthcoming. Until such time, it is important to recognize that serving children and families in their home communities through locally available services, provided before their problems become intractable, is a worthy goal.

We have learned many important (and generalizable) lessons from the conduct of this evaluation. We have come to believe that the extent to which these findings have been perceived as relevant by program managers validates the participatory approach we have followed. Often, research strives toward experimental control and objectivity by building a wall between evaluators and managers; our approach has been oriented in the opposite direction. There are obviously daunting methodological problems that limit causal attributions in relation to this program, but the process of engaging participants in the conceptualization, conduct, and interpretation of the evaluation "breathes life" into the data. The receptivity of program managers to reviewing the data, especially when the results are not compelling in a particular area (or when there are political ramifications), is crucial to the ongoing success of any system of evaluation. Fortunately, we were blessed with a receptive audience that was committed to building evaluation into the routine of the program.

An additional lesson relates to the need to be sensitive to evolutionary program changes, which can change questions, or place them in a different light. Some of our initial questions, including those that focus on outcomes, now appear simplistic and narrow. We have come to understand that the comprehensive system of care we are evaluating is a complex entity. Moreover, the population being served is not unitary, and the service array is idiosyncratic to each recipient. We have completed a number of cluster and discriminant analyses that are useful in describing the complexity within the system, and we expect to publish these elsewhere. We are now in the process of refining our questions and formulating some special studies that may help us further "unpack" process variables that may correlate with outcomes (e.g., family engagement, collaboration, focus, and the helping style of the service coordinator).

The global question as to whether a statewide system of care is "better than" the preceding, more traditional child mental health system is subject to the same limitations as asking whether behavior therapy is preferable to psychoanalysis. As statewide initiatives evolve across the nation, it seems likely that more refined evaluation questions will ask: Which arrays of programs and services work best with which groups of service recipients to facilitate cost-efficient change across one or more outcome areas? No one evaluation can address all the complex questions that will emerge, but we are hopeful that the present evaluation contributes in a credible way to the dialogue.

Endnotes

1. By the December 1, 1994, Kentucky Department of Education child count, the percentage of students with EBD who had been identified and were receiving services had increased to 0.64%.

2. For the 1995–96 fiscal year, $20 million has been allocated for children and families accepted by Kentucky IMPACT.

3. *Emotional and behavioral disorders* is the term used in Kentucky to designate students eligible for special education and related services.

4. See Phillips, Nelson, and McLaughlin (1993) for a description of the changes made in the educational system to better serve students with EBD.

5. IFBSS funds are allocated to be used flexibly for wraparound support of children and families. In the 1995 fiscal year, $2,078,000 has been allocated for this purpose.

6. As of February 21, 1996, 6,926 children and youth have been nominated for IMPACT services since the official start of the program in October 1990. A total of 3,935 of these nominations have been accepted for IMPACT services.

7. A more comprehensive description and discussion of these analyses can be found in Illback, Sanders, & Birkby (1995). It is available from the Kentucky Department of Mental Health, 275 E. Main St., Frankfort, KY 40621.

Authors' Note

Correspondence may be addressed to Robert J. Illback, Executive Director, REACH of Louisville, Inc., 101 E. Kentucky St., Louisville, KY 40203.

References

Achenbach, T. M., & Edelbrock, C. S. (1991). *Child behavior checklist.* Burlington: University of Vermont, Department of Psychiatry.

Cook, T. D., & Campbell, D. T. (1979). *Quasi-experimentation: Design and analysis issues for field settings.* Chicago: Rand McNally.

Dunst, C. J., Trivette, C. M., & Jenkins, R. (1988). The Family Support Scale. In C. J. Dunst, M. Trivette, & A. G. Deal (Eds.), *Enabling and empowering families: Principles and guidelines for practice.* Cambridge, MA: Brookline.

Hawkins, R. P., Almeida, M. C., Fabry, B., & Reitz, A. L. (1992). A scale to measure restrictiveness of living environments for troubled children and youths. *Hospital and Community Psychiatry, 43,* 54–57.

Illback, R. J. (1991, November). *Formative evaluation of the Kentucky IMPACT program for children and youth with severe emotional disabilities.* Frankfort, KY: Cabinet for Human Resources, Division of Mental Health, Children and Youth Services Branch.

Illback, R. J. (1994). Poverty and the crisis in children's services: The need for services integration. *Journal of Clinical Child Psychology, 23,* 413–424.

Illback, R. J., Sanders, D., & Birkby, B. (1995, August). *Evaluation of the Kentucky IMPACT program at year five: Accomplishments, challenges, and opportunities.* Frankfort, KY: Cabinet for Human Resources, Division of Mental Health, Children and Youth Services Branch.

Illback, R. J., Shelton, D., & Birkby, B. (1996). *Medicaid de-certification and aftercare planning within Kentucky's Psychiatric Residential Treatment Facilities (PRTF) and child psychiatric hospitals.* Frankfort, KY: Cabinet for Human Resources, Division of Mental Health, Children and Youth Services Branch.

Institute of Medicine. (1989). *Research on children and adolescents with mental, behavioral, and developmental disorders.* Washington, DC: National Academy.

Kentucky Cabinet for Human Resources. (1990). *Kentucky's comprehensive mental health services plan on behalf of adults with severe mental illness and children and youth with severe emotional problems.* Frankfort, KY: Kentucky Cabinet for Human Resources, Department for Mental Health and Mental Retardation Services, Division of Mental Health.

Kentucky Task Force on the Over and Under Identification of Handicapped Children in Kentucky (1986, August). *Identification of children with handicaps in Kentucky.* Frankfort: Kentucky Department of Education.

Phillips, V., Nelson, C. M., & McLaughlin, J. R. (1993). Systems change and services for students with emotional/behavioral disabilities in Kentucky. *Journal of Emotional and Behavioral Disorders, 1,* 155–164.

Rossi, P. H., & Freeman, H. E. (1993). *Evaluation: A systematic approach.* Newbury Park, CA: Sage.

Systems of Care in California: Current Status of the Ventura Planning Model

7

Craig K. Ichinose, Donald W. Kingdon,
and Randall Feltman

The Ventura County Children's Demonstration Project was initiated in 1985 in an effort to alter fundamentally the delivery of mental health services for children and families in California. The project's mission was to build a child- and family-focused system of care that linked local public agencies with a mandate to serve youths at risk for placement outside their homes. Since the conclusion of the project in 1988, the system has continued to develop fiscally and programmatically in a climate of changing economic conditions and government policy (e.g., Ichinose, Kingdon, & Hernandez, 1994; Ichinose, Kingdon, King, Clark, & Hernandez, 1994; Kingdon, 1994; Kingdon, Ichinose, & Ramirez, 1995; Murphy et al. 1996; Ventura County Mental Health, 1995). Throughout this period of change, the Ventura Planning Model (Jordan & Hernandez, 1990) has remained an essential guide to this ongoing development. The system-building processes addressed in the model reflect the planning and implementation of the county's initial demonstration and provide a framework for the system's growth.

As a prescription for change, the model addresses five basic issues: (a) Whom does the system serve? (b) What outcomes does the system seek to achieve? (c) Who are the public and private partners that participate in the child-serving process and in what ways do they contribute to this process? (d) What services does the system provide? and (e) How is the accountability of the system monitored? Building a system of care requires that these issues be addressed sequentially in a series of steps, each of which is necessary but not sufficient to accomplish the overall result (see Table 7.1). Unlike the process of changing a program, an agency, or a service continuum, this approach seeks to integrate mental health

Table 7.1

Process of Developing a System of Care
as Articulated in the Ventura Planning Model

Sequence	Goal	Focus of Activities
Step One	Identify target population	Specify criteria that identify the individuals whom the system will serve.
Step Two	Define system goals	Specify measurable objectives that the system will achieve in terms of client, consumer, and system outcomes.
Step Three	Develop partnerships	Specify agencies and others that will collaborate in developing and implementing the system and identify their respective roles.
Step Four	Establish services and standards	Specify services that the system will provide and the methods by which they will be delivered.
Step Five	Develop system monitoring and evaluation	Specify methods by which the system's processes and outcomes will be monitored and related information disseminated to system.

services with services provided by other public and private agencies and has been used locally to target selected groups of "high service-users," avoid duplication of services by efficient use of existing resources, and improve outcomes for this group of children and families (Stroul & Friedman, 1986). The latter remain important goals for agencies in the public sector, where the need to recognize the limits of taxpayer resources is ever present.

Previous reports have described the early development of the system of care in Ventura County and the outcomes that were achieved during the Demonstration Project (Jordan & Hernandez, 1990; Ventura County Mental Health, 1987a; 1987b; 1988). The purpose of this chapter is to provide an update of outcomes achieved since the project's conclusion. Where appropriate, outcome data are compared with the corresponding aggregate for all 58 counties in California. Because results for the state as a whole provide an indication of how county systems might fare without system reform, statewide trends in measures such as the number and cost of group home placements are important standards against which the performance of an individual county can be judged. Furthermore, factors that have affected the system's development and outcomes since the end of the project are discussed (e.g., population growth, policy changes). The chapter also reviews recent initiatives that have been adopted to enhance existing services and to expand the population of youths served by the system. Finally, issues related to the system's continuing growth are discussed, including system financing, the demands of managed care, services for juvenile offenders, and ongoing system evaluation.

Overview of the Children's Demonstration Project

Local mental health services for children and families throughout California have been delivered by county mental health departments since 1958 (Short-Doyle Act, Statutes of California, 1957). The Children's Demonstration Project was a response to particular problems in this system of county-delivered services that followed the deinstitutionalization movement of the 1970s and early 1980s. One problem was the limited array of available services, including effective community-based treatment, that resulted in an increased use of costly residential care. Another problem was a general lack of coordination among responsible departments and agencies at state and county levels that resulted in poor service planning and frequent overlap in service delivery. To address these and other problems, the California legislature appropriated funds in 1984 for Ventura County to conduct a three-year project to demonstrate the development of a countywide children's mental health system that could serve as a model for reform throughout the state (Chapter 1474, Statutes of California, 1984).

Description of Ventura County

The principal reasons for the selection of Ventura County as the demonstration site were the existing array of services and a tradition of interagency collaboration in the county. In addition, the county is not considered unique demographically, given the state's size and diversity. Located directly northwest of Los Angeles County, Ventura is a semirural county with a diverse economic base and a predominantly white, middle-class population. With 720,500 residents, the county is the 12th largest in the state (California Department of Finance estimate for January 1, 1995). Of its 10 incorporated cities, four have populations over 100,000 (Oxnard, Thousand Oaks, Simi Valley, and Ventura). Oxnard, the largest city, has a population of 154, 600. Ethnic minorities constitute 34% of the county's population, and Hispanics form its largest ethnic group (26%; U.S. Census, 1990). The Hispanic population is concentrated in the western half of the county, where 61% reside in the cities of Oxnard, Ventura, and Santa Paula. Although the county is relatively affluent (median household income = $45,612), pockets of economic disadvantage exist in the county. According to the latest U.S. census for example, 14% of the persons residing in one Oxnard zip code have incomes below the federal poverty level.

With approximately 27% of its population under 18 years old, Ventura County does not rank extremely high or low on indicators of child well-being compared to other counties in California (Children Now, 1995). For example, the county ranked 17th highest and 28th highest in death by suicide and homicide, respectively, among 0–19-year-olds for the period 1990–93 (indexed to 1993 total county population). Similarly, the county ranked 27th in the dropout rate for public school grades 9–12 for the period 1992–94, 18th in child abuse reports per 1,000 children for the period 1991–94, and 17th in rate of births per 1,000 females between the ages of 15 and 19 for 1993.

Developing the System of Care

The Demonstration Project evolved from a five-step planning process (see Table 7.1). The first of these steps was to define clearly whom the system of care would serve. The process of developing criteria to accomplish this resulted in a decision to target youths for whom the public child-serving system was both legally and fiscally responsible. This group included court wards and court dependents who were placed in out-of-home care by court order, special education students with serious emotional disturbance (SED) for whom eligibility for residential services was established by legislative mandate, and other youths with a functional impairment that put them at risk for out-of-home placement. In the second step, goals were identified and defined in terms of specific outcomes to be achieved by the system. Outcomes for the project included reduction in the use of group homes for court wards, court dependents, and students with SED; reduction in state hospital use; reduction in the reincarceration of court wards; and an increase in school attendance and achievement for students with SED. In the third step, the relationships between the agencies that shared responsibility for serving the system's target population were articulated. In the project, efforts to define these partnerships focused on blending staff and funds into integrated programs for achieving the system's prescribed outcomes and creating written interagency agreements and councils for policy development and interagency case management.

The fourth step in the process involved the development of services. These services were community based, family focused, comprehensive enough to meet the various needs of the population served, and the least restrictive that were clinically appropriate to meet the needs of the child and family. They were capable of achieving specific outcomes and organized around a single point of responsibility. In the final step, procedures were developed to monitor the specified outcomes and provide ongoing feedback to stakeholders at different levels. Existing data from individual agencies participating in the project were used to assess change in measures over time. This was critical to the evaluation process in that it allowed regular reporting of results to public officials, service providers, and clients and their families.

Postproject Outcomes

The effectiveness of the Demonstration Project in achieving its outcomes was assessed by comparing data obtained during the project (i.e., July 1, 1985, through June 30, 1988) with data obtained before the project began. Briefly, final evaluation of the project revealed the following results: (a) out-of-county court-ordered placement for wards and dependents decreased 47%; (b) incarceration for court wards following participation in the system's interagency program for juvenile offenders decreased 22%, though the number of days of incarceration increased 28%; (c) total state hospital patient days decreased 68%; (d) out-of-county group home placement for special education students decreased 21%; (e) 85% of children whose families participated in intensive in-home crisis services remained in their homes 6 months after those services ended; and (f) attendance and academic performance improved significantly for special education students served in the project's day treatment program (Jordan & Hernandez, 1990). The results presented in this chapter are an update of these outcomes in five areas: (a) group home placement for court wards and dependents; (b) group home placement for special education students with SED; (c) state hospital placement; (d) reincarceration of court wards; and (e) school performance of students with SED. In reviewing these data, it should be noted that unlike previous evaluation reports, which compared data obtained before and during the project (e.g., Jordan & Hernandez, 1990), the present report compares outcomes that were obtained during the project with results that have been obtained since its conclusion. Thus, the focus here is whether the gains achieved during the project have been maintained.

Group Home Placement for Court Wards and Dependents

Because of the relative cost and restrictiveness, a major goal of the local system is to minimize the use of group homes and residential treatment centers as out-of-home placements for court wards and dependents. These placements are funded by the federal Aid to Families with Dependent Children-Foster Care program (AFDC-FC) and data from the state Department of Social Services (DSS) are used to monitor their number and cost.

Number and Cost of Placements

Figure 7.1 shows the number (solid lines) and cost of placements (dotted lines) for Ventura County (open circles) and the state of California (closed circles) in successive 6-month periods between July 1985 and June 1995. To facilitate comparison of the county's outcomes over time as well as comparison of outcomes for the county and state, data are shown as the average number of placements

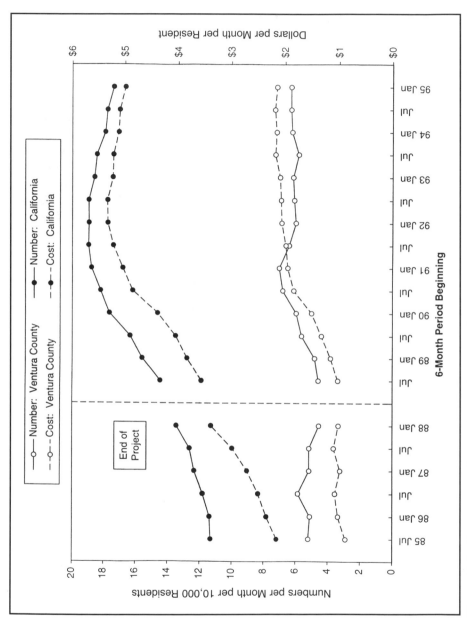

Figure 7.1. Comparison of group home placement for court wards and dependents in Ventura County and the state of California.

per month per 10,000 residents 0–18 years old (left axis) and average cost per month per 0–18 year old resident (right axis). Population estimates used to compute these rates were adjusted each year using census data obtained from the state Department of Finance.

Figure 7.1 reveals three major findings. First, the county's placement rate remained considerably below the state rate throughout the 10-year period. Overall, the county rate was 43% of the state rate during the project and 34% during the 7 years since its conclusion. In general, this result reflects a greater increase in placements statewide than in Ventura County. The county's average placement rate since June 1988 (6.0 per 10,000 residents) was 16% higher than it had been during the project (5.2 per 10,000). In contrast, statewide averages during and after the project were 12.2 and 17.7 per 10,000 residents, respectively.

Second, local and statewide placements leveled off during the second half of the postproject period. County placements reached a peak during the period beginning January 1991 (7.0 per 10,000) and since then have remained below that level. Similarly, statewide placements remained at 18.9 per 10,000 for three consecutive 6-month periods beginning July 1991 and have steadily declined since then. These results coincided with the transfer of nearly all of the state's mental health budget to county departments throughout the state.

Third, placement cost increased for the county and state. Average costs per capita during and after the project were $1.00 and $1.84, respectively, for the county and $2.68 and $4.80 for the state. Furthermore, the county's costs have remained consistently below costs for the state. The county's costs were 37% and 38% of the state's costs during and after the project, respectively. Finally, while the ratio of county to state cost declined through December 1988 (28.5% for the July 1988 period), the ratio has risen steadily since that time. Indeed, the county's per capita cost as a percentage of the state total is now slightly higher than it was when the Demonstration Project began (40.3% for the period beginning July 1985 and 43.2% for the first 6 months of 1995).

Discussion

Local and statewide growth in the 0–18-year-old population and in the cost of group home care make controlling out-of-home placements an increasingly important goal for public mental health systems. Figure 7.1 shows that the local system has been able to maintain placement numbers at levels that are only slightly above those achieved during the Demonstration Project. On the other hand, the county's costs, although they have remained well below state totals, have risen more rapidly than they have statewide since the end of the project. This result is explained in part by the fact that the largest increase in the county's placement cost (22.3%) occurred during the period beginning July 1990, when the method for reimbursing foster care providers (including group homes) under the AFDC-FC program was restructured (Statutes of California, 1989).

Increased costs due to change in the structure that governs reimbursement of providers is noteworthy in two respects. First, it reminds us that number and cost, in part, measure different processes and should not be used interchangeably as measures of placement outcome. Second, it suggests that the efforts of local systems to control placement cost may depend on the effectiveness of their strategies in the area of fiscal innovation and service funding as well as their continuing efforts to develop more effective clinical and therapeutic interventions to keep youths out of placement or to return them to the community.

Group Home Placement for Special Education Students

Enacted during the Demonstration Project, State Assembly Bill 3632 (Chapter 1747, Statutes of California, 1984) directed the state Department of Education to allocate funds to the Department of Social Services for the out-of-home care of special education students with SED. While the introduction of this funding has stimulated residential placement of these youths, the county has sought to minimize these placements, as it has the placement of court wards and dependents. Data obtained from DSS are used to monitor the number and cost of these placements.

Number and Cost of Placements

Figure 7.2 shows placement number (solid lines) and cost (dotted lines) between January 1987 and June 1995 for the county (open circles) and state (closed circles). Placement rates (left axis) during and after the project were 0.3 and 1.3 per 10,000 residents (0–18 years old), respectively, for Ventura County and 0.4 and 1.1 per 10,000 for the state. However, county placements have increased more rapidly since the end of the Demonstration Project than they have for the state. Although the overall county rate was 87.2% of the state rate during the project, it was higher (112.0%) than the state rate after the project's conclusion. Indeed, the county's rate would likely have been even higher had it not been for the impact of a program to increase community alternatives to group home placement (Ichinose, Kingdon, & Hernandez, 1994). The effect of this intervention is seen here in a continuous decrease in the county rate from 1.6 per 10,000 in the July 1992 period to 1.4 for the period beginning January 1995. By comparison, the state rate increased slightly over this period.

Results for placement cost (right axis of Figure 7.2) reveal that the county's per capita cost increased at a rate that was slightly higher than the rate of increase in state cost. Per capita costs during and after the project were $0.07 and $0.37 for the county and $0.10 and $0.36 for the state. The more rapid growth in the county's cost for placement of students with SED is further indicated by the fact that while county costs were 68.1% of the statewide aggregate during the project, they have increased to 103.1% of the state total since the project's conclusion. Also, the impact of the recent effort to strengthen community

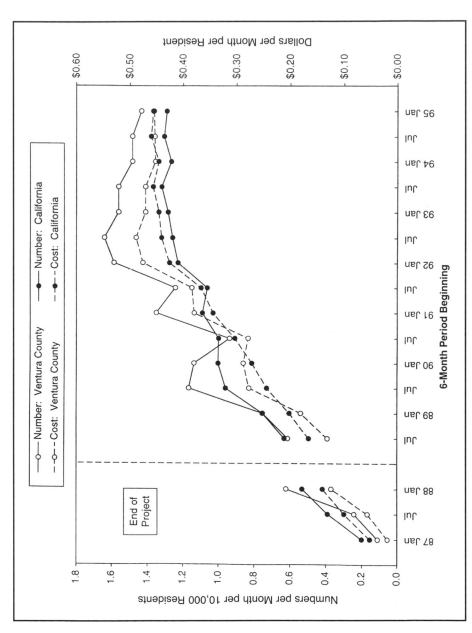

Figure 7.2. Comparison of group home placement for special education students with SED in Ventura County and the state of California.

alternatives to out-of-home placement can be seen in a consistent decrease in the county's cost per capita from $0.49 (July 1992 period) to $0.45 (January 1995 period) compared to an increase in the state's cost from $0.44 to $0.46 over the same period.

Discussion

It is clear that the considerable growth in residential placement of students with SED since 1987 reflects "start-up" activities that followed the initial implementation of AB 3632. It is also noteworthy that this growth has not been uniform across the state in that there has been differential use of AB 3632 funding among California's 58 counties. For example, the DSS Report of Expenditures for SED Children for June 1991 shows that 16 of the counties (32.8%) had no SED payments during the month and that 12 (20.7%) counties had no AB 3632-funded placements during the entire year. These differences suggest that high or low levels of use may in part reflect policy decisions regarding the way special education students in general are served. This result also suggests that while it is informative to compare local and statewide use of AB 3632 funds, it is also necessary to examine a county's unique pattern of use over time in assessing its effectiveness in controlling this source of spending.

It is also important to note that AB 3632 is not entirely consistent with the goals of the local system. Although it provides additional funds to serve students with SED, this legislation also encourages the use of residential services at the expense of services that would divert youths from such placements. Indeed, the pressures of having to absorb AB 3632 placements with no funding to achieve a reduction in out-of-home placements have been considerable as a result of population growth alone. Data obtained from the county Superintendent of Schools Special Education Local Planning Area, for example, reveal that the number of students with SED has increased steadily from 165 in April 1988 to 448 in April 1995. Clearly, the problem of a county's having to control its special education placements without the appropriate resources calls for innovative solutions. In this regard, partners in the local system of care (VCMH, Ventura County Public Social Services Agency [PSSA] and local school districts) have successfully developed new ways of funding nonresidential alternatives for serving this population (Ichinose, Kingdon, & Hernandez, 1994). This effort involves providing specialized school services coupled with improved case management in a way that is designed to maintain youths in their homes or in out-of-home placements that are less restrictive and less costly than group homes or residential treatment centers.

State Hospitalization

According to VCMH treatment guidelines, psychiatric hospitalization should be used only when other less restrictive treatment or residential alternatives are not available. To monitor state hospital use, the number of patient bed days and gross charges for the county's state hospital placements are obtained from the state Department of Mental Health and Department of Developmental Services, respectively.

Number and Cost of State Hospitalizations

Figure 7.3 shows the number of patient days per year per 10,000 residents 0–18 years old (solid lines) and total hospital charges per year per 0–18-year-old residents (dotted lines) since July 1, 1984, for Ventura County (open circles) and the state (closed circles). (Currently, hospital charges for youths are not available on a statewide basis, so comparison between individual counties and the state as a whole cannot be made.) These data show that county's overall utilization (left axis) was lower during (mean = 71.4 days) than after (mean = 80.2 days) the project. However, the trend for patient days reveals that utilization increased during the project and, except for the increase in FY 1991, has declined since the project's end. In contrast, the average annual patient days for the state were 125.9 and 97.0 days during and after the project, respectively, and decreased steadily each year since July 1984. Despite the fluctuations in annual patient days that reflect the admission of difficult cases, these data show that in general the county continues to use state hospital services at a rate that is lower than the statewide rate (56.7% and 82.7% during and after the project, respectively).

Similarly, cost per capita (right axis) was 31.6% lower during the project (mean = $1.69) than after its conclusion (mean = $2.47). However, inspection of trends for per capita cost reveals that, like patient days, cost increased during the project and, except for FY 1991, leveled off following the project's conclusion. These data indicate that the county has maintained its state hospital costs at levels similar to those at the end of the Demonstration Project.

Discussion

One of the major accomplishments of the Demonstration Project was a 68% reduction in the average daily census for children and adolescents in state hospitals compared to a FY 1980 baseline (Ventura County Mental Health, 1988). From a cost analysis perspective, it is important to consider the extent to which statewide implementation of system reform could result in a further reduction of hospital cost for the state as a whole. Because of the absence of cost data that would allow county and state costs to be compared directly, this issue can be addressed only indirectly. In this regard, the similarity between trends in the county's population-adjusted patient days and hospital charges suggests that a similar relationship may well exist between these two indicators statewide. A comparison of patient days for the county and state reveals that the county averaged 27.6% fewer patient days than the state over the 7 years between July 1985 and June 1992. Based on this argument, it is estimated that statewide reform could reduce its costs by an additional 27.6%.

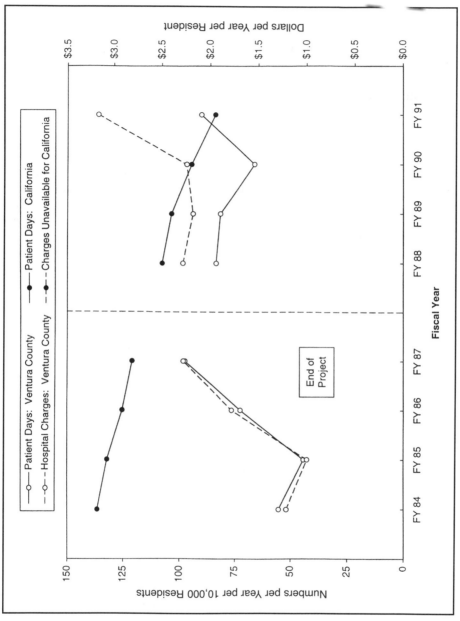

Figure 7.3. Comparison of state hospital placement for children and adolescents in Ventura County and the state of California.

While the reduction in state hospital use and resulting cost remains a priority in the local system, it is important to note that state hospital use is also subject to an artificial control. Specifically, the state provides each county with an annual allocation for state hospital use, and counties are penalized for exceeding that cap. Thus, the system is structured in a way that encourages state hospital use up to the capped amount. Measuring and drawing conclusions from such an artificially delimited variable presents unique problems in policy analysis.

Reincarceration of Court Wards

The Colston Youth Center (CYC) is the county's interagency program for court wards. The program is housed in a 45-bed medium-security coeducational facility. Participants range in age from 13–17 years old and are committed to the program by the Ventura County Juvenile Court for periods of 120–180 days. One of the program's primary goals is to reduce the frequency and seriousness of a youth's criminal behavior after the youth leaves Colston. In this regard, this update compares the number and duration of incarcerations before and after participation in the Colston program.

Selection of Youth Sample

All youths ($n = 131$) who were committed to CYC by the court between July 1, 1989, and June 30, 1990, formed the cohort for the study. A treatment episode was identified for each youth to determine when the youth received Colston services. An episode was defined as a period of at least 80 consecutive days of confinement in CYC or a juvenile detention facility (juvenile hall) that began with the youth's entering CYC and ended with leaving CYC, and included a total of at least 50 days in CYC. Twenty-three youths (17.6%) were removed from the initial list because (a) they had experienced a treatment episode prior to July 1, 1989 ($n = 10$), (b) their CYC commitment order was rescinded and they never entered CYC ($n = 3$), or (c) they did not remain at CYC long enough to satisfy the treatment episode definition ($n = 10$). The remaining 108 youths constituted the final study sample.

Since achievement of Colston's program goals is predicated on youths remaining in the program for the duration of their commitments and because CYC commitments are relatively brief, the amount of time that youths actually spend in confinement is of interest. In this regard, the average duration of the treatment episodes for the 108 youths was 129.4 days, and 92.7% of the episodes lasted longer than 90 days. Thus, it appears that nearly all of the youths remained in Colston long enough to receive maximum benefit from the program.

Incarceration Before and After Treatment Episode

An incarceration was defined as confinement for at least 1 day in any of the following facilities: juvenile hall (any county), CYC, Juvenile Restitution Program (JRP), county jail (any county), California Youth Authority (CYA), or California Department of Corrections (state prison). Furthermore, since the number of days that a youth remains in the community determines opportunities for arrest and incarceration, the duration of the periods preceding and following each youth's treatment episode were equated, and only those incarcerations that occurred within these periods were counted. The average duration of the post-Colston period was 406.9 days.

Table 7.2 shows that the number of incarcerations decreased 7.1% from 294 during the pre-Colston period (2.7 per youth) to 273 during the post-Colston period (2.5 per youth). On the other hand, duration of incarceration increased 56.4% from 6,621 (61.3 days per youth) to 10,356 days (95.8 days per youth). The substantial increase in the duration of incarcerations was due to the fact that 13 (12%) of the youths were committed to the Youth Authority during the post-Colston period. A commitment to CYA is the most severe disposition that can be applied in juvenile cases and typically involves a lengthy period of confinement (CYA commitments ranged from 2 to 10 years for the 13 youths). To determine how the incarcerations of these youths affected the totals for the sample, subtotals for number and duration were computed for the 13 youths who were committed to CYA (CYA Group) and the 95 who were not (No-CYA

Table 7.2

Number of Pre- and Post-CYC Incarcerations and Incarceration Days
by Post-Colston CYA Commitment and Type of Commitment Offense

Commitment	Incarcerations			Incarceration Days		
	Pre-CYC	Post-CYC	Percentage Change	Pre-CYC	Post-CYC	Percentage Change
CYA Group **(n = 13)**	37	46	24.3%	935	4,763	409.4%
New Crime	30	34	13.3%	786	3,977	406.0%
Technical Violation	7	12	71.4%	149	786	427.5%
No-CYA Group **(n = 95)**	257	227	−11.7%	5,686	5,593	−1.6%
New Crime	198	149	−24.7%	4,862	4,326	−11.0%
Technical Violation	59	78	32.2%	824	1,267	53.8%
All Youths (n = 108)	294	273	−7.1%	6,621	10,356	56.4%

Group). This analysis revealed that both the number and duration of post-CYC incarcerations increased for the CYA-committed youths (24.3% and 409.4% respectively). In contrast, youths in the No-CYA Group were incarcerated 11.7% fewer times following their treatment episodes, while the duration of their pre- and post-Colston incarcerations remained the same (−1.6%).

Incarcerations Following New Crimes and Technical Violations

The relationships between the type of charge(s) that led to a youth's being confined and number and duration of incarcerations were also assessed. The issue of whether incarcerations result from youths' commission of new crimes or violation of the terms and conditions of probation is relevant for several reasons. In general, technical violations are used by probation staff as a way of intervening with a youth to reduce the likelihood that the youth will engage in continued or perhaps more serious criminal activity. Thus, the relationship between violations and new crimes is paradoxical in that increased use of violations may be associated with reduced levels of new crimes. Furthermore, the kinds of behaviors for which a youth is "violated" are often not criminal in themselves, and thus are generally considered to be less serious than behavior that violates criminal statutes.

The number of incarcerations that resulted from new crimes increased 13.3% for the CYA Group but decreased 24.7% for the No-CYA Group (see Table 7.2). On the other hand, incarcerations resulting from technical violations increased for both groups (71.4% and 32.2% for CYA and No-CYA Groups, respectively). Similarly, the duration of post-CYC incarcerations that resulted from new crimes increased 406.0% for the CYA Group but decreased 11% for the No-CYA Group. Furthermore, the duration of incarcerations resulting from technical violations increased for both the CYA (427.5%) and No-CYA Groups (53.8%).

These data are significant because they describe two distinct types of outcomes for youths who participated in the Colston program. For youths who were eventually committed to CYA during the post-Colston period, results indicate an increase in both the frequency and duration of incarcerations that resulted from new crimes. On the other hand, youths who were not committed to CYA following their treatment episodes were incarcerated less often and for shorter durations for new crimes than youths in the CYA Group. Furthermore, both the number and duration of incarcerations that resulted from technical violations increased for both groups, though the increases in number and duration were twice and four times as great, respectively, for the committed youths than the youths who were not committed. Finally, of particular interest is that the groups differed slightly in age, gender, and ethnicity. Specifically, the CYA group was older (mean = 16.3 years, versus 15.9 years) and included a higher percentage of males (92% versus 87%) and a higher percentage of white youths (62% versus 51%).

Discussion

Overall, the present results differ in several ways from those reported in the evaluation of the Demonstration Project (Ventura County Mental Health, 1988). First, 75% of the 108 youths in the present study were reincarcerated for at least one day, compared to 44% of 183 youths during the project. Second, the total number of incarcerations decreased 7% in the present study, but 52% during the project. Finally, the number of days of incarceration increased 56% in the present study, but decreased 30% during the project.

In comparing the two sets of data, it is important to note some key differences between the studies. First, the data-collection procedures used in the studies differed in several ways. Particularly significant is that incarcerations in CYA facilities and the county jail were included in this study but not in evaluation of the project. As noted above, CYA commitments result from continuing criminal behavior or commission of more serious criminal offenses; they add significant numbers of incarceration days because they involve lengthy commitment times. Indeed, these results point out the need to distinguish long- and short-term commitments when assessing measures of recidivism. Second, the youths in the two samples appear to differ in certain ways. For example, a review of clinical diagnoses given the youths at admission reveals that 62% of the youths in the study, but only 36% of youths who participated in the project, were diagnosed with conduct disorder (American Psychiatric Association, 1994). Also, 5% of youths in the study, but 24% of those during the project, were diagnosed with substance abuse. Further, anecdotal reports of corrections staff indicate that youths are committing more serious crimes than in the past. Finally, differences in the two sets of results may reflect differences in the sentencing practices of the judges who presided over the juvenile court during and after the project. In practice, judges rotated court assignments every 2 years. Furthermore, in the process of committing a youth, corrections staff provide the judge with a recommendation for disposition that the judge may or may not follow. Anecdotal reports suggest that judges have differed in exercising that discretion.

School Performance of Special Education Students

The Phoenix Day Treatment Program serves the educational and mental health needs of primary- and secondary-aged special education pupils with SED. The program is staffed by personnel from Ventura County Schools and VCMH, and it has a maximum enrollment of 32 youths. Youths who are admitted have a variety of behavioral and academic problems that are addressed using school- and home-based interventions.

School Attendance

Each student's daily attendance is recorded routinely in the Phoenix program. During the Demonstration Project, students at the secondary level attended

88.5% of the possible school days during the 30 months between January 1986 and June 1988 (Ventura County Mental Health, 1988). By comparison, overall attendance was 90.9% (1,987 days attended out of 2,185 possible days) over the 41 weeks that school was in session during FY 1990. Furthermore, attendance increased over the course of the year. This is a significant result because most students enter Phoenix School with serious school attendance problems. Indeed, the lowest monthly attendance occurred in November (78.2%). It is during this period that most students enter the program and that problems in adaptation to the new program are most evident.

Academic Achievement Scores

Student achievement in reading, mathematics, and written language is assessed routinely by administration of the Woodcock-Johnson Psycho-Educational Battery (Woodcock & Johnson, 1977) at admission and at discharge from the Phoenix program. Results for the Demonstration Project indicated a gain in overall test performance of 1.6 grade levels (Ventura County Mental Health, 1988). By comparison, grade equivalent scores for 30 students who were posttested between July 1988 and June 1993 increased in all three areas of performance: 1.3 (Reading), 0.5 (Mathematics), and 0.7 (Written Language). However, since the average duration between pre- and posttests was 9.4 months (0.94 grade level), only the gain in reading represented significant improvement for these students. Furthermore, although their average age at posttest was 15.2 years, the youths' average posttest scores placed them at levels between the sixth and eighth grades (reading, 8.5; mathematics, 6.6; and written language, 6.8). These results indicate that the academic performance of the youths continued to lag behind that of youths of the same age who do not have disabilities, and they suggest the need to develop ways to strengthen academic performance or to consider alternative educational goals for these students.

Summary of Results

The results presented here suggest that the local system has maintained many of the gains that were achieved during the Demonstration Project:

1. The county's group home placement rate for court wards and dependents remained at a level well below the statewide total and increased more slowly than did the state level. However, while the county's expenditures for these placements also remained below state levels, they increased faster than the aggregated expenditure for the state during FY 1994 and 1995.

2. Increases in the number and expense of the county's placements for students with SED were similar to state totals during initial implementation of AB 3632. Furthermore, postproject data indicate that the number and expense of county placements have increased more than they have for the

state, and that this difference has been reduced recently following the implementation locally of increased community-based nonresidential services.

3. State hospital patient days and expenditures increased during the Demonstration Project but have remained generally unchanged since the project's conclusion. While statewide cost data are not available, patient days for the state as a whole have declined steadily over this period.

4. Results for 95 youths who received treatment at the Colston Youth Center in FY 1989 reveal that they were incarcerated for new crimes nearly 25% times fewer following their release, and the duration of their reincarcerations decreased 11%. Data for a comparison group of 13 youths from the same commitment cohort who also received treatment but who were subsequently committed to the California Youth Authority at some point following their release from Colston show that postrelease incarcerations for new crimes increased over 13%, and days of incarceration increased 406% for these youths.

5. Students served by the county's day treatment program attended over 90% of school days during FY 1990, and attendance improved throughout the year. Significant academic gains in the area of reading were achieved by students discharged from the program through June 1992, but only marginal improvement was seen in mathematics and written language.

Changes in the Postproject Environment

The 7 years that have passed since the conclusion of the Demonstration Project have been marked by many changes at the county, state, and national level. While the system has continued to focus on keeping targeted youths at home with their families, attending and progressing in school, and staying out of trouble with the law, these changes have created new challenges for the system of care. For example, the fiscal uncertainty associated with the temporary funding status of the Demonstration Project ended with a rollover of funds into a permanent children's mental health budget. However, this change also created new responsibilities for staff in the areas of quality assurance for Medi-Cal (California's Medicaid program), record-keeping, and revenue generation. The need to become well-versed in funding regulations was particularly important to ensuring an effective transition. Furthermore, factors associated with population growth and increasing costs have created new pressures to expand community-based alternatives to residential placement that are less restrictive and less costly. Finally, a growing realization that reforming a system for delivering services does not ensure the quality of those services has challenged the system to develop new methods for effective case management and treatment processes for keeping children at home, in school, and out of trouble (Kingdon & Ichinose, 1996).

Changes in State-County Relationships

Major changes have also occurred in the fiscal and administrative relationships between the state and county governments since the end of the project. Three changes are of particular significance in this regard. First, effective July 1, 1991, nearly all of the state's mental health budget was transferred to county governments throughout the state. This transfer was accomplished through a landmark process referred to as "realignment" (*State-Local Program Realignment Act,* Statutes of California, 1991). An important result of this change was the creation of mental health and social service "trust funds" in each county to support the operation of existing programs and the development of new ones. With the creation of these funds, county departments gained authority for deciding how dollars are spent.

A second major change that has affected county mental health departments statewide was the implementation of the federal Medicaid Rehabilitation Option and Coordinated Services, effective July 1, 1993. This change has expanded the services that are available to Medicaid recipients and has decentralized service delivery away from clinic settings. It has increased the availability of treatment in local schools and family homes. Under this option, services provided are federally reimbursable even though they are not provided in clinics under the direction of a physician. Additionally, the utilization review (UR) committee, as the point of service authorization and review, has been replaced by a client coordination process. In contrast to UR, client coordination is a clinician-driven service authorization process in which the case coordinator is the broker and monitor of case-related clinical services delivered under the Medi-Cal coordination plan.

Third, counties are currently being affected by a consolidation, under the management of county mental health departments, of funding for services for the chronically mentally ill, and for acute care and outpatient services. Following passage of the Short-Doyle Act in 1958, California has operated two separate systems for reimbursing mental health services through Medi-Cal. One is a fee-for-service system that is composed of private providers, including hospitals, psychiatrists, and psychologists, who bill Medi-Cal directly. The other public system includes county and state-operated programs that provide a continuum of inpatient and outpatient services for clients in the public sector. The current process, known as consolidation, is intended to improve the coordination and delivery of mental health services to families who are eligible for Medi-Cal, by imposing a managed-care framework on service delivery and by introducing efficiencies in the Medi-Cal funding process. Underlying the process is an agreement between the state Health Care Agency and state Department of Mental Health to "carve out" fee-for-service mental health benefits from health care and to transfer to counties the responsibility for integrating and managing these benefits for children and families eligible for Medi-Cal. In the process, there will be a gradual shift of state and federal treatment dollars to each county in the state.

Eventually, the system for fiscal reimbursement will be capitated, with counties receiving a specific sum per member per month and with the state monitoring client outcomes rather than performing service reimbursement. Thus, the shift also involves counties assuming the fiscal risks of exceeding their available funding pool. In a worst-case scenario, a county that exceeds its pool will have to stop delivering services or use county general funds to continue services after the pool is exhausted. Managing this risk effectively will require designing and implementing a managed system of care that focuses on integrating system, client, and fiscal outcomes at the individual county level.

System-of-Care Enhancement

Amid this climate of change, the Ventura Planning Model has provided a rationale and methodology for the ongoing development of the local system of care. With the support of public officials and agency administrators, significant modification in services has been accomplished during a time of uncertain fiscal resources for mental health services. In this section, recent enhancements in the system that address these changes are described. The new initiatives integrate a variety of child- and family-serving processes within the existing system. These processes include the following:

- early identification and referral of at-risk children and adolescents through psychosocial screening in primary health care settings;

- early childhood intervention through collaboration with the countywide Head Start program;

- multiagency assessment and shelter care for abused children through development of a single point of entry to the child protection system;

- family reunification for court-adjudicated children who have been placed in out-of-home care as a result of abuse;

- respite care for the families of children with SED through collaboration with the countywide parent support group; and

- management of acute care services for children and adolescents, including assessment of psychiatric emergencies, diversion to community-based alternatives to hospitalization, and management of the use of inpatient services.

Development and implementation of these initiatives has resulted in expansion of the target population, definition of new outcomes, expansion of partnerships, and development of outcome monitoring through linkages with external evaluation resources.

Early Identification and Intervention

Since its inception, the system of care has served exclusively a target population that includes children and adolescents with a clinical diagnosis (American Psychiatric Association, 1994) that is associated with significant functional impairment and risk for out-of-home placement. Using these criteria, the system serves approximately 1,500 youths, or about 0.8% of the 190,000 county residents 0–18 years old each year. Furthermore, only a handful of the children served are young (see Table 7.3 for a summary of all youths served during calendar year 1994). Finally, emerging patterns of service utilization, particularly in corrections and special education settings, support the view that a small number of youths (approximately 10%) use disproportionately more services than their number would indicate and thus represent a disproportional fiscal risk for public agencies (e.g., Ichinose et al., 1994; Kurz & Moore, 1994).

The narrow definition of the current target population has focused attention on the need to expand the range of children served in the county. Efforts to extend the system to children and youths not previously identified have included screening children and youths in primary health care settings, early child development programs, and at the entry point when children enter the child protection system. Screening in these settings seeks to find individuals who currently meet the criteria for the existing target population or who display "subthreshold" symptoms but are not yet functionally impaired, and thus do not qualify as a target case (Costello & Shugart, 1992). In the former case, screening provides an opportunity to find target population children at a younger age and thus to intervene when problems are more manageable. In the latter case, screening is used to identify individuals for whom implementation of early intervention strategies may prevent eventual entry into the existing target population.

Pediatric Settings

Pediatric primary health care is a process that is closely linked to the overall goal of expanding the population of children and families served in Ventura County. Introducing effective procedures for screening children in pediatric settings and referring those who are experiencing or are at risk for significant functional impairment is viewed as critical to the success of efforts to integrate early intervention processes in the local system of care (Kingdon, 1994). To this end, VCMH is collaborating with the Ventura County Public Health Department (DPH) to develop screening for psychosocial and mental health problems in health care settings. Aided by a grant from the Annie E. Casey Foundation (Ventura County Mental Health, 1995), this effort focused initially on integrating administration of the Pediatric Symptom Checklist (PSC; Jellinek, Murphy, & Burns, 1986) with routine well-child health examinations conducted as part of California's Child Health and Disability Prevention (CHDP)

Table 7.3

Cases Open in Ventura County System of Care by Subsystem During Calendar Year 1994

Characteristic	Corrections Services		Protective Services		Special Education		Mental Health Outpatient	
	Number	Percentage	Number	Percentage	Number	Percentage	Number	Percentage
Number of Youths	417	25.5	296	18.1	190	11.6	731	44.7
Age								
0–6 Years	0	0.0	60	20.3	16	8.4	87	11.9
7–12 Years	9	2.2	113	38.2	97	51.1	345	47.2
13–18 Years	406	97.4	123	41.6	77	40.5	295	40.4
> 18 Years	2	0.5	0	0.0	0	0.0	4	0.5
Sex								
Male	350	83.9	120	40.5	149	78.4	431	59.0
Female	67	16.1	176	59.5	41	21.6	300	41.0
Ethnicity								
Caucasion	164	39.3	167	56.4	153	80.5	374	51.2
Hispanic	202	48.4	94	31.8	26	13.7	278	38.0
African American	32	7.7	25	8.4	4	2.1	45	6.2
Asian	6	1.4	3	1.0	1	0.5	7	1.0
Other	13	3.1	7	2.4	6	3.2	27	3.7

program (the state's implementation of the federal Early and Periodic Screening, Diagnosis, and Treatment program, known as EPSDT). Screenings were performed by DPH in conjunction with two elementary school–based demonstration programs that offered a variety of family-focused services to economically disadvantaged children and their families living within each district.

Between December 1993 and May 1994, parents and caregivers of 310 children aged 3–18 completed the PSC (Murphy, 1994). Of these children, 33 (10.6%) received a score of 28 or higher, indicating that they were at risk for psychosocial problems (Jellinek, Murphy, & Burns, 1986). Furthermore, of 271 children on whom data were available, the parents of 96 (35.4%) reported, apart from the PSC, that their child had a problem with behavior, learning, or emotions. However, only one of these children met the criteria for the existing target population. These results point out the dilemma facing publicly funded systems of care that target high utilizers of service—namely, that children identified through early screening frequently display subthreshold problems that do not reach clinical standards (Costello & Shugart, 1992). Results such as these also point out the need to develop a network of less intensive community services that parallels the delivery of services to targeted youths in the public system (Ventura County Mental Health, 1995).

Head Start

Development of screening for psychosocial and mental health problems in the local Head Start program has proceeded as part of a larger effort to link early childhood services for Medicaid-eligible children with the system of care. Based on a partnership with Child Development Resources of Ventura County, the private, not-for-profit agency that administers the countywide Head Start program, this effort seeks to find Head Start participants who meet target population criteria, as well as to improve services to children who are at risk for involvement with public agencies (Kingdon, Cole, & Ichinose, 1996; Kingdon et al., 1995). Among other things, the collaborative agreement calls for VCMH to dedicate a full-time psychiatric social worker to serve as the mental health consultant for the Head Start program.

Thirty-one referrals were received during the first 5 months following the start of the program in November 1994. Most of the referred children were male (54.8%), Hispanic (67.7%), and eligible for Medi-Cal (70.0%). The extent to which these children are at risk is reflected in the numbers of families that were headed by a single parent (51.6%), were without a wage earner (46.7%), were AFDC eligible (75.0%), and had been investigated previously by the county Child Protective Services Division (28.6%). The added importance of cultural issues in this group is seen in the fact that Spanish was the primary language in the home of 22.6% of the children, and 22.6% resided in homes that were bilingual. Finally, the presenting problems most frequently identified by the referral source were emotional or behavior problems (38.7%), parent concerns

(19.4%), and family problems (16.1%). It is noteworthy that only one of the referred children met criteria for a DSM-III-R Axis I primary diagnosis, and a second could be given a diagnosis on Axis II only.

Casa Pacífica

To further the work in early identification, the system has recently implemented a process of multiagency screening, brief treatment, and referral for all children and youths who have been removed from their homes following an abuse investigation by CPS. A new shelter facility, Casa Pacífica, was opened in August of 1994 to serve as the single point of entry to the countywide child protection system. The facility is a private, not-for-profit agency that is linked by a collaborative agreement with the public agencies that serve abused and neglected children. Based on an intake assessment by a Coordinated Assessment and Response Team (CART) composed of staff from VCMH, CPS, Superintendent of Schools, DPH, and alcohol and drug programs, the program offers early intervention for children and families as they first enter the child protection subsystem, and it tracks their subsequent involvement in the system over time. In addition to the CART assessment, services include liaison with the juvenile court, brief desensitization treatment, and community linkage. A major goal of this process is the early desensitization of children to the traumatic events surrounding their removal and the promotion of coping and adaptive behaviors designed to reduce symptomology and behavioral deterioration.

The program has served 247 children and adolescents in 296 shelter admissions (through July 12, 1995). The average age of the youths at admission was 10.3 years (range: 12 days–17.9 years) and, in contrast to children served in other subsystems, more were female (139, 56.3%) than male. Thirty-eight (15.4%) of the 247 youths were admitted on two or more occasions, and they accounted for 87 (29.4%) of the 296 admissions. Furthermore, 146 (49.3%) of all admissions involved the child's being removed from the home for the first time, while 72 (24.3%) resulted from failed placements (placement no longer available to child protection system) and 78 (26.4%) from placement failures (youth removed from home that can no longer handle the child). Finally, 271 of the 296 admissions were discharged by July 12, 1995, with an average length of stay of 28.4 days.

Several outcomes are associated with the placement of children in shelter care at Casa Pacífica. First, a major goal of assessment and intervention provided at the facility is to determine the most appropriate setting in which the child should be placed upon discharge from shelter care, and to promote the long-term stability of that placement. In this regard, the reunification of children with their families and eventual removal from the child protection caseload is an outcome that the program seeks to achieve. Also, the number and types of placement (including parent's home, shelter care, and psychiatric hospital) in which the child resides following release from shelter care, and the length of time that the child remains in each, are important indicators of placement stability. A second outcome that is relevant to the management of the facility is the duration of shelter care episodes. All things being equal, shorter lengths of stay increase the system's capacity to serve a greater number of children and help to decrease the cost of shelter care per admission. In the latter regard, the average cost for care and supervision for a single shelter episode is $5,084, based on currently available data (i.e., an average cost of $179 per day for board and care, and an average length of stay of 28.4 days).

Family Reunification

Recent growth in the CPS family reunification (FR) caseload has resulted in a collaborative effort by VCMH and CPS to enhance services to families of children adjudicated by the court to foster care because of abuse or neglect. The goal of the new program, Project Impact, is to improve family functioning and reduce the risk of abuse for children who are served. To this end, the program provides home-based, short-term intensive family reunification and family maintenance services to parents and children separated as a result of abuse. The program integrates foster parents in service delivery and is staffed by two full-time clinical social workers, a drug and alcohol specialist on permanent loan from the county Alcohol and Drug Program, a case manager, and a supervisor. Intervention includes the delivery of clinical, drug and alcohol, and case-management services and is guided by a multisystemic approach (Henggeler & Borduin, 1990). Follow-up services are arranged by Interface Child and Family Services, a private, not-for-profit multiservice agency, and provided by established community resources (such as Alcoholics Anonymous). By developing these services as an integrated part of the child protective system, rather than as additional services by an outside provider, many potential boundary conflicts among agencies have been avoided, and a three-way partnership has been formed between CPS, project staff, and the family.

Project Impact has resulted in the identification of four new outcomes for the child protective services subsystem: (a) an increase in the number of children in the FR caseload who are returned to their parents and subsequently dismissed from court dependency status; (b) a reduction in the length of time that children in the FR caseload remain in foster care before being returned to their parents; (c) a reduction in foster care expenditures for the FR caseload; and (d) a reduction in the number of FR cases that are transferred to permanency planning. A total of 61 families have been referred to the project during the 9 months following the program's first referral in November of 1994. Of those, the program assessed 37 families for program services; admitted and provided treatment and family services to 17 families, with a total of 35 children; and reunified five families with a total of 11 children after an average of 2.8 months in out-of-home care per child.

Although the program's caseload in terms of families served is small, the potential for cost savings is magnified by the number of children who are returned from out-of-home care with each successful reunification. Based on (a) the cost of maintaining each of the 11 reunified children in their respective placements for 1 month (sum = $9,189; range = $345–$3,300; 10 were in foster homes, one was in a group home) and (b) an average duration of 2.8 months (range = 0.7–4.6 months) between the date that treatment began and the date the child returned to his/her family, the total cost of out-of-home care that was actually provided for the 11 children was $28,997. This actual cost was $26,137 less than an expected placement cost of $55,134 for 6 months of care at the same rate. (Note that reunification currently occurs most frequently 12 months after initial removal.)

Respite Care

The recent California Systems of Care Grant from the federal Center for Mental Health Services has provided the impetus for the development of respite services for parents and caretakers of youths who are served in the local system of care. The program is the result of a formal partnership between VCMH, United Parents of Ventura County (a parent and family advocacy group), and Interface Child and Family Services. Program services are managed and brokered by the parent group and include respite care delivered in two ways. In one format, Interface-trained respite workers are assigned to individual families for up to 16 hours of care per month. Care focuses on the target child and can be provided in the family's home or the home of the respite worker. In the other format, pairs of families are matched so that, after being trained by Interface staff, each agrees to provide respite support for the other under a "trade-off" arrangement. Backup support of Interface staff is available to both families. In addition to respite care, the program offers training, consultation, and support to affiliated community programs including local Boys and Girls Clubs, YMCA, city parks and recreation departments, and licensed day care programs. The purpose of these efforts is to facilitate the integration and maintenance of children served by the system in community activities.

Managed Care

The 1990s present significant new challenges for countywide systems of care in California. Primary among these is the task of developing systems for managing acute care services for Medicaid-eligible children and adolescents. Success in this endeavor will require balancing client care requirements and fiscal resources. To achieve this, acute care must be redefined as an ongoing activity rather than a single event (i.e., hospitalization). Here, unplanned patterns of expensive crisis-driven services can be managed to create planned access to appropriate levels of care, provided over time. Thus, acute care must be seen as a continuum of services rather than an episode of "four-wall" hospital care. Viewing acute care in this way broadens decision making in the management of care. Rather than deciding only to hospitalize or not, managing care involves considering a range of assessment and intervention activities designed to alleviate the immediate crisis, provide for safety, and ensure appropriate follow-up care to prevent recurrence.

It is important to note that there are important differences between traditional managed care and managed care in a public system of care. In contrast to traditional managed care approaches, that often depend on narrowed access and benefit limitations, a system of care must provide a "safety net" and thereby ensure that no crisis is left without an appropriate response. In an effective safety net, the management of client safety and fiscal resources must be balanced constantly. In such an environment, managing utilization is critical. By providing acute care as an ongoing activity rather than a single event (i.e., hospitalization), unplanned patterns of expensive crisis utilization can be managed to create planned access to appropriate levels of care that is provided over time. Managing utilization in this way can create financial efficiencies without the luxury of benefit caps and limitations on access, which contain risk in the private sector.

The development of processes for managing psychiatric inpatient care for Medicaid-eligible children and adolescents has resulted in the identification of referrals for hospitalization, as well as bed days used and cost of admissions to inpatient facilities, as important new outcomes for the children's system of care. This new effort began with the implementation of a protocol for managing acute care on January 1, 1995 (Ichinose & Randall, 1996). In the protocol, the VCMH Mobile Crisis Team assesses referred children and notifies the VCMH children's medical director when the team's evaluation indicates that the child should be admitted for inpatient services (nonenrolled children are referred to a community inpatient coordinator). Assessment includes use of the SCCARE (Screening Crisis Among Children and Adolescents with Reported Emergencies) to evaluate dangerousness, child coping, and parent competence (Gutterman, Evans, Levine, & Boothroyd, 1995).

Initial data obtained for the first 6 months of 1995 reveal that the Crisis Team completed 269 face-to-face assessments, of which 109 (40.5%) resulted in the youth's being hospitalized. Data for these hospitalizations indicate that the number of bed days actually used during the 6-month period (576 days) was 43.0% lower than projected (1,010 days) prior to the beginning of the year. Similarly, the local matching cost for these bed days ($119,737) was 42.2% lower than projected ($206,992) prior to January 1, 1995.

General Discussion

The outcomes that the county has achieved since the conclusion of the Children's Demonstration Project indicate that the project's original goals continue to be met. However, these results also raise several concerns and thus have implications for the continued development of local systems of care in California. For example, the growth in expenditures for group home care statewide suggests that the goal of controlling residential cost will become increasingly more important. Faced with this prospect, local systems are confronted with two related tasks. From the perspective of systems development, the present trend clearly suggests that new programmatic strategies must be developed to deal with the increasing numbers of youths who appear to be entering the system. In particular, these strategies will need to focus on the development of nonresidential alternatives for youths who are already being served in public systems, and prevention-oriented services designed to serve youths who are at risk for public system involvement.

Given the reality of limited tax-based support for children's services, the outcomes reported here also suggest that existing fiscal resources will become increasingly inadequate to serve targeted youths and their families. Thus, it is critical that new fiscal strategies be developed at the county and state level to fund children's mental health systems, as well as new program strategies for efficiently managing the acute and ongoing care of public-sector clients. Regarding the former, strategies that hold some promise are those that build upon the leveraging of federal dollars and that produce reinvestment capital for new services through the efficient management of fiscal risk (Ichinose, Kingdon, & Hernandez, 1994). It is clear that continued growth and enhancement of an existing system of care can and must proceed without new external funding. Indeed, the ability of the system in Ventura County to achieve cost savings and to reinvest these dollars in developing community-based alternatives to intensive and restrictive deep-end services is vital to the system's future viability.

Financing issues are also central to the current task of developing a process for managing acute and outpatient care for all county residents who are eligible for Medicaid. The goal of this effort is the integration of all aspects of acute care into a well-coordinated process. Important components in this regard are assessment of psychiatric emergencies by the VCMH Crisis Team, crisis stabilization, community- and family-based service alternatives to hospitalization, and inpatient services. Key components in the process are the gatekeeping function provided by the crisis team and the identification of new resources for providing community-based alternatives. An important goal in the latter regard is building an outpatient care process that manages all levels of single- and multi-agency risk for more restrictive and expensive acute care.

Results on the reincarceration of wards who participated in the program at Colston Youth Center highlight another concern for the system. The differences between the most recent results and those obtained during the project can be explained. Nevertheless, the fact that the current outcomes were not more positive suggests that attention needs to focus on strengthening the clinical interventions used with this target group, as well as the mechanisms for delivering them (Kingdon & Ichinose, 1996). The areas that are being considered include: improving screening assessment procedures so that the needs of youths committed to the program are identified more precisely, broadening the focus of services so that all of the identified needs of the committed offenders are met, and strengthening programmatic research and system feedback regarding the characteristics of youths who are most likely to benefit from the program's services.

Finally, the role of ongoing system evaluation in calling attention to these concerns is noteworthy. Ventura County's experiences over the past 10 years reinforce the view that monitoring system outcomes and providing feedback are important elements in the process of maintaining the quality and effectiveness of services. Indeed, these experiences provide several lessons about system evaluation. First, systems must continue to develop ways of measuring and evaluating their operations and outcomes. The practice of treating the number and cost of group home placements as interchangeable measures and as the only measures of a system's effectiveness is a case in point. Clearly, costs are a function of increasing placements as well as changes in rates of payment. On the other hand, the number of placements depends on several factors: the number of youths who enter placement for the first time, the number of youths who leave placement to return to their communities, and the system's effectiveness in maintaining youths in community settings. Complexities such as these require that local systems develop more involved measurement and data-analysis techniques.

Second, outcome evaluation can be made more useful by focusing on clinical and consumer issues as well as system outcomes (Heflinger, 1992). Locally, the development of an evaluation process that is more comprehensive is guided by the notion that outcomes must be defined and measured at the level of taxpayer liability and risk, child and family functioning, and consumer satisfaction. Expanding outcomes is currently being achieved by implementing clinical and consumer measures, including the Child Behavior Checklist (Achenbach, 1991a), Youth Self-Report (Achenbach, 1991b), Child and Adolescent Functional Assessment Scale (Hodges, 1994) and Client Satisfaction Questionnaire 8 (Attkisson & Greenfield, 1995). The long-term goal of this effort is a unified statewide process for measuring clinical, consumer, and system outcomes at the county level.

Third, the evaluation of a system of care can be strengthened by blending internal and external evaluation processes. On one hand, internal evaluation provides information that reinforces a clinician's effort to manage outcomes. Regular feedback at the service-delivery level acknowledges that aggregated outcomes are created one case at a time. Internal evaluation also maintains and reports information that supports management of system operations. Finally, internal evaluation supports advocacy in the political arena of financing for human services by providing regular input and feedback to legislative and funding sources. External evaluation on the other hand provides opportunities to collaborate with experts in particular areas related to implementing a system of care. For example, research involving complex models of service-system evaluation, financing strategies and models, and cultural competence can provide detailed information on specific issues that cannot be routinely obtained in ongoing system operation. Furthermore, external evaluation lends additional credibility to the process of documenting system-of-care outcomes and allows information to be disseminated in ways that local systems would find difficult to accomplish. In this regard, partnerships between local systems and universities have proven beneficial to credibility and broad-based dissemination of outcome data.

In summary, it is clear that the context in which the achievement of the system's current objectives are assessed has changed from previous evaluations of the Children's Demonstration Project. Reform of the system has been accomplished, and current objectives center largely on maintaining the benefits achieved through this previous reform. In this regard, it is important to note that the process of maintaining the gains that have been achieved will be successful to the extent that the system's internal functioning is maintained and to the extent that forces that are external to the system are not allowed to impact the system adversely and thus erode the gains that it is able to achieve.

References

Achenbach, T. M. (1991a). *Manual for the Child Behavior Checklist/4-18 and 1991 profile.* Burlington: University of Vermont, Department of Psychiatry.

Achenbach, T. M. (1991b). *Manual for the Youth Self-Report and 1991 profile.* Burlington: University of Vermont, Department of Psychiatry.

American Psychiatric Association. (1994). *Diagnostic and statistical manual of mental disorders* (4th ed.). Washington, DC: Author.

Attkisson, C. C., & Greenfield, T. K. (1995). The Client Satisfaction Questionnaire (CSQ) scales. In L. L. Sederer & B. Dickey (Eds.), *Outcome assessment in clinical practice.* Baltimore, MD: Williams & Wilkins.

California Department of Finance. (1995). *Population estimates for California cities and counties. Report E-1.* Sacramento, CA: Author.

Children Now. (1995). *California county data book 1995.* Los Angeles: Author.

Costello, E. J., & Shugart, M. A. (1992). Above and below the threshold: Severity of psychiatric symptoms and functional impairment in a pediatric sample. *Pediatrics, 90,* 359–368.

Gutterman, E. M., Evans, M. E., Levine, K. G., & Boothroyd, R. A. (1995, March). *The continuum of care in emergency psychiatric services for children and adolescents: Can we predict clinical decision-making?* Paper presented at the 8th annual Research Conference, Tampa, FL: A system of care for children's mental health: Expanding the research base.

Heflinger, C. A. (1992). Client-level outcomes of mental health services for children and adolescents. *New Directions for Program Evaluation, 14,*(54), 31–45.

Henggeler, S. W., & Borduin, C. M. (1990). *Family therapy and beyond: A multisystemic approach to treating the behavior problems of children and adolescents.* Pacific Grove, CA: Brooks/Cole.

Hodges, K. (1994). *Child and Adolescent Functional Assessment Scale.* Ann Arbor, MI: Author.

Ichinose, C. K., Kingdon, D. W., & Hernandez, M. (1994). Developing community alternatives to group home placement for SED special education students in the Ventura County system of care. *Journal of Child and Family Studies, 3,* 193–210.

Ichinose, C. K., Kingdon, D. W., King, N. E., Clark, S. L., & Hernandez, M. (1994). *An analysis of pre- and post-treatment incarcerations for juvenile offenders in the Ventura County system of care.* Unpublished manuscript, Ventura County Mental Health Department, Ventura, CA.

Ichinose, C. K., & Randall, M. C. (1996, February). Access to acute care in the Ventura County system of care: The crisis team is the first point of contact. In D. W. Kingdon (Chair), *Managing acute care services for children and adolescents in the Ventura County system of care.* Symposium at the 9th annual Research Conference, Tampa, FL: A system of care for children's mental health: Expanding the research base.

Jellinek, M. S., Murphy, J. M., & Burns, B. J. (1986). Brief psychosocial screening in outpatient pediatric practice. *Journal of Pediatrics, 109,* 371–378.

Jordan, D. D., & Hernandez, M. (1990). The Ventura Planning Model: A proposal for mental health reform. *Journal of Mental Health Administration, 17,* 26–47.

Kingdon, D. W. (Chair). (1994, October). *Developing and integrating early identification and referral in the Ventura County system of care.* Symposium at the 4th annual Virginia Beach Conference on Children and Adolescents with Emotional or Behavioral Disorders, Virginia Beach, VA.

Kingdon, D. W., Cole, M. T., & Ichinose, C. K. (1996). Early intervention as a partnership between public mental health and Head Start in the Ventura County system of care. *Child, Youth and Family Services Quarterly, 19,* 3–5.

Kingdon, D. W., & Ichinose, C. K. (1996). The Fort Bragg managed care experiment: What do the results mean for publicly funded systems of care? *Journal of Child and Family Studies, 5,* 191–195.

Kingdon, D. W., Ichinose, C. K., & Ramirez, A. V. (1995). Public mental health and Head Start are partners in the Ventura County system of care. In C. J. Liberton, K. Kutash, and R. M. Friedman (Eds.), *The 8th annual Research Conference proceedings: A system of care for children's mental health: Expanding the research base.* Tampa, FL: University of South Florida, Florida Mental Health Institute.

Kurz, G., & Moore, L. (1994). *The "8% problem": Chronic juvenile offender recidivism.* Unpublished manuscript, Orange County Probation Department, Santa Ana, CA.

Murphy, J. M. (1994, October). Psychosocial screening in pediatric health care settings and development of the Pediatric Symptom Checklist. In D. W. Kingdon (Chair), *Developing and integrating early identification and referral in the Ventura County system of care.* Symposium at the 4th annual Virginia Beach Conference on Children and Adolescents with Emotional or Behavioral Disorders, Virginia Beach, VA.

Murphy, J. M., Ichinose, C., Hicks, R. C., Kingdon, D., Crist-Whitzel, J., Jordan, P., Feldman, G., & Jellinek, M. S. (1996). Utility of the Pediatric Symptom Checklist as a psychosocial screen for EPSDT: A pilot study. *Journal of Pediatrics, 129,* 864–869.

Statutes of California, 1957. Chapter 1989, State Senate Bill 244. Sacramento, CA.

Statutes of California, 1984. Chapter 1474, State Assembly Bill 3920. Sacramento, CA.

Statutes of California, 1984. Chapter 1747, State Assembly Bill 3632. Sacramento, CA.

Statutes of California, 1989. Chapter 1294, State Senate Bill 370. Sacramento, CA.

Statutes of California, 1991. Chapter 89, State Assembly Bill 1288. Sacramento, CA.

Stroul, B. A., & Friedman, R. M. (1986). *A system of care for severely emotionally disturbed children and youth.* Washington, DC: Georgetown University, CASSP Technical Assistance Center.

U.S. Census Bureau. (1990). *Census of population and housing, 1990.* Washington, DC: Author.

Ventura County Mental Health. (1987a). *Two year report on the Ventura Model for interagency children's mental health services.* Ventura, CA: Author.

Ventura County Mental Health. (1987b). *AB377 report on the Ventura County Children's Mental Health Demonstration Project.* Ventura, CA: Author.

Ventura County Mental Health. (1988). *Final report on the Ventura County Children's Mental Health Demonstration Project.* Ventura, CA: Author.

Ventura County Mental Health. (1995). *Child-finding in the Ventura County system of care: Development of a screening protocol for the early identification of mental health problems among economically disadvantaged children.* Final report to the Annie E. Casey Foundation. Ventura, CA: Author.

Woodcock, R. W., & Johnson, M. B. (1977). *Woodcock-Johnson Psycho-Educational Battery.* Allen, TX: DLM Teaching Resources.

Coordinating Care Through Connections' Liaison Staff: Services, Costs, and Outcomes

8

Mary Lynn Cantrell, Robert P. Cantrell,
and Douglas A. Smith

About 7 of every 100 young people live with the effects of serious emotional and behavioral problems, their potentials at risk and their challenges a focus for pain felt by their family members (Kauffman, 1993; Rubin & Balow, 1978). Several authors have been strong proponents for shifting from a pathology-based service system to a strength-based approach, building on families' assets and possibilities (Hobbs, 1982; Burchard, Burchard, Sewell, & VanDenBerg, 1993). Building on the strengths and resources of these children and families requires professional assistance from a variety of service systems in the community. Communication among service systems and families is often sparse or absent, hindering the effective coordination of services (Knitzer, 1982, 1993; Stroul & Friedman, 1986). The current system of child and family care is shredded by territorial protectionism and cost avoidance across overlapping service-system components.

In 1988, service provisions in Cleveland, Ohio, seemed to mirror the problems in other urban settings. Large numbers of children, increased complexities of child-serving systems, and mounting severities of child and family needs exacerbated service coordination problems. The need for a single system of child and family care become even more pronounced. In the absence of jointly funded and coordinated cross-system efforts, the county's mental health board created "Connections" and staffed it with newly funded positions like those of the Liaison Teacher-Counselors (LTCS) operating in the Positive Education Program's Day Treatment Centers since 1975 (Hobbs, 1982, 1994). The LTCs served youth in public schools, primarily those recently returned from day treatment or at risk of referral to the next level of service. The new Connections staff, operating from selected Cleveland City School buildings, made liaison-type service coordination available to children and families most in need of assistance. The intent of the new program was to produce a single, coordinated system of care for each child and family.

The evolution, operations, and descriptive findings of the Connections program are outlined in this chapter. The chapter will present: (a) a description of Connections' operations and development; (b) descriptive data for a sample of over 500 "most in need" children and adolescents served; (c) an overview of the case managers' liaison roles, characteristics, and services; (d) descriptive data for other services; (e) outcomes and subgroup comparisons for the 100 children who left service during that year; (f) costs of service; and (g) implications of these data for work with this population.

Program Development and Operation

Connections staff work with families whose children are "most in need" of mental health services, who are involved in several systems, and who have either been removed from their homes or are in danger of removal. The goals of Connections are to return children to their homes or maintain them there if possible, to increase their functioning in the least restrictive settings possible, and to help them improve in the problem areas they presented at entry. Connections accomplishes these goals through three types of service designed to mobilize family strengths, enhance family functioning, and solve ecological problems. First, liaison staff/case managers assess the ecology and bring all needed parties together each 90 days to survey resources, develop service plans, and assess any changes made since the last team progress review. Second, they provide access to mental health services by means of a voucher payment system created for their use by the Cuyahoga County Community Mental Health Board (CCCMHB). Substantial funds have been made available for these vouchered services, including respite care, independent living, transition services, specialized or therapeutic foster care, group home residency, partial hospitalization, diagnostic assessment, and therapy (family, group, individual, media therapies, sex offender treatment, and in-home therapy). Third, liaison/case managers create "wraparound" services (Burchard et al., 1993) to meet needs traditionally not served by mental health service agencies, but which can make a great difference with relatively small expense; these services are paid for through a small, flexible funding pool.

Connections is operated by the Positive Education Program (PEP), a private nonprofit agency providing integrated mental health and educational services countywide in the greater Cleveland, Ohio area. PEP is a contract agency of the Cuyahoga County Community Mental Health Board (CCCMHB); the Cuyahoga County Board of Education functions as PEP's fiscal agent and as the intermediate unit for educational funds. The Connections component began as the Cleveland school-based case management effort with funding from CCCMHB, expanded with additional human service levy dollars, and then increased considerably in size in 1990 when it became one of the Robert Wood Johnson Foundation's Mental Health Services Programs for Youth (MHSPY), (Cole & Poe, 1993).

Eight county systems were needed as major partners in serving these children: Family and Children's Services, Developmental Disabilities/Mental Retardation, Juvenile Court, Ohio Department of Youth Services, Alcohol and Drug Abuse, Health, Education, and Mental Health. To stimulate community involvement in early Connections development, the county mental health board initiated an ad hoc group in 1988 that represented parents, all eight major public systems, nine nonprofit children's mental health service agencies, and the inner city school districts to form the RWJ Project Group. The group met monthly and functioned as Connections' intersystems advisory and oversight body. Another intersystems committee, the Systems Gatekeepers, was developed to manage the referral stream into Connections. These start-up interactions secured the investment of other programs and agencies in efforts to build a collaborative and comprehensive system of care to serve greater Clevelend's most-in-need youth and their families.

The Connections Steering Committee, composed of staff from PEP and the mental health board's children's services division, met monthly to develop procedures, guide operations, and ensure the resources and support that case managers needed to achieve demanding goals. Initial work included developing structures for case-management functioning and tracking, supervision and training, record-keeping, consultation and support services, and administration and evaluation.

Connections' coordination of services is carried out by 27 liaison staff (case managers), each with 15 to 20 client families at any one time, and serving about 500 young people and their families annually. They are supported by three Connections supervisors, a program director, and three clerical staff, with the backup assistance of PEP central office personnel.

Children and Youth Served by Connections

Descriptive data on the children and families served by Connections in the fiscal year (FY) ending in 1995 are summarized below. Data from FY 93 and FY 94 were roughly similar.

Numbers Served and Length of Service

Connections staff served 517 children, youth, and their families between July 1, 1994, and June 30, 1995. During that time, service was terminated for 19.3% ($N = 100$) of those children. The average length of service for those whose service had been terminated was 722.48 days. This average had increased steadily from

494.71, 2 years before, for two reasons. First, in an effort to ensure that Connections served the county's "most in need," children with less complex needs were discharged with referrals in 1993, and those with less complex needs since then have been referred elsewhere rather than being accepted by Connections. Second, as children with more complex needs and longer service periods terminated services, the average length of service for that year increased.

Time for entry to exit ranged from 3.86 to 258.71 weeks, with a mean of 100.40 weeks (SD = 60.92). Over half of Connections' children (52.1%) left service within 2 years. Of the 100 children who left service during FY 95, 26.5% were in service 12 months or less, 25.6% between 13 and 24 months, 25.6% between 25 and 36 months, and 22.2% for more than 36 months.

Demographic Characteristics

Most children served in FY 95 were males (62% of those served and 55% of those leaving), although females formed a greater proportion than those often cited in the literature (Kauffman, 1993). Perhaps female children served in Connections more closely approximated the need identified by the U.S. Office of Special Education Programs' National Agenda for Children and Youth with Serious Emotional Disturbance (Chesapeake Institute, 1994), when it stated that females were underrepresented in the national service figures.

Most children (82%) were 12 years old or older, and discharges were largely proportional to the age ranges of those served. Age range distributions of children served in FY 95 indicated that 5% of those served were 6–8 years old, 13% were 9–11 years old, 26% were 12–14 years old, 37% were 15–17 years old, and 19% were 18 years old or older.

Racial identifications largely reflected the 1995 census figures of urban Cleveland, where two thirds of the liaisons/case managers worked. Caucasians represented 48%, African Americans 46%, and others 6% of the children served. Sixty-two percent of the children served were Medicaid eligible, which more closely reflects Cleveland's urban than suburban population.

Presenting Problems and Diagnoses

When each child entered Connections, liaisons indicated which of the 58 presenting problems listed in Ohio Department of Mental Health records were reported by the family and referral sources; each problem reported was ranked as severe, moderate, or mild. Each of the 58 presenting problems were associated with one or more of the children served; in addition, 13 "other problems" not on the list were added and specified. No children and youth had only one problem; 84% were listed as having three or more severe problems; 44% were reported with six or more severe problems from this list. The six most frequently identified problems are listed in Table 8.1.

Documented co-existing conditions that fit state definitions in other systems were also found for many of these children; the following percentages included

Table 8.1

Most Frequent Presenting Problems
at Time of Entry

Presenting Problem	Percentage Served (N = 517)	Percentage Discharged (N = 100)
Depressed	30.4	39.0
Defiant Behavior	23.0	18.0
Impulsive Behavior	23.0	22.0
Assaultive	17.4	17.0
Sexually Abused	15.7	16.0
Suicidal Thoughts	13.5	15.0

Note. Since each problem coexisted with others, percentages reflect duplicated counts. Sexual abuse was listed for victims when a severe current service need existed, rather than indicating a past history of abuse.

duplicated counts. A current or past history of being sexually abused was documented for 33% of these children; 33% were identified as being physically abused. Alcohol or drug abuse was identified for 15%. In this same group, 15% met state criteria for having developmental delays, and 3% met state criteria for having severe sensory impairments.

Children served were often given multiple diagnoses on one or more axes used by the American Psychiatric Association's Diagnostic and Statistical Manual. The primary psychiatric diagnoses (DSM IV-Axis I) given were impulse control and disruptive behavior disorders (35.8% of the 517 served and 30% of the 100 leaving); mood disorders (24.8% of those served and 28% of those leaving); anxiety and dissociative disorders (16.0% of both those served and those leaving); attention deficit/hyperactivity disorders (8.5% of those served and 9% of those leaving); schizophrenia and psychotic disorders (7.7% of those served and 12% of those leaving); and the other major categories of DSM Axis I codes (7.3% of those served and 5% of those leaving).

Prior System Involvement and Out-of-Home Placements

All 517 children had been involved with two or more systems and agencies within the system of care. Specifically, 55% were involved with Children and Family Services (25% of all served were in the formal custody of this social service system),

37% with Juvenile Court, and 9% with Developmental Disabilities. Significant medical problems were reported for 79%, and 84% were on psychotropic or other medication. These 517 children and youth averaged three out-of-home placements at the time they entered Connections, with a range of from 0 to 28 out-of-home placements. Prior out-of-home placement settings named at least once for a child included failed adoptive or foster homes (35%), psychiatric hospitals (47%), residential treatment centers (30%), and correctional facilities (12%).

Liaison Services

The Liaison Role

Ecological/case-management services for children experiencing serious emotional disorders were provided in the original Re-ED programs of the early 1960s (Hobbs, 1966, 1982). The goals of staff in the liaison role are clearly congruent with those goals associated with "individualized care" (Burns & Friedman, 1990; Rivera & Kutash, 1994). Recognizing the shaping functions of the titles given professional roles, the term "liaison" was originally chosen to clearly establish the role's functions as facilitator, supporter, mobilizer, and communicator. Avoiding the presumption of managerial authority helped to enhance the involvement of family members and community agents in working toward a common goal. That goal involved empowering families and children to develop more satisfying lives through collaborative, practical problem solving, by recognizing their current strengths and available resources, and by enhancing those resources through learning constructive action.

In this chapter, the terms "liaison" and "case manager" are used interchangeably to designate the ecological facilitation role taken by Connections staff. Our use of these terms assumes that the liaison role exceeds that usually assumed by the "case manager" in a hospital, medical, or insurance setting. Liaison/case managers have at least four major functions.

Ecological Problem Solving

The productivity of ecological problem-solving in the community has been demonstrated in innovative programs across the nation during the last several decades, particularly by Dennis in Chicago's Kaleidoscope, VanDenBerg in Alaska, and Burchard in Vermont with their colleagues (Rivera & Kutash, 1994). PEP has enhanced ecological problem solving through liaison teacher-counselor roles since 1974; since 1984, the Ohio Department of Mental Health has funded 12 of the liaison staff in day treatment centers as case managers. In ecological problem solving, the liaison function goes beyond referral and service brokering to actively structure and coordinate the support that enables an ecosystem to work proactively for a child and family. The liaison person is responsible for helping each family work with extended family members and community agents (involved or available) to answer basic questions and take constructive action. What are our goals for ourselves? What strengths and capabilities do we have and use now? What creates discord in our attempts to meet shared goals? What changes in behaviors would enhance those attempts, and how could those changes be supported? How can we locate and mobilize needed resources? How can we build our capacity to emphasize our strengths and deal with excessive discord in the future? The liaison process involves establishing the trust of the child and family, framing the questions for analysis, identifying involved or helpful individuals, forming a problem-solving team, facilitating mutual decision making in formulating a plan of action, coordinating action, helping evaluate changes, making needed revisions, and suggesting when services are no longer needed.

A grandmother referred to Connections because residential treatment was imminent for her 6-year-old grandson was first given the immediate personal support needed for her to be able to recognize and mobilize her own strength to seek and employ resources. Once she felt confident in the consistent assistance of her case manager, she no longer perceived helping her daughter and grandson simultaneously as impossible. She was then able to set goals, identify individuals who could function on a team to help move toward those goals, and persevere in action even when roadblocks were met.

The degree to which staff can apply caring, ecobehavioral problem-solving skills to ecological problems may be more indicative of success than service-use variables. In a prior study of school support liaisons, Cantrell and Cantrell (1980) found that where problem solving was complete and in sequence (analysis > planning > enactment > revision), more objectives were met in less time across individual liaison staff and all levels of problem complexity.

Mentoring Children and Families

An important part of liaison work is mentoring the liaison function. Empowering extended families requires imparting these skills to whoever is important in the child's life and committed to productive change. For example, the 6-year-old's grandmother learned over time how to advocate for her daughter's and grandson's needs within the community, and how to guide their goal setting and support them in efforts to move toward these goals. The case manager moved from a central coordinating role to an on-demand consulting role. When the child is an adolescent and learning the necessary problem-solving skills, liaison staff structure and support the child's attempts to help the ecosystem function effectively and to meet new crises with less external assistance.

Teamwork Coordination

A primary function of the Connections liaison teacher-counselor is coordinating and facilitating teamwork in planning and review. The Individualized Service

Planning Team (ISPT) that develops quarterly service plans may contain as many as 25 or 30 people, depending on the seriousness and complexity of a child and family's needs and the number of systems involved. Each ecological assessment and enablement plan is a highly specific document worked out through the teamwork of all involved members. The plan emphasizes assets and strengths, defines shared objectives, specifies needed behavior changes and resources to be mobilized, assigns responsibility for actions, tracks progress, and assesses outcomes. As changes in the ecosystem occur, the enablement plan is periodically reviewed and revised. The Connections liaison/case manager is the one person responsible for moving through this process, knowing what everyone else is doing, facilitating communications, and bringing the team together at least quarterly. For the 6-year-old and his grandmother, having the liaison/case manager serve as designated team coordinator decreased the likelihood that action taken would be fragmented and inconsistent.

Fiscally Responsible Decision Making

One important ISPT/case manager responsibility is to make judicious funding decisions in service planning that build on family strengths and fulfill needs. The ISPT members pool their expertise to determine any needed categorical services that may be purchased through vouchers from 14 mental health contract agencies in Cuyahoga County. Connections staff also use the relatively small flexible "WrapAround" funding pool to purchase a variety of resources and noncategorical services needed to help maintain the child at home. For example, wraparound funds were used for a down payment on a car where public transportation to counseling sessions for the family was costing twice as much as a car payment. In another situation, the funds were used to construct a backyard fence that enabled the parents to let the child play outside, made a babysitter willing to supervise him, and gave the parents their first night out in the 6 years since the child's birth. These funds are used only for treatment-related purposes and must be authorized by the ISPT. Availability of these funds can mean a child can remain at home or in a home setting and still obtain the needed assistance (Burchard et al., 1993). Family members are primary members of the ISPT, and often identify needs that can be filled through flexible funding at costs far less than those of traditional services.

Liaison Staff Characteristics and Backgrounds

Staff serving in the liaison roles had an average of 10 years of professional experience (ranging from 3–15 years), with a median salary of $38,223. Sixteen of the 27 had master's degrees, and their average level of university training was a bachelor's degree plus 20 hours. Two thirds were trained in some combination of social work, sociology, or criminal justice coursework; the remaining third were degreed in regular or special education (22.2%), psychology (7.4%), or family/child development (3.7%). The master's degrees of all three supervisors were in psychology, and the Connections program director's graduate degree was in education and administration.

Most of the 27 liaisons/case managers were females (70%), with a racial identification that was approximately equivalent for African Americans (37%) and Caucasians (33%). The 30% of liaison staff who were male were identified as African American (11%), Caucasian (15%), or Hispanic (4%).

Liaison Time Spent on Children's Behalf

Children leaving service in FY 95 received up to 341.6 total hours of direct contact as recorded by their liaison, with a mean of 88.6 hours during their time in service. Included were contacts with the child and family or with others on the child or family's behalf. These figures did not include travel time, trivial contacts, or time spent in individual liaison planning or record-keeping.

Other Services Provided

Individualized Service Planning Teams formulated plans each 90 days after reviewing progress on presenting problems for the prior 90-day period. Services provided were liaison services plus any combination of (a) mental health services purchased from contract agencies through vouchers from the county mental health board; (b) services provided by other systems, such as child welfare or corrections; or (c) less traditional "wraparound" goods or services.

Vouchered Services Provided

Summarized data on vouchered mental health services received are presented in Table 8.2, showing both the number of children leaving who used the service and the numbers of those judged either as "successful" (having met their goals or improved to the point of functioning well with only referral), or "other" (having other reasons for exit). Eight mental health services were used by more than one quarter of the children exiting in FY 95, and all but the crisis service (Safe House) were associated with half or more successful exits. For 20 of the 36 vouchered services used, 50% or more of the children using the service were successful at exit.

Services From Other Child and Family County Systems

Systems other than mental health, such as Children and Family Services or Juvenile Court, paid for a variety of other services for Connections children and families. Their funds purchased foster care, therapeutic foster care, preparation

Table 8.2

Most to Least Used Services by 100 Children Exiting the Program

Service	N Children	(N Successful—N Other)
Family Therapy[a]	79	(42—31)
Safe House	58	(27—31)
Diagnostic Assessment	49	(24—25)
Psychiatric Consultation	41	(20—21)
Home Based Intervention[a]	32	(16—16)
Group Therapy[a]	29	(15—14)
In-Home Respite Care[a]	28	(14—14)
Medical Somatic Service[a]	27	(14—13)
Mentoring	21	(7—14)
Day Treatment[a]	17	(9—8)
Residential Camp[a]	13	(7—6)
Transition School to Work[a]	13	(7—6)
Independent Living Training	12	(5—7)
Group Residence	11	(2—9)
Parent Aide	11	(3—8)
Recreation Program	11	(3—8)
Art/Music Therapy	10	(3—7)
Out-of-Home Respite Care	8	(3—5)
Day Camp	7	(2—5)
Residential Treatment	7	(1—6)
Protective Day Care	7	(2—5)
Tutoring[a]	5	(3—2)

(continues)

Table 8.2 *Continued*

Service	N Children	(N Successful—N Other)
Substance Abuse Outpatient[a]	5	(3—2)
Individual Therapy[a]	4	(2—2)
Group Home[a]	4	(3—1)
Independent Living Residence[a]	4	(2—2)
Specialized Foster Care	3	(1—2)
Psychiatric Hospitalization[a]	3	(2—1)
Runaway Shelter[a]	2	(2—0)
Crisis Stabilization[a]	2	(1—1)
Passages	2	(0—2)
Parent Education	2	(0—2)
Substance Abuse Inpatient[a]	2	(1—1)
Therapeutic Foster Care[a]	2	(2—0)
Weekend Residential Care[a]	1	(1—0)
Big Brother/Big Sister[a]	1	(1—0)

[a]Fifty percent or more of the children served in 1995 using this service were successful at exit.

for independent living, independent living, adoptive subsidy, group home placement, partial hospitalization, and residential treatment for children in their custody.

Services Purchased Through Flexible Funds

Many different types of wraparound services were used for these clients during their time in Connections. These included time for mentors and homemakers, tutoring, memberships in community recreation programs, participation in adolescent rites of passage groups, music lessons, college application fees, down payment on a car, a backyard fence, a prom dress, summer camp fees, transportation, emergency funds, and other items important to children's normal development though not traditional mental health services.

Child and Family Outcomes

Home Maintenance or Return

At entry, one of four master goals was chosen by the Individualized Service Plan Team as appropriate for each client: (a) prevent the child's removal from home, (b) return to family/community, (c) locate alternative permanent placement, and (d) independent living. At the time of exit, liaisons rated the outcome on the client's master goal as (a) achieved, (b) partially achieved, (c) canceled or found to be inappropriate, or (d) failed to achieve. Of the 100 children who left service in FY 95, data on master goals set and their achievement were available for 97 children; no master goals were set for three children who left at the point of the first team meeting, when it was determined that the service was not the one most appropriate for them. A cross-tabulation using master goals by outcomes for those goals produced significant differences, $\chi^2(9, N = 97) = 28.44, p < .001$. Goals set for children to remain in or return to their homes were achieved for 58 children and failed for 11. Goals set for independent living or alternative living placements were met for 7 children but failed for 10 others. The remaining 11 client master goals were either partially achieved or canceled as inappropriate.

At the time of exiting service, 82% of the 100 children remained in or returned to permanent home settings (with biological or adoptive parents, with relatives or surrogate families, or in independent living). The other children were residing either in foster homes (4%), group homes (1%), residential treatment centers (4%), correctional facilities (7%), or were homeless (2%).

Comparisons of Successful and Other Outcome Groups

To investigate the degrees of successful outcomes occurring for the 100 children leaving during FY 95, disposition codes were combined to form two groups: "successful" and "other." Children leaving after having met all their goals, plus those served and then referred to other services considered sufficient to meet their needs, formed the "successful" group ($n = 56$). Exiting children with all other disposition codes were combined to form the "other" group ($n = 44$).

Case managers used disposition codes to record the reason for each child's leaving service. At exit, 56 were considered successful: 30 had met their goals, and 26 were referred to services considered sufficient to maintain their gains. Another 16 were of doubtful success: 13 who had moved and 3 who had left because the service was not appropriate. Just over one quarter (28) resulted in clearly undesirable outcomes: 21 rejected service for a variety of reasons, 4 did not return and avoided contact, 1 requested residential placement, 1 was placed in a correctional facility, and 1 died. Children/families rejecting services were not a homogeneous group, and they are described in detail in a following section.

Liaison Time Intensive Comparisons

Analyses of success rates of children receiving high or low amounts of time from liaisons revealed no significant differences. There was a significant Pearson product moment correlation of .405 ($p < .01$) between total case management costs and ages of children, however. To find if this form of intervention was more time costly with the older children, those 74 children who had successfully met their master goals (by remaining or returning home, achieving a satisfactory alternative living arrangement, or accomplishing independent living status) were compared with the 20 children who had failed to accomplish one of these master goals. The amount of documented case-management time spent either with or on behalf of each of these children was used as the dependent variable. Case managers spent significantly more time with children who ultimately failed to accomplish their master goal successfully, $F(1, 90) = 6.91$, $p = .01$, than they did with children who ultimately succeeded. Case managers also expended significantly more contact time with older children (16.03 years or above) than they did with younger children (below age 16), $F(1, 90) = 18.34$, $p < .001$.

In an attempt to determine some of the other characteristics distinguishing between the successful and nonsuccessful children, stepwise discriminant analysis was used, with group membership (success vs. nonsuccess) as the dependent variable. The following variables significantly discriminated between the two groups in decreasing order of magnitude of effect. The nonsuccessful children were more likely to have (a) spent time in an out-of-home placement in a correctional program, (b) had more group home placement changes, (c) had more placements in residential treatment facilities, and (d) been served by the Bureau of Vocational Rehabilitation. It appears that the significantly extended time that case managers invested in children who already had extensive past histories of contact with service agencies, and who ultimately experienced a much less than satisfactory outcome, were "last ditch" efforts to serve children who had already been failed by multiple, often independently operating components of the system of care.

Liaison Time with Court-Involved Children

For court-involved youth ($n = 25$), case managers spent significantly more time for successful than for nonsuccessfully discharged children. This is probably a function of differential times in service. Mean time in service for nonsuccessful court-involved youth was 70.37 weeks, versus 104.61 weeks for successful court-involved youth. This may indicate that where liaisons were able to advocate for youth and avoid precipitous judicial decisions, the possibility of success increased. In this group, more court-involved youth were unsuccessful ($n = 14$) than were successful ($n = 11$). Nevertheless, liaisons' sustained attention and advocacy appeared to be important, as time spent in service for successful and unsuccessful corrections-involved youth reflected time spent of all 100 leaving.

Time in treatment was significantly longer for the overall group of 56 successfully discharged children and youth than for the 44 in the nonsuccessful group.

Connections Children Who Rejected Services

The unsuccessful exit group included 21 (4% of the 517 served overall) who rejected Connections involvement. This "rejected services" group was of special interest, as they represented that group of children or their families who chose to remove themselves from service. The group was a disparate one: Six reached the age of 18 and chose to leave (two married); four changed custody, and their new caretakers did not feel the need to continue; two decided that Connections was not what they wanted at the point of the first Service Plan; one withdrew because parents wanted residential placement; two parents actively rejected services, perhaps because their own needs were not being met; four youths rejected continuation, and their parents supported them; and two others withdrew for unknown reasons.

Seventy-one of the 100 children discharged during FY 95 had complete service data sets for a discriminate analysis. Whether or not particular services were received was used as predictor variables in a multivariate discriminant analysis against each child's membership in either the "success" ($n = 51$ of 56) discharge category or the "rejected services" ($n = 20$ of 21) category as the dependent variable.

Five service categories significantly discriminated between the success and rejected services outcome groups. These results point to the possible inability of four of the five intervention services to address core issues confronting the 20 children and their families who finally rejected the Connections services. The fifth service was markedly successful for this group. First, parent aide services were provided 4.25 times more frequently to the rejected services group (mean rate = .250, SD = .444) than to the successful outcome group (mean rate = .058, SD = .237). Second, art or music therapy services were provided 3.85 times more frequently to the rejected services group (mean rate = .300, SD = .47) than for the successful outcomes group (mean rate = .078, SD = .27). Third, none of the successful outcomes group received other mental health services. By contrast, the rejected services group received a mean of .10 other mental health services (SD = .308). These services included crisis stabilization and group sessions in a court diversion program. Fourth, children who rejected further services received 2.58 times more residential treatment (rejected services mean rate = .15, SD = .366) than did children in the successful outcomes group (mean rate = .059, SD = .237). As comparison of DSM codes assigned revealed no overall significant differences between the rejecting services and successful services groups, it seemed unlikely that these two groups in residential treatment represented different types of disorders. Fifth, children in the successful discharge group received foster care (mean rate = .039, SD = .196). None of the rejected services group received foster care services.

Service Costs

Mental Health Direct Service Costs Per Child and Family

Mean per child mental health service costs and ranges throughout their time in service are summarized in Table 8.3. The mental health cost for each child was calculated by summing: (a) the accumulated cost of vouchered mental health services delivered by contract agencies from the time of child intake, (b) the wraparound fund expenditures (including child/family transportation costs), and (c) the cost of case manager time (total documented contact hours per child multiplied by $21.52, the mean hourly salary for case managers). This sum was divided by the number of weeks each child was in service to obtain cost per week of Connections services. Indirect costs were not included here. Less than $2,000 each of mental health funds was spent for 32% of this child group, between $3,000 and $10,000 for another 46%, between $10,000 and $20,000 for 15%, and over $20,000 for 7%.

Other System Costs

Systems other than mental health paid for 28 other services that were not trackable costs for the 22 children who received them. Costs paid by other systems for these 22 children might be estimated to equal mental health's costs for the 22 children most expensive to mental health, probably $20,000 or more annually for each of these 22 children.

Table 8.3

Entry to Exit Per Child/Family Mental Health Costs ($N = 100$)

Type of Cost	Mean Cost	Lowest	Highest
Vouchered services[a]	$5,553.34	0	$85,550.59
Wraparound services[b]	$701.80	0	$12,166.32
Liaison time[c]	$1,906.87	$41.32	$7,350.09
Total[d]	$8,162.02	$41.32	$88,734.69
Cost per week[e]	$78.15	$3.14	$938.30

[a]Used for 56 children.   [d]Total mental health costs.
[b]Used for 55 children.   [e]For direct mental health services.
[c]Used for 100 children.

Estimated Annual Per Child Costs

Given an average of 1.98 years in service, total cost per child per year for this group was estimated to be $11,513. Included in this figure are $4,064 for direct mental health service costs (52 weeks at $78.15 per week); $3,049 for indirect Connections cost (e.g., supervision, administration, clerical support, and facilities); and $4,400 for estimated cost paid by other systems ($20,000 each for 22 children, averaged for the group of 100).

Cost Comparisons of Successful/Other Leaving Children

To determine any relationships between cost levels and successful outcomes, the 100 leaving children were divided into four cost groups, and compared for successful versus other outcomes. The four groups were: Very expensive, > $30,000 ($n = 3$), Moderately expensive, $10,000 to $30,000 ($n = 5$), Inexpensive, $4,000 to $10,000 ($n = 43$), and Least expensive, < $4,000 ($n = 48$). No significant differences were found between cost groups in degrees of success obtained, $\chi^2(3, N = 100) = 4.66, p = .19$.

Summary of Child, Service, and Outcome Data

Twenty-seven Connections liaison staff served approximately 500 children each year; about 100 of these completed or left service by the year's end. Over half (52.1%) of Connections children left within 2 years, and 77.7% within 3 years. Since no comparable control groups were available for comparison, conclusions must be tentative.

Whom Did Connections Serve?

Child Demographic Data

Most children served were adolescents, and 62% were males. Over half (51%) were urban, and 62% were Medicaid eligible. Percentages of Caucasians (48%) and African Americans (46%) were roughly equivalent; 6% had other racial identifications. This ethnic makeup reflected more the urban than the suburban population of Cleveland.

Multiple System Involvement

These children and youth had all been previously involved with other agencies in the system of care. One fourth (25%) were in the custody of the child and family services system. They entered with an average of three out-of-home placements, ranging from 0 to 28. Over one third (35%) had been in failed adoptive or foster homes, 47% in psychiatric hospitals, and 30% in residential treatment centers. Juvenile court was involved with 37% at entry, and 12% had been in correctional facilities. Substantiated sexual abuse was reported for 33%, and physical abuse for 33%. Many (79%) had significant medical problems, and 84% received psychotropic or other medications. Only 3% experienced severe sensory impairments, but 15% had serious developmental delays.

Diagnostic Descriptors

Over one third (36%) of the children had been given psychiatric designations grouped within the impulse control and disruptive behavior disorders. At times, designations within this diagnostic group conflicted with the crisis admission policies of traditional psychiatric hospitals, which tended to limit admissions to children experiencing schizophrenic and psychotic disorders (8% of the Connections group). One quarter (25%) experienced mood disorders and another 16% anxiety and dissociative disorders. The most frequently listed presenting problems were depression, defiant behavior, impulsive behavior, assaultive behavior, suicidal thoughts, and sexual abuse (as victims in need of current related services).

What Services Did Connections Provide?

These young people and their families demonstrated significant amounts of resiliency and potential in the face of adversity. They brought these strengths with them to the ISPT and to their services. The individualized service plans developed for each included whatever combination of agency services, nontraditional services, and liaison support were deemed needed by that child and family.

The most frequent combinations of mental health services selected by ISPTs included family or group therapy, home-based intervention and in-home respite care for family needs, Safe House for crisis support, and medical assistance as needed (diagnostic assessment, psychiatric consultation, and medical-somatic services). Other system components outside mental health provided services as well. Over half (55%) of the children received nontraditional services paid for through a flexible funding pool; for most of them, this cost was well under $1,000.

Direct contact time spent on each child's behalf averaged 88.6 hours, not counting time spent in related planning, reporting, or travel. Differential liaison time expenditures with children did not predict differential levels of success. Liaison staff were experienced professionals (mean experience = 10 years). Most had master's degrees in related areas. Supervisory support was strong, and turnover tended to be low. Problem-solving skills, teamwork, and the extent to which significant others were available and ecological resources employable may well have been the more important variables in achieving success.

What Were the Outcomes of Connections Services?

More than three quarters (77%) of the 517 in service, all of whom were formerly removed or in danger of home removal, were being maintained in their homes or a desirable home alternative. More than half (56) of the 100 who terminated service did so because goals were met or referrals were sufficient to meet their continuing needs. One quarter (25) of the children who left (4.8% of all served) actively rejected Connections services or avoided further contact. The remaining 19 moved or were removed from availability. Among those children exiting, 67.0% of the goals set for living arrangements were met; 21.7% of the goals were not met. The remaining 11.3% of goals were either partially achieved or canceled as inappropriate.

What Were the Costs of Connections Services?

Cost per child per year was estimated to be just over $11,500 ($7,113 in mental health costs + an estimated $4,400 paid by other systems = $11,513). These figures compared favorably with the much higher costs of residential care (often over $100,000 per child per year), and the outcomes were comparable or better (Rivera & Kutash, 1994). For example, Hoagwood and Cunningham (1992) studied 114 youth previously in residential treatment; they found that 25% returned to a positive community setting, 11% remained in residential treatment with progress, but over 60% made no progress or were discharged with a negative outcome. Comparable Connections data indicated a much better success rate. Maintaining any significant percentage of these children and youth in their homes and communities at a cost under $12,000 each per year represented a substantial savings in financial costs to the community, as well as in emotional costs to these children and their families.

Discussion

Implications for Practice

1. Evidence for the Value of Persistence

Liaison roles can help meet child and family needs in community settings, and both their results and costs compare favorably with those of residential care. Short term interventions are not likely to be effective in as many cases as we might hope, however. Connections data appear to indicate that longer treatment time for assaultive children resulted in successful outcomes, as did efforts to keep withdrawn children in treatment. Significant liaison time was also required for suicidal children in this sample. Liaison staff can serve as valuable guides in transition from one community-based service to another, but such services are often required throughout the lifespan of an affected individual.

2. "Red Flags" for Service Coordinators

Results from the diverse group of children who rejected services suggested that time-linked feedback loops to supervisors about individual child progress would be helpful. Identification of patterns developing between children and treatment components could be a vital part of a dynamic process evaluation, serving as indicators of more serious problems to come. For example, the average length of time in a particular service needed previously by similarly diagnosed and successfully discharged children, perhaps with an additional standard deviation added in for normal variability, might be used as benchmarks for preventive attention. If progress does not occur after treatment has been ongoing for the benchmark time period, serious deliberations about ceasing or modifying the treatment regimen at that point might avoid some service failures. Maintaining full awareness that standard, traditional interventions may be inappropriate at times for some children appears to be a necessity. Each treatment program might develop its own norms, with milestone markers for reconsideration of treatment strategies based on intraprogram known factors such as skills of staff and characteristics of children.

3. Collaboration with Juvenile Court Personnel

In the 100 FY 95 children who exited service, only one was placed by the court into a correctional facility. This is particularly notable, since 37% of the 517 served in FY 95 were court involved at entry. Certain categories of problem behavior (assaultiveness, defiance, stealing, destructiveness, domestic violence, abuse, sexual offenses, truancy, and vandalism) are potent signals for potential increases in law enforcement involvement. Connections case managers developed strong relationships with court staff and probation officers. They also worked frequently with PEP's juvenile court liaison, a PEP staff member with past experience as a liaison/case manager herself and many networking relationships with court officials and staff. Her law degree and frequent court presence allow her to advocate for more therapeutic court decisions for individual youth. Stable, productive, working relationships with the juvenile court system may do much to prevent abrupt child placements into the justice system.

4. Including All Critical Partners

Teamwork is time-consuming, but the long-term gains make it worth the investment, and persistence is crucial to team effectiveness. Belief in the central role played by family members in any mental health service mandates both training and specific teamwork provisions. Selected family members in Family Service Aide roles are invaluable; they have special reason to understand and care, and they have enormous capacity for support.

5. Continual Training and Support

Selection and training of Connections staff have not been addressed in detail here, but several points should be made. Staff were carefully selected from a wide range of qualified applicants, and turnover has been low. Over the last 5 years, only one liaison has left; three were nonrenewed, and three others were added in newly created positions. Adequate salary scales contributed to this selectivity and longevity.

After initial orientation to Connections philosophy and job procedures, training was provided as staff requested information. One popular training method was cross-training, in which staff, supervisors, and administrators from two (or more) system components met together to inform each other and engage in informal dialogue. Our challenge now is to systematize that wide variety of training experiences, to make it replicable on demand to individuals as needed, and to keep it updated. Another staff development component has been the supportive role taken by Connections supervisors. They see their jobs as helping case managers assist children and youth, support families, and grow professionally. The supervisory role adopted here is not so much a monitoring role as a facilitative one aimed specifically at improving the quality of services that children receive.

6. Consistent Focus on Goals and Language Awareness

Maintaining an orientation based on child and family strengths requires constant vigilance. Procedural structures can be designed as continual reminders that shape this approach through force of habit, until the focus on strength becomes both personal attitude and professional heritage. Streamlining and thoughtfully designing procedures in a highly collaborative effort like Connections requires constant, ongoing attention from every participant. The procedures we use and the labels we assign matter, because they shape both behavior and attitudes.

Implications for Policy

1. Creative Funding Vehicles

Direct service staff in traditionally funded programs can address the ecological problem, solving questions posed by wraparound service providers (Burchard et al., 1993). Even without special funding, creative professionals can often locate sources of support to fill needs on an individual basis. The availability of flexible funding, however, greatly expands the capabilities of service providers to meet serious needs in relatively cost efficient ways.

Service options for Connections children and families, and access to these services, were greatly enhanced by addition of the CCCMHB voucher system and flexible wraparound funding pool. It soon became clear that funds could be wisely used, monitored, and conserved, if staff share the concept that resources are finite and must be spread as far as possible, since needs exceed resources. The flexible fund helped build a group commitment to fiscal guardianship. In addition, the Robert Wood Johnson Foundation's MHSPY project staff and components became an important network for Connections, helping find answers to tough fiscal problems.

2. Need for Early Screening and Response

Most of the Connections children were 15 or older, with many earlier intervention attempts having failed for them. Connections data appear to corroborate the fact that piecemeal, uncoordinated, and sporadic efforts often fail, allowing conditions to worsen as the child ages, until problems are more complex and ecologies less malleable. Connections data underscore the need for systematic and intensive early intervention as a critical part of the system of care. This need was strongly expressed by longitudinal research that found that children not helped until grade four or after had much higher probability of serious life-long problems (Loeber, 1985; Patterson, DeBaryshe, & Ramsey, 1989; Patterson, Reid, & Dishion, 1992). Walker and Severson (1990) have developed and validated a systematic early screening method that is able to identify high-risk students in the early years, when intervention has its highest likelihood of effectiveness.

Implications for Research

1. Early Intervention Efficacy Research

Continued and expanded research on the short- and long-term effects of early intervention efforts could provide the evidence for cost effectiveness needed to advocate for funds for prevention and early intervention efforts.

2. Information Needed To Facilitate Individualized Treatment Planning

Several areas of research could assist in better intervention choices and more individualized decision making. First, analyses of Connections data and other databases with larger numbers of children served, investigating DSM groups by success levels and background variables, might provide us with some intervention hints if tied to successful service combinations for different subgroups. Pairing results of such analyses with cost indicators might be helpful in planning, particularly if other system-component costs can be integrated with those paid by mental health. Also, subgroup comparisons of those rejecting services (e.g., by avoidance, by active withdrawal, or by leaving at some transition point in their lives) may give cues for potential supports that could be provided earlier in service. Are there specific services that are particularly inappropriate matches for some child or family needs? Investigations are needed of different support approaches in relation to different family variables (e.g., constellation, cultural identifications, capabilities, potentials, and need combinations).

Second, additional analyses of service use might look at rates of planned services that are (a) never initiated, (b) initiated and not completed, or (c) completed as planned, to determine how service processes interact with the characteristics of children for optimal results. Service programs and program staff vary in their problem-solving and service skills, in their ability to form positive relationships with children and families, and in other variables that may matter, such as gender or ethnic identification. It does not matter if you *have* it (the service) unless you know *how* to do it (the skills) and *do* it (the process that shapes productive functioning). The more we know about what "it" is in each of these cases, the more child empowering our systems of care can become.

3. Staff and Team Effectiveness

There sometimes appears to be a tendency in mental health to view services as uniform entities, with effectiveness attributable to the type of service or the service system. This view excludes what may be the most critical variables in success, the quality of problem solving performed by the agents of service delivery and their personal ability to develop meaningful relationships with children and family members. Systems may fund and monitor services, but, basically, people deliver services and do not deliver them uniformly. Investigation of the Fort Bragg system of care confirmed that having a coordinated system of community-based care does not in itself guarantee more positive clinical outcomes (Bickman, Bryant, & Summerfelt, 1993; Bickman, Summerfelt, & Bryant, in press). Research on training models, staff/team effectiveness, and both content and process components are paramount needs in our field.

4. Follow-Up Studies Comparing Child-Intervention Effects

Comprehensive, periodic, and long-term follow-up of children in Connections and other service programs is a continuing critical need. More analyses of the children and families who reject services might give us cues for decreasing their numbers by meeting critical needs earlier in the service process. Follow-up information on a program's own child and family graduates can be particularly useful if regularly provided to staff and reviewed to improve processes toward favorable outcomes. The use of measures with high face validity can enhance the interpretability and use of such results to answer important questions. For example, in some situations liaison staff are not able to find or sufficiently support an adult in the child's world who can make "an irrational personal commitment" to the child's development, using Urie Bronfenbrenner's phrase. Investigations of the perceived presence or absence of such an adult and child success over time, across child groups and age blocks, might provide us with additional information about the need for early family support and the forms it should take.

Conclusion

Perhaps it is difficult to extract strong causal support for an ecologically intensive treatment program such as Connections from these data, except for the gentle reminder that these professionals helped most of their departing children succeed. Whatever the argument is likely to be in the future, there is ample support from these results to assert that an ecologically intensive intervention process should be interposed between children in trouble and free-standing institutions of care. Inserted early enough into the troubled situation, Connections-type interventions are less expensive, less intrusive, more congruent with family consolidation, and just maybe, more effective than monolithic programs can be.

Authors' Note

Mary Lynn Cantrell, Ph.D., is director of Training & Evaluation; Robert P. Cantrell, Ph.D., is research consultant; and Douglas A. Smith, Ma. Ed., is Connections program director. All three authors may be contacted at the Positive Education Program in Cleveland, Ohio.

The authors gratefully acknowledge the contributions of the following PEP staff: Kenneth Meyer, systems manager and data system designer; Sandi Lewis and Bruce Greene, data managers; Louis Ford, Nena McCullough, and Donna Allen, data entry staff; Nancy Lowery, Donna Miller, and Claire Shands, supervisors; and most of all the Connections liaisons (case managers) and the family service aides (parent graduates on staff) whose hard work made all the difference for many children, youths, and families.

References

Bickman, L. (1996, May). *The effectiveness of system reform on child and adolescent mental health services.* Presentation to spring research forum of the Cuyahoga County Community Mental Health Research Institute, Case Western Reserve University, Cleveland, OH.

Bickman, L.. Bryant, D., & Summerfelt, T. (1993). *Final report of the quality study of the Ft. Bragg evaluation project.* Unpublished manuscript, Vanderbilt University Center for Mental Health Policy.

Bickman, L., Summerfelt, T., & Bryant, D. (in press). The quality of services in a children's mental health managed care demonstration. In L. Bickman (Ed.), The evaluation of the Ft. Bragg Demonstration [Special issue]. *Journal of Mental Health Administration.*

Burchard, J. D., Burchard, S. N., Sewell, R., & VanDenBerg, J. (1993). *One kid at a time: Evaluative case studies and descriptions of the Alaska Youth Initiative Demonstration Project.* Washington, DC: Georgetown University Press.

Burchard, J. D., & Clark, R. T. (1990). The role of individual care in a service delivery system for children and adolescents with severely maladjusted behavior. *Journal of Mental Health Administration, 17,* 48–98.

Burns, B. J., & Friedman, R. M. (1990). Examining the research base for children's mental health services and policy. *Journal of Mental Health Administration, 17*(1), 87–98.

Cantrell, R. P., & Cantrell, M. L. (1980). Ecological problem solving: A decision making heuristic for prevention-intervention strategies. In J. Hogg & P. Mittler (Eds.), *Advances in mental handicap research: Vol. I.* Chichester, England: Wiley.

Chesapeake Institute. (1994). *National agenda for achieving better results for children and youth with serious emotional disturbance.* Washington, DC: U.S. Department of Education, Office of Special Education and Rehabilitative Services, Office of Special Education Programs.

Cole, R. F., & Poe, S. L. (1993). *Partnerships for care: Systems of care for children with serious emotional disturbances and their families.* Interim report of the Mental Health Services Program for Youth, Robert Wood Johnson Foundation. Washington, DC: Washington Business Group on Health.

Goldman, S. K., & Stroul, B. A. (1991). Descriptive research: One approach to the study of community-based services for children and adolescents who have serious emotional disturbances. In A. Algarin & R. M. Freidman (Eds.), *A system of care for children's mental health: Building a research base* (pp. 195–209). Tampa, FL: University of South Florida, Florida Mental Health Institute, Research and Training Center for Children's Mental Health.

Hoagwood, K., & Cunningham, M. (1992). Outcomes of children with emotional disturbance in residential treatment for educational purposes. *Journal of Children and Family Studies, 1*(2), 129–140. Cited in Rivera, V. R., & Kutash, K. (1994). *Components of a system of care: What does the research say?* Tampa, FL: University of South Florida, Florida Mental Health Institute, Research and Training Center for Children's Mental Health.

Hobbs, N. (1966). Helping disturbed children: Psychological and ecological strategies. *American Psychologist, 21,* 1105–1115.

Hobbs, N. (1982). *The troubled and troubling child.* San Francisco: Jossey-Bass.

Hobbs, N. (1994). *The troubled and troubling child: Second edition.* Cleveland, OH: American Re-Education Association.

Kauffman, J. M. (1993). *Characteristics of emotional and behavioral disorders of children and youth* (5th ed.). New York: Macmillan.

Knitzer, J. (1982). *Unclaimed children: The failure of public responsibility to children and adolescents in need of mental health services.* Washington, DC: Children's Defense Fund.

Knitzer, J. (1993). Children's mental health policy: Challenging the future. *Journal of Emotional and Behavioral Disorders 1*(1), 8–16.

Loeber, R. (1985). Patterns of development of antisocial child behavior. *Annals of Child Development, 2,* 77–116.

Patterson, G. R., DeBaryshe, B. D., & Ramsey, E. (1989). A developmental perspective on antisocial behavior. *American Psychologist, 44,* 329–335.

Patterson, G. R., Reid, J., & Dishion, T. (1992). *Antisocial boys.* Eugene, OR: Castalia Press.

Rivera, V. R., & Kutash, D. (1994). *Components of a system of care: What does the research say?* Tampa, FL: University of South Florida, Florida Mental Health Institute, Research and Training Center for Children's Mental Health.

Rubin, R. A., & Balow, B. (1978). Prevention of teacher identified behavior problems: A longitudinal study. *Exceptional Children, 45,* 102–111.

Strouhl, B. A., & Friedman, R. B. (1986). *A system of care for severely emotionally disturbed children and youth.* Washington, DC: CASSP Technical Assistance Center, Georgetown University Child Development Center.

Walker, H. M., & Severson, H. H. (1990). *Systematic screening for behavior disorders (SSBD): A multiple gating procedure.* Longmont, CO: Sopris West.

Expanding Family Roles in the System of Care: Research and Practice

9

Barbara J. Friesen
and Beverly Stephens

T he involvement of family members in all aspects of services for their children with serious emotional disorders has changed dramatically over the last 15 years. Since 1984, when Congress gave authority to the National Institute of Mental Health to initiate the Child and Adolescent Service System Program, family members have moved "from marginal to central" in the movement to reform children's mental health services (Koroloff, Friesen, Reilly, & Rinkin, 1996, p. 424). Significant participation of family members in planning, implementing, and evaluating services for their own children is now a standard of practice in many parts of the country. Family members, either individually or representing family organizations, are involved in system and policy planning and review. Family advocacy efforts have proved vital to the passage of key legislation affecting children and families at state and federal levels. And family members can now be found as co-teachers in professional training programs (Jivanjee, Moore, Schultze, & Friesen, 1995), as providers of case management and other services (Ignelzi & Dague, 1995), as consultants and trainers for a wide variety of audiences, and as members of research teams (Turnbull & Friesen, 1995).

The movement to expand family roles, decision making, and control, however, has outstripped professional training and practice. The necessary research base for this practice is also underdeveloped. The incorporation of family members into roles and settings that were traditionally the exclusive purview of professionals is sometimes awkward, and there are many questions yet to be answered. For some practitioners, learning to view family members' concerns in new ways and establishing expanded relationships with family members has been transforming, leading to broader views of families' needs (Friesen & Huff, 1996), to practice innovations (Modrcin & Robison, 1991), and to reconsiderations of research approaches (Harry, 1996). For other professionals, however, the call for broader family roles has resulted in confusion and skepticism. Research efforts to describe and understand the impact of expanded family roles have been few and underfunded, resulting in a sparse literature base specific to children's mental health.

In this chapter we address six broad role sets in which family members are involved, summarize research to date, highlight practice examples, and propose next steps for practice and research.

Family Roles

The six broad roles to be examined are presented in Table 9.1. They include family members as context; targets for change and recipients of service; partners in the treatment process; service providers, including consultants and educators; advocates and policymakers; and evaluators and researchers.

Family Members as Context

In this perspective, parents and other family members are viewed as an important part of the environment of a child who has an emotional disorder. Interest is often focused on parents' possible roles as pathogenic agents in the etiology of childhood mental illness and emotional disorders. Much has been written about this perspective both by those who conduct research from this perspective (e.g., Keller et al., 1986; Williams, Anderson, McGee, & Silva, 1990) and by those who question this view (Caplan & Hall-McCorquodale, 1985; Holten, 1990). Since the 1920s, the profound influence of psychoanalytic theory on professional and popular thought in the United States has promoted a general societal response to families whose children exhibit unusual or undesirable behaviors—that is, that virtually all childhood mental problems result from ineffective or malevolent parenting.

In reality, the controversy around parental responsibility and blame is often more political than scientific, partly because it tends to be conducted at a very general level of abstraction. The population of children broadly identified as having "emotional, behavioral, and mental disorders" encompasses a wide variety of emotional and behavioral manifestations, diagnoses, and possible etiological explanations, only some of which emphasize social or psychological variables.

Research Focus

Within this perspective, parents are seen as "independent variables"—that is, as possible causal agents in the mental health problems of their children. Despite

Table 9.1

Family Roles, Research, and Practice Issues

Role of Caregiver and Family	Research Focus/ Concern	Interventions	Research Implications	Practice Challenges
Family members as context	Identifying links between parents' behavior, emotions (especially mother), and child's problems. Current parallel is "risk factors."	Shield child from unhealthy influence by removal from home, introduction of "buffering agents." Intervene to improve parenting, home environment.	Develop improved studies that are longitudinal, include comparison groups, and allow for transactive nature of parent-child relationships.	Reduce blame felt by families. Develop interventions that build on etiological studies that support families.
Family members as targets for change and recipients of service	Developing and validating effective interventions that support parents, promote change.	Provide therapy, parent education, and training to increase competence of parenting, correct unhealthy patterns, support healthy development of child.	Work with practitioners to clarify goals of intervention research. Examine outcomes of single support strategies (e.g., respite care) and combined, "wraparound" approaches.	Develop interventions that address needs of the entire family. Improve professional training to reflect current practice in children's mental health.
Family members as partners in the treatment process	Developing conceptual, philosophical, practice foundations; focus on process, implementation, and (rarely) on outcomes of collaboration.	Engage in flexible relationship, joint planning and decision making, open information sharing, assistance with access to services.	Demonstrate effective strategies for partnership practice. Examine links between collaboration and service appropriateness, outcomes.	Adapt collaborative models to diverse cultures. Manage changing distribution of power and responsibility. Incorporate principles of collaboration into professional education.

(continues)

Table 9.1 *Continued*

Role of Caregiver and Family	Research Focus/ Concern	Interventions	Research Implications	Practice Challenges
Family members as service providers	Describe and evaluate process and outcome of family members in service-provision roles.	Family members work in a variety of service provision roles: case management, case and educational advocacy, training, mediation.	Catalog family service roles. Understand intended and unintended consequences of family service provision; identify effects uniquely related to family member status.	Provide adequate support for family service providers regarding salary training, credentialing, relationships with colleagues. Utilize feedback to improve organization.
Family members as policymakers and advocates	Describing the advocacy activities of family members and family organizations. Understanding the life histories of family advocates. Identifying barriers to participation.	Federal and state mandates and incentives, targeted demonstrations, and direct support for policy-related activities.	Conduct demonstrations that address current barriers, and are adequately supported both financially and administratively.	Provide adequate support to family members in policy roles (e.g., reimbursement, training, mentoring). Adjust expectations of family organizations to match realities of organizational development.
Family members as evaluators and researchers	Small body of conceptual literature; no outcome studies located.	Family members serve as research advisors and consult regarding research priorities, broadening "legitimate" child and family outcomes, peer review, members of research teams.	Describe extent of family involvement, effects on research process and vice versa.	Much education needed for researchers regarding value of family participation in research and evaluation. Family members need greater understanding and skills regarding research process.

the absence of a research base, the work of Sigmund Freud (e.g., Freud, 1952) that emphasized the importance of parental (especially maternal) emotional responses and behaviors in the development of child psychopathology has significantly affected the conceptual frameworks used for both research and practice in children's mental health. Other important influences on the ways that parents were viewed through the 1960s included Frieda Fromm-Reichmann's concept of the "schizophrenogenic mother" (1948) and Bettelheim's (1967) hypotheses about the central role of inadequate mothering in the etiology of autism.

Beginning in the 1970s, a number of studies were published that demonstrated the limitations of some theories that held parents directly responsible for the emotional disorders of their children, and lent credence to Schopler's (1971) suggestion that in the absence of better information, parents were sometimes made scapegoats for their children's mental disorders. Examining the validity of the concept of "schizophrenogenic mother," Arieti (1974) found that no more than 25% of persons with schizophrenia demonstrated such negative maternal relationships. Hingtgen and Bryson (1972) concluded that the research literature on childhood psychosis and family characteristics tended to rule out parental psychopathology as a causative factor. Schreibman's (1988) careful analysis of Bettelheim's parent-causation hypothesis of autism suggests that "the accumulation of more systematically obtained data have contributed to the decline of this hypothesis as viable in the etiology of autism" (p. 51). Although many rather unidimensional theories that implicated parents as causal agents have been shown to be inaccurate or incomplete, many of these ideas persist and are still taught in professional training programs. For example, Wahl (1989) found that the concept of the "schizophrenogenic mother" was included in many psychology textbooks.

Research advances have helped to move thinking about the etiology and treatment of childhood mental disorders from global assumptions about "child mental disorder" to increasingly specific knowledge about the development of particular conditions and to increased attention to the interaction of biological and environmental factors. For example, research findings suggest that a number of child psychiatric disorders including childhood autism, multiple chronic tics and Tourette's syndrome, attention-deficit hyperactivity disorder, and major affective disorders have a strong genetic component (Institute of Medicine, 1989; Rutter et al., 1990). Many of these genetic predispositions are currently thought to interact with environmental conditions to affect both the manifestation and the severity of some childhood disorders.

Thus, as an important part of the child's environment, parenting skills and other family factors continue to receive research attention. Research that emphasizes the emotional and interpersonal contributions of parents to the social and psychological development of their children focuses on characteristics such as maternal warmth (Rohner, Kean, & Cournoyer, 1991), maternal depression (Rutter, 1990; Williams, Anderson, McGee, & Silva, 1990), and on the quality of socioemotional bonds between parent and child (Bowlby, 1988).

Patterson, DeBaryshe, & Ramsey (1989) outline a developmental model of anti-social behavior in children that implicates ineffective parenting practices in early childhood as contributing to the development of conduct disorders. They trace a developmental sequence that includes academic failure, peer rejection, depressed mood, and involvement in a deviant peer group. This research provides a foundation for understanding not only the development of conduct disorder in children, but also a basis for prevention and early intervention.

Attention is also directed to family processes (e.g., family characteristics such as cohesion and adaptability examined by Prange et al., 1992), structure (the concept of family hierarchies explored by Green, Loeber, & Lahey, 1992), conflicts between the child and one or more parent (Eme & Danielak, 1995), or disruptions associated with divorce (Shamsie, 1985). Renewed attention to environmental factors such as poverty (Homel & Burns, 1989; Murphy & Jellinek, 1988) and violence includes investigations of the emotional sequelae of physical and sexual abuse of children (Oliver, 1993) and the negative effects on children of exposure to family and community violence (Fitzpatrick, 1993; McCloskey, Figueredo, & Koss, 1995). Some of this research is limited by a sole focus on clinical populations, designs that are mostly correlational and retrospective, and theoretical frameworks that do not take into account the possible reciprocal effects of parent-child interactions and other alternative hypotheses. For example, although the work of Patterson et al. (1989) makes an important contribution by tracing the development of conduct disorder in children, it does not explain why many children, despite less than ideal parenting practices, do not develop conduct disorder. Thus, it is possible that, in addition to parenting practices, other aspects of the environment, along with certain characteristics of children, interact to produce the set of behavior patterns now called "conduct disorder." Another model that includes the possibility of reciprocal influences is proposed by Thomas and Chess (1984), whose research on temperament spans 25 years of observation. Within this perspective, the behavioral and emotional characteristics of children interact from birth with the characteristics, beliefs, and behaviors of parents to produce behavioral disorders in children. Like Patterson and colleagues (1989), Thomas and Chess have developed an intervention approach designed to support parents as they learn the parenting strategies that are most appropriate for their child's particular circumstances.

Interventions

Treatment strategies based on parental contributions to the emotional, behavioral, or mental disorders of their children employ a variety of interventions. One set is designed to separate the child from the family, thus minimizing the unwanted influence of the parents and allowing the child to build healthy relationships with other adults (Whittaker, 1976). Although this approach has lost favor in light of a renewed emphasis on community-based services, vestiges of this perspective are still present, as in the policies of residential treatment programs that limit contact with parents (Schaefer & Swanson, 1993). Another strategy, often combined with the first, aims to change some aspect of the parents' functioning through teaching new parenting skills, or treating underlying psychopathology. Interventions associated with this approach are more fully discussed in the next section of this chapter, "Family Members as Targets for Change and Recipients of Service." Parental roles within the perspective of "family members as context" are very limited, often restricted to "object of research" or "informant." Parents viewed only from this perspective have tended to feel blamed and stigmatized (Friesen & Huff, 1996).

Research Implications

Much conceptual and empirical work is needed to further understand the etiology of childhood mental disorders. As suggested earlier, the designation "children with emotional disorders" is a very broad category that includes a wide variety of problems, the causes of which are complex and still poorly understood. Research should be conducted that takes into account differences across children and families with regard to issues such as culture, diagnosis or manifestation of the problem, and environmental circumstances, along with inquiry into ways that the actions or omissions of family caretakers may have contributed to their children's problems. There is also a need for additional research that includes nonclinical populations. And, finally, "negative results," such as those reported by Hillman, Sawilowsky, and Becker (1993), should be published. These researchers found no significant effects of maternal employment on the substance abuse and risk-taking behaviors of adolescents.

Although we have an imperfect understanding of the pathways by which problems such as parental mental illness or substance abuse may trigger problems or fail to protect children from the negative consequences of environmental circumstances, a sole focus on these issues does not provide policy-relevant information that advances our understanding about how to improve the lives of children and families. For this reason, and given limited research funds in children's mental health, it seems only humane, and potentially more productive, to include the question "What supports could help families provide an environment that is supportive, nurturing, and developmentally appropriate?" along with a focus on etiology. The work of Patterson and colleagues (1989) constitutes a useful model for combining research about causation with the development and testing of interventions that support parents in their roles. These researchers first identified parenting practices associated with children's poor social skills and aggressive behavior, and then developed and tested interventions designed to help parents learn more effective strategies with their children, and to support the children's psychological, social, and academic development across a variety of settings.

Studies should also examine transactive models, such as those proposed by Thomas and Chess (1984) in their work on temperament and suggested in findings presented by a number of other authors (e.g., Garfinkel et al., 1983; Miller & Keirn, 1978). These models include the assumption that parents and other family members may be affected by child mental health problems, and that "parent pathology" may, at times, be an understandable reaction to extreme duress.

Practice Challenges

Taken alone, a view of family members as "context" does not carry implications for contemporary practice, although the development of knowledge about causation may lead to the development and testing of interventions. Strategies compatible with this perspective are addressed in the next section.

Family Members as Targets for Change and Recipients of Service

In this role, family members are cast as the target of intervention, as patients, clients of service, or learners. This way of viewing parents or other caregivers is compatible with, but not limited to, a view of parents as causal in the development of their children's mental health problems (family as context). Services and supports may also be provided to family members without assuming either that they have contributed to their children's problems, or that a change in their emotional responses or behaviors is indicated.

Research Focus

Overall, the focus of research in this area is on developing and testing the efficacy of interventions. Interventions aimed at providing service to family members, however, come from two very distinct philosophical positions and theoretical assumptions characterized by Marsh (1996) as "pathology-oriented," and "competence-based," as illustrated in Table 9.2. The first focuses on changing the attitudes and behaviors of parents, usually through psychotherapy or parent training, with a central assumption that their emotions or behaviors have contributed to their children's problems, and that changes in the parents are necessary to improve the mental health of the child. This type of research focuses specifically on families whose children have emotional, mental, or behavioral problems (Barber, 1992; Sutton, 1992).

The second approach (i.e., competence-based) was first applied in fields such as developmental disabilities and rehabilitation medicine, where there is no assumption that parents have contributed to their children's disabilities. In addition to a focus on the child with a disability, this approach encompasses concern for the health and well-being of parents and other members of the family as primary considerations, emphasizing family strengths and family

Table 9.2

Families as Recipients of Service
Philosophical/Theoretical Bases

Assumptions	Pathology-Oriented	Competence-Based
Cause of child's emotional disorder	Parents' behavior or emotional responses contribute to child's problems.	Etiology may be multifactorial—biological, psychological, social components.
By whom needs of child/family identified	Assessment, diagnosis developed by professional experts, explained to parents, child.	Needs and goals of service developed by family, professional working together; family definition of need combined with professional assessment.
Purpose of service to child	Remedial, curative; focused on ameliorating, correcting disorder.	Dual focus: (1) Rehabilitative—to directly address, improve child's functioning through treatment, education; (2) to create supportive environment for child (may include intervention with family, school, peer group)
Purpose of service to family	To correct problems of parent that contribute to child's problems so that the child can improve.	On behalf of child: to create supportive environment for child through intervention with family; to address service and support needs of all family members as important in their own right.
Examples of intervention	Individual, couples, family therapy; parent training to improve inadequate parenting skills.	Traditional mental health services may be offered to parents and family. Wide range of services responsive to needs of family, such as support (parent-parent, family/sibling support groups), concrete services (financial aid, transportation, respite/child care); skills training (how to deal with difficult behaviors, address child's low self-esteem, improve sibling relationships).

support strategies. Researchers are concerned both with documenting family needs and experiences associated with living with and caring for a child with an emotional disorder or other childhood disability (Asarnow & Horton, 1990; Friesen, 1989b; Tarico, Low, Trupin, & Forsyth-Stephens, 1989) and in testing specific interventions (Heflinger & Bickman, 1996; Singer et al., 1994).

Because specific services or interventions associated with the pathology-oriented and competence-based approaches may be similar, it is important to emphasize the distinctions between the two. In addition to calling for a broader range of interventions, the competence-based framework encompasses multifactorial causal hypotheses, an attempt to include both professional and family expertise, supportive and rehabilitative, as well as therapeutic interventions, and a clear focus on the health of the entire family. The competence-based approach includes the possibility that some parents need to improve their ability to support their children's development, but does not focus on this issue in the same way as in the pathology-oriented approaches.

Interventions

Strategies for change associated with a view of parents and other family members within the "pathology" perspective include most traditional mental health services (e.g., family therapy, individual or couples therapy for parents) or parent training and education approaches designed to improve the basic parenting skills of caregivers or provide specific behavior management techniques (Sutton, 1992). Competence-based interventions are less frequently emphasized in the mental health literature, although interventions designed to include family support strategies are increasingly found in innovative child mental health practice (Evans et al., 1994; Friesen & Wahlers, 1993). Both research reports and descriptions of family support interventions are abundant in the fields of developmental disabilities and across the rehabilitation literature (Singer et al., 1994). These strategies include the provision of supportive counseling, helping family members increase their range of coping skills, teaching specific stress management techniques, and providing access to a wide range of support services such as respite care; homemaker service; peer, sibling, and parent support groups; transportation; and financial assistance.

Research Implications

One of the most important issues for intervention research involving families is to clarify the goal(s) of such interventions—that is, whether the primary purpose of the intervention is focused on the well-being of the child (e.g., improving the parents' ability to parent more adequately) or more directly on the well-being of the parents or other caregivers, other members of the family, or on the functioning of the family as a whole. Although this point may seem self-evident, in fact, this issue is often murky in research and evaluation efforts, where measures of family functioning are included without specifying whether family functioning is thought to be an explanatory variable or something that is expected to change as the result of intervention. This phenomenon may reflect changing attitudes and theoretical perspectives about families that are not yet integrated, resulting in a somewhat awkward blend of etiological and intervention perspectives. Researchers and evaluators who are conducting field studies can work with service providers to clarify the underlying theory and purpose of their intervention; this clarity is necessary to advance this area of intervention research.

There is also a great need for additional research that both examines the outcomes of single family support strategies such as respite care (Wherry, Shema, Baltz, & Kelleher, 1995) and support groups, and assesses the effectiveness of comprehensive family wraparound strategies (Eber, Osuch, & Redditt, 1996; Evans, Armstrong, & Kuppinger, 1996).

Practice Challenges

A central challenge is to develop family intervention approaches that take the full range of family needs into account. For some practitioners this may involve a shift from specialized to more flexible practice. Addressing the needs of the entire family also involves listening carefully to what families identify as helpful, assessing existing family strengths and resources, and having the organizational flexibility to arrange or provide responsive services (see Friesen & Huff, 1996, for an expanded discussion of family-centered services). This approach to family intervention will challenge many existing mental health organizations as gaps between what families identify as helpful and existing resources become apparent. In many cases, the provision of family-responsive services will involve adding the capacity to provide or arrange family support strategies such as respite care or parent-to-parent support, along with more traditional interventions. It may also include developing new services within agencies, as well as highlighting the need for interagency collaboration when the family's needs are best addressed by multiple organizations.

Professional training curricula must be expanded to ensure that service providers enter the field equipped to function within a family-centered, system-of-care philosophy (Johnson, 1993). Current evidence suggests that relatively few programs provide training that emphasizes competence in providing services within a complex, family-centered environment (Hernandez, Lineberger, & Baimbridge, 1992; Jivanjee, Moore, Schultze, & Friesen, 1995), and that many do not, creating the need for both experienced and entry-level service providers to be retrained in the field (Hanley & Wright, 1995).

Families as Partners in the Treatment Process

Sometimes represented within the children's mental health field by the term "families as allies" (McManus & Friesen, 1986), this notion involves a shift in the relationship between caregivers and professional service providers from the traditional "expert-service recipient" role to one that recognizes the expertise and other potential contributions of family members to the problem-solving process. In this role, family members and professionals work together to identify goals and to develop, implement, and evaluate services for the child and other family members. This emphasis on family-professional partnerships in children's mental health has developed within the last decade, and it is compatible with a competence-based view of families described in the previous section. It is responsive to the stated preferences of parents within the children's mental health field (Friesen & Huff, 1996), influenced by ideas and practice imported from fields such as health, developmental disabilities, and rehabilitation, and it reflects a larger societal trend toward consumerism and increased skepticism of professional expertise, some of which is codified in special education (Education for All Handicapped Children Act of 1975, P.L. 94-142) and early intervention law (Education of the Handicapped Act Amendments of 1986, P.L. 96-272).

Research Focus

Research addressing family-professional collaboration generally addresses three themes: conceptual, philosophical, and practice principles; the process of collaboration; and the implementation of collaborative practice, including evaluation of the outcomes of such an approach. An important early type of research in the area of family-professional collaboration focused on describing the relationships between family members and professionals (Bernheim & Switalski, 1988; Cournoyer & Johnson, 1991; Friesen, 1989b; Johnson, Cournoyer, & Fisher, 1994). This research suggested that family members had a number of concerns about how they were treated by professionals, including feeling blamed, not listened to, and undervalued. In addition, family members and professionals often had quite different views about service needs and priorities (Bernheim & Switalski, 1988; Friesen, Koren, & Koroloff, 1992).

Researchers who examined the outcomes of collaborative practice report that collaborative relationships are related to higher family satisfaction (DeChillo, 1993; DeChillo, Koren, & Schultze, 1994), greater family involvement in discharge planning (DeChillo, 1993), and shorter hospital stays (Williams, 1988). In a follow-up evaluation with professional and family participants in a training program designed to promote parent-professional collaboration, trainees reported that although many barriers to collaborative practice exist, the training had increased their ability to work in partnership and had also increased their ability to serve as advocates for improved services (Williams-Murphy, DeChillo, Koren, & Hunter, 1994).

Interventions

Collaborative practice consists of family members and professionals working as partners in the planning, implementation, and evaluation of services for children who have emotional disorders. A recurrent question about collaboration is how it differs from or is related to standard practice. The findings of DeChillo et al. (1994) provide a framework for examining collaborative practice (i.e., the extent to which it involves a respectful relationship, inclusion in decision-making, help in obtaining services, and responsiveness to feedback). Other objective components that may distinguish collaborative practice from traditional mental health practice include: joint planning and review, where family members (parents and children, when appropriate) are included in all service planning and review meetings; a higher degree of information sharing, bolstered by changing professional attitudes as well as laws and policies that give service recipients access to their medical records; and more attention and responsiveness to consumer feedback about the effectiveness and acceptability of services. Over time, as practice strategies incorporate partnership approaches, standard practice and "collaboration" should become one.

Research Implications

This type of research is still in its infancy. Because a collaborative relationship is preferred by many family members, resources should be devoted to improving and refining the process, as well as to testing whether collaboration contributes to critical outcomes such as improved child behavior, better community adjustment, or cost savings. Important research questions about the process of collaboration include the following: What are the most effective ways to prepare professionals and family members to work in partnership? What are the best choices with regard to the format, length, and content of training? Should family members and professionals be trained together? What organizational policies, procedures, and practices promote and support partnership practice within agencies and systems of care? Questions related to outcome largely revolve around the issue of "added value"—that is, does, and how does, collaborative practice lead to improved child and family well-being, and other valued outcomes?

Also needed are studies of actual efforts to implement collaborative practice such as that reported by Schacht, Pandiani, and Maynard (1996). These researchers elicited reports from staff about the participation of family members in interagency team meetings and reported that parents appeared to feel that they were an equal member of the group less than one third of the time; this proportion did not substantially increase between a survey conducted in 1990 and a second conducted in 1993. These researchers point out that there is a need for additional studies that track parents' responses to collaborative efforts over time, including those that directly ask family members about their experiences. More studies using direct observations of interactions between family members and professionals such as that reported by Curtis and Singh (1995) are also needed.

Practice Challenges

For professionals, the two biggest challenges lie in learning to work in partnership with family members, whose values, culture, attitudes, and behaviors are different from the practitioners', and finding an appropriate balance between sharing power and retaining professional responsibility. Partnership practice requires considerable expertise and flexibility, because appropriate practice will likely vary from family to family and over time within families. Particularly when working with families who are not of the dominant culture, culturally competent practice will require that partnership practice not be implemented in a doctrinaire fashion. This may be especially true around issues such as power-sharing, the degree of formality or informality adopted, and the invocation of professional expertise and authority. While many families may prefer a democratic, egalitarian relationship, others may be more comfortable when the roles are more traditional.

Two of the most frequently misunderstood aspects of partnership practice relate to acknowledging the expertise of family members and shared power in decision-making. Practitioners new to collaborative practice sometimes worry that acknowledging the expertise of family members means that their (professional) expertise is somehow diminished, or is not valued. In fact, the expertise of the professional in collaborative practice is crucial in helping family members make informed decisions; some professionals will need support and assistance in overcoming their traditional training. Managing the distribution of power and responsibility constitutes another important practice challenge. Developing a more egalitarian relationship does not necessarily mean that power and responsibility are equally distributed. The dynamic nature of the issues faced by families who are raising a child with an emotional disorder often means that their preferences and capacity for assuming specific responsibilities vary markedly over time, requiring considerable professional flexibility.

Family Members as Service Providers

Family members operate in a variety of roles that involve the provision of direct services to other family members, as well as functioning as teachers and consultants to families and professionals alike. Koroloff, Friesen, et al. (1996) also point out that family members provide much unpaid service on behalf of their own children; they serve as agents of transition—informal service providers who fill the gaps when no categorical service fits what is needed. These services include service coordination activities (requesting, convening, and often scheduling meetings), transporting their own and others' children to medical and social service appointments, serving as couriers by transporting medical records and other documents between programs, and providing emotional support and information to other family members. Although most of this service is on a volunteer basis, opportunities for family members to be compensated are increasing as their value and expertise are recognized by agencies, as they have become more vocal in their desire to be paid for their work, and as the formal service system enters into contractual arrangements with family organizations to provide a variety of services using family members as employed service providers.

Research Focus

The small body of research in this area includes reports of research demonstration projects involving family members in service provision roles (Koroloff, Elliott, Koren, & Friesen, 1995; Koroloff, Elliott, Koren, & Friesen, 1996; Tannen, 1996) and in program evaluation reports (Murray, 1992). The results of this research suggest that family members can be highly effective in providing such services as information, support, case management, and advocacy for other families. Anecdotal evidence also suggests that family members may be more effective than professional service providers in some circumstances, such as gaining access and establishing trust with families who are reluctant to seek or use services (Ignelzi & Dague, 1995; Leishman, 1995).

Interventions

Family members provide direct services through a variety of organizational configurations. For example, family members may serve as case managers or case aides in mental health or social service agencies, or as employees of family organizations that contract with the formal service delivery system. In Wichita, Kansas, a family organization provides job training for parents who are receiving welfare benefits as part of the state's welfare reform strategy. These family members are trained to become case management aides or educational advocates (Koroloff, Friesen, et al., 1996). Family members participate in all aspects of the program design, implementation, and evaluation within the Finger Lakes Family Support Project in New York State, a program conceived and run as a collaboration between family members and professionals. Family members employed as part-time family support group coordinators also plan and implement periodic family retreats. Volunteer family members screen, hire, train, and supervise respite workers (Friesen & Wahlers, 1993). The Family Council of Stark County, Ohio, employs family members as family advocates, wraparound facilitators, outreach workers, and policy shapers (Stark County Family Council, 1996). In Vermont, the Vermont Federation of Families for Children's Mental Health helped to develop, and currently manages, the respite program for families of children with emotional disabilities (Sturtevant, 1992).

Research Implications

First, there is a need to catalog and describe all of the various roles in which family members are engaged, and the organizational and fiscal arrangements within which they function. This research should also systematically capture the many positive contributions that family members make in their direct service roles and the possible negative consequences for family employees (e.g., constraints on their ability to serve as advocates for the families they serve). With this descriptive research as a foundation, studies can then be designed to explore areas where family members seem uniquely qualified to provide intervention, as well as the outcomes of such intervention. Also, documenting and understanding the reasons why family members are able to gain access and build necessary trust should provide information relevant to improving professional practice, as well.

Practice Challenges

One current challenge lies in clarifying the roles of family members who are providing direct services. Questions from professional colleagues include concerns such as confidentiality, role overlap, and quality and appropriateness of services. Issues for administrators include questions such as how to provide appropriate supervision, support, and training for family members, considerations in establishing equitable salary ranges, and how to incorporate family member contributions as an ongoing part of agency practice. Issues for family members include possible role conflict created when their values and beliefs about what is best for the families that they serve are incompatible with agency policies, practices, or resource constraints. For some family members, issues such as how and whether it is possible to be an employee and a client of the same agency may also arise. Another question for administrators is how best to obtain and use the observations and suggestions for change that come from family member employees, while also supporting their relationships with other staff members. Having family members as employees presents an opportunity for the organization that is seeking ways to become more family centered and responsive.

Family Members as Advocates and Policymakers

Individual family members and representatives of family organizations are now commonly engaged in activities designed to obtain needed services for individual children and families (case advocacy) and to improve services or obtain necessary policy reform for all children with mental health needs (system advocacy). This activity sharply contrasts with that of a decade ago, when there was practically no organization among family members across the country, and parents were largely isolated and disempowered (Friesen, 1991). Family members now engage in advocacy for their own and others' children in order to ensure that appropriate services are planned and provided. They work to change undesirable policies, such as requiring parents to relinquish custody of their children in order to access services (McManus, Reilly, Rinkin, &

Wrigley, 1993), and they promote needed policy development at state and local levels. Individual family members and representatives of family organizations engage in policy-related activity through disseminating information to families, service providers, and policymakers about family perspectives on needed change (e.g., Anderson, 1994), proposing or responding to specific policy initiatives (McManus et al., 1993), and providing case and system-level advocacy training to families (Hunter, 1993; Kelker, 1987).

Research Focus

There has been scant research about parents and other caregivers in family-level or system-level advocacy roles, although there is a small body of conceptual and descriptive literature (Duchnowski, Dunlap, Berg, & Adeighboba, 1994; Fine & Borden, 1989; Friesen, 1989a). Between 1989 and 1994 Koroloff and colleagues (Hunter, 1993; Koroloff, Hunter, & Gordon, 1995; Mayer, 1994), through a project entitled "Families in Action," conducted research that directly addressed family members' participation in policy-level roles. A series of focus groups conducted with family members and professionals (Koroloff, Hunter, & Gordon, 1995) revealed barriers to family member participation in boards, task forces, and advisory groups related to (a) the parents' situation, (b) the structure and process of the decision-making bodies, (c) professional attitudes and behavior, and (d) the service system as a whole. Barriers related to the parents' situation included lack of time and energy (especially if employed), family crises, disruption of family life related to policy involvement, lack of available child care, and concern related to blame and stigma about "going public." Barriers raised by the structure and process of the policy body included time and locations being inconvenient or inaccessible to family members, unreimbursed expenses, issues related to representation, and lack of appreciation for cultural differences. Professional attitudes and behaviors such as merely giving lip service to family participation, condescending behavior, and lack of recognition of parents' expertise also constituted impediments to effective participation. Family members also noted that the professional subculture (opportunities to receive and exchange information and "clubbiness") served to make them feel like less than full members of policy-level groups. Barriers related to the nature of the service system included the slowness of achieving change and lack of available services.

Interventions

Direct efforts to promote family participation at the policy level have included federal and state mandates and incentives, targeted demonstrations, and direct support for policy-related activities. Federal mandates designed to encourage family member participation in policy formation include P.L. 99-660, the State Comprehensive Mental Health Services Plan, which required family

participation in state-level mental health planning processes, and requirements that grants related to Child and Adolescent Service System Program
planning include family participation at all levels of activity (Lourie, Katz-
Leavy, & Jacobs, 1985). A number of states have enacted legislation or implemented administrative rules that require family participation in planning
or decisions about resource distribution (Koroloff, McManus, Pfohl, & Sturtevant, 1996).

A demonstration specifically designed to assist family members' participation at the policy level was reported by Koroloff, Hunter, & Gordon (1995). The
project involved six family groups that developed action goals such as increasing family representation on policy-related bodies or improvement in the quality and effectiveness of their participation. The findings of this project suggest
that family members' optimism about policy participation shifted to "increased
realism" over time. Family participants' perception of the importance of the
work of the policymaking groups in which they were involved changed from
"very important" to "moderately important," and the satisfaction of family
members shifted downward from "much" to "some." Over the 15 months that
data were collected, family members described their participatory behavior in
meetings as moving from "active" to "very active," and saw themselves as gaining increased skills and comfort as participating group members. Many of the
barriers identified by focus group participants will require creative and sustained attention if they are to be overcome. Recommended strategies include
mentoring (by another family member or a professional), focused participation
around specific issues, reimbursement for family participants, and improved
communication and support among parents involved in policy-level activity.
The importance of recruitment, training, and support for family members who
engage in policy-level activities was also noted.

Direct support for policy-related involvement has been available to statewide family organizations since 1988, beginning with five small grants designed
to promote state-level family-run organizations (Koroloff, Stuntzner-Gibson, &
Friesen, 1990). Through 1996, the objectives of statewide family organizations
supported by federal funds included establishment of a mechanism for statewide
communication and dissemination of relevant policy information. Evaluations of
these statewide family efforts revealed a steady increase in policy-related activity over time, as well as a number of important policy initiatives related to the
activity of the statewide family organizations, often through coalitions with
other advocacy organizations (Briggs, Koroloff, & Carrock, 1994; Briggs, Koroloff,
Richards, & Friesen, 1993; Koroloff et al., 1990). These accomplishments include
legislation prohibiting the practice of transferring legal custody of children to the
state merely for the purpose of obtaining reimbursement for services (e.g., in
Minnesota, Georgia, and Oregon). A number of states have passed legislation
calling for the development of a comprehensive system of care for children and
families (Hawaii, Minnesota, Virginia, Wisconsin), at least in part because of the
participation of statewide family organizations.

Research Implications

A foundation of knowledge exists about the experiences of family members who have participated at the policy level. The next logical research step would appear to be demonstrations that are well supported, both financially and administratively. Such projects could systematically implement and test the recommendations proposed in reports of descriptive research (Koroloff, Hunter, & Gordon 1995) such as material supports for families (e.g., reimbursement for costs such as transportation, child care, and lost wages), joint training for family and professional members of policy bodies, and support to organizations in developing the policy skills of members.

Practice Challenges

A central challenge for individual professionals and agencies lies in creating a climate where the potential benefits of family participation in policymaking groups can be realized. In addition to tangible support for family members, strategies may include ongoing training that helps family members, professionals, and other community representatives work together on policymaking bodies. Improving the quantity and quality of family member participation should ultimately improve the effectiveness of the entire process (Jeppson & Thomas, 1995).

Challenges related to family organizations engaged in promoting policy change are related to the current stage of development of family organizations (Koroloff & Briggs, 1996). Many family organizations find themselves trying to "do it all" with inadequate resources: Provide services and supports for individual families, give information and training to families and service providers, serve on boards and commissions, and engage in policy-related dissemination and legislative activity. Funding agencies often expect that strong statewide family organizations will develop, and in turn, use their advocacy skills and clout to garner increased resources and support for children's services. Although this expectation is probably reasonable over the long term, family organizations in many states are struggling to survive, and cannot attend simultaneously to organizational infrastructure requirements, the needs and crises presented by families who seek information and service, and high-profile advocacy activities. Thus, an enormous challenge is to develop strategies that support, but do not control, family organizations, taking into account their development and place in the organizational life cycle (Koroloff & Briggs, 1996).

Family Members as Evaluators and Researchers

In this role, family members participate in the evaluation phase of service implementation and engage in a variety of ways in formal research. The participation of family members in research and evaluation activities is an important but still-developing area. Turnbull and Friesen (1995) presented a continuum of family research participation beginning, at one end, with family members in the traditional role of research respondents and, at the other end, with family members in charge of setting the research agenda and hiring researchers to assist with the technical aspects of research. Although this "idealized" situation is far removed from the current state of affairs, it nevertheless represents a direction toward greater family involvement in research and evaluation both in children's mental health and in other disability fields. As Kutash and Rivera (1996) noted, "Methods of participatory research for parents and consumers should be developed to ensure that they are an integral part of service delivery, the development of systems of care, the development of research design, and the implementation of the design" (p. 205).

Research Focus and Current Practice

The gradual inclusion of family members in research activities is another reflection of a national trend toward the involvement of consumers and their families in all aspects of policy and services (Litvak, Frieden, Dresden, & Doe, 1995). At least one federal agency, the National Institute on Disability and Rehabilitation Research, actively encourages grantees to implement a participatory action research model that includes consumers and family members in all phases of research, orienting research questions to the concerns of consumer participants (Fenton, Batavia, & Roody, 1993). Although there are no studies that examine the roles of families in research and evaluation in children's mental health, family members are now involved in a variety of roles beyond that of research subject or respondent. They serve as members of research advisory committees, consultants regarding research priorities and direction, participants in the peer review process, and as members of the research or evaluation teams.

Family members serve in a wide variety of research advisory capacities in children's mental health. For example, two research and training centers focusing on children's mental health and funded by the Center for Mental Health Services and the National Institute on Disability and Rehabilitation Research (Portland State University and the University of South Florida) have included family members as full participants in their national advisory committees for more than a decade. This activity involves both general review of project plans and progress, and direct input to specific studies. Family members have also been included in the advisory process for the Macro International evaluation of the Child Mental Health Services Program, involving 22 demonstration sites across the country (Stroul, McCormack, & Zaro, 1996).

Family members have also served as consultants about research priorities and directions, allowing them to have considerable influence on research agendas and providing a fresh perspective on the way that researchers think about the entire research process. Family members were key participants in a symposium designed to identify research needs and direction through the 1990s (Friesen, Koroloff, & Koren, 1993). Participants at annual meetings of the Federation of Families for Children's Mental Health have, at the invitation of researchers, responded to questions about their priorities for research. Family members also increasingly participate in research conferences both as audience members and as presenters.

Probably one of the most important contributions of the family perspective in child mental health research has been a broadening of the range of research variables (outcomes and process) that are considered legitimate. This shift has occurred gradually from the early 1980s, when research outcomes tended to be restricted to clinical concerns (e.g., child and family functioning) and a focus on cost and efficiency. Today, research and evaluation studies almost always include measures of family (and sometimes, youth) satisfaction, and often address family empowerment (Koren, DeChillo, & Friesen, 1992; Heflinger & Bickman, 1996), family participation (Stroul et al., 1996), family support (Murray, 1992), and service coordination from the perspective of the family (Koren et al., in press). Attention is also given to the extent to which services are family centered (Allen, Petr, & Brown, 1995) and include concern about phenomena such as family burden (Messer, Angold, Costello, & Burns, 1996).

The practice of including family members on research peer review committees at the Center for Mental Health Services and the National Institute on Disability and Rehabilitation Research constitutes an important statement of values and policy. The process of including nonresearchers (both family members and service providers) on peer review committees required a reexamination of the expectations of reviewers, and some adjustment in the peer review process to capitalize on the strengths of all involved. The inclusion of family members on peer review committees has generally increased the extent to which the importance and feasibility of the research are considered along with other scientific and technical issues.

Family members also serve as employed members of research teams. For example, parents are working as data collectors in several of the 22 service sites participating in the evaluation of the Child Mental Health Services Program (Stroul et al., 1996). Family members are employed by the Research and Training Centers at the University of South Florida and Portland State University, and an increasing number of family members are equipping themselves with formal research training.

Challenges

The major challenges related to fully including family members in the research and evaluation process are related to necessary changes in the attitudes and skills of both researchers and family members. Researchers must first accept the value of family participation, and then learn how to most effectively use it. Turnbull and Friesen (1995) outlined a number of issues related to consumer and family participation in research and evaluation. For example, maximizing the utility of the diverse expertise of researchers and family members may require the education of all parties and the development of clear agreement about how decisions will be made. Logistical considerations include allowing for the additional time required to broaden input into proposal preparation and implementation of research projects, and increased costs (travel and time) associated with increased participation. These barriers are generally believed to be balanced by the greater relevance of research, better dissemination, and more rapid utilization of results (Fenton, Batavia, & Roody, 1993).

Family members, who tend to be impatient with the long-term and abstract nature of much research, must also learn more about research and evaluation in order to most effectively affect the process. Opportunities for family members to gain a working knowledge of the research process are increasingly available at research conferences and in written materials prepared expressively for this purpose (Karp & Nolte, 1990; Nicholson & Robinson, 1996).

Summary and Conclusions

In this chapter, six important roles that family members play in the system of care were reviewed. The first, which emphasizes family members as "context," was included because this perspective and body of research is the subject of much confusion in the field of children's mental health and needs ongoing examination. The second role, that of "target for change," or recipient of service, is conceptually tied to the first, and still probably constitutes the major way that family members are involved in their children's treatment, whether by choice or by cautious acceptance of professional recommendations. The remaining four roles (families as partners, as service providers, as advocates and policymakers, and as participants in the research process) are more innovative, more unevenly implemented, and present more challenges for professionals and family members alike.

The rapid expansion of family roles over the last decade has brought with it important reforms in the planning and operation of services for children with emotional disorders and their families. Changes in how families are viewed and the degree to which parents and other caregivers participate in decisions about their children's education and treatment, and in policy matters, have profoundly altered the nature of services in many parts of the country.

The advent of managed care presents an immediate challenge, and it heightens the importance of developing and maintaining a high level of family participation in all aspects of service. All managed care programs, by definition, emphasize cost containment, and many mental health–managed care programs employ service delivery priorities that parallel those of physical medicine (a focus on the "affected individual" rather than on the needs of the whole family, and an orientation toward acute rather than long-term care). Especially when public mental health services are contracted to not-for-profit or for-profit organizations, care must be taken to ensure that there exist vehicles for family input at all levels and phases of operation, including, but by no means limited to, consumer satisfaction surveys. Guidelines for family participation in managed care have been developed by family organizations (Malloy, 1995; National Coalition for Family Leadership, 1996; Osher, Koyanagi, & Schulzinger, 1996), and, increasingly, family members are becoming well informed about system-of-care and managed-care issues. The combined efforts of service providers, researchers, family members, and advocates are needed to solidify the gains that have been achieved by and on behalf of families whose children have emotional, behavioral, and mental disorders, and to meet the challenges that still remain.

Authors' Note

This chapter was developed with funding from the National Institute on Disability and Rehabilitation Research, United States Department of Education, and the Center for Mental Health Services, Substance Abuse and Mental Health Services Administration (NIDRR grant number H133B900007-96). The contents of this chapter do not necessarily reflect the views or policies of the funding agencies.

References

Allen, R., Petr, C. G., & Brown, B. F. C. (1995). *Family-centered behavior scale and user manual.* Lawrence, KS: Beach Center, University of Kansas.

Anderson, W. C. (1994). *Finding help—finding hope.* Alexandria, VA: Federation of Families for Children's Mental Health.

Arieti, S. (1974). *Interpretation of schizophrenia* (2nd ed.). New York: Basic Books.

Asarnow, J. R., & Horton, A. A. (1990). Coping and stress in families of child psychiatric inpatients: Parents of children with depressive and schizophrenia spectrum disorders. *Child Psychiatry and Human Development, 21*(2), 145–157.

Barber, J. G. (1992). Evaluating parent education groups: Effects on sense of competence and social isolation. *Research on Social Work Practice, 2*(1), 28–38.

Bernheim, K. F., & Switalski, T. (1988). The Buffalo Family Support Project: Promoting institutional change to meet families' needs. *Hospital and Community Psychiatry, 39*(6), 663–665.

Bettelheim, B. (1967). *The empty fortress.* New York: Free Press.

Bowlby, J. (1988). Developmental psychiatry comes of age. *American Journal of Psychiatry, 145*(1), 1–10.

Briggs, H. E., Koroloff, N. M., & Carrock, S. (1994). The driving force: The influence of statewide family organizations on family support and systems of care. *Statewide family advocacy organization demonstration project, 10/90–9/93. Final report.* Portland, OR: Research and Training Center on Family Support and Children's Mental Health, Portland State University.

Briggs, H. E., Koroloff, N. M., Richards, K., & Friesen, B. J. (1993). *Family advocacy organizations: Advances in support and system reform.* Portland, OR: Research and Training Center on Family Support and Children's Mental Health, Portland State University.

Caplan, P. J., & Hall-McCorquodale, I. (1985). Mother-blaming in major clinical journals. *American Journal of Orthopsychiatry, 55,* 345–353.

Cournoyer, D. E., & Johnson, H. C. (1991). Measuring parents' perceptions of mental health professionals. *Research on Social Work Practice, 1*(4), 399–415.

Curtis, W. J., & Singh, N. N. (1995). Family-friendliness of mental health services for children: An observational study of community based family assessment and planning team meetings. In C. R. Ellis & N. N. Singh (Eds.), *Children and adolescents with emotional and behavioral disorders: Proceedings of the Fifth Annual Virginia Beach Conference.* Richmond, VA: Commonwealth Institute for Child and Family Studies, Medical College of Virginia, Virginia Commonwealth University.

DeChillo, N. (1993). Collaboration between social workers and families of patients with mental illness. *Families in Society: The Journal of Contemporary Human Services, 74*(2), 104–115.

DeChillo, N., Koren, P. E., & Schultze, K. H. (1994). From paternalism to partnership: Family/professional collaboration in children's mental health. *American Journal of Orthopsychiatry, 64*(4), 564–576.

Duchnowski, A. J., Dunlap, G. G., Berg, K., & Adeighboba, M. P. (1994). Rethinking the role of families in the education of their children: Policy and clinical issues. In J. Paul, D. Evans, & H. Rosselli (Eds.), *Restructuring special education* (pp. 105–118). New York: Harcourt Brace Jovanovich.

Eber, L., Osuch, R., & Redditt, C. A. (1996). School-based applications of the wraparound process: Early results on service provision and student outcomes. *Journal of Child and Family Studies, 5*(1), 83–99.

Education for All Handicapped Children Act of 1975, PL 94-142 (August 23, 1977). Title 20, U.S.C. 1400 et seq.: U.S. Statutes at Large, 89, 773–796.

Education of the Handicapped Act Amendments of 1986, PL 99-457 (October 8, 1986). Title 20, U.S.C. 1400 et seq.: U.S. Statutes at Large, 100, 1145–1177.

Eme, R. F., & Danielak, M. H. (1995). Comparison of fathers of daughters with and without maladaptive eating attitudes. *Journal of Emotional and Behavioral Disorders, 3*(1), 40–45.

Evans, M. E., Armstrong, M. I., Dollard, N., Kuppinger, A. D., Huz, S., & Wood, V. M. (1994). Development and evaluation of treatment foster care and family-centered intensive case management in New York. *Journal of Emotional and Behavioral Disorders, 2*(4), 228–239.

Evans, M. E., Armstrong, M. I., & Kuppinger, A. D. (1996). Family-centered intensive case management: A step toward understanding individualized care. *Journal of Child and Family Studies, 5*(1), 55–56.

Fenton, J., Batavia, A., & Roody, D. S. (1993). *Constituency-oriented research and dissemination.* A proposed policy statement for the National Institute on Disability and Rehabilitation Research, Washington, DC: National Institute on Disability and Rehabilitation Research.

Fine, G., & Borden, J. R. (1989). Parents Involved Network project: Support and advocacy training for parents. In R. M. Friedman, A. J. Duchnowski, & E. L. Henderson (Eds.), *Advocacy on behalf of children with serious emotional problems* (pp. 68–78). Springfield, IL: Charles C. Thomas.

Fitzpatrick, K. M. (1993). Exposure to violence and presence of depression among low-income, African-American youth. *Journal of Counseling and Clinical Psychology, 61*(3), 528–531.

Freud, S. (1952). Recommendations to physicians. In *Standard edition of the complete works of Sigmund Freud,* Vol. 12. London: Hogarth Press.

Friesen, B. J. (1989a). Parents as advocates for children and adolescents with serious emotional handicaps: Issues and directions. In R. M. Friedman, A. J. Duchnowski, & E. L. Henderson (Eds.), *Advocacy on behalf of children with serious emotional problems* (pp. 28–44). Springfield, IL: Charles C. Thomas.

Friesen, B. J. (1989b). *Survey of parents whose children have serious emotional disorders: Report of a national study.* Portland, OR: Research and Training Center on Family Support and Children's Mental Health, Portland State University.

Friesen, B. J. (1991). *Organizations for parents of children who have serious emotional disorders: Report of a national study.* Portland, OR: Research and Training Center on Family Support and Children's Mental Health, Portland State University.

Friesen, B. J., & Huff, B. (1996). Family perspectives on the system of care. In B. A. Stroul (Ed.), *Children's mental health: Creating systems of care in a changing society* (pp. 41–67). Baltimore: Brookes.

Friesen, B. J., Koren, P. E., & Koroloff, N. M. (1992). How parents view professional behaviors: A cross-professional analysis. *Journal of Child and Family Studies, 1*(2), 209–231.

Friesen, B. J., Koroloff, N. M., & Koren, P. E. (1993). *Family research and demonstration symposium report.* Portland, OR: Research and Training Center on Family Support and Children's Mental Health, Portland State University.

Friesen, B. J., & Wahlers, D. (1993). Respect and real help: Family support and children's mental health. *Journal of Emotional and Behavioral Problems, 2*(4), 12–15.

Fromm-Reichmann, F. (1948). Notes on the development of treatment of schizophrenics by psychoanalytic psychotherapy. *Psychiatry, 11,* 263–273.

Garfinkel, P. E., Garner, D. M., Rose, J., Darby, P. L., Brandes, J. S., O'Hanlon, J., & Walsh, N. (1983). A comparison of characteristics in the families of patients with anorexia nervosa and normal controls. *Psychological Medicine, 13,* 821–828.

Green, S. N., Loeber, R., & Lahey, B. B. (1992). Child psychopathology and deviant family hierarchies. *Journal of Child and Family Studies, 1*(4), 341–349.

Hanley, J. H., & Wright, H. H. (1995). Child mental health professionals: The missing link in child mental health reform. *Journal of Child and Family Studies, 4*(4), 383–388.

Harry, B. (1996). These families, those families: The impact of researcher identities on the research act. *Exceptional Children, 62*(4), 292–300.

Heflinger, C. A., & Bickman, L. (1996). Family empowerment: A conceptual model for promoting parent-professional partnership. In C. A. Heflinger & C. T. Nixon (Eds.), *Families and the mental health system for children and adolescents: Policy, services, and research* (pp. 96–116). Thousand Oaks, CA: Sage.

Hernandez, J. T., Lineberger, H. P., & Baimbridge, T. (1992). Development of an innovative child and youth mental health training and services delivery project. *Hospital and Community Psychiatry, 43*(4), 375–379.

Hillman, S. B., Sawilowsky, S. S., & Becker, M. J. (1993). Effects of maternal employment patterns on adolescents' substance use and other risk-taking behaviors. *Journal of Child and Family Studies, 2*(3), 203–219.

Hingtgen, J. N., & Bryson, C. Q. (1972). Recent developments in the study of early childhood psychoses: Infantile autism, childhood schizophrenia and related disorders. *Schizophrenia Bulletin, 5,* 8–53.

Holten, J. D. (1990). When do we stop mother-blaming? *Journal of Feminist Family Therapy, 2*(1), 53–60.

Homel, R., & Burns, A. (1989). Environmental quality and the wellbeing of children. *Social Indicators Research, 21,* 113–158.

Hunter, R. W. (1993). *Parents as policy-makers: A handbook for effective participation.* Portland, OR: Research & Training Center on Family Support and Children's Mental Health, Portland State University.

Ignelzi, S., & Dague, B. (1995). Parents as case managers. In B. J. Friesen & J. Poertner (Eds.), *From case management to service coordination: Building on family strengths* (pp. 327–336). Baltimore: Brookes.

Institute of Medicine. (1989). *Research on children with mental, behavioral, and developmental disorders: Mobilizing a national initiative.* Washington, DC: National Academy Press.

Jeppson, E. A., & Thomas, J. (1995). *Essential allies: Families as advisors.* Washington, DC: Institute for Family-Centered Care.

Jivanjee, P. R., Moore, K. R., Schultze, K. H., & Friesen, B. J. (1995). *Interprofessional education for family-centered services: A survey of interprofessional/interdisciplinary training programs.* Portland, OR: Research and Training Center on Family Support and Children's Mental Health, Portland State University.

Johnson, H. C. (Ed.). (1993). *Child mental health in the 1990s: Curricula for graduate and undergraduate professional education.* Washington, DC: U.S. Department of Health and Human Services, Public Health Service, Substance Abuse and Mental Health Services Administration, Center for Mental Health Services.

Johnson, H. C., Cournoyer D. E., & Fisher, G. A. (1994). Measuring worker cognitions about parents of children with mental and emotional disabilities. *Journal of Emotional and Behavioral Disorders, 2*(2), 99–108.

Karp, N., & Nolte, C. *Grant writer's guide.* Conference handbook for involving families in the grants process: Developing research skills, Washington, DC. June 21–22, 1990.

Kelker, K. A. (1987). *Making the system work: An advocacy workshop for parents.* Portland, OR: Research and Training Center on Family Support and Children's Mental Health, Portland State University.

Keller, M. B., Beardslee, W. R., Dorer, D. J., Lavori, P. W., Samuelson, H., & Klerman, G. R. (1986). Impact of severity and chronicity of parental affective illness on adaptive functioning and psychopathology in children. *Archives of General Psychiatry, 43,* 930–937.

Koren, P. E., DeChillo, N., & Friesen, B. J. (1992). Measuring empowerment in families whose children have emotional disabilities: A brief questionnaire. *Rehabilitation Psychology, 37*(4), 305–321.

Koren, P. E., Paulson, R. W., Kinney, R. F., Yatchmenoff, D. K., Gordon, L. J., & DeChillo, N. (in press). Service coordination in children's mental health: An empirical study from the caregiver's perspective. *Journal of Emotional and Behavioral Disorders.*

Koroloff, N. M., & Briggs, H. E. (1996). The lifecycle of family advocacy organizations. *Administration in Social Work, 20*(4), 23–42.

Koroloff, N. M., Elliott, D. J., Koren, P. E., & Friesen, B. J. (1995). Connecting low income families to mental health services: The role of the family associate. *Journal of Emotional and Behavioral Disorders, 2*(4), 240–246.

Koroloff, N. M., Elliott, D. J., Koren, P. E., & Friesen, B. J. (1996). Linking low-income families to children's mental health services: An outcome study. *Journal of Emotional and Behavioral Disorders, 4*(1), 2–11.

Koroloff, N. M., Friesen, B. J., Reilly, L., & Rinkin, J. (1996). The role of family members in systems of care. In B. A. Stroul (Ed.), *Children's mental health: Creating systems of care in a changing society* (pp. 409–426). Baltimore: Brookes.

Koroloff, N., Hunter, R., & Gordon, L. (1995). *Family involvement in policy making: A final report on the Families in Action project.* Portland, OR: Research and Training Center on Family Support and Children's Mental Health, Portland State University.

Koroloff, N. M., McManus, M. C., Pfohl, L., & Sturtevant, J. (1996). *How family members participate in policy-making: Legal advocacy models that work.* Presentation at Building on Family Strengths Conference, Research and Training Center on Family Support and Children's Mental Health, Portland, OR, April 11–13, 1996.

Koroloff, N. M., Stuntzner-Gibson, D., & Friesen, B. J. (1990). *Statewide parent organization demonstration project. Final report.* Portland, OR: Research and Training Center on Family Support and Children's Mental Health, Portland State University.

Kutash, K., & Rivera, V. R. (1996). *What works in children's mental health services: Uncovering answers to critical questions.* Baltimore: Brookes.

Leishman, V. (1995). Family members as family advocates. *Building on Family Strengths conference proceedings.* Portland, OR: Research & Training Center on Family Support and Children's Mental Health, Portland State University.

Litvak, S., Frieden, L., Dresden, C., & Doe, T. (1995). *Empowerment, independent living research and participatory action research.* Paper presented at Forging Collaborative Partnerships in the Study of Disabilities: A NIDRR Conference on Participatory Research, Washington, DC, April 18 & 19.

Lourie, I. S., Katz-Leavy, J., & Jacobs, J. H. (1985). *The Office of State and Community Liaison (OSCL) Child and Adolescent Service System Program fiscal year 1985.* Washington, DC: National Institute of Mental Health.

Malloy, M. (1995). *Mental illness and managed care: A primer for families and consumers.* Arlington, VA: National Alliance for the Mentally Ill.

Marsh, D. T. (1996). Families of children and adolescents with serious emotional disturbance: Innovations in theory, research, and practice. In C. A. Heflinger & C. T. Nixon (Eds.), *Families and the mental health system for children and adolescents: Policy, services, and research* (pp. 75–95). Thousand Oaks, CA: Sage.

Mayer, J. A. (1994). From rage to reform: What parents say about advocacy. *Exceptional Parent, 24*(5), 49–51.

McCloskey, L. A., Figueredo, A. J., & Koss, M. P. (1995). The effects of systemic family violence on children's mental health. *Child Development, 66*(5), 1239–1261.

McManus, M. C., & Friesen, B. J. (1986). *Families as Allies conference proceedings.* Portland, OR: Research and Training Center on Family Support and Children's Mental Health, Portland State University.

McManus, M. C., Reilly, L. M., Rinkin, J. L., & Wrigley, J. A. (1993). *An advocate's approach to abolishing custody relinquishment requirements for families whose children have disabilities: The Oregon experience.* Salem, OR: Oregon Family Support Network.

Messer, S. C., Angold, A., Costello, E. J., & Burns, B. J. (1996). *The child and adolescent burden assessment (CABA): Measuring the family impact of emotional and behavioral problems.* Paper submitted for publication. Durham, NC: Department of Psychiatry and Behavioral Sciences, Duke University Medical Center.

Miller, W. H., & Keirn, W. C. (1978). Personality measurement in parents of retarded and emotionally disturbed children: A replication. *Journal of Clinical Psychology, 34*(3), 686–690.

Modrcin, M. J., & Robison, J. (1991). Parents of children with emotional disorders: Issues for consideration and practice. *Community Mental Health Journal, 27*(4), 281–292.

Murphy, J. M., & Jellinek, M. (1988). Screening for psychosocial dysfunction in economically disadvantaged and minority group children: Further validation of the pediatric symptom checklist. *American Journal of Orthopsychiatry, 58*(3), 450–456.

Murray, J. D. (1992). *Analysis of outcome data of the Finger Lakes Family Support Program.* Mansfield, PA: Rural Services Institute, Mansfield University.

National Coalition for Family Leadership. (1996). *The ABCs of managed care: Standards and criteria for children with special health care needs.* Algodones, NM: Family Voices.

Nicholson, J., & Robinson, G. (1996). *A guide for evaluating consumer satisfaction with child and adolescent mental health services.* Boston, MA: Technical Assistance Center for the Evaluation of Children's Mental Health Systems.

Oliver, J. E. (1993). Intergenerational transmission of child abuse: Rates, research, and clinical implications. *Journal of American Psychiatry, 150,* 1315–1324.

Osher, T., Koyanagi, C., & Schulzinger, R. (1996). *Managing behavioral health care for children and youth: A family advocate's guide.* Washington, DC: Bazelon Center for Mental Health Law and Federation of Families for Children's Mental Health.

Patterson, G. R., DeBaryshe, B. D., & Ramsey, E. (1989). A developmental perspective on antisocial behavior. *American Psychologist, 44* (2), 329–335.

Prange, M. E., Greenbaum, P. E., Silver, S. E., Friedman, R. M., Kutash, K., & Duchnowski, A. J. (1992). Family functioning and psychopathology among adolescents with severe emotional disturbances. *Journal of Abnormal Child Psychology, 20*(1), 83–102.

Rohner, R. P., Kean, K. J., & Cournoyer, D. E. (1991). Effects of corporal punishment, perceived caretaker warmth, and cultural beliefs on the psychological adjustment of children in St. Kitts, West Indies. *Journal of Marriage and the Family, 53,* 681–693.

Rutter, M. (1990). Commentary: Some focus and process considerations regarding effects of parental depression on children. *Developmental Psychology, 26*(1), 60–67.

Rutter, M., Macdonald, H., Le Couteur, A., Harrington, R., Bolton, P., & Bailey, A. (1990). Genetic factors in child psychiatric disorders—II. Empirical findings. *Journal of Child Psychiatry and Psychology, 31*(1), 39–83.

Schacht, L., Pandiani, J., & Maynard, A. (1996). An assessment of parent involvement in local interagency teams. *Journal of Child and Family Studies, 5*(3), 349–354.

Schaefer, C. E., & Swanson, A. J. (1993). *Children in residential care.* Northvale, NJ: Jason Aronson.

Schopler, E. (1971). Parents of psychotic children as scapegoats. *Journal of Contemporary Psychotherapy, 4*(1), 17–22.

Schreibman, L. (1988). *Autism.* Newbury Park, CA: Sage.

Shamsie, J. (1985). Family breakdown and its effects on emotional disorders in children. *Canadian Journal of Psychiatry, 30,* 81–287.

Singer, G. H. S., Glang, A., Nixon, C., Cooley, E., Kerns, K. A., Williams, D., & Powers, L. E. (1994). A comparison of two psychosocial interventions for parents of children with acquired brain injury: An exploratory study. *Journal of Head Trauma Rehabilitation, 9*(4), 38–49.

Stark County Family Council. (1996). *A training manual for parent workers.* Canton, OH: Stark County Family Council/FACES.

Stroul, B. A., McCormack, M., & Zaro, S. M. (1996). Measuring outcomes in systems of care. In B.A. Stroul (Ed.), *Children's mental health services: Creating systems of care in a changing society* (pp. 313–336). Baltimore: Brookes.

Sturtevant, J. (1992). Respite for families with children with emotional disabilities. *Access to Respite Care & Help, 2*(3), 2–3.

Sutton, C. (1992). Training parents to manage difficult children: A comparison of methods. *Behavioral Psychotherapy, 20*(2), 115–139.

Tannen, N. (1996). A family-designed system of care: Families First in Essex County, New York. In B. A. Stroul (Ed.), *Children's mental health: Creating systems of care in a changing society* (pp. 375–388). Baltimore: Brookes.

Tarico, V. S., Low, B. P., Trupin, E., & Forsyth-Stephens, A. (1989). Children's mental health services: A parent perspective. *Community Mental Health Journal, 25*(4), 313–326.

Thomas, A., & Chess, S. (1984). Genesis and evolution of behavioral disorders: From infancy to early adult life. *American Journal of Psychiatry, 141,* 1–9.

Turnbull, A. P., & Friesen, B. J. (1995). *Forging collaborative partnerships with families in the study of disability.* Paper presented at Forging Collaborative Partnerships in the Study of Disabilities: A NIDRR Conference on Participatory Research, Washington, DC, April 18 & 19.

Wahl, O. F. (1989). Schizophrenogenic parenting in abnormal psychology textbooks. *Teaching of Psychology, 16,* 31–33.

Wherry, J. N., Shema, S. J., Baltz, T., & Kelleher, K. (1995). Factors associated with respite care use by families with a child with disabilities. *Journal of Child and Family Studies, 4*(4), 419–428.

Whittaker, J. K. (1976). Causes of childhood disorders: New findings. *Social Work, 21*(2), 91–96.

Williams, B. E. (1988). Parents and patients: Members of an interdisciplinary team on an adolescent inpatient unit. *Clinical Social Work Journal, 16,* 78–91.

Williams, S., Anderson, J., McGee, R., & Silva, P. (1990). Risk factors for behavioral and emotional disorder in preadolescent children. *Journal of the American Academy of Child and Adolescent Psychiatry, 29*(3), 413–419.

Williams-Murphy, T., DeChillo, N., Koren, P. E., & Hunter, R. (1994). *Family/professional collaboration: The perspectives of those who have tried.* Portland, OR: Research and Training Center on Family Support and Children's Mental Health, Portland State University.

Including a Family Focus in Research on Community-Based Services for Children with Serious Emotional Disturbance: Experiences from the Fort Bragg Evaluation Project

10

Craig Anne Heflinger,
Denine A. Northrup,
Susan E. Sonnichsen,
and Ana Maria Brannan

W hen research on community-based services for children with serious emotional disturbance (SED) is planned or conducted, the focus must be expanded from the child identified with SED to include the family of that child. Children and adolescents exist within an ecological context (Bronfenbrenner, 1979; Munger, 1991), with the family as the primary structure mediating between them and the larger social environment. Families are the primary caregivers and resources for children (Backer & Richardson, 1989) and the context within which any child-focused intervention or growth takes place. Families are also the primary health/illness defining unit (Matocha, 1995) and directly influence a child's entry into the service system. Children rarely seek health or mental health services on their own; adults, usually family members, refer children for services (Kazdin, 1989) and have a large influence on whether and how long they remain in treatment. In addition, family members, usually parents but sometimes siblings as well, may directly participate in treatment along with the identified child. In community-based interventions, in particular, family members are expected to play an active role in enabling a child with SED to reside at home and function in the community (Hunter & Friesen, 1996). Therefore a family focus also needs to be incorporated into the study of the effectiveness of mental health services for children (Friesen & Koroloff, 1990).

The inclusion of a family focus in research on community-based services involves recognition of the influence of family-related variables on the child, treatment, or treatment outcome, and the effects of the services on the family. Numerous family characteristics may mediate or moderate treatment effects, thus it is crucial to identify and measure these variables. In addition, the impact—both intended and unintended—of the services on aspects of family life should be measured. Although therapists and researchers typically assume that family outcomes improve as a result of participation in services, research now available suggests that this assumption should be questioned (Bernal, Deegan, & Konjevich, 1983; Bernheim, 1989; Dunst, 1986b) and that family measures must be included in evaluations of outcomes. In this chapter we review strategies for measuring family characteristics, promote the use of a theoretical framework to guide research and evaluation, and discuss our experiences in the use of family measures in the evaluation of a community-based mental health demonstration.

Theoretical Framework for Selecting Family Measures

A theoretical framework provides needed structure for selecting specific research variables and measures. By identifying and clarifying the constructs that are considered important as primary influential factors, the researcher can be sure that all of the critical variables have been included in a data collection effort. In research that acknowledges the importance of families, it is important to apply a competence paradigm (Marsh, 1996) that uses a health-based developmental model instead of a disease-based medical model. Such a paradigm emphasizes strengths and resources instead of liabilities, assesses competencies and coping strategies that could lead to positive growth, and recognizes the ecological system in which the child and family are involved and the transactional nature of that ecological system (Hobbs et al., 1984).

Double ABCX Model

A theoretical model that highlights the role that family member perceptions and experiences may play in the child's treatment and outcome is the double ABCX model (see Figure 10.1; McCubbin & Patterson, 1983a). This model draws heavily from physiological (Selye, 1974) and psychological (Mikhail, 1981) concepts of stress and research concerned with family stress (e.g., Figley, 1989), coping and adaptation (e.g., Matheny, Aycock, Pugh, Curlette, & Cannella, 1986), and the family's experience with chronic disease or disability (Wikler, 1986). This model recognizes both the complexity of family life with its multiple influences and the diversity of families and family members that lead them to respond uniquely to situations. This model also recognizes that the child is a member of a family system that has internal and external resources and patterns of appraising and

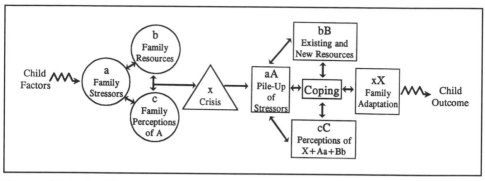

Figure 10.1. Double ABCX model. Adapted from McCubbin, H., & Patterson, J. (1983a). The family stress process: The Double ABCX Model of adustment and adaptation. *Marriage and Family Review, 6,* 14.

coping with stressful events. A stressor (a) is defined as a life event or transition affecting the family unit that has the potential of impacting family well-being. Stressors do not lead directly to the outcome (x: crisis or family adaptation), but are mediated by (b) the level of resources available within the family and (c) the perceptions of the stressors by each and all of the family members. These change and develop over time, thus the double ABCX model is not static but developmental, potentially resulting in a pile-up of stressors (aA), development of family resources (bB), evolution of family perceptions (cC), all of which interact to produce active coping responses, that in turn influence family adaptation (xX), positive or negative. Family adaptation is believed to affect the child's response to treatment as well as the use of community-based services. Thus, family experiences and perceptions are important factors that mediate not only family adaptation but also treatment outcomes.

Stressors (a and aA)

Family stressors consist of those present and past events that potentially impact family life. It is well documented that families experience numerous stressors when living with a child with SED (e.g., McElroy, 1987a,b). Several specific stressors have been identified as common among families with children with SED, including the child's symptoms, disruption of family and social relationships, and strain on family finances. The service system can present additional stressors when families encounter professionals and programs that are insensitive and unresponsive to the family's needs (e.g., Collins & Collins, 1990; Friesen & Koroloff, 1990). The impact of these stressors can be magnified by concurrent life stressors unrelated to the child, as well as by prior events that may have depleted the family's resources.

Resources (b and bB)

There is an extensive literature on resources that can facilitate the coping and adaptation process. Marsh (1996) described eight family resources that were relevant to coping with a child with SED: (a) personal qualities of individual family members, such as overall physical and mental health or self esteem; (b) parental relations, such as marital satisfaction and shared child-rearing responsibilities; (c) family process issues, such as family roles and boundaries; (d) practical resources, including parental level of education and yearly income; (e) family competencies in cognitive, affective, behavioral, and social areas; (f) available coping strategies; (g) social support for families from their informal and formal support networks; and (h) service system resources. Also, the availability of community-based services would be considered a family resource. However, the actual use of those services is a coping response (see below).

Perceptions (c and cC)

In any transactional framework, a life event becomes stressful only after it has been appraised as threatening (Singer & Davidson, 1991). Family members may view a stressor as easy or difficult to manage, as fate, as an act of aggression against the family, or as a challenge or an overwhelming load (Wikler, 1986). The ability to find a sense of meaning and coherence in their lives and the family's attitudes about SED also impact family appraisal (Marsh, 1996). Family values also may be very influential in mediating the effects of the stressful life events involved in living with a child with SED.

Coping

How the family responds to stressors (a and aA) is influenced by the resources present (b and bB) and the family's perceptions (c and cC). The process of coping involves both cognitive responses (e.g., reframing the problem as a challenge that can lead to growth) and behavioral responses (e.g., parent changing a job to allow more time to be spent with the child). These coping responses can in turn influence both resources (e.g., reduction in family income) and perceptions (e.g., shift from appraising the stressor as negative toward seeing the positive aspects of the experience). It has been noted that families tend not to form their coping responses in terms of discrete stressors, but in terms of the constellation of stressors they face (McCubbin & Patterson, 1983a,b). As stated, many aspects of services utilization may be viewed as the family's active coping response interacting with the stressors being faced, the resources available, and the family's perception of the stressors. Whether or not a family accesses services, and the amount or type of service used by the child or family, would be considered a coping response, as would the level of family involvement in all aspects of the treatment process.

Family Crisis (x) and Adaptation (xX)

The initial response (x) is called a "crisis" in this model to depict an initial negative reaction to the stressors. In this dynamic model, this is not a static response, however, and the process continues toward coping and adaptation (xX). Family adaptation results from the coping response and can be characterized as existing on a continuum between bon- and maladaptation. When the coping response leads to bonadaptation, the family adjusts in a way that improves the situation. When the coping response leads to maladaptation, the situation is made worse. Bonadaptation averts further crisis while maladaptation precipitates it. Many family factors can signify adaptation, including family well-being and quality of life (Able-Boone & Stevens, 1994), the level of psychological distress among family members, the caliber of family functioning, and the degree of strain resulting from caregiving responsibilities (Brannan & Heflinger, 1996; Marsh, 1996). If the family's coping response can reduce or avoid caregiver strain, for example, the crisis of having the child placed out of home may be averted.

An illustrative case example may help the reader to better understand the Double ABCX model:

> John and Lisa, in their early 30s, have three children, 10-year-old Ellen, 5-year-old Jeremy, and 3-year-old Beth. Ever since Jeremy was born, Lisa has had increasing difficulty managing his behavior. John does not report as much difficulty, but he is around Jeremy and the other children less, as he travels regularly (Stressors-a). Last week, Jeremy's kindergarten teacher called home to request a parent-teacher conference for Jeremy. At the meeting, the teacher described Jeremy's behavior problems in the classroom and recommended getting help for Jeremy, suggesting that other children with hyperactivity behave much better when they use medication. This news came at a particularly difficult time for the family. John's job had become more stressful, and he was expected to work longer hours to meet the new demands. This put added pressure on Lisa, who was trying to care for her ailing father. She had to quit her part-time job when her father became confined to the home.
>
> (Perceptions-c): John and Lisa were feeling overwhelmed, and despite some understanding of Jeremy's behavior problems they were not prepared to hear that his teacher thought he had a disorder that needed medical treatment. They were also concerned about the school's becoming aware of and involved in Jeremy's problems, as they tended to take care of "family issues" themselves.
>
> (Resources-b): They began to wonder how they could afford to take Jeremy to the doctor to figure out what he needed. They didn't even know where to take him. Should they go to their pediatrician? a psychologist? The family insurance plan did not include coverage for behavioral disorders, and since Lisa had quit her job, there was little money left after paying the monthly bills.
>
> Most of this pressure fell on Lisa, not only because she was more available during the day, but also because she was the "caregiver" for her immediate and extended family. She wanted to learn more about the "problem" Jeremy's

teacher described, but she didn't know where to turn (Crisis-x). (Coping:) She made an appointment with their pediatrician. The pediatrician recommended that they start giving Jeremy daily medication to control his behavior and attention problems, but she also recommended that Lisa and John take Jeremy to see a child psychologist for further evaluation and treatment. (Crisis-x:) Lisa started to feel depressed and found herself taking her frustrations out on Jeremy.

(Pile-up-aA:) Meeting with the psychologist became a weekly appointment, but the clinic office was 40 minutes away. John was never able to go, and although she arranged for Ellen to stay with a friend, Lisa had to take Beth with them each time because she did not have child care. Lisa found herself having to meet with Jeremy's teacher every few weeks to work on a behavior modification program. (Resources-bB:) These new demands on her time took her away from her daughters and father as well. She joined a support group for parents of children with Attention-Deficit/Hyperactivity Disorder. While this group took another two hours out of her week, she began to discover that she was not alone in her experiences. Child care was also provided at the meetings, which served as needed respite for Lisa. (Perceptions-cC:) Because Lisa was the primary caretaker, and because John had not experienced problems with Jeremy's behavior, John began to treat the problems as Lisa's fault, which added strain to their relationship. Lisa began to value the network she had developed at the support group and her beliefs about keeping family issues in the family were changing. (Adaptation-xX:) Lisa, although very worried about Jeremy's progress, began to feel guilty about her neglected family responsibilities. She was regularly asking for support and help from her friends and neighbors but was never able to reciprocate. She began to experience distress and fatigue regularly. (Coping:) Lisa sought out a family therapist at the suggestion of a support group member.

The ABCX model has been used to frame research on families with children with developmental disabilities (Orr, Cameron, & Day, 1991; Smith, Tobin, & Fullmer, 1995; Winton, 1990), autism (Bristol, 1987), learning disabilities (Konstantareas, 1991), and chronic illness (Cherry, 1989), as well as on families with an adult member with cancer (Mullen, Smith, & Hill, 1993) and farm families in financial crisis (Van Hook, 1987). In the study of children with SED, many measures have been used to explore the individual domains highlighted in the ABCX model for the stressor (a and aA) items at the individual child client level (symptom and behavioral checklists, diagnostic inventories, functional assessments), but they are less focused at the family level. Family resource instruments (b and bB) are becoming more prominent (e.g., family resource inventories, parental or family functioning questionnaires, indices of social support), as are those of family adaptation (x and xX; e.g., parental distress, caregiver burden or strain). However, at the level of family perceptions of the stressors (c and cC) and the role they play in child and family outcomes, few instruments available are designed for the target population of families of children with SED. Those that are available are very limited in their foci, generally assessing negative attributions. What is lacking is a broader understanding of family experiences that considers family perceptions, values, and goals. These would include the opportunity for families to talk about the positive attributions they make about their children that also influence their experiences and subsequent adaptation (Turnbull, Summers, & Brotherson, 1986). Our experience in applying this model to community-based mental health services research is described below.

Experiences in the Fort Bragg Evaluation Project

As part of the start-up of the Fort Bragg Evaluation Project (FBEP) in 1989, the decision to include measures on family characteristics was made early in the process. The FBEP was designed to assess the effectiveness of a managed continuum-of-care approach to the delivery of mental health services to children and adolescents through the Fort Bragg Child and Adolescent Mental Health Demonstration Project (Demonstration; Bickman et al., 1995).[1] Located in the Fort Bragg, North Carolina, catchment area, the Demonstration offered a broad array of community-based mental health services. The FBEP used a quasi-experimental design to compare the impact of the Demonstration on the cost and utilization of services, quality of care, and client outcomes. Two comparison sites (Fort Stewart, Georgia, and Fort Campbell, Kentucky) were chosen in which services were delivered in a more traditional fee-for-service system.

As a longitudinal study, data were collected at multiple time points. The first wave of data was collected within 30 days of the child's entry into treatment with the child's current therapist. The follow-up data collection points came at 6-month intervals. All descriptive statistics, subscale reliabilities, and intercorrelation matrix values presented in this chapter were derived from Wave 1 data. The analyses of change over time were limited to data collected at Waves 1 through 3 (12 months after intake). For the purposes of this description of family measures, data from all sites have been combined.

Participants

The current sample was drawn from families who participated in the FBEP and has been described in detail elsewhere (see Bickman et al., 1995). In order to be eligible for the FBEP, families had to have a child in formal mental health treatment at one of the sites who was a Civilian Health and Medical Program for the Uniformed Services (CHAMPUS) beneficiary. Informants for these data were the primary caregiver, as designated by the family, of the identified child client. Caregivers who served as informants were primarily women (83%), the biological mothers of the children in treatment. The caregivers were between

the ages of 20 and 62, with the majority being white (70%) and having completed high school (94%). The majority of children in treatment were boys (63%)
between the ages of 5 and 17 with an average age of 11 years. Approximately
half of the families had incomes between $20,000 and $40,000; 89% of the
households included two adults.

Family Measures for the Fort Bragg Evaluation Project

The double ABCX model was used as a framework for selecting family measures
for the FBEP. Given the limitations of available instruments, no measures of
family perceptions (cC) were found to be appropriate and a full test of the model
was not possible, however this model provided the theoretical framework needed
to select measures for data collection.

Stressors

Child symptoms and poor social functioning are stressors for many families. In
the FBEP, the severity of the child's emotional and behavioral problems were
measured with a battery of checklists, structured interviews, and interviewer
ratings (see Bickman, Heflinger, Pion, & Behar, 1992, for a discussion of all
FBEP data-collection measures). In addition, a measure of family life events
was included. The Family Inventory of Life Events and Changes (FILE)
(McCubbin & Patterson, 1983b, 1987) is a 71-item self-report instrument designed
to record normative and nonnormative life events and changes experienced by
a family unit (e.g., a family member lost or quit a job; a family member was
married). Although originally designed to record events that occurred in the
past year, in this study, the FILE was limited to events in the past 6 months
to correspond with the data-collection periods. Though weights are available to
differentially weight various stressors, the authors of the FILE suggest that
an unweighted sum of stressors is as useful as any weighting procedure. The
authors of the measure have shown adequate internal consistency (i.e., Cronbach's alphas ranging from .79 to .82). Although subscales exist for the FILE,
they have not been demonstrated to be very reliable. Construct validity has
been demonstrated when comparing the FILE to other family measures
(McCubbin & Patterson, 1987).

Resources

Dimensions of family resources included in the FBEP were social support, concrete resources, and family functioning. These were considered factors that could
potentially influence the family's coping response to their child's special needs.

Social Support

For the purposes of the FBEP, subscales were selected from two measures of family support and coping, the Family Index of Regenerativity-General version (FIRA-G) and Military version (FIRA-M). In order to minimize informant burden, only two subscales of the FIRA-G were used (Relative and Friend Support Index and Social Support Index), in addition to one subscale from the FIRA-M (Family Index of Coherence).

The Relative and Friend Support Index (McCubbin, Larsen, & Olson, 1982) is an 8-item subscale of the FIRA-G, designed to assess the degree to which the informant relies on family members as a coping strategy in times of stress (e.g., We cope with family problems by . . . sharing problems with neighbors; . . . seeking advice from relatives). This subscale has good internal reliability (Cronbach's alpha = .82) for this subscale. This subscale was also found to correlate strongly (r = .99) with a measure of family coping strategies. The Social Support Index (McCubbin, Patterson, & Glynn, 1982) is a 17-item subscale of the FIRA-G that was designed to assess the extent to which the informant perceives the community as a source of potential support and feels a part of the community. Sample items include the following: People can depend on each other in this community; living in this community gives me a secure feeling. The FIRA-G demonstrated good internal reliability (Cronbach's alpha = .82) and a moderate relationship (r = .40) was found between this subscale and the family well-being subscale of the FIRA-G. The Family Index of Coherence (FIC; McCubbin & Patterson, 1982) is a 17-item scale that was designed specifically for military families to assess the informant's ability to predict future work demands, sense of commitment to military life, control of the family's future in the military community, and the likelihood that the military will support the family in times of need. Sample items include the following: Our family can pretty well plan in advance for military assignments; the Military treats its members and their families justly and fairly. The FIC demonstrated good internal consistency (Cronbach's alpha = .85).

Concrete Resources

The Family Resource Scale (FRS; Dunst & Leet, 1987) was selected for the FBEP to assess the extent to which concrete material resources available to the family were perceived as adequate by the primary caregiver (e.g., heat for your house or apartment; medical care for your family). This 30-item scale assesses the adequacy of eight dimensions of family resources, reflecting basic needs (health, shelter, nutrition), financial resources (income, communication, and employment), childcare, and higher order needs (growth and support, intrafamilial support). The FRS authors found the total scale to demonstrate good internal consistency (Cronbach's alpha = .92; Dunst & Leet, 1987). Availability of resources as measured by the FRS has been found to be associated with both personal well-being (Dunst, 1986a) and parental commitment to follow through with child treatment recommended by professionals (Dunst, 1986b).

Family Functioning

Family functioning was assessed using the Family Assessment Device (FAD; Epstein, Baldwin, & Bishop, 1983). The FAD is a 60-item, self-report inventory based on the McMaster model of family functioning. Within that model and reflected in the FAD are seven mutually exclusive dimensions around which family functioning is assessed by subscale scores: Problem Solving, Communication, Roles, Affective Involvement, Affective Responsiveness, Behavior Control, and General Functioning. Respondents rate the extent to which each statement describes their family (e.g., We resolve most everyday problems around the house; when someone is upset the others know why). Higher scores on the FAD subscales indicate a greater number of problems within the dimension. The original authors also developed clinical cutoffs for each of the scales. The FAD has been used to measure family functioning in mental health services research (e.g., Cohen, Coyne, & Duvall, 1993; King, Segal, Naylor, and Evans, 1993).

A number of researchers have examined the psychometric properties of the FAD (e.g., Kabacoff, Miller, Bishop, Epstein, & Keitner, 1990; Miller, Epstein, Bishop, & Keitner, 1985; Perosa & Perosa, 1990). Reliability estimates of internal consistency have ranged from a Cronbach's alpha of .72 to .92 for the different subscales, with the general functioning subscale being the most reliable. Test-retest reliability was examined with a 1-week delay between reports, and subscale correlations ranged from $r = .66-.76$. In addition, researchers have found that the FAD was able to adequately differentiate between clinical and nonclinical families, correctly identifying 64% and 67% of families, respectively. The FAD was also compared with family therapists' ratings on each of the dimensions of family functioning. Families rated by clinicians as unhealthy on a dimension had significantly higher scores on that dimension of the FAD. Finally, evidence of good predictive validity has been demonstrated in predicting morale and health (Bishop, Epstein, Baldwin, Miller, & Keitner, 1988), service utilization (Browne, Arpin, Corey, Fitch, & Gafni, 1990), alcohol use (McKay, Murphy, Rivinus, & Maisto, 1991), social competence (Portes, Howell, Brown, Eichenberger, & Mas, 1992), and eating disorders (Waller, Slade, & Calam, 1990).

Family Adaptation

A family's adaptation to stressors can be manifested in a number of ways. In the FBEP, two variables of family adaptation were included: parental distress and caregiver strain. Low levels of distress and strain in the face of stressful life events and child behavior problems are considered examples of effective family adaptation.

Parental Distress

Parental distress was measured in the FBEP using the Brief Symptom Inventory (BSI; Derogatis & Melisaratos, 1983), an abbreviated form of the Symptom Checklist (SCL-90-R). The BSI is a 53-item self-report checklist designed to measure psychological symptoms experienced over the previous 7 days. Sample items include feeling lonely, feeling fearful, trouble falling asleep, and difficulty making decisions. These items can be summarized into the following nine symptom profiles: somatization, obsessive-compulsive, interpersonal sensitivity, depression, anxiety, hostility, phobic anxiety, paranoid ideation, and psychoticism. In addition, the BSI offers three global indices of psychological distress, including the Global Severity Index, the Positive Symptom Distress Index, and the Positive Symptom Total. The BSI has been normed based on scores from a community sample of nonpatients (Derogatis & Melisaratos, 1983), with clinical cutoff scores derived from outpatient and inpatient samples. Evidence of the BSI's validity and reliability has been provided in several publications (e.g., Boulet & Boss, 1991; Derogatis & Melisaratos, 1983). Due to its ease of administration and its purported psychometric properties, the BSI has been used widely to assess psychopathology and psychological distress in patient and nonpatient samples alike. It has been used frequently to describe patient samples (e.g., Witztum, Brown, & De-Nour, 1987), to detect changes in symptoms as a result of psychological intervention (e.g., Piersma, Reaume, & Boes, 1994), and to assess the psychological impact of stressors (e.g., Worby, Altrocchi, Veach, & Crosby, 1991). The BSI also has been used widely with nonpatient caregivers of children and adults with special needs, ranging from developmental delay to dementia related to aging (e.g., Knight, 1992; Sanger, MacLean, & Van Slyke, 1992). Because the BSI was used in the FBEP as a measure of distress, reporting scores for the symptom profiles is not appropriate for this paper. Only the Global Severity Index (GSI) scores have been reported here.

Caregiver Strain

The strain experienced by caregivers relative to their child with SED was measured through the Burden of Care Questionnaire (BCQ), a 21-item self-report instrument developed specifically for the FBEP (Brannan, Heflinger, & Bickman, 1994). Relying on the work of previous researchers (e.g., Montgomery, Gonyea, & Hooyman, 1985; Thompson & Doll, 1982) six areas of caregiver strain were included: disruption of family life and relationships, demands on time, negative mental and physical health effects for any member, financial strain, disruption of social/community life for any member, and worry, emotional strain, and embarrassment. Sample items include the following: How much of a problem was your missing work or neglecting other duties because of your child's illness? How tired or strained did you feel as a result of your child's illness?

Confirmatory factor analyses conducted on a subset of the FBEP sample (N = 392) have supported the existence of three related dimensions of the BCQ (Brannan, Heflinger, & Bickman, 1994). Objective strain refers to the informant's perception that observable, negative events (e.g, difficulty with the community, disrupted family relationships) resulting from the child's SED have been a problem. Subjective externalized strain refers to negative feelings directed at the child, such as anger, resentment, and embarrassment. The dimension of subjective internalized strain captures negative feeling directed inwardly, such as worry and fatigue.

Analyses and Results

For the purpose of describing the family context for this sample of children and families in need of mental health services and comparing to existing norms and samples, descriptive statistics on the various family measures used in the FBEP are presented. As mentioned above, many of these family measures were developed based on different samples (e.g., FRS was based on families with a child with a developmental disability; FIRA was based on a "normal" family) and for alternative purposes. For this reason, it is necessary to demonstrate how the measures perform on a sample of families of children with SED who are receiving mental health services. The internal consistency of the scale is presented for each of the measures. Descriptive statistics for each scale are compared with other samples that have been assessed using the same measures. Intercorrelations between the different scales are discussed with regard to expected relationships based on the theoretical model. Finally, the reported change in each measure from intake into services to a 12-month follow-up is described.

Internal Consistency

Cronbach's alpha was calculated for this sample for each of the author-defined subscales for each measure, and the results are reported in Table 10.1.[2] With regard to the estimates of internal consistency based on this sample of families with SED children, all of the family measures yielded adequate reliability estimates ranging from .71 to .97 that were comparable to those demonstrated by each of the respective authors. The Burden of Care Questionnaire was the only measure developed for the FBEP and not previously published, yet it also yielded acceptable levels of internal consistency.

Descriptive Statistics

To assess the family context within which a child functions, this sample of families was compared to other investigations using the same measures. Through

Table 10.1

Cronbach's Alpha Coefficients
for Family Measures at Baseline

Instrument	Alpha
BSI (GSI T-score)	0.97
FAD (Problem Solving)	0.78
FAD (Communication)	0.78
FAD (Roles)	0.71
FAD (Affective Responsiveness)	0.79
FAD (Affective Involvement)	0.74
FAD (Behavior Control)	0.73
FAD (General Functioning)	0.88
FILE	0.77
FIRA (Relative and Friend Support)	0.81
FIRA (Family Index of Coherence)	0.81
FIRA (Social Support)	0.81
FRS	0.94
BCQ (Objective Strain)	0.91
BCQ (Subjective-Externalized)	0.73
BCQ (Subjective-Internalized)	0.84

comparison with other samples, it is feasible to examine how similar families with a child receiving mental health services are to other families in terms of stressors, resources, and adaptive factors. Descriptive statistics for the family measures used for this sample, including means, standard deviations, and ranges, are provided in Table 10.2.

Life Stressors

The FILE was utilized to describe the stressors experienced by a family just prior to a child's being referred for mental health services. As shown in Table 10.3, the mean count of stressors for the sample was 11.6, with a range from 0 to 37. This number of stressors is higher than the national norms reported by the instrument authors, in which the mean number of stressors endorsed was 8.8 with a standard deviation of 5.9 (McCubbin & Patterson, 1987). Other samples of families without a child with a medical or mental health concern have also reported fewer stressors than reported by the families in the FBEP (e.g., Anderson & Leslie, 1991). This indicates that these families are experiencing more stress than the average family. Additionally, the FILE has been used extensively with

Table 10.2

Descriptive Statistics for Family Measures at Baseline

Measure	N	Mean	Standard Deviation	Min	Max
FILE	965	11.59	6.18	0	37
FIRA (Relative and Friend)	952	24.28	5.84	8	40
FIRA (Family Index of Coherence)	703	52.77	9.87	23	79
FIRA (Social Support)	949	58.53	8.27	25	85
FRS	917	122.30	18.44	51	150
FAD (Problem Solving)	959	2.19	0.45	1	4
FAD (Communication)	961	2.27	0.43	1	4
FAD (Roles)	961	2.34	0.36	1	4
FAD (Affective Responsiveness)	958	2.11	0.53	1	4
FAD (Affective Involvement)	959	2.21	0.45	1	4
FAD (Behavior Control)	959	1.80	0.38	1	3
FAD (General Functioning)	960	2.14	0.49	1	4
BSI (GSI T-score)	857	56.07	10.94	33	80
BCQ (Objective Strain)	955	2.05	0.91	1	5
BCQ (Subjective-Externalized)	932	2.29	0.94	1	5
BCQ (Subjective-Internalized)	945	3.40	1.03	1	5

families of children with various medical conditions (e.g., Walker, Garber, & Greene, 1993) and only occasionally with families of children with mental health concerns (e.g., Reis & Heppner, 1993). However, many of these studies neglect to report the mean number of life events endorsed, making comparison difficult.

Social Support

McCubbin and colleagues generated norms for the subscales of the FIRA-G and FIRA-M, using three samples: two nonmilitary, $n = 1000$ and $n = 300$ (as cited in McCubbin, 1987), and one military, $n = 1036$ (McCubbin, Patterson, & Lavee, 1983). Norms for the Social Support and Family Index of Coherence subscales were generated from the military sample using a Department of the Army sample of families stationed in Western Europe (McCubbin et al., 1983). McCubbin and colleagues claimed that their sample was representative of U.S. army

Table 10.3

Intercorrelations Among FBEP Family Characteristics

	BSI (GSI T-score)	FAD (General Functioning)	FILE	FIRA (Relative and Friend Support)	FIRA (Family Index of Military Coherence)	FIRA (Social Support Index Strain)	FRS	BCQ (Objective Strain)	BCQ (Subjective Internalized)	BCQ (Subjective Externalized)
BSI (GSI T-score)	1.00									
FAD (General Functioning)	-.338**	1.00								
FILE	.405**	-.365**	1.00							
FIRA (Relative and Friend Support)	-.043	.128**	.078*	1.00						
FIRA (Family Index of Military Coherence)	-.230**	.264**	-.233**	.005	1.00					
FIRA (Social Support Index)	-.344**	.472**	-.262**	.257**	.409**	1.00				
FRS	-.393**	.248**	-.390**	.027	.435**	.392**	1.00			
BCQ (Objective Strain)	.341**	-.202**	.494**	-.003	-.189**	-.184**	-.230**	1.00		
BCQ (Subjective Internalizing)	.228**	-.218**	.276**	-.022	-.110**	-.159**	-.114**	.540**	1.00	
BCQ (Subjective Externalizing)	.372**	-.270**	.413**	.009	-.196**	-.181**	-.258**	.656**	.565**	1.00

Note. The FAD was reverse-scored such that higher scores indicate better family functioning.

*p < .05. **p < .01.

families. Normative data for the Relative and Friend Support subscale is available based only on the nonmilitary sample ($n = 1000$; McCubbin et al., 1982).

The means and standard deviations for the FBEP sample matched McCubbin and colleagues' norms only on the Relative and Friend Support Subscale, which was normed on a nonmilitary sample. While it can be inferred that the FBEP sample is comparable to the nonmilitary norms for Relative and Friend Support, there is no way to determine how similar to nonmilitary populations the FBEP sample is on the social support subscale. The maximum possible score on the Social Support subscale is 85. Means from the original authors' normative sample were approximately 46, or about 1.5 standard deviations lower than the means for the complete FBEP sample (58.6).

Means from the FBEP sample were significantly higher than the norms from the authors' military sample for the Family Index of Coherence and Social Support subscales (McCubbin et al., 1983). The maximum possible score on the Family Index of Coherence subscale is 85. The mean for 1,036 military families was approximately 30, more than 2 standard deviations lower than the mean for the FBEP sample (52.8). Of the 974 respondents, 260 (27%) reported not having a family member employed by the military, and were instructed to skip this subscale. Since the Family Index of Coherence was designed specifically for military populations, it is appropriate to compare the FBEP sample means to those from the McCubbin, Patterson, and Lavee (1983) sample. Families in the FBEP sample report higher ratings of coherence within the military community than families stationed at a base in Western Europe in 1982.

Concrete Resources

Dunst and Leet (1987) reported norms for the FRS when completed by a sample of 45 mothers of children with handicaps or developmental delays. The FBEP sample was remarkably similar in terms of their reports of concrete resources available. Of a maximum possible score of 150, the average score from the Dunst and Leet (1987) sample was 116.54, $SD = 17.76$, while the mean of the FBEP sample for Wave 1 was 122.30, $SD = 18.44$ (see Table 10.3). This similarity suggests that the parents in the two samples, despite the differences in the nature of their children's special needs, perceived comparable amounts of resources, generally describing their resources as "somewhat adequate" to "usually adequate." However, so many of the FBEP respondents reported their resources to be "almost always adequate" at Wave 1 that the scale resulted in a distribution of scores that were negatively skewed, rather than normally distributed. This evidence could be suggestive of a ceiling effect in the scale, insufficient to fully illustrate a broad range of families.

Family Functioning

In this study, the FAD was one of many instruments employed to describe the family context and resources available to children who were referred for mental health services. The services the children received covered the gamut of mental health services for children from outpatient treatment to intermediate services to inpatient treatment. While many of the subscale means from the FBEP were near the clinical cutoffs, of particular importance is the indication of greater problems in general family functioning, higher than the clinical cutoff. This suggests that families with a child with special mental health needs may need additional supports and services to enhance family functioning as well as addressing the individual needs of the child. In addition, when subscale means for this sample were compared with other samples, some trends emerged. The FBEP sample of families demonstrated more problems than families in the community and families who had had a family member referred for medical services, but fewer problems than families who had had a family member admitted to an inpatient psychiatric hospital (Kabacoff et al., 1990; King et al., 1993). Cohen et al. (1993) assessed a group of families with adopted and biological children who were referred to mental health services and treated in community mental health agencies. In comparison with the Cohen et al. sample, the FBEP sample reported more problems in functioning across all the domains of family functioning. This result is likely because the FBEP sample consisted of children with a variety of mental health concerns with varying levels of severity, whereas the Cohen et al. sample contained children requiring only outpatient services.

Parental Distress

Although developed to assess psychopathology in adult psychiatric patients, the BSI has been widely used as a measure of psychological distress among nonpatient samples. Based on the scores of 719 respondents from community samples, the BSI authors developed nonpatient norms (Derogatis & Melisaratos, 1983). The FBEP sample's GSI score (mean T-score = 56) fell between the normative sample scores reported for the outpatient sample (mean T-score = 63) and the nonpatient sample T-score of 50.

In addition to other nonpatient samples, the BSI has been used with samples of caregivers. GSI scores for the FBEP sample were very similar to the scores reported for other nonpatient caregiver samples. For example, parents of children dependent on medical technology reported GSI T-scores of between 55 and 64 (Leonard, Brust, & Patterson, 1991). In this study, lower scores were reported by parents who were receiving enhanced economic and support services, and higher scores were reported by parents receiving only traditional insurance reimbursement. In a sample of mothers of children referred to a behavioral pediatric clinic, the mean GSI T-score was 55 (Sanger et al., 1992). Because the BSI is the abbreviated form of the SCL-90-R, comparison with those scores is also appropriate. Parents of children with insulin-dependent diabetes mellitus reported SCL-90-R global scores of 51 (Kovacs et al., 1990). Similarly, parents of children in treatment for fire-setting reported SCL-90-R global scores of 54 (Kazdin & Kolko, 1986). In sum, the caregivers in the FBEP sample reported levels of psychological distress similar to those reported by other samples of parents caring for children with chronic illnesses, other medical problems, and emotional and behavioral problems. Mean scores from these samples tend to be higher than scores from community nonpatient samples, but lower than scores from patient samples.

Caregiver Strain

The BCQ was developed for the FBEP and has not been used in any other studies. For that reason, BCQ scores from the FBEP sample cannot be compared to scores from any other sample. In this sample, the mean of 2.05 for the objective strain subscale reflects those items (e.g., family member doing without things, child having trouble with the community, financial strain) as "a little of a problem." The subscales reporting subjective strain received higher ratings. In the area of subjective-internalized strain, caregivers tended to respond that they had "some" or "quite a bit" of a problem, with the highest reports of strain being feelings of sadness, worry about the child's and family's future, feeling tired, and the toll taken on the family (see Brannan et al., 1994).

Family Measure Intercorrelations

Exploration of an intercorrelation matrix of all the family characteristics measured in FBEP was a preliminary attempt to assess the relationships (presented in Table 10.3) between family characteristics. It was hypothesized that some significant intercorrelations would be demonstrated between the measures because they were all measuring family characteristics and they were all being completed by a single respondent, the primary caregiver. Despite the anticipated level of overlap, the authors were interested in measures that would assess distinct aspects of the family, without unnecessary redundancy. Correlations in the hypothesized directions and levels (high, moderate, low) were accepted as general evidence of the specificity of the measures in assessing the unique constructs they were designed to measure. For ease of interpretation of the intercorrelation matrix, the FAD was reverse-scored so that across all family measures, higher scores would be indicative of more of the characteristic being measured (e.g., high BSI—more parental distress, high FAD—better family functioning).

Positive, moderate relationships were hypothesized between social support (FIRA) and both concrete resources (FRS) and family functioning (FAD). These reflect the similarities among support and resources, the bB components of the ABCX model. Additionally, life stress (FILE) was expected to correlate positively with caregiver strain (BCQ) and parental distress (BSI). Parental distress (BSI) and caregiver strain (BCQ) were also expected to be positively correlated, as both were conceptualized as representing the family adaptation (xX) factor.

In general, negative, moderate relationships were predicted between stressors (aA) and resources (bB). Life stressors (FILE) were expected to be negatively related to social support (FIRA), concrete resources (FRS), and family functioning (FAD). In other words, higher levels of life stressors would be related to lower levels of social support, fewer concrete resources, and greater problems with family functioning. Both parental distress (BSI) and caregiver strain (BCQ) were expected to be negatively related to social support (FIRA), concrete resources (FRS), and family functioning (FAD), suggesting that reduced support and resources were indicative of poorer adaptation (increased parental distress and caregiver strain).

It was expected that significant relationships among these measures of family characteristics would be low to moderate, but not high, indicating that although the constructs could be interrelated, no single measure was duplicative of another instrument.

In the Wave 1 FBEP sample, most of the hypothesized relationships were confirmed, with a few exceptions (see Table 10.4). Those predicted moderate,

Table 10.4

Change of Family Variables Over Three Waves

Family Variable	N	Wave 1	Wave 2	Wave 3
BSI (GSI T-score)	422	58.09	54.07	51.82
FAD (Problem Solving)	613	2.20	2.16	2.14
FAD (Communication)	614	2.28	2.23	2.19
FAD (Roles)	614	2.35	2.32	2.28
FAD (Affective Responsiveness)	612	2.11	2.11	2.08
FAD (Affective Involvement)	613	2.21	2.17	2.13
FAD (Behavior Control)	611	1.80	1.80	1.77
FAD (General Functioning)	614	2.14	2.10	2.05
FILE	616	11.53	8.61	8.05
FIRA (Relative and Friend Support)	601	24.61	24.13	24.41
FIRA (Family Index of Coherence)	354	52.70	54.06	54.12
FIRA (Social Support Index)	589	58.59	59.06	59.59
FRS	538	120.93	123.73	123.89
BCQ (Objective Strain)	610	2.06	1.78	1.58
BCQ (Subjective Externalized)	567	2.30	2.05	1.91
BCQ (Subjective Internalized)	594	3.41	2.98	2.57

positive correlations were found, with the exception of the Relative and Friend Support subscale of the FIRA. While anticipated to correlate positively with other resource factors and negatively with stressor factors, only two significant correlations were found (FIRA-Relative and Friend Support with the FAD with the FILE), but the correlations were very small ($r = .128$ and $r = .078$ respectively). The negatively correlated relationships were also supported with the exception of the unpredicted behavior of the FIRA subscale on Relative and Friend Support. This subscale was uncorrelated with the FILE and the BCQ, contrary to expectations. Implications for this subscale are discussed below.

Stressors (aA) as measured by the FILE were expected to be negatively associated with the components of the resource category and positively associated to maladaptation. These relationships were found suggesting that higher levels of stress are associated with more reported parental distress and caregiver strain. As predicted, most of the characteristics representing resources were positively related to each other, at moderate levels. This suggests that the measures selected to represent the resource component (bB) of the Double ABCX model demonstrated rudimentary convergent validity but were not redundant in the latent constructs they measured. The finding that resources (with the exception of the FIRA Relative and Friend Support subscale) were negatively related to indicators of maladaptation (xX; i.e., parental distress and caregiver strain) suggests that positive family functioning, adequate levels of concrete resources, and social support are associated with more adaptive outcomes.

Describing Change Over Time

Measures used in a longitudinal study should be sensitive enough to detect real change in the variables of interest. Change in scores on measures of family variables can reflect treatment effects, normative family development, instability of constructs, regression to the mean, unreliability of measures, and other measurement error. Conversely, no observed change in scores can indicate that the measure was not sensitive enough to detect change that truly occurred, or that there was, in fact, no change to detect. An in-depth technical study of change in family variables is beyond the scope of this chapter. However, the change in scores on the family measures used in the FBEP over time can be examined in a preliminary fashion. For the reasons discussed above and the lack of a guiding conceptual model of change, this preliminary examination will be descriptive in nature and will not statistically test the changes in the family characteristics over time. This description should be viewed as the first step toward understanding change in key variables among families with children receiving formal mental health services.

Little empirical research has been conducted that models the normative developmental path of family-related constructs such as social support, life events, concrete family resources, or family functioning. Nor has the literature provided guidance regarding how much change in family variables should be expected in families caring for children with SED. Although it has been theorized that families change in order to adapt to the demands of caring for a child with special needs (e.g, Kazak, 1989; Newbrough, Simpkins, & Maurer, 1985), little empirical research has described that change in terms of key family variables. Gallimore, Weisner, Bernheimer, Guthrie, and Nihira (1993) addressed this question in a retrospective study in which parents were asked to describe the changes made by the family to accommodate a child with developmental disabilities. However, the researchers focused on describing activities of accommodation, not on measuring change in family factors longitudinally.

In another study, researchers followed caregivers for 6 years after their child's diagnosis of diabetes in order to assess the psychological impact on mothers over time (Kovacs et al., 1990). The authors showed that just after being informed of their child's diagnosis, mothers reported moderate psychological distress. Ten to 24 months after the diagnosis, caregivers' psychological distress mean scores (measured with the SCL-90-R) initially decreased and then incrementally increased over the next 5 years. Although psychological distress was predicted by the perceived difficulty of managing the diabetes, the mother's initial level of psychological distress was also a strong predictor of later distress. Mothers who experienced high levels of distress directly following the diagnosis were more likely to experience distress at some point over the next 6 years. Kovacs and colleagues (1990) interpret these finding in light of the relevant theoretical literature, and concluded that "individual differences in the degree of symptomatology . . . appeared to be a fairly stable aspect of mothers' functioning" (p. 194).

The few remaining studies that assessed change in family factors focused on changes in families who were receiving some form of family intervention (e.g, Scherer, Brondino, Henggeler, Melton, & Hanley, 1994; Willett, Ayoub, & Robinson, 1991). Although several researchers have found small to moderate improvements in families receiving family therapy, similar findings should not be expected for families who are not in treatment.

Expected Change

Recall that eligibility for the FBEP was based on the family's having a child in formal mental health treatment, and that the families were not identified through family intervention programs but rather sought treatment on their own. Although families may have received some family therapy or other support service in connection with their child's treatment, family services and outcomes were not of primary interest in the FBEP. Nonetheless, mental health treatment for the child may be expected to exercise an indirect influence on some family variables. Hence, for this sample, change in scores on some family measures should be expected to fall somewhere between normative family development and change resulting from participation in family treatment.

In general, little change was expected to be observed for the FBEP sample in the family variables of interest. For family variables that are more stable and not likely to be affected by the child's involvement in formal mental health services, minimal change was predicted. In the current study, family characteristics that were expected to be stable included life events, concrete resources, and social support. The variables that may be less stable (including caregiver strain, parental distress, and family functioning) and more likely to be affected (at least indirectly) by the child's involvement in mental health services were expected to change slightly.

Other researchers have reported correlations between client symptomatology and caregiver strain (Baker & McCal, 1995; Montgomery et al., 1985; Noh & Turner, 1987). Thus, to the extent that mental health services actually reduce the child's symptoms, caregiver strain (as measured with the BCQ) would be expected to change somewhat. Because caregiver strain and distress have been found to be related in previous research (Brannan & Heflinger, 1996; Noh & Turner, 1987), parental distress (measured with the BSI) was also expected to demonstrate slight change. Finally, family functioning (measured with the FAD) should change slightly to the extent that mental health treatment improves child functioning, leading to improved family interactions.

Describing Change Over a 1-Year Period

As discussed earlier, the data for this study were collected for a longitudinal study with multiple data collection points, approximately 6 months apart. Data collected during the first three waves have been reported here. In addition, only cases with summary scores for each of the three waves have been included. This strict missing value criterion was considered appropriate because the purpose of this effort was to describe real change. Imputing missing data, by any method, would have had the effect of making the missing data look like the data that was present, potentially reducing variance. This is of particular concern because, depending on the measure, 37–64% of the cases did not have summary scores at each of the data collection points. In order to determine whether the cases included in the description of change were similar to those excluded, additional analyses were conducted. Some significant differences between the present and missing groups were found with Wave 1 data. Specifically, the group of cases missing from the description of change on the BSI reported significantly less distress and caregiver strain (all dimensions), fewer life stressors, and more resources at Wave 1. Cases who were missing follow-up data on the FRS were also likely to have more resources at Wave 1.

The data reported at each wave for each variable reflect mean scores for the portion of the sample with no missing scores for that subscale across waves. The number of cases and the mean sample score on the measures for three waves of data are shown in Table 10.4.

In general, very little change occurred in any of the variables of interest over the 12-month period. As predicted, the greatest change was found for the BCQ, with the greatest reduction observed in Subjective Internalized Strain (e.g., worry, fear, tiredness), from 3.41 at Wave 1 to 2.57 at Wave 2. Small reductions were also found for the mean BSI Global Severity Index, with an average reduction of more than six symptoms, and for the FILE, with an average reduction of 3.48 life events between Waves 1 and 2. The scores of the remaining variables stayed essentially the same, including the FAD subscale scores, the FIRA subscale scores, and the FRS total score.

One question that arises in the exploration of change is the extent to which initial scores allow for subsequent change to be detected—that is, the absence of ceiling and floor effects. For the most part, the initial mean scores on these family variables were near enough to the middle of the possible range of scores (see Table 10.3) so that movement up or down the scale would be possible. However, there are three exceptions to this general observation. The initial mean FRS score of 120.93 is considerably closer to the top of the range (150) than it is to the bottom of the range (51). Similarly, the initial Objective Strain (2.05) and Subjective Externalized Strain (2.30) of the BCQ were much closer to the bottom of the range of scores (ranging from 1 to 5). It is possible that the lack of improvement in these variables observed over time was due, at least in part, to these initial scores being too close to the limits of the scale ranges.

Summary and Implications Regarding Family Measures

All the family measures described in this section demonstrated evidence of internal consistency. The descriptive statistics for each measure were presented to provide information about how each of the measures performs with a sample of families whose children were receiving a wide variety of community-based mental health services. For each measure, the Wave 1 means were compared with existing norms and literature to provide perspectives about the characteristics of these families. In general, these families had more difficulties with family functioning and more life event stressors than the average family. The FBEP families also reported more social support resources and coherence with the military than the military families in the FIRA authors' sample. Caregivers in the FBEP sample reported levels of psychological distress between those found among clinical outpatient samples and nonpatient community norms, and similar to the levels reported for other nonpatient caregiver samples. Finally, an intercorrelation matrix was presented to examine expected relationships among family characteristics based on the ABCX model. Most of the anticipated relationships were demonstrated.

The finding of little or no change in the family measures over time is difficult to interpret. Given that little empirical research has indicated how much change should be expected in families with a child receiving mental health services, there are no benchmarks to which these findings can be compared. It cannot be determined with these data whether the lack of observed change was due to the measures' failure to detect the actual magnitude of the change, or whether little change actually occurred. These data do, however, provide a baseline for future studies. Further analyses must be conducted with the FBEP data to explore the extent to which these family variables co-vary over time.

Based on the results, some implications for the use of these family measures are evident. First, it is clear from the comparison with existing studies that have used these measures that, although the majority of these measures perform well on this sample of families, standard norms focusing on the average family may not provide an appropriate "yardstick" for evaluating these families. These families have special strains and resources that need to be considered carefully before immediately applying clinical cutoffs or norms. The application of these clinical cutoffs, for instance on the FAD or the BSI, can be detrimental if a family is labeled on the basis of a score. This is of concern as the average family with a child in the FBEP scored in the "clinical" range of family functioning on the FAD. While this is clearly an indication that such a family may need additional supports and resources, it is not appropriate to label the family as "dysfunctional" or "abnormal" or to provide a unidirectional causation for the mental health concerns of the child. Several researchers have interpreted elevated scores on the FAD or BSI as indicating psychopathology among caregivers of children with SED (e.g., Kazdin & Kolko, 1986). The ABCX model specifically presents a transactional relationship, and indicates that the stressors associated with caring for a child with SED may result in elevated problems in family functioning or parental distress. For a more thorough discussion of the use of symptom checklists with nonpatient caregiver samples, see Brannan and Heflinger (1996).

Second, some concerns exist about the applicability of these measures for this population of children with SED and their families. In terms of the assessment of internal consistency on the FILE, while it was adequate for this sample, as it was by the scale authors, this result should be viewed cautiously. Many life event scales have substantive subscales for various types of stressors; however, these subscales often do not demonstrate adequate internal consistency (McCubbin & Patterson, 1987). Based on the different types and potential impact of the various life events or stressors, it may be inappropriate to assume that different life events should yield a cohesive, internally consistent scale and that this form of reliability may not be applicable to life event inventories. The estimate of internal consistency, rather, may have been an artifact of the number of items (71) contributing to the scale and may not be indicative of reliability. As a complement to the collection of normative life event stressors, it may be beneficial also to collect information about family stressors that are more directly relevant to this sample of families. Families with a child with SED may encounter many stressors in addition to those associated with the problems of that child or other life events. Specifically, stressors associated with obtaining mental health services often have been mentioned by families of individuals with mental health needs.

Some concern exists whether the Relative and Friend Support subscale of the FIRA (McCubbin, Larsen, & Olson, 1982) is assessing the type of social support it was designed to measure based on the lack of predictability in relationships with other factors. This could be due to the nature of the subscale in its combination of items measuring intrafamilial support and items assessing informal support from friend networks. These two groups have been considered separate in the social support literature (e.g., Coyne, Ellard, & Smith, 1990; Dunst, Trivette, & Deal, 1988), and their inclusion in the same subscale could be responsible for its poor performance. For a more detailed discussion of the use of the FIRA in the FBEP, see Sonnichsen and Heflinger (1996).

The FRS was included in the FBEP to measure the amount of concrete, basic resources to which families had access. In the FBEP, most parents reported adequate to very adequate levels of resources and that resulted in limited variance in the sample. The FRS may yield a more normal distribution of scores in a more heterogenous sample. A measure more suited to the FBEP, and other insured mental health service consumers, would better differentiate differing levels of resources by expanding the range of response set to include more specific descriptors, and by including more items assessing resources to meet higher level needs (e.g., time for medical appointments, money or insurance for special needs services).

Implications for Future Research on Community-Based Services

In this chapter, we have reviewed our experiences of including family measures in the evaluation of community-based mental health services. Using the double ABCX model as a theoretical framework to inform the research process resulted in the recognition and inclusion of specific family constructs: family stressors, family resources, family perceptions, family coping, and family adaptation. This model reflects a competence-based paradigm and provides researchers with a framework to guide research design that recognizes the importance of family factors in the community-based treatment of children with SED, the complex nature of family reactions and interactions, the diversity of family experiences, and the potential impact of service delivery on the family.

Use of the double ABCX model also introduces several challenges, including the consideration of family participation in the research process, construct measurement, and analytic strategies for future research endeavors. As in other aspects of community-based services for children with SED, family participation in research should be integral to the process. Both family members and researchers will need education and support to make this a productive partnership. Resources with which to educate family members about research are becoming more accessible, for example the provision of parent-focused research method sessions at recent conferences sponsored by the Research and Training Centers for Children's Mental Health in Tampa and Portland. Models and methods for researchers to use to engage in participatory research are also becoming more prominent (Cousins & Earl, 1992; Weiss & Greene, 1992).

Next, finding family measures for the ABCX constructs that are available, appropriate for use, and have adequate, demonstrated performance with this population is a gargantuan task that will require careful thought, much searching, and likely frustration. As mentioned above, the search for FBEP measures in 1989 resulted in one measure of family stressors, several measures of family resources, not one measure of family perceptions, and limited measures of family adaptation. Surely a current search would yield more fruitful results; the literature on services for children with SED to date, however, has provided only limited examples of either the inclusion of a competence-based family focus or the development of measures of family stressors, resources, perceptions, or adaptation. Examples of areas in need of measurement development include: the rewards of having a child with special needs; cognitive-behavioral aspects of family coping, such as family involvement in services; family values and attitudes that influence their perceptions of the stressors they encounter; and family quality of life.

These measurement development initiatives need to employ state-of-the-art methods for test design, construction, and revision (DeVellis, 1991; Ghiselli, Campbell, & Zedeck, 1981) so that reliable and valid measures result (Halvorsen, 1991). In addition, the sensitivity to change of the measurement instruments selected must be carefully considered. Factors that may influence sensitivity should be examined, including characteristics of the target population, length of time between data-collection intervals, and the number of participants needed for adequate statistical power (Lipsey, 1990).

In addition to development of reliable and valid measures for certain constructs, other measurement issues must be addressed. First, it is important to define the unit of analysis. The unit in family-focused research is not a specified individual as in other outcome research but a system, "a group of individuals and the patterns of relationships between them" (Patterson, 1996, p. 118), which consists of both structural elements (family composition) and functioning (patterns of relationships).

This approach raises another measurement challenge, namely obtaining and integrating reports from more than one family member about family issues. To obtain the most representative view of the family, multiple family members' reports are necessary, which requires additional time and resources invested into data collection. Additionally, while the different perspectives are valuable, they can also complicate the assessment procedure. Often there are only low to moderate levels of agreement between family members reporting on family issues (Barnes, 1988; Jessop, 1981). The researcher is confronted with the problem of how best to integrate or learn from the varying perspectives, which can be a complicated and elusive endeavor (for a more extensive discussion of this issue, see Northrup, 1995).

The methods for assessing patterns of relationships in families and related family characteristics have taken on a variety of forms, including observational coding schemes, global rating scales, structured interviews, experimental tasks, and self-report questionnaires. Most services research has used an insider approach, with the self-report questionnaire as the primary method. From a practical standpoint, self-report questionnaires require far fewer resources than other methods, take less time to complete than interviews or experimental tasks, and require less training to administer and score than observational or interview methods. However, the investment of resources into observational or interview methods is worthwhile, given the resulting rich descriptive information that can enhance our understanding of interactional patterns within families.

An additional challenge of adopting a comprehensive, developmental, and transactional theoretical framework such as the double ABCX is in finding and applying suitable analytic techniques. Traditional descriptive statistics and multivariate techniques barely begin to test the relationships in such a model. The application of path analysis (see Mullen et al., 1993) and structural equations modeling (see Brannan & Heflinger, 1996; Smith, Tobin, & Fullmer, 1995) techniques hold promise, yet tests of the complete double ABCX model have not yet appeared in the literature as guides.

Despite the challenges posed by a family-oriented approach to evaluating community-based services, the ultimate goal is to yield greater understanding of the effects of services for children with SED. The importance of contextual factors in the study of multidimensional interventions with families can not be overstated. Despite the additional resources necessary, we suggest the use of multiple methods of data collection, measurement, and analysis. We recognize the strengths as well as many of the limitations of quantitative approaches in distilling useful answers to the complex questions that demand the attention of researchers of community-based services. We encourage the application of rigorous qualitative methods to the study of families within the context of community service delivery. Moreover, we recommend focusing on the interactions between service providers and family members. If community-based services research is intended to improve services and outcomes for children and families, it is critical that the research lens capture the day-to-day experiences of the professionals and families engaged in this endeavor.

Endnotes

1. The Demonstration and FBEP were both funded by the U.S. Army Health Services Command. The FBEP received additional support from the National Institute of Mental Health.

2. Because in most cases the authors did not intend for the subscales to reflect a single unidimensional construct, calculating Cronbach's alpha on a "total item score" would not be logical

and would likely result in a low reliability coefficient estimate. Furthermore, test-retest reliability from Wave 1–Wave 2 was not considered an appropriate method for assessing reliability for these instruments because data were collected 6 months apart and, in the interim, services intended to improve child and family functioning had been provided.

Authors' Notes

This research was supported by the U.S. Army Health Services Command (DA-DA10-89-C-0013) as a subcontract from the North Carolina Department of Human Resources/ Division of Mental Health, Developmental Disabilities and Substance Abuse Services, and grants from the National Institute of Mental Health (RO1MH-46136 and MH-19544, principal investigator Leonard Bickman, and R29MH50101, principal investigator, Craig Anne Heflinger). Special thanks go to all the families who participated in this project for giving their time and describing their lives in order to promote a better understanding of the needs of children with emotional and behavioral disturbance and their families.

The authors may be contacted at the Center for Mental Health Policy, Vanderbilt Institute for Public Policy Studies, 1207 18th Avenue, South, Nashville, TN 37212; (615) 322-8435.

References

Able-Boone, H., & Stevens, E. (1994). After the intensive care nursery experience: Families' perceptions of their well-being. *Children's Health Care, 23*(2), 99–114.

Anderson, E. A., & Leslie, L. A. (1991). Coping with employment and family stress: Employment arrangement and gender differences. *Sex Roles, 24,* 223–237.

Backer, T. E., & Richardson, D. (1989). Building bridges: Psychologists and families of the mentally ill. *American Psychologist, 44,* 546–550.

Baker, D. B., & McCal, K. (1995). Parenting stress in parents of children with attention-deficit hyperactivity disorder and parents of children with learning disabilities. *Journal of Child and Family Studies, 4*(1), 57–68.

Barnes, H. L. (1988). Cross-generational coalitions, discrepant perceptions and family functioning. *Journal of Psychotherapy and the Family. 4*(1–2), 51–78.

Bernal, G., Deegan, E., & Konjevich, C. (1983). The EEPI family therapy outcome study. *International Journal of Family Therapy, 5,* 3–21.

Bernheim, K. F. (1989). Psychologists and families of the severely mentally ill: The role of family consultation. *American Psychologist, 44,* 561–564.

Bickman, L., Guthrie, P. R., Foster, E. M., Lambert, E. W., Summerfelt, W. T., Breda, C. S., & Heflinger, C. A. (1995). *Managed care in mental health: The Fort Bragg Experiment.* New York: Plenum Press.

Bickman, L. B., Heflinger, C. A., Pion, G., & Behar, L. (1992). Evaluation planning for an innovative children's mental health system. *Clinical Psychology Review, 12,* 853–865.

Bishop, D. S., Epstein, N. B., Baldwin, L. M., Miller, I. W., & Keitner, G. I. (1988). Older couples: The effect of health, retirement, and family functioning on morale. *Family Systems Medicine, 6*(2), 238–247.

Boulet, J., & Boss, M. W. (1991). Reliability and validity of the Brief Symptom Inventory. *Psychological Assessment, 3,* 433–437.

Brannan, A. M., & Heflinger, C. A. (1996). *Caregiver strain as a mediator between child's symptoms and caregiver's distress: Modeling the relationships between child, family, and caregiver variables.* Nashville, TN: Vanderbilt Center for Mental Health Policy.

Brannan, A. M., Heflinger, C. A., & Bickman, L. B. (1994). *The Burden of Care Questionnaire: Measuring the impact on the family of living with a child with serious emotional problems.* Nashville, TN: Vanderbilt Center for Mental Health Policy.

Bristol, M. M. (1987). Mothers of children with autism or communication disorders: Successful adaptation and the double ABCX model. *Journal of Autism and Developmental Disorders, 17,* 469–486.

Bronfenbrenner, U. (1979). *The ecology of human development.* Cambridge, MA: Harvard University Press.

Browne, G. B., Arpin, K., Corey, P., Fitch, M., & Gafni, A. (1990). Individual correlates of health service utilization and the costs of poor adjustment to chronic illness. *Medical Care, 28*(1), 43–58.

Cherry, D. B. (1989). Stress and coping in families with ill or disabled children: Application to a model of pediatric therapy. *Physical and Occupational Therapy in Pediatrics, 9*(2), 11–32.

Cohen, N. J., Coyne, J., & Duvall, J. (1993). Adopted and biological children in the clinic: Family, parental and child characteristics. *Journal of Child Psychology and Psychiatry, 34*(4), 545–562.

Collins, B., & Collins, T. (1990). Parent-professional relationships in the treatment of severely emotionally disturbed children and adolescents. *Social Work, 35,* 522–527.

Cousins, J. B., & Earl, L. M. (1992). The case for participatory evaluation. *Educational Evaluation and Policy Analysis, 14*(4), 397–418.

Coyne, J. C., Ellard, J. H., & Smith, D. A. F. (1990). Social support, interdependence, and the dilemmas of helping. In B. R. Sarason, I. G. Sarason, & G. R. Pierce (Eds.), *Social support: An interactional view.* (pp. 129–149). New York: John Wiley, & Sons.

Derogatis, L. R., & Melisaratos, N. (1983). The Brief Symptom Inventory (BSI): An introductory report. *Psychological Medicine, 13,* 595–605.

DeVellis, R. F. (1991). Scale development: Theory and applications. *Applied Social Research Methods Series* (Vol. 26, pp. 51–90). Newbury Park, CA: Sage.

Dunst, C. J. (1986a). A short form scale for measuring parental health and well-being. Unpublished paper, Family, Infant and Preschool Program, Western Carolina Center, Morganton, NC.

Dunst, C. J. (1986b). Measuring parent commitment to professionally prescribed, child-level interventions. Unpublished paper, Family, Infant and Preschool Program, Western Carolina Center, Morganton, NC.

Dunst, C. J., & Leet, H. E. (1987). Measuring the adequacy of resources in households with young children. *Child Care, Health and Development, 13,* 111–125.

Dunst, C. J., Trivette, C. M., & Deal, A. (1988). *Enabling and empowering families: Principles and guidelines for practice.* Cambridge, MA: Brookline Books.

Epstein, N. B., Baldwin, L. M., & Bishop, D. S. (1983). The McMaster Family Assessment Device. *Journal of Marital and Family Therapy, 9*(2), 171–180.

Figley, C. R. (1989). *Helping traumatized families.* San Francisco: Jossey-Bass.

Friesen, B. J., & Koroloff, N. M. (1990). Family-centered services: Implications for mental health administration and research. *Journal of Mental Health Administration, 17*(1), 13–25.

Gallimore, R., Weisner, T. S., Bernheimer, L. P., Guthrie, D., & Nihira, K. (1993). Family responses to young children with developmental delays: Accommodation activity in an ecological and cultural context. *American Journal of Mental Retardation, 98*(2), 185–206.

Ghiselli, E. E., Campbell, J. P., & Zedeck, S. (1981). *Measurement theory for the Behavioral Sciences.* New York: W. H. Freeman.

Halvorsen, J. G. (1991). Self-report family assessment instruments: An evaluative review. *Family Practice Research Journal, 11,* 21–54.

Hobbs, N., Dokecki, P. R., Hoover-Dempsey, K. V., Moroney, R. M., Shayne, M. W., & Weeks, K. H. (1984). *Strengthening families.* San Francisco: Jossey-Bass.

Hunter, R. W., & Friesen, B. J. (1996). Family-centered services for children with emotional, behavioral, and mental disorders. In C. A. Heflinger & C. T. Nixon (Eds.), *Families and the mental health system for children and adolescents: Policy, services, and research* (pp. 18–40). Thousand Oaks, CA: Sage.

Jessop, D. J. (1981). Family relationships as viewed by parents and adolescents: A specification. *Journal of Marriage and the Family, 43,* 95–107.

Kabacoff, R. I., Miller, I. W., Bishop, D. S., Epstein, N. B., & Keitner, G. I. (1990). A psychometric study of the McMaster Family Assessment Device in psychiatric, medical and nonclinical samples. *Journal of Family Psychology, 3*(4), 431–439.

Kazak, A. E. (1989). Families of chronically ill children: A systems and social-ecological model of adaption and challenge. *Journal of Consulting and Clinical Psychology, 57*(1), 25–30.

Kazdin, A. E. (1989). Developmental psychopathology: Current research, issues, and directions. *American Psychologist, 44,* 180–187.

Kazdin, A. E., & Kolko, D. J. (1986). Parent psychopathology and family functioning among childhood firesetters. *Journal of Abnormal Child Psychology, 14*(2), 315–329.

King, C. A., Segal, H. G., Naylor, M., & Evans, T. (1993). Family functioning and suicidal behavior in adolescent inpatients with mood disorders. *Journal of the American Academy of Child and Adolescent Psychiatry, 32,* 1198–1206.

Knight, B. (1992). Emotional distress and diagnosis among helpseekers: A comparison of dementia caregivers and older adults. *Journal of Applied Gerontology, 11,* 361–373.

Konstantareas, M. M. (1991). Autistic, learning disabled and delayed children's impact on their parents. *Canadian Journal of Behavioural Science, 23,* 358–375.

Kovacs, M., Iyengar, S., Goldston, D., Obrosky, D. S., Stewart, J., and Marsh, J. (1990). Psychological functioning among mothers of children with insulin-dependent diabetes mellitus: A longitudinal study. *Journal of Consulting and Clinical Psychology, 58*(2), 189–195.

Leonard, B. J., Brust, J. D., & Patterson, L. (1991). Home care reimbursement for technology-dependent children: Its impact on parental distress. *Lifestyles: Family and Economic Issues, 12*(1), 63–76.

Lipsey, M. W. (1990). *Design sensitivity: Statistical power for experimental research.* Newbury Park: Sage.

Marsh, D. T. (1996). Families of children and adolescents with serious emotional disturbance: Innovations in theory, research, and practice. In C. A. Heflinger & C. T. Nixon (Eds.), *Families and the mental health system for children and adolescents: Policy, services, and research* (pp. 75–95). Thousand Oaks, CA: Sage.

Matheny, K. B., Aycock, D. W., Pugh, J. L., Curlette, W. L., & Cannella, K. A. (1986). Stress coping: A qualitative and quantitative synthesis with implications for treatment. *Counseling Psychologist, 14,* 499–549.

Matocha, L. (1995). Families and health crises. In R. Day, K. Gilbert, B. Settles, & W. Burr (Eds.), *Research and theory in family science.* Pacific Grove, CA: Brooks/Cole.

McCubbin, H. I. (1987). The family index of regenerativity-military. In H. McCubbin & A. Thompson (Eds.), *Family assessment for research and practice.* Madison: University of Wisconsin.

McCubbin, H., Larsen, A., & Olson, D. (1987). F-COPES family crisis oriented personal scales. In H. McCubbin & A. Thompson (Eds.), *Family assessment for research and practice.* Madison: University of Wisconsin. (Original work published 1982)

McCubbin, H. I., & Patterson, J. (1982). Family index of coherence. In H. I. McCubbin & A. I. Thompson (Eds.), *Family assessment inventories for research and practice.* Madison: University of Wisconsin. (Original work published 1982)

McCubbin, H., & Patterson, J. (1983a). The family stress process: The Double ABCX Model of adjustment and adaptation. *Marriage and Family Review, 6,* 7–37.

McCubbin, H., & Patterson, J. M. (1983b). Stress: The family inventory of life events and changes. In E. Filsinger (Ed.), *Marriage and family assessment* (pp. 275–297). Beverly Hills, CA: Sage.

McCubbin, H. I., & Patterson, J. M. (1987). FILE: Family inventory of life events and changes. In H. I. McCubbin & A. I. Thompson (Eds.), *Family assessment inventories for research and practice.* Madison: University of Wisconsin.

McCubbin, H. I., Patterson, J. M., & Glynn, T. (1987). Social support index (SSI). In H. McCubbin & A. Thompson (Eds.), *Family assessment inventories for research and practice.* Madison: University of Wisconsin. (Original work published 1982)

McCubbin, H., Patterson, J., & Lavee, Y. (1983). *One thousand army families: Strengths, coping, and supports.* St. Paul: University of Minnesota.

McElroy, E. (Ed.). (1987a). *Children and adolescents with mental illness: A parents guide.* Kensington, MD: Woodbine House.

McElroy, E. M. (1987b). The beat of a different drummer. In A. B. Hatfield & J. P. Lefley (Eds.), *Families of the mentally ill: Coping and adaptation* (pp. 225–243). New York: Guilford Press.

McKay, J. R., Murphy, R. T., Rivinus, T. R., & Maisto, S. A. (1991). Family dysfunctioning and alcohol and drug use in adolescent psychiatric inpatients. *Journal of the American Academy of Child and Adolescent Psychiatry, 30,* 967–972.

Mikhail, A. (1981). Stress: A psychobiological conception. *Journal of Human Stress, 7,* 9–15.

Miller, I. W., Epstein, N. B., Bishop, D. S., & Keitner, G. I. (1985). The McMaster Family Assessment Device: Reliability and validity. *Journal of Marital and Family Therapy, 11*(4), 345–356.

Montgomery, R. J. V., Gonyea, J. G., & Hooyman, N. R. (1985). Caregiving and the experience of subjective and objective burden. *Family Relations, 34,* 19–26.

Mullen, P. M., Smith, R. M., & Hill, E. W. (1993). Sense of coherence as a mediator of stress for cancer patients and spouses. *Journal of Psychosocial Oncology, 11*(3), 23–46.

Munger, R. L. (1991). *Child mental health practice from the ecological perspective.* Lanham, NY: University Press of America.

Newbrough, J. R., Simpkins, G., & Maurer, H. (1985). A family development approach to studying factors in the management and control of childhood diabetes. *Diabetes Care, 8*(1), 83–92.

Noh, S., & Turner, R. J. (1987). Living with psychiatric patients: Implications for the mental health of family members. *Social Science Medicine, 25*(3), 263–271.

Northrup, D. A. (1995). The relationship between adolescent and parent reports about family issues (Doctoral dissertation, Vanderbilt University, 1995). *Dissertation Abstracts International.*

Orr, R. R., Cameron, S. J., & Day, D. M. (1991). Coping with stress in families with children who have mental retardation: An evaluation of the Double ABCX model. *American Journal on Mental Retardation, 95,* 444–450.

Patterson, J. M. (1996). Family research methods: Issues and strategies. In C. A. Heflinger & C. T. Nixon (Eds.), *Families and the mental health system for children and adolescents: Policy, services, and research* (pp. 117–144). Thousand Oaks, CA: Sage.

Perosa, L. M., & Perosa, S. L. (1990). Convergent and discriminant validity for family self-report measures. *Educational and Psychological Measurement, 50,* 855–868.

Piersma, H. L., Reaume, W. M., & Boes, J. L. (1994). The Brief Symptom Inventory as an outcome measure for adult psychiatric inpatients. *Journal of Clinical Psychology, 50,* 555–563.

Portes, P. R., Howell, S. C., Brown, J. H., Eichenberger, S., & Mas, S. A. (1992). Family functions and children's post divorce adjustment. *American Journal of Orthopsychiatry, 62*(4), 613–617.

Reis, S. D., & Heppner, P. P. (1993). Examination of coping resources and family adaptation in mothers and daughters of incestuous versus nonclinical families. *Journal of Counseling Psychology, 40*(1), 100–108.

Sanger, M. S., MacLean, W. E., & Van Slyke, D. A. (1992). Relation between maternal characteristics and child behavior ratings: Implications for interpreting behavior checklists. *Clinical Pediatrics, 31*(8), 461–466.

Scherer, D. G., Brondino, M. J., Henggeler, S. W., Melton, G. B., and Hanley, J. H. (1994). Multisystemic family preservation therapy: Preliminary findings from a study of rural and minority serious adolescent offenders. *Journal of Emotional and Behavioral Disorders, 2*(4), 198–206.

Selye, H. (1974). *Stress without distress.* New York: Lippincott & Crowell.

Singer, J. E., & Davidson, L. M. (1991). Specificity and stress research. In A. Monat & R. S. Lazarus (Eds.), *Stress and coping: An anthology* (3rd ed., pp. 36–47). New York: Columbia University Press.

Smith, G. C., Tobin, S. S., & Fullmer, E. M. (1995). Elderly mothers caring at home for offspring with mental retardation: A model of permanency planning. *American Journal on Mental Retardation, 99,* 487–499.

Sonnichsen, S. E., & Heflinger, C. A. (1996). *Reliability, validity and sample findings for the Family Index of Regenerativity in the Fort Bragg Evaluation Project.* Nashville, TN: Vanderbilt Center for Mental Health Policy.

Thompson, E. H., Jr., & Doll, W. (1982). The burden of families coping with the mentally ill: An invisible crisis. *Family Relations, 31,* 379–388.

Turnbull, A. P., Summers, J. A., & Brotherson, M. J. (1986). Family life cycle: theoretical and empirical implications and future directions for families with mentally retarded members. In J. Gallagher & P. Vietze (Eds.), *Families of handicapped persons: Research, programs, and policy issues.* Baltimore: Brookes.

Van Hook, M. P. (1987, May). Harvest of despair: Using the ABCX model for farm families in crisis. *Social Casework: The Journal of Contemporary Social Work,* 273–278.

Walker, L. S., Garber, J., & Greene, J. W. (1993). Somatic complaints in pediatric patients: A prospective study of the role of negative life events, child social and academic competence, and parental somatic symptoms. *Journal of Consulting and Clinical Psychology, 62*(6), 1213–1221.

Waller, G., Slade, P., & Calam, R. (1990). Who knows best? Family interaction and eating disorders. *British Journal of Psychiatry, 156,* 546–550.

Weiss, H. B. & Greene, J. C. (1992). An empowerment partnership for family support and education programs and evaluations. *Family Science Review, 5,* (1&2).

Wikler, L. M. (1986). Family stress theory and research on families of children with mental retardation. In J. J. Gallagher & P. M. Vietze (Eds.), *Families of handicapped persons: Research, programs, and policy issues* (pp. 167–195). Baltimore: Brookes.

Willett, J. B., Ayoub, C. C., & Robinson, D. (1991). Using growth modeling to examine systematic differences in growth: An example of change in the functioning of families at risk of maladaptive parenting, child abuse, or neglect. *Journal of Consulting and Clinical Psychology, 59*(1), 38–47.

Winton, P. J. (1990). Promoting a normalizing approach to families: Integrating theory with practice. *Topics in Early Childhood Special Education, 10,* 90–103.

Witztum, E., Brown, J. P., & De-Nour, A. K. (1987). Psychological distress in medical patients referred for psychiatric consultation. *Psychosomatics, 28,* 425–428.

Worby, C. M., Altrocchi, J., Veach, T. L., & Crosby, R. (1991). Early identification of symptomatic post-MI families. *Family Systems Medicine, 9,* 127–135.

Evaluation Approaches III

Methods for System-Level Evaluations of Child Mental Health Service Networks

11

Joseph P. Morrissey, Matthew C. Johnsen,
and Michael O. Calloway

Throughout the United States, services for children and adolescents with serious emotional disturbances (SEDs) have traditionally been in scarce supply, operated by a patchwork of public and private agencies, and inadequately financed. These services include not only those offered by traditional mental health providers, but also what appears to consumers as a bewildering array of support services provided by welfare and social service agencies, schools, health departments, juvenile and family courts, juvenile detention and training centers, and substance abuse agencies. Each of these programs has its special purpose, its unique sources of funding, its particular eligibility requirements, its own mode and standards of operation, and sometimes, its own geographic catchment area. Together, these features define system fragmentation, a situation in which responsibility is divided "among multiple, separate individuals and agencies, each with a categorical purpose," with "the whole lacking a coherent policy, an integrated direction, and coordinated relationships" (Roemer, Kramer, & Frink, 1975, p. 3). As a result, families are faced with barriers, gaps, and inadequacies in caring for children who have SEDs (Knitzer, 1982).

In the past 15 years, an advocacy movement has been mobilized to overcome these deficiencies (Duchnowski & Freidman, 1990). The guiding premise is that children and adolescents with SED require a range of mental health and other support services (see Chapter 1). The challenge is for mental health agencies to collaborate with educational, health, social service, child welfare, and juvenile justice agencies to provide comprehensive services. Two principles guide these efforts. First, a "continuum of care," or a range of services at varying levels of intensity, is required to meet the multiple needs of these youths and their families. Second, if this continuum is to be truly effective, it must be transformed into a "system of care," that is, a "comprehensive spectrum of mental health and other necessary services that are organized into a coordinated network to meet the multiple and changing needs of severely emotionally disturbed children and adolescents" (Stroul & Friedman, 1986, p. 3). The concept of a system of care connotes not only a range of particular service elements, but also the mechanisms, arrangements, incentives, structures, and processes needed to ensure that these individual elements work together as a coordinated and cohesive whole. So conceived, a system of care is the antithesis of services fragmentation.

A key insight of work that takes a systems perspective begins with the recognition that to understand an organization's behavior, and the impact of that behavior on its clients, you must understand the context of that behavior (Pfeffer & Salancik, 1978). Organizations are inescapably bound up with the conditions of their environments. Human service organizations are dependent on people and other organizations in their environments for the resources that make up their lifeblood. For a human service agency, these material resources include staff, clients, information, capital, facilities, and support. In addition, cultural and normative aspects of an organization are profoundly influenced by the interorganizational environment (DiMaggio & Powell, 1983).

As system-of-care concepts have become more central in the design and implementation of child mental health interventions over the past decade, efforts to design ways of studying and evaluating service system performance have become equally important. Stroul (1993) reviewed 30 community-level initiatives and discovered positive outcome trends as indicated by less restrictive residential placements and improved child and youth functioning. Glisson and James (1992) found that children served by interagency coordination teams in Tennessee were placed in less restrictive and more appropriate placements after 6 months than children not served by these teams. This study also reported greater improvement in child functioning for seriously disturbed children in the intervention group. In contrast, Bickman (1995) found no differences in client outcomes between intervention and control communities in the Fort Bragg demonstration, an innovative system of care for military dependents in one area of North Carolina.

Several studies of adult mental health service delivery networks are instructive in their approaches to defining these systems. Provan and Milward (1991, p. 394) have studied "service implementation networks" where "no single agency provides the entire package of services often needed by clients"; rather, "multiple services are best delivered interorganizationally through a coordinated and integrated network of organizations offering components of the complete service." There often is a lead or coordinating agency in these networks, and member organizations are only partially or segmentally involved. The findings suggest that not all forms of service network integration are alike (Provan & Milward, 1991; Provan & Milward, 1995). Networks organized and coordinated centrally, through a single core agency, are likely to be more effective than are denser, cohesive networks integrated in a decentralized way. Centralization appears to facilitate both integration and coordination, something that decentralized systems have a difficult time accomplishing because of the number of organizations and linkages involved. Morrissey and colleagues examined mental health systems, focusing on the performance of local mental health authorities (Morrissey et al., 1994). The main premise of this work was that urban mental health systems serving adults with serious mental illness would be more effective if funding were provided through, and primary services arranged by, a single mental health authority. While considerable changes in system performance occurred at several sites during the demonstration, these changes did not lead to consistent or significant improvements in client outcomes (Lehman, Postrado, Roth, McNary, & Goldman, 1994).

The study of interorganizational networks flows quite naturally from the increasing recognition of resource dependency as a prime determinant of organizational behavior. An interorganizational network perspective can also be used to assess service system structure and change. These methods have been increasingly applied to the evaluation of mental health (Morrissey, Tausig, & Lindsey, 1985; Morrissey et al., 1994; Provan & Milward, 1995) and other human services (Alter & Hage, 1993; Bolland & Wilson, 1994; Van de Ven & Ferry, 1980). The premise underlying this work is that service systems can be conceptualized as networks of interacting organizations and that the integration and coordination of these systems can be inferred from the patterns of interagency relationships involving client referrals, information flows, and resource exchanges.

Studies of interorganizational relations can focus on several levels of analysis. The simplest level is the dyad, or pairwise relationship. A basic question about a dyad is whether or not a direct tie exists between two actors. Typical dyadic analyses seek to explain variations in ties as a function of joint characteristics of the pair—for example, the degree of similarity of their attribute profiles. At the next highest level of analysis is the triad, where organizations are considered three at a time. Across all triads, a census is made of the 16 possible nonredundant types of directed relationships that may occur among three entities, A → B → C (Wasserman and Faust, 1994). These types range from the null set (no linkages at all) to the densely connected set where each entity is connected by double-headed arrows. For example, a major question asked of a triad analysis is the extent to which the triad patterns in the network are nonrandom—that is, how they compare to some known distribution of relationships.

The third level of analysis focuses on organization sets that consist of a focal organization and all of the other organizations with which it has input or output relations (Evan, 1972). Here, rather than examining relations two or three at a time, the focus is on the set of multiple relationships and how they, both individually and collectively, influence the behavior of the focal organization. At this level of analysis it is possible to consider characteristics of these sets, such as number of organizational links, as attributes of a focal organization, much as one might consider gender an attribute of a person. Beyond the set level, the next most important level of analysis is the complete network, or system (Knoke & Kuklinski, 1982; Scott, 1991). In these analyses, a researcher uses information about the patterning of ties among all actors in a system to identify distinct positions or roles within the system and to describe the nature of relations among these positions. There is no one focal organization, nor are there specific dyads or triads in these analyses; relationships among all organizations are considered simultaneously. Analyses at this level may involve examining structures within these networks based on cohesion (using cliques or k-cores) or structures based on role similarity (using structural equivalence). A distinctive feature of the network level of analysis is the requirement that there be no missing data; information must be available about the relationship between each actor and every other actor in the network. In contrast, analyses of dyads, triads, and sets can often be performed with incomplete data.

In this chapter we provide an overview of several methods of data collection and analysis for studying mental health and related service systems. These methods are informed by interorganizational theory and social network data analysis techniques. The authors have used these methods to assess a variety of urban and rural service systems for both adults and children. The primary focus of this program of research has been on two of the four levels of analysis: sets and networks. These two levels will be the ones emphasized in this chapter as well. Four distinct but interrelated methods will be reviewed. First, a key informant approach to developing global measures of service system performance will be described. Second, an organization-set approach to assessing the relations of a lead agency in a system of care will be presented. The third and fourth approaches, blockmodels and k-cores, are based on the complete network level of analysis. Each approach will be illustrated and references to published studies will be provided. The intent in this chapter is to provide readers with (a) a user-friendly, schematic overview of each method; (b) some guidelines for thinking about how to use these methods as part of their own service system research and evaluations; and (c) some references to published literature where more technical details about the logic and implementation of these methods can be found. Readers who want a fuller treatment of the conceptual and methodological issues underlying this work are encouraged to consult the citations to this now rapidly expanding literature.

Method 1: Key Informant Ratings of Service System Performance

Background and Main Concepts

Over the past two decades, the practice of implementing "system of care" concepts for children and youth—or "community support systems" as they are referred to for adults with serious mental illnesses (Turner & TenHoor, 1978)—has developed much more rapidly than has the capacity of the research community to measure and assess the performance of these initiatives. The service system concept encompasses a much more complex reality both for providers and researchers because of the sheer numbers and types of agencies and associated service programs involved (e.g., mental health, social welfare, employment, housing, rehabilitation, and criminal justice). Although systems concepts for describing service delivery (such as availability, accessibility, accountability, adequacy, quality, continuity, comprehensiveness, and viability) have become well ensconced in mental health services jargon, methods for assessing the capacity and performance of service systems has lagged behind.

Two contrasting strategies for developing system performance measures have been tried—direct and indirect. The direct approach seeks to construct measures from operational data about the utilization and impact of services provided by individual agencies or service sectors within the service system. Possible data sources include agency management information systems, record abstracts, or national data bases. Social indicator strategies are one example of this approach (Ciarlo, Tweed, Shern, Kirkpatrick, & Sachs-Ericsson, 1992; Goldsmith et al., 1984). Some of the problems encountered in implementing this approach are the limited availability or quality of data, which often do not consistently or uniformly encompass the service sectors of interest. Key concepts are often only obliquely or tangentially measured by the available data (i.e., poor epistemic correlations between concept and measure), and numerous assumptions have to be made about need, quality, effectiveness, and other dimensions of services for which there is little support or guidance in the published literature.

The indirect approach relies upon surveying knowledgeable persons or "experts" about the performance of the service system. The idea of expert opinion polling has a long tradition in the mental health needs assessment literature (Attkisson, Hargreaves, Horowitz, & Sorensen, 1978; Lauffer, 1978). The strategy relies upon principles of psychological scaling (Nunnally & Bernstein, 1994) and a survey research logic in which the investigator develops a series of statements about system performance and, either in an interview or questionnaire format, asks a sample of respondents to rate the local service system's level of performance on each item. Average ratings on individual items or sets of items (e.g., unidimensional scales) are then used to compare and contrast system performance between communities at a particular point in time (cross-sectional analysis) or for the same communities at two or more points in time (longitudinal analysis). Two advantages of this approach are that it is relatively inexpensive and it can be well focused on the particular concepts or performance dimensions of interest in a particular study. Its limitations turn in part on how knowledgeable the respondents really are and how valid and reliable their "perceptions" are vis-à-vis the "actual" performance of the service system.

The latter strategy was used in the evaluation of the Robert Wood Johnson Foundation's Program on Chronic Mental Illness, a nine-city demonstration that sought to enhance the organization and financing of service systems for this target population (Goldman et al., 1990; Morrissey et al., 1994). After looking for an established instrument without success, the investigators developed a "key informant survey" to obtain performance ratings of local service systems from knowledgeable persons at each of the demonstration sites. Subsequent iterations of the instrument have been used to assess children's mental health systems (Morrissey, Johnsen, et al., 1997) and systems for persons who are homeless and mentally ill (Morrissey, Calloway, et al., 1997).

The development and scale composition of the original instrument for adult services is described elsewhere (Morrissey, Ridgely, Goldman, & Bartko, 1994), as is its adaptation to child mental health services (Morrissey, Calloway, et al., 1997). The key informant survey yields four multi-item scales that measure the following dimensions of children's service system performance:

- *Adequacy of services:* The extent to which youths needing each of 20 system-of-care (SC) services actually receive them;

- *Quality of services:* The extent to which each of the 20 SC services meets current professional standards on interpersonal, technical, and physical location considerations;

- *Availability of services:* The extent to which each of the 20 SC services exists in the local community;

- *Coordination of services:* The extent to which the local service system performs 11 activities reflecting joint planning and decision making between agencies to achieve shared goals.

Data Collection and Analysis

Initially, a mailed questionnaire format was used to implement this key informant survey. Respondents included two groups: a representative from each of the agencies in the service network and a snowball sample (i.e., a sample made by asking respondents to nominate other respondents to complete the survey; see Sudman, 1976) of other stakeholders (e.g., advocates, government officials, private practitioners, and interested citizens) who were nominated by the agency representatives as persons making important contributions to the local service system (Morrissey, Ridgely, et al., 1994; Morrissey, Johnsen, et al., 1997). Response rates in the adult study were in the 59–73% range across nine communities, while those in the children's study were 51 and 80% for the two time periods. These experiences indicated that many respondents (especially those in the snowball samples) were not familiar enough with the operations of the overall service system to rate many of the items. Subsequently, an in-person interview format was developed that combined the key informant and interagency network surveys into a single instrument. Much higher response rates (≥ 95% in two multicounty children's studies and an 18-site adult homeless study) have been obtained with the latter format, along with much more complete patterns of responses across scale items. Admittedly, the interview approach involves trading-off a broader sample of community stakeholders for a narrower but more complete agency-based sample of informants.

Data analyses follow standard survey research methods. These include an analysis of nonrespondents to assess the representativeness of the respondent sample, reliability analyses to establish the unidimensionality of scales, and statistical tests to assess significant differences between sites and time periods (Morrissey, Calloway, et al., 1994; Morrissey, Johnsen, et al., 1997). The nonresponse analyses for these data showed that there were no significant differences between respondents and nonrespondents. In both studies, reliabilities for the four scales were in the .70–.92 range. Scale scores averaged across respondents for adequacy, quality, availability, and coordination provide measures of system performance. Statistical analyses were then performed with T-tests and one-way analysis of variance procedures.

Illustration

An illustration of the key informant approach to a system-level evaluation is presented in Table 11.1. The data are from two counties in western North Carolina that participated in the Robert Wood Johnson Demonstration Program for

Table 11.1

Key Informant Ratings of Children's Service System Performance
for an Urban and a Rural County at Two Time Points

System Performance Indices	Urban County			Rural County		
	T1 (1991)	T2 (1993)	T2–T1 Difference	T1 (1991)	T2 (1993)	T2–T1 Difference
Adequacy of Services	2.80	3.05	0.25*	2.94	3.00	0.06
Quality of Services	2.75	3.20	0.45	3.13	3.06	− 0.07
Availability of Services	2.56	2.85	0.29**	3.05	3.24	0.19
Coordination of Services	2.54	2.92	0.38*	3.10	2.91	− 0.19

Note. From Morrisey, J., Calloway, M., Johnsen, M., & Ullman, M. (1997). Service system performance and integration: A baseline profile of the ACCESS demonstration sites. *Psychiatric Services, 48*(3), 374–380.

* $< .05$. ** $< .01$.

Youth (England & Cole, 1992; Morrissey et al., 1997). Key informant ratings on the four system dimensions discussed above are displayed at two time points: T1 (1991), which occurred at the end of the demonstration's 2-year planning phase, and T2 (1993), which came close to the end of the 3-year implementation phase. System performance measures were rated on a 5-point Likert scale ranging from low (1) to high (5).

At T1, the ratings for the rural site on each system performance measure tended to be higher than the ratings for the urban site. However, the overtime changes are much greater and more consistent across indices for the urban system. The T2–T1 changes for the rural site show slight improvements for the adequacy and availability of services, but corresponding decreases for the quality and coordination indices. Thus, the performance of the rural system as perceived by the key informants remained basically the same between 1991 and 1993, but the performance of the urban system increased considerably over the same time interval.

Comments

Key informant surveys provide a relatively inexpensive and focused way of obtaining data on the performance of child mental health and other similar service systems. This approach is quite flexible in that constructs of interest can be measured so long as multiple items or questions presumed to tap key aspects of the underlying construct can be posed and meaningfully answered by the respondents. As with any survey research procedure, key informant ratings are susceptible to systematic biases such as those that might occur in government or foundation demonstrations when multiple respondents choose to present the service system in an excessively positive light. (The in-person interview format helps to minimize, but does not totally eliminate, such biases.) Ratings from such surveys also may be sensitive to immediate sociopolitical events and, as a result, they might not be highly correlated with measures based on network data. In the RWJ/PCMI, for example, system performance at one site was downrated, apparently in response to media attention about fiscal and management problems at the newly created local mental health authority, even though the network data indicated that the structure of its service system had moved much closer to the goals of the demonstration than other sites with higher key informant ratings (Morrissey, Calloway, et al., 1994).

Another limitation of these measures is their global nature and inability to identify specific ways in which the service system is deficient, or ways in which it might be improved. The system is treated essentially as a "black box," making it difficult to infer anything about the organization of the service system based solely on these ratings. Systems rated at the same performance level, for example, might have quite different patterns of "systemness" as indicated by network properties (e.g., centralization, density, fragmentation). The network approaches described below open up this black box by providing a much clearer picture of these organizational and interorganizational arrangements.

Method 2: Organization-Set Analysis

Background and Main Concepts

Much of the research on mental health service systems has been carried out in the context of service demonstration programs that are attempting to deliberately alter interagency relationships in a community care system by making them more coordinated and more responsive to meeting the multiple needs of clients with serious mental disabilities. Often these demonstrations are organized with one agency or small group of agencies assigned the role of change agent relative to all of the other organizations in the service system. This type of arrangement was a central component of the NIMH Community Support Program (Turner & TenHoor, 1978), the NIMH Child and Adolescent Service Program (Stroul & Friedman, 1986), the Robert Wood Johnson Foundation's Program on Chronic Mental Illness (Shore & Cohen, 1990), the Mental Health Program for Youth (England & Cole, 1992), and more recently, the Center for Mental Health Services' ACCESS demonstration for persons who are homeless and mentally ill (Randolph, 1995). One issue that arises in evaluating the success of these demonstrations is the role of the lead agency: Does it serve as the coordinating hub of the service system? Is the lead agency well connected to the other member agencies? Does the density of these connections increase over time?

The system-level method that is best suited to answering these types of questions is organization-set analysis (Evan, 1972; Wasserman & Faust, 1994). For the most part, the major focus of an organizational-set analysis is not on the attributes of the organizations but rather on the relationships of a focal organization to other organizations with which it maintains input or output relations. Several network-based measures are available to indicate the focal organization's activity with the rest of the service system, particularly across several specific dimensions (Minor, 1983), for example the relationship's existence, direction, context (positive versus negative valence), and extensity. The following list presents some of these measures and their definitions:

- *Range:* The number of ties that exist between a focal organization and all others in the service system. This number can also be calculated across particular sets of organizations rather than the whole network. The two specific range measures used in the illustration below are organizational linkage (the number of agencies within the network with which an organization has at least one tie) and service linkage (the number of distinct relations an organization has with all other organizations within the network).

- *Multiplexity:* The extent to which an organization's relationships exist across three dimensions—that is, funding, clients, and information. Multiplexity is computed as the ratio of service linkages to organizational linkages. Values range from a low of 0 to a high of 6 (three relations—clients, funds, information x two directions—send vs. receive) reflecting the average multibonded content of each relationship.

- *Multiplex Density:* The proportion of agencies that have multiplex ties; values range between 0 and 1. This can be thought of as a measure of the extensiveness of multibonded ties among agencies in each network. The multiplexity measure ignores all 0 values (absent ties), whereas the multiplex density measure score includes all organizations in the calculation, whether they have an exchange relationship or not.

While the above list is not exhaustive of the types of analysis that can be done using a focal organization and all other organizations in its environment (further information is provided in Wasserman & Faust, 1994), it is illustrative of the simplicity and versatility of this approach to characterizing the focal organization within its environment. If these measures are calculated over time, indications of the organization-set's stability or instability can be determined.

Data Collection and Analysis

The data requirements for an organizational-set analysis are different from those associated with the key informant survey. The data required in this instance are relational, measuring the existence or strength of relationships connecting a focal organization to other organizations in the network. For a stand-alone organization-set analysis, only information about the links between the focal organization and each of the other organizations is required. (Relations between the latter group of organizations are usually ignored.) For the purposes of this chapter, however, we will present this method in the context of a full network study of the children's mental health systems in two North Carolina counties. (This background will apply to the blockmodel and k-core presentations as well.) The content and format of data collection are very much the same regardless of whether one is considering sets, networks, or k-cores. (The differences occur primarily in data analysis.)

Data collection for the child system study involved three steps. First, a list of agencies and major subprograms was developed to define the boundaries of the two children's service systems. These lists were prepared in consultation with staff of the two community mental health centers that served as the lead agencies for the local RWJF demonstration program. The member agencies of the interagency councils created under the demonstration became the seeds on our list; other agencies and subprograms were added on the basis of discussions with lead agency staff, inspection of local human service directories, and preliminary interviews with a representative from selected agencies on each council. For the initial survey at T1 (1991), a list of 68 agencies was used; this number grew to 82 at T2 (1993).

Second, a representative from each agency (usually a program or agency director) was identified to serve as a source of information about the agency and its relationships with the other organizations on the list. Third, data were collected both in the form of a personal interview and a self-administered questionnaire. The 45-minute interview focused on characteristics of the agency (e.g., services, staffing, budgets) and the nature of its involvement (if any) with the local RWJF demonstration. At its conclusion, the respondent was presented with a questionnaire that asked for information about the agency's working relationships with the other agencies on the list with regard to client referrals, funding exchanges, and information flows. Respondents were asked to complete the questionnaire and to return it in a postage-paid envelope within two weeks of the interview date. After several written and telephone follow-ups, a 98% response rate on these questionnaires was obtained.

Data obtained from the questionnaires were arrayed into square agency-by-agency matrices constructed for each of the three types of resource exchanges: client referrals, funding, and information flows (Morrissey, 1992; Morrissey, Johnsen, et al., 1997). The ij cells of the matrices reflect the presence and strength of the interorganizational links between each pair of agencies across these three relationships. The use of these particular items is based on a well-established tradition of interorganizational network research (Levine & White, 1961; Van de Ven & Ferry, 1980). Several steps were taken to maximize reliability of these items in data collection: (a) the instrument used presents respondents with a list of organizations bounded within their child mental health service systems (rather than relying on the respondent's memory to generate such a list); (b) a conservative approach is used to identify interagency links by constructing matrices composed of confirmed ties only (those for which the sending and the receiving organization both acknowledge); and (c) the analyses utilize three relations (client referrals, funding, and information flows) rather than a single tie, thereby adding stability to the estimates. In addition, the analyses reported here consider only relatively intense relationships (i.e., those with a value of 3 or 4 on a 0–4 scale), expecting that generation of such strong ties would be a more demanding test of system change. It has been demonstrated elsewhere that these procedures do yield reliable estimates of interagency relationships (Calloway, Morrissey, & Paulson, 1993; Marsden, 1990).

Once these data have been collected and arrayed, an organizational-set analysis can proceed by "stripping out" the rows and columns of the matrices that contain the focal organization's responses to the other N-1 organizations (row vector) and the other organization's responses about the focal organization (column vector). For calculation of the network measures as described above, sums and proportions can be determined using network analysis packages, spreadsheets, or popular statistical packages (e.g., SPSS, SAS). In fact, some of the measures are so simple in calculation that paper and pencil techniques can be used, provided the network size is small enough to be manageable. These measures can be taken across multiple relationships (indeed, multiplexity requires it) in order to determine network activity across multiple relationships.

These network measures can be based on assessments reflecting the extent of change in the focal organization's relationships over time. In addition, most of these change measures can be tested for statistical significance using a proportional means test (Blalock, 1972). In the same manner, different focal organizations can be compared in terms of their change profile. While there are no statistical tests associated with centrality, it is still possible to determine which focal organization is the most central actor comparatively, and how that centrality might change over time.

Illustration

The following example will serve to illustrate the use of an organization-set analysis. The data come from the study of two western North Carolina counties that participated in the RWJ Youth demonstration (England & Cole, 1992). One of the counties was predominantly rural and the other was urban. Data were collected at two points in time for both service systems. One goal of the demonstration was to provide case-management services (including the development of child specific interagency treatment teams) for children with SED served under the auspices of the demonstration (Burns et al., 1994). The lead agencies were two community mental health centers for which several child-specific programs were included in the network study. For purposes of illustration, the case-management subunit is selected as the focal organization in each system.

The organization-set indices for the two case management programs at the two time points are provided in Table 11.2. The measure of organizational linkage indicates slight improvement over time in each network. The measure of service linkage indicates mixed trends in the two networks, and the measures of multiplexity indicate slightly fewer multiplex ties over time. The overall change appears to be mixed at best, until one interprets the findings in light of the size of the organizational networks. Within each network at T1, the case-management services were almost fully linked in terms of organizational connections (39 of 41 organizations in the urban site, and 24 of 27 in the rural site). Under these circumstances the two sites were close to a ceiling effect, as much improvement was difficult given the initial very high levels of linkage at T1. Similarly, the measure of multiplex density began at such a high level (very close to 1) that the addition of several new agencies within the networks at T2 created some downward movement for this indicator.

Discussion

Organization-set analysis allows for a micro-view of service system organization. Conceptually, it is a step down from the macro-level perspective of the key informant or blockmodel methods (see below). One advantage of an organization-set approach over other methods that focus on a broader or more complete sample of organizations is its simplicity and ease of use. These analyses can be done quickly with the help of existing network analysis packages. Indeed, because many of the network measures that are used to analyze organization-sets consist of summa-

Table 11.2

Organization-Set Indices for Case Management Units
at Urban and Rural Sites for T1 and T2

Organization-Set Indices	Urban		Rural		Percentage Change	
					Urban	Rural
	T1 $n = 41$	T2 $n = 49$	T1 $n = 27$	T2 $n = 34$	T2–T1	T2–T1
Organization Links	39	41	24	25.21	5.1%	4.2%
Service Links	137	132	80	83.21	−3.6%	3.8%
Multiplexity	3.61	3.30	3.48	3.46	−8.5%	−0.6%
Multiplex Density	0.98	0.85	0.92	0.76	−12.4%	−17.9%

tions of different types of relationships, many of them can be derived by pencil and paper techniques, spreadsheet programs, or generally available statistical packages. The presentation of findings is also straightforward and requires only an understanding of the measures themselves (and less so the math underlying them). Findings can be presented in simple table formats or graphical depictions. A second important advantage of organization-set analysis is that it allows for a detailed understanding of a focal organization as it relates to its environment through other organizations. Organization-set analysis relies upon relational data, therefore it is less susceptible to the individual response biases, limited understanding, or misunderstandings inherent in key informant ratings. Finally, organization-sets can be compared statistically with simple difference of proportions or means tests.

Its strength is also a disadvantage, in that an organization-set analysis says little about the overall system of care. Underlying social groupings or structures (e.g., coalitions or cliques) cannot be detected or compared because the technique ignores the lateral connections between set members. In this sense, the organization-set approach requires other contextual data to make it possible to understand why relationships do or do not exist.

Method 3: Blockmodel Analysis

Background and Main Concepts

As described earlier, there are specific situations in which evaluators may be interested in assessing a service system and its change over time or in comparing it with other systems cross-sectionally. Examples are evaluating programs that are specifically intended to alter the structure of an existing system over time (e.g., Morrissey, Calloway, et al., 1994), or comparing systems where a demonstration is underway at one site and a comparison site has no systems intervention (e.g., Randolph, 1995). Because the data used to assess systems of care are gathered on organizational interactions, a focus on systems and their structural profiles requires first that the data be aggregated in some manner. In short, a mathematical or graphical method is needed to transform the information about relationships among all of the organizations into system-level attributes or characteristics.

Within the broader context of network analyses, such an aggregation method exists; it is called blockmodeling (White, Boorman, & Breiger, 1976). Wasserman and Faust (1994) describe blockmodels as "hypotheses about the structure of relations in a social network. These hypotheses refer to positions of actors rather than to individuals, and they summarize features of the entire network in a multi-relational system" (p. 408). The strength and distinctiveness of a blockmodel approach is its ability to aggregate organizations into social positions wherein member organizations have similar relationships within the system. It summarizes the complexity found in a system by focusing on a smaller number of social positions and their interconnections. One of the prerequisites for this approach is that the relationships to be analyzed should involve the patterns of connections among actors in exchange relationships (Emerson, 1972; Turner, 1986). First, the blockmodel approach groups a large number of service organizations into a smaller number of social positions or blocks. It then assesses the existence of important service linkages among the identified positions. By focusing on social positions and their multiple ties across exchange relationships, blockmodels provide a way to develop a structural profile of a given service system. This depiction of systems as relationships among positions, rather than as averages across all organizations in a system, distinguishes a blockmodel approach from other network approaches.

Data Collection and Analysis

The first stage in a blockmodel approach is determining the number and composition of system positions based on interorganizational exchange relationships (see for review Borgatti, Everett, & Freeman, 1992; DiMaggio, 1987; Mizruchi & Galaskiewicz, 1993). Traditionally, blockmodel approaches view social actors or groups that are involved in similar relationships with all others in their network as enacting similar or equivalent roles. Structural equivalence (SE), being a proxy for similar status or role sets, has become an often used criterion for grouping social actors in network studies (see Burt, 1982, p. 271; Burt & Minor, 1983, p. 330).

Multirelational data, like those used in the organization-set analysis, are likewise used in a blockmodel approach. Computationally, equivalent positions are identified by developing a distance score between each actor pair taken across all other actors in the network, across all relationships (Burt, 1982). Those organizations with similar distance scores are considered role equivalent. These distance scores are then clustered, resulting in groups of actors that are very similar to all other organizations (role equivalent) in their group in their day-to-day exchange relationships. For example, it could be argued that inpatient and outpatient units have very different sets of organizations they routinely interact with, suggesting that each unit plays a distinct role in the service-delivery system.

A second stage in a blockmodel approach is the determination of the relationships among the positions, or blocks, that have been empirically identified through structural equivalence. The patterns of structural equivalence among organizations within defined networks can be analyzed as "stacked" networks (Schott, 1991). That is, multiple networks can, and should, be used in the determination of the positions. The computational algorithm constrains organizational occupants to be structurally equivalent in all relational networks. The end result of computing SE across multiple exchange networks in a system is an S by S nonsymmetric matrix (where S is the number of derived positions) of 0/1 data for each individual exchange network and, if multiple time points are used, for each time point. Thus, in the context of an analysis over time, the number and composition (member agencies) of the positions remain constant across networks and time points; only the relationships between the positions vary, as a function of the specific interactions enacted in each network. Structural profiles are then constructed based on the relational characteristics of the SE positions found across multiple networks and possibly multiple time points.

The S by S matrix is a "blockmodel" of the system of relationships. This image matrix is the data source for developing systems profiles. Profiles are constructed using traditional network measures that assess characteristics of the relationships, such as strength, mutuality, and direction, using the blockmodels as input data. Three particular measures have been used extensively to characterize the structure of a network as depicted by blockmodels:

- *Density:* The extent of linkage or connectivity among social positions, measured as the proportion of actual links among positions over the total possible links (Knoke & Kuklinski, 1986). The density index ranges from 0 (absence of links) to 1 (all possible links present).

- *Centralization:* The extent of hierarchy in the system or the degree to which a social position dominates the receiving or sending of valued resources available to the network. Centrality scores of network organizations are routinely normalized by the most central actor (Burt, 1982), so that the centralization index varies from 0 (no hierarchy) to 1 (complete hierarchy).

- *Fragmentation:* The tendency for agencies to cluster together into cohesive subsystems (cliques) without many ties to agencies in other positions in the same network. Fragmentation is characterized by the majority of network ties being intrapositional rather than interpositional. It is measured by a special clique detection algorithm (Bolland & Wilson, 1994). Like density and centralization, the fragmentation index varies from 0 (positions completely integrated) to 1 (positions completely isolated).

The choice of measures is at the discretion of the researcher, depending upon the situation at hand. The point to be made here is that the profiles are a rich source of information (taken directly from the blockmodels); they are representations of the system based on multiple relationships comparable across systems, from which a host of network measures can be derived and compared (see Calloway et al., 1993, for a thorough discussion).

Illustration

The following illustration of a blockmodel approach is taken from a study of the Robert Wood Johnson's Children's Initiative, a project aimed at improving mental health service systems for children. The data come from a two-county area of North Carolina, and the details of the study are given elsewhere (Johnsen, Morrissey, and Calloway, 1996; Morrissey et al., 1997). Given the major goal of the demonstration of integrating service sectors, it was anticipated that the systems of care would change structurally over time. The structural change anticipated was for the systems to become more densely connected, less fragmented across service sectors, and a centralization of activity around the lead mental health providers.

The major focus of the evaluation was on measuring changes in two systems of care over time. This was accomplished by using the interorganizational relationships across three exchanges of critical organizational resources: clients, funding, and information for two time periods (Johnsen et al., 1996). Use of these particular relationships is based on a well-established tradition of interorganizational network research (Levine & White, 1961; Van de Ven & Ferry, 1980), whose metric properties have been extensively discussed elsewhere (Calloway et al., 1993; Marsden, 1990). To maximize reliability of these items in data collection, several steps were taken, including an instrument that provided respondents with a complete list of organizations composing their local service systems, matrices composed of confirmed ties only, and the use of multiple relations (client referrals, funding, and information flow).

Using a distance score calculated on the relational data, a structural equivalence analysis was conducted resulting in identification of structural positions in both systems (see Table 11.3). Using these blockmodels, the relationships among and between the positions in each of the systems were examined using traditional network measures: density, centrality and fragmentation. A brief look at the results in Table 11.3 demonstrates the ability of network analyses and blockmodeling to quantify and compare system-level profiles both across systems and across time.

Table 11.3

Structural Comparison of Two County Service Networks
Serving Children with SED

	Urban		Rural	
	T1	T2	T1	T2
Total Number of Agencies	41	49	27	33
Number of Structural Positions	7	6	7	3
Number of Residual Agencies	0	0	4	2
Density				
Client Referral	.51	.53	.48	.60
Funding	.18	.25	.04	.20**
Information	.57	.53	.49	.68*
Centralization				
Client Referral	.45	.46	.39	.28
Funding	.64	.68	1.00	.81**
Information	.96	1.00	.38	.28
Fragmentation				
Client Referral	.29	.13*	.41	.38
Funding	1.00[1]	1.00[1]	1.00[1]	.93*
Information	.63	.67	.27	.75**

Note. From "Structure and Change in Child Mental Health Service Delivery Networks," by M. C. Johnsen, J. P. Morrissey, and M. O. Calloway, 1996, *Journal of Community Psychology,* 24(3), pp. 275–289. Reprinted by permission.

[1]Funding exchanges are so infrequent that calculation of fragmentation involves division by 0.
*$p < .05$. **$p < .01$.

Although there were many more organizations in the urban system providing services to children with SED, the blockmodel results identified an equal number of structural positions in both systems at T1 (7). The positions identified were typical for these systems and included case management services, social services, school-based services, community residential services, community mental health services, residential treatment services, and an isolate group (see Figure 11.1a and b for the urban system). Looking at each of the three relationships (clients, funds, and information) and the three network indicators (density, centralization, and fragmentation), there appears to be significant change in the structure of the rural system of care, particularly in the funding and information exchanges. This change is also indicated by a fewer

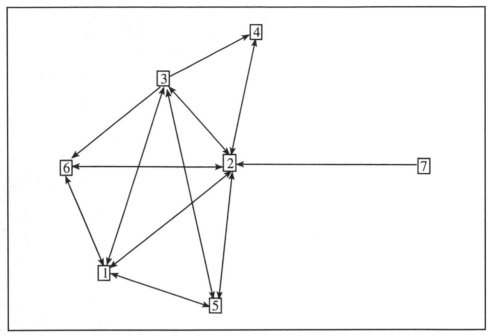

Figure 11.1a. Urban client referral blockmodel T1: 1. Schools 2. Case management 3. Social services 4. Residential (group homes) 5. Community mental health 6. Residential (treatment) 7. Isolates. From "Structure and Change in Child Mental Health Service Delivery Networks," by M. C. Johnsen, J. P. Morrissey, & M. O. Calloway, 1996, *Journal of Community Psychology, 24*(3), 275–289. Copyright 1996 by M. C. Johnsen et al. Reprinted with permission.

number of social positions at T2 in the rural system. The only notable change in the urban system was that it became significantly less fragmented in the client exchanges over time. While there were changes in the patterning of client exchanges in the rural system, they were not statistically significant as determined by difference-of-proportions tests. In short, both systems experienced structural changes over the life of the demonstration, but the rural system underwent relatively more change than did the urban system.

Discussion

The blockmodel approach is a very powerful and parsimonious method for characterizing and assessing system change. This focus on the system-level distinguishes a blockmodel approach. It is capable of reducing the amount of information significantly for presentation, even though it uses all the network activity to find results. Furthermore, blockmodels allow for assessment over

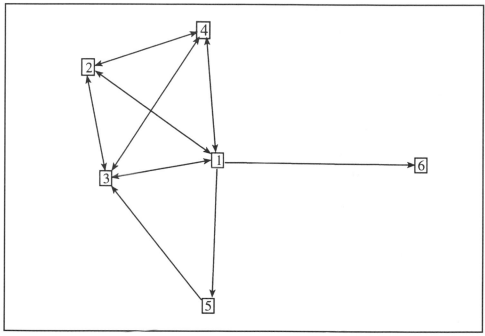

Figure 11.1b. Urban client referral blockmodel T2: 1. Social services 2. Juvenile detention 3. CMH/Schools/Case management 4. Residential (emergency) 5. Mixed clinical services 6. Residential. From "Structure and Change in Child Mental Health Service Delivery Networks," by M. C. Johnsen, J. P. Morrissey, & M. O. Calloway, 1996, *Journal of Community Psychology, 24*(3), 275–289. Copyright 1996 by M. C. Johnsen et al. Reprinted with permission.

time in a more straightforward way than some network procedures. The results of blockmodels can also be used as data input for calculating traditional network indices in order to build system profiles for comparisons over time. The method has theoretical linkages to a well-established sociological and anthropological literature that focuses on characterizing social systems. Also, the data used for the analysis are the same as those used in other network analyses (e.g., organization-set and k-core analyses) and therefore is an extension of less complex analyses of system participants. Further, the findings of the blockmodel can be used to impute attributes to organizations based on their location in the system that help identify causes for behavior at the organizational level. Finally, blockmodels have accompanying "goodness of fit" statistics that allow for testing of the observed data to some hypothesized or expected data (Wasserman and Faust, 1994, pp. 679–692).

A major disadvantage to a blockmodel approach is its focus. It does not allow an easy method for depicting an organization's linkages to other organizations. While one can make statements about the centrality of a position, one does not have this information for particular organizations. Additional knowledge about the organizations in the system is required in order to understand and name the positions that are found. The results of a blockmodel analysis do not stand on their own. Also, a blockmodel approach requires the use of special social network packages along with other available statistical packages. While this process is manageable, the analysis does require more time than a typical network analysis based on organization sets, or even other network-based techniques like k-cores. The algorithm uses structural equivalence based on similarity or dissimilarity measures and is therefore not based on cohesion (this may or may not be a disadvantage). The derived structure of a system is dependent upon this understanding. Finally, an analysis over time based on blockmodels must either use a positional approach, in which organizations are allowed to move freely across positions over time, or a relational position, in which the organizations are fixed in a position over time and only their relationships are allowed to vary. The analyst must choose one or the other approach—both cannot be done simultaneously.

Method 4: K-Core Analysis

Background and Main Concepts

One of the practical issues that can arise in service system demonstration studies is whether the criterion for measuring the success of the demonstration should be based on the entire network or only on some smaller constellation of agencies. For example, mental health "system-of-care" service networks in large urban areas may include more than 80 agencies and organizational subunits. Among the goals of an intervention such as the Johnson Foundation's Mental Health Program for Youth (England & Cole, 1992) might be to increase the integration and performance of the participating systems over time. This goal may be unrealistic, however, given the relatively small amount of grantee funds provided. A more viable approach may be for the lead agency to channel efforts at a smaller subset of agencies and the integration of this subnetwork. Under these circumstances, the basis for performance and impact evaluations may be the subset of agencies rather than the whole network.

To evaluate these differences, it may be important for a services network researcher to understand how the relations in a particular network are structured into core and periphery. Intuitively, the core is an area of a network in which agencies are more cohesive and richly connected than in other areas of the network. The core is defined by the presence of many ties between organizational members to a relatively greater degree than are organizations in the periphery. The periphery of a network consists of isolated or disconnected organizations. Peripheral organizations are characterized not by the presence of ties, but rather by their absence. In the current operationalization of periphery, organizations within that network zone have either no ties with other organizations in the network or are included in only one significant relation. Finally, the term *semiperiphery* is used to represent organizations whose relations are somewhat ambiguous and not easily placed in either the core or periphery. As defined here, to identify areas of core, semiperiphery, and periphery within networks requires a way of assessing cohesion and the lack of it within areas in these networks.

A mathematical approach to identifying cohesive subgroups that allows for distinctions between core and periphery is known as k-core analysis (Seidman, 1983). A k-core is analogous to the concept of "social circle" (Kadushin, 1966). It provides a method for identifying cohesive subsets of actors in a network of relations among whom there are relatively strong, direct, intense, frequent, or positive ties (Wasserman & Faust, 1994). A k-core defines areas or zones of a network of relations in terms of the minimum number (k) of adjacencies (links) that must be present within a subset of agencies (denoted C). The value of k may vary from 0 (no nodes connected) to N-1 (all nodes directly linked to each other within one step). As a formal definition:

> Let the set of nodes C_k denote a k-core. The set of organizations C_k is a k-core if, when attention is restricted to them and the ties connecting them (without going outside it), each node receives at least k ties.

Thus, each member of a C_3 k-core must have at least three ties with other members of the C_3 core set of nodes. Members of this core may have more than three ties, but all members must have at least three ties. In sum, in the present application, the core is the set of organizations with the highest k-value, the periphery is the set with the smallest k-values, and the semiperiphery refers too all the k-values in between.

Data Collection and Analysis

The data requirements for a k-core analysis are the same as those described for sets and blockmodels elsewhere in this chapter. K-core analysis uses the complete set of network data. The analyses begin with data matrices in which the *ij* cells indicate "send" or "receive" relationships from organization *i* to organization *j* (for *i* and *j* = 1 to *N*) in the network. K-cores are identified in each independent exchange network (clients, funds, and information) at two points in time (T1, 1991; T2, 1993) and are then used to map the structure of core and peripheral agencies within the child SED service systems. The requirement is for square matrices, so missing data are unacceptable. Furthermore, currently available software (UCNET-IV) works only with symmetric matrices (Borgatti et al., 1992).

Within a particular analysis, system structure and change can be detected by looking at differences in k-cores between time points in relation to three indices:

- *Core extensity:* This measure is a simple count of the number of organizations included within the k-cores of the service system. Increases in these counts at a given k-value are one indication of improvement in system cohesion.

- *Interactive intensity:* This measure is inferred from the highest k-value attained by a system. As k increases there is evidence of more intense levels of interaction within a system of relations. In the present context, comparisons of the k-values of the innermost k-cores is used to assess differences in interactive intensity within and between the two county systems of care.

- *System concentration:* This is another index for comparing systems. It is based on the proportion of organizations in the system that are located within the highest valued k-core. As this proportion increases, systems are becoming more concentrated as more and more of the network activity (e.g., referring clients, exchanging funds, sharing information) is spread across a broader range of agencies.

Illustration

To illustrate the use of k-cores, we provide findings from the study of child mental health services in two western North Carolina counties that participated in the RWJF Children's Initiative, designed to improve system integration (Morrissey et al., 1997). One county was predominantly rural, while the other was urban. Data were collected at two points in time, once early in the demonstration and one near the end of the demonstration.

Given the demonstration's goal of developing a more cohesive service system, it is hypothesized that core extensity, interactive intensity, and concentration will increase in both systems from T1 to T2. In addition, successful implementation of the demonstration should also result in a repositioning of agencies such that community-based services (e.g., case management) are drawn into higher k-cores, whereas others (e.g., inpatient hospitalization and institutional services) gravitate to lower and more peripheral k-cores. To test the significance of changes in core extensity, a Z-test for difference of proportions is employed with the number of agencies in the county at each time period as the denominator for the core extensity tests, and the core extensity value reported in the table as the numerator.

Table 11.4 presents the quantitative results of the k-core analysis for the urban and rural system at each time point. At T1, the rural system (27 organizations) is both smaller and more cohesive than the urban system (41 organizations). The urban system (k = 7) has a slightly higher intensity than the rural system (k = 6), but the latter has a much higher extensity within its highest k-cores. The highest k is 13, in the rural system; it is only 10 in the urban system. The rural system is also much more concentrated than the urban system, with a significantly larger proportion of agencies in its highest k-core (.24 vs. .48, $p < .01$).

Table 11.4

Size and Cohesiveness of Two Networks for Children with SED

	Urban			Rural		
	T1	**T2**	**Diff**	**T1**	**T2**	**Diff**
Total number of agencies	41	49	+8	27	33	+6
System Concentration Index	.24	.45	+.21	.48	.42	−.06
Interactive Intensity Index (K-value of maximum K-core)	7	9	+2	6	8	+2
K-core Extensity						
K = 9	0	22	22**	0	0	0
K = 8	0	24	24**	0	14	14**
K = 7	10	26	16**	0	14	14**
K = 6	18	29	11	13	16	3
K = 5	26	31	5	14	20	6
K = 4	29	33	4	18	23	5
K = 3	35	38	3	21	25	4
K = 2	37	40	3	22	27	5
K = 1	38	46	8	25	28	3

Note. From Morrisey, J. P., Johnsen, M.C., & Calloway, M. O. (1997). Evaluating performance and change in mental health systems serving children and youth: An interorganizational network approach. *Journal of Mental Health Administration, 24*(1), 9.

$**p < .01$.

The agency composition of the k-cores in the two systems are quite similar. The cores are populated by agencies that are key members of the interagency councils (mental health, social services, juvenile justice, schools, residential) developed by the RWJF initiative. The periphery contains agencies with no or few ties (e.g., Alliance for the Mentally Ill, state hospital adolescent unit, other private agencies). Thus, the key differences between the two systems at T1 appear to be in overall size and concentration, rather than in the core/periphery structure of the systems of care for children and youth with a SED.

By T2, significant changes had occurred in the interagency relationships within and between the two child SED systems. First, in both counties, there are notably more organizations and organizational subunits in the child SED system. This growth (about a 20% increase for each county) is consistent with the RWJF demonstration's goal of developing a broader continuum of care for children and families in these communities. Second, within the urban system, there is also evidence of greater cohesiveness between organizations on the three measures of extensity, interactive intensity, and system concentration. At each k-value, there are more organizations represented within the k-cores at T2 than at T1. Further, there is an indication that at every level of the network the urban system became more extensive, with more agencies drawn into contact with one another. In terms of interactive intensity, the core agencies have even more connections with each other at T2 (indicated by the fact that the highest k-level at T1 was 7 and included 10 agencies, while at T2 the highest k-level was 9 and included 22 agencies). In addition, as can be seen from Table 11.4, the overall system in the urban county became significantly more concentrated at T2 (.45 vs. .24, $p < .01$).

While the core of the urban system at T1 consisted of units of the host mental health center and the local social services department, by T2 this core had expanded to include the schools, many other units of the mental health center, units of the county department of social services, the sheriff, police, juvenile detention and juvenile counseling, as well as several residential programs (Morrissey et al., in press). The tremendous expansion of the core suggests that the overall network of services became better connected and that the system was characterized by a larger core of organizations over the course of the demonstration.

In contrast, the structure of the rural system changed little between the two time points. As can be seen from Table 11.4, there was a slight decrease in the overall concentration of the system between T1 and T2 (.48 vs. .42) and a slight increase in interactive intensity (from $k = 6$ to $k = 8$). The agency composition of the core was already quite comprehensive at T1, and it remained so between T1 and T2. In effect, the intensity of interaction among agencies in this zone increased only somewhat. At the same time, the periphery of the system expanded because a number of the new agencies added at T2 fell into the outermost or isolate area (i.e., $k = 0$). Finally, while many community-based organizations are included near the network core, regional resources such as the state psychiatric hospital and other regional private psychiatric hospitals became more peripheral at T2. In a sense, then, as the system became more adept at dealing with children with SED within community-based settings, the importance of these regionally based organizations declined.

A graphic representation of the k-core analysis is presented in Figure 11.2. Here k-cores are depicted as concentric circles with the size of the outermost circles proportionate to the overall size of each system. Both the T1 (1991) and T2 (1993) networks for the urban and rural sites are displayed. The band width of these circles is proportionate to the number of organizations within each k-core. What is notable in these diagrams is the extent of system concentration, or the size of the highest k-core (the innermost circle) relative to the size of the overall network (the outermost circle). At T1, the rural system was smaller (27 vs.

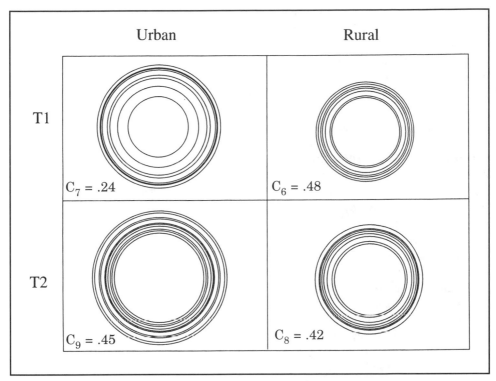

Figure 11.2. Graphic representation of system change using k-cores in an urban and a rural child mental health service system.

41 organizations) but more structurally concentrated (.48 vs. .24) than the urban system. Over time, the rural system grew slightly in overall size (by 6 organizations, or 20%), but its structural concentration (.42) remained about the same. The urban system experienced a proportionate growth in size (by 8 organizations, or 20%), but, in contrast, it experienced a significant increase in its structural concentration (from .24 to .45). Over time, there was evidence for the convergence of the two systems toward a moderate level of system concentration, with more than 40% of the agencies participating in the core sector of the overall systems. Further, the urban system at T2 mirrored the structure of the rural system at T1.

Discussion

The measures derived from k-cores represent a valuable additional tool for researchers interested in understanding and characterizing mental health service systems and their associated patterns of system integration. In addition, these tools can be particularly helpful in studies that are looking for similarities and differences across several systems.

K-cores appear to have some advantages over other methods of network analysis. They provide an intuitive way of understanding and describing the core and periphery of a network. Unlike an organization-set approach, the k-core approach provides researchers with a clear sense of an organization's place within a network—that is, whether a particular focal organization is located in the core or periphery of the network. Like the blockmodel approach, and unlike the key informant approach, k-core analysis relies on relational information about interorganizational service networks, and arguably may be less susceptible to individual response biases or misunderstanding of key informant ratings. Compared with blockmodel analytic approaches, k-cores have the advantage of relative ease of conceptualization and computation. Once data about network relations have been arrayed in matrix form, network analysis software programs can easily be used to conduct these analyses. Simple difference-of-proportions tests can be employed on the k-core indices to compare several different systems or the same systems across time.

There are also several limitations of this approach. Because k-cores have not been used much in describing human service networks, it is not yet clear what typical patterns of concentration, extensity, and reach within mental health service delivery systems are, much less what levels would be associated with ideal system performance. Further work is needed to understand more fully the characteristics associated with such performance using cohesion-based measures like k-cores. Similar to blockmodel approaches, k-core analysis requires relational information about the complete network, and therefore is somewhat more labor intensive (and expensive) in its application than either key informant or organization-set approaches. The use of k-cores helps an investigator to distinguish between system core and periphery in graphic relief. However, it does not describe the roles of organizations or clusters of organizations (positions) within these structures. Approaches involving blockmodels and structural equivalence analysis are better prepared to address questions about particular patterns of interactions that distinguish subsets of actors within the core and peripheral areas of a network.

Summary and Conclusions

In this chapter we have presented an overview of several methods for conducting system-level evaluations of children's mental health services. These methods are based upon the application of interorganizational theory and social network analysis techniques. Although each method can be used as a stand-alone evaluation technique, the presentations in this chapter highlight the utility of using them as an overall strategy for a more complete analysis of system organization and performance. Each method elucidates certain aspects of these systems that are opaque or only partially observable through the use of the other methods. When employed together, the four methods provide a telescoping capacity to view service systems from their global performance (key informant approach) to their macrostructures (blockmodels) and micro-structures (focal organizations and k-cores).

Thus there are many advantages to integrating network and survey research methods in research and evaluations of service systems. Key informant ratings can measure a set of global performance attributes (adequacy, quality, availability, and coordination) applicable to any service system. These measures provide information that cannot be ascertained with network approaches. Items can be inserted in a key informant survey that can be used to assess the quality of the day-to-day activity that goes beyond the mere existence of interagency linkages. Information about a wide range of topics dealing with services, administrative procedures, financing, and program philosophies can supplement network measures based on the relational properties of the system. Such measures can then be used to validate, corroborate, or extend findings obtained from network approaches.

There are a number of advantages to using interorganizational network methods for the description and assessment of multiagency service-delivery systems. K-cores can identify zones within the system of care that demarcate groups of agencies with increasing density of linkages. Measures of k-core extensity, intensity, and concentration can be used to compare and assess the scope of linkage formation and its changes over time within and between systems of interest. A defining feature of k-cores is the ability to display results in an intuitively appealing graphic form.

A multimethod approach that includes the collection of informant ratings and interorganizational network data may open the black box of system performance and ultimately permit the development of a more explicit understanding of the connections between systems change and client outcomes. To date, none of the large-scale mental health demonstrations for children or for adults have found a close connection between service system improvements and client outcomes. The jury is still out as to whether the absence of client-level effects in these studies represents a failure of theory, of method, or of implementation (Bickman, 1996; Friedman & Burns, 1996). The conclusion derived from the evaluation of the RWJ Program for Chronic Mental Illness is that service system change is a necessary, but not a sufficient, condition for improving client-level outcomes (Goldman, Morrissey, & Ridgely, 1994). Rather, improvements at the client level require service system change in combination with consistent treatment interventions. Studies to demonstrate the validity of this conclusion for children's services have yet to be undertaken, but the ACCESS evaluation (Randolph, 1995) will test this hypothesis for adults who are homeless and severely mentally ill.

The goal that still remains elusive in services research is a set of empirically based principles for the design and management of mental health service systems. The methods described in this chapter provide one set of tools for describing and assessing the organization and performance of systems of care. The challenge for the research community is to identify opportunities whereby the interface between systems and client outcomes can be better articulated and evaluated. Whether system change, in combination with consistent treatment interventions, can also enhance client outcomes is one of the major unanswered questions in this field. While obtaining clear answers may be difficult to accomplish in the current political climate of retrenchment in human services, it is an agenda that is absolutely crucial for the design and management of mental health services to ensure beneficial outcomes for children and youth. What are most needed to advance this agenda are improved clinical interventions for children who are seriously emotionally disturbed and opportunities to evaluate their joint impacts in field situations.

Authors' Note

The work upon which this chapter is based has been supported by research grants from the National Institute of Mental Health (MH44839; MH48053; MH51410) and the Robert Wood Johnson Foundation (12558).

Correspondence may be sent to Joseph P. Morrissey, Cecil G. Sheps Center for Health Services Research, University of North Carolina at Chapel Hill, 725 Airport Road, Chapel Hill, NC 27599-7590; (919) 966-5829; Fax (919) 966-3811; joe_morrissey@unc.edu.

References

Alter, C., & Hage, J. (1993). *Organizations working together.* Newbury Park: Sage.

Attkisson, C., Hargreaves, W., Horowitz, M., & Sorensen, J. (Eds.). (1978). *Evaluation of human service programs.* San Francisco: Academic Press.

Bickman, L. (1995). A continuum of care: More is not always better. *American Psychologist, 51*(7), 689–701.

Bickman, L. (1996). Reinterpreting the Fort Bragg Evaluation findings: The message does not change. *Journal of Mental Health Administration, 23*(1), 137–145.

Blalock, H. M. (1972). *Social statistics* (2nd ed.). New York: McGraw-Hill.

Bolland, J., & Wilson, J. (1994). Three faces of integrative coordination: A model of interorganizational relations in community-based health and human services. *Health Services Research, 29*(3), 341–366.

Borgatti, S., Everett, M., & Freeman, L. (1992). *UCINET IV, 1.0.* Columbia, SC: Analytic Technologies.

Burns, B., Farmer, E. M. Z., Morrissey, J., Angold, A., Costello, J., & Behar, L. (1994). Effects of case management from the RWJ children's initiative in North Carolina. Paper presented at the annual meeting of the American Public Health Association, Washington, DC.

Burt, R. (1982). *Toward a structural theory of action.* New York: Academic Press.

Burt, R., & Minor, M. (1983). *Applied network analysis: A methodological introduction.* Beverly Hills: Sage.

Calloway, M., Morrissey, J., & Paulson, R. (1993). Accuracy and reliability of self-reported data in interorganizational networks. *Social Networks, 15,* 377–398.

Ciarlo, J. A., Tweed, D. L., Shern, D. L., Kirkpatrick, L. E., & Sachs-Ericsson, N. (1992). Validation of indirect methods to estimate need for mental health services: Concepts, strategy, and general conclusions. *Evaluation and Program Planning, 15,* 115–131.

DiMaggio, P. (1987). Structural analysis of organizational fields: A blockmodel approach. *Research in Organizational Studies, 2,* 229–247.

DiMaggio, P., & Powell, W. (1983, April). The iron cage revisited: Institutional isomorphism and collective rationality in organizational fields. *American Sociological Review, 48,* 147–160.

Duchnowski, A., & Freidman, R. (1990). Children's mental health: Challenges for the nineties. *Journal of Mental Health Administration, 17*(1), 3–12.

Emerson, R. (1972). Exchange theory, part II: Exchange relations and networks. In J. Berger & B. Anderson (Eds.), *Sociological theories in progress,* (Vol. 2). Boston: Houghton Mifflin.

England, M. J., & Cole, R. F. (1992). Building systems of care for youth with serious mental illness. *Hospital and Community Psychiatry, 43*(6), 630–633.

Evan, W. (1972). An organization-set model of interorganizational relations. In M. Tuite & R. K. Chisholm (Eds.), *Interorganizational decision making* (pp. 181–200). New York: Aldine-Atherton.

Friedman, R. M., & Burns, B. J. (1996). The evaluation of the Fort Bragg demonstration project: An alternative interpretation of the findings. *Journal of Mental Health Administration, 23*(1), 128–136.

Glisson, D., & James, L. (1992). The interorganizational coordination of services to children in state custody. *Administration in Social Work, 16*(3/4), 65–80.

Goldman, H., Lehman, A., Morrissey, J., Newman, S., Frank, R., & Steinwachs, D. (1990). Design for the national evaluation of the Robert Wood Johnson Foundation program on chronic mental illness. *Hospital and Community Psychiatry, 41*(11), 1217–1230.

Goldman, H., Morrissey, J., & Ridgely, M. (1994). Evaluating the Robert Wood Johnson Foundation Program on chronic mental illness. *Milbank Quarterly, 72*(1), 37–47.

Goldsmith, H. F., Jackson, D. J., Doenhoefer, S., Johnson, W., Tweed, D. L., Stiles, D., Barbaro, J. P., & Warheit, G. (1984). *The Health Demographic Profile system's Inventory of Small Area Social Indicators.* Washington, DC: Superintendent of Documents, U.S. Government Printing Office.

Johnsen, M. C., Morrissey, J. P., & Calloway, M. O. (1996). Structure and change in child mental health service delivery networks. *Journal of Community Psychology, 24*(3), 275–289.

Kadushin, C. (1966). The friends and supporters of psychotherapy: On social circles in urban life. *American Sociological Review, 31,* 786–802.

Knitzer, J. (1982). Unclaimed children. Washington, DC: Children's Defense Fund.

Knoke, D., & Kuklinski, J. (1982). *Network analysis.* Beverly Hills: Sage.

Lauffer, A. (1978). *Social planning at the community level.* Englewood Cliffs, NJ: Prentice Hall.

Lehman, A., Postrado, L., Roth, D., McNary, S., & Goldman, H. (1994). An evaluation of continuity of care, case management, and client outcomes in the Robert Wood Johnson Program on chronic mental illness. *Milbank Quarterly, 72*(1), 105–122.

Levine, S., & White, P. (1961). Exchange as a conceptual framework for the study of interorganizational relationships. *Administrative Science Quarterly, 5,* 583–601.

Marsden, P. V. (1990). Network data and measurement. In W. R. Scott & J. Blake (Eds.), *Annual Review of Sociology* (pp. 435–463). New York: Annual Reviews.

Minor, M. (1983). Panal data on ego networks: A longitudinal study of former heroin addicts. In R. Burt & M. Minor (Eds.), *Applied network analysis: A methodological introduction.* Beverly Hills, CA: Sage.

Mizruchi, M. S., & Galaskiewicz, J. (1993). Networks of interorganizational relations. *Sociological Methods and Research, 22*(1), 46–70.

Morrissey, J. (1992). An interorganizational network approach to evaluating children's mental health service systems. In L. Bickman & D. Rog (Eds.), *New directions for program evaluation.* San Francisco: Jossey-Bass.

Morrissey, J., Calloway, M., Johnsen, M., & Ullman, M. (1997). Service system performance and integration: A baseline profile of the ACCESS demonstration sites. *Psychiatric Services, 48*(3), 374–380.

Morrissey, J., Ridgely, S., Goldman, H., & Bartko, W. T. (1994). Assessments of community mental health support systems: A key informant approach. *Community Mental Health Journal, 30*(6), 565–579.

Morrissey, J., Tausig, M., & Lindsey, M. (1985). Network analysis methods for mental health service system research: A comparison of two community support systems. (DHHS Publication No ADM 85-1383). National Institute of Mental Health. BN No. 6. Washington, DC: Government Printing Office.

Morrissey, J. P., Calloway, M., Bartko, W. T., Ridgley, S., Goldman, H., & Paulson, R. I. (1994). Local mental health authorities and service system change: Evidence from the Robert Wood Johnson Foundation Program on Chronic Mental Illness. *Milbank Quarterly, 72*(1), 49–80.

Morrissey, J. P., Johnsen, M. C., & Calloway, M. O. (1997). Evaluating performance and change in mental health systems serving children and youth: An interorganizational network approach. *Journal of Mental Health Administration, 24*(1), 4–22.

Nunnally, J. C., & Bernstein, I. H. (1994). *Psychometric Theory* (3rd. ed.) New York: McGraw-Hill.

Pfeffer, J., & Salancik, G. R. (1978). *The external control of organizations: A resource dependence perspective.* New York: Harper and Row.

Provan, K. G., & Milward, H. B. (1991). Institutional-level norms and organizational involvement in a service-implementation network. *Journal of Public Administration Research and Theory, 1*(4), 391–417.

Provan, K. G., & Milward, H. G. (1995). *Toward a theory of network effectiveness: A comprehensive study of network structure, context, and outcomes in community mental health.* Unpublished manuscript, University of Kentucky, Lexington.

Randolph, F. (1995). Improving service systems through systems integration: The ACCESS program. *American Rehabilitation, 21*(1), 36–38.

Roemer, R., Kramer, C., & Frink, J. (1975). *Planning urban health services: From jungle to system.* New York: Springer.

Schott, T. (1991). Network models: Structural equivalence. In R. Burt (Eds.), *STRUCTURE: Version 4.2 Reference Manual.* New York: Columbia University.

Scott, J. (1991). *Social network analysis: A handbook.* London: Sage.

Seidman, S. B. (1983, September). Network structure and minimum degree. *Social Networks, 5,* 269–287.

Shore, M., & Cohen, M. (1990). The Robert Wood Johnson Foundation program on chronic mental illness: An overview. *Hospital and Community Psychiatry, 41*(11), 1212–1216.

Stroul, B. A. (1993). *Systems of care for children and adolescents with severe emotional disturbances: What are the results?* Washington, DC: Georgetown University Child Development Center, CASSP Technical Assistance Center.

Stroul, B., & Friedman, R. (1986). *A system of care for severely emotionally disturbed children and youth.* Tampa: University of South Florida, CASSP Technical Assistance Center.

Sudman, S. (1976). *Applied Sampling.* New York: Academic Press.

Turner, J. (1986). *The structure of sociological theory.* Homewood, IL: Dorsey.

Turner, J., & TenHoor, W. (1978). The NIMH community support program: Pilot approach to a needed social reform. *Schizophrenia Bulletin, 4*(3), 319–408.

Van de Ven, A., & Ferry, D. (1980). *Measuring and assessing organizations.* New York: Wiley.

Wasserman, S., & Faust, K. (1994). *Social network analysis: Methods and applications.* New York: Cambridge University Press.

White, H. C., Boorman, S. A., & Breiger, R. L. (1976). Social structure from multiple networks I: Blockmodels of roles and positions. *American Journal of Sociology, 81,* 730–780.

Assessing the Child and Family Outcomes of Systems of Care for Youth with Serious Emotional Disturbance

12

Abram Rosenblatt

As chronicled throughout this book, innovative care systems and service interventions designed to address and remedy the plight of children and adolescents with serious emotional disturbance (SED) spread exponentially in the last decade, through both local and federal initiatives. There is considerable excitement, enthusiasm, and hope regarding the potential of these innovations to provide better care for children and their families. Nonetheless, there is also considerable dread, doubt, and worry about the future of reform efforts. Federal, state, and local human services budgets are facing the closest scrutiny in years as resources become increasingly scarce. New models of health care delivery generally subsumed under the rubric of managed care are creating uncertainty regarding the future of reform efforts in children's services (Stroul, 1996).

It is just this trepidation about the future that is feeding a groundswell of interest in whether systems of care are an effective and efficient model of service delivery that can survive in a rapidly changing human service delivery environment. Although a number of research programs deriving from investments in child services research capacity over the last several years are beginning to yield results, the research findings remain limited. Few of the research results are published (Burns & Friedman, 1990; Stroul, 1993), making an evaluation of the quality of the findings difficult. Consequently, in spite of a number of notable local and state attempts to reform service systems, critically needed information regarding effective treatment and service system strategies was either unavailable or incomplete during the recent federal health care reform process of 1993–94 (McGuire, Frank, & Goldman, 1992; National Advisory Mental Health Council, 1993; Scallet, 1994).

In part, the lack of information on systems of care for youth with SED derives from the difficulty in conducting outcome studies of these multilayered systems. In this chapter the outcomes of system-of-care research are reviewed in the context of the central challenges to assessing the effectiveness of these reform efforts. These challenges are grouped into three core questions pertaining to outcomes research: (a) What is the independent variable (in this case, a system of care)?; (b) What is an "outcome"?; and (c) How are the independent variable and the outcomes linked, and what is the methodology? The chapter concludes with an overview of the strengths and weaknesses of the knowledge base regarding child and family outcomes of systems of care for children with SED. Implications for the future are also discussed.

The Problem of the "Independent Variable": What is a System of Care?

By any definition, a system of care is a complex intervention, and this chapter does not attempt to comprehensively define a system of care (see instead National Institute of Mental Health [NIMH], 1983; Stroul & Friedman, 1986). Nonetheless, an understanding of the levels of a system of care is essential to assessing the outcomes of a system of care. Although human service systems can be analyzed from a wide range of perspectives, current research on systems of care tends to focus on three levels of analysis: the systems level, the programmatic level, and the clinical level.

The Systems Level: Structure, Organization, and Financing

System level reforms deriving initially out of the mental health sector in the last decade have been dominated by two emergent concepts: the systems-of-care approach described initially by Stroul and Friedman (1986), and the wraparound approach (Burchard & Clark, 1990), associated with pioneering work by Dennis, VanDenBerg, Burchard, Tannen, Lourie, and others and most frequently exemplified by the Kaleidescope program in Chicago, the Alaska Youth Initiative, and project wraparound in Vermont.

The systems of care approach, spearheaded through the National Institute of Mental Health (NIMH) and Center for Mental Health Services (CMHS) Child and Adolescent Service System Program (CASSP), was designed to provide assistance to states and communities in the development of comprehensive, coordinated systems of care for children and adolescents (Day & Roberts,

1991; National Institute of Mental Health, 1983). Local examples of programs firmly rooted in this tradition include Ventura County, California (Jordan & Hernandez, 1990), and North Carolina (Behar, 1985; 1992).

Systems of care place a special emphasis on linkages between child-serving agencies such as mental health, juvenile justice, social welfare, and education, on community-based care in lieu of restrictive placements, on developing a continuum of services, and, in some cases, on measuring the costs and outcomes of care. All of these elements are also essential to the wraparound process (Van-DenBerg & Grealish, 1996). Analogously, although wraparound efforts are historically known for their emphasis on individualized services, on the unconditional provision of care, and on flexible funding, many locales following the systems-of-care approach incorporate these ideals and services into their service arrays. Both systems of care and the wraparound process fully share the principles of involving parents in all aspects of service delivery. They also emphasize providing culturally competent, community-based, integrated care. Results from research on reform efforts that are most firmly rooted in the system-of-care approach to service delivery will be presented in this chapter.

The Program Level: Components of a System of Care

A system of care is composed of programmatic components that can include traditional clinical services such as outpatient and inpatient care or can include more innovative, blended services such as therapeutic foster care, case management, and individualized care. In theory, a system of care should be composed of component services that are themselves effective. However, the overall effectiveness of any of these individual components is not well documented (Kutash & Rivera, 1996). Although some findings are promising, on the whole the evidence is nonexistent, sparse, or not encouraging regarding the positive effectiveness of most individual program components. It is still important to note that the general lack of encouraging findings regarding the components of a system of care does not necessarily preclude discovering more encouraging results for an entire system of care. The whole may be greater than the sum of its parts. Different components may interact with each other to produce effective change.

The Clinical Level: Caseworker Behaviors, Skills, and Tools

Regardless of the level of innovation at the program or system levels, the ultimate success of any care is dependent on what occurs at the "clinical" level. This level refers to the ways in which a caseworker (or a team of caseworkers) interacts directly with children, their families, and their support systems. Clinical interventions in a system of care may include a range of office-based psychotherapeutic approaches such as cognitive-behavioral therapy, family therapy, and play therapy. In a system of care, however, interventions at the clinical level also encompass the interactions of line-level staff with children and families across a continuum of settings and interventions. These settings may include the home, the school, the juvenile courts, and the foster care system. The interventions used in these settings are often loosely articulated and consist of the capacity of line-staff to collaborate successfully with probation officers, teachers, and foster parents in providing services to the child and family.

Considering the range of skills required to work in the natural environments in which children and families live, it is not entirely paradoxical that the voluminous and relatively sophisticated literature on the outcomes of psychotherapy does not adequately inform the development of a system of care, because of a lack of external validity (Weisz, 1988; Weisz, Donenberg, Han, & Kauneckis, 1995). Research on mental health services to children and adolescents at the clinical level has focused on the efficacy of various treatment interventions for a variety of specific disorders. Based on a metaanalysis of outcome studies of psychotherapy for children age 4–18, Weisz, Weiss, Alicke, & Klotz (1987) concluded that the average treated individual was better adjusted after treatment than 79% of those not treated. This cumulative finding may provide support for the efficacy of outpatient psychotherapy interventions provided to children presenting with specific mental health problems and behavioral disorders. In fact, when results from clinic-based trials are examined, the findings are less positive than those conducted in university-based laboratories (Weisz et al., 1995).

Historically, clinical interventions were designed to reside in only one programmatic component of a system of care: outpatient therapy. A similar body of knowledge does not exist regarding more novel treatment approaches such as therapeutically enhanced foster care or individualized service programs. Remarkably little is empirically known about what clinicians actually do when they provide many of the services within more novel care modalities. An exception to this tradition is the work conducted by Henggeler and colleagues on developing Multi Systemic Therapy (MST; Henggeler & Bourduin, 1990; Henggeler, Melton, & Smith, 1992). This treatment approach is consonant with the principles of a system of care and focuses on interventions that are tied to the multiple environments or systems in which a child lives.

Assessing the Intervention: The Strength, Integrity, and Ecology of a System of Care

Given the multilayered nature of systems of care, assessing whether a system can or should be called a "system of care" is a difficult task. Concepts deriving out of program evaluation, such as the strength and integrity of an intervention, can be applied to help understand the dimensions that need to be assessed to determine whether a system of care follows the intent of the model. In addition, complex social interventions such as systems of care evolve and change over time, requiring an ecological approach to understanding the evolution of the care systems.

Strength and Integrity

In order for a program to be effective, it must be implemented with sufficient strength and integrity (e.g. Sechrest, West, Phillips, Redner, & Yeaton, 1977; Sechrest & Rosenblatt, 1987). The most straightforward analogy is to medicine: Penicillin may cure an infection, but if it is administered in an insufficient dose (strength) or on an irregular schedule (integrity), it will not be effective. Similarly, systems of care may constitute a completely correct theory of service delivery. Nonetheless, if the intensity of services that are provided in a given community is insufficient, if interagency coordination is not complete, if staff commitment is lacking, and if programs within a continuum of care are ineffective, then the system of care may not be strong enough to impact on the children and families served. Likewise, if treatment teams are not composed of the people necessary to create change for a child and family, if treatment plans are poorly conceived, if children and families irregularly receive needed services, if target populations are not clearly specified, and if interagency coordination does not exist, then the program as implemented may not have sufficient integrity to the treatment model to achieve results.

The lack of strength and integrity in the implementation of a program can lead to erroneous conclusions regarding whether a program can be effective. As one example, less than a decade ago the general conclusion was that community-based diversion programs for juvenile delinquency did not work (Quay, 1987)—that is, they were no more effective in preventing re-arrests than jail or no treatment. At that point, we examined the literature and found that little attention had been paid to the strength and integrity of the so-called ineffective treatments. In one instance, children and families rarely attended the group therapy sessions that were at the core of a diversion program (Sechrest & Rosenblatt, 1987). As a result, we concluded that the hypothesis of whether community-based treatments could reduce rates of relapse into the juvenile justice system had not been tested, and that little could really be concluded about the effectiveness of community care with this population.

Evaluation and the Ecology of Systems of Care

Ensuring that a system of care has sufficient strength and integrity to create outcomes requires ongoing evaluation of which elements of the care system are effective. Historically, studies that evaluate the implementation of a program were called process (after Cronbach, 1964) or formative (Scriven, 1967) evaluations. These kinds of evaluations stood in contrast to outcome (Cronbach, 1964) or summative (Scriven, 1967) evaluations. Close to two decades ago, however, Tharp and Gallimore (1979) broke down the distinction between these two types of evaluations by applying the language of ecology to social programs. Although these concepts were designed to describe the development of programs, they are perhaps even more applicable to the development of systems. Tharp and Gallimore argued that social programs evolve over time through a series of relatively transitory stages until they reach a stable condition. This stable condition is described as "an association of program elements, organized for and producing a defined social benefit, which will continue to exist, and in which there will not be a replacement by other element types, so long as social values, goals and supporting resources remain constant" (Tharp & Gallimore, 1979, p. 43). They further describe four conditions required for a program to reach this stable state: (a) longevity—stability requires time, (b) stability of values and goals—the program must meet a stable value, (c) stability of funding—a program must remain consistently funded in order to survive, and (d) power of the evaluator—the influence of an evaluator must be maintained to influence the integrity of program research and development.

Taken seriously, the implications for outcomes research of considering the evaluation of systems of care from this ecological framework are profound. Most systems of care are relatively new, and few could meet the aforementioned four conditions for program stability. In particular, few systems of care have an integrated evaluation process that influences system development. Conducting "outcome" evaluations of such programs is liable to produce premature and erroneous results. Put another way, systems that are not in a stable condition are unlikely to have sufficient strength and integrity to achieve results.

The Dependent Variable: Measuring Outcome

A system of care is obviously a complex intervention that attempts to achieve positive change in children and families across a range of behaviors, settings, and contexts. Consequently, the goals of a system of care are highly varied. Ideally, the outcomes of a system of care ought to derive directly from the goals of the care system. Because care systems do not have a single goal, a single outcome can not capture the desired effects of the care system. Just as several authors have pointed out the need for multiple measures and approaches to measuring outcomes both for persons suffering from the most severe disorders (Attkisson et al., 1992; Hargreaves & Shumway, 1989; NIMH, 1991) and for persons suffering from a range of mental disorders (Ciarlo, Brown, Edwards, Kiresuk, & Newman, 1986), so too do outcomes need to be considered from a multidimension framework with respect to children with SED.

The potential list of outcome indicators for children with SED could easily number in the hundreds. It is therefore helpful to have a mechanism for grouping measures on some set of criteria. A model that can be used to stratify the various kinds of measurement that may be undertaken in outcome research on systems of care is summarized below. This model consists of four treatment outcome domains (what is measured), five respondent types (who participates as a respondent), and four behavioral contexts of measurement (where the measured phenomena occur). The model is presented more fully elsewhere (Rosenblatt & Attkisson, 1993).

Systematic Domains of Service Outcome

The first question is the content areas or outcome domains that are included in the conceptual framework. We derive four domains of treatment outcome. In Table 12.1, each of these domains along with examples of measures or indicators of that domain are presented. The first is called the clinical status domain. This domain encompasses the dual concepts of mental and physical health and includes measurement and indices of psychopathology and symptomatology encompassing both classification and severity. The domain thereby focuses on impairments in both psychological and physical status. Measures of clinical status are defined as processes that document and assess the physical, emotional, and cognitive and behavioral signs and symptoms related to disorder. Common measures of clinical status in children include the problem domains of the Child Behavior Checklist (CBCL; Achenbach & Edelbrock, 1993), the Child Depression

Table 12.1

Examples of Measures and Indicators of Outcome Domains

Clinical Status	Functional Status	Life Satisfaction and Fulfillment	Safety and Welfare
• CBCL/YSR Problem Scales	• CBCL/YSR Competency Scales	• Child and parent satisfaction with services	• Presence of abuse or neglect
• Child Depression Inventory	• CAFAS Role Performance Scales	• Family Empowerment Scale	• Presence of criminal victimization.
• CAFAS Moods and Emotions Scale	• Educational attendance and achievement	• Satisfaction with living situation	• Presence of communicable disease
• Diagnostic Interview Schedule for Children (DISC)	• Juvenile justice arrest rates	• Satisfaction with school or work	• Drug or alcohol abuse
		• Self-esteem and happiness	

Inventory (Kovacs, 1991), and the Diagnostic Interview Schedule for Children (DISC; Shaffer, Fisher, Piacentini, Schwab-Stone, & Wicks, 1989).

The second domain, called functional status, captures the ability to effectively fulfill social and role-related functions. This area includes measures of ability to function in a variety of life settings. These functions include the maintenance of interpersonal and familial relationships and the development of school, employment, and vocational capacities. Examples of functional adaptation include the ability to work, attend school, learn, remain in home or maintain independent living, and maintain positive and enhancing social relationships. Common measures or indictors of functional status include the competency domains of the Child Behavior Checklist (Achenbach & Edelbrock, 1993), the role performance scales of the Child and Adolescent Functional Assessment Scale (CAFAS; Hodges et al. 1994), and functional indicators such as re-arrest rates and educational attainment.

The third dimension is called life satisfaction and fulfillment. Contained within this dimension is an attempt to capture the human struggle to achieve some level of personal fulfillment during the course of a life. This domain, in many ways the most conceptually intricate, relies on prior work that defines the meaning of terms such as well-being, life satisfaction, objective quality of life, subjective quality of life, and happiness. The life satisfaction and fulfillment domain focuses on the subjective appraisal of well-being. This is distinguished from subjective quality of life in that subjective quality of life is usually understood to encompass both subjective appraisal of well-being and also positive and negative affect. Affective and mood states are included as part of the clinical status domain within our model and do not need to be included again in this domain. In our model, quality of life and well-being measures will often span the two domains of functional status and life satisfaction. Importantly, life satisfaction may include satisfaction with services, as measured by instruments such as the Client Satisfaction Questionnaire (Attkisson & Greenfield, 1995). Life satisfaction may also include a family's sense of empowerment, as measured by instruments such as the Family Empowerment Survey (Koren, DeChillo, & Friesen, 1992).

The final domain, welfare and safety, encompasses the safety and welfare problems posed by SED to the individual, the family, their social network, and the community in which they live. Such problems include self-injurious behaviors and acts such as suicide, substance abuse, and lack of basic sanitation; infectious diseases such as AIDS, other sexually transmitted diseases, and tuberculosis; abuse, neglect, or other forms of violence suffered by the youth; and violent and illegal acts committed by the youth.

Type of Respondent

Measures of outcome must reflect a range of social perspectives. The range of respondent types in the outcome frame can include: (a) the client, (b) family members, (c) members of the social network, (d) clinical practitioners, and (e) scientists. These can be operationalized as varying sources of outcome information. The perception of psychopathology, for instance, may vary depending on the source of the information. The method of data collection can also vary within and between respondent types. Self-reports, interviews, behavioral observations and other types of assessments can all be used to collect data from different respondent types. The scales developed by Achenbach and colleagues (Achenbach & Edelbrock, 1993), for example, collect a range of perspectives on the functioning of the child, including those of the teacher, parent or caregiver, researcher or independent rater, and the child.

Social Contexts in the Measurement of Outcomes

The cost-outcome model stipulates four social contexts of measurement: (a) the individual/self, (b) the family, (c) the work setting or school, and (d) the community. The levels move from the individual unit to the broader scope of individual life contexts.

Measures taken within the individual/self context focus on the characteristics, symptoms, and adaptational responses of the youth. Examples of this context would include presence or absence of physical disease in the individual, presence or absence of a clinical diagnosis for the individual, and level of symptomatology for an individual. However, most human abilities and characteristics vary across social contexts. Some children function well at school but not at home, for example. Others function well in the presence of their family but are unable to function socially in the broader community. Measures within the family context focus on the child in the context of family life. Importantly, "family life" is broadly defined to include a range of persons with whom the child may live and may be considered part of a "family" social structure or environment. Measures within the school or work context focus on the youth in the work or educational setting. Measures at the level of the community context focus on youths in the context of the broader community in which they live. One example, the CAFAS, measures role performance (functioning domain) at the school, community, and family (termed home on the CAFAS) contexts.

Integration of Cost, Service Use, and Outcome Data

Outcome information, regardless of its quality, is an insufficient basis of sound public policy in mental health. Cost data are equally essential for public mental health policy—as well as for managing and marketing systems of care in mental health. Research and evaluation efforts that integrate cost, service use, and outcome data are those that are most likely to have an impact on practice, administration, and policy (Phillips & Rosenblatt, 1992). Costs and outcomes are usually combined in two separate types of analyses: cost-effectiveness analysis and cost-benefit analysis.

Cost-effectiveness analysis (CEA) traditionally combines cost measures with measures of effectiveness or outcome (Sorensen & Grove, 1978). For example, one program may cost less than another but demonstrate roughly equivalent reductions in symptomatology. In such a case, one program may be considered more cost effective than another. In cost-benefit analysis (CBA), dollar values are assigned to the cost of delivering services in the same manner as in cost-effectiveness analysis. In CBA, however, dollar values are also assigned to outcomes or benefits. Total dollar costs are subtracted from total benefit costs to provide the net benefit of a program. In these analyses, one program, for example, may have a net benefit of $100 for each person served when compared to another program. Such studies have typically assigned dollar values (such as lost earnings) to mortality and morbidity. Assigning dollar values to other types of outcomes such as happiness or well-being are extremely difficult.

In both types of studies, the measurement can be classified within the framework according to the measure of "effectiveness" or "benefit." Thus, studies that combine assessment of costs with the measurement of psychopathology might fall into the clinical status domain. Similarly, if benefits are measured in terms of dollar values associated with decreased job productivity, then the outcome measure would fall into the functional adaptation domain at the work/school context. Better classification and understanding of which dimensions are being measured is critical in cost studies. This is especially the case when attempts are made to synthesize the results from several cost-effectiveness, cost-benefit, or other cost studies.

There are, however, practical difficulties in applying these methods to children enrolled in systems of care. These problems revolve largely around the capacity to collect detailed utilization data regarding a specific time span or episode of treatment. Many of the children enrolled in systems of care receive services from multiple child-serving sectors (e.g., mental health, juvenile justice, and social welfare). Each of these sectors may contain within them a wide range of programs. A significant and clinically important proportion of these children will likely have complex treatment histories that span a number of different care sectors. Existing automated records do not typically track children across these multiple care systems, either making a labor intensive review of charts necessary for constructing treatment history careers or requiring complex and often difficult linkages across care sector data systems.

Selecting Outcome Measures

As our conceptual model illustrates, there are a wide range of outcome measures from which to choose in determining the results of a system of care. Resources rarely exist to collect all possible kinds of outcome data, and even when resources do exist, it may not be desirable to do so. Difficult decisions must be made about which measures need to be included in an outcome study. A number of strategies, or perhaps more accurately approaches, can be described for selecting measures, including: (a) selecting all possible measures (the Kitchen Sink approach), (b) selecting measures by what is available, (c) selecting measures that best match the goals of a program, (d) selecting measures according to their desired impacts or purpose, and (e) selecting measures by some combination of the above strategies. Each of these strategies is discussed below.

The Kitchen Sink Approach

It is tempting to measure virtually all possible domains with all possible youth when conducting outcome research on systems of care. This approach appears the most certain way to find some kind of significant change on at least one of the measures. The potential does exist for capitalizing on chance (for example, if 20 measures are administered, the odds are that one of the measures will be significant at the .05 probability level just by chance). It is usually, however, neither possible nor wise to select all possible measures. If, for example, six critical outcomes are significantly positive out of the 20 that were measured, conclusions regarding the effectiveness of the program can be confusing. Multiple measure can distract from more central indicators of effectiveness.

This dilemma for program evaluators is magnified in the case of evaluating a system of care. Historically, programs designed to focus on a single problem (e.g., teen pregnancy) are relatively more focused in their intended outcomes when compared to many systems of care. Both statistical and methodological strategies exist for determining whether an intervention "succeeds" from a range of potentially contradictory outcomes, although these strategies require skill to properly apply them. There is considerable ongoing debate, for example, about a portion of findings from a major recent study of a continuum of care in which 3 of 12 tests were found to be significant (Friedman & Burns, 1996; Lambert & Guthrie, 1996). One set of authors consider this to be somewhat discouraging, whereas others consider the findings to be somewhat encouraging. Of course, selecting too few measures can give the appearance of measuring too few domains.

Availability

Systems of care are a relatively new approach to serving youth with SED. Many of the key aspects of these systems deviate from more traditional modes of treatment. Most well-validated measures were developed to assess the kinds of domains and perspectives found in more traditional treatment approaches (e.g., the clinical or scientific perspective on clinical status such as depression inventories developed to assess changes in level of depression among adolescents). For example, a range of long-standing service models focus on the alleviation of psychopathology and reduction of symptoms. Many measures, consequently, exist for measuring psychopathology and symptoms. Systems of care, however, are often based on building strengths as opposed to alleviating weaknesses, and they may focus more directly on improving social and academic functioning. Few strength-based measures, however, exist, and measures of social and even academic functioning are not always included in studies of systems of care.

The present situation places the researcher in a considerable quandary regarding the selection of measurement tools: Should selection focus on more psychometrically sound measures that do not directly match the goals of the care system, or should selection focus on less psychometrically sound measures that more directly match the goals of the care system? Relying on unproven measures is clearly risky for any large-scale evaluation. Any results are subject to extensive reinvestigation regarding the reliability and validity of the measure. Many measures of functional status and of safety and welfare can be collected as concrete indictors with limited "measurement" error (Rosenblatt, 1993). Youth either are arrested or they are not, they either live in the community or in a hospital, they are in school or they are not, they are the victim of a crime or not. Although considerable subtlety and effort is required to collect this type of information, doing so is not necessarily dependent on the creation of psychometric tools.

Matching of Goals

Measures that fail to match the goals of a system of care may be inappropriate to assessing the outcomes of a system of care. In the field of services to adults with severe mental illness, for example, vocational programs may improve the level of employment of individuals enrolled in the program without reducing psychiatric symptomatology. A service system designed to promote keeping youth in the most homelike environment may improve the stability of a youth's residential location without significantly improving levels of depression or anxiety. Although most systems of care have wide-ranging goals for the youth they serve, and many measures and domains are intercorrelated, priorities often need to be established regarding which of these goals are going to be the subject of ongoing evaluation.

Desired Impact

We have presented a model of outcome assessment that delineates five domains of outcome measurement: clinical status, functional status, service satisfaction, life satisfaction and fulfillment, and safety and welfare. Different domains of outcome measurement will likely have different kinds of impacts or will be targeted toward varying audiences. Ultimately, the utilization of outcome results rests on the matching of outcome domains with the desired arenas of impact.

Data collected in the clinical status domain is most likely to appeal to clinical practice or the research community. Many clinicians are conversant with the language of test scores and clinical assessment devices. Clinicians often must work at the symptom level, attempting to reduce the occurrence of more harmful thoughts and behaviors and increase the occurrence of more beneficial ways of acting in the world. Clinical status measures may have some utility to program administrators if the data are quickly scored and analyzed. Clinical status measures, taken alone, will likely have relatively less impact on organization, financing, and policy. Such measures are less likely to reflect the more concrete and practical considerations faced by those who work in the political and regulatory arenas (Rosenblatt, 1993).

Data collected in the functional status domain will appeal to a number of audiences. Clinicians, especially those working within a strength-based model, are likely to be especially concerned about the ability of their clients to remain in school, to stay out of trouble, or to continue living at home. Administrators are also likely to find functional status data valuable. Information, for example, on work and school performance can point to vocational or academic programs that need to be integrated with the care system. Similarly, the public and hence politicians and legislators are often concerned that all members of society engage in productive roles.

One of the more subtle areas of data collection pertains to life satisfaction and fulfillment. This domain can potentially impact on a wide range of audiences. Job or educational satisfaction, service satisfaction, satisfaction with the home environment, and the like have obvious value to administrators and clinicians who provide a range of services. Satisfaction or dissatisfaction with services can, when voiced by consumers and consumer advocates, be a powerful agent for political change (Attkisson & Greenfield, 1994, 1995).

Finally, measures of safety and welfare are especially germane to the policy arena. Public perceptions of safety and public health undeniably drive part of the mental health policy debate. Interventions that are able to reduce public fears will likely be more easily embraced by policymakers from the "grass roots" to the elected level. As a result, interventions that hope to impact on policy need to strongly consider measuring variables such as arrest rates, suicide rates, and rates of co-morbid conditions such as drug use.

Mixing Strategies

In reality, the ultimate choice of which outcome measures to select will rest on some combination of the goals of the service system, the desired impacts, the availability of measures, and the available resources. However, the success of outcome studies relies on the congruence between goals, desired impacts, and the availability of quality measures or indicators. As care systems evolve, so too must measurement strategies. For example, system reform may begin by focusing on creating interagency teams and placement screening processes. The goal of these new interventions may be to reduce placements in restrictive levels of care. Consequently, the ability of youth in the care systems to remain in home becomes a critical measure of system outcome given these new interventions. Although it may be desirable to measure other outcome domains, reductions in rates of placements may not translate into reductions in symptomatology. As the care system evolves, however, and begins interventions at the level of the child and family that are designed to reduce problematic behaviors in youths so that they can be maintained in their homes, measures of symptoms may become important outcomes.

Table 12.2 draws from our experiences to illustrate how the goals, programs or services, target populations, outcomes, and audiences or stakeholders can interrelate (Rosenblatt, 1993). The table demonstrates that it is important to achieve consistency between the goals, the target populations, and the outcomes of a care system. Choices regarding the selection of any of these individual components impacts on other components. For example, if a care system is attempting to keep youth in school, then there ought to be programs targeted specifically toward helping a defined group of children reach that goal. Further, measures need to be incorporated into an ongoing evaluation of the care system to ensure that the goal is met and that relevant audiences can be convinced of the utility of the program. In the case of keeping youth in school, such audiences might naturally include board of education members. Of course, although not illustrated in the table for purposes of simplicity, many measures may be suitable across a range of target populations and may have multiple impacts beyond those specified in the table.

System of Care Outcomes by Domain

There is a paucity of published, peer reviewed research on the outcomes of systems of care for children and youth with serious emotional disturbance. A majority of the work in this area is available only as technical reports or as brief professional conference proceedings. Fortunately, Stroul (1993) undertook the task of summarizing the outcomes of systems of care to that point. This review relies on Stroul's (1993) work along with newly published documents and reports obtained by the author to overview the current status of system-of-care outcomes research. Because some documents could not be obtained and because unpublished reports often do not provide sufficient information regarding study design and methods, a review of this material can be neither critical nor comprehensive. Rather, the review demonstrates the focus of systems-of-care research to this point. Finally, this review does not examine the outcomes of various components within a system of care (for a complete review of system-of-care component outcomes, see Kutash & Rivera, 1996).

Table 12.2

Example of Matching Goals, Populations, Measures, and Impacts

Goal	Target Population	Program	Measure	Desired Audience
In Home	Youth at risk of out-of-home placement	Interagency placement screening team	Placements and expenditures in restricted levels of care	Program managers Board members State policy
In School	Youth enrolled in special education programs	Special day schools	School attendance School achievement	County supervisors Board of education
Out of Trouble	Wards of the court	Juvenile hall support	Re-arrest rates	State policy County supervisors Judges
Healthy	Younger youth with multiple risk factors	Outpatient therapy	Child Behavior Checklist	Clinical line staff Program managers

The results of the outcomes of 20 community-based systems of care by outcome domain are summarized in Table 12.3. The knowledge base is expected to grow further in the future as results from new systems of care become available. This is especially the case given the awarding, through the Center for Mental Health Services, of 22 grants across the nation designed to implement systems of care for youth with SED (McCormick, 1994).

As illustrated in Table 12.3, a range of studies have demonstrated reductions in either the cost of care or utilization of restrictive levels of care as measured through hospital admissions, inpatient lengths of stay, state hospital expenditures, and residential treatment center placements (e.g., Behar, 1992; Burchard & Clarke, 1990; Goldman, 1992; Illback, 1993; Jordan & Hernandez, 1990; Lourie, 1992; Rosenblatt & Attkisson, 1992; Stroul, 1992, 1993). Researchers have also shown improvements in clinical and functional status. For example, results from the Kentucky IMPACT project indicate reductions in internalizing and externalizing problem behaviors (Illback, 1993), as measured by the Child Behavior Checklist (Achenbach & Edelbrock, 1993). Using the same instrument, evaluators in Tennessee found improved functioning of children involved in the AIMS Project after 1 year (Glisson, 1992). Improvements in the safety and welfare domain have also been demonstrated. A range of studies demonstrated reduced juvenile justice recidivism, incarceration rates, or school achievement and attendance (e.g. Jordan & Hernandez, 1990; Rosenblatt & Attkisson, 1977; Rugs, 1992). Investigators in North Carolina report moderate to substantial improvements in functioning, as demonstrated by scores on the Child and Adolescent Functioning Scale (Hodges, Bickman, Kurtz, & Reiter, 1992) after 1 year (Behar, 1992). A component of life satisfaction and fulfillment, satisfaction with services, was also assessed in half a dozen of the studies, with generally high levels of satisfaction being reported.

However, a major recent and important study reported less positive results. The Department of Defense CHAMPUS program funded the creation of a continuum of care in Fort Bragg, North Carolina. Through this demonstration, military families in Fort Bragg were allowed to receive virtually any type of mental health service rather than more traditional inpatient, outpatient, and residential care (Behar, Macbeth, & Holland, 1993). An evaluation was conducted that compared the costs and outcomes of care for children and families who received services in Fort Bragg to the costs and outcomes of care for children and families who received a limited range of outpatient and inpatient care at a comparison site. Evaluators from the Fort Bragg Project found no differences between the intervention and no-intervention groups in terms of child adaptive functioning, child psychopathology, or degree of family burden (Bickman et al., 1995). Differences were found in the Fort Bragg study for levels of family satisfaction in favor of the intervention group. This study, the most comprehensive child services research effort to date, is the subject of ongoing scientific discussion and debate (e.g. Bickman, 1996b, 1996c; Friedman & Burns, 1996).

Table 12.3

Outcomes of Community Based Systems of Care

Study (Primary Reference)	Clinical Status	Functional Status	Life Satisfaction/ Fulfillment	Safety/ Welfare	Cost/ Utilization
New Directions, VT (Vermont DMHMR, 1993)	Improved	Improved	"Extremely Satisfied"		Reduced
Ventura CA (Jordan & Hernandez, 1990)		Improved		Reduced Arrests	Reduced
Children's Initiative, NC (Behar, 1992)	Improved	Improved	"Very Satisfied"	Reduced Arrests	Reduced
Stark, OH (Stroul, 1992)					Reduced
Bennington, VT (Stroul, 1993)	Improved	Improved			Reduced
Dubuque, IA (Iowa DHS, 1992)					Reduced
Mountain State Network, WV (Rugs, 1992)				Reduced Arrests	Reduced
Impact, KY (Illback, 1993)	Improved	Improved	Increased	Improved	Reduced
Fort Bragg, NC (Bickman, 1995)	Same as Comparison	Same as Comparison	Higher in Demonstration		Higher in Demonstration
Demonstration Projects, VA (Virginia DMHMRSA, 1992a)			"Excellent or Good"		Reduced

(continues)

Table 12.3 *Continued*

Study (Primary Reference)	Clinical Status	Functional Status	Life Satisfaction/ Fulfillment	Safety/ Welfare	Cost/ Utilization
AB377 Counties, CA (Rosenblatt et al., 1992)					Reduced
Northumberland, PA (Lourie, 1992)					Reduced
Augusta, GA (Georgia DMHMRSA, 1992)					Reduced
FMP CA (Martinez & Smith, 1993)		Improved		Reduced Detention	Reduced
Lucas, OH (Keros, 1993)					Reduced
AIMS, TN (Glisson, 1992)	Improved	Improved			Reduced
LIS Projects, VA (Virgina DMHMRSA, 1992b)	Improved	Improved			
Connections, OH (Hanna-Williams, 1993)	Improved	Improved			
North Idaho (Lubrecht, 1993)	Improved	Improved	"Good or Very Good"		
Franklin, OH (McCoard, 1993)					Reduced

A number of trends in system-of-care research to date emerge from the studies described in Table 12.3. The majority of the research has focused on demonstrating reductions in cost or utilization of restrictive service options, with all but five studies presenting findings in this domain. In some cases these reductions were translated into dollar amounts. Less than half of the studies presented results on clinical or functional status, as typically measured on the CBCL, the CAFAS, or other scales. Direct indicators of safety and welfare such as educational status and law enforcement status were each assessed by fewer than 20% of the studies. Aside from client satisfaction, only a few of the investigators attempted to measure other indicators of satisfaction and fulfillment, such as family participation in services, amount of abuse or neglect inflicted upon the child, spousal and other family violence, and family burden.

Linking the Independent and Dependent Variable: The Quality of the Research Design

The results from system-of-care research illustrate that youth and families enrolled in systems of care do show improvements in a range of outcome domains. Making the causal link, however, between the implementation of these complex interventions and the outcomes achieved can be difficult. The capacity to draw these conclusions is at least in part a function of the research design of each study. The current attention focused on the Fort Bragg study is due largely to the inclusion of outcome measures that covered the range of domains typically considered relevant for assessing the effectiveness of systems of care along with the use of a comparison group. In this study, the results would have appeared completely positive if it were not for the inclusion of the comparison group. Youth in the demonstration site did show improvement, but youth in the comparison site showed similar levels of improvement on most measures (Bickman et al., 1995; Lambert & Guthrie, 1996).

Importantly, a distinction exists between making a causal link and making a plausible link between an intervention and an independent variable. Inferring causality (i.e., Did the intervention cause the outcome?) is largely a function of the internal validity (i.e., the strength of the design and the measures) of the research (Campbell & Stanley, 1966). The plausibility of a research finding to various audiences such as scientists, program administrators, legislators, and clinicians is a more complex matter that involves an interplay between the internal and external (i.e., generalizability to other populations and interventions) validity of the design along with how findings are presented. Weiss and Bucuvalas (1980), for example, found that methodological rigor was only one of several other factors (e.g., a perceived lack of bias in the conclusions) related to the judged utility of research findings. Similarly, Holland (1984) found that mental health providers did not distinguish between the "truthfulness" and the "usefulness" of research results.

It is possible to have a well-conducted research project that demonstrates a causal, but implausible, link between an intervention and an outcome. The most simple examples are internally valid studies that have little external applicability. An intervention may "cause" situationally depressed college students to feel better, but clinicians or program administrators would be unlikely to implement the intervention with persons who have major affective disorder. More subtle examples exist. Considerable debate exists regarding why clinicians tend not to use the results of psychotherapy outcomes research in their practice. Weisz et al. (1995) offer a likely solution by noting that even though an extensive and sophisticated literature on psychotherapy outcomes with children exists in controlled settings, the literature on the "real world" outcomes of psychotherapy is sparse. Most psychotherapists practice outside of the university-based clinics where most psychotherapy research is conducted, making many of the results from the psychotherapy outcomes literature remote, not relevant, unconvincing, or implausible compared to their own clinical experiences.

Inferring causality without randomized experiments is problematic (Sechrest, 1984), and, even when randomized experiments are conducted, inferring causality may still not be possible. Randomized studies are rarely perfectly conducted, and deviations from treatment or intervention protocols combined with inevitable disruptions in the random assignment process can wreak havoc on sophisticated research designs conducted in applied settings. Although a randomized design was implemented in one study of a system of care in Ohio (Bickman, 1996a), results from that study are not yet available. It is highly unlikely that many further randomized trials will be implemented anytime in the near future. A system of care is an extensive intervention, usually aimed at counties, catchment areas, or communities. In all cases, it is unlikely that alternate care systems can be implemented within such geographical or regional boundaries. Although alternate systems may exist in neighboring communities, it is certainly not feasible, nor ethical, to randomly request youth and families to move to a different county just so they can participate in a research study.

Consequently, the barriers to implementing a randomized design of a system of care are extensive, at least equal to those found in other social interventions (Weiss, 1972). Randomized designs of components of a system of care are feasible, have been conducted, and are yielding results (Kutash & Rivera, 1996). These studies can compare two different treatment options within a care system and randomly assign youth to two potentially equally attractive treatment options. Opportunities may exist in the future to conduct randomized designs of contrasting system models if multiple providers begin to move into communities and compete for public funds. The dawning of managed mental health care in both the private and public sectors may create scenarios where multiple providers exist in communities, each providing full arrays of services under different models. In such instances, random assignment, or a close variant of random assignment, may be feasible.

Nonetheless, research on systems of care has relied on quasi-experimental designs and will most likely continue to rely on more refined variants of these designs in the future. The wide range of potential research designs still used by most of the evaluation research world have changed little since the seminal work by Campbell and Stanley (1966) and Cook and Campbell (1979). Although innovations in research designs appear periodically, most quantitative evaluation work still draws on refinements of designs that originated over a decade ago. The major nonexperimental research designs pertinent to systems of care are described below.

Pre-Post Designs

Pre-post designs contain no comparison to a nontreatment group. In these designs, measurements are taken before and after an intervention. In some cases, these designs create relatively weak arguments for the link between an intervention and a set of outcome findings. However, these designs can have importance in relatively young fields, such as children's mental health services. Pre-Post designs can be the blocks upon which more sophisticated research builds. They can demonstrate the possibility of change for populations where change is not a given, such as in the case of children with SED. In doing so, these designs can change the research and policy agenda from questions of whether youth can improve to questions of which factors or interventions lead to improvement. Further, these designs may become the basis of policy formulation. For example, as illustrated earlier in this chapter, the majority of research on systems of care has focused on whether youths can be maintained in homelike environments. One research and policy question that derives from these studies is whether the youth who are either removed or diverted from residential care suffer poor outcomes as a result of controls on utilization. Pre-post designs can make plausible arguments that youth are faring well even when utilization of restrictive levels of care is controlled. These designs also have some value in the policy arena because of the relative simplicity and intelligibility of the results that derive from these studies.

Non-Equivalent Comparison Group Designs

Non Equivalent Comparison Group Designs (NECGD) are likely to become the mainstay of research on systems of care as the field builds upon simple pre-post designs. These designs use a nonrandomly assigned comparison group to compare to a group receiving an intervention. The quality of these designs rests largely on the capacity to find or create two or more comparison groups that are as similar as possible. A range of techniques exist for equating the two groups either statistically (e.g., analysis of covariance, forced entry regression) or as design features (e.g., matching strategies).

Time Series and Multiple Time Series Designs

Interrupted time series designs can, if properly conducted, provide highly defensible conclusions regarding the effects of an intervention (Judd & Kenney, 1981). These designs require ongoing measurement of the variable of interest both before and after a specified intervention. They are distinguished from repeated measures designs in that they require a relatively large number of pre- and post-measurement intervals. Consequently, these designs are often used to analyze data such as cost, utilization, and community indicators such as crime rates that are collected repeatedly over extended periods of time. Time series designs can be used to compare multiple series, such as crime rates in one community versus another. The statistical treatment of these designs is well established (McCleary & Hays, 1980) and can help create relatively powerful and plausible arguments regarding an intervention. The major limitation of these designs is the relatively large number of observations required over time to permit successful analyses.

Regression Discontinuity Designs

Regression discontinuity designs can be a fairly powerful design option (Trochim, 1984) that has not been used to date in system-of-care research. These designs require that youths be assigned to conditions on the basis of some cut point or cutting score. For example, if youths with a reading score below 80 are assigned to a remedial class while youths with a score of 81 or above remain in a regular class, then it is possible to assess the relative effectiveness of each treatment option. These designs can also be used when youths are assigned to a treatment condition on the basis of age. For example, youths under 17 may be eligible for "children's" services, whereas youths 18 and over may be eligible only for "adult" services. Natural cut points may also occur on the basis of service utilization. It is common, for example, in managed care to allocate a set number of sessions (e.g., eight outpatient sessions) to anyone who requests care, but to also then require utilization reviews for persons who wish to receive more than the allowed number of sessions (e.g., nine or more). Although regression-discontinuity designs can be difficult to implement and analyze (the cutting score may often not be exact or precise), the design is nonetheless a potentially rigorous option whenever youth are assigned to services on the basis of some type of "cutting" score.

Mixing Designs

In many cases, research on systems of care can be composed of a series of substudies, which may feature varying design strategies. A randomized design of case-management strategies may be nested as a separate, more intensive study, contained within a broader, nonequivalent comparison group study of the system as a whole. Alternately, time series techniques may be used to compare cost data across systems while pre-post designs are used to evaluate the effectiveness of specific programs within a system.

Review of Systems of Care and Research Designs

A summary of the research designs used to achieve the results summarized earlier in this chapter is presented in Table 12.4. At this writing, there are no results available from randomized research designs of systems of care, and only one such design is being implemented (Bickman, 1996a). The most frequent research design used across these studies is a pre-post design. Time series designs of varying quality are also frequently used in assessing service use outcomes. Three studies used nonequivalent group comparison designs to measure child and family outcomes.

Research designs vary considerably by the type of outcome variable analyzed. Several of the studies apply a range of time series methods to cost and utilization data, and some type of external comparisons are utilized with these types of outcome indicators more frequently than other outcomes. Cost and utilization data are frequently found in a variety of management and billing information systems and have been collected and stored over time in a wide range of locales, making the application of time series and multiple time series designs feasible. Client outcome data are not as readily available as certain types of cost and utilization data and, consequently, often require more time, effort, and resources to collect. As a result, time series designs are not typically used with these types of variables.

When considered in the context of the research designs, the positive findings presented in Table 12.3 for systems of care present a far less consistent picture. The findings are universally positive with the critical exception of the Fort Bragg study, which included a comparison group. In terms of scientific and political significance, the reality that the results from the Fort Bragg study can overshadow the results from 19 other research efforts is largely a testimony to the power of more sophisticated research designs. Clearly, more studies that find ways to utilize some types of comparisons to communities implementing systems of care are needed.

Conclusions

Changes in child and adolescent mental health care are occurring in the context of dramatic shifts in the organization and financing of public mental health services, including (a) shifts toward managed care, resource capping, and capitation models (Hoge et al., 1994; Mechanic & Aiken, 1989); (b) increasing movement toward local control and responsibility for public mental health

Table 12.4
Research Designs of Community Based Systems of Care Studies

Study (Primary Reference)	Clinical Status	Functional Status	Life Satisfaction/ Fulfillment	Safety/ Welfare	Cost/ Utilization
New Directions, VT	Pre-Post	Pre-Post	Post		Pre-Post
Ventura, CA	Pre-Post	Pre-Post		Pre-Post	Post/Time Series
Children's Initiative, NC	Pre-Post	Pre-Post	Post	Pre-Post	Pre-Post/NECGD
Stark, OH					Time Series
Bennington County, VT	Post	Post			Time Series
Dubuque, IA					Time Series
Mountain State Network, WV				NECGD	NECGD
Impact, KY	Pre-Post	Pre-Post	Pre-Post		Pre-Post/Time Series
Fort Bragg, NC	NECGD	NECGD	NECGD	NECGD	NECGD
Demonstration Projects, VA			Post		NECGD/Pre-Post
AB377 Counties, CA					Mult. Time Series
Northumberland, PA					Repeated Measures
Augusta, GA					Time Series/NECGD
FMP, CA		Post		Pre-Post	Pre-Post
Lucas, OH					Pre-Post
AIMS Project, TN	NECGD	NECGD			NECGD
LIS Projects, VA	Pre-Post	Pre-Post			
Connections, OH	Post	Post			
North Idaho	Pre-Post	Pre-Post	Post		
Franklin, OH					Pre-Post

Note. NECGD is Non-Equivalent Comparison Group Design.

programs and systems; and, (c) movement toward the privatization of what previously were public mental health services. All of these changes are occurring in the context of greatly diminished public resources and with the imperative to "do more with less."

In such an environment, documenting the outcomes of care systems can determine whether models and systems continue to survive. Given the sociopolitical context in which the systems-of-care movement now exists, there is a strong tendency for a "rush to judgment." As argued elsewhere (Rosenblatt, 1996), quick and easy answers to whether "systems of care" or other complex social programs are working do not provide the basis for sound policy development.

Nonetheless, the first decade of research on the outcomes of systems of care for youth with SED did yield a knowledge base that researchers can build upon. This base includes the following broad conclusions:

- Across a range of outcome domains, youth with SED who are enrolled within innovative systems show improvement.

- The Fort Bragg study (Bickman et al., 1995) raises the question of whether these improvements are due to being enrolled in a system of care, are simply the result of obtaining any kind of services, or constitute the natural course of SED (youth would get better without any intervention). Given the severity of the problems faced by children and families who receive these services, as well as numerous reports citing the unfortunate plight of children and families, the latter conclusion is highly implausible.

- With the exception of the Fort Bragg study, the research demonstrates that systems of care can manage costly out-of-home placements. The research methods for these studies are consistently more convincing than the methods for assessing child and family outcomes, with a number of studies utilizing time series methods or comparisons of some type. Consequently, there is substantial evidence that communities implementing systems of care can control residential placements (either lower or reduce the rate of increase). This finding is consistent with the concept of utilization and cost as an indicator of change at the system level.

Still, as would be expected given the relative youth of the field, the existing literature has its share of weaknesses:

- The existing research on systems of care is extremely difficult to evaluate critically. Most studies are not published in scientific journals and thus are not subject to peer review; descriptions of methodology are generally inadequate; and statistical analyses are often either inappropriate or incomplete.

- The research methods used in evaluating the child and family outcomes of systems of care vary considerably but are all quasi-experimental. Pre-post designs are the norm. There is a need for more sophisticated research designs.

- Measure selection for evaluating systems of care is difficult both because of the range of outcomes that systems are designed to influence and because of limitations in measurement. Few measures exist that are designed specifically out of the values and goals of the system-of-care approach.

- Care systems are complex interventions occurring at many levels. Relatively little is empirically known regarding how different levels of a system of care can interact to produce change across a range of potential outcome domains.

- Given the complexity of multilayered systems, it is not entirely surprising that the term "system of care" is often used loosely and is not objectively defined. This makes it difficult to distill whether the care systems studied in the literature truly embody the concepts or theory behind the system-of-care movement.

Linking Systems of Care and Outcomes

As this chapter emphasized, research on the outcomes of systems of care rests on making plausible links between a multilayered social intervention and a multidimensional set of potential outcomes. The relationships between these two multidimensional constructs is likely to be neither direct nor linear. Rather, the ultimate effectiveness of a system of care relies on the independent and interactive effectiveness of systemic, programmatic, and clinical reforms. Changes at different levels of the systems may correspond to changes in different types of outcomes. The quality of clinical interventions, for example, may be most directly related to changes in symptomatology, while the quality of system organization may be most directly related to improvements in the efficiency of service delivery. It is tempting to view any outcome of a system of care as a function of system change alone, which can be expressed as:

$$O_i = f(S) \tag{1}$$

where O_i is the outcome for an individual, i, and S represents some kind of system level reform. A great deal of the current research essentially relies on this level of model, for example whether systems of care can reduce utilization of out-of-home placements or improve clinical status. A slightly more complex version of the line of thought in model (1) can be expressed as:

$$O_{itdcp} = f(S) \tag{2}$$

where O_{itdcp} is the outcome for an individual at time t for clinical domain d, in context c and by perspective p. This model acknowledges that changes may occur in a range of different types of outcomes and may vary by the outcome domain, the perspective on outcome measurement, and the context in which outcomes are assessed as well as by the time interval during which change in an outcome is assessed. A few researchers of systems of care followed this type of model by studying a range of outcomes of system level reform efforts without explicitly or clearly attending to reform at programmatic and clinical levels. This model, therefore, is overly simplistic given the multiple levels found within a system of care. The more inclusive, and more appropriate, way of envisioning the relationships between levels of care and outcome expands on (2) above and can be expressed as:

$$O_{itdcp} = f(S, P, C) \tag{3}$$

where P reflects some constellation of programmatic reforms and C some constellation of clinical reforms. Systemic, programmatic, and clinical changes may interact with one another within this framework to produce different types of outcomes. This perspective also allows for the exploration of how specific types of outcomes may relate only to specific combinations of system, program, and clinical interventions. The research on systems of care reviewed in this chapter does not fully embrace this last perspective, no doubt in part because of the difficulty of conducting such research.

The direct implications of this model for analyzing the outcomes of a system of care are threefold: (1) Systems of care need to be created, understood, studied, and described, their strength and integrity assessed, at multiple levels; (2) Outcomes within a system of care need to be thought of as multidimensional and multidetermined; and (3) The relationships between levels of intervention delivered within a system of care and the multiple outcomes of the system of care can be interactive as well as additive.

Even this final model is over-simplified. Many factors can mediate the relationship between multiple levels of a system of care and multiple outcome domains. The characteristics of the children, their families, and the communities in which they live are bound to mediate the relationships between systems and outcomes. Similarly, different research designs may yield different levels of confidence in the strength of the linkages between system change and child and family outcomes. The quality of the data-analytic strategies are yet another factor in understanding outcomes that are not discussed in this chapter.

The Future

Although models like the one presented above can lead to applied research problems that rapidly approach a level of incomprehensible complexity, they are important to keep in mind in evaluating and discussing the current state of systems-of-care outcomes research. Even the most sophisticated existing studies relevant to systems of care focus almost exclusively on either the system, the program, or the clinical levels. Most system-of-care studies do not measure outcomes across a range of measurement domains, perspectives, and contexts. Too often, results are presented as though system change can be expected to lead directly to changes in individual level outcomes. The strength and integrity of a system of care needs to be better elucidated and ensured. Finally, relatively new systems are often prematurely expected to produce a range of outcomes, before they have reached a sufficient level of maturity. Additional multidimensional models need to be developed that acknowledge the complexities inherent in the relationships between systems and outcomes, and these kinds of models need to be kept in mind in interpreting the existing literature.

Although the challenges are clearly great, the future of research on systems of care for youths with SED can be bright. Already, researchers involved at the systemic, programmatic, and clinical levels of a care system are exchanging ideas regarding how research at different levels can be more coherently conducted. As an example, attention is now being focused on how clinical efficacy research can bridge the gap into effectiveness research (Hoagwood, Hibbs, Brent, & Jensen, 1995b; Weisz, Donenberg, Han, & Kauneckis, 1995). A model of clinical intervention that is based on the multisystemic needs of youth is being implemented in a range of "systems of care" and may provide one bridge between the clinical, programmatic, and systemic levels of care systems (Henggeler & Borduin, 1990; Henggeler et al., 1992). The components of systems of care are receiving increasing levels of attention, and individualized service approaches are being integrated into systems of care (VanDenBerg & Grealish, 1996).

The first generation of research on the outcomes of systems of care for youth with serious emotional disturbance did yield the beginnings of a knowledge base. The research also, however, yielded something else: an evolutionary revolution in how research can be conducted on human service systems and how researchers can cross their own disciplinary and topical boundaries to produce more integrative, holistic, and, it is hoped, ultimately meaningful research. It is appropriate that a service reform movement based on principles of collaboration and integration should encourage collaboration and integration among researchers working in often disparate traditions.

Finally, from a broader perspective, systems of care for youth with SED are one of a number of efforts to better integrate services for children and families. Although a range of attempts at service integration date to the 1970s, there remains precious little information on the costs and effects of these efforts (Kagan & Neville, 1993). The current wave of interest in service integration provides an opportunity to begin to answer a host of questions about the ultimate success of service integration. Without these answers, the social and political pendulum will certainly swing in other directions as dictated by the fashions and forces of the times. Without these answers, it will be impossible to know whether the pendulum is swinging in a benign and beneficial direction, or whether it is headed on a collision course with families and children.

Author's Notes

Preparation of this chapter was supported in part by evaluation research contracts from the Center for Mental Health Services and the California State Department of Mental Health (89-70225, 90-70195, 91-71106, 92-72090, 92-72347, 93-73346, 94-74252, 94-74285, and 95-75217) and a center grant from the National Institute of Mental Health (P50MH43694).

Correspondence may be addressed to Abram Rosenblatt, the University of California, San Franciso, Child Services Research Group, Department of Psychiatry, 44 Montgomery, Suite 1450, San Francisco, CA 94104.

References

Achenbach, T. M., & Edelbrock, C. S. (1993). *Manual for the Child Behavior Checklist and Revised Child Behavior Profile.* Burlington: University of Vermont, Department of Psychiatry.

Attkisson, C. C., Cook, J., Karno, M., Lehman, A., McGlashan, T. H., Meltzer, H. Y., O'Connor, M., Richardson, D., Rosenblatt, A., Wells, K., Williams, J., & Hohmann, A. (1992). Clinical services research. *Schizophrenia Bulletin, 18*(4), 561–626.

Attkisson, C. C., & Greenfield, T. K. (1994). Client Satisfaction Questionnaire-8 and Service Satisfaction Scale-30. In M. E. Maruish (Ed.), *The use of psychological testing for treatment planning and outcome assessment.* Hillsdale, NJ: Lawrence Erlbaum.

Attkisson, C. C., & Greenfield, T. K. (1995). The Client Satisfaction Questionnaire (CSQ) Scales. In L. L. Sederer & B. Dickey (Eds.), *Outcome assessment in clinical practice.* Baltimore: Williams & Wilkins.

Behar, L. (1985). Changing patterns of state responsibility: A case study of North Carolina. *Journal of Clinical Child Psychology, 14,* 188–195.

Behar, L. (1992). *The children's initiative, North Carolina mental health services program for youth.* Raleigh: North Carolina Division of Mental Health, Developmental Disabilities, and Substance Abuse Services, Child and Family Services Branch.

Behar, L. B., Macbeth, G., & Holland, J. M. (1993). Distribution and costs of mental health services within a system of care for children and adolescents. *Administration and Policy in Mental Health, 20,* 283–295.

Bickman, L. (1996a). Preliminary findings from a randomized trial in Stark County, Ohio. Paper presented at an NIMH-sponsored workshop, "Moving from Efficacy to Effectiveness in Children's Research," Washington, DC.

Bickman, L. (1996b). The evaluation of a children's mental health managed care demonstration. *Journal of Mental Health Administration, 23,* 7–15.

Bickman, L. (1996c). Reinterpreting the Fort Bragg evaluation findings: The message does not change. *Journal of Mental Health Administration, 23,* 137–145.

Bickman, L., Guthrie, P., Foster, E. M., Lambert, E. W., Summerfelt, W. T., Breda, C., & Heflinger, C. A. (1995). *Managed care in mental health: The Fort Bragg experiment.* New York: Plenum.

Burchard, J. D., & Clarke, R. T. (1990). The role of individualized care in a service delivery system for children and adolescents with severely maladjusted behavior. *Journal of Mental Health Administration, 17,* 48–98.

Burns, B. J., & Friedman, R. M. (1990). Examining the research base for child mental health services and policy. *Journal of Mental Health Administration, 17,* 87–98.

Campbell, D. T., & Stanley, J. C. (1966). *Experimental and quasi-experimental designs for research.* Skokie, IL: Rand McNally.

Ciarlo, J. A., Brown, T. R., Edwards, D. W., Kiresuk, T. J., & Newman, F. L. (1986). *Assessing mental health treatment outcome measurement techniques.* National Institute of Mental Health. Series FN No.9. DHHS Publication No. (ADM)86-1301. Washington, DC: Superintendent of Documents, U.S. Government Printing Office.

Cook, T. D., & Campbell, D. T. (1979). *Quasi-experimentation design: Design and analysis in field settings.* Skokie, IL: Rand McNally.

Cronbach, L. J.(1964). Evaluation for course improvement. In R. W. Heath (Ed.), *New Curricula* (pp. 231–248). New York: Harper & Row.

Day, C., & Roberts, M. C. (1991). Activities of the Child and Adolescent Service System Program for improving mental health services for children and families. *Journal of Clinical Child Psychology, 20,* 340–350.

Friedman, R. M., & Burns, B. J. (1996). The evaluation of the Fort Bragg demonstration project: An alternative interpretation of the findings. *Journal of Mental Health Administration, 53,* 128–136.

Georgia Division of Mental Health, Mental Retardation, & Substance Abuse (DMHMRSA). (1992). *A report on the August SED project.*

Glisson, C. (1992). *The adjudication, placement, and psychosocial functioning of children in state custody.* Knoxville: University of Tennessee College of Social Work.

Goldman, S. (1992). Ventura County, California. In B. Stroul, S. Goldman, I. Lourie, J. Katz-Leavy, & C. Zeigler-Dendy (Eds.), *Profiles of local systems of care for children and adolescents with severe emotional disturbances* (pp. 287–337). Washington, DC: CASSP Technical Assistance Center.

Hanna-Williams, F. (1993). [Connections project data]. Unpublished raw data. Cleveland: Cuyahoga County Community Mental Health Board. Cited in B. Stroul, *Systems of care for children and adolescents with severe emotional disturbances: What are the results?* Washington, DC: CASSP Technical Assistance Center, Georgetown University Child Development Center.

Hargreaves, W. A., & Shumway, M. (1989). Effectiveness of mental health services for the severely mentally ill. In C. A. Taube, D. Mechanic, & A. Hohmann (Eds.), *The future of mental health services research.* DHHS Publication No. (ADM)89-1600. Washington, DC: U.S. Government Printing Office.

Henggeler, S. W., & Borduin, C. M. (1990). *Family therapy and beyond: A multisystemic approach to treating the behavior problems of children and adolescents.* Pacific Grove, CA: Brooks/Cole.

Henggeler, S. W., Melton, G. B., & Smith, L. A. (1992). Multisystemic treatment of serious juvenile offenders: An effective alternative to incarceration. *Journal of Consulting and Clinical Psychology, 60,* 953–961.

Hoagwood, K., Hibbs, E., Brent, D., & Jensen, P. (1995a). Efficacy and effectiveness studies of child and adolescent psychotherapy. *Journal of Consulting and Clinical Psychology, 63,* 683–687.

Hoagwood, K., Hibbs, E., Brent, D., & Jensen, P. (1995b). Introduction to the special section: Efficacy and effectiveness in studies of child and adolescent psychotherapy. *Journal of Consulting and Clinical Psychology, 63*(5), 683–687.

Hodges, K. (1994). *The Child and Adolescent Functional Assessment Scale.* Available from Kay Hodges, Eastern Michigan University Psychology Department, Ypsalanti, MI 48197.

Holland, R. S. (1984). *Perceived truthfulness and perceived usefulness of program evaluations by direct services staff.* Unpublished doctoral dissertation, University of Michigan.

Hoge, M. A., Davids, L., Griffith, E. E., Sledge, W. H., et al. (1994) Defining managed care in public sector psychiatry. *Hospital and Community Psychiatry, 45,* 1085–1089.

Illback, R. (1993). *Evaluation of the Kentucky Impact program for children and youth with severe emotional disabilities, year two.* Frankfort, KY: Division of Mental Health, Children and Youth Services Branch.

Iowa Department of Human Services (DHS). (1992). *Dubuque County progress report.* Dubuque: Iowa Department of Human Services, Dubuque Area Office.

Jordan, D. D., & Hernandez, M. (1990). The Ventura Planning Model: A proposal for mental health reform. *Journal of Mental Health Administration, 17,* 26–47.

Judd, C. M., & Kenny, D. A. (1981). *Estimating the effects of social interventions.* New York: Cambridge University Press.

Kagan, S. L., & Neville, P. R. (1993). *Integrating services for children and families: Understanding the past to shape the future.* New Haven, CT: Yale University Press.

Katz-Leavy, J. W., Lourie, I. S., Stroul, B. A., & Zeigler-Dendy, C. (1992). Individualized services in a system of care. Washington, DC: CASSP Technical Assistance Center, Georgetown University Child Development Center.

Keros, J. (1993). [Unpublished data]. Toledo: Lucas County Mental Health Board. Cited in B. Stroul, *Systems of care for children and adolescents with severe emotional disturbances: What are the results?* Washington, DC: CASSP Technical Assistance Center, Georgetown University Child Development Center.

Koren, P. E., DeChillo, N., & Friesen, B. J. (1992). Measuring empowerment in families whose children have emotional disabilities: A brief questionnaire. *Rehabilitation Psychology, 37,* 305–321.

Kovacs, M. (1991). *The Children's Depression Inventory.* North Tonawanda, NY: Multi-Health Systems.

Kutash, K., & Rivera, V. R. (1996). *What works in children's mental health services? Uncovering answers to critical questions.* Baltimore: Brookes.

Lambert, W. E., & Guthrie, P. R. (1996). Clinical outcomes of a childrens' mental health managed care demonstration. *Journal of Mental Health Administration, 53,* 51–68.

Lourie, I. (1992). Northumberland County, Pennsylvania. In B. Stroul, S. Goldman, I. Lourie, J. Katz-Leavy, & C. Zeigler-Dendy (Eds.), *Profiles of local systems of care for children and adolescents with severe emotional disturbances* (pp. 87–149). Washington, DC: CASSP Technical Assistance Center, Georgetown University Child Development Center.

Lubrecht, J. (1993). Coeur d'Alene, ID: Region I Health and Welfare, Family and Children's Services. Cited in Stroul, B. A. (1993). Systems of care for children and adolescents with severe emotional disturbances: What are the results? Washington, DC: CASSP Technical Assistance Center, Georgetown University Child Development Center.

Martinez, M., & Smith, L. (1993). *The Family Mosaic project, Report submitted to the Washington Business Group on Health.* San Francisco: Family Mosaic Project.

McCleary, R., & Hays, R. A., Jr. (1980). *Applied time series analysis for the social sciences.* Beverly Hills, CA: Sage.

McCoard, D. (1993). *10 KIDS: An interprofessional managed care approach to returning SED youth placed out-of-county using nontraditional cross-system collaborative strategies.* Paper presented at the 6th annual Research Conference, A System of Care for Children's Mental Health: Expanding the Research Base, Tampa, FL.

McCormick. (1994). Measuring outcomes of systems of care. Paper presented at 1994 CASSP Biennial Training Institutes, Traverse City, MI.

McGuire, T. G., Frank, R. G., & Goldman, H. H. (1992). Designing a benefit plan for child and adolescent mental health services. *Administration and Policy in Mental Health, 19,* 151–157.

Mechanic, D., & Aiken, L. H. (1989). Capitation in mental health: Potentials and cautions. *New Directions for Mental Health Services, 43,* 5–18.

National Advisory Mental Health Council. (1993). Health care reform for Americans with severe mental illness: Report of the National Advisory Mental Health Council. *American Journal of Psychiatry, 150*(10), 1447–1465.

National Institute of Mental Health. (1983). Program announcement: Child and Adolescent Service System Program. Rockville, MD: Author.

National Institute of Mental Health. (1991). Caring for people with severe mental disorders: A national plan of research to improve services. DHHS Publication No. (ADM)91-1762. Washington, DC: Superintendent of Documents, U.S. Government Printing Office.

Phillips, K. A., & Rosenblatt, A. (1992). Speaking in tongues: Integrating psychology and economics into health and mental health services outcomes research. *Medical Care Review, 49*(2), 191–230.

Quay, H. C. (1987). *Handbook of juvenile delinquency.* New York: John Wiley.

Rosenblatt, A. (1996). Bows and ribbons, tape and twine: Wrapping the wraparound process for children with multi-system needs. *Journal of Child and Family Studies, 5,* 101–116.

Rosenblatt, A. (1993). In home, in school, and out of trouble. *Journal of Child and Family Studies, 2*(4), 275–282.

Rosenblatt, A., & Attkisson, C. C. (1992). Integrating systems of care in California for youth with severe emotional disturbance—I: A descriptive overview of the California AB377 Evaluation Project. *Journal of Child and Family Studies, 1,* 93–113.

Rosenblatt, A., & Attkisson, C. C. (1993). Assessing outcomes for sufferers of severe mental disorder: A review and conceptual framework. *Evaluation and Program Planning, 16*(4), 347–363.

Rosenblatt, A. & Attkisson, C. C. (1997). Integrating systems of care with severe emotional disturbance IV: Educational attendance and achievement. *Journal of Child and Family Studies, 6*(1), 113–129.

Rosenblatt, A., Attkisson, C., & Mills, N. (1992). *The California AB377 evaluation, three year summary report.* San Francisco: University of California.

Rugs, D. (1992). *Mountain state network project.* Unpublished report. Tampa: Florida Mental Health Institute, Department of Child and Family Studies.

Scallet, L. J. (1994). The unintended consequences of health care reform for children's mental health services. *Behavioral Healthcare Tomorrow, 3*(2), 68–69.

Scriven, M. (1967). The methodology of evaluation. In R. W. Tyler, R. M. Gagne, & M. Scriven (Eds.), *Perspectives of curriculum evaluation.* Chicago: Rand McNally.

Sechrest, L. (1984). *Evaluating health care.* Unpublished manuscript, University of Arizona.

Sechrest, L., & Rosenblatt, A. (1987). Research methods. In H. C. Quay (Ed.), *Handbook of juvenile delinquency* (pp. 81–101). New York: John Wiley.

Sechrest, L., West, S. G., Phillips, M. A., Redner, R., & Yeaton, W. (1977). Some neglected problems in evaluation research: Strength and integrity of treatments. In L. Sechrest, S. G. West, M. A.

Phillips, R. Redner, & W. Yeaton (Eds.), *Evaluation studies review annual*. (Vol. 4, pp. 15–35). Beverly Hills, CA: Sage.

Shaffer, D., Fisher, P., Piacentini, J., Schwab-Stone, M., & Wicks, J. (1989). *Diagnostic Interview Schedule for Children (DISC-2.1)*. New York: New York State Psychiatric Institute.

Sorensen, J. E., & Grove, H. D. (1978). Using cost-outcome and cost-effectiveness analyses for improved program management and accountability. In C. C. Attkisson, Q. A. Hargreaves, M. J. Horowitz, & J. E. Sorensen (Eds.), *Evaluation of human service programs*. New York: Academic Press.

Stroul, B. A. (1992). Stark County, Ohio. In B. Stroul, S. Goldman, I. Lourie, J. Katz-Leavy, & C. Zeigler-Dendy (Eds.), *Profiles of local systems of care for children and adolescents with severe emotional disturbances* (pp. 211–286). Washington, DC: CASSP Technical Assistance Center, Georgetown University Child Development Center.

Stroul, B. A. (1993). *Systems of care for children and adolescents with severe emotional disturbances: What are the results?* Washington, DC: CASSP Technical Assistance Center, Georgetown University Child Development Center.

Stroul, B. A. (1996). *Managed care and children's mental health: Summary of the May 1995 state managed care meeting.* Washington, DC: Georgetown University Child Development Center, National Technical Assistance Center for Children's Mental Health.

Stroul, B. A., & Friedman, R. M. (1986). *A system of care for seriously emotionally disturbed children and youth.* Washington DC: CASSP Technical Assistance Center, Georgetown University Child Development Center.

Tharp, R. G., & Gallimore, R. (1979). The ecology of program research and evaluation: A model of evaluation succession. In L. Sechrest, S. G. West, M. A. Phillips, R. Redner, & W. Yeaton (Eds.), *Evaluation studies review annual* (Vol. 4, pp. 39–60). Beverly Hills, CA: Sage.

Trochim, W. M. K. (1984). *Research design for program evaluation: The regression discontinuity approach.* Beverly Hills, CA: Sage.

Trupin, E. W., Forsyth-Stephens, A., & Low, B. P. (1991). Service needs of severely disturbed children. *American Journal of Public Health, 81,* 975–980.

VanDenBerg, J. E., & Grealish, E. M. (1996). Individualized services and supports through the wraparound process: Philosophy and procedures. *Journal of Child and Family Studies, 5,* 7–22.

Vermont Department of Mental Health & Mental Retardation. (1993). *Vermont new directions evaluation of children and adolescent services.* Waterbury, VT: Division of Mental Health.

Virginia Department of Mental Health, Mental Retardation, & Substance Abuse Services (DMHMRSA). (1992a). *Demonstration project interim evaluation results.* Richmond, VA: Office of Research and Evaluation.

Virginia Department of Mental Health, Mental Retardation, & Substance Abuse Services (DMHMRSA). (1992b). *Local interagency service projects initiative.* Richmond, VA: Office of Research and Evaluation.

Waskow, I. E., & Parloff, M. B. (Eds.), (1974). *Psychotherapy change measures.* DHEW Publication No. (ADM)74-120. Washington, DC; Superintendent of Documents, U.S. Government Printing Office.

Weiss, C. H. (1972). *Evaluation research: Methods of assessing program effectiveness.* Englewood Cliffs, NJ: Prentice-Hall.

Weiss, C. H., & Bucuvales, M. J. (1980). Truth tests and utility tests: Decision makers frames of reference for social science research. *American Sociological Review, 45,* 302–313.

Weisz, J. R., Donenberg, G. R., Han, S. S., & Kauneckis, D. (1995). Child and adolescent psychotherapy outcomes in experiments versus clinics: Why the disparity? *Journal of Abnormal Child Psychology, 23*(1), 83–106.

Weisz, J. R., Weiss, B., Alicke, M. D., & Klotz, M. L. (1987). Effectiveness of psychotherapy with children and adolescents: A meta-analysis for clinicians. *Journal of Consulting and Clinical Psychology, 55*(4), 542–549.

Weisz, J. R., Weiss, B., & Donenberg, G. R. (1992). The lab versus the clinic: Effects of child and adolescent psychotherapy. *American Psychologist, 47,* 1578–1585.

The Role of the Case Study in the Evaluation of Individualized Services

13

John D. Burchard and Eric J. Bruns

During the past 12 years there has been a paradigm shift in the field of children's mental health. In 1982 it was determined that two thirds of the 3 million children with serious emotional disorders in this country were not receiving the services they needed, and many more were receiving inadequate care (Knitzer, 1982). The predominant services at the time were two categorical types of service: outpatient therapy and residential treatment. These services were categorical in the sense that the children had to fit the service. Children had to meet specific referral criteria in order to receive the service, and if their behavior was not appropriate they could be either expelled or discharged. Most children did not fit the service.

Over the past decade, remarkable efforts have been made to develop a more comprehensive continuum of services that would meet the needs of children and families (Stroul & Friedman, 1994). One of the fundamental principles of this alternative approach to delivering mental health services has been the focus on the individual child and family. As stated by Stroul & Friedman (1994), "Children with emotional disturbances should receive individualized services in accordance with the unique needs and potentials of each child and guided by an individualized plan" (p. xxiv).

The most developed use of the individualized service approach has been the wraparound process (Burchard & Clarke, 1990, VanDenBerg & Grealish, 1996). Basically, the process involves working with the people who are most influential in the life of the child and family, agreeing on what that particular child and family most need to live a stable and productive life, devising and implementing individualized, positive ways to meet those needs, and never giving up on the child and family. Instead of having professionals try to fit the child into existing categorical services, the people who are the most influential to the child and family tailor the services to fit the child and family.

While this shift to individualized services has become very popular and has spread to many parts of the country, it has created a significant challenge in the area of research and evaluation. Most of the research strategies that have dominated the field of mental health have focused on groups of individuals and have produced findings that are based on group differences. Group research strategies are not well suited for the evaluation of individualized services.

The purpose of this chapter is to describe and illustrate the use of the case study in the evaluation of individualized services. Following a brief discussion of the limitations of the more traditional methods of evaluation, case study methods will be presented. This will be followed by a discussion of the role of the case study in the evaluation of a service delivery system.

The Limitations of Group Designs

Experimental group designs have dominated the research efforts in the field of mental health. Rossi (1992) has argued that the preferred strategy for the assessment of the impact of any social program is the randomized controlled experiment. In such a study subjects are assigned randomly, either to an experimental group, where a standardized treatment is administered, or to a control group (i.e., comparison group), where the treatment is withheld. A fundamental assumption of the study's design is that all subjects, especially those within the experimental group, receive the same treatment. Because of the practical and political difficulties in conducting the randomized controlled experiment, there are many quasi-experimental research designs that involve creating comparison groups through means other than random assignment. Examples include comparisons of subjects receiving treatment versus those who have been put on a waiting list, or comparisons of treatment A versus treatment B. These designs also may be used to compare a group of individuals who received the treatment in question with a group that did not. The primary difference is that the subjects are not assigned randomly to the different groups.

A primary condition of these experimental and quasi-experimental group designs is the control of the independent variable. In many group designs, a specific experimental treatment is experienced by all the individuals in the experimental group and none of the individuals in the comparison group. For example, in a clinical trial study, children in the experimental group may receive a combination of Ritalin and behavior therapy, while children in the control group would receive no treatment (Pelham et al., 1990). The experimental group design has also been helpful in investigating the effectiveness of more complex categorical interventions. For example, in a study of the Homebuilders model for preventing out-of-home placements, the experimental group received intensive, family-based intervention while the children in a comparison group did not receive such services (Feldman, 1990). In each case, the study is designed to investigate the relationship between a specific intervention and a treatment outcome. Since the intervention is intended to achieve a specific outcome for each child, the comparison of group means on one or more predetermined variables is appropriate.

Group designs applied to individualized services, however, produce very little information on the relationship between intervention and treatment outcome. It is not possible to isolate the effect of any specific service because every child in the experimental group receives a different array of services. If the intervention were rigidly controlled and standardized for each child, the services could not be considered truly "individualized." In order to analyze the effect of a specific intervention within the experimental group, it would be necessary to utilize statistical, rather than experimental, controls. For example, a regression analysis could be conducted to determine which variables (e.g., hours of case management, therapy, respite) were associated with good outcomes. However, this would involve a situation in which there was variability in the utilization of a service (i.e., the individualized service model), as opposed to a situation in which all subjects received the same service (i.e., the clinical trial research design).

If an experimental group study were used to investigate outcomes associated with individualized services, the common denominator for the children in the experimental, individualized service group would be the process by which services were identified, rather than the services themselves. While it would be helpful to compare the individualized and the categorical service-delivery process, this has not been the focus of the studies that have been conducted. A case in point is the Fort Bragg study (Bickman, 1996). This study was a 5-year, $80-million effort to evaluate the cost-effectiveness of a full continuum of care that delivered services on an individualized basis. Through the use of a quasi-experimental design, it was concluded that there were no clinical or functional differences between the children and families in the experimental and control groups. In other words, individualized services were no better than categorical services.

But is the Fort Bragg study an adequate test of individualized services? In spite of the $80 million cost of the project, there are several reasons why this study provides very little useful information about individualized services (Burchard, 1996). First, there is little evidence that the process for identifying and delivering services was individualized. The evaluators acknowledged that they did not have adequate measures that assessed the process of care and that they were not able to show that the assessment or treatment planning processes in the experimental group were any better than those in the control group. Second, there is considerable evidence that many of the children in the experimental group did not receive individualized services (Summerfelt, Foster, & Saunders, 1996). Only 48% of the parents indicated that they were "very involved" in treatment planning, fewer than 15% of the children received inter-mediate-level services (e.g., group homes, foster homes, wilderness camps, in-home services, day treatment, after-school care), and there was no mention of the use of respite care, child mentors, professional roommates, or parent support groups, services that were an important part of the individualized services in other studies (Burchard, Burchard, Sewell, and VanDenBerg, 1993; Bruns, Burchard, and Yoe, 1995). Given that the predominate service in both groups was outpatient therapy (received by 87% of the experimental group and 86.8% of the comparison group), it appears that the operational definition of individualized services was the addition of a few more categorical services, which were received by 15% of the children and families.

A third reason the Fort Bragg study is of little help in the evaluation of individualized services is the nature of the experimental group design. Experimental group designs establish relationships that apply only to many individuals, *on the average,* and not to any given individual. In this case it was concluded that, on the average, the children who received "individualized services" improved, but no more so than the children who did not. Because of the many differences inherent in the delivery of individualized services, this type of evaluation is of very limited help. Those individuals working directly with children and families want to know what services are likely to be most effective with a child and family, and whether the services they are providing are making a difference. Although the Fort Bragg study has generated numerous books and articles, there is little information in the study that will answer such questions about individual children and families.

The Case Study Design

While it is important to pursue experimental group research, particularly to compare the individualized and the categorical service-delivery process, much can be learned about individualized services through the careful study of individual cases (Kazdin, 1992; Kratochwill & Levin, 1992). The different methods of individualized case study can be conceptualized in terms of a continuum of scientific rigor. The extreme points of the continuum would be represented by the qualitative case study at one end and the true experimental case study at the other. In the middle would be the quasi-experimental case study (Table 13.1 provides an outline of these different methods).

Most experimental case study designs, such as the reversal design, the changing criterion design, and the simultaneous treatment design, involve controlled manipulations of the intervention in an effort to isolate an effect on a behavior. Such designs are not suitable for evaluating individualized services, where the changes that are made in the intervention are made for research rather than clinical purposes. The one exception is the multiple baseline design, where it would be possible to administer individualized services to

Table 13.1
Case Study Methods for Evaluating Individualized Services

Research Design	Distinguishing Characteristics
Qualitative Designs	
Type A	Nonempirical, subjective data with Phase A representing either traditional services or individualized services
Type A-B	Nonempirical, subjective data with Phase A representing traditional services and Phase B representing individualized services
Quasi-Experimental Designs	
Type A	Empirical data with Phase A representing either traditional or wraparound services
Type A-B	Empirical data with Phase A representing traditional services and Phase B representing individualized services
Experimental Designs	
Multiple Baseline	Empirical data obtained on three or more subjects with a transition from traditional services to individualized services at different points in time.

multiple clients at different points in time. This was actually done in a recent study by Myaard (1996), in which the positive effects of wraparound services were replicated across four very challenging juvenile offenders. In the remainder of this chapter, however, only the qualitative and quasi-experimental case study methods will be described and illustrated.

The Qualitative Case Study Design

The purpose of the qualitative case studies that are discussed in this chapter is to make inferences about the effects of services by looking for changes in performance that are associated with different services within the same subject. The defining characteristic of these qualitative case studies is the use of uncontrolled observations. In most cases the data is obtained through open-ended interviews or written documents. While there is no empirically based data-collection process, an important component of the qualitative case study is the use of multiple sources of information to establish chains of evidence (Yin, 1989). Therefore, when inferences are made, they are not based on a single informant or source of information. Also, the process for obtaining data from interviews and documents should be consistent across people and time. See Epstein & Quinn (1996) and Schaefer, Burchard, & Rick (1992) for additional information concerning the data collection process.

Some of the benefits of the qualitative case study are that (a) it can be applied retrospectively to a time period when empirically based data were not obtained, (b) it requires less control of the variables being studied, and (c) it can provide a rich array of information that is not available through predetermined, empirically based data-collection instruments. On the other hand, the absence of empirically based data also creates its major limitation. Because the study relies on anecdotal reports and subjective impressions, interpretations of the data are subject to alternative explanations.

Type A Qualitative Case Study Design

The type A design is the most basic form of the qualitative design. It focuses on the relationship between services and patterns of behavior over a period of time when a particular service or delivery model is in place. The design is usually employed to determine whether or not the child is making progress. However, such a design also may be used to gain insight into the service-delivery process. For example, research in Vermont and Illinois used retrospective, qualitative case studies to provide insight into the types of services that might have prevented repeated placement failures.

In the Vermont study, the subjects were 10 children who were residing in out-of-state residential treatment centers, and the sources of information were child and parent interviews and the review of multiple agency records. Although only one of the case studies was published (Schaefer et al., 1992), all 10 cases revealed a trail of sparse, fragmented, categorical services and pointed to the need for more individualized services early in the child's life, when significant at-risk indicators were present. The Illinois study focused on eight children who were or previously had been placed outside of their homes and were regarded as the most challenging to the placement agency. A very thorough case study was presented on one of the children that also revealed many ways in which services could have been improved (Epstein & Quinn, 1996).

While the case studies describe what has and has not happened to children who have experienced repeated failures in the service-delivery system, it is important to treat the findings with caution. These are uncontrolled case studies that are based on subjectively filtered descriptions of services, events, and behaviors that have occurred in the absence of experimental control. Therefore, it is not possible to determine the effect of the presence or absence of any particular service. Nevertheless, the case studies do serve as a source of ideas about how the failures might have been prevented and how the service-delivery system can be improved.

Type A-B Qualitative Case Study Design

The A-B qualitative design is used to evaluate the relationship between services and patterns of performance before and after a major change in the way services are delivered. Rather than looking for change over time, this design uses qualitative data to investigate the impact of a specific change in an intervention.

In Vermont, the A-B qualitative design was used in a demonstration project in which four very challenging children were moved from long-term residential treatment into community-based, individualized services (Burchard et al., 1991). The children averaged 14 placement failures prior to the demonstration project. The results of the case studies showed that after 1 year of individualized services, all four children continued to display a relatively stable adjustment in the community. In addition, the findings of the case studies helped promote a change in the overall service-delivery system. At the present time, more than 100 of the most challenging children in Vermont are now receiving individualized services.

In Alaska, the qualitative case study was used to evaluate a radical shift from categorical to individualized services in an entire service-delivery system (Burchard, Burchard, Sewell, & VanDenBerg, 1993). As part of the shift, 39 of the 40 children in out-of-state residential treatment were returned to their communities and villages. After approximately 1 year of individualized services, case studies were conducted on 10 of the more successful and innovative cases. In general, the case studies revealed a very creative process of tailoring different services to each child; the consensus from approximately 75 interviews was that the individualized-service approach represented a marked improvement in the delivery of mental health services to children and families. The following is a more detailed description of one of those cases.

 Mary: An Example of the Retrospective Case Study Design

The case of Mary represents a retrospective study of an extremely challenging child who, after many years of receiving very traditional, categorical services, began receiving individualized services. Because the case exemplifies some of the major distinctions between traditional and individualized services, it will be described in some detail (see Burchard et al., 1993, for the complete case study).

A multiaxial timeline documenting major events, behaviors, and services from Mary's birth until the time the study was conducted are presented in Figure 13.1. To the left of the vertical dotted line is condition A, the period of approximately 16½ years when Mary received traditional, categorical services. The right of the dotted line represents condition B, the period of approximately 1 year when she received individualized services from the Alaska Youth Initiative (AYI).

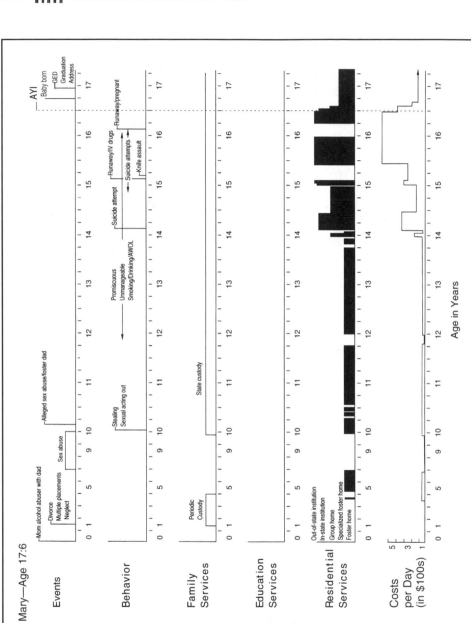

Figure 13.1. Multiaxial life events timeline.

As can be seen, Mary experienced much trauma and instability during her early life. Her parents were divorced when she was approximately 1 year old, and her mother had a severe alcohol problem that periodically demanded she place Mary for short periods of time with her maternal grandparents, a boyfriend, and a receiving home for abused and neglected children. By age 4½, Mary's mother had faded out of the picture, leaving only periodic reports of chronic drinking, alcohol overdoses, suicide attempts, and hospitalizations.

Over the next several years, Mary experienced multiple placements with different foster parents, her father, and her grandparents. At age 9, Mary reported to her stepmother that her father had been having violent sexual intercourse with her on a regular basis over the previous 18 months. The allegations included being beaten and tied up as well as being sexually assaulted. The stepmother confronted her husband, who denied the allegations. She then reported Mary's allegations to the paternal grandparents, who called Mary a liar and made her apologize. Approximately 2 months later the stepmother notified the child welfare agency, whereby the allegations were substantiated. Several years later, Mary disclosed to a counselor that the sexual abuse had begun when she was 3 years old.

From age 9 until she was accepted into AYI at age 16, Mary experienced 13 additional placement changes. This included six foster home placements, a placement with her stepmother, two group home placements, a placement in a detention center, a stay in a psychiatric hospital, and two placements in out-of-state, residential treatment centers.

In general, the restrictiveness of Mary's placements increased with the severity of her behavior problems. Each placement change resulted from an inability of service providers to cope with various forms of acting-out behavior. In the early stages of the struggle to obtain a suitable placement for Mary, she was transferred from one foster home to another for such behaviors as noncompliance, theft, and inappropriate interactions with men that ranged from fears of being raped to sexual provocations with strangers. Over time she "behaved" her way into more restrictive placements through a variety of more severe incidents involving aggression, running away, sexual promiscuity, drug abuse (marijuana, LSD, cocaine, PCP, and heroin), suicide attempts, and expressions of homicidal intent. This culminated, at age 16, in her being sent to a second out-of-state residential treatment center. Upon admission, Mary was given the following diagnosis:

> *borderline personality disorder because of a long history of unstable relationships, self-damaging impulsiveness, affective instability, self-mutilating behavior, a lack of meaningful sense of self and conduct disorder, solitary aggressive type, with mixed substance abuse.*

She was placed on a locked unit in which she received frequent psychiatric counseling and the antidepressant medication Nortriptyline. A major focus of treatment was to help her develop trust in adult caretakers. After 6 months it was determined she had made sufficient progress to be transferred to an unlocked psychiatric wing. One week later, in response to punishment for smoking, she ran away to a large nearby city where she lived with a boyfriend she had met during a 3-month runaway from her first out-of-state placement. After she had spent 3½ months in the city, her boyfriend, in a fit of anger, reported her to the authorities.

Upon her return to the institution, it was found that Mary was approximately 2 months pregnant. The pregnancy necessitated an abrupt change in her treatment plan. Since the state of Alaska could claim custody of her baby only if the birth took place in Alaska, officials at the treatment center began to prepare Mary and the child welfare agency in Alaska for an eventual discharge and return to Alaska. At this point, the child welfare agency in Alaska referred Mary's case to AYI.

While developing an individualized service plan for Mary, AYI arranged for an independent psychiatric evaluation prior to her return to Alaska. The recommendations from the nine-page report included the following:

> It is clear that (Mary) will continue to need long term inpatient psychiatric treatment for an extended period of time. . . . She will need a minimum of 6 months and possibly up to a year of continued inpatient treatment in a locked facility in order to prevent her from impulsively eloping as she has in the past.
>
> It is highly likely that the prospect of becoming a mother will reawaken unresolved conflicts. . . . The patient's psychiatric symptoms will be exacerbated as the pregnancy progresses.
>
> It would be highly dangerous to both her and her baby to have this treatment take place outside of a locked, inpatient psychiatric unit.
>
> The optimal solution would be for the patient to voluntarily relinquish the baby. Hopefully, in intensive therapy should could come to recognize that it would not be in her best interest or that of the fetus for her to assume caretaking responsibility for it. One of the goals in such a therapy would be to help her recognize that she could interrupt the terrible cycle in her family of abuse and neglect that resulted in her own unhappiness and severe dysfunction.

The ecologically based treatment approach adopted by AYI differed radically from the more traditional, clinically based approach modeled after the medical profession. The traditional approach would hold that the child has a "disorder" and that the physical environment within which the child is "treated" plays a minor role with respect to their adjustment. From this perspective, the objective in treating someone like Mary would be to first get her (and the baby) in a safe place and then provide "treatment."

The approach that was taken by AYI was somewhat the opposite. It assumed that the environment played a much more significant role, both with respect to the problem and the solution. The objective was to achieve a greater balance between the restrictiveness of the environment and the safety of the child. Instead of placing Mary on a locked ward with many other "severely disturbed" children, AYI focused on creating a community placement whereby staff could be "wrapped around" the child to achieve safety. The AYI approach began by assuming Mary's needs, attitudes, motivations, and strengths from a broad *ecological perspective and then added safety, rather than starting with safety and then adding the treatment.*

After the birth of her child and a brief placement in a group home, Mary was placed with a foster family with a 2-year-old child. Some of the character- istics that led to the selection of this particular family were the foster parents' minority status, their unconditional commitment to help Mary, one parent's experience and skill as a mental health professional, and the opportunity for the foster parents to model appropriate parenting skills on an everyday basis.

The evaluation of the case took place approximately 5 months after Mary had been placed into her specialized foster home. At that time her adjustment continued to be remarkable. She was relating to her baby in a very appropriate manner; she was receiving counseling at the community mental health center; she completed her GED and gave the commencement address at the graduation ceremonies; and she was developing a small network of friends in the commu- nity. In addition, Mary was actively planning to attend college in the fall.

Once again, it is necessary to qualify the findings of this case study. While it appears Mary's progress was a function of her transition to individualized ser- vices, the study leaves many important questions unanswered. What caused the improvement in Mary's performance? What were the specific effects of different services that Mary received? What would be Mary's current level of adjustment had she been sent to a locked psychiatric hospital? Would the outcome that is associated with the individualized services be the same for children who are com- parable to Mary? These questions cannot be answered without further research.

Nevertheless, this case study makes a valuable contribution to the field of children's mental health. While it is unclear what would have happened had Mary been sent to a psychiatric hospital, two things are clear: First, outcomes associated with the use of individualized services often are more positive than professionals predicted. While Mary's adjustment could change overnight, the collective opinion of several professional experts had been that progress could be achieved only through long-term, inpatient psychiatric treatment. Second, because of this case study, the outcomes are much more visible than any that would have been associated with further inpatient psychiatric treatment. Due to confidentiality laws and a dearth of credible follow-up studies, it is difficult to determine what happens to children who grow up in the service-delivery sys- tem. Since what we do know is very discouraging, it is valuable to see the results of a case study like Mary's, which describes a positive outcome from an approach that is radically different from traditional services.

Type A Quasi-Experimental Case Study Design

The quasi-experimental case study design is the next on the continuum of sci- entific rigor. This design features increased rigor because it uses quantitative measures that are repeated over time. While the quasi-experimental design narrows the focus on the study, the repeated use of quantitative measures enhances the reliability of the data. Nevertheless, the design is not a true experimental design because it does not isolate the effect of an intervention by systematically withdrawing and presenting alternative interventions (Kazdin, 1992).

The simplest form of the quasi-experimental design involves tracking performance and services over time and documenting changes in the stability of behavior (type A design). For example, if the child was receiving individualized services, a change in the stability of performance could be used to demonstrate that progress was being made.

Samantha: An Example of a Type A Quasi-Experimental Case Study Design

This is the case of Samantha, a 15-year-old adolescent who was receiving individualized services in Vermont (Burchard et al., 1995). Samantha was removed from her mother's custody before she was 2 years old as a result of neglect and probable physical abuse. She was placed in two foster homes and adopted at age 5. She was the victim of sexual abuse by one of the foster parents and by her neighbor while she was living in her adoptive home.

By the time Samantha was 10, her behavior had become so problematic that her adoptive parents felt they were unable to manage her alone. She was extremely aggressive with peers and adults, indulged in repeated and prolonged temper tantrums, inappropriate sexual behavior, attempts at suicide, self-injurious gestures (e.g., biting and swallowing broken light bulbs and other sharp objects), and smearing of feces and menstrual blood. Her thinking was incoherent at times, she was rejected by her peers, and she suffered a very poor self-image and depressed mood. She was placed in a residential treatment center for children and youth, where she remained for 6 months before beginning a series of unsuccessful placements in group homes and foster homes.

When Samantha was 14 years old, she was removed from a group home, placed in a therapeutic foster home, and began receiving individualized wrap-around services. At that time her caretakers began completing the Weekly Adjustment Indicator Checklist (WAIC; Burchard & Bruns, 1993). Using the WAIC, her caretakers indicated how many days per week the 22 behaviors listed in Table 13.2 occurred.

The 10 severe negative behaviors were regarded as those behaviors that would place the child most at risk of being removed from the community.

Four behaviors were determined to be the most problematic for Samantha:

1. Physical aggression: hitting, striking, biting, or scratching a person with intent to harm (includes hitting with an object).

Table 13.2

WAIC Indicators

Severe Negative	Moderate Negative	Positive
Physical aggression	Alcohol/drug use	Self-confidence
Property damage	Cruelty to animals	Compliance
Theft	Sad	Peer interaction
Running away	Anxious	School attendance
Life threat	Self-injury	Work attendance
Sexual abuse	Extreme verbal abuse	
Fire-setting	Sexual acting out	
Suicide attempt		
Police contact		

2. *Sad: sad, withdrawn, or depressed to a degree that significantly interfered with participation in an important activity.*

3. *Anxious: fearful, anxious or worried to a degree that interfered with participation in an important activity.*

4. *Self-injury: attempt to harm herself.*

The frequency of Samantha's exhibition of the four behaviors is illustrated in Figure 13.2. As shown, progress was made with all four behaviors. Physical aggression stopped after the 11th week; depression and anxiety continued throughout the year but at a reduced rate, and no self-injury was observed after week 3. Because of the repeated use of quantitative measures, the change in behavior can be established more reliably than with qualitative measures. In this example, the positive change in the stability of the behavior is apparent through visual inspection.

Although the quasi-experimental design can establish an association between a service and an outcome, demonstration of change during an intervention does not establish a causal relationship. The current case demonstrates that Samantha made significant progress while she was receiving individualized services, but not necessarily because of it. Nevertheless, given the multitude of

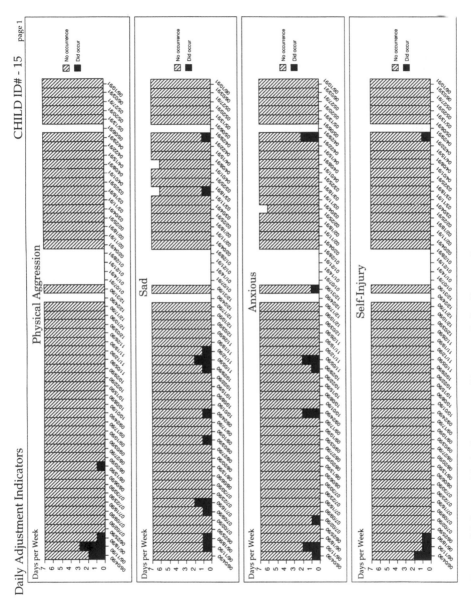

Figure 13.2. Weekly behavior tracking graph for Samantha.

failures she had previously experienced, this type of demonstration can be very helpful to an agency trying to improve services for children and families.

In using the quasi-experimental design with individualized services, it is not uncommon to obtain data that are difficult to analyze through visual inspection. In such cases it may be helpful to employ a statistical test to determine if there is a trend in the stability of the behavior. The Kendall Tau statistic is an easily calculated measure of association that can be used to test for a trend in time-series data (Daniel, 1990). Kendall Tau can be used as an index on which a positive value indicates an upward trend of behavioral occurrences, and a negative value indicates a downward trend. It also can be used as the basis for testing the null hypothesis, that there is no behavioral trend (Tau = 0) in a series of observations, against the alternative of either upward or downward trend (Tau > 0 or Tau < 0) in the series. With regard to behavioral tracking data, Tau may be interpreted as the probability that the behavioral score for each week will be greater than the score for the week immediately preceding.

Figure 13.3 exemplifies how a test for trend was applied to WAIC data to help determine if a child made progress in a program in South Dakota (Froelich, 1995). From a visual inspection of the graph for severe negative behaviors (solid line), a downward trend seems clearly apparent. This conclusion is supported by the statistically significant Tau coefficient (−0.526; p < .05). It is more difficult to

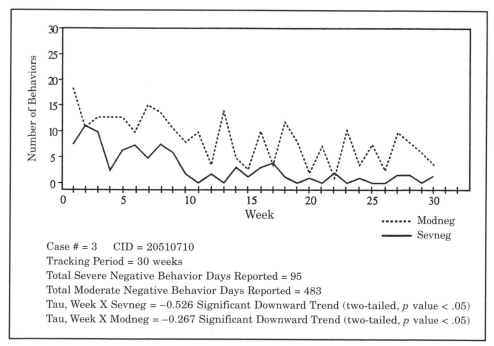

Figure 13.3. Behavioral trend analysis using Kendall's Tau.

visually discern a trend for moderate negative behaviors, which might lead one to conclude that no progress was made on those particular problem behaviors. The Tau coefficient (-0.267; $p < .05$), however, indicates that, for moderate behaviors, a relatively weak but statistically significant downward trend is present.

While this information may be of limited use to a child and family team that is striving for more obvious progress, this type of statistical yardstick can be very helpful for an agency that is trying to assess progress across a large number of cases. This systems use of the Kendall Tau analysis will be discussed further below.

Type A-B Quasi-Experimental Design

The A-B quasi-experimental is used to focus greater attention on the potential behavioral effects of a specific change in service. This is done by looking for a noticeable change in the stability of a behavior or a pattern of behavior that coincides with an abrupt change in service. If the study included two or three additional changes in services, it would be referred to as an A-B-C or an A-B-C-D respectively.

While A-B quasi-experimental design still cannot be used to establish a causal relationship, it does have the potential to strengthen an inference that a service had a particular effect on behavior (Kazdin, 1992). If the relationship between the service and behavior was of primary concern, the inference would be further strengthened if a particular finding were replicated across subjects or settings.

The case of Samantha will be used to illustrate the use of an A-B-C-D quasi-experimental design. In the study, the effect of three planned placement changes on the frequency of specific positive and negative behaviors was analyzed. The positive and negative behaviors were recorded daily by Samantha's caretakers, using the WAIC (for a more detailed description of this case and the data-collection process, see Burchard et al., 1995). The planned placement changes involved a transfer from a residential treatment center to a staffed apartment, from the staffed apartment to a specialized foster home (also referred to as therapeutic foster home), and from the foster home to a supervised apartment. The four placements are referred to as conditions A, B, C, and D.

The results of the analysis are shown in Figure 13.4. In order to increase stability and facilitate the analysis, the data is plotted across months rather than weeks. Because school attendance is graphed separately, it is not included in the aggregate of positive behaviors. Each graph covers a time period of 2 years and 2 months.

In general, the graphs demonstrate that remarkable progress was made with Samantha over the 2-year period. The transition from the residential treatment center to the staffed apartment resulted in a sharp decline in the frequency of negative behaviors, followed by additional decline to almost nonoccurrence at the end of the year. (This time period coincides with the time period

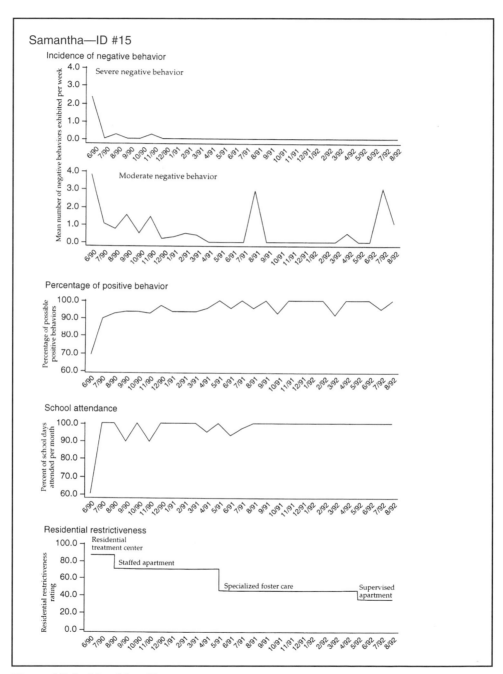

Figure 13.4. Monthly adjustment summary.

covered in the bar graphs of four of the behaviors shown in Figure 13.2). In addition, the increase that took place in the occurrence of positive behaviors over this same time period is shown in this graph.

Also of interest in this case study is the sharp, temporary increase in moderate negative behaviors that followed Samantha's next two placement changes. The specific behaviors that contributed most to these increases were anxiety ("anxious to a degree which significantly interfered with participation in an important activity") and extreme verbal abuse ("speaking to another person in an extremely malicious, abusive or intimidating manner"). The occurrence of these behaviors appeared to be a function of the decreased supervision and the increase in responsibility associated with each placement change. In response to these reactions, the staff provided additional one-to-one contact with Samantha, which was then gradually reduced.

There were two important benefits of this case study. First, the use of quantitative measures demonstrated that significant progress had occurred over the 2-year period of the study. Such documentation was helpful feedback for the service providers as they attempted to wrap services around other children exhibiting challenging behaviors. Such evidence of success also was rewarding to the team members. As one provider put it, "I feel like this shows my life's work." Second, the data revealed an important relationship between a change in service and an increase in negative behaviors that can now be examined in further case studies.

Evaluating the Impact of Individualized Services With a Group of Children

Thus far, examples of the case study design have been used to draw inferences about the impact of individualized services on the individual child. It is also possible to use case study data to evaluate the behavioral changes experienced by a group of children receiving individualized services. In one method, an objective criterion for behavioral change can be applied across a group of children who are receiving individualized services. This method was used in a South Dakota study involving 292 children who were receiving home-based therapy over a period of 20 weeks (Froelich, 1995). Although the study did not focus on individualized services, the methodology would be the same.

In this study, all children were tracked using the WAIC. Using the Kendall Tau statistic, as illustrated in Figure 13.3, and two-tailed tests, each case was classified as "downward" ($p < .05$), "upward" ($p < .05$) or "no trend" on severe moderate negative behaviors. Using a chi-square test, it was then shown that there were significantly more downward than upward trends for both types of behavior. While it could not be concluded that the intervention caused the positive change in behavior, it did provide objective, quantified evidence that progress was being made with a large group of children.

In the South Dakota study, progress was defined in terms of a significant decline in negative behaviors. A second way to evaluate groups of children would be to establish a more comprehensive definition of progress, which considers performance across several domains, and then present the results in the form of a report card. This procedure was used in Baltimore in a 1–2-year follow-up study of 45 youth who had been receiving individualized services as an alternative to residential treatment (Hyde, Burchard, & Woodworth, 1996).

Progress was operationally defined in terms of a youth's performance in four areas: school attendance, work attendance, the frequency of severe negative behaviors, and the restrictiveness of the living environment. Based on data collected over a 30-day period, each child was classified into one of three levels of community adjustment: "good," "fair," or "poor." For example, for a child's adjustment to be classified as "good," that child must have been living with a family or in an apartment, must have attended school 85% of the time or worked 35 hours per week (or a lesser combination of the two), and must have had no more than 2 days during which there was an occurrence of a severe negative behavior. Using this classification system, the levels of adjustment for the 45 youth were approximately 50% good, 25% fair, and 25% poor.

This type of analysis presents progress information in a very user friendly format, while utilizing empirically based data. The community adjustment report card could be used to compare a group with itself (within-group analysis) or for comparing two groups that are receiving different services (between-group analysis).

Conclusion

The purpose of this chapter has been to describe and illustrate how the case study method can be used to study individualized services. Given the complex, ever-changing nature of the individualized service method, it is believed that the case study can generate and test inferences about services and outcomes that are not achievable through the more traditional methods of research and evaluation.

It has been argued that the large, expensive, experimental group studies, like the Fort Bragg study, has provided us with relatively little information about individualized services. If such studies are to be conducted in the future, it is highly recommended that they systematically incorporate case study approaches into the evaluation, so that the flexibility and creativity of the services can be described and the potential impact on individual clients can be documented.

References

Bickman, L. (1996). The evaluation of a children's mental health managed care demonstration. *Journal of Mental Health Administration, 23,* 6–147.

Bruns, E. J., Burchard, J. D., & Yoe, J. T. (1995). Evaluating the Vermont system of care: Outcomes associated with community-based wraparound services. *Journal of Child and Family Studies, 4,* 321–339.

Burchard, J. D., (1996). Evaluation of the Fort Bragg managed care experiment. *Journal of Child and Family Studies, 5,* 173–176.

Burchard, J. D., & Bruns, E. J. (1993). *User's guide to the Weekly Adjustment Indicator Checklist.* Burlington: University of Vermont, Department of Psychology.

Burchard, J. D., Burchard, S. N., Sewell, R., & VanDenBerg, J. (1993). *One kid at a time: The case study evaluation and implementation of the Alaska Youth Initiative Demonstration Project.* Washington, DC: Georgetown University Press.

Burchard, J. D., & Clarke, R. T. (1990). The role of individualized care in a service delivery system for children and adolescents with severely maladjusted behavior. *Journal of Mental Health Administration, 17,* 48–60.

Burchard, J. D., Hinden, B., Carro, M., Schaefer, M., Bruns, E., & Pandina, N. (1995). Using case-level data to monitor a case-management system. In B. J. Friesen & J. Poertner (Eds.), *From case management to service coordination for children with emotional, behavioral, or mental disorders: Building on family strengths* (pp. 169–187). Baltimore: Brookes.

Burchard, J. D., Schaefer, M., Harrington, N., Rogers, J., Welkowitz, J., & Tighe, T. (1991). An evaluation of the community integration demonstration project. Unpublished report, Vermont Department of Mental Health and Mental Retardation.

Daniel, W. W. (1990). *Applied nonparametric statistics.* Boston: PWS-Kent.

Epstein, M. H., & Quinn, K. P. (1995). A case study approach to analyze the relationship between children and services in a system of care. *Journal of Emotional and Behavioral Studies, 4,* 21–29.

Feldmen, L. (1990). Evaluating the impact of family preservation services in New Jersey. Draft document, Bureau of Research, Evaluation and Quality Assurance, New Jersey Division of Youth and Family Services.

Froelich, P. (1995). Evaluation of home-based family therapy: First steps in building South Dakota's Child and Adolescent Service System. Unpublished report, South Dakota Division of Mental Health Child and Adolescent Service System Program, Pierre, SD.

Hyde, K. L., Burchard, J. D., & Woodworth, K. (1996). Wrapping services in an urban setting. *Journal of Child and Family Studies, 5,* 67–82.

Kazdin, A. K. (1992). *Research in design in clinical psychology.* Boston: Allyn and Bacon.

Knitzer, J. (1982). *Unclaimed children: The failure of public responsibility to children and adolescents in need of mental health services.* Washington, DC: Children's Defense Fund.

Kratochwill, T. R., & Levin, J. R. (1992). *Single-case design and analysis: New directions for psychology and education.* Hillsdale, NJ: Lawrence Erlbaum.

Myaard, M. J. (1996). The effects of wraparound services on the adjustment of four severely emotionally disturbed youth: A controlled multiple-baseline study. Unpublished doctoral dissertation, Western Michigan University, Kalamazoo.

Pelham, W. W., Schnedler, R. W., Bender, M. E., Nilson, D. E., Miller, J., Budrow, M. S., Ronnel, M., Paluchowski, C., & Marks, D. A. (1990). The combination of behavior therapy and methylphenidate in the treatment of attention deficit disorders: A therapy out-come study. In L. Bloomingdale (Ed.), *Attention deficit disorders* (Vol. 3). New York: Pergamon Press.

Rossi, P. H. (1992). Assessing family preservation programs. *Children and Youth Services review, 4,* 77–97.

Schaefer, M., Burchard, J. D., & Rick, K. (1992). A case study of a child in out-of-state residential care: An in-depth analysis of what didn't work. In A. Algarin, R. M. Friedman, A. F. Duchnowski, K. M. Kutash, S. Silver, & M. K. Johnson (Eds.), *Proceedings of the 3rd annual*

Research Conference: A System of Care for Children's Mental Health: Building a Research Base (pp. 211–226). Tampa: Florida Mental Health Institute.

Stroul, B. A., & Friedman, R. (1994). *A system of care for severely emotionally disturbed children and youth.* Washington, DC: CASSP Technical Assistance Center, Georgetown University Child Development Center.

Summerfelt, W. T., Foster, E. M., & Saunders R. C. (1996). Mental health services utilization in a children's mental health managed care demonstration. *Journal of Mental Health Administration, 23,* 80–91.

VanDenBerg, J. E., & Gealish, E. M. (1996). Individualized services and supports through the wraparound process: Philosophy and procedures. *Journal of Child and Families Studies, 5,* 7–21.

Yin, R. (1989). *Case study research: Design and methods.* Beverly Hills, CA: Sage.

Designing Economic Evaluations To Measure Societal Costs

14

Nancy Wolff

Introduction

The nation's single largest investment is in our children. Families and the government annually spend billions of dollars to meet the developmental, educational, and social needs of the youngest generation (Kronebusch & Schlesinger, 1994). Investments in youth are expected to yield future societal returns in the form of reduced private and public spending on health and social problems, as well as to contribute to higher worker productivity (National Commission on Children, 1991). Not surprisingly, families constitute the largest investors in our children (Morgan, 1978). Kronebusch and Schlesinger (1994) estimate that families spend over $500 billion annually for individuals younger than age 20. Although most Americans believe that families should bear most of the responsibility for meeting the needs of children (Bales, 1993), some families are not able to meet these responsibilities. Too few private dollars are likely to be invested in children who live in poverty or who have extraordinary needs because of health or behavioral problems (Edelman, 1987; Gottschalk & Danziger, 1993; Klerman, 1991).

Programs for children funded by federal, state, and local governments complement the investments made by families. Some of these programs are designed and targeted for children of poor or medically needy families (e.g., food programs for Women, Infant, and Children; Medicaid), while others benefit all children independent of their family's economic situation (e.g., public education). It is estimated that federal spending for children amounted to $94 billion in 1990 (Kronebusch & Schlesinger, 1994). State and local governments fund a wide range of children's services. Approximately $200 billion was spent on public primary and secondary education by state and local governments in

385

1990 (U.S. Bureau of the Census, 1994). Based on 1984 estimates (the most recent data) adjusted to 1990 prices, an additional $10 billion was spent on health-related programs for children (Larson,1990).

The needs of children are diverse and span the boundaries of many service systems, including health and mental health care, social service, education, and juvenile justice. Contemporary social problems such as AIDS, substance abuse, and violence are altering the nature of these needs and are reshaping the relationships among the systems designed to meet them (Hawkins, 1985). The lack of investment in children by one system may increase the demands placed on other systems. Moreover, inadequate investment in the health or well-being of a child at any point in time may result in loss of functional capacities, which may increase the future needs of children or decrease their future productivity.

Increasing demands for public-sector services by children who are poor or medically needy has drawn attention to the growing public costs associated with these services (General Accounting Office, 1994). Combined with fiscal and political pressures on the government to contain costs, the growing need for services is creating tensions between the private and public sectors, among different service systems, and among the different levels of government (Huston, 1991). One way to lessen the tensions between and among these groups is to discover ways to use public monies more efficiently.

As policymakers have struggled to get the most out of each public dollar, economic evaluations of public-sector investments have become more important. In the case of children, policymakers need to know how much the public is spending for each special needs group. This information is useful in determining how to allocate public monies fairly among groups and across service systems. In addition, policymakers are interested in knowing the relative cost of competing interventions so that they can promote those interventions that are most efficient. The first set of issues is addressed by cost identification studies, the second by cost-effectiveness/benefit evaluations.

In this chapter economic evaluations will be examined, with special emphasis on the methods used to estimate costs. The discussion draws on my experiences with estimating the societal costs associated with programs for persons with serious mental illness. Choosing the appropriate structure for an economic evaluation hinges on several choices that are discussed in the next section. Then, the chapter focuses on the cost-benefit framework, the "ledger" of costs and benefits, as a set of input-output relationships associated with each program or investment. In the last section, costing methods are reviewed with an emphasis on how to collect and use data to produce reliable and consistent estimators of resource costs.

Purpose of Economic Evaluations

Economic evaluations are a tool for assessing specific investments (e.g., treatment settings, purchases of equipment, staffing structures, medications, system designs). The two major forms are cost identification studies, which focus exclusively on resource costs measured in dollars, and cost-benefit, cost-effectiveness, or cost-utility studies, all of which measure both costs and benefits, but differ from each other in the way that benefits are valued. The number of published studies of each type has been growing in recent years. Of particular note are the cost-of-illness studies by Frank (1985), Rice, Kelman, & Miller (1991), Rice, Kelman, & Miller (1992), and Rice, Kelman, Miller, & Dunmeyer (1990); the cost-of-treatment studies by Dickey et al. (1989), Dickey, Cannon, McGuire, & Gudeman (1986a), Dickey, McGuire, & Gudeman (1986b), Jerrell and Hu (1993), and Wolff, Helminiak, & Diamond (1995); and the cost-benefit studies by Bond, Miller, Drumwied, & Ward (1988), Jerrell (1995), Jerrell and Hu (1989), Reed, Hennessey, Mitchell, & Babigian (1994), Weisbrod (1983), and Wolff et al. (1995).[1]

Cost identification or cost-of-illness studies ask this question: What is the cost of a particular illness or treatment strategy? The simplest cost identification study estimates the costs of resources used to produce the services (or goods) used by persons who have an illness or who are targeted to receive a particular type of treatment. A more comprehensive cost study (usually referred to as "cost-of-illness") also includes the costs associated with lost productivity for people who are too sick to work (or who die prematurely) or who must give up jobs to take care of a person who is ill. The findings from cost-based evaluations traditionally have been used to assess whether a particular health problem is important and deserving of increased research or public attention. In this way, cost-based evaluations can be used to inform and rationalize macrolevel fiscal planning. For example, in allocating research dollars among different types of physical and mental health problems, policymakers could use information from cost-of-illness studies to rank health problems in accordance to the potential savings from dollars invested in certain types of clinical research. These same results also could be used to examine issues of funding equity among illnesses by examining current public spending on specific health and mental health problems in proportion to their respective illness costs. The distribution of health costs among persons with different health problems is becoming more valuable to private and public insurers who are paying providers a capitated rate (i.e., a fixed prospective payment received per enrolled person that is designed to cover the expected costs of health care over a predefined time period) for their services in order to encourage greater efficiencies. For a capitated payment system to work equitably, health care providers ought to be paid roughly what particular patients can be expected to cost. How good these rates are depends on the accuracy of the underlying cost data.

The more common form of economic evaluation is the cost-effectiveness, cost-utility, or cost-benefit study. These studies evaluate the relative efficiencies of two or more possible investments by comparing the net gains (benefits minus costs) among various investment options. The principal difference between cost-effectiveness, cost-utility, and cost-benefit studies involves the measurement of benefits. Benefits in cost-benefit studies are measured in dollars, whereas benefits are measured in clinical terms (e.g., years of life saved or mgs of cholesterol reduction) in cost-effectiveness studies, or in utility terms (e.g., quality adjusted life years) for cost-utility studies.

Evaluations of this type provide a criterion for determining which of many investments is the most efficient—that is, the one that yields the greatest net benefits. This approach will result in an optimal allocation of resources only if there has been a comprehensive accounting of all benefits and costs for all relevant investment options. Cost-benefit analysis may order investments incorrectly if either some benefits or costs that vary among the different investment options are excluded from the analysis or if some relevant investment options are excluded from the analysis. Ultimately, the quality of the resulting ranking hinges on whether the researcher used the analytical tool appropriately.

Information from cost-benefit or cost-effectiveness analyses is valuable to policymakers who need to make choices. For example, Oregon attempted to apply a form of cost-benefit analysis to rank the health care service priorities covered by Medicaid (Eddy, 1991; Hadorn, 1991). Congress is considering a bill that would require environmental regulations to pass a cost-benefit test (Cushman, 1995). New medications are increasingly expected to demonstrate their cost-effectiveness prior to approval in many European countries and prior to being included on the formulary lists of many managed care organizations (Hillman et al., 1991). And the Government Accounting Office is increasingly using cost-benefit analysis to support public spending on children's programs (General Accounting Office, 1992, 1993).

Key Research Design Issues

Cost-benefit is often used to refer generically to cost-effectiveness, cost-benefit, or cost-utility studies, an approach that will be followed in this chapter. Increasingly, cost-benefit analysis is being used to guide decisions that have significant consequences. Unfortunately, policymakers are often unaware of how the results of these studies depend on decisions made by researchers regarding (a) analytical perspective, (b) study duration, and (c) estimation precision.

Analytical Perspective

A central principle of cost-benefit analysis is to include all relevant costs and benefits associated with an investment option. The scope of relevancy for costs and benefits will differ, however, depending on the perspective used in the study. Five perspectives are common: society, government, provider, payer, and individual. These options are listed from most to least in terms of comprehensiveness.

The choice of perspective influences which costs and benefits are included in the cost-benefit analysis, as well as the value assigned to the resources that are used to produce the investment and the effects caused by the investment. Much of the theoretical exposition on cost-benefit analysis is framed in terms of the societal perspective. This employs the broadest definition of costs and benefits; this perspective includes all costs and benefits associated with an investment, regardless of the segment of the society that bears the costs or receives the benefits. Resources are valued at their opportunity costs—that is, their value based on their best alternative use.

The other four perspectives use a narrower range of benefits and costs. The government (federal, state, local, or all levels) perspective, for example, may exclude costs that are external to the government's budget, such as costs and benefits that are borne by individuals or private organizations. The separate "government" perspective is discussed because the government is both a provider of and payer for services. And the government perspective is generally more inclusive than those of other providers or payers given its broader organizational mission. Because different levels of government are typically responsible for different needs, it is quite possible that a cost-benefit analysis using a state government perspective may yield a different ordering of programs than one using a federal government perspective. Even narrower views of relevant costs and benefits are associated with (private) provider, payer, and individual perspectives. Private organizations that provide or pay for services predominantly define benefits by their revenues and costs by their accounting ledgers. In contrast, a cost-benefit analysis using an individual perspective would include the individual's out-of-pocket costs related to treatment, plus productivity losses or gains, pain and suffering costs, as well as the perceived benefits from treatment. Once the scope of costs and benefits has been defined, the period of time for which they will be measured must be chosen.

Study Duration

Any program will have some costs and benefits incurred in the present; others are delayed into the future. For example, a program designed to keep teenagers from dropping out of school may yield some immediate benefits (reduced delinquency) and some long-term benefits (increased productivity from a better-educated workforce). Single-period studies, which focus only on present benefits and costs, may yield different investment decisions if one of the investments has greater net benefits in the future. To compare two programs over several time periods, it is necessary to "discount" future costs and benefits. Discounting takes into account that a dollar valued today is worth more than the same dollar valued in the future, as the former can be invested to yield some return. The estimated value of future costs and benefits is thus lower the higher the discount rate used in the study. This effect will be particularly pronounced for studies with longer time horizons, those comparing programs that are likely to save costs or reap benefits far in the future. This is common for programs targeted for children.

Estimation Precision

Researchers use two different techniques to estimate costs and benefits. The first is a "macro" estimation technique. A good illustration of the macro estimation technique is found in Dorothy Rice's work estimating the cost of mental illness (Rice et al., 1990, 1991). Macro estimation involves dividing a population into a set of subgroups, and then estimating the costs and benefits for each subgroup based on results in the literature (using meta-analysis). The total costs and benefits of the program depend on the researcher's estimates of the number of people in each subgroup and the cost (benefit) experiences of each subgroup. Because this approach assumes that the population can be divided into subgroups, the quality of the total cost estimate is sensitive to the parameters used to estimate the cost experiences of each subgroup. Sensitivity analysis is typically used to test how sensitive the outcome estimates are to small changes in the values for key parameters.

While macro estimation techniques are appropriate for some macro-level investment decisions, these techniques become more suspect when policymakers are considering more disaggregated choices. "Micro-level" studies rely on data collected at the individual level on the costs and benefits of an intervention. This type of analysis is more appropriate for investment decisions, where the benefits and costs are systematically influenced by local conditions or diffused unevenly among many individuals and organizations. Most cost-benefit studies are based on micro estimation techniques. One of the best examples of a societal cost-benefit analysis using micro estimation techniques is the Weisbrod (1983) study of the Program of Assertive Community Treatment (PACT).

Designing a Cost-Benefit Framework

The cost-benefit framework is analogous to an accountant's ledger. Each investment or program is a column of the ledger, whether it involves competing drugs (Meltzer et al., 1993; Revicki et al., 1990), treatment settings (Bond et al., 1989; Creed, 1990; Dickey et al., 1989; Rappaport et al., 1987), staffing compositions (Wolff et al., 1995), packages of services (Bond, Miller, Drumwied, & Ward, 1988; Jerrell, 1995; Jerrell & Hu, 1989; Reed et al., 1994; Weisbrod, 1983), or service systems (Behar, Macbeth, & Holland, 1993). The comparison is usually confined to two investments—an existing treatment protocol (the usual care investment) and a new protocol (the innovative investment). The two may differ according to who provides a service, where the service is provided, or how the service is administered.

The "rows" of the ledger are the costs and benefits. This section of the chapter discusses how the rows of the ledger—that is, the different categories of costs and benefits and the relationships among these categories—are determined. This discussion of designing a cost-benefit framework is divided into three parts. In the first part, the categories of costs and benefits—these can be thought of as the menu of possible costs and benefits that could be incorporated into the framework—are discussed. In the second part, I discuss two production "models" through which investments are thought to create costs and benefits. These "models" describe the underlying theoretical process by which costs and benefits are produced and identify which costs and benefits are appropriate for inclusion in the cost-benefit framework. Described in the third part is how research design choices define the final structure of the cost-benefit framework.

Menu of Costs and Benefits

It is possible to divide costs and benefits into three categories: service-related, productivity-related, and intangible.[2] This categorization scheme deviates somewhat from the more standard language of direct, indirect, and intangible benefits and costs. The standard schema was rejected because the "direct" and "indirect" labels have been used in ambiguous and inconsistent ways in the literature. The three categories of service, productivity, and intangibles can be further classified as either internal or external. An internal cost or benefit accrues directly to the producing or consuming unit. For example, immunizing a child against polio reduces the child's risk of the disease. Risk reduction for the immunized child is an internal benefit. In contrast, an external effect involves costs or benefits that are experienced by others as a result of the internal effect. In this example, immunizing children benefits the rest of society because the inoculated child is not spreading a contagious disease. Some studies may include only internal costs and benefits, while others will include both internal and external costs and benefits. This distinction may have important behavioral implications: Decision makers respond more to internal costs and benefits because they directly experience them, not the costs and benefits that are external.

Service-Related Costs and Benefits

Service-related costs refer to all relevant resource consumption associated with the interventions. These include the internal costs associated with the resources used to produce medical services that are provided to the individual, such as diagnosis, treatment, and rehabilitation services, as well as additional costs associated with food, lodging, and transportation that are borne by the treated individual. External costs are costs that spill over onto family members (e.g., aftercare responsibilities) and other service providers (e.g., social service, education, law enforcement) as a result of the individual's treatment. Internal and external benefits are defined in a comparable manner. The former include averted costs of treatment and tests for the individual who is treated. External benefits refer to cost savings that are realized by others in society.

Productivity-Related Costs and Benefits

Investments often will affect an individual's ability to work. For example, the productivity effects of health care services often are linked to changes in morbidity or mortality. Productivity effects are internal if they are realized by the treated individual in the form of increased (or decreased) income or productivity, and external if they are garnered by other parties (e.g., family members).

Two quite different approaches have been used to measure productivity losses and gains. The human capital method measures the change in the discounted value of the future stream of earnings lost due to premature mortality or morbidity. It involves valuing the period of lost (or gained) work time by the individual's wage rate. The willingness-to-pay method attempts to measure what individuals would be willing to pay for a pre-specified health improvement or an averted health deterioration. It involves valuing the individual's loss by the amount the individual would pay to reduce the risk of such an experience. While the methodology for estimating the human capital approach is straightforward, it has an ethical disadvantage of valuing lives according to their economic productivity (Hodgson & Meiners, 1982). The willingness-to-pay method, while theoretically appealing, is more difficult to estimate since individuals must provide consistent and reliable responses to hypothetical questions about future probabilities (Gafni, 1991).

Intangible Costs and Benefits

Intangible effects commonly include inconvenience, pain, loss of self-esteem, disfigurement, suffering, fear, enjoyment, loss of companionship, and other nonfinancial impacts. The value placed on feeling healthy also is an important intangible benefit. These (internal and external) benefits and costs are often difficult to quantify and value, but they are nonetheless important. The willingness-to-pay method could be used to value these effects.

To put the types of costs into some perspective, the estimated costs distributions for service- and productivity-related activities for alcohol abuse, drug abuse, and mental illness is shown in Table 14.1 (Rice et al., 1990). While the percentage of costs for services varies by disorder, these costs account for less than 45% of the aggregate costs of each disorder. Forgone productivity as a result of morbidity and mortality accounts for the larger share of the costs associated with each disorder. Intangible costs have not been estimated in cost-of-illness studies.

Modeling the Production Process

To estimate costs accurately, it is important to carefully describe or "model" the relationships that determine a program's outcome. Economists describe these relationships in terms of inputs and outputs. When designing a cost-benefit

Table 14.1

Percentage Distribution of Costs
by Cost Category for Alcohol Abuse, Drug Abuse,
and Mental Illness, 1985

Cost Category	Mental Illness (%)	Alcohol Abuse (%)	Drug Abuse (%)
I. Service-Related	42.6	22.2	36.9
II. Productivity-Related			
a. Internal			
1. morbidity	45.7	38.9	13.6
2. mortality	8.9	34.1	5.8
b. External	2.7	4.5	43.7

Note. From "Estimates of Economic Costs of Alcohol and Drug Abuse and Mental Illness," by D. P. Rice, S. Kelman, and L. S. Miller, 1991, *Public Health Reports, 106*(3), Tables 73, 74, and 75.

framework, two types of input-output relationships are important to explore. The first involves the input-output relationships within the organization providing services. Different programs, for example, may involve using different types of clinical staff to produce a mental health service. The second production relationship concerns the way in which the treatment affects the client. In this production relationship, the individual is the unit of analysis. The client contributes certain inputs—time, effort, resources—to the production process at this level. The behavioral effects may be internal or external to the client, including changes in service consumption, productivity, pain, suffering, or well-being. Modeling the production process involves both examining the input-output relationships within organizations that produce the investments and the tracking of the internal and external effects caused by the investment.

Organizational Input-Output Relationships

Services, be they medical, mental health, social, law enforcement, or educational, are produced using scarce resources. Organizations (including households) use various types of labor, equipment, buildings, and supplies to produce outputs, such as services. Estimating costs is a complex task because most organizations produce many outputs simultaneously; this makes it difficult to determine which resources (costs) are appropriately linked to which outputs (services).

Describing the production relationships within an organization begins with a series of investigative questions. The central question on the output side is: What outputs are produced by the organization? For example, if a community mental health center (CMHC) produces individual therapy and group therapy in three different programs—A, B, and C, as well as research and community education services—the investment profile of this CMHC is as follows: It produces five investments—Programs A, B, and C; research; and community education, in addition to two measured outputs, individual and group therapy. For most CMHCs the program activities are billable, but the other two are not billable. The organization thus has an incentive to load all its costs into these billable activities. Because organizations typically fail to account for all the outputs of their investments, it is common for costs to be incorrectly linked to outputs.

Once the investments and their corresponding outputs are defined, they must be characterized by the resources used to produce them. The central question to be answered at this stage is this: What inputs are consumed by each investment? This question quickly leads to more specific questions regarding the characteristics of the professional staff, the sharing of staff among different investments, the allocation of administrative staff, the value of owned buildings and equipment, the division of building space and supplies, and so forth. These questions necessarily follow because outputs are eventually valued in terms of their costs of production. How much it costs to produce an output is inextricably tied to how much of each type of resource input goes into producing it. To unbundle the organization's set of resources requires detailed information about its internal structure and operation.

Individual Input-Output Relationships

The organization's productive effort can induce behavioral changes that produce both internal and external effects. For example, the mental health treatment provided to a child with a serious emotional disturbance may stabilize the child's behavior and increase his quality of life—internal benefits of treatment. This internal effect has external correlates. Improvements in the child's behavior may reduce family stress, discipline problems at school, and truancy interactions with the police. These are the external effects associated with the treatment services provided by the community mental health center.

Mapping out the production effects associated with treatment is complex. Any treatment may have multiple internal effects, and each internal effect can induce multiple external effects. Outside mediating factors also may enhance or inhibit the internal effects as well as augment the interaction between internal and external effects. For example, the expected effect of a treatment may be mediated by the dysfunction within the child's family, the housing and economic stability of the family, or the mental health status of the parent. In addition, the special treatment received by one child within the family may create tensions and rivalry within the family that adds to the treated child's stress level and affects his receptiveness to treatment. These residual effects may offset the expected effects of treatment. In addition, programs may differ in terms of how long it takes to produce an effect and how long the effect lasts once it is produced. For example, a program that removes a child from an unhealthy family environment may have immediate internal benefits, but these benefits may evaporate the longer the child is separated from his family. Overlooking any of the output effects, their mediators, or their timing patterns can result in a misspecification of the cost-benefit framework.

Structuring the Cost-Benefit Framework

In theory, the cost-benefit framework should include all internal and external costs and benefits relevant to the investments. Which of the internal and external effects are incorporated into the framework, however, depends less on theory and more on the research design choices. The choice of analytical perspective determines (a) which costs and benefits are included in the cost-benefit framework and (b) how resources are valued. How long data on costs and benefits are collected is determined by the choice of study duration. And the choice regarding estimation precision dictates the methodological technique used to estimate costs and benefits.

To illustrate how the analytical perspective influences the design of the cost-benefit framework, consider the following example of a cost identification study. Assume that a policymaker is considering two treatment programs for children with serious emotional disturbances: an assertive community treatment (ACT) program and a traditional case management (TCM) program. Each investment is expected to reduce the child's symptoms and improve his functioning ability. Children in the ACT program are expected to receive more treatment services than children in the TCM program. Also, the TCM program is expected to cost less than the ACT program because TCM employs social workers with baccalaureate degrees, while the ACT program employs only social workers with master's degrees. Improvements in the child's functioning and the reduction of symptoms are expected to lower rates of hospitalization, learning problems, truancy, foster care, and family burden. A set of representative costing frameworks that could be used to compare the ACT and TCM programs are shown is Table 14.2. All perspectives would include the internal costs associated with producing the ACT and TCM programs. Only the societal and individual perspectives include the intangible costs of treatment borne by the individual.

The selection of a particular analytical perspective affects the definition of external effects. The spillover effects from an investment are included in the costing framework only if the decision unit (e.g., society, government, provider, payer, or individual) is held accountable for those costs. For example, because private insurers are not held fiscally responsible for the client's use of law enforcement, residential, and family resources, these costs are not included in the costing framework when a private payer perspective is adopted. Note: An individual perspective would include external service, productivity, and intangible costs if individuals were concerned with the effects of treatment on

Table 14.2

Influence of Analytical Perspective on Costing Framework

Research Perspective	Cost Framework			Interpretation of Findings	
	Included Categories	Definition of Categories	Definition of Price	Economic Efficiency	Cost-Shifting

Societal	I. Service-related
	  a. internal
	  b. external
	II. Productivity-related
	  a. internal
	  b. external
	III. Intangible
	  a. internal
	  b. external
		Services include:
		mental health
		general health
		social/human
		residential
		law enforcement
		court system
		family
			"Opportunity cost" associated with resources used in production process	Yes	Yes

Government	*Public Payer*
	I. Service-related
	  a. internal
	  b. external
	II. Productivity-related
	  a. internal
	  b. external
		Only the service costs and productivity losses paid for by the government.	"Payments" Amount paid by public insurers and public agencies	No	No

	Public Provider I. Service-related a. internal	Only the medical and nonmedical service costs that are borne by the provider.	"Average Budgeted Costs"	No	No

(continues)

Table 14.2 *Continued*

Research Perspective	Cost Framework Included Categories	Definition of Categories	Definition of Price	Interpretation of Findings Economic Efficiency	Interpretation of Findings Cost-Shifting
Private Payer	*Private Insurance* I. Service-related a. internal	Only the services that must be paid for by the private insurer.	"Payments" Amount paid by private insurers	No	No
Private Provider	*Private Provider* I. Service-related a. internal	Only the medical and non-medical service costs that are borne by the provider	"Payments" Amount paid to the factors of production.	No	No

Individual	I. Service-related
	   a. internal
	II. Productivity-related
	   a. internal
	III. Intangible
	   a. internal
		Only the service and productivity costs borne by the individual.
		
		Include external service, productivity, and intangible costs if individuals consider others in their decisions.
			"Uninsured Costs"	No	No

their family. It is important to keep in mind that the relative costs and bene-fits between programs may change when one perspective is used instead of another. For this reason, the study perspective must be chosen within the con-text of the research question so as to ensure that the estimated outcomes pro-vide information that is useful to researchers and decision makers.

Clearly, the categories and definitions of costs included in the costing framework change with the viewpoint of the study. But so does the definition of "price." From a societal perspective, all internal and external effects are cap-tured in the costing framework, and all resource inputs identified through the organizational input-output analysis are valued at their opportunity costs. In societal studies, prices are constructed such that all society's resources are assigned their highest value, even though some of the resources may be donated to or owned by an organization or contributed by unpaid individuals.

In sharp contrast, the other analytical perspectives value outputs in terms of their payments or average budgeted costs. "Prices" based on payments, in general, are not equal to prices based on costs of production. For example, Med-icaid and Medicare payments cover less than 60% of the costs of production (Pear, 1994). Indeed, a provider may agree to accept many different payments for the same service. It is a common practice for large private and public insur-ers to negotiate favorable payment arrangements with providers (Dranove, 1988). Payment reductions received by one insurer for one consumer, however, lead to higher payments by less competitive insurers or individuals. Payment rates, therefore, may bear little or no relationship to resource costs, but rather reflect the negotiation skills and historical practices of payers and providers (Finkler, 1982).[3]

Estimating costs using the societal perspective is more difficult than doing so from other perspectives. By definition, societal cost-benefit studies involve the activities of many public and private organizations. This breadth increases the data collection effort. Perhaps more troublesome is the technical effort required to construct prices that fully capture the social costs of production. This task would be simplified if competitive markets existed. Under such con-ditions, market prices are equivalent to social opportunity costs. Unfortu-nately, competitive markets do not exist for mental health and health care ser-vices, and no markets exist for services and functions performed by law enforcement and social services agencies. The only option, in such cases, is to derive these costs using one's understanding of the input-output relationships within organizations.

The difficulties associated with a societal cost-benefit perspective, how-ever, should not overshadow its many advantages. Only the societal frame-work allows inquiry into two important issues. The first concerns efficiency changes within the economy. The stated goal of cost-benefit analysis is to iden-tify the most efficient investment from a set of choices. By definition, the most efficient investment yields the largest change in economic activity or health outcome for the lowest cost. But the cost-benefit tool fails, just as markets fail, to identify the most efficient investments when costs are incorrectly specified. For example, private providers will value more highly any treatment that shifts caregiving costs to the family (because they treat family costs as zero in their calculations). Because family inputs are undervalued, providers may select socially inefficient investments—causing the misallocation of resources. Studies using the government, payer, provider, or individual perspectives may lead to the selection of an inefficient investment because these studies do not fully measure resource consumption changes, nor do they accurately value these resource changes. Therefore, the results based on these perspectives cannot be interpreted in terms of economic efficiency.

A second related issue concerns changes in the distribution of costs. Cost savings may be confused with cost shifting if external costs are partially or fully excluded from the costing framework. For example, suppose an insurer negotiates lower prices with a mental health care provider (e.g., a CMHC). From the perspective of the insurer, this appears as a cost saving even if the provider in turn raises its prices to other payers (Dranove, 1988). Because the societal framework incorporates the costs borne by all sectors of society, the realignment of costs among sectors caused by the investments will be fully monitored and internalized in the cost-benefit calculation, ensuring that real costs are not hidden from the decision process.

The aforementioned decisions regarding study perspective and duration have the effect of altering the cost-benefit framework in ways that affect both the reliability of the rank ordering of the investments and the interpretation of how the investments influence the economy. Because research choices can affect the meaningfulness of the study findings, these pivotal choices need to be made in the context of their intended policy implications. Which framework is correct depends on who is making the choice.

Procedures for Calculating Cost Estimates

Once the cost-benefit framework has been customized to the interests of the decision makers, the framework must be estimated. In this section, the focus is on estimating the service-related costs associated with an investment using a micro-estimation approach. Estimating productivity-related costs is conceptually straightforward and has been described in detail elsewhere (Hodgson & Meiners, 1982; Rice et al., 1990). Changes in productivity can be counted as either a benefit or a cost in economic evaluations of mental health interventions. For example, if a study subject is unemployed prior to the intervention and the treatment increases the person's involvement in sheltered or competitive employment, the productivity changes are measured as an internal benefit. However, suppose the intervention increases the demands placed on family members, causing them to miss work; such productivity losses are measured as an external cost.

Intangible costs, while important, are difficult to measure and value in dollars. Only a few investigators have attempted to account for these costs by measuring the percentage of individuals who experience certain losses (Reed et al., 1994; Weisbrod, 1983; Wolff & Helminiak, 1992). Some examples of reported intangible costs are percentage of families experiencing emotional strains (physical illnesses) caused by the client's illness (Weisbrod, 1983), sleep disruption caused by the client, anxiety related to the client's illness, and family disharmony caused by the client (Wolff & Helminiak, 1992). The intangible benefits that have been reported in the literature include assessments of quality of life, contribution to home or community (Reed et al., 1994), and improvements in consumer decision making (Weisbrod, 1983).

The distribution of service and productivity costs for two (societal) economic evaluations of mental health programs for adults with serious mental illness is shown in Table 14.3. Less than 10% of the estimated costs were a result of lost earnings associated with family members spending time helping their adult child or their inability to work because of the adult child's mental illness. Although productivity costs may be less important in studies of seriously mentally ill adults, this area of costs should not be overlooked when designing a cost framework for interventions for children. Lost productivity for parents may be nontrivial in interventions for children, given the more instrumental and active roles of parents in the lives of youth and adolescents.

Although most societal costs involve services, little attention has been focused on how to estimate service-related costs accurately. This oversight reflects the

Table 14.3

Percentage Distribution of Societal Costs by Cost Category

	Weisbrod[a]		
Cost Category	Experimental (%)	Control (%)	Wolff, et al.[b] (%)
I. Service-Related			
a. Internal	43.0	59.3	19.2
b. External			
1. formal	55.3	39.8	64.8
2. family	—	—	7.4
II. Productivity-Related			
a. External	1.6	0.9	8.6

[a]Calculations based on data regarding societal costs for adults with serious mental illness enrolled in either a PACT program or usual care program, published in Weisbrod (1983).

[b]Calculations based on similar data for adults with serious mental illness enrolled in a mobile ACT program, published in Wolff et al. (1995).

fact that service cost estimation appears, on its face, to be simple: The total cost for any service is just the price (P) of the service multiplied by the number of service units (Q) consumed. Indeed, estimating service costs would be quite easy if units of services and competitive prices were readily available. Unfortunately, this is not the case. Organizations vary in their data-collection efforts; some collect detailed service utilization data disaggregated by client name, while others collect aggregate level data on only some services. Also, as mentioned earlier, because of market failures and the lack of markets for some services, competitive prices do not exist. How to handle these limitations is discussed in this section.

Structure of the Cost Estimation Process

Estimating the cost of services is seemingly straightforward. The total costs (TC_s) for the services provided by a CMHC (or any provider) to a sample of subjects is calculated by the following:

$$TC_S = \sum_{i=1}^{n} P_{ti} \times Q_{si} \qquad (1)$$

where P_{ti} equals the CMHC's price for service type i, Q_{si} equals the quantity of service i used by the study sample (s), and n is the number of different types of services provided by the CMHC. The "t" subscript denotes a population variable, which is based on all patients served by the CMHC. (Total costs for an individual would be calculated by defining Q_{si} as Q_{jsi}, which equals the quantity of service i used by subject j of study s.)

For each service type, i, an average cost price is calculated by the following:

$$P_{ti} = AC_{ti} = TC_{ti} \div Q_{ti} \qquad (2)$$

where AC_{ti} equals average cost associated with service type i, TC_{ti} equals the total costs associated with producing service type i, and Q_{ti} equals the total volume of service type i produced by the center. This average cost price is an estimate of the market price, which does not exist.

Data on service utilization is needed to estimate the actual services received by study subjects (Q_{si}) and total number of services provided by the CMHC (Q_{ti}). Expenditure data are needed to estimate the total costs (TC_{ti}) associated with each of the services.

Methodological Issues Related to Service Utilization Data

Four issues are central to the estimation of service quantities (Q): (a) identifying the service providers and payers, (b) choosing a data source, (c) requesting service utilization data, and (d) defining a unit of service.

Identifying Providers and Payers

Micro level costing studies are data intensive, particularily those involving children with special needs. A complex array of private and public agencies provide services to these children and their families. The first challenge is to identify all relevant agencies providing services to study subjects (and their families) and then to organize them under each of the main cost category headings (e.g., mental health, law enforcement) of the costing framework. Typically, agencies are identified by asking study subjects and their families for the names of the individuals or organizations who provide them with services.[4]

The responses from all study subjects are used to compile an exhaustive list of service providers. This list is then augmented by information obtained from payers of services and systemwide case managers (if they are available). For example, Medicaid and Medicare claims records reveal the names of hospitals and provider groups. In some states, there are special county agencies that contract with nonprofit agencies to deliver services to target populations. These county agencies can provide listings of organizations that have contracts with the county. It is important to augment the list of self-reported agencies for several reasons, which are discussed further below.

In the end, the list of service providers for a study conducted in a community of moderate size typically includes a hundred or more public and private agencies. In most cases, the sheer number of agencies will necessitate the development of a priority scheme for choosing which agencies should be contacted for data. To make this assessment, it is necessary to understand the input-output relationships, which identify the essential inputs and effects for an intervention. Any internal or external cost that is expected to significantly change as a result of the investment should be given greater weight when assigning priorities for data collection. For example, if an experimental intervention was expected to reduce the number of foster care days for children with SED (an external cost), obtaining data from the foster care system would be given a high priority. On the other hand, foster care data would be assigned a low priority if the intervention was not expected to change the relative use of foster care services between the control and experimental groups.

Obtaining data from any agency requires a release of information form signed by study subjects (or their guardians). Agencies scrutinize these forms very carefully since releasing individual-level data raises issues of confidentiality. There is considerable variability among agencies regarding their degree of sensitivity to privacy issues and their protocols for releasing individual-level information to researchers. Some agencies, as a matter of policy, simply choose not to honor the release of information forms (designed by researchers) that are signed by study subjects (e.g., child, adult, parent, or guardian). They may release information only if study subjects have signed the agency's release of information form. For example, the Social Security Administration has been known to honor only its own release of information form. Private hospitals may require that their internal review committee approve the reseacher's release form. Some police departments have required that the subject's primary therapist sign a separate "state of mind" form that certifies that the subject is able to give informed consent. Issues of privacy are especially relevant for research on children. Special legal protections are granted to children, as well as to particular types of data that may be potentially stigmatizing (e.g., substance abuse, psychiatric, and criminal justice involvements).

For these reasons, researchers are advised to review the state and federal laws regarding access to medical, psychiatric, educational, and juvenile justice information for children as well as the release requirements for public data collected by the Social Security Administration, intermediaries for Medicaid and Medicare, law enforcement, and legal authorities. This review should be done before developing a release of information form. Future problems with public and private agencies can be minimized by asking them for comment on the form during its development.

Choosing a Data Source

Data on service utilization could be obtained from the client (self-report), from service records maintained by providers (primary), or from claims records kept by payers (secondary). Each data source has advantages and disadvantages. Self-report data are the easiest to collect but are subject to unpredictable reporting errors. Respondents may unintentionally (or intentionally) under- or overreport service use by incorrectly recalling events, forgetting that service use occurred, or adding service use to the recall period that occurred in earlier periods. For reasons discussed more fully below, it is recommended that service use data derived from informants be used only as a last resort—that is, when there are no alternative data sources.

The alternatives to self-report data are primary and secondary data sources. It is undoubtedly more efficient to use secondary data (e.g., claims data) sources because these computerized claims records include service information on many providers. But information in claims records is restricted to those services that are covered by the payer and billed for by the provider. Consequently, secondary data sources are likely to be less reliable if (a) few study subjects are covered by the payer, (b) few services provided by the provider are reimbursed by the payer, or (c) few bills are submitted by the provider or subject.

Before secondary data sources are substituted for primary data, their representativeness should be assessed (Wolff & Helminiak, 1996). One way to do so is to examine the proportion of the provider's costs that are reimbursed by the payer. For example, Medicaid claims data are a principal data source in many mental health costing studies. While many persons with serious mental illness are covered by Medicaid, the services covered by Medicaid and their payment rates vary by state. Medicaid records will provide less complete service utilization profiles in those states with less generous Medicaid payment rates, narrow benefit packages, or more stringent eligibility requirements. To illustrate this, cost data for three community mental health centers (CMHCs) located in different states were used to calculate Medicaid reimbursement to CMHC cost ratios for each CMHC. Overall, Medicaid reimbursement covered only a modest proportion of the CMHCs' costs. Two of the CMHCs received less than 15% of their funding from Medicaid, compared to approximately 40% for the third CMHC. This suggests that even if all study subjects were covered by Medicaid, the Medicaid records may show only a small fraction of the services that were provided by the CMHC. In addition, the representativeness of the records for control and experimental subjects may be biased if the comparison programs offer different service mixes that are differentially covered by Medicaid.

In general, secondary data sources should be used with caution for two reasons. First, underreporting of service use misrepresents the service activities of providers and produces an underestimation of service-related costs if correction factors are not constructed. Second, the reporting error within the data source may interact with the treatment effect. That is, in some cases, the goal of an experimental program is to affect the percentage of study subjects who are enrolled in various public programs, especially Medicaid. If the program is successful, more of the study subjects in the experimental program than those in the control group will be enrolled in Medicaid by the end of the study. Now, if service utilization data are drawn from Medicaid claims records, Medicaid records will report services for subjects in the experimental program more accurately than for those in the control group. In this case, the goal of the program affects the amount of data appearing in the data source. Because of the more complete measurement of services received by subjects enrolled in the experimental program, this program appears more expensive relative to the control program.

Reporting bias can be examined in two ways. The simplest method involves comparing the percentage of subjects in each group covered by the payer. The second method involves a cross-validation substudy based on a random sample of 10–20% of clients drawn from each comparison group. The test involves comparing the two groups in terms of their ratio of total services reported in the secondary data base to that reported in the primary data base. Significant differences between groups (using either the percentage covered or ratio of services) should lead to the rejection of the secondary data source, or to the development of a strategy for supplementing the secondary data source with some other data source.

Primary data sources, in many cases, have their own limitations. This is perhaps best illustrated by examining the jail data for 94 seriously mentally ill adults shown in Table 14.4. The naive estimates are based on a printout obtained from the computerized records of the sheriff's department. These estimates aroused suspicion after it was noticed that several subjects were reported to be in jail and other facilities simultaneously. The final estimates are based on information contained in the log books, which record booking and

Table 14.4

Comparison of Reported Jail Days Data
Obtained from Sheriff's Department
Computerized Record System and Log Books

Jail Contact Information	Data from Sheriff's Department	
	Computerized Record System	Log Books
Number of Clients Booked	17	16
Total Jail Bookings	36	31
Total Jail Days	491	184

Note. Unpublished data from an economic evaluation of a
mobile ACT program located in Madison, WI (Wolff et al., 1995).

release dates. As shown, the computerized reports overstated the number of clients booked, bookings, and jail days. Jail costs would have been grossly overestimated for this sample if the data from the computerized report system had been indiscriminately used.

In many cases, the researcher chooses primary data from several alternatives. This can be illustrated by examining the different data sources available for community mental health centers (CMHCs). Most CMHCs record service utilization data in three places: (a) logs, which are data-reporting forms developed by the agency and completed by staff; (b) clinical charts, which summarize providers' interactions with clients and list some of the services that have been provided to them; and (c) management information systems, which are computerized data bases that include information on service utilization, demographics, payment arrangements, and, in some cases, costs. Any of these data sources could be used to obtain information on the services received by study subjects. This information also may be complemented by service data collected separately by the research staff.

As in the case of secondary data sources, there is an efficiency advantage to using the management information system. But the advantages of efficiency may be offset by less complete data. Which of the three data sources is most complete can be tested in several ways. The first entails constructing a ratio of recorded hours by direct service staff to total work hours of direct service staff.[5] The closer this ratio is to one, the more complete is the data source in capturing staff activities. In a recent comparison of two (fully employed) programs (A and B) offered by a CMHC serving a catchment area of 175,000, it was found that in the first year of the study less than 5% of each program's direct staff time was reported in the CMHC's management information system (MIS). Reporting completeness increased markedly the next year because of an organizational change at the CMHC. The recorded hours ratio for the second year of the study equalled .21 for Program A and .34 for Program B; over 50% more service activity was reported by the staff of Program B relative to that of Program A. If a study were to compare the two programs relying only on data from the MIS, Program A would erroneously appear to provide fewer services to its clients because of its greater underreporting of its service activities by the staff.

For longitudinal studies, incomplete reporting produces additional problems if the quality of data reporting changes during the study and if these changes vary among comparison groups. Improvements in data reporting are expected to occur over the life of most new programs because providers initially will be more concerned with adapting to the new program than with reporting client contacts. But, over time, enthusiasm for the new program may prompt staff to report their activities more carefully. As a result, more assiduous reporting of services by the staff in the new program over the duration of the study could lead researchers to conclude that the study subjects were receiving more services as a result of the intervention when in fact they did not.

If the MIS is found to be incomplete, greater consideration should be given to using logs and charts. Both of these data sources, especially charts, are used in economic evaluations of clinical interventions. But these data sources also have important limitations. This can be seen by using the second test of reporting completeness. In this test, for a sample of subjects, the information on client encounters found in the charts (or logs) and the MIS are merged without duplication of entries. The total number of unduplicated client encounters for the sample is represented by the number of matched services found in both data sources, plus the unique encounters found in either data source. A matching ratio is constructed by expressing the unique encounters for (say) the chart data source as a proportion of the total unduplicated encounters from both chart and MIS data sources. Reporting completeness increases the closer the matching ratio is to 1.

As part of a study of multisite cost estimates, matching ratios were calculated for two CMHCs. At site A, matching ratios based on chart and MIS service use data were constructed for a 6-month period using a sample of 32 randomly selected clients. The matching ratio for the MIS was .82, compared to .59 for the charts. In other words, the charts underrepresented the total recorded services by 42%—over twice the rate for the MIS. At the second CMHC, there had been a dramatic improvement in the MIS midway through the study. Because of this change in data quality, log and MIS data sources were compared before and after the change. For a sample of 30 clients, service entries appearing on log forms were compared to those appearing in the MIS. During the first half of 1991, approximately 11% of the logged services for these clients were uniquely matched to services reported in the MIS. But by the second half of 1991, over 80% of the client's logged services were matched to MIS entries. Here, again, service reporting changes could easily have been misinterpreted as a treatment effect.

Examining the relative completeness of service reporting among primary data sources leads to a more informed choice. However, one other factor is important to consider in the selection of a data source for service utilization data—which data source will be used to enumerate services provided to all CMHC clients (Q_{ti}) in the price estimation step. Using the same data source for calculating sample (Q_{si}) and population (Q_{ti}) estimates of service quantities eliminates another source of potential inconsistency. This point is discussed further in the next section on price estimation.

Requesting Service Utilization Data

Once access has been approved and a data source has been selected, service utilization data are requested from each agency for all study subjects regardless of whether the study subject (or family informant) indicated contact with the agency. Self-report data about service contact may not be reliable. The subject may have had contact with the agency and either have forgotten about the contact or may not want to reveal information about the contact to the interviewer. And, for those who do report contact, their ability to recall the volume of services may be unreliable. Underreporting is especially likely for contacts that indicate wrongdoing. Drake, Alterman, & Rosenberg (1993) found that dually diagnosed clients systematically underreport their use of illegal drugs and alcohol. Subjects also are likely to underreport contacts with the police. Self-report data on police contact are compared to actual encounter data obtained from law enforcement agencies in Table 14.5. Police records show that 65 of the 94 clients had had an encounter with the police over a 12-month period, but fewer than 50% of the clients reported that they had had contact. The reliability of self-report responses increased for contacts related to any arrest and any time in jail, but the underreporting still equaled 25% or more.

Whether missing information on 25–50% of the clients who had contact with the agency is acceptable depends in part on whether the error is equal between comparison groups and if the underreporting is random among study subjects. If, for example, the experimental program is expected to differentially affect the use of criminal justice resources, then self-report bias may seriously compromise the comparison. Nonrandom reporting error casts further doubt on self-report data. Reporting error would be nonrandom if subjects who had more frequent contact with the police were more likely to report that they had no such contact. Omitting high-cost users from the analysis would bias the law enforcement cost estimate toward zero. To illustrate this point, the reporting patterns of clients by the number of actual contacts they had with the police in 1988 is shown in Table 14.6. Those clients with the most frequent contact with police were the least likely to report that they had any such contact in 1988.

Table 14.5

Comparison of Client Responses to Actual Police Contact Information

Contact and Reporting Status	Any Police Encounter	Any Arrest	Any Days in Jail
Clients with Known Contact[a]	65 clients	21 clients	16 clients
Percent Who Reported—Yes	46.0	71.0	75.0
Percent Who Reported—No	51.0	24.0	19.0
Percent Who Reported—Don't Know	3.0	5.0	6.0
Clients with No Known Contact[a]	29 clients	73 clients	78 clients
Percent Who Reported—Yes	17.0	3.0	1.0
Percent Who Reported—No	76.0	93.0	96.0
Percent Who Reported—Don't Know	7.0	4.0	3.0

Note. Unpublished data from an economic evaluation of a mobile ACT program located in Madison, WI (Wolff et al., 1995).

[a]Based on police and jail administrative records.

Table 14.6

Comparison of Client Responses to Actual Police Contacts
by Number of Contacts

Recorded Contacts for Year		Client Response to "Any Police Contact" Question		
Number of Police Contacts	Total Number of Persons	Percentage Reported "Yes"	Percentage Reported "No"	Percentage Reported "Don't Know"
1	27	48.0	48.0	4.0
2	14	57.0	36.0	7.0
3 or more	24	38.0	63.0	0.0

Note. Unpublished data from an economic evaluation of a mobile ACT program located in Madison, WI (Wolff et al., 1995).

Reporting errors are minimized by asking agencies to search their data bases for all clients in the comparison groups. Their searches will be more complete if agencies are given a full set of information for cross-referencing clients: first and last names, with a middle initial; aliases (or name changes due to marriage or adoption); first and last names of both parents (in the case of children); date of birth; social security number; and Medicaid number.

Measuring a Unit of Service

Services units can be measured in terms of outputs or inputs. An output measure counts outpatient services in either hours, visits, or clients, whereas an input measure counts the number of hours that staff spend with clients. These alternative measures are likely to yield different estimates of service utilization for services produced using more than one staff member or delivered to two or more clients simultaneously. For example, group therapy involves one provider seeing more than one patient. If (say) one provider saw five clients during a group session, the group session could be counted either as 5 client visits, 5 group hours, or 1 group hour using an output metric, or 1 staff hour if an input metric is used. Service use measurement becomes more complicated if more than one provider leads a group session.

How different service unit metrics affect service measurement is shown in Table 14.7. In this example, service use data are presented for a CMHC and the Unified Services Board (the county funder of the CMHC's services). Service data appearing in the county data base had been downloaded from the CMHC's management information system. Note, however, that the total number of service units reported by the Unified Services Board (USB) was 20% less than that reported by the CMHC. The primary source of the discrepancy was the definition of service units. The CMHC reported staff time, whereas the USB reported

Table 14.7

Comparison of Reported Mental Health Services
for the Community Mental Health Center According
to the Unified Services Board (USB)
and CMHC Management Information System

Service Characteristics	CMHC MIS Data	USB Data
Number of Clients with Records	94	93
Hours of Service Reported	7,658	6,135

Note. Unpublished data from an economic evaluation of a mobile ACT program located in Madison, WI (Wolff et al., 1995).

client time. Indeed, after further inspection, five different definitions of service units were found in the CMHC's data base.

The issue of metric selection is complicated by the fact that agencies do not have codebooks for their management information systems, nor are their data specialists sensitive to definitional differences among variables. This information is typically acquired through a combination of trial and error and exploratory discussions with administrative staff.

Either measure could be used and both are in practice. However, the selection of a service unit metric raises several concerns about consistency. A study will be internally consistent if the same metric is used to enumerate the services received by subjects and to derive service prices. Problems of internal inconsistency arise when different data sources are used to measure services received by experimental and control subjects. For example, data for subjects enrolled in the experimental program may be based on reporting forms created by researchers and completed by research staff, whereas the data for the control group are based on agency data sources. Inconsistencies arising from using different metrics to measure sample and population service volume (Q_{si} and Q_{ti}) are explored in the next section.

Additional problems emerge in multisite studies since different agencies may have developed different ways of measuring services and different classifications for types of services. Consequently, a unit of "case management" at one agency may mean something quite different at another agency; even if the two agencies define the service comparably, one may measure it in terms of hours of staff time, another in terms of number of client contacts.

Estimating Per-Unit Costs

Prices measure the value of resources used to produce outputs (in this case, services). When competitive prices are unavailable, they must be independently estimated. This is a complicated task because some costs associated with the resources used by an agency appear on its budget (on-budget), some may be paid for by some other agency (off-budget), and some may not be directly paid for by any agency or individual (unbudgeted; Wolff, Helminiak, & Tebes, 1997). Estimating equation (2) for the societal perspective requires that all costs, independent of who bears them, be identified and then accumulated into a summary measure—total costs (TC_i). Resource costs will be underrepresented if any resources are omitted. Costs determined through established accounting processes are likely to differ appreciably from economic costs. The divergence results in part from the use of standard accounting procedures that supply necessary financial information but do not accurately identify the opportunity cost of resources used in the production process. Financial accounting procedures generally do not include the opportunity cost of owned land (i.e., the value of the land in its next best use). Capital depreciation usually represents historical, rather than replacement, cost. Also, the opportunity cost of volunteer labor and other donated resources is typically ignored by accounting conventions.

Average cost "prices," however, play another important role. When prices are calculated for each service type using equation (2), they automatically adjust for measurement error associated with the service use data source (Wolff & Helminiak, 1996). Undermeasurement of total services (Q_{ti}) reduces the denominator in equation (2), which, in turn, increases the quotient—the average cost for the service (AC_{ti}). This means that average cost "prices" will yield unbiased estimates of total sample costs (TC_s) if Q_{si} and Q_{ti} are based on the same data sources and the measurement errors are equal between the sample and the population (i.e., that service staff do not alter their reporting patterns for study subjects).

Estimating Total Costs (TC_t)

To illustrate how total costs for outpatient services are estimated, a numerical example is given using cost data for a multiservice and multiprogram community mental health center (CMHC). A societal costing perspective is assumed. The total cost estimation process is divided into four steps. The cost numbers corresponding to the steps appear in Table 14.8.

Table 14.8

Isolating the Total Costs Associated With Outpatient Mental Health Services

Cost Category	Dollar Value in Millions
Total CMHC Budgeted Costs	$22.2
Step One: Identifying all Outpatient On-budget Costs	−$8.8 (inpatient & day)
Total "On-budget" CMHC Costs—Outpatient only	$13.4
Step Two: Identifying all the Off-budget Costs	
Total "Off-budget" CMHC Costs	$6.3
Explicit Costs	$3.8
Implicit Costs	$2.5
Gross Resource Costs	$19.7
Step Three: Deducting Unrelated Costs	
Unrelated On-budget Explicit Costs	−$6.6
Unrelated Off-budget Explicit and Implicit Costs	−$2.5
Net Resource Costs	$10.6

Note. Unpublished data from an economic evaluation of respite services for persons with severe mental illness (Sledge, Tebes, Wolff, & Helminiak, 1995).

Step 1 involves examining the CMHC's budget and identifying all resource cost categories that relate to outpatient services. The center's budget statement (equalling $22.2 million) consists of 650 separate cost categories, including salaries and wages, fringe benefits, medications, supplies, equipment, building space, and utilities. Because this center produces inpatient, day hospital, and outpatient services, all resource costs related to inpatient and day hospital services must be subtracted. On-budget costs for outpatient services equals $13.4 million. (They would be the only costs included in the definition of total costs if the provider perspective were assumed.) These on-budget expenses are explicit costs borne by the CMHC.[6]

Step 2 adds on explicit costs that are borne by other collateral agencies (other than the center itself) and implicit costs borne by the CMHC and collateral agencies. These are referred to as off-budget items. Off-budget explicit costs refer to resources hired or purchased by the CMHC but that are fully or partially paid for by another agency. There were two off-budget explicit costs for the center: fringe benefits and grants. First, employees of the CMHC are hired by the state (since the CMHC is a state facility). The state provides funding to the CMHC to cover staff wages; their fringe benefits are paid for by the state and this cost item appears on the state's budget. Second, the CMHC received service and research grant funding to provide some additional outpatient services. These additional payments received from government agencies or private foundations are not captured in the CMHC's budget. These explicit off-budget items added $3.8 million dollars to total costs.

Implicit costs (or unbudgeted costs) refer to the value of resources for which no explicit monetary payments are made for resources used by an agency. The most common examples of implicit costs are owned (or donated) land, building, and equipment, as well as donated labor. This state-operated CMHC received many resource subsidies. First, some of its administrative services and all of its legal services were donated by collateral state agencies (e.g., State Attorney's Office, State Comptroller's Office, and Department of Mental Health Central Office). Second, some of its employees were on contract from other (nonprofit cooperating) agencies. The center was required to pay only the contracted workers' wages and fringe benefits; it did not pay the administrative costs associated with hiring employees or the processing costs associated with their compensation. Third, as a state agency, the CMHC did not have to pay local property taxes, which finance fire and law enforcement (as well as other local) services that the CMHC benefits from. Fourth, the buildings and equipment owned by the center were not assigned an economic value. Imputed values were constructed for the owned and donated resources using fiscal data from state and private agencies. Imputed implicit costs were valued at $2.5 million.

In aggregate, the gross total value of all resources devoted to outpatient services equaled $19.7 million. This is roughly 50% higher than the on-budget costs. But some of the resources included in this estimate are unrelated to the outpatient services used by study subjects and so must be eliminated from the cost estimate.

Step 3 of the estimation process involves making a series of deductions from the gross total cost estimates to derive the value of the resources used to produce Q_s. Three types of services must be excluded from the definition of total costs. The first type are nonclient services. The CMHC, like some multiservice community mental health centers, is involved in research, community education, and training activities. Because study subjects received only client services from nonresearch programs and they did not directly benefit from community education activities, the resource costs attributed to these ancillary outpatient activities were deducted. (Research costs would not be totally subtracted if sample clients received services that were fully or partially funded by research grants.) Most training costs were not deducted because some of the staff who were treating sample clients were students enrolled in internship programs.

The second type of deduction relates to contract services. It is not uncommon for mental health centers to contract with another service agency to produce some specialized services (e.g., social rehabilitation). Contracted services involve money transfers only. The resource costs associated with contract services must be removed from the estimate of TC_t because the corresponding information on service volume (Q_t) is not recorded in the CMHC's data management systems (i.e., the quantity information is missing). The costs for social rehabilitation should be estimated separately, using service use and cost data from the contractor agency.

Unrelated patient services are the third type of services deducted from gross total costs. The CMHC produced some outpatient services for special populations, for example forensic patients, elderly persons, and children. Because of the special needs of these populations, the cost functions associated with producing these services are likely to be different from that for services provided to a general class of adult patients (the population from which our study sample was drawn). Because none of our subjects used these special services, their costs were deducted from gross total costs.

Deductions for on-budget explicit costs equaled approximately $6.6 million. Comparable deductions were made to off-budget explicit ($1.8 million) and implicit ($0.7 million) costs that were unrelated to outpatient services received by study subjects. The final value of the resources used to produce outpatient services used by the study sample of patients is $10.6 million.

Step 4 involves mapping outputs to individual programs (investments) within the CMHC. Costs must be matched to the programs (and then to services) before equation (2) can be calculated. This step requires developing a method for integrating the services measured in the management information system (MIS) and the costs identified in steps one through three. This is a challenging step because the two data systems are not formally integrated (and have been developed without regard for the other).

The allocation of costs to the different program investments (or "cost centers") and then to the different outputs of the investments is summarized in Figure 14.1. The MIS symbol indicates the use of the agency's management information system to identify the different cost centers and outputs.

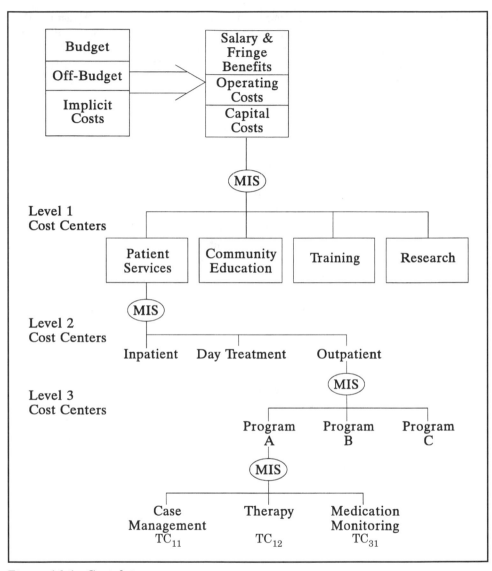

Figure 14.1. Cost data.

For this particular CMHC, services recorded in the MIS were assigned by staff name to the different program cost centers (which were defined by the geographic location of their different treatment programs). Services within each (program-specific) cost center were then aggregated by service type (e.g., case management, individual therapy, medication checks). The enumerated services by program cost center measure the total number of patient services that are provided by each program cost center. Since the enumeration of service types and the patient service costs are uniquely identified by staff member, the two different data sources can be combined.

Estimating the Average Costs (AC$_t$)

Average cost estimates for outpatient services (AC$_t$) are derived by dividing the estimate of total cost by the volume of recorded services for all patients serviced by the included programs.[7] Price estimates are needed for each unique service (e.g., individual therapy, group therapy) provided by each program (e.g., assertive community treatment program, community support program, vocational rehabilitation program) if the production relationships differ by program within the CMHC or by service within a program.

The derivation of average prices and sample total costs for one of the CMHC's programs is shown in Table 14.9. Multiplying each of the service prices (P$_{ti}$) by the corresponding number of service units consumed by the study sample (Q$_{si}$) and then dividing by the sample size ($n = 300$) yields the average cost (AC$_{si}$) of each service category. The average cost of all services received by study subjects was $13,753.

Recall, average costs can be expressed per staff unit or per client unit. Whichever metric is used to calculate average costs must be used to measure the sample's service volume (Q$_{si}$) or vice versa. The importance of metric consistency within a cost-benefit study is illustrated in Table 14.10. If the sample of study subjects received 1,000 client hours, their value would be set at $254,880 using the average cost per staff hour estimate, but at $141,710 if the average cost per client hour was used. Also, total sample costs are underestimated if Q$_{si}$ is measured in staff hours but valued using an average cost expressed per client hour. Avoiding this problem is surprisingly difficult because most agencies are not accustomed to scrutinizing their data for definitional nuances of this sort.

Adjusting the Cost Estimates

Thus far, only present costs have been considered. This section explores several issues related to future costs. It concludes with a discussion of how to test for how sensitive the cost estimates are to choices regarding how costs are measured and valued.

Adjusting for the Effects of Time

Cost estimates frequently need to be adjusted for the effect of time. Because programs, particularily those aimed at children, may have delayed costs or benefits, studies collect data over several years. The value of the estimated costs and benefits is adjusted to account for inflation and time preference.

Table 14.9

Calculating Cost Estimates for Outpatient Mental Health Services

Type of Service	Population Estimates				Sample Estimates ($n = 300$)			
	Q_{ti}	TC_{ti}	P_{ti}		Q_{si}	P_{ti}	TC_{si}	AC_{si}
Case Management	10,600	$1.060m	$100		5,732	$100	$0.573m	$1,910
Individual Therapy	65,200	$10.106m	$155		10,528	$155	$1.632m	$5,439
Group Therapy	121,900	$5.486m	$45		32,458	$45	$1.461m	$4,869
Individual-other	9,300	$1.056m	$114		3,392	$114	$0.387m	$1,289
Group-other	3,889	$0.194m	$50		1,476	$50	$0.073m	$246
Total								$13,753

Note. Unpublished data from Sledge et al. (1995).

Table 14.10

Effect of Service Metric on Average Cost

Service Unit Definition	Quantity of Services (Q_{ti})	Total Costs (TC_{ti})	Average Cost (AC_{ti})
"Staff" hours	34,479	$8.788m	$254.88
"Client" hours	62,013	$8.788m	$141.71

Note. Unpublished data from Sledge et al. (1995).

Inflation Adjustments

With inflation, future costs are likely to be higher. Costs incurred over many time periods must be deflated to the present so that all costs are expressed in the value of the dollars to be invested. There are two methods used to standardize prices. The first method simply uses the prices of one year (a base year) to value future services. That is, all costs would be valued in real terms. But this method holds price, productivity, and quality changes constant—that is, it does not allow for real changes in the value of the inputs. A more serious limitation of this method relates back to the issue of data completeness. Improvements in data reporting typically increase the number of services reported for the study subjects (Q_{si}) and the population estimate of service use (Q_{ti}). But if the base year's average costs are reflecting the level of reporting completeness of the base year, future costs will be biased upward.

The second method involves using a price index to adjust for price changes. Future costs, expressed in nominal terms, are converted into constant dollars by dividing the cost estimate for that year by a price index, which expresses how much prices have changed between that year and the base year. There are separate indices for consumer and medical prices. Using the price index method to adjust for inflation also has its limitations. The meaningfulness of the medical price index has been strongly questioned in recent years because it imperfectly captures changes in the price of medical care (Huskamp & Newhouse, 1994). Future costs will be distorted if the price index misspecifies the inflation rate for the services included in the cost framework. A second problem relates to the availability of a price index. There is a separate price index for each year up to the present. But for costs that occur 5, 10, or 20 years from the present, real price changes must be projected. This is a notably difficult and inaccurate process.

Time Preference Adjustments

As noted earlier, it is also necessary to "discount" future benefits and costs to their present value. Discounting is necessary because future dollars are not as valuable as present dollars. That is, having a dollar today is not equal to having the same dollar a year from now (even if inflation is assumed to be zero). The reason is that today's dollar could be invested to yield a future return equal to the interest rate paid on the investment. The opportunity cost of present dollars is defined in terms of its investment yield. Future dollars are brought into the present by discounting them by the same investment yield. Essentially "discounting" future dollars to the present is the transpose of calculating the future return of current investments.

Selecting the appropriate rate at which to discount future costs is controversial (Warner & Luce, 1982). But there are two general guidelines for selecting a discount rate. First, if costs are expressed in constant dollars, a real discount rate (inflation-free) is used to discount future costs to the present. On the other hand, if costs are measured in nominal terms, the discount rate must reflect the inflation assumptions built into the cost estimates (i.e., a nominal discount rate is used). Second, the most appropriate discount rate is that used in similar studies. Standardizing the discount rates among studies enhances the ability to compare findings among studies (Russell, 1987).

Sensitivity Analysis

As we have illustrated in this chapter, many assumptions are made in the process of estimating costs. Choices of data sources, inflation rates, discount rates, and so forth may have a nontrivial influence on the value of costs assigned to a particular investment. Moreover, these assumptions may have an uneven influence on the different investments being compared. One can be more confident in a ranking of programs if that ranking remains the same even if one substitutes alternative values for the variables involving important assumptions. This process is referred to as sensitivity analysis.

Different techniques are used for the selection of values to be employed in sensitivity analysis. One might compare high and low values for a variable, essentially assessing the worst case or best case. Another approach is to calculate the break-even value for a critical assumption—that is, the point where the ranking of the two programs reverses.

Uncertainty regarding the appropriateness of various key assumptions permeates all cost-benefit and cost-identification studies. The more the researcher is uncertain about a particular input-output relationship or the accuracy of a measured value, the more important it becomes to test the results of the evaluation for sensitivity to those uncertain parameters.

Discussion and Conclusions

Economic evaluations have become a popular analytic tool in recent years. Because policymakers and the public are increasingly intent on controlling public spending and on spending public (as well as private) dollars more wisely, it is likely that the use of economic evaluations will continue. But, as these studies have grown in number, more attention has focused on the meaningfulness of such information. Issues of reliability, accuracy, and internal consistency have been raised with greater force, casting a shadow of uncertainty on the findings from these studies (Wolff & Helminiak, 1993). This is particularly true with estimates of costs. Such criticisms can be deflected only by improving the application and methodological rigor of the economic evaluations and by subjecting the estimates to sensitivity analysis.

This chapter focused on how to customize the cost-benefit tool to address particular types of policy-relevant questions. Emphasis was placed on research design choices and their influence on the cost estimation process, and on estimating costs using a microestimation technique. It has been shown through a series of illustrative examples that choices regarding the analytical perspective, study duration, source of data, definition of the service unit, and specification of "price" can produce results that are misleading and that may be confounded with the treatment effect. Awareness of how these choices influence the study outcomes is the first step in repairing and preserving the reputation of cost-benefit analysis. Failing to take this step increases the likelihood that funding decisions may rest on unreliable and potentially inaccurate cost-benefit estimates. Indeed, there is no guarantee that the relative merits of two (or more) programs will be proven by cost-benefit analysis unless the process of estimating the costs (as well as benefits) meets certain reliability and validity standards, and these methods are documented.

Estimating societal costs is a complex process. This chapter touched on many of the complicated issues that arise in the process of designing a cost analysis, collecting data on service utilization, and estimating the economic value of these services. This complexity, however, is exacerbated in the case of research on children. It is more difficult to conduct economic evaluations of investments for children because the benefits and costs associated with these investments accrue over many years, there are greater protections placed on data related to children, children are involved with more public and private service systems, and the behavior of treated children affects the activities, productivity, and well-being of parents and other siblings. Precisely because of these challenges it is important to conduct (societal) economic evaluations of interventions designed for children with SED. However, it is in the best interest of children that these studies be conducted carefully and completely. A few carefully designed and well-documented scientific studies evaluating the (societal) costs and benefits of innovative treatment programs for children with SED may do more to ensure the availability of cost-effective care for children than a large number of quick studies of uncertain quality. Advocates for reform must accurately represent to policymakers the full costs and benefits associated with public policy options for these children. Omitting either the future or external costs and benefits related to such investments will bias policy choices in favor of quick fix policies that either shift costs to hidden sectors (e.g., families or juvenile justice) or to the future. In addition, findings based on studies of unreliable quality may inadvertently promote the selection of less cost-effective programs. Because children cannot effectively advocate for their present or future needs, it is all the more important to have well-informed policymakers who can examine the trade-offs of paying now or paying later for our nation's most valuable asset.

Endnotes

1. These studies are based on adult populations with serious mental illness. Economic evaluations of programs for children with serious emotional disturbances (SED) have been initiated only recently. One notable published economic evaluation based on children with SED is that by Behar et al. (1993). This is a cost identification study that examines the mental health care costs associated with a system of care. There have, however, been a number of cost-benefit and cost-effectiveness studies of early childhood and educational interventions for children (Barnett, 1985; Levin et al., 1987; Ruopp, Travers, Glantz, & Coelen, 1979). Reviews of these studies appear in Barnett and Escobar (1987) and Levin (1988).

2. My thinking on this section has benefited greatly from reviewing a draft chapter of a book being written by the Panel on Cost-Effectiveness in Health & Medicine (Office of Disease Prevention and Health Promotion).

3. There is an enormous conceptual difference (and often a substantial practical difference) between economic costs, charges, and payments. Charges are costs only to those who pay them; they may not depend on output level, and they are not determined by the costs of the resources used to produce them. Instead, they are determined by negotiation, regulation, and convention (Finkler, 1982). Payments refer to the amount of the charge actually paid for by the insurer. In a recent study, I compared the cost-to-charge ratios for three different CMHCs. These ratios varied from 0.99 to 9.5. Moreover, the cost-to-charge ratios varied for programs within a CMHC and over time. For example, cost-to-ratio ratios equaled 9.5 for one program and 7.8 for another; but the next year the ratios decreased to 0.9 and 1.5, respectively (Wolff & Helminiak, 1995).

4. The question is typically divided in two parts. The first part asks if the study subject (family member) has had any contact with a hospital (physician, social worker, law enforcement agency, social service agency, and so forth) over the past few months. If the answer is "yes," then the second part of the question asks the subject to disclose the name of the provider or agency.

5. The denominator in the recorded hours ratio represents aggregate working hours that are available for outpatient client services. That is, it first excludes all time off from work (e.g., vacation, sick leave, holidays) and time devoted to supervision of other staff, research responsibilities, training duties related to inpatient care or (nonrecorded) day hospital activities and other responsibilities unrelated to the delivery of outpatient services.

6. Resource costs are divided into explicit and implicit. The differences between these two types of costs center on whether an actual payment is made by the firm for the use of the resource. If the firm pays for the use of a resource (say, a salary to a worker), the payment is regarded as a cost, or more particularly, as an explicit cost. But, if resources are used without some form of payment, the opportunity costs associated with these resources are referred to as an

Gumberg Library
Duquesne University

(412) 396-6130

Patron's Name

Shah, Darshini Dhanraj (

TITLE   **DUE**

Outcomes for children and   12/6/2012,23:5
35282005296416

You have checked out 1 book(s) today.

implicit cost. These are costs because the production opportunity associated with the unpaid resources are lost even though they are treated as "free" by the user. Examples of implicit costs are owned buildings and donated labor.

7. In this section, I discuss how to calculate average costs. Average costs include both fixed and variable costs. Fixed costs are those costs that exist independently of the specific level of service production. Costs related to buildings, administrative overhead, and basic equipment are typically referred to as fixed in the short run. Variable costs are those that are dependent on the level of service production—for example, personnel time devoted to meeting with clients. Marginal costs refer to the incremental costs of producing an additional service. Only variable costs are included in the calculation of marginal costs.

   Whether a given economic evaluation should employ average unit costs or marginal costs depends on the question being asked. If one is looking at extending or contracting an activity that is already in place, marginal cost is the appropriate measure. On the other hand, if one is looking at a major new activity in a time frame that includes the associated fixed-cost investments, average costs may be an appropriate measure. The convention in the literature is to use average costs, which means that either a long-time horizon is being assumed or that the organization is assumed to be producing at its lowest per-unit cost.

Author's Note

Correspondence may be addressed to Nancy Wolff, Institute for Health, Health Care Policy and Aging Research, Rutgers University, 30 College Avenue, New Brunswick, NJ 08903; (908) 932-6635; e-mail: nwolff@rci.rutgers.edu.

References

Bales, S. N. (1993). Public opinion and health care reform for children. *Future of Children, 3*(2), 184–197.

Barnett, W. S. (1985). Benefit-cost analysis of the Perry Preschool program and its long-term effects. *Educational Evaluation and Policy Analysis, 7*(4), 333–342.

Barnett, W. S., & Escobar, C. M. (1987). The economics of early childhood intervention: A review. *Review of Educational Research, 57*(4), 387–414.

Behar, L. B., Macbeth, G., & Holland, J. M. (1993, March). Distribution and costs of mental health services within a system of care for children and adolescents. *Administration and Policy in Mental Health, 20*(4), 283–295.

Bond, G. R., Miller, L. D., Drumwied, R. D., & Ward, R. S. (1988). Assertive case management in three controlled studies. *Hospital and Community Psychiatry, 39*(4), 411–418.

Bond, G. R., Witheridge, T., Wasmer, D., Dincin, J., McRae, S., Mayes, J., & Ward, R. (1989). A comparison of two crisis housing alternatives to psychiatric hospitalization. *Hospital and Community Psychiatry, 40*(2), 177–183.

Creed, F. (1990). Randomized controlled trial of day patient versus psychiatric treatment. *British Medical Journal, 300,* 1033–1037.

Dickey, B., Binner, P., Leff, S., Uyeda, M., Schlesinger, M., & Gudeman, J. (1989). Containing mental health treatment costs through program design: A Massachusetts study. *American Journal of Public Health, 79*(7), 863–867.

Dickey B., Cannon, N., McGuire, T., & Gudeman, J. (1986). The quarterway house: A two-year cost study of an experimental residential program. *Hospital and Community Psychiatry, 37*(11), 1136–1143.

Dickey, B., McGuire, T., & Gudeman, J. (1986b). Mental health cost models: Refinements and applications. *Medical Care, 24*(9), 857–867.

Drake, R. E., Alterman, A. I., & Rosenberg, S. R. (1993). Detection of substance disorders in seriously mentally ill patients. *Community Mental Health Journal, 29*(2), 175–192.

Dranove, D. (1988). Pricing by non-profit institutions: The case of hospital cost-shifting. *Journal of Health Economics, 7,* 47–57.

Eddy, D. M. (1991). Oregon's methods: Did cost-effectiveness analysis fail? *Journal of the American Medical Association, 266*(15), 2135–2141.

Edelman, M. W. (1987). *Families in peril: An agenda for social change.* Cambridge, MA: Harvard University Press.

Finkler, S. (1982). The distinction between cost and charges. *Annals of Internal Medicine, 96,* 102–109.

Frank, R. G. (1985). Direct costs and expenditures for mental health care in the United States in 1980. *Hospital and Community Psychiatry, 36*(2), 165–168.

Gafni, A. (1991). Willingness-to-pay as a measure of benefits. *Medical Care, 29*(12), 1246–1252.

General Accounting Office. (1992, April). *Early intervention: Federal investments like WIC can produce savings.* (GAO-HRD-92-18). Washington, DC: United States General Accounting Office.

General Accounting Office. (1993, March). *Opportunities to improve immunization rates at lower cost.* (GAO-HRD-93-41). Washington, DC: United States General Accounting Office.

General Accounting Office. (1994, April). *Infants and toddlers, dramatic increases in numbers living in poverty.* (GAO-HEHA-94-74). Washington, DC: United States General Accounting Office.

Gottschalk, P., & Danziger, D. (1993). Family structure, family size, and family income: Accounting for changes in the economic well-being of children, 1968–1986. In S. Danziger & P. Gottschalk (Eds.), *Uneven tides: Rising inequality in America* (pp. 167–193). New York: Russell Sage Foundation.

Hadorn, D. C. (1991). Setting health care priorities in Oregon: Cost-effectiveness meets the rule of reason. *Journal of the American Medical Association, 265*(17), 2218–2225.

Hawkins, J. (1985). Executive summary. In *Drug abuse, mental health, and delinquency.* Washington, DC: U.S. Department of Justice.

Hillman, A. L., Eisenberg, J. M., Pauly, M. V., Bloom, B. S., Glick, H., Kinosian, B., & Schwartz, J. S. (1991). Avoiding bias in the conduct and reporting of cost-effectiveness research sponsored by pharmaceutical companies. *New England Journal of Medicine, 324*(19), 1362–1365.

Hodgson, T. A., & Meiners, M. R. (1982). Cost-of-illness methodology: A guide to current practices and procedures. *Milbank Memorial Fund Quarterly, 60*(3), 429–461.

Huskamp, H. A., & Newhouse, J. P. (1994). Is health spending slowing down? *Health Affairs, 13*(4), 32–38.

Huston, A. (1991). Antecedents, consequences, and possible solutions for poverty among children. In A. C. Huston (Ed.), *Children in poverty: Child development and public policy* (pp. 282–315). Cambridge: Cambridge University Press.

Jerrell, J. M. (1995). Toward managed care for persons with severe mental illness: Implications from a cost-effectiveness study. *Health Affairs, 14*(3), 197–207.

Jerrell, J. M., & Hu, T. (1989). Cost-effectiveness of intensive clinical and case management compared with an existing system of care. *Inquiry, 26,* 224–234.

Jerrell, J. M., & Hu, T. (1993). Service variations and costs of case management for severely mentally ill clients. *Institute for Mental Health Services Research, 14*(5), 4–13.

Klerman, L. V. (1991). The health of poor children: Problems and programs. In A. C. Huston (Ed.), *Children in poverty: Child development and public policy* (pp. 79–104). Cambridge: Cambridge University Press.

Kronebusch, K., & Schlesinger, M. (1994). Intergenerational transfers. In V. Bengtson & R. A. Harootyan (Eds.), *Intergenerational linkages, hidden connections in American society* (pp. 112–151). New York: Springer.

Larson, M. S. (1990). A children's health care budget. In M. J. Schlesinger & L. Eisenberg (Eds.), *Children in a changing health system, assessments and proposals for reform* (pp. 67–88). Baltimore: Johns Hopkins University Press.

Levin, H. M. (1988). Cost-effectiveness and educational policy. *Educational Evaluation and Policy Analysis, 10*(1), 51–69.

Levin, H. M., Glass, G. V., & Meister, G. R. (1987, February). A cost-effectiveness analysis of computer-assisted instruction. *Evaluation Review, 11*(1), 50–72.

Meltzer, H. Y., Cola, P., Way, L., Thompson, P. A., Bastani, B., Davies, M. A., & Snitz, B. (1993). Cost effectiveness of clozapine in neuroleptic-resistant schizophrenia. *American Journal of Psychiatry, 150*(11), 1630–1638.

Morgan, J. (1978). Intra-family transfers revisited: The support of dependents inside the family. In G. Duncan & J. Morgan (Eds.), *Five thousand American families—Patterns of economic progress* (Vol. 10, pp. 1–59). Ann Arbor, MI: Institute for Social Research.

National Commission on Children. (1991). *Beyond rhetoric, a new American agenda for children and families: Final report of the National Commission on Children.* Washington, DC: U.S. Government Printing Office.

Pear, R. (1994, April 5). Medicare paying doctors 59 percent of insurers' rate, panel finds. *New York Times,* Section A, p. 16.

Rappaport, M., Goldman, H., Thornton, P., Stegner, B., Moltzen, S., Hall, K., Gurevitz, H., & Attkisson, C. (1987). A method for comparing two systems of acute 24-hour psychiatric care. *Hospital and Community Psychiatry, 38*(10), 1091–1095.

Reed, S. K., Hennessey, K. D., Mitchell, O. S., & Babigian, H. M. (1994). A mental health capitation program: II. Cost-benefit analysis. *Hospital and Community Psychiatry, 45*(11), 1097–1103.

Revicki, D., Luce, B. A., Weschler, J. M., Brown, R. E., et al. (1990). Cost effectiveness of clozapine for treatment-resistant schizophrenic patients. *Hospital and Community Psychiatry, 41*(8), 850–854.

Rice, D. P., Kelman, S., & Miller, L. S. (1991). Estimates of economic costs of alcohol and drug abuse and mental illness, 1985 and 1988. *Public Health Reports, 106*(3), 280–292.

Rice, D. P., Kelman, S., & Miller, L. S. (1992). The economic burden of mental illness. *Hospital and Community Psychiatry, 43*(12), 1227–1232.

Rice, D. P., Kelman, S., Miller, L. S., & Dunmeyer, S. (1990). The economic costs of alcohol and drug abuse and mental illness, 1985. Report submitted to the Office of Financing and Coverage Policy of the Alcohol, Drug Abuse, and Mental Health Administration, U.S. Department of Health and Human Services. San Francisco: Institute for Health & Aging, University of California.

Russell, L. (1987). *Evaluating preventive care.* Washington, DC: Brookings Institute.

Ruopp, R., Travers, J., Glantz, F., & Coelen, C. (1979). *Children at the center: Summary findings and policy implications of the national day care study.* Cambridge, MA: Abt.

Sledge, W., Tebes, J., Wolff, N., & Helminiak, T. W. (1995). Day hospital/crisis respite care vs. inpatient care, part II: Service utilization and costs. *American Journal of Psychiatry 153*(8), 1074–1083.

U.S. Bureau of the Census. (1994). *Statistical abstract of the United States* (114th ed., Table 227, p. 154). Washington, DC.

Warner, K. E., & Luce, B. R. (1982). *Cost-benefit and cost-effectiveness analysis in health care: Principles, practice, and potential.* Ann Arbor, MI: Health Administration Press.

Weisbrod, B. A. (1983). A guide to benefit-cost analysis, as seen through a controlled experiment in treating the mentally ill. *Journal of Health Politics, Policy and Law, 7*(4), 808–845.

Wolff, N., & Helminiak, T. W. (1992). Measuring the societal costs of community mental health care. Unpublished manuscript, Rutgers University, Institute for Health, Health Care Policy and Aging Research.

Wolff, N., & Helminiak, T. W. (1993). The anatomy of cost estimates—the "other" outcome. In R. Scheffler & L. F. Rossiter (Eds.), *Advances in health economics and health services research* (Vol. 14, pp. 159–179). Greenwich, CT: JAI Press.

Wolff, N., & Helminiak, T. W. (1995, May). Improving the effectiveness of multi-site cost effectiveness analysis. Paper presented at the 148th annual meeting of the American Psychiatric Association, Miami, Florida.

Wolff, N., & Helminiak, T. W. (1996). Nonsampling measurement error in administrative data: Implications for economic evaluations. *Health Economics, 5,* 501–512.

Wolff, N., Helminiak, T. W., & Diamond, R. (1995). Estimated societal costs of assertive community mental health care. *Psychiatric Services, 46*(9), 898–906.

Wolff, N., Helminiak, T. W., & Tebes, J. K. (1977). Getting the cost right in cost-effectiveness analyses. *American Journal of Psychiatry, 154*(6), 736–743.

Cultural Diversity: A Challenge for Evaluating Systems of Care

15

Nirbhay N. Singh

A number of systems of care for children and adolescents with emotional and behavioral disorders have been initiated over the last decade. As defined by Stroul and Friedman (1986, p. 3), a system of care is "a comprehensive spectrum of mental health and other necessary services which are organized into a coordinated network to meet the multiple and changing needs of severely emotionally disturbed children and adolescents." Although overlapping in many respects, the systems of care in many states and localities vary in terms of their conceptual models, as well as in their service-delivery systems. The systems of care in North Carolina (Behar, 1996), the four-county California systems of care (Attkisson, Dresser, & Rosenblatt, 1996), the Fort Bragg Continuum of Care (Bickman, Heflinger, Lambert, & Summerfelt, 1996), the Robert Wood Johnson Foundation's Mental Health Services Program for Youth (Saxe, Cross, Lovas, & Gardner, 1996), and the various wraparound models (Clark & Clarke, 1996; VanDenBerg & Grealish, 1996) provide specific examples of systems of care for integrating services for children and adolescents with emotional and behavioral disorders (EBD).

The proliferation of systems of care suggests that policymakers and service providers do not believe that any one model fits the needs of all children in all settings. Indeed, models of systems of care vary along several dimensions, including conceptual and service goals, target populations, service-delivery systems, degree and types of interagency collaboration, governance structures, state and local financing of services, and outcomes. Given that most of these models have been initiated within the last few years, we have minimal information regarding how well these models are implemented in different localities and the nature of the outcomes for children with EBD who are provided the services. However, the current political and fiscal policies mandate that the service-delivery process, as well as outcomes for children with EBD and their families, be evaluated empirically. Thus, evaluation of current practices and outcomes is critical in the future development of systems of care.

Program Evaluation

There has been substantial growth in the nature and functions of program evaluation since this field began evolving in the 1960s. The early models of program evaluation were developed from quantitative research methods, emphasizing robust experimental designs, standardized data collection methods, objective and reliable data from large subject samples, and statistical analyses of the data. These early models were intended to provide information on the relationship between service programs and their outcomes. The recognition that these models did not account for the unique characteristics, contexts, and processes of individual programs as perceived by the programs' developers, the recipients of the program services, and the various stakeholders of the programs led to the development of evaluation models that replaced quantitative with naturalistic, qualitative research methods. While being useful in the evaluation of specific programs, these qualitative models were of limited value in terms of generalizing the findings across programs or for comparative evaluations of different programs. More recently, program evaluation models have begun to use both quantitative and qualitative approaches, depending on the nature of the questions being asked.

Along with the development of different methods for evaluating programs, there was a growing recognition that program evaluations served an increasing number of functions. For example, program evaluation data could be used in a dynamic fashion as formative information to facilitate the modification and refinement of program structures, processes, and functions or as summative information to judge a program's accomplishments. Further, evaluation data could be used by policymakers and funding agencies to ensure accountability of the program. A related development was the recognition that the role of the evaluator varied, depending on the proposed use of the evaluation findings. While a general discussion of these issues is beyond the scope of this chapter, Table 15.1 presents a brief summary of different approaches to program evaluation, the specific role of the evaluator, the particular emphasis of each approach, and the issues that are most pertinent for each approach. In addition, Table 15.1 also includes a summary of specific types of information needed to undertake each type of program evaluation.

All of the approaches to evaluation presented in Table 15.1 provide an overall framework for gathering pertinent information for any system of care. The needs of the stakeholders (e.g., funding agency, service providers, service

Table 15.1

Approaches to Program Evaluation

Approach	Evaluator's Role	Emphasis	Focusing Issues	Information Needed
Experimental	Expert/scientist	Research design	What effects result from program activities, and can they be generalized?	Outcome measures Client characteristics Variation in treatments Other influences on clients Availability of control groups
Goal-oriented	Measurement specialist	Goals and objectives	What are the program's goals and objectives, and how can they be measured?	Specific program objectives Criterion-referenced outcome measures
Decision-focused	Decision support person	Decision making	Which decisions need to be made, and what information will be relevant?	Stage of program development Cycle of decision making Data gathering and reporting routines
User-oriented	Collaborator	Information users	Who are the intended information users, and what information will be most useful?	Personal and organizational dynamics Group information needs Program history Intended uses of information
Responsive	Counselor/facilitator	Personal understanding	Which people have a stake in the program, and what are their points of view?	Variation in individual and group perspectives Stakeholder concerns Program history Variation in occasions and sites

Note. Adapted from *How to Focus an Evaluation*, by B. M. Stecher and W. A. Davis, 1987, Thousand Oaks, CA: Sage. Copyright 1987 by B. M. Stecher and W. A. Davis.

recipients), the program objectives, and the evaluator's role often combine to determine the specific nature of the information to be collected. However, regardless of the particular approach chosen, most program evaluations provide data on five key aspects of a service-delivery system. First, the evaluation must describe the characteristics of the context in which the services are delivered, because context provides the framework or constraints within which the program's services and outcomes must be evaluated. For example, sociopolitical, financial, and program-specific factors play critical roles in determining not only the nature of the services delivered within a program but also the outcomes of the services provided. Second, the evaluation must describe the characteristics of the service recipients because these variables are correlated to outcomes. Third, a description of the process for implementing the program goals is necessary because it provides the basis for comparison with other programs that may have similar goals. Fourth, the evaluation must document the extent to which the goals of the program are achieved. And, fifth, the evaluation must include an analysis of the program in terms of financial, human, and time costs. The evaluation may include data from cost-benefit, cost-effectiveness, cost-utility, and cost-feasibility analyses (Levin, 1983).

In this chapter, I will discuss selected aspects of cultural diversity as they impact on services and program evaluation in systems of care. I will focus substantially on three of the five key aspects of program evaluation—namely, context, participants, and outcomes. Although they are equally important, less emphasis will be placed on process and costs because of space limitations. Readers interested in costs should consult an excellent review by Ruiz, Venegas-Samuels, and Alarcon (1995). Finally, I will briefly discuss issues related to the competencies needed by program evaluators in cultural diversity to ensure appropriate program evaluations in the future.

Context

In terms of program evaluation, context can be defined in a number of ways. For example, it has been referred to as the web of experience that includes thoughts, acts, and the past (Kuhns & Martorana, 1982), and as the general framework that influences a person's current decision making about specific issues (Welshimer & Earp, 1989). Miles and Huberman (1984) defined context as the immediately relevant aspects of a situation in which a person functions. Context provides the framework for the prediction, explanation, and understanding of the phenomenon of interest. However, the use of context in program evaluation ranges from nonuse, as in context stripping, to extensive use in the assessment and interpretation of the findings. Context stripping is used in quantitative research when the researcher is interested in the misguided notion of discovering universal, context-free laws of human behavior. In program evaluation, context stripping assumes that the context of the participant's life and well-being is irrelevant to his or her current functioning. Typically, contextual aspects of systems of care have been described as the background or backdrop to the program evaluation, and the impact of the context is not subsequently considered in terms of the evaluation methodology or the interpretation of the findings; the context is divorced from the process and outcomes of the evaluation. However, nothing in systems of care is acontextual, and a program evaluation makes sense only when the process and outcomes of a service-delivery system are understood within its context.

Cultural Context of Systems of Care

Differences in the culture of the service recipients, the service providers, and the program evaluators can have a profound impact on the outcome of systems of care. The rapidly changing demographic composition of the United States will be reflected in the children and adolescents with EBD and their families in systems of care across this country. Cultural differences in values, approaches to child rearing and education, views of mental illness, and the seeking of services for their children undoubtedly influence many aspects of the involvement of families in systems of care. Further, the cultural competence and sensitivity of service providers will impact not only the nature of the services sought and received by these families but also the level of their involvement with different sectors of the service system. Finally, how well our program evaluations truly reflect the well-being and improvements in the quality of life of diverse children with EBD and their families is dependent on the evaluators understanding and valuing the cultural world views of the families served within the systems of care being evaluated.

Culture

No single definition of culture is likely to be universally accepted; it is a dynamic conceptual abstraction that has been socially constructed by groups of people, and it is continually modified and transmitted across generations. Broadly defined, culture is "the shared values, traditions, arts, history, folklore, and institutions of a group of people that are unified by race, ethnicity, nationality, language, religious beliefs, spirituality, socioeconomic status, social class, sexual preference, politics, gender, age, disability, or any other cohesive group variable" (Singh, 1995b). Clearly, this definition recognizes that all of us simultaneously belong to more than one cultural group and that each person is in a complex dynamic relationship with others from overlapping cultural traditions.

The components of a culture can be classified across several dimensions. For example, aspects of a culture can be classified as objective, which refers to its tangible or observable aspects, or subjective, which refers to its invisible or mental aspects (Triandis, 1977). The objective aspects of a culture, which include such things as its members' clothing, food, and artifacts, are relatively easily seen, understood, and accepted by people of other cultures. Although the basis of many cultural stereotypes originate at this level, few cross-cultural misunderstandings occur at the objective cultural level. The subjective aspects of a culture, which refer to values, ideals, attitudes, roles, and norms, are less easily understood by people of other cultures and provide the basis for much misunderstanding between people of different cultures. Understanding and appreciating the subjective aspects of another culture often pose the greatest challenge to service providers and evaluators in systems of care, because this requires a nonjudgmental acceptance of the nuances of that culture.

Cultural Awareness, Sensitivity, and Competency

As with the term "culture," there are many definitions of cultural awareness, sensitivity, and competency. Cultural awareness is a general term used to indicate that a person is conscious of the similarities and differences within, between, and among cultures. Awareness is a necessary but not sufficient condition for a person to behave in a culturally appropriate manner toward others from different cultures. Cultural sensitivity is a more specific term used to indicate that a person not only has an awareness of the nuances of one's own culture as well as those of other cultures, but also that he or she does not assign a negative or positive value to the differences within, between, and among cultures. Sensitivity means that the person accepts cultural differences nonjudgmentally. Cultural competency is a term used to indicate that a person has "knowledge and skills that enable him or her to appreciate, value and celebrate similarities and differences within, between and among culturally diverse groups of people" (Singh, 1996, p. 124). Competency is a dynamic concept and does not imply that a person ever reaches a state of being universally culturally competent; rather, it implies that the person has the knowledge and skills for displaying and increasing his or her understanding and appreciation of the changing nature and nuances of his or her own cultures as well as those of others.

Diversity in the United States

In 1990, the population of the United States consisted of 75% Anglo Americans (non-Hispanic white), 12% African Americans, 9% Hispanics, 3% Asians and Pacific Islanders, and 0.8% Native Americans (American Indian; U.S. Bureau of Census, 1992a). By the year 2000, African Americans will constitute 13.1% of the total population, Hispanics 9.4%, Asians and Pacific Islanders 3.5%, and Native Americans 1% (U.S. Department of Health and Human Services, 1990). By the year 2050, the composition of the different ethnic groups in the United States will change dramatically. The percentage of Anglo Americans will decrease to

52.7%, and African Americans, Hispanics, Asians and Pacific Islanders, and American Indians will increase to 16.2%, 21.1%, 10.7%, and 1.2% of the population, respectively (O'Hare, 1992; U.S. Bureau of Census, 1992b). The largest proportional increase will be seen in Hispanic and Asian and Pacific Islander groups.

Although the U.S. Bureau of Census and the Office of Civil Rights officially recognize five racial/ethnic groups (i.e., American Indian, Asian, Hispanic, black, and white), there is great diversity within these groups. For example, African Americans may differ in terms of cultural heritage, ethnic identity, family structure, religious affiliation and spirituality, and socioeconomic status. Hispanics may have different ancestral heritage, originating from Mexico, Puerto Rico, Central and South America, or Cuba. Asian Americans include the Chinese, Filipinos, Japanese, Koreans, Asian Indians, Vietnamese, Cambodians, and Laotians. Pacific Islanders include those who come from the dozens of countries and thousands of islands in the Pacific Ocean. Native Americans include people from more than 200 tribes who speak one or more of the 200 tribal languages (LaFromboise, 1988). Finally, there is diversity within each of these groups as well. As diversity increases in our society, the diversity of children and adolescents with EBD and their families in our systems of care will inevitably increase.

Diversity in Systems of Care

The prevalence of EBD in school children has been estimated to be anywhere between 2 and 12% (Office of Technology Assessment, 1986). However, Kauffman (1997) has suggested that probably 3–6% of students in our schools probably have emotional and behavioral disorders that require some form of intervention. Although the data are limited, there is a good general indication that children with EBD form a culturally diverse group. For example, an analysis of nine recent studies on the characteristics of children in systems of care shows that, on average, the age of the children ranges from about 8 to 16 years, about 70–75% of them are boys, and between 50 and 75% are Caucasians, followed by about 25–30% African Americans, 10% Hispanic Americans, and others, including Native Americans, Asians, Pacific Islanders, and those of mixed races (Barber, Rosenblatt, Harris, & Attkisson, 1992; Cullinan, Epstein, & Quinn, 1996; Epstein, Cullinan, Quinn, & Cumbald, 1994, 1995; Landrum, Singh, Nemil, Ellis, & Best, 1995; Quinn et al., 1996; Quinn, Newman, & Cumbald, 1995; Silver et al., 1992; Singh, Landrum, Donatelli, Hampton, & Ellis, 1994).

These data indicate that even when only three indicators of cultural diversity (age, gender, and ethnicity/race) are taken into account, there is a broad spectrum of children with EBD who are being served in various systems of care in this country. Of course, virtually no data are available on some of the other aspects of cultural diversity in these children and their families, such as their nationality, language, religious beliefs, spirituality, socioeconomic status, social class, sexual preference, politics, and disability, among others. The reporting of these data are crucial in future research because it may well be that some of these variables will be found to be highly correlated not only with the nature of the services needed or sought by children with EBD and their families but also with the types of services that are most appropriate.

A related issue is the lack of similar data reported in outcome studies from various systems of care. First, such data provide an indication of cultural diversity of the sample being provided services. Second, the reporting of these data indirectly indicates that evaluators and, perhaps, the service providers are aware of the unique needs of children and families from different cultural groups. For example, it is well established that evaluators may need to use assessment instruments and diagnostic methods that are culturally appropriate for children from different racial and ethnic groups. Further, children from diverse cultural backgrounds may need additional interventions that are different from the generic programs used with white, middle-class children and their families (Singh, Ellis, Oswald, Wechsler, & Curtis, in press; Singh, Williams, & Spears, in press). Third, these data alert the reader to look for cultural influences on the research methods and statistics used in the outcome analysis.

The changing cultural demographics of our society are reflected in the demographics of children with EBD and their families in systems of care. As the numbers of children from culturally diverse families increase in systems of care, the context in which services are being delivered is also changing. This change has immense implications for the nature and effectiveness of the services delivered in systems of care.

Participants

Data on the participants or the recipients of the services are of prime importance to both the service providers and the evaluators. Depending on the program evaluation model chosen (see Table 15.1), the evaluator may either simply access the data on the characteristics of the participants from the service providers or the evaluator may collaborate with the service providers in setting up the process for obtaining the information on the participants. In either case, the information to be collected will include the customary sociodemographic as well as assessment and diagnostic data.

Socio-Demographic and Intake Information

The sociodemographic and intake data will include the contextual information discussed above, with the caveat that data are collected on only those variables that are directly relevant to service delivery and outcomes. Service providers and evaluators should remember that collecting data even on sociodemographic variables is an intrusive process that affects the children as well as their family members. The degree of intrusiveness experienced by families is dependent on a number of factors, including their cultural heritage, social customs, and expectations of outcome.

Children with EBD and their families participate in the intake interview and data-collection process because they view their participation as serving a legitimate purpose—that is, in return for providing the requested data, they will receive needed services. Given that initial interviews are used not only to gather factual sociodemographic data and to determine the nature of the services sought, but also to establish a working relationship with the children and their families, the information provided by the families is contextually grounded and jointly constructed by the families and the interviewer. That is, the child and the family are strongly influenced by the interviewer and, at the same time, the interview is strongly influenced by the child and his or her family.

Inherent in the transactional relationship between the participants and the service providers or evaluators are potential iatrogenic effects of the data collection that are akin to the demand characteristics (Orne, 1962) and experimenter expectancies (Rosenthal, 1969) in subject-researcher interaction systems. We know, for example, that the interviewer's age, demeanor, gender, race/ethnicity, professional experience, and interpersonal style, among other variables, may affect the subjective responses of the participants. Further, some service recipients, particularly those from holistic cultures, such as American Indian, African American, Asian, and Puerto Rican (see Singh et al., in press), may experience embarrassment or distress in revealing intimate aspects of their family to a complete stranger, especially in view of the fact that it is a one-sided exchange of personal and family information. Participants from cultures in which telling others about disruptions in one's family life or mental illness in a family member is seen as a loss of face (Zane, 1991) may provide information that is sanitized for public consumption. Finally, participants from the dominant, Anglo American culture may also have an acute emotional response to answering seemingly innocuous questions, such as those about one's social networks and social support (Anglin, 1996).

The impact of collecting participant sociodemographic and intake data on the well-being of children with EBD and their families has not been considered in the evaluation of systems of care. In the context of family therapy, it has been shown that the mere asking of questions is a form of intervention because it invariably results in some change in family transactions (Bussell, Matsey, Reiss, & Hetherington, 1995). The situation is further complicated when cultural variables interact with the need to collect data regarding the child with EBD and his family. Service providers and program evaluators need to be aware of the obvious conflict between gathering enough data on which to base appropriate interventions and protecting the participants' welfare, particularly if the participants are from cultures that are sensitive to some of the questions being asked. We need to have a better understanding of culturally diverse participants' reactions to questions typically asked in sociodemographic and related questionnaires. At the very least, we will need to understand the data-collection experience from the perspective of the participants (Singh, 1995a).

Finally, we need to consider whether the standard questions in our sociodemographic forms and intake interviews tap into the issues and experiences of culturally diverse families. Most of the questions typically included in these forms and interviews are based on our experiences with Anglo American children with EBD and their families, or they are based on a priori notions of inquiry into areas that will lead to more detailed assessments on standardized instruments. It is unlikely that these questions will include the experiences of culturally diverse families that they deem important to their child and to themselves. A more compelling alternative would be to use "client-based" methodologies (Kuehl, Newfield, & Joanning, 1990) and ethnographic interviews (Lincoln & Guba, 1985), which would enable the participants and service providers to collect the appropriate information that can then be used to collaboratively construct the service needs and culturally appropriate interventions for the child with EBD and his or her family.

When service providers and evaluators collaborate with the service recipients to construct a family's sociodemographic profile, the contour of the cultural characteristics of the family is very rich. In addition to the standard demographic variables traditionally highlighted in Western systems-of-care evaluations, many families will include information on their family origins, migration patterns, and location of significant family members in this country and in their country of origin. These data can used by service providers to determine the availability as well as the strength of the family's support systems, a major moderating variable in intervention outcome.

Other issues that families will raise include the social roles of extended family members, general health status of each member, their holistic perspective on what constitutes illness, their attitudes and responses to illness, and help-seeking behavior with regard to health and mental health services. Rosado (1980) has suggested that the following variables be discussed with families because they provide the basis for assessing their mental health needs: their perceptions of the etiology of psychiatric and psychological problems, psychological support systems, verbal and nonverbal communication patterns within the extended family, the language spoken most often in the family home, time orientation (linear vs. circular), spiritual resources, and their conceptions of physical and mental well-being.

Finally, the coping experiences of people from cultures that have traditionally been marginalized in this country also have a bearing on their mental health and help-seeking behavior. Thus, information on their adaptation to a majority, Anglo American culture that has different values and practices discrimination is very important. This type of information can be obtained in terms of a family's assimilation, acculturation, biculturalism, and multiculturalism (Dana, 1993). Clearly, culturally sensitive sociodemographic information can be gathered only through collaborative constructions with the family members. The critical importance of sociocultural information in the planning of culturally sensitive services and in minimizing institutional barriers in service provision cannot be overstated.

Assessment

In systems of care, service providers and program evaluators use the assessment process as a systematic method for learning about the characteristics and needs of children with EBD and their families. In the psychiatric model, one of the anticipated outcomes of clinical assessment is that it will lead to a diagnosis of psychopathology, if present. Diagnostic assessment has been seen as an important part of the process for providing services because there is an assumption that the better the goodness-of-fit between the assessment and the proposed interventions, the better will be the outcomes (Meyer, 1989).

Assessment of Ability and Achievement

Standardized tests of ability and achievement are used with children for a number of reasons. For example, the results of these tests can be used by teachers for making curricular decisions—that is, they can determine in which subject areas the child needs instructional attention. Similarly, the test data can be used for placing students in special programs, such as special education or gifted programs. Further, the same test data can be used within the context of accountability to assess the effectiveness of teachers, schools, and school districts. While ability and achievement tests are not standard components of an intake assessment in system of care, often the test data are requested from the school system and incorporated in the child's profile. Further, in many cases, children are referred to different service agencies depending on the grouping in which they have been placed in school as a consequence of their performance on these tests.

One of the assumptions in standardized testing is that, regardless of their personal life experiences, all children taking the test understand the meaning of a question or test item in exactly the same way. However, this assumption ignores contextual factors and is not supported by data (Glick, 1985). Research has not produced any evidence for a generalized cognitive processor in children or adults that operates across knowledge domains; rather, the data strongly support the notion that learning is predominantly context-specific (Scribner & Cole, 1981). As most tests have culture-specific items, tests of ability and achievement are context-specific with culture-specific items. In addition, there are other more general factors that may affect test outcome. For example, when compared to the normative sample for a test, factors such as language differences, urban and rural subcultures, exposure to specific test materials or test formats, cultural differences in a testing situation, socioeconomic status, and social desirability, among others, will affect test outcome

(Bond, 1990; Brescia & Fortune, 1989; Groth-Marnat, 1990; Neisser et al., 1996). The critical issue for service providers and evaluators is that if ability and achievement test data are to be used for the purpose of determining any aspect of service provision, they must be aware of the fact that sociocultural contexts significantly influence cognitive performance.

Assessment Methodology

There arc few standardized assessment instruments that may have universal application—that is, they can be used with all children or adults, regardless of their cultural heritage and personal life experiences. Typically, the assessment instruments used in assessing children with EBD in various systems of care have been developed in this country from an Anglo American perspective. Although the developers of some instruments have attempted to include normative samples that include participants from diverse cultures, rarely have these instruments fulfilled the methodological requirements for a valid instrument that can be used with participants from different cultures. For example, few developers of instruments have factor analyzed their normative samples separately for the different subgroups to see if they all have the same factor structure.

Service providers and program evaluators may begin with a choice between an emic (indigenous) or an etic (universal) orientation in their assessment methods, if they are at all aware of the methodological problems inherent in participant populations that involve multiple cultures. In cross-cultural research, emic refers to the perspective of the people within the culture, and etic refers to a universal perspective that applies across cultures. In working within the emic perspective, the service providers or evaluators elicit meaning, experiences, and perceptions from the participant's rather than from their own point of view. Thus, they are more interested in understanding the participant's beliefs and values that underlie the psychopathology or psychological distress rather than imposing their own beliefs and theoretical perspectives on the assessment data. Clearly, the emic perspective is closely aligned with qualitative methods of inquiry because these methods focus on understanding phenomena from the viewpoint of the participants; that is, these methods of inquiry emphasize understanding the transactional processes between the participants and their environments rather than in controlling and predicting outcomes.

Etic methodologies require the use of instruments that are valid and reliable, and the data are evaluated and interpreted by the evaluator in terms of current theories of the phenomena of interest. Thus, the etic perspective is closely aligned with quantitative methods of inquiry that are based on accepted conceptual frameworks and hypothesis testing. Further, quantitative methods are based on a deductive approach, in which the meaning of the phenomena of interest is not understood until the data collection is complete and the data are statistically analyzed. In contrast, qualitative methods rely on inductive analyses of the data, letting the meaning of the phenomena emerge as the evaluator interacts with the participants. Thus, in this approach, the meaning of the phenomena is socially constructed by the participants and the evaluator.

What is the implication of the emic-etic distinction for program evaluation in systems of care? The main implication is that data based on the etic method of inquiry does not provide a complete understanding of the participants if the assessment and outcome instruments used are not valid and reliable for the participant's culture. A related issue is that there are hardly any clinical assessment instruments that have been developed from an emic perspective. The traditional solution to this problem has been to translate and adapt standard Western assessment instruments and structured interviews to different cultures using the forward-back translation format. Thus, for example, a standardized rating scale in English is translated into Japanese and then back-translated into English. The accuracy of the Japanese version is assessed by correlating the back-translated English version with the original English version. However, this is not a satisfactory solution because it presumes universality of symptom patterns across cultures (Fegert, 1989), an assumption that is clearly at variance with the research data (Mezzich, Kleinman, Fabrega, & Parron, 1996). Further, the manner in which psychiatric or psychological problems or distress is expressed varies within, between, and among cultures, and this is not reflected in the instruments constructed in this manner.

Another solution has been to develop assessment instruments and structured interviews de novo for a specific culture using Western concepts of psychopathology, psychological distress, and behavior disorders. The new scale is assumed to be valid if its factor structure is similar to those found in Western cultures (Elton, Patton, Weyerer, Diallina, & Fichter, 1988). One assumption of this method of developing new instruments is that similar factor structures will emerge in different cultures only if similar behaviors or beliefs exist in these cultures. Thus, the similarity of the factor structure of a rating scale in two or more cultures is assumed to be evidence for the cross-cultural utility of the scale. However, this approach also has its problems, including the fact that it does not take into account "culture-specific" disorders (Mezzich et al., 1996).

Selecting Culturally Appropriate Instruments

Flaherty et al. (1988, p. 258) have suggested that instruments intended for use across cultures can be selected according to the following priorities: (a) instruments already proven to be cross-culturally equivalent, (b) instruments that have been extensively tested and found to be psychometrically sound in one culture but have not been tested in other cultures, and (c) instruments that have high face validity but require further psychometric testing in the country of origin followed by cross-cultural validation. Of course, a fourth option is to develop a new instrument if none are available to measure the phenomenon of interest. The likelihood of finding an instrument that has already been proven to be cross-culturally equivalent is very slim at the present time. The second option, to use an extensively tested and well-validated instrument from one culture and test it in another, has been chosen most often in cross-cultural research in mental health and psychological distress. Typically, these instruments are translated into the language of another culture, if necessary, and tested for their usefulness in the second culture. This option has had negligible use in program evaluation in systems of care.

When working in Peru with a Spanish translation of the NIMH Diagnostic Interview Schedule, Gaviria et al. (1984) detected five kinds of validity problems in using a forward-back-translated instrument. These included content validity, semantic validity, technical validity, criterion validity, and conceptual validity. These five psychometric dimensions of cultural equivalence can be used as the basis for testing an existing instrument with participants from another culture, or for developing and evaluating an instrument for assessing in a new culture a phenomenon that exists in another culture. An instrument is culturally equivalent in two cultures if it meets the criterion on one or more of the five dimensions of validity. Thus, an instrument can be considered to have content equivalence if its items are relevant to the phenomena in the two cultures.

Flaherty et al. (1988) have developed a taxonomy of issues that need to be considered in assessing instruments for cross-cultural validation in psychiatric research. However, their taxonomy applies equally well to systems-of-care evaluations. In their taxonomy, each dimension of cultural equivalence is mutually exclusive of others, and the best instrument would possess equivalence on all five dimensions. For content equivalence, each item included in the scale being assessed must describe a phenomenon that is present and relevant in the culture that the instrument is to be used in. When developing an instrument by forward-back-translation, each item from the original instrument must be checked by a team of content raters for its relevance to the new culture. Only those items that are culturally relevant are kept, new culture-specific items may be added, and then the new scale is subjected to psychometric examination, including internal consistency, reliability and validity, and factor structure.

For semantic equivalence, the meaning of each item in the scale must remain the same after translation into the language of the new culture. Simply translating a well-validated scale from one culture into the language of another does not guarantee that the translated scale will be reliable or valid. Semantic equivalence can be achieved through the forward-back-translation method. The three-phase development of the scale includes the following: (a) forward-translation from the language of culture A to the language of culture B by a bilingual person or a team of bilingual translators, (b) back-translation of the scale from the language of culture B to the language of culture A by a second bilingual person or another team of bilingual translators, and (c) ratings by a panel of bilingual experts on the concordance in meaning between the original and back-translated versions. Items must not only retain the same meaning as in the original scale but also use the idiom (i.e., the characteristic forms of expression) of the culture in which it is to be used or else a response bias may be evident. If an instrument is translated into more than two languages, it is critical that there is semantic concordance among the different language versions of the scale.

Technical equivalence requires demonstration of the fact that the mode of data collection has not differentially affected the participants' responses in the two cultures. This can be somewhat problematic because many oral cultures are not proficient at using pencil-and-paper tests (Vernon & Roberts, 1981). In some cultures, one-on-one interviews with females is proscribed, particularly if the interviewer is a male. The repetitive questions and probing typical in semistructured interviews and questionnaires commonly used in Western research is seen as coercive in developing countries (Flaherty et al., 1988). Further, in some Asian and Native American cultures, people do not ask known-answer questions and do not take kindly to being asked such questions. One method for assessing technical equivalence requires the demonstration of concurrent validity when data on the same phenomenon in a culture are collected through two different modes (e.g., a paper-and-pencil test and an interview format) by different data collectors. Further, the technical equivalence of an instrument may be compromised if the participants from different cultures have differing response tendencies (e.g., need for social approval, trait desirability, and acquiescence).

Criterion equivalence requires the demonstration that responses to similar items on an instrument relate to the same normative concept or independent criteria in the two cultures. According to Flaherty et al. (1988), criterion equivalence refers to "the instrument's capacity to assess the variable (i.e., phenomenon) in both cultures studied and to the fact that the interpretation of the results from the instruments is the same in both cultures" (p. 261). This means that an instrument with a high degree of sensitivity and specificity in one culture would show similar rates of sensitivity and specificity in the second culture. If not, it may be an indication that the cutoff scores for the instrument in the second culture may need recalibration. If recalibration does not solve the problem, then the most likely interpretation is that, in the two cultures, either the instrument does not measure the target phenomenon in the same manner or the target phenomenon does not exist in a similar manner. However, it must be remembered that the critical issue in criterion equivalence is "not whether the phenomena or symptoms occur, but whether the diagnostic criteria actually measure the same phenomena" (Flaherty et al., 1988, p. 262) in the two cultures.

Conceptual equivalence is demonstrated if an instrument measures the same basic construct or concept in two or more cultures. In systems of care, it would be expected that conceptually equivalent instruments would measure the same psychiatric disorders, psychiatric distress, or emotional problems across cultures. This would presume that the disorders are conceptualized and quantified in a similar manner across target cultures.

Finally, service providers and evaluators need to understand that even if cross-cultural equivalence of instruments has been satisfactorily resolved, there is the issue of intracultural diversity, which increasingly poses problems in assessment. For example, intergenerational differences in assimilation, acculturation, language use, and world views pose assessment problems within a culture similar to those posed by differences between cultures. That is, we do not know much about how multiple generations within a culture formulate their expressions of psychiatric or psychological distress, nor do we know if standard assessment measures of mental health are reliable and valid across multiple generations within a culture.

Clearly, the adequacy of the assessment instruments and methodology are at the heart of any program evaluation. In current systems of care, the majority of the instruments being used were developed for Anglo Americans, and few, if any, of the instruments were developed from the service recipients' perspectives. The assessment instruments reflect the cultural bias of the Anglo American culture, and may not be totally appropriate as measures of psychiatric illness or psychological distress in children from other cultures.

Diagnosis

Recent studies of children and adolescents in systems of care show that they suffer from a wide range of psychiatric disorders (Barber et al., 1992; Epstein et al., 1995; Quinn, Epstein, Cumbald, & Holderness, 1996; Singh et al., 1994). Of the many diagnostic issues that are important, two deserve special attention. The first issue is whether the DSM-IV nosology (American Psychiatric Association [APA], 1994) provides a valid formulation of the mental health of children and adolescents who are not Anglo American. The second issue stems from the fact that psychiatric disorders, psychological distress, and behavior problems occur in the context of the child's family, friends, and community. Thus, the issue is whether we should be using a relational nosology in addition to the individually focused system of DSM-IV.

Culturally Formulated Diagnosis

There is extensive evidence to show that people from diverse cultures are more frequently misdiagnosed than Anglo Americans (Good, 1993; Lin, 1996). Some of the reasons for the misdiagnosis include problems of language, cultural nuances, and biases of the clinicians. Further, until the publication of the DSM-IV, clinicians did not have the benefit of cultural formulation guidelines for psychiatric diagnosis. The DSM has always been about treating mental disorders rather than about the people who have these disorders (Strauss, 1992), and, when the focus is on people, it is clear that their culture has a tremendous impact not only on the experience and manifestation of mental disorders, but also on its assessment, course, and response to treatment (Fabrega, 1987; Hooper, 1991; Kleinman, 1988; Rogler, 1989). The recent addition of cultural formulation guidelines has increased the cultural validity and suitability of the DSM-IV (see Table 15.2).

Although current research with children and adolescents with EBD has not focused on the cultural aspects of their psychiatric disorders and emotional problems, extrapolation from the adult literature suggests that non–Anglo American children may well be misdiagnosed. Further, we know from recent descriptive and epidemiological research on children with EBD in systems of care that a large percentage of them are on psychotropic medication for their psychiatric problems (Epstein et al., 1995; Landrum et al., 1995; Singh et al., 1994). However, the research also shows that no attention has been paid to the fact that there are cross-ethnic and cross-national variations in the dosing and side-effect profiles of psychotropic medications (Lin, Anderson, & Poland, 1995). In addition, recent work in pharmacokinetics, pharmacogenetics, and pharmacodynamics shows that culture and ethnicity greatly influence the disposition and effects of many psychotropic drugs that these children are prescribed (Lin, Poland, & Nakasaki, 1993). Service providers and program evaluators must be cognizant of these findings because culturally diverse children may be (a) misdiagnosed and therefore may be receiving inappropriate treatment, and (b) on doses of psychotropic medication that are not optimal for them. Both of these scenarios may lead to negative outcomes for the children.

Relational Diagnosis

The focus of the DSM as a nosological system has always been on the individual's mental disorders. In the DSM-IV, it is stated quite clearly that "each of the mental disorders is conceptualized as a clinically significant behavioral or psychological syndrome or pattern that occurs in an individual. . . . It must currently be considered a manifestation of a behavioral, psychological, or biological dysfunction in the individual (APA, 1994, pp. xxi–xxii). However, as family members and service providers, we know that the emotional and behavioral disorders of children and adolescents with EBD are associated more with interpersonal problems than with intrapsychic distress. When the cultural context is overlaid on the relational nature of children's emotional and behavioral disorders, it makes sense to diagnose a child's problems in terms of the context in which they occur.

Further, children and adults from holistic cultures view themselves as being a part of the whole; they see themselves in relational terms. That is, they are interdependent and interconnected with all others in their family, community, and the cosmos (Singh, 1995b, 1995c). They are a part of an interpenetrated collective that is defined by kinship, and they tend to value harmony with their environment, holistic thinking, group identity, cooperation, and cohesiveness above mastery of and control over their environment, dualistic

Table 15.2
The DSM-IV Cultural Formulation Guidelines

The following outline for cultural formulation is meant to supplement the multiaxial diagnostic assessment and to address difficulties that may be encountered in applying DSM-IV criteria in a multicultural environment. The cultural formulation provides a systematic review of the individual's cultural background, the role of the cultural context in the expression and evaluation of symptoms and dysfunction, and the effect that cultural differences may have on the relationship between the individual and the clinician. . . . In addition, the cultural formulation suggested below provides an opportunity to describe systematically the individual's cultural and social reference group and ways in which cultural context is relevant to clinical care. The clinician may provide a narrative summary of the following categories:

Cultural identity of the individual

Note the individual's ethnic or cultural reference groups. For immigrants and ethnic minorities, note separately the degree of involvement with both the culture of origin and the host culture (where applicable). Also, note language abilities, use, and preferences (including multilingualism).

Cultural explanations of the individual's illness

The following may be identified: the predominant idioms of distress through which symptoms or the need for social support are communicated (e.g., "nerves," possessing spiritus, somatic complaints, inexplicable misfortune), the meaning and perceived severity of the individual's symptoms in relation to norms of the cultural reference group, any local illness category used by the individual's family and community to identify the condition, the perceived causes or explanatory models that the individual and the reference group use to explain the illness, and current preferences for and past experience with professional and popular sources of care.

Cultural factors related to psychosocial environment and levels of functioning

Note culturally relevant interpretations of social stressors, available social supports, and levels of functioning and disability. This would include stresses in the local social environment and the role of religion and kin networks in providing emotional, instrumental, and informational support.

Cultural elements of the relationship between the individual and the clinician

Indicate differences in culture and social status between the individual and the clinician and problems that these differences may cause in diagnosis and treatment (e.g., difficulty in communicating in the individual's first language, in eliciting symptoms or understanding their cultural significance, in negotiating an appropriate relationship or level of intimacy, in determining whether a behavior is normative or pathologic).

(continues)

Table 15.2 *Continued*

Overall cultural assessment for diagnosis and care

The formulation concludes with a discussion of how cultural considerations specifically influence comprehensive diagnosis and care.

Note. From *Diagnostic and Statistical Manual of Mental Disorders* (4th ed., pp. 843–844), American Pyschiatric Association, 1994, Washington, DC: Author. Copyright 1994 by the American Psychiatric Association. Adapted with permission of the author.

thinking, individualism, and competition. Further, people from holistic cultures value the relational context in their lives, and they find comfort in extended family relationships. They are likely to place the well-being of the extended family above their own; when one member of their family has a problem, the problem is seen as belonging to the entire family.

Service providers and evaluators must be cognizant of the world views of children and families from different cultures. Thus, using a linear diagnosis that is focused clearly on an individual may not sit well with people who come from holistic cultures and who see the problem as affecting all members of the family rather than just the child with EBD. With all families, service providers should use an emic perspective and view the problem from the perspective of the family members. Thus, if a diagnosis is to be made, it must be relational rather than individualistic. Similarly, an emic perspective should be taken for developing a treatment program. In the absence of family involvement and ownership of the treatment program, there is an excellent chance that the prescribed treatment will be assessed by the family as being inappropriate and subsequently will prove to be ineffective. Indeed, service providers may wish to use group and family modes of treatment because these methods may be culturally aligned with the family's strong sense of interconnectedness of all family members.

Outcomes

In systems of care, the measures used to determine the need for services as well as baseline assessments of psychopathology, psychological distress, and behavior problems are also used to provide data on outcomes. With the exception of an instrument to measure consumer satisfaction with the services, additional instruments are rarely needed just for evaluating outcomes. Nonetheless, if additional instruments are needed, the principles enumerated for selecting assessment instruments will apply. In addition to the appropriate choice of measures, an appreciation of cultural influences on methods, data analysis, and interpretation of the findings is of prime importance.

Consumer Satisfaction

The general issues involved in assessing consumer satisfaction in systems of care have recently been reviewed by Young, Nicholson, and Davis (1995). Perhaps the only critical issue that they did not include was a cultural perspective in understanding and evaluating consumer satisfaction. Current consumer satisfaction measures assume that the participant belongs to a homogeneous group called "consumers," and that all consumers behave in the same way and have the same expectations of outcome. The emic perspective suggests that consumer satisfaction may be affected to a large extent by the participant's explanatory models of causation and symptomatology of illness, experiences of the illness, preference for different forms of treatment (e.g., allopathy vs. folk healing), view of the therapist or healer, and expected outcomes. These issues are rarely, if ever, considered when selecting or designing a measure of consumer satisfaction.

A cultural perspective suggests that to fully assess the consumer's satisfaction with the services we need an insider's view or, in the parlance of anthropology, we need the "native point of view" (Geertz, 1983). A culturally valid consumer satisfaction instrument must be based on the participant's personal perspective, and there are a number of issues that will determine the nature of the items that should be included in such an instrument:

Cultural Identity

The participant's cultural identity (e.g., ethnicity, religious and spiritual beliefs) provides the context within which the illness or disorder is viewed. For example, Asian Indian Hindus believe in karma, destiny, and fate, and this provides the context within which they view their illness and its outcome. Believing that their illness is karmic, they may not have any expectations regarding either the treatment or the outcome of such treatment. Thus, they may rate their satisfaction with the services as high regardless of the nature or quality of the services offered. The ethnomedical context of Navajo Indians provides another example of the importance of cultural identity. Navajo Indians identify illnesses by the agents that cause them, rather than by symptom identification as in the Western culture (Adair & Deuschle, 1970). Thus, they may rate satisfaction with services in a Western system of care as low because they would have a hard time understanding why a therapist would spend hours taking down their history or giving them a physical examination prior to treatment. Knowing the cultural identity of the participant will assist the service providers and evaluators to understand how that person will react to the services offered.

Cultural Idioms

Cultural factors that are pertinent to the participant's psychiatric disorder or psychological distress will have an impact on his or her rating of consumer satisfaction. These cultural factors may include culture-specific illnesses, explanatory models for their disorders, cultural significance of the symptoms, and patterns and rates of seeking services. Hallucinations provide an excellent example of the cultural significance of symptoms. For example, it is a normative experience for Plains Indians to hear the voices of recently deceased family members calling them from the spirit world (Kleinman, 1996). If the same experience is reported by someone from a Western culture, the experience would be considered hallucinatory, and the person would be deemed in need of mental health services.

Differential rates of help seeking behavior have been found to be related to culture and ethnicity (Snowden & Cheung, 1990). Asians, Pacific Islanders, and Hispanics appear to seek the services of mental health providers at lower rates than Anglo Americans because it is customary in these cultures to maintain the mentally ill family member at home. They utilize Western mental health services only when all traditional/folk measures have failed, and they will do so with some degree of shame because of the stigma that is attached to having a family member with mental illness. In such cases, services are sought only when the family feels that the problem is intractable, and their satisfaction with the services will be influenced by this context.

Participant's Relationship and Expectations of the Therapist

There are great cultural variations in consumer-therapist relationships, and issues associated with these relationships influence consumer satisfaction with the overall services. For example, Italians place a much greater emphasis on the character and humanitarian attitude than on the medical or psychiatric skills of the therapist, especially physicians (Zborowski, 1969). In contrast, Jewish patients place a greater emphasis on the therapist's quality of training and professional experience than on personal qualities (Zborowski, 1969). Thus, in addition to other variables, consumer satisfaction ratings will differ depending on the patient-therapist relationship desired and achieved by the consumers.

Other cultural variables that influence consumer satisfaction with services include, but are not limited to, cultural expectations of clinical decision making (Schreiber & Homiak, 1981), the therapist's understanding of the consumer's language and his or her ability to communicate clearly with the consumer, cultural variations in levels of symptom reporting, degree of rapport and confidentiality established with the therapists, and cultural expectations of treatment outcome. The implication for service providers and evaluators is that no single global measure will encompass these variables or provide a reliable and valid measure of consumer satisfaction. The use of a simple, unidimensional rating scale, as is popular in the mental health field today, is probably an indication of our ignorance of or insensitivity to cultural perspectives in consumer satisfaction in systems of care.

Cultural Influences on Methods, Data Analysis, and Interpretation of Findings

Standard program evaluation methods may be used when the evaluator, service providers, and participants in a service-delivery system are all from the same ethnic and racial group. However, even belonging to the same racial and ethnic group does not preclude differential cultural influences within the group. Thus, cultural influences need to be considered whenever differences between two groups of people are being investigated.

Cultural Influence of the Evaluator

The nature of the questions asked in a program evaluation is determined by a number of factors, including the cultural background of the evaluator. Formulation of the questions is dictated, in part, by the personal experiences and cultural bias of the evaluator and others who are involved in determining the evaluation methodology. From an emic perspective, it is reasonable to assume that not all recipients of the services, or even the service providers, will view the program evaluation questions as equally important or relevant to them as they may be to the evaluator, because there will be cultural and personal differences in how issues regarding evaluation are viewed.

In many cases, because of their presumed importance, the evaluation questions are simply imposed on the service recipients and the service providers. The evaluator makes the decision regarding what and how to assess. In a practical sense, the evaluator's level of rapport with the participants will affect their responses, especially if they are from socioeconomically disadvantaged groups (Fuchs & Fuchs, 1986). Further, culturally relevant feedback provided by the evaluator typically improves performance, particularly on achievement and ability tests (Groth-Marnat, 1990). Interpretation of test results and other data are strongly influenced by the evaluator's cultural attitudes, traditions, ideals, subjective predisposition, and personal and moral convictions (Kaplan & Saccuzzo, 1989).

Sampling of Participants

Typically, the evaluator has no control over sampling issues, unless the evaluation is driven by a research hypothesis and the participants are randomly assigned to predetermined conditions. In such cases, evaluators have the opportunity to decide whether the sample included in the program evaluation will be representative of a given culture or will be based on other considerations, such as the participant's need for services and availability. Evaluators need to be aware that, in the absence of some formal sampling procedures being used, the service recipients in most systems of care typically do not constitute a representative sample of their cultures, and that findings of intergroup differences in such samples should not necessarily be ascribed to cultural differences.

In many program evaluations, the pool of service recipients from different cultures is not large enough to analyze in terms of the cultural influences on outcome. Further, even if the numbers of service recipients from each culture are large enough, the evaluator may still not be able to make intercultural judgments because the samples across cultures may not be equivalent. That is, just because there are 100 African American children and 100 Anglo American children in a wraparound program (VanDenBerg & Grealish, 1996), that does not necessarily mean that the two samples are equivalent. For example, the children in the two samples could differ on a number of variables, including socioeconomic status, educational achievement, disability status, social experiences, exposure to technology, resilience to life stressors, and social support. Thus, program evaluators must consider not only differences arising from culture but also other plausible variables that may account for the observed differences between the two groups.

Cultural Influences on Data Analysis

Many instruments used in program evaluations include some form of rating for each item (e.g., 1 = strongly disagree, 5 = strongly agree). Cross-cultural research shows that there is a tendency in some cultures to respond in terms of a "cultural response set" to such items in rating scales. For example, when requested to rate consumer satisfaction on a 7-point scale, service recipients from culture A may rate either 6 or 7 and those from culture B may rate either 4 or 5. The evaluator may interpret these data as showing that consumers from culture A are generally more satisfied than those from culture B. All things being equal, this is a reasonable interpretation of the data. However, what if further research shows that people from culture B actually rate everything a few points lower than the people from culture A? This cultural response set in people from culture B means that they have a cultural tendency to use the middle part of the scale most often. When the cultural response set is taken into account, the program evaluator may now conclude that people in the two cultures are generally equally satisfied with the services.

Program evaluators should be aware of the possibility that cultural response sets may confound the cultural differences in the data. In addition, they need to be aware of the possibility that there may be cultural differences as well as cultural response sets, or either may be present by itself. Finally, it should not be forgotten that cultural response sets are also a part of cultural differences.

Cultural Influences on Interpreting the Data

As in life itself, data from program evaluations are open to multiple plausible interpretations. For example, the data may reflect true cultural differences, cultural response sets, or an interaction of the two. In many cases, other alternative interpretations will also be possible. Because program evaluation deals with people in the context of their lives and few, if any, intervening variables are controlled, the data may be only suggestive of a cultural difference. This ambiguity in the data leaves open the possibility for biased interpretation by the evaluator. For example, if the evaluator is looking for cultural differences, the ambiguity may allow him or her to interpret the data as showing a cultural difference. Indeed, we all interpret our data through our own cultural lenses. Further, as consumers of program evaluation data, we should not forget that regardless of their nature, all data are biased in some way.

In summary, we need to be aware of the importance of cultural influences on the nature and conduct of program evaluations. These influences are in addition to those that are inherent in the manner service providers deliver services to culturally diverse children with EBD and their families.

Cultural Competencies

It is almost de rigueur in any discussion of cultural diversity to refer to the need for training in cultural competency. The seminal work of Cross, Bazron, Dennis, and Isaacs (1989) on culturally competent systems of care for children with EBD from diverse cultures provided the guiding principles for cultural competency training. Concurrently, researchers and policy analysts noted that there was a significant underutilization of mental health and related services by culturally diverse families, especially those with low incomes, when compared to Anglo American families (Ruiz et al., 1995). The lack of cultural competency in service-delivery systems was viewed as a major barrier to accessing services by culturally diverse families.

Although a small cottage industry has developed to enhance cultural competency in systems of care, there is little evidence to suggest that these efforts have had a major impact in our service-delivery system, including program evaluation. Nonetheless, some progress has been made. For example, we now have a number of tools that can be used to measure the cultural competency of agencies (e.g., Dana, Behn, & Gonwa, 1992) as well as that of individual service providers (e.g., Sodowsky, Taffe, Gutkin, & Wise, 1994). These tools can be used to determine training needs as well as progress made in cultural competency by both agencies and individual service providers.

A number of guidelines and principles have been enumerated by several investigators regarding cultural competencies that service providers and therapists should possess (e.g., Hinkle, 1994; Kalyanpur & Harry, in press; Sue, Arredondo, & McDavis, 1992). These guidelines and principles are broad enough that they would also be useful for program evaluators.

Further, program evaluators can go through a series of steps to ensure that their evaluations are culturally competent. First, they must ensure that they have a good understanding of program evaluation models and methods that transcend particular cultures. Second, this knowledge must be complemented with competency training in their own culture as well as those of others. Third, as one cannot have a good grasp of the cultural nuances of all cultures in our society, program evaluators will need to collaborate with informed people from the target cultures, including the service recipients, service providers, representatives from funding agencies, and other professionals. This collaborative effort should yield the basic design, choice of culturally appropriate instruments, methods, and the process of program evaluation for a particular culture. Fourth, the planned evaluation should be tested in a pilot project and extensive feedback obtained from the service recipients, service providers, collaborators, and other significant personnel (e.g., from funding agencies, program evaluation experts). The feedback is used to revise and strengthen the evaluation plans. Fifth, the evaluation is undertaken and data analytic plans are developed that take into account potential cultural influences in data analysis and interpretation. Sixth, the data are analyzed and informed members of the target culture as well as of different cultures provide feedback on the data analysis and interpretation of the findings. Finally, the program evaluation findings are revised in accordance with the feedback.

In summary, culturally competent program evaluation is a complex endeavor that should be performed by those who are trained in program evaluation and have some degree of cultural competency.

Conclusions

Cultural influences are pervasive in human society and need to be taken into account when we provide and evaluate mental health and related services. Regardless of whether our own definitions of culture are narrow or broad, we all belong to multiple cultures and, therefore, we all have to transcend overt or covert cultural barriers in our daily lives. One of the most important things we can do as people is to develop cultural self-awareness so that we are aware of the hidden cultural assumptions that influence our interactions with others. Further, such awareness will assist us in clarifying our own biases and prejudices, which we may have tacitly accepted as a part of who we are.

In this chapter, I have raised some issues that deal explicitly with cultural influences on service delivery and its evaluation. The broad definition of culture that I have used is derived from our understanding of the complexity of human society as viewed by social scientists.

Issues of culture go well beyond the mere enumeration of race, creed, and gender; it encompasses the breadth of diversity witnessed in our world today. However, because of space considerations, the focus of this chapter has been limited to issues that deal mainly with race and ethnicity. Even with issues regarding race and ethnicity, I have not covered some essential ground (e.g., biracial, multiracial, and multiethnic people) for the same reason. Other issues of diversity (e.g., age, gender, sexual orientation, socioeconomic status, religion) are equally important and no less worthy of our attention.

When dealing with cultural influences on assessment, the focus has been on children and adolescents with EBD. While similar issues arise in the assessment of their families, there are numerous assessment issues that are specific to the culturally appropriate assessment of families that need to be addressed. Issues regarding cultural influences on service delivery, and the wider context of culturally responsive systems of care, need to be addressed as well.

Given the pervasive effects of culture on human behavior, accounting for the influence of all cultural variables in every facet of program evaluation can be quite daunting. Obviously, the effects of even the major cultural variables can neither be assessed meaningfully nor controlled in any one program evaluation. Indeed, it would be folly to attempt to do so, not only because of the size of the task but also because of the dynamic nature of cultural influence in the lives of the service recipients, service providers, and program evaluators. Our energies may be better directed at finding program evaluation principles and methods that are universal and would apply across cultures, and those that are specific to different cultural groups.

References

Adair, J., & Deuschle, K. (1970). *The people's health: Medicine and anthropology in a Navajo community*. New York: Appleton-Century-Crofts.

American Psychiatric Association. (1994). *Diagnostic and statistical manual of mental disorders* (4th ed.). Washington, DC: Author.

Anglin, J. P. (1996). Eureka! Bathed in transformation. In L. Heshusius & K. Ballard (Eds.), *From positivism to interpretivism and beyond* (pp. 19–25). New York: Teachers College Press.

Attkisson, C. C., Dresser, K. L., & Rosenblatt, A. (1996). Service systems for youth with severe emotional disorder: System-of-care research in California. In L. Bickman & D. J. Rog (Eds.), *Children's mental health services* (pp. 236–280). Thousand Oaks, CA: Sage.

Barber, C. C., Rosenblatt, A., Harris, L. M, & Attkisson, C. C. (1992). Use of mental health services among severely emotionally disturbed children and adolescents in San Francisco. *Journal of Child and Family Studies, 1*, 183–207.

Behar, L. B. (1996). State-level policies in children's mental health: An example of system building and refinancing. In L. Bickman & D. J. Rog (Eds.), *Children's mental health services* (pp. 21–41). Thousand Oaks, CA: Sage.

Bickman, L., Heflinger, C. A., Lambert, E. W., & Summerfelt, W. T. (1996). The Fort Bragg managed care experiment: Short term impact on psychopathology. *Journal of Child and Family studies, 5*, 137–160.

Bond, L. (1990). Understanding the black/white student gap on measures of qualitative reasoning. In F. C. Serafica, A. I. Schwebel, R. K. Russell, P. D. Isaac, & L. B. Myers (Eds.), *Mental health of ethnic minorities* (pp. 89–107). New York: Praeger.

Brescia, W., & Fortune, J. C. (1989). Standardized testing of American Indian students. *College Student Journal, 23*, 98–104.

Bussell, D. A., Matsey, K. C., Reiss, D., & Hetherington, M. (1995). Debriefing the family: Is research an intervention? *Family Process, 34*, 145–160.

Clark, H. B., & Clarke, R. T. (1996). Research on the wraparound process and individualized services for children with multi-system needs. *Journal of Child and Family Studies, 5,* 1–5.

Cross, T. L., Bazron, B. J., Dennis, K. W., & Isaacs, M. R. (1989). *Towards a culturally competent system of care* (Vol. 1). Washington, DC: CASSP Technical Assistance Center, Georgetown University Child Development Center.

Cullinan, D., Epstein, M. H., & Quinn, K. P. (1996). Patterns and correlates of personal, family, and prior placement variables in an interagency community based system of care. *Journal of Child and Family Studies, 5,* 299–321.

Dana, R. H. (1993). *Multicultural assessment perspectives for professional psychology.* Boston, MA: Allyn & Bacon.

Dana, R. H., Behn, J. D., & Gonwa, T. (1992). A checklist for the examination of cultural competence in social service agencies. *Research on Social Work Practice, 2,* 220–233.

Elton, M., Patton, G., Weyerer, S., Diallina, M., & Fichter, M. (1988). A comparative investigation of the principal component structure of the 28-item version of the General Health Questionnaire (GHQ). *Acta Psychiatrica Scandinavica, 77,* 124–132.

Epstein, M. H., Cullinan, D., Quinn, K. P., & Cumbald, C. (1994). Characteristics of children with emotional and behavioral disorders in community-based programs designed to prevent placement in residential facilities. *Journal of Emotional and Behavioral Disorders, 2,* 51–57.

Epstein, M. H., Cullinan, D., Quinn, K. P., & Cumbald, C. (1995). Personal, family, and service use characteristics of young people served by an interagency community-based system of care. *Journal of Emotional and Behavioral Disorders, 3,* 55–64.

Fabrega, Jr., H. (1987). Psychiatric diagnosis: A cultural perspective. *Journal of Nervous and Mental Disease, 175,* 383–394.

Fegert, J. M. (1989). Bias factors in the translation of questionnaires and classification systems in international comparative child and adolescent psychiatric research. *Acta Paedopsychiatrica, 52,* 279–286.

Flaherty, J. A., Gaviria, F. M., Pathak, D., Mitchell, T., Wintrob, R., Richman, J. A., & Birz, S. (1988). Developing instruments for cross-cultural psychiatric research. *Journal of Nervous and Mental Disease, 176,* 257–263.

Fuchs, D., & Fuchs, L. S. (1986). Test procedure bias: A meta-analysis of examiner familiarity effects. *Review of Educational Research, 56,* 243–262.

Gaviria, M., Pathak, D., Flaherty, J., Garcia-Pacheco, C., Martinez, H., Wintrob, R., & Mitchell, T. (1984). *Designing and adapting instruments for a cross-cultural study on immigration and mental health in Peru.* Paper presented at the American Psychiatric Association Meeting.

Geertz, C. (1983). *Local knowledge.* New York: Basic Books.

Glick, J. (1985). Culture and cognition revisited. In E. D. Neimark & R. De Lisi (Eds.), *Moderators of competence* (pp. 99–144). Hillsdale, NJ: Erlbaum.

Good, B. J. (1993). Culture, diagnosis and comorbidity. *Culture, Medicine and Psychiatry, 16,* 427–446.

Groth-Marnat, G. (1990). *Handbook of psychological assessment* (2nd ed.). New York: Wiley.

Hinkle, J. S. (1994). Practitioners and cross-cultural assessment: A practical guide to information and training. *Measurement and Evaluation in Counseling and Development, 27,* 103–115.

Hooper, K. (1991). Some old questions for the new cross-cultural psychiatry. *Medical Anthropology, 5,* 299–330.

Kalyanpur, M., & Harry, B. (in press). A posture of reciprocity: A practical approach to collaboration between professionals and parents of culturally diverse backgrounds. *Journal of Child and Family Studies.*

Kaplan, R. M., & Saccuzzo, D. P. (1989). *Psychological testing: Principles, applications, and issues*. Pacific Grove, CA: Brooks/Cole.

Kauffman, J. M. (1997). *Characteristics of emotional disorders of children and youth* (6th ed.). Upper Saddle River, NJ: Merrill.

Kleinman, A. (1988). *Rethinking psychiatry: From cultural category to personal experience*. New York: Free Press.

Kleinman, A. (1996). How is culture important for DSM-IV? In J. E. Mezzich, A. Kleinman, H. Fabrega, & D. L. Parron (Eds.), *Culture and psychiatric diagnosis: A DSM-IV perspective* (pp. 15–25). Washington, DC: American Psychiatric Press.

Kuehl, B. P., Newfield, N. A., & Joanning, H. (1990). A client-based description of family therapy. *Journal of Family Psychology, 3,* 310–321.

Kuhns, E., & Martorana, S. (1982). *Qualitative methods for institutional research*. San Francisco: Jossey-Bass.

LaFromboise, T. D. (1988). American Indian mental health policy. *American Psychologist, 43,* 388–397.

Landrum, T. J., Singh, N. N., Nemil, M. S., Ellis, C. R., & Best, A. M. (1995). Characteristics of children and adolescents with serious emotional disturbance in system of care. Part II: Community-based services. *Journal of Emotional and Behavioral Disorders, 3,* 141–149.

Levin, H. M. (1983). *Cost-effectiveness: A primer.* Thousand Oaks, CA: Sage.

Lin, K. M. (1996). Cultural influences on the diagnosis of psychotic and organic disorders. In J. E. Mezzich, A. Kleinman, H. Fabrega, & D. L. Parron (Eds.), *Culture and psychiatric diagnosis: A DSM-IV perspective* (pp. 49–62). Washington, DC: American Psychiatric Press.

Lin, K. M., Anderson, D., & Poland, R. E. (1995). Ethnicity and psychopharmacology. *Psychiatric Clinics of North America, 18,* 635–647.

Lin, K. M., Poland, R. E., & Nakasaki, G. (1993). *Psychopharmacology and psychobiology of ethnicity*. Washington, DC: American Psychiatric Press.

Lincoln, Y. S., & Guba, E. G. (1985). *Naturalistic inquiry*. Thousand Oaks, CA: Sage.

Meyer, R. G. (1989). *The clinician's handbook: The psychopathology of adolescence and adulthood*. Needham Heights, MA: Allyn & Bacon.

Mezzich, J. E., Kleinman, A., Fabrega, H., & Parron, D. L. (1996). *Culture and psychiatric diagnosis: A DSM-IV perspective*. Washington, DC: American Psychiatric Press.

Miles, M., & Huberman, A. (1984). *Qualitative data analysis: A sourcebook of new methods*. Thousand Oaks, CA: Sage.

Neisser, U., Boodoo, G., Bouchard, T. J., Boykin, A. W., Brody, N., Ceci, S. J., Halpern, D. F., Loehlin, J. C., Perloff, R., Sternberg, R. J., & Urbina, S. (1996). Intelligence: Knowns and unknowns. *American Psychologist, 51,* 77–101.

Office of Technology Assessment (1986). *Children's mental health: Problems and services. Background paper* (Pub. No. OTA-BP-H-33). Washington, DC: U.S. Government Printing Office.

O'Hare, W. P. (1992). America's minorities: The problem of diversity. *Population Bulletin, 47*(4), 1–47.

Orne, M. T. (1962). On the social psychological experiment: With particular reference to demand characteristics and their implications. *American Psychologist, 17,* 776–783.

Quinn, K. P., Epstein, M. H., Cumbald, C., & Holderness, D. (1996). Needs assessment of community-based services for children and youth with emotional or behavioral disorders and their families: Part 2. Implementation in a local system of care. *Journal of Mental Health Administration, 23,* 432–446.

Quinn, K. P., Epstein, M. H., Dennis, K., Potter, K., Sharma, J., McKelvey, J., & Cumbald, C. (1996). Personal, family, and service utilization characteristics of children served in an urban family preservation environment. *Journal of Child and Family Studies, 5,* 469–486.

Quinn, K. P., Newman, D. L., & Cumbald, C. (1995). Behavioral characteristics of children and youth at risk for out-of-home placements. *Journal of Emotional and Behavioral Disorders, 3,* 166–173.

Rogler, L. H. (1989). The meaning of culturally sensitive research in mental health. *American Journal of Psychiatry, 146,* 296–303.

Rosado, J. W., Jr. (1980). Important psychocultural factors in the delivery of mental health services to lower-class Puerto Rican clients: A review of recent studies. *Journal of Community Psychology, 8,* 215–226.

Rosenthal, R. (1969). Interpersonal expectations: Effects of the experimenter's hypothesis. In R. Rosenthal & R. L. Rosnow (Eds.), *Artifact in behavioral research* (pp. 181–227). New York: Academic Press.

Ruiz, P., Venegas-Samuels, K., & Alarcon, R. D. (1995). The economics of pain: Mental health care costs among minorities. *Psychiatric Clinics of North America, 18,* 659–670.

Saxe, L., Cross, T. P., Lovas, G. S., & Gardner, J. K. (1996). Evaluation of the mental health services program for youth: Examining rhetoric in action. In L. Bickman & D. J. Rog (Eds.), *Children's mental health services* (pp. 206–235). Thousand Oaks, CA: Sage.

Schreiber, J., & Homiak, J. (1981). Mexican Americans. In A. Harwood (Ed.), *Ethnicity and medical care.* Cambridge, MA: Harvard University Press.

Scribner, S., & Cole, M. (1981). *The psychology of literacy.* Cambridge, MA: Harvard University Press.

Silver, S. E., Duchnowski, A. J., Kutash, K., Friedman, R. M., Eisen, M., Prange, M. E., Brandenburg, N. A., & Greenbaum, P. E. (1992). A comparison of children with serious emotional disturbance served in residential and school settings. *Journal of Child and Family Studies, 1,* 43–59.

Singh, N. N. (1995a). In search of unity: Some thoughts on family-professional relationships in service delivery systems. *Journal of Child and Family Studies, 4,* 3–18.

Singh, N. N. (1995b, June). *Living from our center: Consciousness, spirituality and exceptionality.* Paper presented at the Colloquium on Spirituality, Consciousness and Exceptionality, Sugarloaf Conference Center, Temple University, Chestnut Hill, PA.

Singh, N. N. (1995c, October). The quest for wholeness: Personal growth in daily life. In C. R. Ellis & N. N. Singh (Eds.), *Children and adolescents with emotional and behavioral disorders: Proceedings of the Fifth Annual Virginia Beach Conference* (p. 150). Richmond, VA: Commonwealth Institute for Child and Family Studies, Medical College of Virginia, Virginia Commonwealth University.

Singh, N. N. (1995d, November). *Unity in diversity.* Keynote address presented at the 18th annual conference of the Teacher Education Division of the Council for Exceptional Children, Honolulu, HI.

Singh, N. N. (1996). Cultural diversity in the 21st century: *Beyond E Pluribus Unum. Journal of Child and Family Studies, 5,* 121–136.

Singh, N. N., Ellis, C. R., Oswald, D. R., Wechsler, H. A., & Curtis, W. J. (in press). Addressing and valuing diversity. *Journal of Emotional and Behavioral Disorders,*

Singh, N. N., Landrum, T. J., Donatelli, L. S., Hampton, C., & Ellis, C. R. (1994). Characteristics of children and adolescents with serious emotional disturbance in system of care. Part I: Partial hospitalization and inpatient psychiatric services. *Journal of Emotional and Behavioral Disorders, 2,* 13–20.

Singh, N. N., Williams, E., & Spears, N. (in press). Value and address diversity: From policy to practice. In U.S. Department of Education, OSEP (Ed.), *Improving results for children and youth with serious emotional disturbance.* Washington, DC: Chesapeake Institute.

Snowden, L. R., & Cheung, F. K. (1990). Use of inpatient mental health services by members of ethnic minority groups. *American Psychologist, 45,* 347–355.

Sodowsky, G. R., Taffe, R. C., Gutkin, T. B., & Wise, S. L. (1994). Development of the multicultural counseling inventory: A self-report measure of multicultural competencies. *Journal of Counseling Psychology, 41,* 137–148.

Stecher, B. M., & Davis, W. A. (1987). *How to focus an evaluation.* Thousand Oaks, CA: Sage.

Strauss, J. S. (1992). The person—Key to understanding mental illness: Towards a new dynamic psychiatry, III. *British Journal of Psychiatry, 161*(Suppl. 18), 19–26.

Stroul, B. A., & Friedman, R. M. (1986). *A system of care for severely emotionally disturbed children and youth.* Washington, DC: CASSP Technical Assistance Center, Georgetown University Child Development Center, National Technical Assistance Center for Children's Mental Health.

Sue, D. W., Arredondo, & McDavis, R. J. (1992). Multicultural counseling competencies and standards: A call to the profession. *Journal of Counseling and Development, 70,* 477–486.

Triandis, H. C. (1977). *Interpersonal behavior.* Pacific Grove, CA: Brooks/Cole.

U.S. Bureau of Census. (1992a). *Census of population and housing—Summary tape file 1: Summary population and housing characteristics.* Washington, DC: U.S. Government Printing Office.

U.S. Bureau of Census. (1992b). *Current population reports, P25-1092: Population projections of the United States by age, sex, race, and Hispanic origin: 1992–2050.* Washington, DC: U.S. Government Printing Office.

U.S. Department of Health and Human Services. (1990). *Healthy people 2000* (PHS 91-50213). Washington, DC: Government Printing Office.

VanDenBerg, J. E., & Grealish, E. M. (1996). Individualized services and supports through the wraparound process: Philosophy and procedures. *Journal of Child and Family Studies, 5,* 7–21.

Vernon, S. W., & Roberts, R. E. (1981). Measuring nonspecific psychological distress and other dimensions of psychopathology: Further observations on the problem. *Archives of General Psychiatry, 38,* 1239–1247.

Welshimer, K., & Earp, J. (1989). Genetic counseling within the context of existing attitudes and beliefs. *Patient Education and Counseling, 13,* 237–255.

Young, S. C., Nicholson, J., & Davis, M. (1995). An overview of issues in research on consumer satisfaction with child and adolescent mental health services. *Journal of Child and Family Studies, 4,* 219–238.

Zane, N. (1991, August). *An empirical examination of loss of face among Asian Americans.* Paper presented at the annual meeting of the American Psychological Association, San Francisco.

Zborowski, M. (1969). *People in pain.* San Francisco: Jossey-Bass.

Measuring Consumer Satisfaction with Children's Mental Health Services

16

Jeffrey A. Anderson, Vestena
Robbins Rivera, and Krista Kutash

O ne of the major shifts in belief and practice since the implementation of the community-based services initiative in the early 1980s has been the view that parents of children with serious emotional disturbances (SED) should be viewed as partners in the helping process rather than the traditional view that parents are part of the "problem" (Knitzer, 1993). This shift in belief and practice has influenced how services and programs are delivered and evaluated. Researchers and practitioners have recognized that children and family members can provide critical information for treatment planning as well as for program evaluation efforts. Moreover, including the family members' perspectives of service delivery in evaluation is part of the growing holistic, family-centered, participatory approach to evaluation in the children's mental health field (Duchnowski & Kutash, 1996; Young, Nicholson, & Davis, 1995). Having family members (both child and parent) complete opinionnaires about their satisfaction with services is one evaluation technique that has been used to capture the family's perspective of service delivery.

When providers embrace a family-focused philosophy of service delivery, information from satisfaction surveys can provide valuable information for improving program performance in both the process and outcomes of care (McNaughton, 1994). Additionally, in a recent review of studies conducted on consumers' satisfaction with services, Young et al. (1995) concluded that many of the efforts in the past 5 years have used consumers' ratings of satisfaction in understanding both specific services and entire systems of care. In the state of Texas, for example, child and parent satisfaction-with-services data is routinely collected and analyzed as part of the process of evaluating the state's array of mental health services for children (Berndt, 1995; Rouse, MacCabe, & Toprac, 1996).

However, consumer satisfaction, as a component of program evaluation, has been described as being in its infancy (McNaughton, 1994). Despite some attempts to understand and assess consumer satisfaction with children's mental health services, this area of inquiry has been largely neglected (Byalin, 1993; Stüntzner-Gibson, Koren, & DeChillo, 1995). Young et al. (1995) point out that "there are no extensive discussions in the literature about the ideal role of children's mental health services consumer satisfaction data, nor are there any accounts of consumer satisfaction data being used to make practical changes in programs or services systems" (p. 235). Because of the paucity of research on measuring consumer satisfaction with children's mental health services, much of the current knowledge base has evolved out of the adult mental health services literature (Rosen, Heckman, Carro, & Burchard, 1994). Recently, however, there have been some advances in the measurement and utilization of consumer satisfaction in the children's mental health field.[1] In this chapter, we will synthesize the available literature on consumer satisfaction in the children's mental health field, discuss issues that confound the assessment of satisfaction, describe several currently used instruments, and explore emerging trends in assessing families' perspectives of service delivery.

Definitions and Models

Consumer satisfaction has tended to be conceptualized broadly where "few have attempted to elaborate satisfaction conceptually or to place the concept within any larger psychological theory" (Young et al., 1995, p. 221). However, efforts to differentiate consumer satisfaction with services from other types of service and treatment outcomes have resulted in closer attention to how consumer satisfaction is defined and subsequently measured. This section discusses definitions and conceptual models of consumer satisfaction, beginning with the literature on adults and their satisfaction with mental health services.

Working in a relatively new area, Larsen, Attkisson, Hargreaves, and Nguyen (1979) reported on the development of a general satisfaction instrument (Client Satisfaction Questionnaire) designed to measure client/patient satisfaction with mental health services. Previously, the role of client satisfaction with services had been either ignored or relegated to a subjective rating of improvement—that is, whether clients perceived that their functioning had improved as a result of receiving services. However, Larsen et al. (1979) suggested that consumer satisfaction should extend beyond service-provider definitions of satisfaction to include consumer expectations about services and the extent to which these expectations are fulfilled.

It is currently acknowledged that consumer satisfaction is a multidimensional construct that may be related to various service factors, such as a consumer's satisfaction with outcomes, the relationship with the practitioner, confidentiality issues, the accessibility of services, pharmacological issues, and the adequacy of facilities (Lebow, 1983; Young et al., 1995). Additionally, there are factors specific to the children's mental health field that may affect a consumer's level of satisfaction with services, including family burden, parental collaboration, treatment effectiveness, and degree of family participation (Young et al., 1995). Thus, levels of reported satisfaction may be determined by factors outside the direct control of the service program. For example, Brannan and Heflinger (cited in Young et al., 1995) have proposed a model in which in addition to the family's actual experiences with service providers and programs, parental satisfaction may be associated with several interrelated concepts, including a family's resources, the mental health status of their child, and prior expectations about the nature of services.

Development and Rationale

Historically, consumer satisfaction has been used as an indicator of the quality of mental health care (Nicholson & Robinson, 1996). Results from satisfaction surveys provided an opportunity for program managers to obtain information about program effectiveness as well as consumers' perspectives on service delivery. This process served as an evaluative function that administrators could use to improve programs. These efforts to gather satisfaction data, however, were often informal, without consistent implementation and structure. Recently, there has been an increased recognition of the need to develop and implement systematic procedures to assess consumer satisfaction with services and to include these results in evaluation efforts. As families become more involved in their children's mental health services and more vocal in expressing their needs (Northrup, Bickman, & Heflinger, 1994), the development and utilization of effective methods for including the family's perspective gain importance.

In one of the first papers on the importance of consumer satisfaction, Larsen et al., (1979) identified three reasons for assessing client satisfaction that remain applicable to the field of children's mental health. First, as the family's role in service provision expands, it becomes increasingly important for agencies to understand the family's perspective (Moynihan, Forward, & Stolbach, 1994). Without this perspective, service evaluation is incomplete and also may be biased. Second, many social service–delivery agencies have experienced mandates either from state or federal agencies or other external funding sources to include the clients' viewpoint as part of outcome evaluations (Heflinger, Sonnichsen, & Brannan, 1996; Plante, Couchman, & Diaz, 1995). Finally, publicly funded mental health services predominantly are "supplier dominated." Often individuals who access and use public services have a limited choice of providers, thus reducing their purchasing power. Therefore, there is little or no financial incentive for service providers to ensure service quality and adequacy. However, examining consumer satisfaction with services provides a mechanism for overcoming this challenge. When consumers have a limited choice of service programs or providers, obtaining the consumer's perspective is a method program staff can use to capture the consumer's estimate of the quality and adequacy of service delivery (McNaughton, 1994).

McNaughton (1994) also provided several reasons for assessing parents' opinions of satisfaction. In his work with early intervention programs, he found that (a) parents have the primary control and responsibility for their child's well-being, making their input critical, (b) data from parent satisfaction scales can be used to improve services, (c) including parents in the evaluative process may increase parent participation in programs, and (d) information can be used to inform policymakers and other stakeholders about a program's importance.

Another reason for assessing satisfaction with services is to use this information as a measure of treatment acceptability. Treatment acceptability has been defined as the consumer's and potential consumer's judgment of a treatment, including whether the treatment is appropriate to the problem, reasonable, fair, and consistent with the expectations of what the treatment should provide (Kazdin, 1980). Moreover, there may be a link between treatment acceptability and satisfaction with services (Heflinger et al., 1996). That is, treatment acceptability may be related to a consumer's compliance with treatment requirements, and this compliance may lead to improved outcomes, and thus, greater satisfaction with services.

Treatment Outcomes

It is important for practitioners and researchers to recognize that satisfaction with services and treatment effectiveness represent different types of outcomes of service delivery. Traditionally, the consumer's perspective was assessed to gain information about treatment effectiveness (e.g., asking the question, Are you better?), with little attention given to how consumers perceived the treatment process (e.g., Did the services offered meet your expectations?; McMahon & Forehand, 1983). When the focus of evaluation is solely on impact, other significant aspects of a consumer's experience with services may be ignored or devalued. Moreover, while it generally has been thought that consumer satisfaction is related to treatment effectiveness (Sabourin et al., 1989), scant data exist to support this position. Factors indicating that individuals are satisfied with services may differ from factors related to treatment effectiveness (Nicholson & Robinson, 1996). For example, satisfaction with a treatment, because it is readily available or inexpensive, does not automatically translate to functional improvements.

In an attempt to better understand the construct of satisfaction, Rosen et al. (1994) conducted an investigation of the relationship between youths' overall satisfaction with wraparound services, satisfaction with their own progress, and an objective measure of functional improvement. Overall satisfaction was related to subjective ratings of improvement (i.e., youths' satisfaction with their own progress), but not with functional improvement. These findings are consistent with the results reported by Lambert (1996), who examined the relationship between satisfaction, parental reports of their child's improvement, and changes in levels of psychopathology. Again, subjective reports of improvement were more highly associated with measures of satisfaction than with changes in psychopathology. These two studies lend empirical support to the notion that consumer satisfaction and treatment effectiveness are different constructs.

Summary

Satisfaction with services is a recently acknowledged construct in the children's mental health field, is multidimensional in nature, and may be connected to factors outside a program's direct control. Moreover, researchers and practitioners increasingly recognize that satisfaction data are important to internal program improvement as well as in serving as a mechanism to address concerns from external audiences. Finally, researchers are beginning to explore whether there are relationships between distinct treatment outcome domains (e.g., behavioral improvement, level of psychopathology) and levels of consumer satisfaction.

Issues in the Role and Measurement of Consumer Satisfaction

Like many constructs in the human services field, consumer satisfaction with services delivery is difficult to assess. This section discusses several criticisms of measures of consumer satisfaction, including bias due to inflated responses, inadequate evidence of reliability and validity, and the need for instruments that are sensitive to cultural diversity. Additionally, issues specific to measuring children's perceptions of satisfaction are addressed.

The Nature of Responses

The majority of the professional literature has reported elevated levels of satisfaction with services (Brannan, Sonnichsen, Heflinger, in press), with three theories forwarded as accounting for the positive results. First, the influence of social desirability (Rosen et al., 1994) can confound the assessment of consumer satisfaction with services such that reported levels of satisfaction are greater than true levels of satisfaction. Socially desirable responses occur when respondents answer items in ways they believe others would want them to. Participants may respond positively despite their true opinions because they believe that negative responses could jeopardize their relationship with their practitioner, or out of a desire to make a program or provider "look good" because they fear losing services (Nicholson & Robinson, 1996; Bailey, 1987).

Second, attrition rates in mental health programs can inflate reported levels of satisfaction, as satisfaction data may be obtained only from those consumers who complete a course of treatment (Lebow, 1983). Individuals who are not satisfied with services may be more likely to withdraw prematurely from treatment, and thus not provide input into satisfaction data at discharge (Brannan et al., in press). They also may be less likely to respond to mailed follow-up questionnaires inquiring about their satisfaction with services (Lebow, 1982).

Third, providing feedback on service delivery may represent a new role for consumers. This new role, developed by providers, may not have been adequately explained to consumers. Data provided by consumers who are not sure why they are being queried about their degree of satisfaction may not reflect their accurate perceptions and possibly inflate responses.

Reliability and Validity

As with any construct, evidence of adequate reliability and validity of the instruments employed are important factors in measuring consumer satisfaction with services. Reliable instruments produce consistent scores over time or across people, while validity refers to the extent that an instrument measures what it is intended to measure. It should, for example, differentiate satisfied consumers from dissatisfied consumers (Nicholson & Robinson, 1996). Unfortunately, many of the instruments measuring consumer satisfaction with children's mental health services do not have data on reliability and validity available for inspection, and it appears that some researchers are taking these constructs for granted (Young et al., 1995). It is important for researchers and practitioners to understand the limitations of instruments currently being used to measure satisfaction, because without evidence of validity and reliability, scales may be inadequate for their intended purpose. However, by using instruments with documented evidence supporting reliability and validity, researchers can be more confident of their findings.

Sensitivity to Diversity

The measurement of satisfaction, like mental health services in general, should be sensitive to the diversity of individuals who complete the scales (Nicholson & Robinson, 1996), as individuals from ethnically and culturally diverse backgrounds may perceive satisfaction differently. The reading level of an instrument and other literacy issues also can add to the complexity of assessing consumer satisfaction with services. Additionally, the influence of socioeconomic status (SES) may complicate the measurement of satisfaction, because SES may be related to whether consumers have a choice of providers. It is important to recognize that the influence of ethnicity, educational level, and SES can remain undetected when using measures that are not sensitive to these areas.

Issues Specific to Measuring Satisfaction with Children's Services

There are several factors in the children's mental health field that distinguish it from the adult field that should be addressed when measuring consumer satisfaction. First, whereas adults tend to self-refer to mental health services (Schwab & Stone, 1983), most often it is a parent or custodial adult who is responsible for a child's receipt of services. Often children are excluded from decision making that leads to treatment; therefore, they may not perceive the need for services or understand why they are receiving treatment (Young et al., 1995). Second, the treatment process in children's mental health may involve others in addition to the child receiving treatment. For example, parents and siblings may be active participants in the treatment process. Thus, measuring satisfaction with services will extend beyond the child receiving treatment to include the family members who also are involved in the process. Third, younger children are cognitively immature in comparison to adolescents and adults and may be unable to look beyond treatment-related discomforts to see long-term goals and possibilities (Young et al., 1995). Finally, program managers should realize that while it has been assumed that the parents' reported level of satisfaction with services provides an adequate proxy for their child's perception of satisfaction, children's perceptions may differ substantially from adult perceptions (Stüntzner-Gibson et al., 1995). Thus, while it is important to include the unique perspectives of children in program evaluation, satisfaction instruments should be age appropriate, and data should be interpreted carefully, attending to the developmental context of the child (Young et al., 1995).

Summary

Researchers and service providers need to understand the challenges inherent in the assessment of satisfaction with services. Foremost, distributions of satisfaction with services data historically have been skewed, making consumers appear more satisfied than they actually may have been with programs and services. Moreover, these positive findings may limit the desire of program managers to probe into a consumer's actual experiences with services. Additionally, several other issues currently influence how satisfaction instruments are designed, including the need to be sensitive to diversity, the need for demonstrated evidence of reliability and validity, and factors that are specific to measuring satisfaction with children's services. It is important to recognize that information from the consumer's perspective provides valuable insight about mental health service delivery, information that may not be uncovered otherwise. Thus, the field should continue to strive to overcome these challenges by developing scales that are responsive to the criticisms presented here.

A Selection of Currently Used Satisfaction Scales

A number of consumer satisfaction measures have been reported in the research literature on children's mental health services (see Nicholson & Robinson, 1996). However, because no standardized measure of satisfaction exists, there has been a tendency for researchers and service providers to develop their own questionnaires (Heflinger, 1992) and, to date, the majority of studies are based on instruments whose psychometric properties have not been reported (Young et al., 1995). In this section, a brief review of some of the currently used measures of satisfaction with children's mental health services is provided and summarized in Table 16.1. These scales were chosen for review because psychometric properties have been established. The section begins with a brief description of the Client Satisfaction Questionnaire (CSQ; Larsen et al., 1979), considered the first standardized satisfaction survey to assess adult mental health services (Young et al., 1995). The CSQ scales have been used in evaluative studies across an array of health and human services (Attkisson & Greenfield, 1994). Moreover, the CSQ has served as a foundation for the development of a number of instruments used to assess satisfaction with both adult and child/adolescent mental health services (e.g., DeChillo, 1990; Stüntzner-Gibson et al., 1995). Following the discussion of the CSQ and the related Youth Satisfaction Questionnaire (YSQ; Stüntzner-Gibson et al., 1995), five satisfaction instruments used with children and families are presented; two are designed to survey parents and families, and three are designed to survey children and adolescents. For each instrument there is a description of the scale, available data on the scale's psychometric properties, and a review of a study in which the instrument was used.

Client Satisfaction Questionnaire

The Client Satisfaction Questionnaire (CSQ; Larsen et al. 1979) was designed to be easily administered and completed across a variety of settings. The scale was developed in the following manner. First, the scale was constructed from information gathered from a review of the literature, containing nine categories, each with nine items. Then, mental health professionals ranked these 81 items as to how well each measured the dimension under investigation, and 45 items were retained. Next, mental health board members from throughout California rank-ordered the 45 items (based on areas they believed would yield

Table 16.1

Overview of Consumer Satisfaction Scales Used
in the Children's Mental Health Field

Instrument and Author	Description	Evidence of Reliability (Coefficient Alpha)	Evidence of Validity
Youth Satisfaction Questionnaire (YSQ; Stüntzner-Gibson et al., 1995)	Five (3-point) general satisfaction Likert items, and blank lines for children to grade services and activities received.	.80[a]	—
Family Satisfaction Questionnaire (FSQ; Rouse et al., 1994)	12 (5-point) Likert items, a multiple choice question about treatment obstacles, and an open-ended item for comments.	0.89	Factor analysis indicated three dimensions of satisfaction.
Parent Satisfaction Scale (PSS; Brannan et al., in press)	Covers nine service-specific modules with each model generally covering nine content areas. Number of items varies for each content area.	$\geq .70$[b]	Confirmatory factor analysis of the outpatient module indicated four dimensions of satisfaction.
Child/Adolescent Satisfaction Questionnaire (CASQ; Rouse et al., 1994)	12 (5-point) Likert questions, a multiple-choice question about treatment obstacles, and an open-ended item for comments.	0.88	Factor analysis indicated three dimensions of satisfaction.
Adolescent Satisfaction Survey (ASS; Brannan et al., in press)	Covers nine service-specific modules with each model generally covering nine content areas. Number of items varies for each content area.	$>.70$[c]	—
Youth Satisfaction Survey (YSS; Rosen et al., 1994)	Number of items varies; youth rate satisfaction with services and providers relevant to their individualized treatment plan.	.88	—

[a]Coefficient alphas calculated only for the three items thought to measure general satisfaction.

[b]Coefficient alphas analyzed for eight of nine modules (one module was not analyzed because of limited sample size).

[c]Coefficient alphas reported only for three modules because of limited sample size of the remaining modules.

useful feedback), resulting in the retention of 31 items. This version was field tested with 248 individuals who were receiving mental health treatment. Using a principal-component factor analysis, without rotation, eight items with the highest loadings on the general satisfaction factor were selected for the current scale, the CSQ-8 (see Attkisson & Greenfield, 1994; Larsen et al., 1979; and Nguyen, Attkisson, & Stegner, 1983 for a thorough discussion of this process).

The instrument has met acceptable psychometric standards. A coefficient alpha of .93 was reported for the CSQ-8 (Attkisson & Zwick, 1983; Larsen et al., 1979), demonstrating a high degree of internal consistency. Additionally, evidence of construct validity has been reported for the CSQ-8, as it has been found to correlate well with other satisfaction instruments. Currently, there are two alternative forms of the CSQ-8, an 18-item CSQ (CSQ-18) and a four-item version (CSQ-4). However, the CSQ-8 remains the most widely used version (Attkisson & Greenfield, 1994).

Youth Satisfaction Questionnaire

The Youth Satisfaction Questionnaire (YSQ; Stüntzner-Gibson et al., 1995) was based partially on the original CSQ by modifying the wording to make the items understandable to children. The YSQ measures children's perspectives about services received during the previous 6 months and can be used with children 9 years old and older. The instrument consists of five general questions addressing how satisfied the children are with the services they received (e.g., "Did you like the help you were getting?"). The respondents rate each item along a 3-point Likert scale consisting of "Yes"—"Somewhat"—"No." The remaining portion of the form provides an area where the staff lists specific services a child received, so the child can grade them (A, B, C, D, F). Listed services may include clubs, school activities, and sports, as well as mental health services.

Psychometric Properties

For three of the five items dealing directly with satisfaction, a coefficient alpha of .80 was obtained. The remaining two items were dropped because of a low correlation with the other items. The authors suggest that the two dropped items, unlike the other three, pertain to quantity rather than quality of services. While the YSQ is based partially on the CSQ, which has been validated for adults, data have not been reported on the validity of the YSQ with children.

Research Findings

Data from the YSQ were used to assess the impact of the Robert Wood Johnson Foundation's Mental Health Services Program for Youth (Beachler, 1990) in Multnomah County, Oregon. The evaluation focused on the effects of a case-management program that used a flexible funding approach to provide individualized services for children and adolescents who were experiencing substantial limitations in various life domains (e.g., home, school) and had a DSM-III-R diagnosis. Participants ranged from 5–18 years of age and had been involved with at least two service agencies in the community. Data were collected at program admission and at 6-month intervals.

The response rate was 66% ($N = 165$). Item numbers 1, 2, and 5 were totaled to provide a global satisfaction score. The theoretical midpoint for the range of possible scores was 6.0 and the average score was 6.5 ($SD = 1.9$). Thus, the distribution was skewed in a direction that indicated high satisfaction; however, the authors reported that 49% of the subjects had scores at or below the midpoint. An analysis was conducted to examine age, minority status, gender, problem behavior, and the relationship of each to the level of satisfaction reported by participants. The only statistically significant relationship was found between the age of the subjects and the subjects' reported level of satisfaction with the services. This relationship ($r = -.26, p < .001$) indicated that as the age of the child increased, level of satisfaction decreased.

For the second section of the scale, in which youths graded services and activities, a system was developed to classify the types of services and activities reported ($N = 22$). For each service or activity in which at least 25 youths reported participating, an average grade was calculated. Services that strongly correlated with general satisfaction included day treatment ($r = .66, p < .001$), special education ($r = .49, p < .001$), general education ($r = .47, p < .001$), and counseling ($r = .45, p < .001$). Less formal activities (e.g., clubs, sports) produced weaker correlations, suggesting that children did not perceive these activities to be as helpful with their problems as the more formal activities (for a detailed explanation, see Stüntzner-Gibson et al., 1995).

Family Satisfaction Questionnaire

The Family Satisfaction Questionnaire (FSQ; Rouse et al., 1994) is a self-administered measure designed to survey parental satisfaction with services, provider characteristics, consumer participation, direct products of treatment (i.e., knowledge and skills learned during treatment), and treatment outcomes (e.g., decreased symptomatology). The questionnaire, written at a 6th-grade reading level, consists of 12 (5-point) Likert questions, one multiple choice question about obstacles to services, and an open-ended question requesting additional comments about the program.

Psychometric Properties

A coefficient alpha of .89 was reported for the FSQ (Rouse et al., 1994), with item-total correlations ranging from .30 (How much family participation) to .83 (Program helped deal with problems). Thus, the FSQ appears to be internally consistent, as most items correlated well with the total score. An exploratory factor analysis indicated that the instrument appears to measure three dimensions of parents' perception of services: Treatment Effectiveness (Factor I), with factor loadings ranging from .85 (Program helped deal with problems) to .88 (How child is doing); Satisfaction with Services (Factor II), with factor loadings ranging from .77 (Would return for services) to .86 (Was staff helpful); and Family Participation (Factor III), with a factor loading of .97 for one item (How much family participation). This analysis suggests that satisfaction is composed of a number of closely related components. Concurrent validity was established by correlating the FSQ with other measures. The instrument was found to be significantly (although not highly) positively correlated with child satisfaction scores from the parallel child/adolescent version of the scale ($r = .61$, $p < .0001$); the service providers' satisfaction with the case ratings ($r = .40$, $p < .0001$); Global Assessment of Functioning (GAF) change scores ($r = .23$, $p < .0007$); and ratings by service providers of whether treatment goals were met ($r = .28$, $p < .0001$).

Research Findings

The FSQ was developed as a measure of consumer satisfaction within the evaluation of the Texas Children's Mental Health Plan (TCMHP), an interagency effort to provide an array of community-based mental health services to children and youth with severe emotional disturbance (SED) and their families. Individuals were referred to the program by participating agencies, a family member, or by self-referral. To qualify, referred children must have had a DSM-III-R diagnosis and have met one of the following conditions: (a) a GAF score of 50 or less, (b) being at risk for out-of-home placement, or (c) being eligible for special education services. Parents who returned the FSQ ($N = 354$; 21%) were found to be similar to the total TCMHP sample. With a range of possible scores of 12–60 with higher scores equaling greater satisfaction, the average satisfaction score ($M = 51.3$, $SD = 7.01$) indicated a mostly positive response. No differences were found in average scores on the basis of respondent, participation in public assistance, or type of treatment received. Consistent with previous findings, those who completed treatment reported significantly higher satisfaction scores on the average than those who did not complete treatment. Further, average satisfaction scores were similar to the parallel child/adolescent version of the scale.

Parent Satisfaction Scale

The Parent Satisfaction Scale (PSS; Brannan et al., in press), developed as part of the Fort Bragg Child and Adolescent Mental Health Demonstration Study (see Bickman, 1996; Bickman et al., 1995), is a self-administered questionnaire designed to assess parent satisfaction with mental health services. Rather than limiting assessment to global satisfaction, the instrument is unique in that a "service-specific" approach is taken. Nine service-specific modules include (a) intake and assessment, (b) outpatient therapy, (c) inpatient hospital/residential treatment center, (d) case management, (e) day treatment, (f) therapeutic group home, (g) therapeutic family home, (h) after-school services, and (i) in-home counseling. In addition, within each module, several aspects of the treatment process referred to as "content areas" (Brannan et al., in press) are included. Although content areas vary across modules, they generally include (a) access and convenience, (b) child's treatment, (c) parent services, (d) family services, (e) relationship with therapist, (f) staff responsiveness, (g) financial charges, (h) discharge/transition services, and (i) global satisfaction.

Psychometric Properties

To assess the internal consistency of each content area for eight of the nine modules, coefficient alphas were reported. Generally, all coefficient alphas were greater than .70, indicating high internal consistency. Within the day treatment module, two content areas had a reported alpha coefficient of less than .70 (i.e., parent services, .57; family services, .68). The after-school service module was not assessed because of the limited sample size.

To detect possible correlates of satisfaction and to determine whether the PSS replicated the results of other satisfaction measures, correlational analyses were conducted for the outpatient therapy and inpatient hospital/residential treatment center modules. For the outpatient module, only two content areas were found to be significantly related to the demographic characteristics of parent age, gender, race, educational level, and income. Older parents indicated greater satisfaction with access to and convenience of outpatient services, and fathers reported less satisfaction with their child's treatment than mothers. With regard to treatment characteristics, longer length of treatment was associated with greater satisfaction with the parent-therapist relationship as well as the explanation of the financial charges/payment. Finally, parent-provider agreement about treatment termination was moderately related to satisfaction with most content areas of outpatient services.

Correlational analyses of the inpatient hospital/residential treatment center module yielded no significant relationships between content areas and demographic variables. Only parent services and family services were significantly related to the treatment characteristics included in the analyses. Parents whose children received treatment longer and those with high confidence in the treatment reported greater satisfaction with parent services. Those with a greater number of persons residing in the household reported less satisfaction with family services than those with smaller households. Finally, the longer a child had received residential services, the higher the parents' reported satisfaction with parent services. Thus, these results are consistent with previous findings and suggest that the PSS measures service satisfaction similarly to other measures in the literature (see Brannan et al., in press, for a comprehensive overview of these analyses).

The validity of the PSS was assessed through a confirmatory factor analysis (CFA) using data from the outpatient module. Results indicated the existence of four dimensions of satisfaction including (a) access and convenience, (b) child's treatment process and relationship with therapist, (c) parent and family services, and (d) global satisfaction. Fit index for this four-factor model was .974 with a chi-square of 82.50 ($df = 29$, $p < .001$). Factor loadings ranged from .82 to .98 with error terms ranging from .20 to .54.

Research Findings

The PSS was developed as part of the Fort Bragg Evaluation Project (Bickman, 1996; Bickman et al., 1995), an independent evaluation of a children's mental health managed care demonstration site developed for military families at Fort Bragg, North Carolina. The demonstration site offered a continuum of mental health services, including nontraditional services (e.g., day treatment, crisis intervention) and case management for children in need of intensive services. Two similar U.S. Army posts, offering only traditional mental health services, served as the comparison site for the evaluation.

A total of 984 families participated in the study, each of which used CHAMPUS mental health benefits for their children. Children and youth were between the ages of 5 and 18 and had received treatment from their current mental health service provider for less than 1 month prior to participation in the study (see Breda, 1996, for a discussion of the demographics of the total sample). Satisfaction data were collected from the child's primary caregiver at intake (within 30 days of admission) and at follow-up (every 6 months).

Heflinger et al. (1996) presented parent ratings of satisfaction for the following services provided at both the demonstration and comparison sites: intake assessment during admission to any service setting, outpatient therapy, and inpatient hospitalization and residential treatment centers. In the area of intake/assessment, parents at the demonstration site reported significantly higher levels of satisfaction globally and for 11 of the 16 content areas measuring specific dimensions of satisfaction. Regarding satisfaction with outpatient services, parents at the demonstration site reported significantly higher levels of satisfaction than the parents at the comparison site across all content areas. In the inpatient hospitalization/residential treatment center module, significantly higher levels of parent satisfaction with two content areas (i.e., access to services and financial charges) were noted at the demonstration site. Consistent with the previous findings, global satisfaction scores with outpatient services were significantly higher at the demonstration site, while no difference between sites in global satisfaction scores with inpatient hospitalization/residential treatment center services was noted.

Child/Adolescent Satisfaction Questionnaire

The Child/Adolescent Satisfaction Questionnaire (CASQ; Rouse et al., 1994), the parallel version of the FSQ, is a self-administered measure designed to survey children and adolescents as to their satisfaction with services, provider characteristics, consumer participation, direct products of treatment, and treatment outcomes. The questionnaire, written at the 6th grade reading level, consists of 12 (5-point) Likert questions, one multiple choice question about obstacles to services, and an open-ended question requesting additional comments about the program.

Psychometric Properties

A coefficient alpha of .88 was reported for the CASQ. Item-total correlations ranged from .38 (How much family participation) to .80 (How happy with progress). Thus, the instrument demonstrates adequate internal reliability. As was evident with the parent version of this scale, an exploratory factor analysis indicated that the instrument seems to measure the following three dimensions: Treatment Effectiveness (Factor I), with factor loadings ranging from .82 (How happy with progress, How family is doing, and Program helped deal with problems) to .75 (How much learned about problems); Satisfaction with Services (Factor II), with factor loadings ranging from .64 (Was staff helpful) to .81 (How happy with time with provider); and Child and Provider Relationship (Factor III), with factor loadings ranging from .61 (Was staff helpful) to .82 (Was staff nice). Again, as with the parent version, this analysis suggests that satisfaction is composed of a number of closely related components. Concurrent validity was established by correlating the CASQ with other measures. The instrument was found to be significantly (although not highly) correlated with parent scores from the parallel parent version of the scale ($r = .61, p < .0001$); service providers' satisfaction with case ratings ($r = .27, p < .002$); Global Assessment of Functioning (GAF) change scores ($r = .27, p < .0004$); and ratings by service providers of whether treatment goals were met ($r = .24, p < .002$).

Research Findings

As with the parallel parent version of this scale, the CASQ was developed to serve as a measure of child/adolescent satisfaction within the evaluation of the Texas Children's Mental Health Plan (TCMHP). The sample for this investigation was the same as for the parent version. The number of youths responding to the questionnaires ($N = 266$; 18%) was similar to the total TCMHP sample. With a range of possible scores from 12 to 60, with higher scores equaling higher satisfaction, the CASQ yielded an average score of 50.2 ($SD = 7.16$), suggesting that most respondents were satisfied with the services. No differences were noted in average satisfaction scores on the basis of gender, ethnicity, participation in public assistance, or type of treatment received. However, average scores did differ by level of program completion, as higher satisfaction scores were correlated with treatment completion. Finally, scores on the CASQ and the parallel parent version of this scale were similar.

Adolescent Satisfaction Survey

The Adolescent Satisfaction Survey (ASS; Brannan et al., in press), developed as part of the Fort Bragg Child and Adolescent Mental Health Demonstration Study (Bickman, 1996; Bickman et al., 1995), is a self-administered questionnaire designed to assess adolescent satisfaction with mental health services. The ASS, the parallel version of the previously described FSS, contains the same nine service-specific modules as the parent version. As with the parent version, each module contains several content areas; however, those areas considered inappropriate (e.g., satisfaction with explanation of financial charges/payment) were eliminated from the adolescent version.

Psychometric Properties

Coefficient alphas were reported for three of the nine modules contained in the ASS—that is, the intake assessment, outpatient therapy, and inpatient hospital/residential treatment center modules. In general, the content areas for all three modules demonstrated high internal consistency, with most having alpha coefficients of .70 or greater. Only three content areas had alpha coefficients lower than .70. In the outpatient module, the area of satisfaction with discharge/transition services ($r = .61$) and satisfaction with therapist relationship ($r = .68$) demonstrated lower internal consistency, while in the inpatient hospital/residential treatment center module, satisfaction with access and convenience yielded a coefficient alpha of .63. Thus it appears that these three modules of the ASS have acceptable internal consistency, with alphas ranging from .61 to .91. Data examining the validity of the ASS were not reported.

Research Findings

As was true for the parallel parent version, the ASS was developed as part of the Fort Bragg Evaluation Project (see earlier discussion of the PSS). Ratings of satisfaction with outpatient and inpatient hospitalization/residential treatment center services were gathered for the demonstration and comparison sites (Bickman et al., 1995). For the outpatient module, adolescents at the demonstration site reported significantly higher levels of satisfaction with two of the eight content areas, including access to and convenience of services and relationship to the therapist. No significant differences were noted between sites on any areas in the inpatient hospitalization/residential treatment center module; however, the authors caution that these results may be the result of small sample sizes. Consistent with findings from the parent version, global satisfaction scores with outpatient services were significantly higher at the demonstration site, while there were no differences in global satisfaction scores across sites for the area of inpatient hospitalization/residential treatment centers.

Youth Satisfaction Survey

The Youth Satisfaction Survey (YSS; Rosen et al., 1994) was developed to serve as one component of an evaluation of outcomes for youth receiving community-based wraparound services in Vermont (see Burchard & Clarke, 1990). The survey contains questions about the amount of contact youngsters have with each of their service providers (e.g., case worker, therapist), their satisfaction with each component of their service plan, and satisfaction with their own progress. Using a 5-point Likert scale, respondents rate their level of satisfaction with the services and service providers relevant to their individualized treatment plan, including the (a) treatment team, (b) residential treatment, (c) case worker, (d) case manager, (e) therapist/counselor, (f) school program, (g) vocational program, (h) respite care, and (i) an overall rating of services. In addition, youth rate their level of satisfaction with their own progress.

Psychometric Properties

The overall satisfaction scale, obtained by averaging each respondent's ratings across all services/service providers and across six data-collection points, yielded an alpha coefficient of .88, suggesting high internal reliability. No information on the validity of this scale was reported.

Research Findings

Using the YSS as one component of an evaluation of outcomes for youth receiving wraparound services in Vermont, a study was conducted to investigate youths' satisfaction with wraparound services, explore possible correlates of youth satisfaction, and further examine the relationship of youth satisfaction, sense of involvement, and perception of unconditional care to behavioral adjustment. The YSS was completed by 20 youths identified as having emotional and behavioral problems and in need of intensive services who received wraparound services in Vermont. The youths lived in placements of varying levels of restrictiveness, ranging from independent living to residential treatment centers, and they received a number of community and family-based interventions (e.g., therapeutic case management, individual and family therapy).

Overall satisfaction with services and service providers yielded a mean of 4.16 (SD = .64, range 2.5–5.0), indicating a high level of satisfaction with wraparound services. For specific services and service providers, an average satisfaction score of 4.02 or higher was obtained for all areas except satisfaction with case worker ($M = 3.47$, $SD = .83$). Satisfaction with case manager yielded the highest average score ($M = 4.37$, $SD = .87$).

An examination of the correlates of satisfaction indicated that an increase in the youths' sense of involvement, perception of unconditional care, and satisfaction with their own progress was associated with higher overall satisfaction, while an increase in restrictiveness of placement was related to a decrease in overall satisfaction. Partial correlational analyses revealed that youths who felt a sense of involvement in their treatment and perceived their care as unconditional appeared to be highly satisfied with services. Further, even when placed in a highly restrictive setting, youth were more satisfied if they felt a sense of involvement in their treatment.

Correlations among satisfaction, sense of involvement, and unconditional care with behavioral adjustment revealed that overall satisfaction and sense of involvement generally were not correlated with behavioral adjustment. Perception of unconditional care was strongly associated with behavioral adjustment. Correlations between behavioral adjustment and satisfaction with specific services indicated that while youths' satisfaction with their case manager was unrelated to behavioral adjustment, greater satisfaction with their case worker was associated with less depressive or self-abusive behavior (see Rosen et al., 1994, for a discussion of other correlations of marginal significance).

Moving Beyond the Construct of Consumer Satisfaction

The interaction between families and the children's mental health service-delivery system has changed dramatically over the last decade (Knitzer, 1993). Increasingly, it is recognized that the needs and desires of the family should guide the way in which services are provided. Additionally, services that embrace family-oriented values (e.g., family-centeredness) are believed to impact functional outcomes positively, and thus also may increase satisfaction with services. Therefore, the essence of consumers' satisfaction with services may lie in the ability of service providers to adhere to these family-oriented values. Researchers and practitioners have moved beyond solely assessing global satisfaction and developed instruments that attempt to measure family-oriented values, including (a) family centeredness (i.e., the degree to which a service is oriented toward meeting the needs of the family, rather than requiring the family to conform to the nature of the program); (b) family empowerment (i.e., enabling families to influence how their child's mental health services are delivered); (c) service coordination (i.e., the match between the services provided and the family's needs);

(d) family supportiveness (i.e., the family's perception of the level of support provided by a program); and (e) cultural competence (i.e., the cultural and ethnic sensitivity of providers, programs, and the instruments used to assess principles of service delivery).

Family-Centeredness

Family-centered practices have been defined as those practices that (a) involve the family in assessment, decision making, planning, and service delivery at all levels, including family, agency, and system levels; (b) develop services not just for the child, but also for the whole family; (c) use the family's priorities for services and goals to guide service provision; (d) respect the family's choice as to their level of involvement and participation with child and family service agencies (Murphy, Lee, Turnbull, & Turbiville, 1995); and (e) embrace a strengths-based focus. The goal is to enable the family to make "fully informed" decisions about the direction of their child's treatment (Allen, 1996).

The Family Centered Program Rating Scale (FamPRS; Murphy et al., 1995) assesses and monitors the degree of family-centeredness in programs for children and their families. The FamPRS has demonstrated some evidence of reliability and validity (see Murphy et al., 1995). Another scale, the Family-Centered Behavior Scale (FCBS; Allen, 1996), gathers information from parents of children with special needs about desirable and undesirable behaviors exhibited by professionals during treatment. The FCBS allows parents to rate the degree to which professionals perform specific family-centered behaviors during treatment (Allen, Petr, & Cay Brown, 1995). The FCBS has shown some evidence of reliability and validity (see Allen, 1996).

Family-Empowerment

Family empowerment is viewed as an important outcome by many child and family service agencies (Koren, DeChillo, & Friesen, 1992). Empowerment has been described as the ability of parents to "become collaborators in their children's mental health treatment" (Heflinger, Anderson, Digby, Grubb, & Williams, 1994, p. 1). There is, however, little research on how empowerment can be enhanced in families (Northrup et al., 1994), little agreement about what distinguishes empowerment from other constructs, and a lack of systematic methods for assessing whether empowerment has been enhanced (Koren et al., 1992).

The Vanderbilt Mental Health Services Efficacy Questionnaire (Heflinger et at., 1994) was created to measure whether empowerment was enhanced for a group of parents, following a parent-empowerment training program. The questionnaire assessed whether parents believed that they could act in ways that would impact their child's mental health treatment and that if they did act in such ways, the treatment process would be more appropriate for their child. Findings revealed that participating in the parent empowerment group led to a significant increase in both mental health services knowledge and self-efficacy (Heflinger, 1995). A second scale, the Family Empowerment Scale (FES; Koren et al., 1992), was designed to assess empowerment at three levels (Family, Service System, and Community/Political). Research on the FES suggests that these levels of empowerment can be assessed in reliable and valid ways (see Elliot, Koroloff, Koren, & Friesen, this volume; Koren et al., 1992).

Service Coordination

Service coordination has been broadly defined as "service providers working together on behalf of children, regardless of the formal (e.g., case management) or informal processes that cause this to happen" (Koren, Paulson, Kinney, Yatchmenoff, Gordon, & DeChillo, in press). As treatments become more individualized, increased numbers of agencies may have to work together, and it is more likely that children's needs will be identified and addressed when services are coordinated. In a recent study, the Service Coordination Scale (Koren et al., in press) was used to assess parental perceptions of whether they believed that agencies and organizations were working together to coordinate services for their children. Parents were asked about the conditions or activities that promote or limit integration among organizations and agencies, such as availability of services, communication among providers from different agencies, duplication of paperwork, and agreement about a single service plan across providers. The Service Coordination Scale has shown adequate internal reliability, but validity data has not been reported.

The Supportiveness of Services

The Kentucky Interagency Mobilization for Progress in Adolescent and Child Treatment (IMPACT) required that state and federal funds be used to provide appropriate community-based services for children and adolescents with severe emotional disabilities (Illback, Fitzgerald, Call, & Andis, 1994). The IMPACT program was evaluated on a number of process and outcome variables, including assessing the extent to which families experienced higher levels of both formal and informal social support and were satisfied with both the timeliness and responsiveness of support received from those services. Findings from the Inventory of Social Support (Illback et al., 1994) and the Family Support Satisfaction Scale (Illback, Nelson, & Sanders, this volume) suggest that IMPACT has provided participants with a source of social support and that families are satisfied with this social support (see Illback et al., 1994; Illback, Nelson, & Sanders, this volume).

Cultural Competence

Satisfaction with services also may be related to the respect and understanding of cultural differences providers demonstrate when working with families from ethnically and culturally diverse backgrounds. Cultural competence can influence how individuals from diverse backgrounds access and utilize mental health services, and additionally, it can impact treatment outcomes (Mason, Benjamin, & Lewis, 1996). Scales currently are being developed to address these issues—for example, the Parent Satisfaction Questionnaire (Johnson & Hall, 1992) assesses the degree to which practitioners understand the values and ethnic beliefs held by a family, asks if the language in which services were provided was appropriate, and inquires about the ethnic background of service providers. Marfo, Brieda, Witty, and Bobo (1995) developed the Service Satisfaction Scale, designed to measure the extent to which African-American parents are satisfied with the early intervention services their child received. In addition to statements that investigate the consumer's level of satisfaction with services in areas such as respect, relationship quality, and involvement with decision making, this instrument includes a statement specific to African Americans (i.e., "The extent to which services are provided in a culturally appropriate way to ensure that your needs as African-American families are met."). Psychometric properties have not yet been reported for these scales.

Summary

In an effort to attain more precise data about a family's experience with the service-delivery system, mental health services researchers have moved beyond measuring the construct of global satisfaction with services and currently are exploring several distinct but related constructs in the children's mental health field (i.e., family centeredness, family empowerment, service coordination, service supportiveness, cultural competence). In the children's mental health field, researchers have ventured into the parallel activities of assessing global satisfaction as well as adherence to the specific values inherent in providing family-oriented services. The predominant challenge facing researchers is to link the implementation of family-oriented values to global satisfaction as well as positive functional outcomes for children and families.

Discussion and Implications

In this chapter, we have described the historical context for the assessment of consumer satisfaction with mental health services and the current research findings in the children's mental health services field. Changes in public policy and the philosophy that consumers should have input into service delivery have made the assessment of consumer satisfaction a critical component of program evaluation. While acceptance of the role of consumer satisfaction has gained momentum, the parallel activities of developing models, instruments, and methods for measuring satisfaction have not kept pace. Enthusiasm for the adoption of the construct has outstripped the research realities regarding how to best assess satisfaction with services and the role consumer satisfaction data has in providing feedback to program staff and external audiences. In a review by Nicholson and Robinson (1996) of 16 instruments that measure satisfaction with children's mental health services, only half reported any psychometric data available for inspection. Additionally, several of these scales were adaptations of the instrument developed by Larsen et al. (1979) that measured adult perspectives on satisfaction with mental health services and have not been tested in the children's area.

There have, however, been some notable exceptions in the measurement of satisfaction with mental health services for children and families. Most notable is the work conducted as part of the Ft. Bragg Child and Adolescent Mental Health Demonstration Project (Bickman et al., 1995; Brannan et al., in press; Heflinger et al., 1996) in which a model of satisfaction was theorized as being determined by factors both internal and external to the services received. In developing the scales, researchers acknowledged that both global and service-specific factors of satisfaction should be assessed. In the comparison of two service delivery systems, the results indicated significantly higher levels of satisfaction with both the intake and treatment process for outpatient services as well as some of the components within the inpatient/residential services in the delivery system that provided a comprehensive and coordinated array of service options. However, it should be noted that high levels of satisfaction were reported by parents in both delivery systems, indicating that a wide range of responses were not captured. This points to the need to refine the measurement system to capture the apparently subtle dimensions of consumer satisfaction with services.

This review of the research literature on consumer satisfaction in the children's mental health services field has direct implications for consumers, researchers, service providers, and policymakers. While the desire to have consumer input into service delivery provided the impetus for the assessment of consumer satisfaction with services, the lack of consumer and advocacy group involvement in the development of this area is striking. None of the authors described the involvement of consumers in the development of their instruments and instead often have relied on the work of Larsen et al. (1979), whose scale was developed with professional involvement and may have had some consumer involvement. This input, however, is now dated. Likewise, researchers in this area have relied on factor analytic techniques to support the validity of consumer satisfaction scales. While this technique is useful from a statistical standpoint of understanding the underlying dimensions of a scale, the knowledge of the construct may best be advanced by testing a scale that is based on a model or theory. Until models and theories concerning satisfaction with services are developed, the results from consumer satisfaction scales may not lead to improvement of services. With the current emphasis to create partnerships between consumers of services and services researchers (Greene, 1988), an opportunity exists to bring both together to fully explicate the areas of satisfaction that consumers want explored and the best methods to gather this information.

A major finding from this review is that consumers of services report positive levels of satisfaction irrespective of scale or setting. This skewed distribution has implications for consumers, service providers, and researchers. These positive results seem to suggest that the majority of consumers report high satisfaction with services and that service providers are offering services that satisfy consumers. As research on outcomes of children's mental health services are mixed at best, one may infer that at present families appear to value any type of service as more beneficial than no service at all. One could speculate that when asked to evaluate satisfaction, vulnerable family members may be biased in reporting higher satisfaction because of the misperception that lower reports of satisfaction may affect the receipt of services. Service providers and policymakers also should be aware that the positive results of consumer satisfaction surveys may not reflect accurately the perceptions of consumers, and they should attempt to increase the validity of these results by using other methods to collect supplementary information from consumers (e.g., focus groups, interviews, case-study investigations).

An important implication for policymakers is that we must continue to strive to develop family focused, family friendly systems of care in which consumers will be empowered and confident enough to give honest and valid feedback to program staff. The concept of developing treatment teams in which family members are viewed as equal decision-making partners is an important step in this direction. The field needs a critical number of such programs so that valid evaluation of program efficacy and consumer satisfaction can be reliably tested.

The use of consumer satisfaction scales has become a popular method for collecting information from consumers in the hope of improving service delivery. From the results of the research literature reviewed in this chapter, the majority of scales commonly used in this area appear to be reliable, but validity has yet to be established. Therefore, the various users of the information from these scales (i.e., consumers, advocates, researchers, service providers, and policymakers) should be aware of the potential weaknesses of this approach and should work together in establishing the validity of the existing scales and in developing a new generation of measures that tap into the multiple aspects of a family's experience with the service-delivery system. There is reason to be optimistic that such an initiative will emerge in the near future because of the rapidly expanding services research field, the demands for consumer evaluation in managed care systems, and the ever-increasing family empowerment movement.

Endnote

1. This 1996 monograph, *A guide for evaluating consumer satisfaction with child and adolescent mental health services,* by J. Nicholson & G. Robinson, is available from the Technical Assistance Center for the Evaluation of Children's Mental Health Systems, Judge Baker Children's Center, 295 Longwood Avenue, Boston, MA 02115.

Authors' Note

Correspondence may be addressed to the authors at the Research and Training Center for Children's Mental Health, Florida Mental Health Institute, University of South Florida, 13301 Bruce B. Downs Blvd., Tampa, FL 33612; (813) 974-4661.

References

Allen, R. I. (1996). *The family-centered behavior scales: A report on the validation study.* Lawrence: University of Kansas, Beach Center on Families & Disabilities.

Allen, R. I., Petr, C. G., & Cay Brown, B. F. (1995). *Family-centered behavior scale and user's manual.* Lawrence: University of Kansas, Beach Center on Families & Disabilities.

Attkisson, C. C., & Greenfield, T. K. (1994). Client Satisfaction Questionnaire-8 and Service Satisfaction Scale-30. In M. E. Maruish (Ed.), *The use of psychological testing for treatment planning and outcome assessment.* Hillsdale, NJ: Lawrence Erlbaum.

Attkisson, C. C., & Zwick, R. (1983). The Client Satisfaction Questionnaire: Psychometric properties and correlations with service utilization and psychotherapy outcome. *Evaluation and Program Planning, 5,* 233–237.

Bailey, D. B. (1987). Collaborative goal-setting with families: Resolving differences in values and priorities for services. *Topics in Early Childhood Special Education, 7*(2), 59–71.

Beachler, M. (1990). The mental health services program for youth. *Journal of Mental Health Administration, 17,* 115–121.

Berndt, D. (1995). Symposium: Results from the process and outcome evaluations of the Texas children's mental health plan three. In C. Liberton, K. Kutash, & R. Friedman (Eds.), *The 7th Annual Research Conference Proceedings, A System of Care for Children's Mental Health: Expanding the Research Base, February 28 to March 2, 1994* (pp. 3–5). Tampa: University of South Florida, Florida Mental Health Institute, Research and Training Center for Children's Mental Health.

Bickman, L. (1996). The evaluation of a children's mental health managed care demonstration. *Journal of Mental Health Administration, 23*(1), 7–15.

Bickman, L., Guthrie, P. R., Foster, E. M., Lambert, E. W., Summerfelt, W. T., Breda, C. S., & Heflinger, C. A. (1995). *Evaluating managed mental health services: The Fort Bragg experiment.* New York: Plenum Press.

Brannan, A. M., Sonnichsen, S. E., & Heflinger, C. A. (in press). Measuring satisfaction with children's mental health services: Validity and reliability of the satisfaction scales. *Evaluation and Program Planning.*

Breda, C. S. (1996). Methodological issues in evaluating mental health outcomes of a children's mental health managed care demonstration. *Journal of Mental Health Administration, 23*(1), 40–50.

Burchard, J. D., & Clarke, R. T. (1990). The role of individualized care in a service delivery system for children and adolescents with severely maladjusted behavior. *Journal of Mental Health Administration, 17,* 48–59.

Byalin, K. (1993). Assessing parental satisfaction with children's mental health services. *Evaluation and Program Planning, 16,* 69–72.

DeChillo, N. (1990). Client Satisfaction Questionnaire. In K. Kutash & V. R. Rivera (Eds.), *Measures of satisfaction with child mental health services.* Unpublished manuscript, University of South Florida, Florida Mental Health Institute, Research and Training Center for Children's Mental Health, Tampa.

Duchnowski, A. J., & Kutash, K. (1996). The mental health perspective. In C. M. Nelson, R. B. Rutherford, & B. I. Wolford, (Eds.), *Comprehensive and collaborative systems that work for troubled youth: A national agenda* (pp. 90–110). Richmond, KY: National Coalition for Juvenile Justice Services.

Elliot, D. J., Koroloff, N. M., Koren, P. E., & Friesen, B. J. (this volume). Improving access to children's mental health services: The family associate approach. In M. H. Epstein, K. Kutash, & A. J. Duchnowski (Eds.), *Community-based programming for children with serious emotional disturbances and their families: Research and evaluation.* Austin, TX: Pro-Ed.

Greene, J. C. (1988). Stakeholder participation and utilization in program evaluation. *Evaluation Review, 12*(2), 91–116.

Heflinger, C. A. (1992). Client-level outcomes for mental health services for children and adolescents. *New Directions for Program Evaluation, 54,* 31–45.

Heflinger, C. A. (1995). Studying family empowerment and parental involvement in their children's mental health treatment. *Focal Point, 9*(1), 6–8.

Heflinger, C. A., Anderson, J., Digby, J., Grubb, C., & Williams, C. (1994). *Vanderbilt family empowerment project: Family group curriculum manual.* Nashville, TN: Vanderbilt University Center for Mental Health Policy.

Heflinger, C. A., Sonnichsen, S. E., & Brannan, A. M. (1996). Parent satisfaction with children's mental health services in a children's mental health managed care demonstration. *Journal of Mental Health Administration, 23*(1), 69–79.

Illback, R. J., Fitzgerald, E. M., Call, J., & Andis, P. (1994). Evaluation of Kentucky Impact at year two: A summary of the findings. In C. Liberton, K. Kutash, A. Algarin, & R. Friedman (Eds.), *The 6th Annual Research Conference Proceedings, A System of Care for Children's Mental Health: Expanding the Research Base, March 1 to March 3, 1993* (pp. 13–18). Tampa: University of South Florida, Florida Mental Health Institute, Research and Training Center for Children's Mental Health.

Illback, R. J., Nelson, C. M., & Sanders, D. (this volume). In M. H. Epstein, K. Kutash, & A. J. Duchnowski (Eds.), *Community-based programming for children with serious emotional disturbances and their families: Research and evaluation.* Austin, TX: Pro-Ed.

Johnson, M., & Hall, K. S. (1992). *Parent Satisfaction Questionnaire.* Tampa: University of South Florida, Florida Mental Health Institute, Research and Training Center for Children's Mental Health.

Kazdin, A. E. (1980). Acceptability of alternative treatments for deviant child behavior. *Journal of Applied Behavior Analysis, 13*(2), 259–273.

Knitzer, J. (1993). Children's mental health policy: Challenging the future. *Journal of Emotional and Behavioral Disorders, 1*(1), 8–16.

Koren, P. E., DeChillo, N., & Friesen, B. J. (1992). Measuring empowerment in families whose children have emotional disabilities: A brief questionnaire. *Rehabilitation Psychology, 37*(4), 305–321.

Koren, P. E., Paulson, R. W., Kinney, R. F., Yatchmenoff, D. K., Gordon, L. J., & DeChillo, N. (in press). Service coordination in children's mental health: An empirical study from the caregiver's perspective. *Journal of Emotional and Behavioral Disorders.*

Lambert, E. W. (1996, February). *Psychopathology change, consumer satisfaction, and parent-reported improvement.* Paper presented at the 9th annual research conference, A System of Care for Children's Mental Health: Expanding the Research Base, Tampa, FL.

Larsen, D. L., Attkisson, C. C., Hargreaves, W. A., & Nguyen, T. D. (1979). Assessment of client/patient satisfaction: Development of a general scale. *Evaluation and Program Planning, 2,* 197–207.

Lebow, J. L. (1982). Consumer satisfaction with mental health treatment. *Psychological Bulletin, 91*(2), 244–259.

Lebow, J. L. (1983). Research assessing consumer satisfaction with mental health treatment: A review of the findings. *Evaluation and Program Planning, 6,* 211–236.

Marfo, K., Brieda, M., Witty, J., & Bobo, M. (1995). *Service Satisfaction Scale.* Unpublished instrument, University of South Florida, Department of Special Education, Tampa.

Mason, J. L., Benjamin, M. P., & Lewis, S. A. (1996). The cultural competence model: Implications for child and family mental health services. In C. A. Heflinger & C. T. Nixon (Eds.), *Families and the mental health system for children and adolescents* (pp. 165–190). Thousand Oaks, CA: Sage.

McMahon, R. J., & Forehand, R. L. (1983). Consumer satisfaction in behavioral treatments of children: Types, issues, and recommendations. *Behavior Therapy, 14,* 209–225.

McNaughton, D. (1994). Measuring parent satisfaction with early childhood intervention programs: Current practice, problems, and future perspectives. *Topics in Early Childhood Special Education, 14*(1), 26–48.

Moynihan, M. H., Forward, J. R., & Stolbach, B. (1994). Colorado's Parents' Satisfaction Survey: Findings and policy implications for local systems of care. In C. Liberton, K. Kutash, & R. Friedman (Eds.), *The 6th Annual Research Conference Proceedings, A System of Care for Children's Mental Health: Expanding the Research Base, February 28 to March 2, 1993* (pp. 69–79). Tampa: University of South Florida, Florida Mental Health Institute, Research and Training Center for Children's Mental Health.

Murphy, D. L., Lee, I. M., Turnbull, A. P., & Turbiville, V. (1995). The family centered program rating scale: An instrument for program evaluation and change. *Journal of Early Intervention, 19*(1), 24–42.

Nguyen, T. D., Attkisson, C. C., & Stegner, B. L. (1983). Assessment of patient satisfaction: Development and refinement of a service evaluation questionnaire. *Evaluation and Program Planning, 6,* 299–314.

Nicholson, J., & Robinson, G. (1996). *A guide for evaluating consumer satisfaction with child and adolescent mental health services.* Boston: Judge Baker Children's Center.

Northrup, D., Bickman, L., & Heflinger, C. A. (1994). *The family empowerment project: A theory-based family intervention and evaluation.* Unpublished manuscript, Vanderbilt University, Center for Mental Health Policy, Nashville.

Plante, T. G., Couchman, C. E., & Diaz, A. R. (1995). Measuring treatment outcome and client satisfaction among children and families. *Journal of Mental Health Administration, 22*(3), 261–267.

Rosen, L. D., Heckman, T., Carro, M. G., & Burchard, J. D. (1994). Satisfaction, involvement, and unconditional care: The perception of children and adolescents receiving wraparound services. *Journal of Child and Family Studies, 3*(1), 55–67.

Rouse, L. W., MacCabe, N., & Toprac, M. G. (1994, February). *Measuring satisfaction with community-based services for children with severe emotional disturbances: A comparison of questionnaires for children and parents.* Paper presented at the 7th annual research conference, A System of Care for Children's Mental Health: Expanding the Research Base, Tampa, FL.

Rouse, L. W., MacCabe, N., & Toprac, M. G. (1996). Measuring satisfaction with community-based services for children with severe emotional disturbances: A comparison of questionnaires for children and parents. In C. Liberton, K. Kutash, & R. Friedman (Eds.), *The 8th Annual Research Conference Proceedings, A System of Care for Children's Mental Health: Expanding the Research Base, March 6 to March 8, 1995* (pp. 69–79). Tampa: University of South Florida, Florida Mental Health Institute, Research and Training Center for Children's Mental Health.

Sabourin, S., Laferriere, N., Sicuro, F., Coallier, J., Cournoyer, L., & Gendreau, P. (1989). Social desirability, psychological distress, and consumer satisfaction with mental health treatment. *Journal of Psychology, 36*(3), 352–356.

Schwab, M. E., & Stone, K. (1983). Conceptual and methodological issues in the evaluation of children's satisfaction with their mental health care. *Evaluation and Program Planning, 6*, 283–289.

Stüntzner-Gibson, D., Koren, P. E., & DeChillo, N. (1995). The Youth Satisfaction Questionnaire: What kids think of services. *Families in Society, 76*(10), 616–624.

Young, S. C., Nicholson, J., & Davis, M. (1995). An overview of issues in research on consumer satisfaction with child and adolescent mental health services. *Journal of Child and Family Studies, 4*(2), 219–238.

Applied Research

IV

Multisystemic Therapy: Changing the Natural and Service Ecologies of Adolescents and Families

17

Sonja K. Schoenwald, Charles M.
Borduin, and Scott W. Henggeler

In a recent monograph examining the mental health needs of youths charged with status offenses or delinquent acts who show a range of behavioral or emotional problems, Cocozza (1992) concluded that the extant system of care fails to address the complexity of these youths' needs. Despite system-of-care initiatives to increase interagency collaboration in the treatment of such youth (Barnum & Keilitz, 1992), extant services and interventions remain, with rare exceptions, "based on premises that bear little resemblance to what either common sense or empirical research suggests is likely to be effective" (Melton & Pagliocca, 1992, pp. 107–139). Treatment efforts are generally individually oriented, narrowly focused, and delivered in settings that bear little relation to the problems being addressed (e.g., residential treatment centers, outpatient clinics). Given overwhelming empirical evidence that serious antisocial behavior (chronic criminal offending; adolescent substance abuse) is determined by the interplay of individual, family, peer, school, and neighborhood factors (for reviews, see Henggeler, 1991, in press), it is not surprising that treatments for serious antisocial behavior have been largely ineffective (Lipsey, 1992; Mulvey, Arthur, & Reppucci, 1993). In light of the failure of most treatments of serious antisocial behavior, systems-level reforms (e.g., interagency coordination and cooperation, flexible funding) should not, in and of themselves, be expected to favorably impact clinical outcomes for these youth (Henggeler, Schoenwald, & Munger, 1996). Rather, such reforms might be expected to facilitate the work of clinical teams providing "effective" treatments—treatments that address the multidetermined nature of serious clinical problems in an individualized yet comprehensive fashion.

The purpose of this chapter is to describe one treatment model that has a well-documented capacity to address the aforementioned difficulties in providing effective mental health services for juvenile offenders. Multisystemic Therapy (MST; Henggeler & Borduin, 1990; Henggeler, Schoenwald, Borduin, Rowland, & Cunningham, in press) is an intensive, time-limited, family- and community-based treatment approach that has demonstrated effectiveness in randomized trials with chronic and violent juvenile offenders and their families (Borduin et al., 1995; Henggeler, Melton, & Smith, 1992; Henggeler, Melton, Smith, Schoenwald, & Hanley, 1993; Scherer, Brondino, Henggeler, Melton, & Hanley, 1994). In these studies, MST has been equally effective with families of different cultural backgrounds (African American and Caucasian) and socioeconomic status. Current projects are examining its effectiveness with juvenile offenders diagnosed as substance abusing and substance dependent (Henggeler, Pickrel, & Brondino, 1995), with gang-affiliated juvenile offenders, many of whom are Hispanic American (Thomas, 1994), and as an alternative for youths about to be hospitalized for homicidal, suicidal, or psychotic behavior (Henggeler & Rowland, in press). MST has also been effective with small samples of maltreating parents (Brunk, Henggeler, & Whelan, 1987) and adolescent sex offenders (Borduin, Henggeler, Blaske, & Stein, 1990).

In addition to describing the theoretical, clinical, and research-related features of MST, a second goal of this chapter is to discuss the implications of the emergent success of MST for the development of effective community-based mental health programming for youths and families. It is suggested that, to have a positive clinical impact on clinical outcomes for youth and families, changes in the service ecology (e.g., increases in accessibility and array of services, increased interagency collaboration, and flexible funding) should be matched with changes in the youth's natural ecology. Changes in the natural ecologies of youths, in turn, are most likely to occur when service providers alter their clinical practices to include empirically validated treatment models that address the multiple correlates and causes of serious clinical problems in youths (Henggeler et al., in press).

The Multisystemic Therapy (MST) Model of Treatment

Multisystemic Therapy (MST; Henggeler & Borduin, 1990; Henggeler et al., in press) is an intensive, time-limited, home- and family-focused treatment approach predicated on socioecological (Bronfenbrenner, 1979) and family systems models of behavior. Similarly, MST is supported by findings from causal modeling studies of serious antisocial behavior (delinquency, adolescent substance abuse) that indicate that a combination of family (low warmth, high conflict, harsh or inconsistent discipline, low monitoring of youth whereabouts, parental problems, low social support), peer (association with deviant peers), school (low family-school bonding, problems with academic and social performance), and neighborhood (transiency, disorganization, criminal subculture) factors predict the development of serious antisocial behavior in adolescents. Thus, consistent with socioecological theory and the empirically established determinants of antisocial behavior in youth, MST directly targets for change those factors within the youth's family, peer group, school, and neighborhood that are contributing to his or her antisocial behavior. Moreover, to optimize the ecological validity of interventions (Henggeler, Schoenwald, & Pickrel, 1995), MST is conducted directly in the natural ecologies (home, school, community) of the youth and family.

Rationale for the Model

A brief description of the major theoretical, empirical, and service-delivery underpinnings of MST are presented below. For a more extensive discussion of these issues, see a clinically oriented volume that describes MST in detail (Henggeler et al., in press) and presents specific guidelines for implementing MST for serious problems in youth.

Theory of Social Ecology

Consistent with Bronfenbrenner's (1979) theory of social ecology, MST views individuals as being nested within a complex of interconnected systems that encompass individual (e.g., biological, cognitive), family, and extrafamilial (peer, school, neighborhood) factors. Behavior problems can be maintained by problematic transactions within or between any one or combination of these systems. Thus, MST targets identified child and family problems within and between the multiple systems in which family members are embedded.

Empirical Underpinnings

Importantly, this ecological view of child behavior problems is strongly supported by research on causal modeling in the areas of adolescent substance use/abuse (Brook, Nomura, & Cohen, 1989; Dishion, Reid, & Patterson, 1988; Elliott, Huizinga, & Ageton, 1985; Oetting & Beauvais, 1987), delinquency (for a review, see Henggeler, 1991), and child psychopathology, where virtually all types of serious problems have been shown to be multidetermined (e.g., Belsky, 1993; Elliott et al., 1985; Henggeler, in press). Moreover, mounting evidence from this research suggests that antisocial behavior, substance abuse, academic failure, and other risk-taking behaviors (e.g., cigarette smoking, high-risk sexual behavior) co-vary (Ary, Duncan, Biglan, Metzler, Noell, et al., 1994; Donovan, Jessor, & Costa, 1988; Elliott, Huizinga, & Menard, 1989) and implicate the same constellation of factors as "common causes" (White, Pandina, & LaGrange, 1987) in the development of antisocial behavior.

Model of Service Delivery

The provision of MST is consistent with the family preservation model of service delivery. Family preservation is based on the philosophy that the most effective and ethical route to helping children and youth is through helping their families. Thus, families are seen as valuable resources, even when they are characterized by serious and multiple needs. While the particular "practice models" that characterize family preservation programs vary (for a review see Nelson, 1994), critical service-delivery characteristics are shared (Nelson & Landsman, 1992). These characteristics include low caseloads, delivery of services in community settings (e.g., home, school, neighborhood center), time-limited duration of treatment, 24 hour/day and 7 day/week availability of therapists, and provision of comprehensive services. With respect to MST, specifically, caseload size has averaged from four to six families per counselor, and duration of treatment has ranged from 3–5 months. Thus, a team of three counselors provides service for approximately 50 families each year. Depending on the stage of treatment and extant crises, sessions may be held every day or as infrequently as once a week. Emphasis is placed on the efficient use of treatment sessions, each typically lasting 30–75 minutes and concluding with the assignment of explicit tasks related to the identified goals.

Principles and Components of MST Interventions

Principles

Detailed descriptions of the MST principles enumerated below, and examples that illustrate the translation of these principles into specific intervention strategies, are provided in a clinical volume for practitioners (Henggeler et al., in press). Note that these principles are consistent (Santos, Henggeler, Burns, Arana, & Meisler, 1995) with the guiding principles of the "system of care" (Stroul & Friedman, 1994).

1. The primary purpose of assessment is to understand the "fit" between the identified problems and their broader systemic context.

2. Therapeutic contacts should emphasize the positive and should use systemic strengths as levers for change.

3. Interventions should be designed to promote responsible behavior and decrease irresponsible behavior among family members.

4. Interventions should be present-focused and action-oriented, targeting specific and well-defined problems.

5. Interventions should target sequences of behavior within and between multiple systems.

6. Interventions should be developmentally appropriate and fit the developmental needs of the youth.

7. Interventions should be designed to require daily or weekly effort by family members.

8. Intervention efficacy is evaluated continuously from multiple perspectives.

9. Interventions should be designed to promote treatment generalization and long-term maintenance of therapeutic change.

These principles inform therapists' efforts to set the stage for lasting therapeutic gains by focusing on the empowerment of families through the mobilization of indigenous child, family, and community resources. Thus, the overriding goal of MST is to empower parents (parent [and family] is broadly defined to include the adult [or adults] who serves as the youth's primary parent figure or guardian) with the skills and resources needed to independently address the inevitable difficulties that arise in raising teenagers and to empower youth to cope with family, peer, school, and neighborhood problems.

Interventions

The choice of modality used to address a particular problem is based largely on the empirical literature on its efficacy. As such, MST interventions are usually adapted and integrated from pragmatic, problem-focused treatments that have at least some empirical support. These include strategic family therapy (Haley, 1976), structural family therapy (Minuchin, 1974), behavioral parent training (Munger, 1993), and cognitive behavior therapies (Kendall & Braswell, 1993). In addition and as appropriate, biological contributors to identified problems are identified and psychopharmacological treatment is integrated with psychosocial treatment.

Initial therapy sessions identify the strengths and weaknesses of the adolescent, the family, and their transactions with extrafamilial systems (e.g., peers, friends, school teachers, principals, parents' workplace, and social service agencies, where applicable). The treatment plan is designed in collaboration with family members and is, therefore, family-driven rather than therapist-driven. Problems identified conjointly by family members and the therapist are explicitly targeted for change, and the strengths of each system are used to facilitate such change. Although specific strengths and weaknesses can vary widely from family to family, one or more of the aforementioned determinants of serious behavior problems (see "Empirical underpinnings") are usually implicated in the identified problems. Within a context of support and skill building, the therapist places developmentally appropriate demands on the adolescent and family for responsible behavior. Treatment sessions focus on facilitating attainment of goals that were defined conjointly by family members and the therapist. As substantive progress is made toward meeting one goal, treatment sessions incorporate additional goals. In addition, treatment interventions have the flexibility to be relatively intense, in terms of both time in treatment (e.g., multiple sessions per week) and task orientation of treatment sessions (e.g., explicit goal setting and extensive homework assignments).

At the family level, adolescents presenting serious clinical problems and their parents frequently display high rates of conflict and low levels of affection. Similarly, parents (or guardians) frequently disagree regarding discipline strategies, and their own personal problems (e.g., substance abuse, depression, marital problems) often interfere with their ability to provide necessary parenting. Family interventions in MST often attempt to provide the parent(s) with the resources needed for effective parenting and for developing increased family structure and cohesion. Such interventions might include introducing systematic reward and discipline systems (e.g., Munger, 1993), prompting parents to communicate effectively with each other about adolescent problems, solving day-to-day conflicts, addressing marital problems that interfere with parenting practices, and developing social support networks in the parents' natural ecology (neighborhood, workplace, church, extended family, community organizations). The key to effective interventions, however, is determining and addressing the barriers to effective parenting. Although typical mental health services address parenting difficulties by providing structured parenting classes to enhance parental knowledge, such interventions rarely address the core barriers to effective parenting. In families of youth presenting serious clinical problems, the more substantive core barriers are likely to include parental substance abuse, parental psychopathology, low social support, high stress, marital (or adult relationship) conflict, and poverty. These barriers must be successfully resolved before enhanced parenting knowledge can be used to influence youth behavior.

At the peer level, a frequent goal of treatment for adolescents presenting serious clinical problems is to decrease their involvement with deviant and drug-using peers and to increase association with prosocial peers (e.g., through church youth groups, organized athletics, afterschool activities, employment). Consistent with MST principles, even peer interventions are usually designed to facilitate the capacity of the parent or caregiver to initiate and monitor changes in the youth's peer interactions over time (see principle #9, regarding treatment generalization). Thus, interventions aimed at changing peer groups or peer interactions often consist of helping parents to actively support and encourage associations with nonproblem peers (e.g., meeting peers and their parents, monitoring peer activities, facilitating opportunities to meet prosocial peers, providing transportation, privileges for increased contact with prosocial peers) and to strongly discourage associations with deviant peers (e.g., applying significant sanctions). Likewise, with the assistance of the therapist, the parents develop strategies to monitor and promote the youth's school performance and vocational functioning. Typically included in this domain are strategies for helping parents to open and maintain positive communication lines with teachers, and to restructure afterschool hours to promote academic efforts.

Finally, although the emphasis of treatment is on systemic change, there are also situations in which individual interventions can facilitate behavioral change in the adolescent or parents. Interventions in these situations generally focus on modifying the individual's social perspective-taking skills, belief system, and motivational system, and encouraging the youth to deal assertively with negative peer pressures. Similarly, individual interventions for parents may address depression, lack of positive social support, and so forth.

Treatment is terminated when evidence from multiple sources (youth, parent, school, probation officer, etc.) indicates that: (a) the youth has no significant clinical problems and the family has been functioning reasonably well for at least a month; (b) the youth is making reasonable educational and vocational efforts; (c) the youth is involved with prosocial peers and is minimally involved with problem peers; and (d) the clinician and supervisor feel that the parent(s) has the knowledge, motivation, and resources needed for handling subsequent problems. Treatment may also be terminated when some of the preceding goals have been met but treatment has reached a point of diminishing returns for therapy time invested.

The Case Study of Jamie

A case example is presented to illustrate the principles and practices of MST. Jamie, a 14-year-old 7th grader, was referred for MST by a public mental health agency. Jamie had displayed significant behavioral problems since the age of 10, had been suspended from school many times for disruptive and aggressive behavior, and had failed the 7th grade. Having recently been arrested for vandalism and car theft, Jamie was court-ordered to receive outpatient mental health treatment. At the school's recommendation, Jamie had received such treatment for several months during each of the 3 previous years. Jamie's therapist reported some improvements in Jamie's within-session behavior; his teacher and mother, however, reported no improvement at school and at home. Recognizing that family factors might contribute to Jamie's problems, the counselor scheduled several office-based family therapy sessions. Because of conflicts with her work schedule and lack of reliable transportation, Jamie's mother often canceled these appointments. Jamie lived with his mother, two younger siblings, an 18-year-old sister, and her 6-month-old infant. His mother was employed at minimum wage as a cook's assistant in a local hotel; his father lived in another state and had no contact with his children.

In assessing the "fit" between Jamie's problems and the broader systemic context (principle #1), the therapist identified several significant strengths that could be used as levers for therapeutic change (principle #2). On the family front,

Jamie's mother cared for him, wanted him to finish school, had sought treatment for him previously, and held a job. Jamie and his siblings "covered" for one another when trouble was brewing. At school, one teacher and one guidance counselor were willing to "give Jamie another chance." Two teachers observed that Jamie interacted with one or two prosocial peers in several classes. As for individual strengths, Jamie demonstrated athletic skill, was attractive, and had been a "C" student in most subjects until middle school. Several weaknesses were also apparent, however. On the family front, Jamie's mother's rotating work schedule often kept her away from home during after-school and evening hours. Jamie's mother was chronically fatigued, mildly depressed, and often overwhelmed by the demands of work, single parenthood, and Jamie's problems.

There was no extended family in the vicinity, and Jamie's mother could not identify any sources of social support (e.g., church, a friend at work or outside of work, a neighbor). Jamie and his younger siblings often engaged in verbal and physical conflicts, and while his mother had asked the 18-year-old sister to intercede while she was at work, the sister had neither the authority nor the skills to do so. In his mother's absence, Jamie sought out peers who had begun to experiment with drug use and other delinquent acts. At school, two teachers and the principal saw expulsion as a desirable solution to the problems Jamie's behavior caused in class. The therapist also assessed the real and potential impact of other agencies on the family and on the treatment plan the MST therapist and family would develop together. The mental health counselor, probation officer, and family court judge were players in the "service ecology" surrounding Jamie and his family. That is, the behavior of these individuals and the mandates of their agencies influenced the family, and, therefore, could influence the treatment plan in more or less desirable ways. The judge had ordered Jamie to outpatient treatment, and the mental health counselor was mandated to follow the court's treatment plan. Jamie's mother reported feeling blamed by the court, the schools, and the mental health agency.

Having obtained this initial assessment of the natural and service ecologies in which Jamie and his family were nested, the therapist solicited the mother's goals for treatment. Her overarching goals were to get Jamie to school on time and keep him in school all day, every day; to stop Jamie's criminal activity; and, to decrease Jamie's involvement with antisocial peers and increase his involvement with prosocial peers. Next, the therapist began to identify the interim steps to the attainment of these overarching goals. These interim steps, or intermediary goals, are logically linked to the overarching goals, and constitute the focus of therapeutic interventions. In Jamie's case, initial interim steps focused on the most obvious factors preventing his mother from consistently engaging in the monitoring and discipline practices—namely, her rotating work schedule, mild depression, social isolation, and limited skill with discipline techniques likely to be effective with adolescents. In addition, because Jamie was about to be permanently expelled from school, an immediate priority was to reestablish a workable relationship between Jamie's mother and school personnel.

As treatment progressed, the therapist sought feedback from Jamie's mother, school teachers, a neighbor who had agreed to assist with monitoring, and the probation officer, regarding Jamie's attendance, whereabouts after school, and criminal activity (principle #8). After 5 days of school attendance without truancy or suspension, several teachers reported that Jamie had arrived late to class and displayed disruptive behavior. In trying to understand the "fit" of this behavior with Jamie's changing ecology, the therapist learned that Jamie's mother had relaxed her monitoring plan when her work schedule changed and that she sometimes "gave in" to Jamie's pleas and demands. Moreover, her disappointment with the reemergence of Jamie's problem behavior amplified her fatigue and mild depression. Thus, the therapist redoubled efforts to identify people in the natural environment (e.g., neighbors, co-workers, church members) who could support his mother's monitoring and discipline plan and provide some pleasant adult interaction. The MST therapist also recognized that she, herself, had to provide the daily reinforcement for Jamie's mother's parenting efforts until the new supports were in place.

Treatment was terminated 4 months after referral. During the course of treatment, Jamie attended school regularly, had been truant 3 times, and had not been suspended. He received three disciplinary warnings and an in-school suspension on two occasions. Following these incidents, his mother, though frustrated and fatigued, talked with school personnel about the incidents and reinstituted the daily school-home communication plan that had been implemented during the early weeks of treatment, delivering agreed-upon consequences at home. By the 2nd month of MST treatment, she had been able to take such action with little, if any, assistance from the therapist. Thus, while Jamie continued to demonstrate some behavioral problems, his mother was usually able to manage them, and she and school personnel were able to work together as needed. On the other hand, Jamie's mother was still fatigued often, relatively socially isolated, and mildly depressed on occasion. Jamie's mother concurred that she would have some difficulty maintaining treatment gains without support from other adults. She identified her work schedule and fatigue as primary barriers to obtaining such support, and she had begun to seek alternative employment when treatment ended.

Facilitating Successful Implementation of MST

Each of the following factors is believed to be critical to the successful implementation of MST (see Henggeler, Smith, & Schoenwald, 1994):

1. The empirically derived correlates/determinants of serious clinical problems must be addressed in a comprehensive yet individualized protocol.

2. Services must be provided in the natural environment of the youth and family.

3. Therapists must be well trained and supported, and therapist adherence to the treatment model must be monitored.

4. Substantial efforts must be directed toward the development and maintenance of positive interagency relationships.

Because the first two issues have already been addressed, the focus of this section is upon the supervisory and administrative practices used to facilitate the successful implementation of MST in completed and ongoing trials of MST, and in partnerships with community-based providers of child and family mental health services in South Carolina, Texas (Thomas, 1994), and Tennessee.

Training, Clinical Supervision, and Monitoring of Treatment Fidelity

Clinical training and supervision in the MST model of family preservation is provided in four ways. First, 5 days of intensive training are provided to all staff who will engage in treatment or clinical supervision of MST cases. The initial training includes didactic and experiential components. Didactic components include: (a) instruction in systems theories, social learning theory, and the major psychological and sociological models and research regarding serious emotional disturbance in youth; (b) research relevant to problems experienced by targeted youth (e.g., learning disabilities, substance abuse); and (c) research on interventions used in MST (e.g., empirically validated family and marital therapy approaches, parenting behavioral training, cognitive behavior therapy, and school consultation).

Experiential components include roleplays on engagement, assessment, and intervention strategies and exercises designed to stimulate critical thinking about the treatment process (e.g., what evidence therapists use to draw conclusions about the correlates/causes of a problem, to determine whether their interventions are effective, etc.). Second, as therapists gain field experience with MST, quarterly booster sessions are conducted on site. The purpose of these 1½ day boosters is to provide additional training in areas identified by therapists (e.g., marital interventions, treatment of parental depression in the context of MST) and to facilitate in-depth examination, enactment, and problem-solving of particularly difficult cases. Third, treatment teams and their supervisors receive weekly telephone consultation from Family Services Research Center faculty, who are experts in MST. The purpose of the consultation is to assist the team and supervisor in conceptualizing cases from an MST point of view, clearly articulating treatment priorities and obstacles to success and developing intervention strategies for addressing those obstacles, and to reinforce critical thinking throughout the treatment process (e.g., asking what evidence indicates that the mother is depressed, and that this depression is correlated with her child's behavior problem; how does the therapist know that a child is no longer associating with deviant peers, or whether marital interventions are "working"?, etc.). Fourth, an on-site clinical supervisor trained in the model provides weekly group supervision that mirrors the consultation process described above. Group supervision is problem focused, active, and time efficient (12–15 cases are addressed within a 1½–2 hour group supervision session). The supervision focuses on ensuring the multisystemic focus of therapists' intervention strategies, identifying strategies for overcoming obstacles to successful engagement of key participants (e.g., family members, school personnel, sources of parental social support), and implementing interventions successfully.

In general, group supervision sessions proceed as follows: Whenever a therapist begins work with a family, the therapist presents a 10–15 minute summary of the strengths and weaknesses in each system, the overarching goals identified by family members and key figures in other systems, and the therapist's understanding of the "fit" between the identified problems and these systems. Then, intermediary goals are identified, and strategies for attaining the intermediary goals are discussed. Subsequent supervision sessions focus on advances toward completion of those goals and barriers to their attainment, and on designing strategies for overcoming these barriers.

To illustrate the nature of supervision, the example of Jamie is revisited briefly here. Within the first 3 days after Jamie was referred for MST, the therapist had met with Jamie's family at his home and with his mother at her workplace, had observed neighborhood activities after school, and had met with several teachers and the school principal. The therapist presented the team with most of the strengths and needs in the ecology described earlier. Clear overarching treatment goals had not yet been established. The therapist reported, with a sense of urgency, that the principal had stated that Jamie's next suspension would result in permanent expulsion. The therapist had therefore suggested to Jamie's mother that they schedule a meeting with school officials posthaste, and offered to transport Jamie's mother to the meeting. Jamie's mother refused. The therapist was puzzled by the refusal, and asked the team about techniques she might use to help Jamie's mother change her mind about the meeting. The clinical supervisor observed that the therapist appeared to have insufficient evidence with which to make sense of Jamie's mother's refusal. The therapist learned that a history of negative parent-school communications (notes, phone calls, and meetings), doubt about her ability to advocate for Jamie, and concerns about missing work all contributed to Jamie's mother's initial refusal to attend the meeting. Thus, the therapist met individually with Jamie's mother, each of the teachers, and the principal. The objectives of these meetings were to reduce negative attributions, identify the goals of the first meeting, establish a meeting protocol that would minimize opportunities for conflict, and obtain several possible times at which the meeting could be held.

To track adherence to MST treatment principles and practices, therapists record each treatment contact using a structured treatment session log (Henggeler & Borduin, 1992) designed to track direct (youth and family) and indirect (school, employer, peer) contact. The logs specify frequency and duration of contact, systems addressed (e.g., marital, family, peer, school, etc.), problem areas within each system addressed, homework assigned and completed, and so forth. In addition, clinical supervisors periodically review audiotaped treatment sessions to assess adherence to the MST principles and to identify aspects of therapist-family interactions and interventions that either facilitate or complicate the advancement of therapeutic progress.

Therapist Variables

In clinical trials of MST, therapists have generally been master's level clinicians (social workers, counselors), with some experience in family and community-based work; motivated bachelor's-level therapists have also been involved in these trials and in collaborative projects with service providers in South Carolina and other states. In clinical trials, therapists were selected by project coordinators and clinical supervisors in the community clinics from which MST was being conducted. Outside of the context of clinical trials, public and private service providers seeking to establish home-based services using MST either hire specifically for these positions, or seek volunteers from among the ranks of clinicians currently employed by the provider.

In general, MST service providers and supervisors are held accountable for family engagement and therapeutic outcome. This stance contrasts rather sharply with traditional models of treatment, which tend to blame families and parents (i.e., "resistance") for treatment failure. To sustain such levels of accountability, the therapist and the clinical supervisor accept responsibility for effecting therapeutic change. Thus, for example, Jamie's mother's refusal to attend a meeting was not interpreted as resistance to treatment; instead, the behavior, and the therapist's confusion about it, indicated that more information was needed regarding the "fit" of that behavior with the mother's experiences with her child, the school, her work schedule, and other service providers. Similarly, when confronted with "no shows," reluctance to participate in treatment, statements indicating that a caregiver is "fed up," and so on, the MST therapist's task is to gather the information needed to understand how the behavior makes sense. Families are not blamed for failing to change and social systems are not blamed for their failure to support therapeutic change. Instead, it is the responsibility of the treatment team to find a strategy or approach that will work. If Plan A is unsuccessful, the treatment team identifies the barriers to success and develops Plan B, and so on. Supervisory experiences with MST suggest that sustaining such an iterative process (e.g., designing interventions, identifying barriers to the successful implementation of these interventions, developing strategies to address those barriers) requires that therapists possess a high level of commitment to the family, the capacity to identify and capitalize on family and individual strengths, social and interpersonal flexibility (because different treatment situations may require different therapeutic responses, ranging from humor and warmth to confrontation), and sensitivity to cultural and ethnic issues.

To help therapists sustain such high levels of activity and responsibility, clinical supervisors and treatment team members track process and outcomes for each family on an ongoing basis. In addition, team members engage in MST-informed clinical problem solving as needed (e.g., between weekly group supervision sessions) and provide weekend and vacation relief to one another. In addition, agency policies may need to be adjusted to facilitate the practice of MST (e.g., through implementation of flexible time and comp time policies; scheduling weekly group supervision and phone consultation time, and so forth).

Interagency Collaboration

MST treatment staff meet with personnel from child-serving agencies (e.g., child welfare, mental health, juvenile justice, education, substance abuse) to communicate regarding a variety of issues, and make every effort to cultivate parent/service provider partnerships that can be sustained without therapist involvement. Families are encouraged to sign release of information agreements that allow such communication between treatment staff and other agencies. MST therapists coordinate (and often help change) agency plans for a particular child and family with MST treatment goals and intervention strategies. To this end, staff work to understand the mandates, philosophies, and decisions that characterize various agencies, and particular individuals within agencies, and to coordinate agency and MST activities in ways that facilitate favorable long-term outcomes for the youth and his or her family. As suggested earlier, a treatment team that is accountable not only for engaging in the therapeutic process, but also for obtaining positive outcomes, can ill afford to blame families or other agencies for poor outcomes. From the MST perspective, a premium is placed on therapist engagement of all parties—individuals in the youth's indigenous contexts and service agency personnel—in behavior that will increase the likelihood of attaining and maintaining positive clinical outcomes.

The Long-Term Effectiveness of MST

As described next, our emphasis on obtaining clinical outcomes and the capacity of MST to accomplish them is documented in the findings from recent clinical trials examining the long-term effectiveness of MST with serious juvenile offenders. In a randomized trial conducted in a community mental health center in collaboration with the South Carolina Department of Mental Health and South Carolina Department of Juvenile Justice, and funded by the National Institute of Mental Health, Henggeler and colleagues (Henggeler et al., 1992; Henggeler et al., 1993) examined the effectiveness of MST with violent and chronic juvenile offenders at imminent risk of incarceration. MST was more effective than usual services at reducing rates of incarceration, self-reported delinquent acts, and out-of-home placements more than 1 year after completion of treatment. In addition, MST sustained reductions in re-arrest more than 2 years after completion of treatment. Such long-term success has recently been replicated and extended by Borduin and his colleagues at the University of Missouri.

The Missouri Delinquency Project:
Long-Term Prevention of Criminality
and Violence in Serious Juvenile Offenders

The Missouri Delinquency Project was developed through the cooperation of the Missouri Department of Social Services (Division of Youth Services), the Missouri Thirteenth Judicial Circuit Juvenile Court, and the University of Missouri at Columbia to deliver treatments to juvenile offenders and their families in the natural environment and to train mental health professionals to provide such treatments (Borduin et al., 1995). In addition to providing a needed replication of the recent MST trial described above (Henggeler et al., 1992, 1993), the present study of MST contained several important methodological improvements including (a) a relatively large sample size to permit subgroup analyses (e.g., recidivism for MST completers vs. MST dropouts); (b) a longer follow-up period for re-arrest; (c) observational measures of family relations; and (d) a comparison group that received a roughly equivalent number of treatment hours.

Design and Participants

A pretest-posttest control group design, with random assignment to conditions and a 4-year follow-up for arrests, was used to compare the effectiveness of MST with that of individual therapy (IT). Two hundred families with a 12- to 17-year-old adolescent offender were referred to the project by juvenile court personnel and agreed to participate in a pretreatment assessment session. Referrals included all families in which the youth had had at least two arrests and was currently living with at least one parent figure. The youths averaged 4.2 previous arrests ($SD = 1.4$), and the mean severity of the most recent arrest was 8.8 ($SD = 1.5$) on a 17-point seriousness scale (e.g., 1 = truancy, 4 = disorderly conduct, 8 = assault/battery, 11 = grand larceny, 13 = unarmed robbery, 17 = murder) developed by Hanson, Henggeler, Haefele, and Rodick (1984). All of the youths had been detained previously for at least 4 weeks. The mean age of the youths was 14.8 years ($SD = 1.5$); 67.5% were male; 70% were Caucasian, and 30% were African American; and 53.3% lived with two parental figures (biological parents, stepparents, foster parents, or grandparents). Families averaged 3.1 children ($SD = 1.5$), and 68.8% of the families were of lower socioeconomic class (Class IV or V; Hollingshead, 1975).

Of the 200 families who completed pretreatment assessments, 24 (12%) subsequently refused to participate in treatment (hereafter referred to as "refusers"). The remaining 176 families were randomly assigned to MST ($n = 92$) or individual therapy (IT; $n = 84$). Of these, 140 (79.5%) completed treatment (hereafter referred to as "completers"), and 36 (21.5%) dropped out, defined as unilaterally terminating after the first session (with the youth/family) and before the seventh. Of the 36 youths and their families who dropped out of treatment (hereafter referred to as "dropouts"), 15 were from the MST condition and 21 were from the IT condition (drop-out rates for MST [16.3%] and IT [25%] were not significantly different). It was not possible to obtain posttreatment assessment data from the 36 dropouts or the 24 refusers; however, arrest data were obtained over the follow-up period for these youths. Analyses of variance (ANOVAs) and chi-square tests showed no between-groups differences in the criminal histories or demographic characteristics of MST completers, MST dropouts, IT completers, IT dropouts, and treatment refusers.

Treatment Conditions

Families who completed the pretreatment assessment and agreed to participate in treatment were randomly assigned to conditions and to therapists within each condition. The mean numbers of hours of treatment were 23.9 ($SD = 8.2$) for the MST completers, and 28.6 ($SD = 9.8$) for the IT completers; these means were significantly different, $F(1, 139) = 9.67$, $p <. 01$. The MST dropouts and IT dropouts averaged 4.07 hr ($SD = 0.70$) and 4.29 hr ($SD = 1.01$), respectively, of treatment; these means did not differ significantly.

MST was provided using the principles and intervention stategies described earlier. The therapy provided in the IT condition was selected to represent the usual community treatment for juvenile offenders in the judicial district, and perhaps in many other judicial districts as well (see Henggeler, 1989). The offenders in this condition received individual therapy that focused on personal, family, and academic issues. The therapists offered support, feedback, and encouragement for behavior change. Their theoretical orientations were an eclectic blend of psychodynamic (e.g., promoting insight and expression of feelings), client-centered (e.g., building a close relationship, providing empathy and warmth), and behavioral (e.g., providing social approval for school attendance and other positive behavior) approaches. Although there were some variations in treatment strategies used by the therapists (e.g., some therapists provided less empathy or were more directive than other therapists), the common thread of their approaches was that interventions focused on the individual adolescent rather than on the systems in which the adolescent was embedded.

Therapists

MST was provided by three female and three male graduate students (ages 23–31 years, $M = 26$) in clinical psychology. One of the therapists was Native American, and the others were Caucasian. Each had approximately 1.5 years of direct clinical experience with children or adolescents before the study. Therapist supervision was provided in a 3-hour weekly group meeting and continued throughout the investigation. During these meetings, the therapists and supervisor reviewed the goals and progress of each case, observed and discussed selected videotaped therapy sessions, and made decisions about how best to facilitate the family's progress.

Interventions in the IT group were provided by three female and three male therapists (ages 25–33 years, $M = 28$) at local mental health outpatient agencies, including the treatment services branch of the juvenile court. One therapist was African American, and the others were Caucasian. Each therapist had a master's degree (or equivalent training) in counseling psychology, social work, or a related field, and had approximately 4 years of direct clinical experience with adolescents. These therapists attended 2.5-hour weekly case reviews with the treatment coordinator from the juvenile court to discuss the goals and progress of each case.

Treatment Integrity

To sustain the integrity of MST, therapists documented each therapeutic contact, and ongoing clinical supervision and feedback were provided throughout the investigation. To monitor the integrity of IT, therapists were required to provide monthly reports summarizing the nature of therapeutic contacts, and the project director met periodically with therapists to review session videotapes and to ensure that therapists adhered to treatment plans. The juvenile court treatment coordinator also met weekly with the IT therapists to promote adherence to treatment plans. In addition, therapists in both conditions completed a checklist for each of their cases to indicate the systems directly addressed during the course of treatment (i.e., individual, marital, family, peer, school) and the general issues addressed in each system. The checklists revealed that MST therapists always addressed multiple systems, whereas the interventions of IT therapists rarely extended beyond the individual youth.

Outcome Measures

A multiagent, multimethod assessment battery was used to obtain outcome measures related to the instrumental and ultimate goals (Rosen & Proctor, 1981) of MST. Instrumental goals, which are theory driven, included improved individual adjustment of the adolescent and parent(s), improved family relations, and improved adolescent peer relations. Ultimate goals, which are common to all treatments of juvenile offenders, included decreases in the rate and seriousness of adolescent criminal activity.

Individual Adjustment

Symptomatology in mothers, fathers (when present), and adolescents was assessed through self-reports on the Symptom Checklist-90-Revised (SCL-90-R;

Derogatis, 1983). The Global Severity Index, which represents the best single indicator of the respondent's psychiatric functioning, was used to provide an overall symptom score for each family member. Behavior problems in adolescents were assessed through mothers' reports (total score) on the 89-item Revised Behavior Problem Checklist (RBPC; Quay & Peterson, 1987). This measure discriminates between violent and nonviolent delinquents (Blaske, Borduin, Henggeler, & Mann, 1989) and predicts serious offense history in delinquents (Hanson et al., 1984).

Family Relations

Parental and adolescent perceptions of family relations were evaluated with the 30-item Family Adaptability and Cohesion Evaluation Scales-II (FACES-II; Olson, Portner, & Bell, 1982), which assesses the constructs of cohesion and adaptability. Following the recommendations of Henggeler, Burr-Harris, Borduin, & McCallum (1991), adaptability and cohesion were treated as linear scales in subsequent statistical analyses. Family composite ratings of adaptability and cohesion were created by averaging together the scores of the individual family members on each scale. Observational measures of family relations were based on the family members' videorecorded discussion on the 9-item Unrevealed Differences Questionnaire-Revised using procedures described in previous publications (Blaske et al., 1989; Mann, Borduin, Henggeler, & Blaske, 1990). Three dimensions of family interaction derived from factor analysis were assessed: supportiveness (encouragement and respect between members of a family dyad), verbal activity (amount of verbal activity within a dyad), and conflict-hostility (emotional negativity resulting from clashing interests or ideas within a dyad).

Peer Relations

Maternal and teacher perceptions of the youth's peer relations were evaluated with the 13-item Missouri Peer Relations Inventory (MPRI; Borduin, Blaske, Cone, Mann, & Hazelrigg, 1989), which measures three factor-analytically derived dimensions of peer relations: emotional bonding, aggression, and social maturity.

Criminal Activity

Juvenile court, local police, and Department of Public Safety (state police) records, collected over an average of 3.95 years ($SD = 1.03$; range = 2.04 to 5.41) from the time of the adolescent's release from juvenile court supervision (i.e., probation), were used to obtain data on postprobation arrests. Arrest data for each offender were anchored by the point of release from probation (i.e., within 2 weeks of treatment termination for 96% of completers and an average of 6 months from the time of referral for dropouts and refusers) to provide a distinct beginning for the follow-up period for treatment completers, dropouts, and refusers.

Results

Instrumental Outcomes

Table 17.1 summarizes the results of multivariate analyses of variance (MANOVAs) and ANOVAs used to evaluate whether significant changes were experienced between the pretreatment and posttreatment assessment by youths and families in the MST and IT conditions.

Individual Adjustment

Significant treatment effects were found for mothers' and fathers' reports of psychiatric symptomatology (SCL-90-R). Mothers and fathers in the MST group showed decreases in their symptoms from pre- to posttreatment, whereas their counterparts in the IT group showed either an increase (mothers) or no change (fathers) in their symptoms. A significant treatment effect also emerged for mothers' reports of adolescent behavior problems. Mothers in the MST group reported a decrease in adolescent behavior problems from pre- to posttreatment, whereas mothers of youths receiving IT reported an increase in behavior problems.

Family Relations

Significant treatment effects were observed for both measures of perceived family functioning (FACES-II). Families receiving MST reported increases in family cohesion and adaptability at posttreatment, whereas reported family cohesion and adaptability decreased in the IT condition.

On the observational measures, the analyses generally indicated that families in the MST group evidenced many more positive changes in their dyadic interactions than did families in the IT group. Specifically, in the MST group, mother-adolescent dyads, father-adolescent dyads, and mother-father dyads showed increased supportiveness and decreased conflict-hostility from pre- to posttreatment. In contrast, dyadic relations for families in the IT group either deteriorated (decrease in mother-adolescent supportiveness, increase in father-adolescent conflict-hostility) or showed no change (on measures of supportiveness and conflict-hostility).

Peer Relations

Measures of adolescent peer relations (MPRI) did not show any significant treatment effects.

Table 17.1

Group Means, Standard Deviations, and F Values for Treatment Completers
on Measures of Instrumental Outcomes

Measure	Multisystemic therapy completers ($n = 70$)		Individual therapy completers ($n = 56$)		Repeated ANOVA F	
	Pre	Post	Pre	Post	Time	Group X Time

Individual Adjustment

SCL-90-R (z scores)

Mother

M	0.12	-0.15^a	0.04	0.20^b	0.31	4.16*
SD	1.02	0.97	1.17	1.26		

Father

M	0.06	-0.07^a	0.06	0.19	0.05	4.44*
SD	0.90	0.77	1.05	1.09		

Adolescent

M	0.03	-0.15	-0.05	-0.07	6.02*	0.36
SD	0.94	0.79	0.98	1.03		

RBPC (z scores)

M	0.17	-0.54^a	-0.15	0.64^b	0.33	4.97*
SD	0.74	0.81	0.80	0.85		

Family Relations

FACES-II (mean of mother, father, and adolescent z scores)

Cohesion

M	-0.11	0.14^b	0.11	-0.08^a	0.42	3.83*
SD	0.86	0.88	0.82	0.74		

Adaptability

M	-0.03	0.13^b	0.04	-0.16^a	0.58	5.49*
SD	0.72	0.86	0.85	0.71		

Observational measures (factor scores)

Mother–adolescent Supportiveness

M	-0.09	0.23^b	0.10	-0.14^a	1.78	6.42**
SD	1.01	0.90	0.99	0.93		

Verbal activity

M	-0.05	-0.16	0.05	0.26	2.65	3.07
SD	1.03	1.05	0.97	0.94		

Conflict-hostility

M	0.09	-0.54^a	-0.11	-0.22	14.13***	5.30*
SD	1.01	0.76	0.98	0.85		

(*continues*)

Table 17.1 *Continued*

Measure	Multisystemic therapy completers (n = 70)		Individual therapy completers (n = 56)		Repeated ANOVA F	
	Pre	Post	Pre	Post	Time	Group X Time
Father-adolescent Supportiveness						
M	0.06	1.06[b]	−0.07	0.23	19.91***	9.18**
SD	1.03	1.27	0.97	0.90		
Verbal activity						
M	0.10	0.70	−0.12	0.26	13.01***	1.31
SD	1.07	1.04	0.90	0.94		
Conflict-hostility						
M	0.15	−0.63[a]	−0.18	0.27[b]	0.68	6.66**
SD	0.93	0.82	1.06	0.79		
Mother-father Supportiveness						
M	−0.01	0.79[b]	−0.09	0.31	17.49***	6.33**
SD	1.00	1.03	1.06	0.82		
Verbal activity						
M	0.12	0.10	−0.15	−0.22	0.85	1.65
SD	0.94	0.86	1.07	1.03		
Conflict-hostility						
M	0.27	−0.54[a]	−0.04	−0.03	2.24	4.34*
SD	0.96	0.57	1.11	1.03		

Peer relations

MPRI (mean of mother and teacher factor scores)

Measure	Pre	Post	Pre	Post	Time	Group X Time
Peer bonding						
M	0.24	0.34	0.41	0.44	0.34	0.76
SD	1.52	1.07	1.24	1.13		
Peer aggression						
M	−0.15	−0.11	0.10	0.32	0.08	1.56
SD	2.02	1.88	1.74	1.65		
Peer maturity						
M	0.04	0.17	−0.07	0.24	0.92	0.14
SD	1.87	1.81	2.19	1.88		

Note. SCL-90-R = Symptom Checklist-90-Revised; RBPC = Revised Behavior Problem Checklist; FACES-II = Family Adaptability and Cohesion Evaluation Scales-II; MPRI = Missouri Peer Relations Inventory. The univariate *df*s for each measure are as follows: mother SCL-90-R and observed mother-adolescent relations (1, 123); father SCL-90-R and observed father-adolescent relations (1, 64); adolescent SCL-90-R, RBPC, FACES-II, and MPRI (1, 125); observed mother-father relations (1, 62). From Borduin, C. M., Mann, B. J., Cone, L. T., Henggeler, S. W., Fucci, B. R., Blaske, D. M., & Williams, R. A. (1995). Multisystemic treatment of adolescent sexual offenders: Long-term prevention of criminality and violence. *Journal of Counseling and Clinical Psychology, 63,* 569–578. Copyright © 1995 by the American Psychological Association. Reprinted with permission.

[a]Significant decrease from pretreatment to posttreatment.
[b]Significant increase from pretreatment to posttreatment.
*p < .05. **p < .01. ***p < .001.

Ultimate Outcomes

As noted earlier, measures of ultimate outcome were based on arrest data that were collected an average of 3.95 years from the time of the adolescents' release from juvenile court supervision.

Survival Functions

Survival analysis (based on the LIFETEST procedure; SAS Institute, 1991) was used to obtain the cumulative survival functions (or survival curves) for MST completers (M follow-up = 1446.5 days), MST dropouts (M follow-up = 1452.0 days), IT completers (M follow-up = 1428.6 days), IT dropouts (M follow-up = 1414.3 days), and treatment refusers (M follow-up = 1492.5 days). The cumulative survival function represents the proportion of subjects surviving arrest (i.e., not arrested) in each group by the length of time (in days) from release from probation. The overall set of differences between the survival functions for the five groups was highly significant. Pairwise comparisons of the survival curves shown in Figure 17.1 revealed that the MST completers were at lower risk of arrest (i.e., more likely to "survive") during follow-up than were IT completers, MST dropouts, IT dropouts, or treatment refusers. MST dropouts also were at lower risk of arrest during follow-up than were treatment refusers, or IT dropouts, although the latter comparison only approached significance. IT completers were not significantly different from IT dropouts, MST dropouts, or refusers. At 4 years after follow-up, the overall recidivism rate for MST completers (22.1%) was less than one third the overall rate for IT completers (71.4%), IT dropouts (71.4%), or treatment refusers (87.5%), and approximately one half the overall rate for MST dropouts (46.6%).

Number and Seriousness of Arrests

Additional analyses examined the number of arrests and the seriousness (based on the 17-point seriousness scale, Hanson et al., 1984) of those arrests among recidivists only in the MST completer (n = 17), MST dropout (n = 7), IT completer (n = 45), IT dropout (n = 15), and treatment refuser (n = 21) groups. The first set of analyses revealed that recidivists who had completed MST had fewer arrests (M = 1.57, SD = 0.85) during follow-up than did recidivists who had completed IT (M = 4.41, SD = 3.89). The second set of analyses indicated that recidivists who had completed MST had been arrested for less serious offenses (M = 6.35, SD = 4.67) than recidivists who completed IT (M = 9.67, SD = 3.38). Thus, MST was more effective than IT in reducing the number and seriousness of crimes among those youths who were arrested. Moreover, and importantly, youths who participated in MST were less likely to be arrested for violent crimes following treatment than were youths who participated in IT.

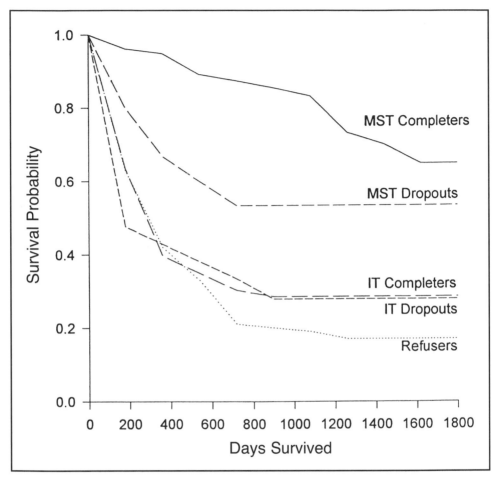

Figure 17.1. Survival functions for multisystemic therapy (MST) completers, MST dropouts, individual therapy (IT) completers, IT dropouts, and treatment refusers. Copyright © 1995 by the American Psychological Association. Reprinted with permission of the author.

Factors Associated with Ultimate Outcome

Hierarchical multiple regression analyses were used to evaluate the effects of potential moderators (age, race, social class, gender, pretreatment arrests) of MST effectiveness. Findings showed that MST outcome did not vary as a function of these different potential moderators. Consistent with findings from an earlier clinical trial (Henggeler et al., 1992; Henggeler et al., 1993), MST was equally effective with youths of different gender, ethnic backgrounds, and social class.

Summary of Findings

The findings demonstrated the impact of MST on key family correlates of antisocial behavior and on individual adjustment in family members. At post-assessment, MST had very positive effects on perceived family relations (increased cohesion and adaptability) and on observed family interactions (increased supportiveness and decreased conflict-hostility across family dyads). In addition, MST resulted in decreased symptomatology in parents and decreased behavior problems in youth. Most important, however, MST produced long-term change in youths' criminal behaviors. Youths treated with MST were much less likely than comparison counterparts to be re-arrested within 4 years of treatment termination, and, when re-arrested, had committed less serious offenses. Although arrest data can be an unreliable measure of criminal activity because of the low probability of being arrested for a criminal act (Henggeler, 1989), the conclusion that MST reduced criminal activity is supported by observed effects of MST on factors linked with criminal activity (i.e., family relations, youth behavior problems) and by the large between-groups differences observed for re-arrest. Moreover, as noted previously, an earlier randomized trial with violent/chronic juvenile offenders (Henggeler et al., 1992; Henggeler et al., 1993) demonstrated the capacity of MST to reduce criminal behavior based on both arrest data and self-reports of criminal behavior (Elliott et al., 1985). Thus, the capacity of MST to reduce the criminal activity of serious juvenile offenders is relatively well established (see e.g., Tate, Reppucci, & Mulvey, 1995).

Discussion

The findings regarding short- and long-term reductions in recidivism and the improvements in family functioning and caregiver symptomatology suggest that MST is effective in changing the natural ecologies in which chronic juvenile offenders are embedded, and in enabling families to sustain those changes over time. We suggest that several factors contribute to the apparent success of MST in treating serious juvenile offenders, a population for whom treatment approaches and service systems (Melton & Pagliocca, 1992) have historically failed (Borduin, 1994; Lipsey, 1992; Mulvey et al., 1993). These factors, described in greater detail elsewhere (Henggeler et al., in press), include: (a) the focus of MST on a comprehensive array of factors contributing to the etiology of serious antisocial behavior; (b) the ecological validity of MST (e.g., treatment occurs within the settings in which problems occur); (c) its reliance on problem-focused, present-focused, and active intervention techniques that have some empirically demonstrated validity; (d) the provision of training, clinical supervision, and monitoring of implementation of MST by therapists;

and (e) the considerable energies devoted to the development and maintenance of positive interagency collaborative relations across MST projects.

In light of the failure of even well-conceptualized, well-structured treatment approaches that target limited aspects of the youth's natural ecology (e.g., parent behavior training, social skills training for youth, etc.) to obtain favorable long-term outcomes with youth in the juvenile justice system and given recent findings suggesting that systems-of-care initiatives may not, in and of themselves, succeed in improving clinical outcomes for youth (Bickman, Heflinger, Lambert, & Summerfelt, in press), it seems reasonable to suggest that progress in the development of effective, innovative, community-based services for youth and families would be greatly enhanced by paying increased attention to the nature of the treatment implemented by service providers and by examination of treatment outcomes. That is, the implementation of services changes (e.g., introduction of wraparound services, home-based services, school-based mental health services, mentoring programs, etc.) and service system changes (increased access, availability, and array of services) are not likely to result in changes in clinical outcome unless services effectively alter those aspects of the youth's and family's natural ecology that are contributing to identified problems.

Authors' Note

Preparation of this manuscript was supported in part by National Institute on Drug Abuse Grant DA-08029 and by National Institute of Mental Health Grants MH-51852 and R24MH53558-01.

Correspondence concerning this chapter should be addressed to Sonja K. Schoenwald, Family Services Research Center, Department of Psychiatry & Behavioral Sciences, Medical University of South Carolina, 171 Ashley Avenue, Charleston, SC, 29425; (803) 792-8003.

References

Ary, D. V., Duncan, T. E., Biglan, A., Metzler, C. W., Noell, J. W., & Smolkowski, K. (1994, November). *A social context model of the development of adolescent problem behavior.* Paper presented at the annual convention of the Association for the Advancement of Behavior Therapy, San Diego, CA.

Barnum, R., & Keilitz, I. (1992). Issues in systems interactions affecting mentally disordered juvenile offenders. In J. J. Cocozza (Ed.), *Responding to the mental health needs of youth in the juvenile justice system* (pp. 49–87). Seattle, WA: National Coalition for the Mentally Ill in the Criminal Justice System.

Belsky, J. (1993). Etiology of child maltreatment: A developmental-ecological analysis. *Psychological Bulletin, 114,* 413–434.

Bickman, L., Heflinger, C. A., Lambert, W. E., & Summerfelt, W. T. (in press). The Fort Bragg managed care experiment: Short-term impact on psychopathology. *Journal of Child and Family Studies.*

Blaske, D. M., Borduin, C. M., Henggeler, S. W., & Mann, B. J. (1989). Individual, family, and peer characteristics of adolescent sex offenders and assaultive offenders. *Developmental Psychology, 25,* 846–855.

Borduin, C. M. (1994). Innovative models of treatment and service delivery in the juvenile justice system. *Journal of Clinical Child Psychology, 23 (suppl.),* 19–25.

Borduin, C. M., Blaske, D. M., Cone, L., Mann, B. J., & Hazelrigg, M. D. (1989). *Development and validation of a measure of adolescent peer relations: The Missouri Peer Relations Inventory.* Unpublished manuscript, University of Missouri, Department of Psychology, Columbia.

Borduin, C. M., Henggeler, S. W., Blaske, D. M., & Stein, R. (1990). Multisystemic treatment of adolescent sexual offenders. *International Journal of Offender Therapy and Comparative Criminology, 34,* 105–113.

Borduin, C. M., Mann, B. J., Cone, L. T., Henggeler, S. W., Fucci, B. R., Blaske, D. M., & Williams, R. A. (1995). Multisystemic treatment of serious juvenile offenders: Long-term prevention of criminality and violence. *Journal of Consulting and Clinical Psychology, 63,* 569–578.

Bronfenbrenner, U. (1979). *The ecology of human development:* Experiences by nature and design. Cambridge, MA: Harvard University Press.

Brook, J. S., Nomura, C., & Cohen, P. (1989). A network of influences on adolescent drug involvement: Neighborhood, school, peer, and family. *Genetic, Social, and General Psychology Monographs, 115,* 125–145.

Brunk, M., Henggeler, S. W., & Whelan, J. P. (1987). A comparison of multisystemic therapy and parent training in the brief treatment of child abuse and neglect. *Journal of Consulting and Clinical Psychology, 55,* 311–318.

Cocozza, J. J. (Ed.). (1992). *Responding to the mental health needs of youth in the juvenile justice system.* Seattle, WA: National Coalition for the Mentally Ill in the Criminal Justice System.

Derogatis, L. R. (1983). *The SCL-90-R: Administration, scoring, and procedures manual-II.* Towson, MD: Clinical Psychometric Research.

Dishion, T. J., Reid, J. B., & Patterson, G. R. (1988). Empirical guidelines for a family intervention for adolescent drug use. *Journal of Chemical Dependency, 2,* 189–224.

Donovan, J. E., Jessor, R., & Costa, F. M. (1988). Syndrome of problem behavior in adolescence: A replication. *Journal of Consulting and Clinical Psychology, 56,* 762–765.

Elliott, D. S., Huizinga, D., & Ageton, S. S. (1985). *Explaining delinquency and drug use.* Beverly Hills, CA: Sage.

Elliott, D. S., Huizinga, D., & Menard, S. (1989). *Multiple problem youth. Delinquency, substance use, and mental health problems.* New York: Springer-Verlag.

Haley, J. (1976). *Problem solving therapy.* San Francisco: Jossey-Bass.

Hanson, C. L., Henggeler, S. W., Haefele, W. F., & Rodick, J. D. (1984). Demographic, individual, and family relationship correlates of serious and repeated crime among adolescents and their siblings. *Journal of Consulting and Clinical Psychology, 52,* 528–538.

Henggeler, S. W. (1989). *Delinquency in adolescence.* Newbury Park, CA: Sage.

Henggeler, S. W. (1991). Multidimensional causal models of delinquent behavior and their implications for treatment. In R. Cohen & A. W. Siegel (Eds.), *Context and development* (pp. 211–231). Hillsdale, NJ: Lawrence Erlbaum.

Henggeler, S. W. (in press). The development of effective drug abuse services for youth. *Treating drug abusers effectively—Milbank Foundation and NIDA.* New York: Blackwells–North America.

Henggeler, S. W., & Borduin, C. M. (1990). *Family therapy and beyond: A multisystemic approach to treating the behavior problems of children and adolescents.* Pacific Grove, CA: Brooks/Cole.

Henggeler, S. W., & Borduin, C. M. (1992). *Multisystemic therapy adherence scales.* Unpublished instrument, Department of Psychiatry and Behavioral Sciences, Medical University of South Carolina, Charleston.

Henggeler, S. W., Burr-Harris, A. W., Borduin, C. M., & McCallum, G. (1991). Use of the Family Adaptability and Cohesion Evaluation Scales in child clinical research. *Journal of Abnormal Child Psychology, 19,* 53–63.

Henggeler, S. W., Melton, G. B., & Smith, L. A. (1992). Family preservation using multisystemic therapy: An effective alternative to incarcerating serious juvenile offenders, *Journal of Consulting and Clinical Psychology, 60,* 953–961.

Henggeler, S. W., Melton, G. B., Smith, L. A., Schoenwald, S. K., & Hanley, J. (1993). Family preservation using multisystemic therapy: Long-term follow-up to a clinical trial with serious juvenile offenders. *Journal of Child and Family Studies, 2,* 283–293.

Henggeler, S. W., Pickrel, S. G., & Brondino, M. J. (1995). *Multisystemic treatment of substance abusing/dependent delinquents: Outcomes for drug use, criminality, and out-of-home placement at posttreatment and 6-month follow-up.* Manuscript under review.

Henggeler, S. W., & Rowland, M. D. (in press). Investigating alternatives to hospitalization of youth presenting psychiatric emergencies. *Emergency Psychiatry.*

Henggeler, S. W., Schoenwald, S. K., Borduin, C. N., Rowland, M. D., & Cunningham, P. B. (in press). *Multisystemic treatment of antisocial behavior in youth.* New York and London: Guilford Press.

Henggeler, S. W., Schoenwald, S. K., & Munger, R. L. (1996). Families and therapists achieve clinical outcomes, systems of care mediate the process. *Journal of Child and Family Studies, 5,* 177–183.

Henggeler, S. W., Schoenwald, S. K., & Pickrel, S. G. (1995). Multisystemic Therapy: Bridging the gap between university- and community-based treatment. *Journal of Consulting and Clinical Psychology,* 709–717.

Henggeler, S. W., Smith, B. H., & Schoenwald, S. K. (1994). Key theoretical and methodological issues in conducting treatment research in the juvenile justice system. *Journal of Clinical Child Psychology, 23,* 143–150.

Hollingshead, A. B. (1975). *The four-factor index of social status.* Unpublished manuscript, Yale University, New Haven, CT.

Kendall, P. C., & Braswell, L. (1993). *Cognitive-behavioral therapy for impulsive children,* (2nd ed.). New York: Guilford.

Lipsey, M. W. (1992). Juvenile delinquency treatment: A meta-analytic inquiry into the variability of effects. In T. D. Cook, H. Cooper, D. S. Cordray, H. Hartmann, L. V. Hedges, R. J. Light, T. A. Louis, & F. Mosteller (Eds.), *Meta-analysis for explanation: A casebook* (pp. 83–127). New York: Russell Sage Foundation.

Mann, B. J., Borduin, C. M., Henggeler, S. W., & Blaske, D. M. (1990). An investigation of systemic conceptualizations of parent-child coalitions and symptom change. *Journal of Consulting and Clinical Psychology, 58,* 336–344.

Melton, G. B., & Pagliocca, P. W. (1992). Treatment in the juvenile justice system: Directions for policy and practice. In J. J. Cocozza (Ed.), *Responding to the mental health needs of youth in the juvenile justice system* (pp. 107–139). Seattle, WA: National Coalition for the Mentally Ill in the Criminal Justice System.

Minuchin, S. (1974). *Families and family therapy.* Cambridge, MA: Harvard University Press.

Mulvey, E. P., Arthur, M. W., & Reppucci, N. D. (1993). The prevention and treatment of juvenile delinquency: A review of the research. *Clinical Psychology Review, 13,* 133–167.

Munger, R. L. (1993). *Changing children's behavior quickly.* Lanham, MD: Madison Books.

Nelson, K. E. (1994). Family-based services for families and children at risk of out-of-home placement. In R. Barth, J. D. Berrick, & N. Gilbert (Eds.), *Child welfare research review: Vol. 1* (pp. 83–108). New York: Columbia University Press.

Nelson, K. E., & Landsman, M. J. (1992). *Alternative models of family preservation: Family-based services in context.* Springfield, IL: Charles C. Thomas.

Oetting, E. R, & Beauvais, F. (1987). Peer cluster theory, socialization characteristics, and adolescent drug use: A path analysis. *Journal of Counseling Psychology, 34,* 205–213.

Olson, D. H., Portner, J., & Bell, R. (1982). *FACES-II.* In D. H. Olson, H. I. McCubbin, H. L. Barnes, A. Larsen, M. Muxen, & M. Wilson (Eds.), *Family inventories* (pp. 5–24). St. Paul: University of Minnesota, Family Social Science.

Quay, H. C., & Peterson, D. R. (1987). *Manual for the Revised Behavior Problem Checklist.* Coral Gables, FL: University of Miami.

Rosen, A., & Proctor, E. K. (1981). Distinctions between treatment outcomes and their implications for treatment evaluation. *Journal of Consulting and Clinical Psychology, 49,* 418–425.

Santos, A. B., Henggeler, S. W., Burns, B. J., Arana, G. W., & Meisler, N. (1995). Research on field-based services: Models for reform in the delivery of mental health care to difficult clinical populations. *American Journal of Psychiatry, 152,(8),* 1111–1123.

SAS Institute. (1991). *SAS user's guide: Statistics.* Cary, NC: Author.

Scherer, D. G., Brondino, M. J., Henggeler, S. W., Melton, G. B., & Hanley, J. H. (1994). Multisystemic family preservation with rural and minority families of serious adolescent offenders: Preliminary findings from a controlled clinical trial. *Journal of Emotional and Behavioral Disorders, 2,* 198–206.

Schoenwald, S. K., Scherer, D. G., & Brondino, M. J. (in press). Effective community-based treatments for serious juvenile offenders. In S. W. Henggeler & A. B. Santos (Eds.), *Innovative services for "difficult to treat" populations.* Washington, DC: APA Books.

Stroul, B. A., & Friedman, R. M. (1994). *A system of care for children and youth with severe emotional disturbance.* Washington, DC: Georgetown University Child Development Center.

Tate, D. C., Reppucci, N. D., & Mulvey, E. P. (1995). Violent juvenile delinquents: Treatment effectiveness and implications for future action. *American Psychologist, 50,* 777–781.

Thomas, C. R. (1994). *Island youth programs,* University of Texas Medical Branch, Galveston.

White, H. R., Pandina, R. J., & LaGrange, R. L. (1987). Longitudinal predictors of serious substance use and delinquency. *Criminology, 25,* 715–740.

An Individualized Wraparound Process for Children in Foster Care with Emotional/Behavioral Disturbances: Follow-up Findings and Implications from a Controlled Study

18

Hewitt B. Clark, Mark E. Prange, Barbara Lee, Elizabeth Steinhardt Stewart, Beth Barrett McDonald, and L. Adlai Boyd

The child welfare and mental health systems have not adequately served many of their dependent children and families during the past decade. From 1984 to 1989–90, the number of foster homes in America decreased 27%, while the number of children in foster care increased 48% (Terpstra & McFadden, 1993). Faced with recession-pinched resources, most states had been struggling simply to provide "three hots and a cot" for a great many children in out-of-home placements, only responding as required to class action lawsuits favoring more and better services for such children and their families (Boyd, 1992; Knitzer & Yelton, 1990). Inexcusable deaths and other horrors perpetrated on abused and neglected children, either while in care or shortly thereafter, were more and more in the public eye and conscience. Add to those factors the rising costs and the limited effectiveness of institutional care for the children in greatest need, and the situation appeared increasingly hopeless.

While some critics of the systems have called for a return to orphanages, some advocates and service providers have insisted on trying new, creative ways of meeting child and family needs, such as professionalized group care, intensive family preservation, and family reunification models (e.g., Terpstra & McFadden, 1993). Still other professionals and advocates were convinced that an individualized system of care involving family-centered, case-managed, integrated services would effectively serve these children (Boyd, 1992; Stroul & Friedman, 1986; Wynn, 1995). Meanwhile, all concerned individuals preached the gospel of the illusive "best interests of the child" (Lambiase & Cumes, 1987; Solnit, 1987). At best, the field had been in some confusion as to what really worked, was cost effective, and accountable.

In September of 1989, an Intensive Family Preservation Services Research Conference was held to propose a research agenda for the 1990s. As the final report suggested (Wells & Biegel, 1990), family preservation programs (e.g., Homebuilders) had been widely replicated during the past decade, but few of the important questions surrounding this type of intervention had been studied scientifically. A subsequent call for research on alternative systems of care (e.g., case management, home-based treatment) was articulated by Burns and Friedman (1990). They emphasized the importance of such research in guiding service innovation and policy in children's mental health, although the need is felt equally urgently within child welfare (Landsverk, Madsen, Ganger, Chadwick, & Litrownik, in press; Shealy, 1995).

One of the most pressing social problems connected with child abuse has been its concomitant risk for severe emotional and behavioral disturbances. It is estimated that between 35 and 63% of children in the foster care system have emotional or behavioral disturbances or are at critical risk of such (Boyd, Struchen, & Panacek-Howell, 1989, 1990; Groves, 1993; Landsverk et al., in press; Widom, 1989). These data described the context of risk in the nation's overtaxed systems of care for children and families; yet it remained unclear what some of the more harmful aspects of the system might be, much less what to do about them.

Common sense holds that few abused or neglected children can be expected to adapt readily to being removed from their homes. Their emotional and behavioral disturbances may be exacerbated by frequent placement changes within the dependency system, by lengthy stays away from family and friends, by no longer being wanted by parents, by ill treatment or abuse within foster homes, or by the inadequacy or absence of mental health and related services for these children.

Consequently, the mental health of children with emotional or behavioral disturbances who are in foster care has become a major concern and focus within Florida and many other states. As a result of this recent interest, it has become clear that the children's mental health and foster care systems, already overtaxed by greater need than resources, are severely limited in addressing these issues. Given the scope and focus of the problems delineated above, it was obvious that these children, in need of mental health and related services, composed a critical population for study and for interagency collaboration.

In response to the documented need, and to calls for additional research in the area of home-based, individualized interventions for children with emotional or behavioral disturbance, and for those at risk of such, we saw a need to investigate the effects of individualized wraparound services for children who have had extended exposure to the dependency system. The Fostering Individualized Assistance Program (FIAP) study was designed to investigate the effects of a case-managed, individualized, collaborative intervention with these children in the child welfare system (Clark & Boyd, 1990, 1992). This chapter provides (a) a description of the recommended practices of this intervention, (b) outcome data from a randomly selected group of children in foster care who received the intervention and a comparable group of children who received practices standard to the foster care system, (c) follow-up data on permanency status at 6 to 12 months following any contact with the family specialists of the wraparound intervention, and (d) implications of these findings for wraparound interventions for children with emotional or behavioral disturbances in the dependency system.

Method

Subjects and Setting

Children in the state foster care system were eligible for inclusion in this study if they were (a) in temporary custody of the state because of having been abused or neglected; (b) 7 through 15 years of age; (c) living in a regular foster home or in an emergency foster shelter facility; and (d) experiencing behavioral or emotional disturbances, or at risk of such, as defined by screening indicators (Boyd et al., 1989, 1990; Sullivan, Henley, & Williams, 1988). Foster care caseworkers periodically completed a brief screening form for all children on their caseloads who were within this age range and who did not have a primary diagnosis of mental retardation. An at-risk screening form instructed the caseworkers to indicate the presence or absence of behavioral and situational indicators. For inclusion in the at-risk pool, a child had to be exhibiting, within the 2 months prior to the screening, at least 2 of 18 behavioral indicators (e.g., harm to self or other, used drugs and/or alcohol, engaged in abnormal sexual behavior) and had to meet at least 1 of 7 situational indicators (e.g., long-term dependency status, failed home placement, placed in a more restrictive setting in the past 6 months).

Children from the at-risk pool were randomly selected and assigned to the FIAP group or the standard practice (SP) control group using a computer-generated random-number system. To compensate for a predicted higher attrition rate within the SP group, (e.g., because of extended runaways, voluntary dropouts), approximately 50% more subjects were randomly assigned to the SP group than to FIAP. The subjects for both groups were phased in to the study over a 15-month period. The pace and schedule with which subjects were included were determined by the capacity of the FIAP case managers (i.e., family specialists) to initiate new cases.

A total of 131 children in the foster care system participated in this study,[1] of whom 39.7% were female and 60.3% male. The ethnic distribution was 61.8% Caucasian, 33.6% African American, 2.3% Hispanic, and 2.3% biracial. At the time of assignment to the study, the subjects had spent an average of 2.6 years in out-of-home placements (i.e., adjudicated dependent) and had an average annualized rate of 4.0 placement changes, across a range of settings varying from foster home and emergency shelter care to psychiatric hospital units and detention centers. The FIAP and SP groups did not differ statistically on any of these descriptive variables.

At entry to the study, all of the subjects were residents of either a county encompassing a large urban area or a county that was predominantly rural, with a few small towns. The per capita incomes for the two counties were $16,044 and $14,246, and the high school graduation rates were 82.8% and 73.1%, respectively (Weitzel, Friedman, Shanley, & Levine, 1993). The interventions for these subjects were delivered in the context of the children's homes (i.e., foster, biological, relative, adoptive), schools, and communities.

Standard Practice Foster Care

All of the children entering this study, whether assigned to the SP group or the FIAP group, were recipients of the standard practices of the foster care system. Standard practice foster care refers to the prevailing care, support, and services that the state system provides to its children who have been adjudicated dependent and placed in the child welfare system. These children may be placed in foster homes holding up to 12 other children, in group emergency shelter facilities for extended periods, or transferred to one of a broad range of group home, residential treatment, detention, or other private child-care facilities.

The statutes regarding the child dependency system mandate that the state is responsible for meeting the welfare needs of all of its children. However, not all services and supports needed by children in foster care are "entitlements" guaranteed by the state. Services such as outpatient counseling, respite care, home-based interventions, and crisis counseling for foster parents are not "entitled," as are the more basic services of safety and out-of-home placements. Although some improvements in allocations for mental health and related services did occur during the course of this study, there continued to be inadequate funding to pay for specialized services, as well as insufficient numbers of professionals to address the broad array of unique services required by children in foster care and their families.

All children in the study had permanency plan statements in their child welfare case records. However, these plans often appeared to exist only to "meet the letter of the law" rather than to serve functional purposes. This situation was often evidenced when foster caseworkers were questioned about their children's permanency plans, and they did not know or remember what was designated.

Overview of the FIAP Intervention

The basic goals of the Fostering Individualized Assistance Program (FIAP) model were to stabilize placement in foster care and develop viable permanency plans and, secondly, to improve the behavior and emotional adjustment of the children receiving FIAP services. The achievement of these goals was sought through the four major intervention components of FIAP: strength-based assessment, life-domain planning, clinical case management, and follow-along supports and services. The recommended practices for our FIAP intervention are described briefly in this chapter and in greater detail elsewhere (McDonald, Boyd, Clark, & Stewart, 1995). However, it is important to understand that the FIAP intervention underwent development and modifications over the course of the study.

The four components of FIAP intervention were implemented by the Family Specialists (FSs) who served as family-centered, clinical case managers and home-based counselors, collaborating with foster caseworkers, other providers (e.g., teachers, therapists, scout leaders), foster parents, and natural families. FSs followed and served their children across all settings, providing individually tailored services for them, as needed (Burchard & Clarke, 1990; McDonald et al., 1995; VanDenBerg & Grealish, 1996). Each of the FSs held a bachelor's or master's degree and had between 3 and 12 years of experience working with troubled youth and families, within treatment programs such as family preservation, therapeutic foster care, and group homes for children with emotional or behavioral disorders. The FSs were selected for their expertise, as well as their demonstrated histories of caring about, and respecting children and families. Each specialist eventually carried about 12 active cases and up to 10 maintenance-level cases that were monitored monthly and reactivated when necessary. The FSs and their supervisor met weekly to discuss their cases.

Strength-Based Assessment

Strength-based assessment focuses on the strengths and potentials of the children and their families, while recognizing the problems that exist in their lives. Although the strength-based philosophy upon which this assessment operates does not discount the usefulness of traditional psychological assessment information, it "asserts that strengths and capacities are the building blocks for change and should receive primary emphasis" (Duchnowski & Kutash, 1996, p. 102).

As children entered the study, they were assigned to one of the four FSs. The FSs initiated their cases by assessing the need for mental health and related overlay services for the children, their biological families, and to some extent, even their foster families. This assessment process involved studying the child welfare case records and interviewing the child's foster caseworker, foster parent, biological parent, teacher, guidance counselor, and other adults (e.g., provider agency therapist) who were relevant to the child's situation. The FSs attempted to gather information from each of the relevant adults to provide an understanding of the child and the family's past and current problems, and more important, to learn about their past successes and present strengths and potentials.

As the FSs reviewed external case records and interviewed the relevant adults, they framed their search for strengths, needs, and potentials across several life domains that relate to basic human needs that individuals of this age typically have or experience (VanDenBerg, 1993). The life domains were (a) residence; (b) family or surrogate family; (c) social competencies and relationships; (d) educational or vocational training; (e) health and medical care; (f) psychological well-being and emotional support; (g) legal or social system assistance; (h) safety knowledge and security from harm; (i) community involvement, mobility skills, and transportation resources; and (j) cultural/ethnic/spiritual interests and involvement.

The FSs attempted to meet each child's relevant adults in their own settings, to make it convenient for these individuals. Efforts were made to provide opportunities for meeting and observing the child in the foster home (or emergency shelter), during home visits with the family of origin, at school, and in other situations involving activities such as recreation or peer interactions. These numerous and varied contacts during the assessment process provided the FSs opportunities to (a) get to know the children and relevant adults, as well as their circumstances; (b) begin developing personal and professional relationships with these individuals; and (c) acquaint themselves with the roles that they might play as support team members for the children. Assessment work also provided the FSs with much of the information needed for the planning process and for guiding the team toward a proactive service plan.

Life-Domain Planning

A FIAP team was established for each child, composed of as many of the relevant adults as would participate. Each team typically met monthly, depending on the changing needs of the child and circumstances regarding natural, adoptive, extended, or foster family. The goal of the FIAP team was to formulate, and revise as necessary, a life domain plan, addressing child/family priority needs within each of the domains, and processing the most viable permanency plan through the child welfare system and the courts.

The FS typically served as the facilitator for the initial team meetings, with the goal of gradually transferring this responsibility to a parent, other relative, adoptive parent, or case manager who would play a consistent role in the child's life on a long-term basis. The facilitator's role was to (a) guide the meeting, encouraging members to listen to and respect each other's points of view, particularly the input of those who were closest to the child (e.g., foster parents, biological parents, relatives, and teachers); (b) formulate or revise the life domain plan; and (c) bring topics to a level of consensus that would lead to fulfillment of this action plan.

Following each team meeting, the FS (or facilitator) contacted, by telephone or in person, the relevant adults who were not able to attend the meeting and discussed what had evolved. Their input and assistance were solicited in accomplishing the tasks that the team had identified as important to the implementation of the life domain plan. The FS then sent out a copy of the plan with the tasks, persons responsible, and target dates specified to all team members.

Strength-based assessment and life-domain planning build on the consumer's interests and strengths, and identify and provide supports for possible limitations. An example is reflected in the situation of a 16-year-old boy in the foster care system who ran away from every foster home, group home, emergency shelter, and residential center placement, and had dropped out of school after a history of difficulty and poor performance. During his extensive runaway periods, he seemed to manage well in protecting himself and keeping out of serious trouble. The FS and the wraparound team, to whom this youth was assigned, used a strength-based assessment to identify his interests and competencies. They found that he related quite well to strong male figures, and although he had very limited reading and writing skills, he followed their instructions well. The team also learned that he owned a bicycle that he kept in good repair, even though he lived on the streets. The plan they developed with him involved his getting a job at a bicycle shop, being mentored by one of the repairmen, and living on his own in a small apartment with his FS working closely with him, teaching community-life skills as necessary.

It is important to note that, for all FIAP subjects, attention was given to matching the youths to settings that took advantage of their individual interests and strengths. This is not to say that initial plans did not address all aspects of these children's needs, but exposure to, and success with, these life experiences were designed to set the stage for these youths to tackle other areas of skill development.

Clinical Case Management

Home/community-based services. The FIAP model emphasized the provision of intensive, individualized services and supports in the context of the child's home and community settings, to the extent possible. The FSs and other professionals associated with FIAP clients attempted to work with families at times and in locations that were convenient to the family members (e.g., evening hours or while transporting a child).

Delivery of services. In their role as home-based counselors, the FSs often instituted child counseling, family preservation interventions, or family therapy themselves. These services were initiated to ensure that the children and adults began these services with professionals whom they already knew and to avoid delays caused by the funding and bureaucratic approval process. Because of the FSs' caseloads, they could only occasionally continue highly time intensive interventions for extended periods. Thus, services that required long-term and extremely demanding levels of involvement were initially set up with other professionals, or gradually transferred to them, as funding and appropriate providers were secured.

In their case management roles, the FSs coordinated and monitored services that they brokered. Services and supports were tapped from those available through the social services systems (e.g., child dependency, mental health, juvenile justice), the educational system, community provider agencies (e.g., adoptive parent support groups), and community service organizations (e.g., Big Brothers/Big Sisters). Services included such things as providing a mentor for a child after school and on weekends, family systems therapy, grief counseling, joint sibling visits or therapy, and vocational training for youths or parents.

The FSs also facilitated or provided some services and supports that were critical to the life-domain plan for a child or family, but which were not eligible expenditures within traditional funding mechanisms (Dollard, Evans, Lubrecht, & Schaeffer, 1994). The FSs had flexible funding available to them, averaging $200 per month per case for the first 6 months, and $75 for each of the next 12 months. This flexible funding enabled the FSs to address such critical needs as (a) obtaining child abuse counseling with a qualified therapist; (b) purchasing a refrigerator for a mother, in order for her to qualify for family reunification; (c) purchasing a flute, bicycle, or computerized game for children who wanted to pursue their interests; or (d) arranging for a tutor to assist a child with schoolwork. Appropriate accounting and audit trails were in place regarding these flexible funds.

Accountability. In their role as case managers, the FSs had primary responsibility for actively involving and communicating with all of the relevant adults on an ongoing basis. Initially, the FS was responsible for ensuring that all of the team members clearly understood their roles and tasks and for following up with them to ensure completion. The FSs also tracked the child's and family's progress across all of the targeted areas of the life domain plan. They also were responsible for periodically bringing the team together to review the status of the case and to revise the plan, as necessary, to ensure that clinical goals were being addressed, and that necessary supports and services were in place.

Child/family advocacy. Another major aspect of the FSs' activities related to advocacy for their children and families. This advocacy was evidenced in activities ranging from involvement with, and input from, both foster and biological parents, to bringing an issue to a court hearing in order to impel the child welfare system to address some critical needs regarding a child's permanency plan.

Follow-Along Supports and Services

Linkage with natural supports. The FIAP model encouraged FSs to link children and families to natural supports within their homes, schools, and community settings, whenever possible. Although an FS might initially have hired a Big Brother for an adolescent who needed more recreational involvement and mentoring, this role was often shifted to a cousin or uncle as the child moved into a permanency setting in closer proximity to his extended family. The use of natural supports involved situations in which the FSs gradually were able to establish a biological parent as the child's case manager, who could then deal with issues such as the child's therapy, school, or transportation needs.

Self-advocacy. One of the goals pursued with many families was to assist parents to become empowered to advocate and address issues regarding theirs and their children's rights and needs and provision of essential services and supports. FSs frequently worked with youth, foster parents, biological parents, and adoptive parents to teach and encourage self-advocacy.

Tracking. As the FSs and FIAP teams were successful in addressing critical life domain needs, children moved to a maintenance rather than an active case status. However, during maintenance, the FSs continued regularly scheduled tracking and monitoring of these children and their families, in attempts to prevent or remediate new or recurring serious problems. For example, an FS had to reactivate a case, briefly, to provide a youth with transportation to a place of employment, in order to avoid loss of a job. In another situation, an FS reactivated a case, on a long-term basis, because the permanency plan was jeopardized by recurring child abuse reports and parental resistance to family preservation intervention.

Research Methods

Measurement Domains

The child research data were collected by trained interviewers across a number of important measurement domains and from multiple sources. Information was systematically gathered from the children and caregivers (i.e., foster parent, biological parent, adoptive parent, or agency staff) through interviews and from foster care case records, and from computerized placement and school records. The interviews were conducted in the field (e.g., at the child's residence), separately with the child and caregiver at entry to the study (Wave 1), and at each 6-month interval thereafter (Waves 2–8). The dependent measures are described below in three measurement domains: emotional or behavioral adjustment, placement, and school.

Placement Measurement Domain

Placement settings and change rates. The out-of-home placement history and ongoing placement data were available through the computerized foster care record system used for placement payments. Placement days for each child were tracked across settings, such as foster homes, group homes, group emergency shelter facilities, residential treatment centers, and psychiatric hospitals. Information regarding time spent living alone or with adoptive families, relatives, and parents was collected by the interviewers when the children and caregivers (or foster caseworkers) were interviewed or when they were contacted to schedule interviews.

A placement change was defined as movement from one provider to another or in the case of an extended runaway of more than 30 days (a shorter runaway was not logged as a placement change). The days during which a child was on an extended runaway, was incarcerated, or the days following an adoption were excluded from the calculations of the annualized rate of placement change, as the child was not available for a change in placement during those periods.

Runaway status. The number of runaways and days on runaway status also were logged in the foster care payment record. When calculating the annualized rate of all runaways and days on runaway, the time during which a child was incarcerated was excluded because it was unlikely that this was a possibility from the secure facilities of detention, jail, corrections, or prison (and, if a runaway occurred, it would not have been logged on the foster care payment record).

Incarceration. The time during which a child was incarcerated was not logged specifically on the payment record but, rather, included under an "other" notation. The interviewers secured detailed information regarding these notations through computerized records of arrests and incarceration, their interviews, and contacts with foster care caseworkers.

School Measurement Domain

Data were collected from computerized school records regarding each of the following school-related variables: (a) attendance, operationalized as the percentage of days absent per school year for those subjects who had not dropped out or graduated; (b) suspensions, operationalized as the percentage of days suspended per school year; and (c) school-to-school movement, operationalized as the average number of changes from one school to another per school year. For youths who moved out of the counties being studied, their current school districts were contacted, with guardian consent, for release of information.

Emotional and Behavioral Adjustment Measurement Domain

Youth Self Report and Child Behavior Checklists. The Child Behavior Checklist (CBCL; Achenbach, 1991a) and the Youth Self Report (YSR; Achenbach, 1991b) are measures for describing the behavior of children from the perspective of the caregivers and of the youth themselves. These instruments provide a total problem score, eight narrow-band factors (i.e., withdrawn, somatic complaints, anxious/depressed, social problems, thought problems, attention problems, delinquent behavior, aggressive behavior), and two broad-band factors (i.e., internalizing and externalizing). The internalizing score is based on the narrow-band factors of withdrawn, somatic complaints, and anxious/depressed, and the externalizing score is based on the narrow-band factors of delinquent and aggressive behaviors. Standardization of the CBCL and YSR was done using geographically matched children, clinically referred and not clinically referred, and representative of national socioeconomic, ethnic, regional, and urban/suburban/rural factors. Inter-interviewer reliabilities for the YSR and the CBCL were both above .90 for total scores. The 1-week test-retest reliabilities for the total scores averaged .93, and the subscale scores ranged from .82 to .95.

Conduct disorder score. The Diagnostic Interview Scale for Children (DISC; Fisher, Wicks, Shaffer, Piacentini, & Lapkin, 1991) is a structured interview that contains items reflecting the presence of current and past symptoms, emotions, and behaviors that correspond to DSM III-R criteria. One section of the DISC is the conduct disorder interview protocol, which yields a conduct disorder diagnosis. The conduct disorder instrument was added to the interview protocol for Waves 6, 7, and 8 of this study. The subscale scores from these waves were averaged to provide a single conduct disorder score for each subject.

Official delinquency score. The counties maintain computerized records of official criminal charges against juveniles. The number of criminal charges prior to entry to the study was used as a prescore for each subject, and the number of charges after entry was used as a postscore. The criminal charges were separated into five categories by type of offense (i.e., theft, drugs, assaults, sexual crimes, and other) and also were combined to provide an official delinquency score for each subject.

Total delinquency score. A composite delinquency score, referred to as total delinquency, was derived from the dependent measures of the delinquency items on the CBCL and YSR, the conduct disorder score, and the official delinquency score. A total delinquency score was computed for each of the 131 subjects. This score was calculated by converting each of the scale scores available for this particular individual into Z scores and averaging them to establish a total delinquency score.

Data Collection and Management

Interview Procedures

The research interviews with the children and caregivers were conducted at entry to the study and at 6-month intervals for a maximum of eight possible interviews over a 3½ year period. The interviews were conducted in the field by trained, supervised interviewers. When children moved further than 75 miles from the research site, the interviews were conducted using the Telephone Interview Process established by the Florida Research and Training Center on Children's Mental Health (Prange et al., 1992). The child interviews generally took from 45 to 75 minutes, and the caregiver interviews typically lasted 30 to 60 minutes. All interviews were conducted on a voluntary basis and included the appropriate provisions for informed consent and the rights of subjects. Subjects and caregivers were provided a cash gratuity for participating in each interview (i.e., children $15 and caregivers $20). The information was collected, managed, and analyzed by research personnel and was shared with FIAP intervention personnel only in the aggregate, as a function of presenting research findings.

Data Management

Raw data from the interviews and records were entered by trained personnel into specifically designed computer databases. Independent reliability checks were made on a randomly selected 20% of each of the data sets. If fewer than 1% of the digits were incorrect, the reliability level was considered acceptable. However, if a larger proportion of the digits of this sample was found to be incorrect, another 20% of the data set was checked. This process continued until two consecutive 20% checks yielded the acceptable reliability rate. Throughout this process, data entry errors were corrected from the raw data forms as the errors were identified.

Experimental Design

The FIAP study used a repeated-measures between-groups design, with at-risk children in the foster care system who were randomly assigned either to continue in standard practice foster care (SP group, $n = 77$), or to participate in the Fostering Individualized Assistance Program (FIAP group, $n = 54$). The children of both groups were exposed to the care and treatment practices that were usual to foster care, with the FIAP group receiving intensive case management and services.

Description of Statistical Analyses

Several types of analyses were used to explore group (condition) differences on placement outcomes, school outcomes, and emotional and behavioral adjustment outcomes. A list of the dependent measures related to each of these outcome domains and the availability of pre- and postperiod data is provided in Table 18.1. The same types of data from the same sources were collected for each subject in both groups (i.e., FIAP condition and SP condition).

Table 18.1

The Outcome Domains and Related Dependent Measures

Outcome Domain	Dependent Measure	Pre Period	Post Period
Placement	Permanency and Placement Changes	Adjudicated dependent to entry into study	Status at end of study or at point aged out of system
	Runaway	Same as above	Entry to study
	Incarceration	Lifetime	Entry to study through entire post period
School	Absences	Adjudicated dependent to entry into study	Entry to study through to exit from school
	Dropouts	None occurred	Same as above
	Suspensions	Same as "absences" above	Same as above
	School-to-school Movement	Same as above	Same as above
Emotional and Behavioral Adjustment	YSR	Wave 1	Waves 2–8
	CBCL	Wave 1	Waves 2–8
	Conduct Disorder	Not measured	Waves 6, 7, 8
	County Delinquency	Lifetime history to entry into study	Entry to study through remainder of study period

Data from interval scales, such as T-scores (YSR and CBCL) or time, were analyzed using analysis of variance (ANOVA). If both pre- and post-period data were available, these were analyzed in a repeated measures ANOVA model. For data in the form of categorical variables (e.g., proportion of time in incarceration, percentage of children in clinical range), nonparametric odds ratio analyses were used to assess differences between conditions.

Many of the analyses involved descriptive variables related to the subjects. When these were used, they were defined as follows: (a) age involved a median split at entry to the study, which established two groupings—children 7–11.5 years and youths 11.5–16 years of age; (b) gender was male or female; (c) ethnicity was Caucasian or African American/Hispanic, combined due to the small number of Hispanic and biracial subjects in this sample; and (d) condition was defined as the FIAP group or SP group to which each subject had been randomly assigned. The number of subjects included within each analysis was determined by the availability of a complete and reliable data set for the subject on the particular measure(s) involved. Negative, as well as positive, findings regarding condition effects are reported throughout the results section. Interactions that did not involve condition are not presented since they had the same effects on both the FIAP and SP groups. An alpha level of .05 was used for all statistical tests, but the lowest probability levels obtained are shown.

Results

Permanency Status Outcomes

At entry to the FIAP study, all of the children were in regular foster care or emergency shelter care. A follow-up examination of the final placements of children and youth was conducted to determine the proportion residing in permanency-type settings, such as with parents, relatives, or adoptive homes, or who were living independently. An analysis of these categorical data suggested that a child in FIAP was 2.0 times more likely to be in permanency than was a child in SP, odds ratio = 2.0, $p < .05$. This difference was not found to be statistically significant for the younger subset but, rather, was a function of the greater success of FIAP in achieving permanency for the older subset of youth, odds ratio = 4.5, $p < .05$.

In order to examine changes in the proportion of time spent in permanency placements over the course of the study, the post period was divided into seven equal 6-month intervals. The percentage of time spent in permanency in each post period was analyzed in a repeated measures ANOVA. The results from this analysis revealed an effect related to age; thus, the two age subsets were analyzed in separate repeated measures ANOVAs.

A visual portrayal of the age subset results is provided in Figure 18.1 across each of the seven postperiod intervals. There were no significant main effects or interactions for the younger subset except for time alone, $F(6, 57) = 8.98, p < .001$, showing that the younger subjects in both conditions had significantly greater time in permanency. For the older subset, there was a comparable effect for time alone, $F(6, 60) = 5.54, p < .001$, and there were significant effects both for condition alone, $F(1, 65) = 4.04, p < .05$, and for condition by time, $F(6, 390) = 5.49, p < .001$. These findings suggest that, overall, youth in the FIAP group had significantly more time in permanency during the post period than did the SP group, and that the pattern of change over time for the two groups was different. For

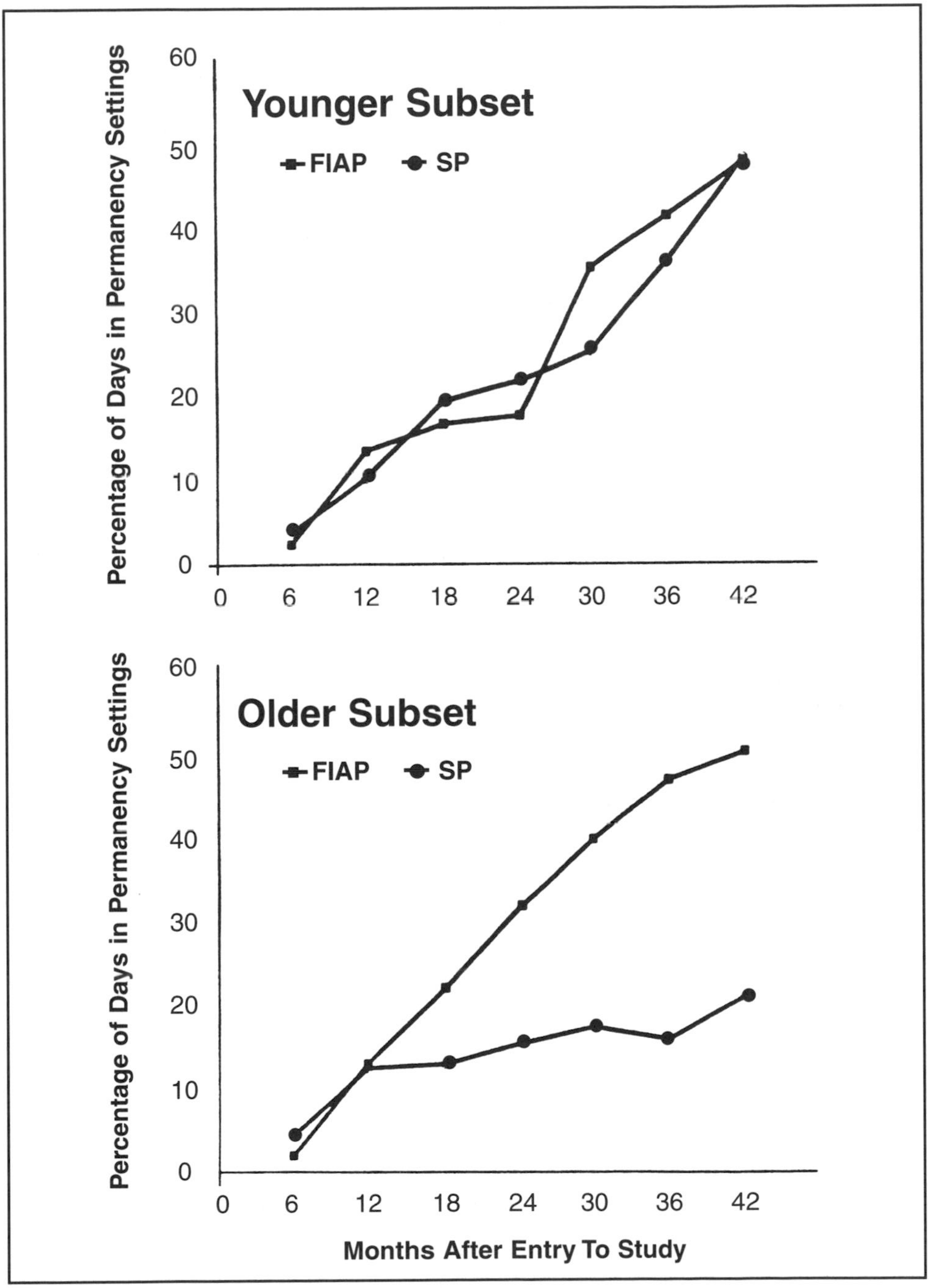

Figure 18.1. The percentage of days FIAP and SP subjects spent in permanency settings across seven equal 6-month intervals covering the post period. The upper graph represents the pattern for the younger subset ($n = 64$), and the lower graph represents the pattern for the older subset ($n = 67$).

the first two intervals of the post period, there was no difference between the two conditions in average time spent in permanency. From the third through the seventh intervals, the percentage of time in permanency continued to increase steadily, and by the end of the sixth interval, the SP and FIAP percentages of time in permanency were separated by an amount greater than that predicted by the 95% confidence interval. Subsequent analyses included gender and then ethnicity along with the condition factor, but there were no additional significant effects or interactions for either gender or ethnic group.

Other Placement and School Outcomes

Repeated measures ANOVAs were performed on three placement variables (i.e., rate of placement change, days on runaway, days in incarceration) and on four school variables (i.e., days absent, days since dropping out, days suspended, and the rate of school-to-school movements). Across these dependent variables, the only condition by time effect was that of days on runaway, $F(1, 130) = 7.59$, $p < .01$, showing that the FIAP group had a lower annualized proportion of time on runaway during the post period.

Twenty-two percent of the children had spent time incarcerated in detention, jail, correctional centers, or adult prisons during the pre or post periods, or both. For this subset of 29 youths (13 FIAP, 16 SP), a repeated measures ANOVA was conducted and a significant difference was found, showing that the FIAP youth spent fewer days in incarceration during the post period than did the SP youth, $F(1, 27) = 4.68$, $p < .05$.

Across three placement and four school variables, no interaction effects involving gender and ethnicity were significant. However, age was found to be significant, or marginally significant, across many of these dependent variables. An examination of the range of scores across the placement and school variables showed that the FIAP youth had fewer extreme scores during the post period when compared with SP youth. In an exploratory analysis, each of the placement and school variables was categorized to analyze the likelihood of a FIAP versus an SP subject's, being in the extreme category. An odds ratio was calculated first for all the subjects and then for the subsets of younger children and older youth. The results of these categorical analyses are shown in Table 18.2. The general pattern across the variables is that there were differences for all subjects and for the older subset, but not for the younger subset.

Emotional and Behavioral Adjustment Outcomes

In order to examine the changes in emotional and behavioral adjustment over the entire course of the study, subsets of children for whom interview data were secured on all eight waves were selected for this next series of analyses (YSR $n = 43$; CBCL $n = 41$). Repeated measures ANOVAs were performed on both

Table 18.2

Analyses of Condition Effects for Categorical Extremes
Across Placement and School Variables During Post Period
for All Children and for Both Age Subsets

Likelihood of SP vs. FIAP Child Experiencing an Extreme Rate of Placement Changes (> 12 changes/year)

SUBJECTS	ODDS RATIO	
All subjects	2.8	$p < .05$
Younger subset		ns
Older subset	3.3	$p < .05$

Likelihood of SP vs. FIAP Child Engaged in Extreme Proportion of Days on Runaway (> 50% of time/year)

SUBJECTS	ODDS RATIO	
All subjects	2.5	$p < .05$
Younger subset		ns
Older subset	2.9	$p < .05$

Likelihood of SP vs. FIAP Child Experiencing Extreme Proportion of Days in Incarceration (> 50% of time/year)

SUBJECTS	ODDS RATIO	
All subjects	3.7	$p < .05$
Younger subset		ns
Older subset	4.0	$p < .05$

Likelihood of SP vs. FIAP Child Engaged in Extreme School Absences (> 40% of school days missed)

SUBJECTS	ODDS RATIO	
All subjects		ns
Younger subset		ns
Older subset	2.6	$p < .05$

Likelihood of SP vs. FIAP Child to Drop Out of School

SUBJECTS	ODDS RATIO	
All subjects		ns
Younger subset		ns
Older subset		ns

(continues)

Table 18.2 *Continued*

Likelihood of SP vs. FIAP Child Engaged in Extreme Proportion of Days on Suspension (> 1% of school days)

SUBJECTS	ODDS RATIO	
All subjects	2.5	$p < .05$
Younger subset		ns
Older subset	4.3	$p < .05$

Likelihood of SP vs. FIAP Child Experiencing Extreme Number of School-to-School Movements (> 3/year)

SUBJECTS	ODDS RATIO
All subjects	ns
Younger subset	ns
Older subset	ns

YSR and CBCL broad- and narrow-band factors for Waves 1 through 8 with condition, age, and gender as independent factors. These analyses on the YSR and CBCL scores revealed no within-subject effects for internalizing or any internalizing narrow-band factors for condition, condition by age, or condition by gender.[2] Both groups showed improvement over time, and there were several gender by time and age by time interactions.[3]

For externalizing factors, repeated measures analyses for YSR scores on Waves 1 through 8 revealed a condition by gender interaction for externalizing, $F(7, 245) = 2.53$, $p < .01$, delinquency, $F(7, 245) = 2.90$, $p < .001$, and a marginal effect for aggression, $F(7, 245) = 1.84$, $p < .08$. No other externalizing effects over time with condition, condition by age, or condition by gender were found. A positive effect for time occurred for both conditions, and several gender by time and age by time interactions were found.

Subsequent Fisher's Least Significant Difference (LSD) tests were performed to assess mean differences on YSR externalizing and YSR delinquency scores for Waves 1 through 8 for FIAP versus SP males and females, separately. On the externalizing broad-band factor, a significant interaction showed that FIAP males had significantly lower scores than SP males during Waves 4, 7 and 8, and FIAP females had significantly higher scores compared to SP females during Waves 1, 2 and 3. On the delinquency narrow-band factor, the same significance pattern emerged across the waves.

Repeated measures analyses for CBCL scores on Waves 1 through 8 revealed a condition by gender interaction over time for both externalizing and delinquency. No other externalizing or delinquency effects with condition, condition by age, or condition by gender were found. No significant effect was found for aggression. For the two narrow-band and the broad-band externalizing factors, the only additional findings were positive time effects for both conditions and several interactions of time with age.

Subsequent LSD tests were performed to assess mean differences on CBCL externalizing and CBCL delinquency scores for Waves 1 through 8 for FIAP versus SP males and females, separately. The FIAP males had higher externalizing scores compared to SP males only at Wave 1. However, FIAP females had significantly higher externalizing scores compared to SP females during Waves 2, 3, and 7. For CBCL delinquency, the FIAP males had higher scores during Waves 1 and 2 than did SP males. FIAP females had significantly higher scores than SP females during Waves 1 and 3.

Official Delinquency

A $2 \times 2 \times 2$ (condition $\times$ gender $\times$ age) pre-post repeated measures ANOVA of official delinquency data, $F(1, 124) = .64, p > .05$, revealed no significant main effects or interaction effects.

Conduct Disorder

ANOVAs performed on the conduct disorder data (condition $\times$ gender $\times$ age) yielded no main effect for condition, gender, or age. However, a significant gender by condition interaction was found, $F(1, 124) = 5.41, p < .05$. Subsequent LSD tests of the gender by condition interaction demonstrated that FIAP males reported less conduct disorder behavior than SP males, whereas FIAP females showed significantly greater conduct disorder behavior than their SP counterparts.

Total Delinquency

An ANOVA for the total delinquency data demonstrated an effect for gender by condition, $F(1, 124) = 5.41, p < .05$. Subsequent LSD tests of the gender by condition interaction revealed that FIAP males reported less delinquent behavior than SP males. No effect was found for FIAP females compared to SP females. No other effects involving condition were significant.

YSR and CBCL: Percentage of Children in Clinical Range

The percentages of the FIAP group ($n = 54$) and of the SP group ($n = 77$) in clinical and clinical border-line range on the YSR and the CBCL were evaluated using a T-score of 60 or higher. The mean percentages of children in this clinical range are shown on Table 18.3 for the total score and for the broad-band factors of externalizing and internalizing. The two groups were not shown to be significantly different at pre, however, at post the FIAP group shows a significantly smaller percentage of children in the clinical range on externalizing.

Table 18.3

Percentages of All Children in Clinical Range
on the YSR and/or CBCL (FIAP $n = 54$, SP $n = 77$)

Factor and Group	Pre: Wave 1 Interviews	Post: Last-Wave Interviews	Significant Difference Between Groups at Post
Total Score			
FIAP	85.2	59.3	*ns*
SP	90.9	70.1	
Externalizing			
FIAP	88.9	64.8	Odds ratio
SP	84.4	80.5	$= 2.2, p < .05$
Internalizing			
FIAP	75.9	64.8	*ns*
SP	80.5	72.7	

The percentages of children in clinical range on the YSR and CBCL were then examined between the two groups at pre and post for the variables of age, gender, and ethnicity. The only systematic finding occurred for gender. As shown in Table 18.4, the percentage of FIAP males, versus SP males, was significantly lower for the total score and the two broad-band factors. The females did not show any significant differences, pre or post.

YSR and CBCL: Score Changes Over Time

A repeated measures ANOVA was conducted on both the YSR and CBCL total T-scores, and on the broad-band factor T-scores, for Wave 1 (pre) and for the last wave of interview data (post) gathered from each of the 54 FIAP children and the 77 SP children. There was a significant time effect with both groups showing improvement over time on total scores for both the YSR, $F (1, 129) = 82.6, p < .001$, and the CBCL, $F (1, 129) = 20.9, p > .001$. Similar time effects were found for both broad-band factors of externalizing and internalizing.

Discussion

Summary of Findings

The results of this controlled experiment for children with emotional or behavioral disturbance, who have had histories of extended stays within the depen-

Table 18.4

Percentages of Males and Females in Clinical Range
on the YSR and/or CBCL (FIAP $n = 54$, SP $n = 77$)

Factor and Group	Pre: Wave 1 Interviews	Post: Last-Wave Interviews	Significant Difference Between Groups at Post
Total Score			
FIAP males	81.3	50.0	Odds ratio
SP males	89.4	70.2	= 2.4, $p < .05$
FIAP females	90.9	72.7	ns
SP females	93.3	70.0	
Externalizing			
FIAP males	87.5	53.1	Odds ratio
SP males	83.0	76.6	= 2.9, $p < .05$
FIAP females	90.9	81.8	ns
SP females	86.7	86.7	
Internalizing			
FIAP males	75.0	53.1	Odds ratio
SP males	78.7	70.2	= 2.1, $p < .05$
FIAP females	77.3	81.8	ns
SP females	83.3	76.7	

dency system suggest that the FIAP wraparound process assisted in improving the externalizing and delinquency behaviors for males, and increasing the likelihood of permanent placement for older youths.

The analyses regarding emotional and behavioral adjustment suggest that the most consistent finding is that the FIAP intervention seems to have improved the FIAP males' externalizing and delinquency behavior, when compared with that of the SP males. These condition-related findings occurred in the context of (a) the emotional and behavioral adjustment scores (YSR and CBCL), which improved significantly for both groups over time; and (b) the composite delinquency score, which showed significantly more delinquent behaviors for both groups as the subjects got older.

During the 2.6 years prior to entry into the study, the children had been changing placements an average of 4.0 times per year. One of the major goals of the FIAP intervention was to secure viable permanency placements with parents, relatives, adoptive homes, or in independent living arrangements for these children. We previously reported that a significantly greater proportion of FIAP versus SP individuals achieved permanency status at both the 2.5- and 3-year points after entry into the study (Clark, Lee, Prange, & McDonald,

1996). The permanency findings presented in this chapter are based on follow-up data from an average of 3.5 years after entry to the study, and they continued to show that a significantly greater proportion of the FIAP versus SP individuals achieved permanency status. It also was shown that this effect was related to the success of FIAP in securing permanency settings for older youth. It appears that the family specialists as well as the foster care counselors were equally successful in securing permanency placements for the younger children, but the family specialists were even more effective in securing permanency for the older youths.

Other placement and school indicators showed increasing problems for both groups as they got older, with greater proportions of time on runaway, time incarcerated, absences from school, and days on suspension. However, a repeated measures analysis showed that the mean annualized days on runaway status increased substantially less for the FIAP group than for the SP individuals. A similar finding was identified for the subset of youths with a history of incarceration, revealing that the FIAP subset had a lower proportion of days in incarceration than the SP subset. Both of these results were related primarily to the differential effects for the older youths in FIAP and SP.

Based on an exploratory analysis of extremes in rates of maladaptive behaviors and extended proportions of time exposed to negative consequences, a trend emerged that suggests that the FIAP wraparound process was effective in moderating the extremes of some older FIAP youth, in contrast to the SP youth, in (a) engaging in extended time on runaway and school absences, and (b) experiencing extreme rates of placement change and school-to-school movement as well as extended time in incarceration and on school suspension. This slight advantage afforded the older FIAP youth is consistent with the permanency status results discussed previously.

Implications for Effectively Serving These Youth

The estimates that we obtained from protective service records suggest that about 76% of the children had confirmed histories of physical or sexual abuse, with the remaining children either having been witness to abuse or having been neglected. From other interview and clinical record sources, it was estimated that approximately 77% of the FIAP girls had been sexually abused. It is likely that the percentage would have been similar for the SP girls.

Histories of severe maltreatment in childhood have been shown to be associated with poor developmental social processing patterns and later externalizing behaviors (Dodge, Pettit, Bates, & Valente, 1995); adverse academic outcomes related to standardized test scores, grade point averages, absenteeism, and rates of grade retention (Leiter & Johnsen, 1994); and adulthood depression and self-destructive behaviors (Boudewyn & Liem, 1995). In a comparison of clinic-referred children, ages 5–15, with and without histories of sexual abuse, Oates, O'Toole, Lynch, Stern, and Cooney (1994) found that the group with a sexual abuse history were more dysfunctional at intake and at an 18-month follow-up evaluation, particularly as related to the measures of self-esteem and depression. All of these children were referred for treatment at a variety of clinics; however, for those children who received therapy, there was no relationship between therapy and outcome. Where improvement did occur for the children with sexual abuse histories, it was related to the adequacy of family functioning.

Although both the FIAP and SP groups improved over time on the YSR and CBCL measures of emotional and behavioral adjustment, the girls, most of whom had experienced sexual abuse, showed differential effects indicating that the SP girls had lower externalizing scores during several early waves of the study. In part, these may constitute pre differences, as they were evident primarily during Waves 1 and 3. The percentages of FIAP and SP girls in the clinical range on their last interviews revealed no significant differences. It appears that the FIAP process had no positive, and possibly a slightly detrimental, differential effect on the girls' emotional and behavioral adjustment as measured by YSR and CBCL.

In contrast, the FIAP boys did show greater improvement in externalizing and delinquency adjustment than did their SP counterparts. However, the internalizing adjustment was not consistently better among either the FIAP boys or girls than for their SP counterparts. This finding is consistent with the relatively weak treatment effects on psychopathology found in one of our preliminary FIAP studies (Clark et al., 1994).

Greater therapeutic interventions may be needed to successfully treat individual therapy to address issues related to sexual abuse trauma. These girls with extensive sexual abuse histories may require more specific and sophisticated therapeutic interventions, including family therapy, to improve the adequacy of family functioning, and extensive individual therapy to address issues related to sexual abuse trauma.

Behavior problems have been found to occur more frequently among children who have experienced many family moves than among children who have never or infrequently moved (Wood, Halfon, Scarlata, Newacheck, & Nessim, 1993). Their study, as well as several others, demonstrated strong correlations between frequent mobility and lower school achievement, increased dropout rates, poorer psychological adjustment, and adverse effects on maintenance of friendships (Eckenrode, Rowe, Laird, & Brathwaite, 1995; Haggerty, Roghman, & Pless, 1975; Nelken & Gallo, 1978; Paiz, 1985; Stokols & Shumaker, 1982). Regarding out-of-home placements, studies have reported that children with behavior problems have longer stays (Lawder, Poulin, & Andrews, 1986); that the number of placement changes is linked to emotional and behavioral disturbances (Cooper, Peterson, & Meier, 1987); and that the more extended are the out-of-home placements and the more externalizing types of problems displayed, the lower the probability of reunification (George, 1990; Landsverk, Davis, Ganger, Newton, & Johnson, 1995). The greater percentage of FIAP individuals in permanency status with family and independent-living settings would appear to have favorable implications for overall adjustment.

The children and youth in our study were placed at substantial risk for the development or exacerbation of emotional or behavioral disturbances while in the dependency system. The results of our study suggest that the participants displayed more delinquent behaviors, school absences, suspensions, and incarceration as they grew older. Although it is not feasible to determine the cause of these problems, the relationship between high rates of placement change and poorer child outcomes suggests that the system may be a contributing factor.

The findings regarding the FIAP intervention are encouraging in two fronts: (a) improved externalizing and delinquency adjustment for males, and (b) improved placement outcomes for older youths (i.e., a larger percentage in permanency status, and lower proportions of time on runaway and in incarceration). Another series of controlled studies, which have shown encouraging results both on emotional and behavioral adjustment and on a community adjustment indicator of arrests, have been conducted by Henggeler and his associates (Henggeler, Melton, Smith, Schoenwald, & Hanley, 1993; Scherer, Brondino, Henggeler, Melton, & Hanley, 1994). Using a wraparound-type process with conduct disordered youth referred to as Multisystemic Therapy, they have reported improvement in both emotional and behavioral adjustment and arrests rates. It appears that Henggeler and his associates have emphasized an intensive family systems therapeutic component and ensured the integrity of the delivery of their individualized intervention to a greater extent than any of the other individualized wraparound process studies to date. This may partially account for the superiority of their findings across both categories of outcomes.

Implications for the Field

Our findings, in conjunction with those of Henggeler and his associates, as well as other individualized wraparound initiatives (Clark and Clarke, 1996), lend growing, but limited, support to the superiority of individualized strategies of service delivery for children with the severest of emotional and behavioral disturbances and their families. The magnitude of the effects across these studies would suggest that only a portion of the children are reaching the levels of clinical improvement that would indicate that they were treated adequately (Bickman, 1996; Cunningham-Howard, 1994). However, some of these initial small effects are somewhat understandable in light of the fact that the field is still defining and refining the wraparound process and children's systems-of-care strategies for these extremely challenging children and their families. These children and their families with complex, multisystem needs may require an intensity of intervention that is difficult to achieve unless a service-delivery system can be developed to ensure the adequacy of match between child and family needs and services, and ensure that the fidelity of the interventions can be maintained.

Limitations of the Study and Future Research Strategies

From a research perspective, the FIAP study has an advantage over many others in that it was a controlled experiment with at-risk children having been randomly assigned to a usual services condition versus a wraparound condition. Nevertheless, the descriptor "controlled" did not guarantee that the FIAP study was exempt from sources of confound, such as: (a) the fidelity of the intervention varying because of the wraparound process having to be modified over time as weaknesses were found in our original model; (b) the fidelity of the intervention weakening, at times, because of variations across the family specialists and their supervisor; (c) the lack of consistent field supervision for the family specialists; (d) the high rate of caseworker turnover caused by low salaries, large case loads, inadequate supervision and guidance, and the reorganization of the state foster care system; (e) the unanticipated delays in securing permanency plans through the foster care system and the courts; and (f) the threat of a lawsuit, which caused the governor and legislature to appropriate millions of new dollars to the foster care and adoption system midway through our study, thus enhancing "standard practice."

The challenge to system-of-care researchers is to minimize as many confounding variables as possible, while designing measures that will allow them to adequately describe the intervention and the systemic context in which it is being employed. However, the "gold standard" of the experimental design based on the random assignment of clients to either a control or experimental group may be premature for much of the current work on individualized systems of care (Friedman, 1997). Due to the complexity of determining individualized child/family needs and strengths and the multiple sources of supports and services that are often required to address these needs, prerequisite work in program development and measurement instrumentation would appear to be essential before definitive tests of wraparound processes should be undertaken. Burns and her associates have proposed a developmental research process that encourages researchers and funding agencies to begin exploring innovative service strategies with program development efforts that can lead to the application of more sophisticated quasi-experimental designs as the knowledge base is expanded regarding the intervention and the measurement of its outcomes (Burns, 1996; Burns, Hoagwood, & Maultsby, this volume). Burns and her associates suggest that the use of large-scale, controlled experimental studies should be reserved for high-cost or high-risk interventions, and then used only after adequate developmental work has been undertaken. We are confident that the fidelity of the FIAP intervention and the differential outcomes from our controlled study would have been strengthened had we had an initial year or two to: (a) establish a broader base of community ownership regarding this initiative; (b) pilot test and refine our wraparound processes for this challenging population; and (c) identify measures that would be most reliable, valid, and sensitive for the types of outcomes that this intervention targeted.

The fact that at least moderate levels of superiority are being reported for individualized strategies, as applied to the most challenging of children, should be seen as encouraging. As these wraparound and systems-of-care strategies are refined, as the process for determining child/family needs and associated services becomes more reliable, as family systems therapy is incorporated more adequately, and as personnel training and field supervision methods are standardized to ensure the consistency of application of the intervention, the fidelity of the individualized approach to children with emotional and behavioral disturbances should be strengthened greatly (Clark & Clarke, 1996; Rosenblatt, 1996).

Endnotes

1. One of the 132 subjects was dropped because he was returned to his home the day after he entered our study and was not exposed to either treatment condition of this study.

2. An analysis shows that the subjects with complete data (i.e., 1 through 8) from both groups were younger and had lower Wave 8 scores than their counterparts. However, no differential loss in subjects for any of the demographic factors was found for FIAP versus SP. Despite the notable drop in the number of subjects included in this analysis, the lack of differential loss of subjects provides support for the findings reported in this section on emotional and behavioral adjustment.

3. Throughout this section, interactions that did not involve condition are not presented, as they had the same effects on both the FIAP and SP groups.

Authors' Note

This study would not have been possible without the continuing support and collaborative efforts of Edward Howell, Joseph Tagliarini, Sylvia Thomas, Adrienne Holderith, and Ann Hipson of Florida's Child and Family Services Program Office; Celeste Putnam Tanzy, DeVon Hardy, Evelyn Shelley, Debbie Spellman, and Peg Stateler of Florida's Children's Mental Health Program Office; and Colleen Bevis of the Children's Committee of the Health & Human Services Board of District Six. The authors also wish to express their appreciation to Mark Rose for the excellent assistance he provided in statistical analyses; Martin Factor and Richard Foster for their expertise in data management; Kristin Knapp for her excellent supervision of the interview and data-collection process; and to Susan Guttentag, Joyce Lum, Rosalyn Malysiak, and Kristin Knapp for their dedication and sensitivity as interviewers and data collectors.

The FIAP study, which is a collaborative research demonstration project between the Florida Mental Health Institute at the University of South Florida and the Florida Health & Rehabilitative Services Department, was funded, in large part, by the Child, Adolescent, and Family Branch of the Center for Mental Health Services (Grant No. 9 HD5 SM51328) and the Child and Family Support Branch of the National Institute of Mental Health (Grant No. 1-R18-MH47910).

Correspondence regarding this study should be sent to Dr. Hewitt B. "Rusty" Clark, Department of Child & Family Studies, Florida Mental Health Institute, University of South Florida, Tampa, FL 33612.

References

Achenbach, T. M. (1991a). *Manual for the Child Behavior Checklist/4-18 and 1991 Profile.* Burlington: University of Vermont, Department of Psychiatry.

Achenbach, T. M. (1991b). *Manual for the Youth Self-Report and 1991 Profile.* Burlington: University of Vermont, Department of Psychiatry.

Bickman, L. (1996). A continuum of care: More is not always better. *American Psychologist, 51,* 689–701.

Boudewyn, A. C., & Liem, J. H. (1995). Childhood sexual abuse as a precursor to depression and self-destructive behavior in childhood. *Journal of Traumatic Stress, 8,* 445–459.

Boyd, L. A. (1992). *Integrating systems of care for children and families: An overview of values, methods and characteristics of developing models, with examples and recommendations.* Tampa: University of South Florida, Department of Child and Family Studies, Florida Mental Health Institute.

Boyd, L. A., Struchen, W. L., & Panacek-Howell, L. J. (1989). *A study of the mental health and substance abuse service needs of Florida's foster children: A report to HRS.* Tampa: University of South Florida, Department of Child and Family Studies, Florida Mental Health Institute.

Boyd, L. A., Struchen, W. L., & Panacek-Howell, L. J. (1990). *A comparison of foster parent and foster caseworker survey results in studies of the mental health and substance abuse needs of Florida's foster children: A report to HRS.* Tampa: University of South Florida, Department of Child and Family Studies, Florida Mental Health Institute.

Burchard, J. D., & Clarke, R. T. (1990). The role of individualized care in a service delivery system for children and adolescents with severely maladjusted behavior. *Journal of Mental Health Administration, 17,* 48–60.

Burns, B. J. (1996). What drives outcomes for emotional and behavioral disorders in children and adolescents? In D. M. Steinwachs, L. M. Flynn, G. S. Norquist, & E. A. Skinner (Eds.), *Using outcomes information to improve mental health and substance treatment: New directions for mental health services.* (pp. 89–102). San Francisco: Jossey-Bass.

Burns, B. J., & Friedman, R. M. (1990). Examining the research base for child mental health services and policy. *Journal of Mental Health Administration, 17,* 3–12.

Burns, B. J., Hoagwood, K., & Maultsby, L. T. (this volume). Improving outcomes for children and adolescents with serious emotional and behavioral disorders. In M. Epstein, K. Kutash, & A. Duchnowski (Eds.), *Community based programming for children with serious emotional disturbances and their families: Research and evaluation.*

Clark, H. B., & Boyd, L. A. (1990). *Fostering individualized mental health care: A study* (Grant No. 1-R18-MH47910). Rockville, MD: Child and Family Support Branch of the National Institute of Mental Health.

Clark, H. B., & Boyd, L. A. (1992). *Fostering individualized mental health care: Follow up* (Grant No. 9 HD5 SM51328-04). Rockville, MD: Child, Adolescent, and Family Branch of the Center for Mental Health Service.

Clark, H. B., & Clarke, R. T. (Eds.). (1996). Research on the wraparound process and individualized services for children with multi-system needs [Special issue]. *Journal of Child and Family Studies, 5*(1).

Clark, H. B., Lee, B., Prange, M. E., & McDonald, B. A. (1996). Children lost within the foster care system: Can wraparound service strategies improve placement outcomes? *Journal of Child and Family Studies, 5,* 39–54.

Clark, H. B., Prange, M. E., Lee, B., Boyd, L. A., McDonald, B. A., & Stewart, E. S. (1994). Improving adjustment outcomes for foster children with emotional and behavioral disorders: Early findings from a controlled study on individualized services. *Journal of Emotional and Behavioral Disorders, 2,* 207–218.

Cooper, C. S., Peterson, N. L., & Meier, J. H. (1987). Variables associated with disrupted placement in a select sample of abused and neglected children. *Child Abuse and Neglect, 11,* 75–86.

Cunningham-Howard, M. V. (1994). *School-based histories and educational outcomes of children and youth receiving community mental health services through the Texas Children's Mental Health Plan. Final report.* Austin: University of Texas, Department of Educational Psychology.

Dodge, K. A., Pettit, G. S., Bates, J. E., & Valente, E. (1995). Social information-processing patterns partially mediate the effect of early physical abuse on later conduct problems. *Journal of Abnormal Psychology, 104,* 632–643.

Dollard, N., Evans, M. E., Lubrecht, J., & Schaeffer, D. (1994). The use of flexible service dollars in rural community-based programs for children with serious emotional disturbance and their families. *Journal of Emotional and Behavioral Disorders, 2*(2), 117–125.

Duchnowski, A. J., & Kutash, K. (1996). The mental health perspective. In C. M. Nelson, R. B. Rutherford, & B. I. Wolford (Eds.), *Comprehensive and collaborative systems that work for troubled youth: A national agenda* (pp. 90–110). Richmond, KY: National Coalition for Juvenile Justice Services.

Eckenrode, J., Rowe, E., Laird, M., & Brathwaite, J. (1995). Mobility as a mediator of the effects of child maltreatment on academic performance. *Child Development, 66,* 1130–1142.

Fisher, P., Wicks, J., Shaffer, D., Piacentini, J., & Lapkin, J. (1991). *A users' manual for the Diagnostic Interview Schedule for Children (DISC 2.3).* New York: New York State Psychiatric Institute.

Friedman, R. M. (1997). Services and service delivery systems for children with serious emotional disorders: Issues in assessing effectiveness. In C. T. Nixon & D. A. Northrup (Eds.), *Evaluating mental health services: How do programs for children "work" in the real world?* (pp. 16–44). Thousand Oaks, CA: Sage Publications.

Goerge, R. M. (1990). The reunification process in substitute care. *Social Service Review, 64,* 422–457.

Groves, I. (1993). *Creating a new system of care: Building a stronger child and family partnership: Needs assessment: Children, family & systems.* Tampa: University of South Florida, Department of Child and Family Studies, Florida Mental Health Institute.

Haggerty, R., Roghman, K., & Pless, I. B. (1975). *Child health and the community.* New York: John Wiley & Sons.

Henggeler, S. W., Melton, G. B., Smith, L. A., Schoenwald, M. A., & Hanley, J. H. (1993). Family preservation using multisystemic treatment: Long-term follow-up to a clinical trial with serious juvenile offenders. *Journal of Child and Family Studies, 2,* 283–293.

Knitzer, J., & Yelton, S. (1990). Collaboration between child welfare and mental health: Both systems must exploit the program possibilities. *Public Welfare, 48,* 24–33.

Lambiase, E. A., & Cumes, J. W. (1987). Child custody decisions: How legal and mental health professionals view the concept of "best interests of the child." *South African Journal of Psychology, 17*(4), 127–130.

Landsverk, J., Davis, I., Ganger, W., Newton, R., & Johnson, I. (1995). *Impact of child psychosocial functioning on reunification from out-of-home placement.* Manuscript submitted for publication.

Landsverk, J., Madsen, J., Ganger, W., Chadwick, D., & Litrownik, A. (in press). Mental health problems of foster children in three California counties. *Child Abuse and Neglect.*

Lawder, E. A., Poulin, J. E., & Andrews, R. G. (1986). A study of 185 foster children 5 years after placement. *Child Welfare, 65*(3), 241–251.

Leiter, J., & Johnsen, M. C. (1994). Child maltreatment and school performance. *American Journal of Education, 102,* 154–189.

McDonald, B. A., Boyd, L. A., Clark, H. B., & Stewart, E. S. (1995). Recommended individualized wraparound strategies for serving foster children with emotional or behavioral disturbances and their families. *Community Alternatives: International Journal of Family Care, 7(2),* 63–82.

Nelken, I., & Gallo, K. (1978). *Factors influencing migrant high school students to drop out or graduate from high school* (ERIC Document Reproduction Service No. ED 164 245). Chico, CA: Nelken and Associates.

Oates, R. K., O'Toole, B. I., Lynch, D. L., Stern, A., & Cooney, G. (1994). Stability and change in outcomes for sexually abused children. *Journal of the American Academy of Child and Adolescent Psychiatry, 33,* 945–953.

Paiz, R. (1985). *Correlates contributing to the school success or failure of Mexican-American students.* Oroville, CA: Region II Migrant Education Service Center.

Prange, M. E., Greenbaum, P. E., Silver, S. E., Friedman, R. M., Kutash, K., & Duchnowski, A. J. (1992). Family functioning and psychopathology among adolescents with severe emotional disturbances. *Journal of Abnormal Child Psychology, 20,* 83–102.

Rosenblatt, A. (1996). Bows and ribbons, tape and twine: Wrapping the wraparound process for children with multi-system needs. *Journal of Child and Family Studies, 5,* 101–116.

Scherer, D. G., Brondino, M. J., Henggeler, S. W., Melton, G. B., & Hanley, J. H. (1994). Multisystemic family preservation therapy: Preliminary findings from a study of rural and minority serious adolescent offenders. *Journal of Emotional and Behavioral Disorders, 2,* 198–206.

Shealy, C. N. (1995). From *Boys Town* to *Oliver Twist:* Separating fact from fiction in welfare reform and out-of-home placement of children and youth. *American Psychologist, 50,* 565-580.

Solnit, A. J. (1987). Child placement conflicts: New approaches [Special issue]. *Child Abuse and Neglect, 11,* 455–460.

Stokols, D., & Shumaker, S. A. (1982). The psychological context of residential mobility and well-being. *Journal of Social Issues, 38,* 149–171.

Stroul, B. A., & Friedman, R. M. (1986). *A system of care for severely emotionally disturbed children & youth.* Washington, DC: CASSP Technical Assistance Center.

Sullivan, H., Henley, C., & Williams, C. W. (1988). *A study of changing trends in foster family care in the southeast.* Chapel Hill: University of North Carolina, School of Social Work, National Child Welfare Leadership Center.

Terpstra, J., & McFadden, E. J. (1993). Looking backward: Looking forward—new directions in foster care. *Community Alternatives: International Journal of Family Care, 5(1),* 115–134.

VanDenBerg, J. E. (1993). Integration of individualized mental health services into the system of care for children and adolescents. *Administration and Policy in Mental Health, 20,* 247–257.

VanDenBerg, J. E., & Grealish, E. M. (1996). Individualized services and supports through the wraparound process: Philosophy and procedures. *Journal of Child and Family Studies, 5,* 7–22.

Weitzel, S., Friedman, R., Shanley, K., & Levine, J. (1993). *Key facts about the children: The 1993 Florida kids count data book.* Tampa: Florida Mental Health Institute.

Wells, K., & Biegel, D. E. (1990). *Intensive family preservation services: A research agenda for the 1990's final report.* Cleveland, OH: Intensive Family Preservation Services Research Conference.

Widom, C. S. (1989). *Pathways to criminal violence.* Newbury Park, CA: Sage.

Wood, D., Halfon, N., Scarlata, D., Newacheck, P., & Nessim, S. (1993). Impact of family relocation on children's growth, development, school function, and behavior. *Journal of the American Medical Association, 270,* 1334–1338.

Wynn, J. (1995). Enhancing social services for children and families. *Public Welfare, 53,* 12–23.

Preliminary Outcomes of an Experimental Study Comparing Treatment Foster Care and Family-Centered Intensive Case Management

19

Mary E. Evans,
Mary I. Armstrong, Anne D.
Kuppinger, Steven Huz,
and Thomas L. McNulty

O ver the past 15 years, a number of national studies on children's mental health services have concluded that major changes need to occur in how services are planned, provided, and delivered to children and adolescents with serious emotional disturbance (SED) and their families. Jane Knitzer's *Unclaimed Children* (1982) decried the overreliance on inpatient care as well as the failure of state mental health authorities to take responsibility for developing and funding programs and services that are family centered and community based. Several other reports also have focused national attention on children with SED. For example, the Office of Technology Assessment's report on children's mental health problems and services (Dougherty, Saxe, Cross, & Silverman, 1987) reached conclusions similar to Knitzer's about the need for improvements, including better access to care, an adequate array of services, and better coordination between mental health and other child-serving systems. As recently as 1993, Cole and Poe, in *Partnerships for Care: Interim Report of the Mental Health Services Program for Youth* (1993), reiterated these same concerns and additionally called for movement toward an individualized care approach and parent-professional partnerships.

In 1984 the Child and Adolescent Service System Program (CASSP) was created to provide states with technical assistance and financial aid to foster the restructuring of their systems of care by redirecting public resources from inpatient and residential programs to community-based services (Stroul & Friedman, 1986). Like other states, New York has benefited from CASSP funding, technical assistance, and ideological leadership. The New York State Office of Mental Health, the state mental health authority, is guided by a set of core principles in the development and delivery of services to children and their families. Chief among these principles are that the family is the most desirable setting in which to raise children and that clinical practice, policy direction, and funding must support raising children in family and familylike settings (New York State Office of Mental Health, 1992). These principles were operationalized by the establishment of community-based services, such as therapeutic foster care, psychiatric emergency services, and intensive case-management programs that were child centered and family focused. While these programs were positively received by providers and parents, the mental health authority's early experiences with community-based services convinced policymakers that a number of additional individualized supports (e.g., respite care, behavior management skills development, peer support groups) would be necessary if children were to remain in family settings.

To address the need for continued innovation in services for children with SED and their families as well as to add to the research knowledge base (Friedman & Duchnowski, 1990; Saxe, Cross, & Silverman, 1988), the New York State Office of Mental Health successfully responded to a request for applications from the National Institute for Mental Health (Evans, 1990) for a research demonstration grant. The proposal was designed to compare the child, family, and service-system outcomes of New York's treatment foster care program, Family-Based Treatment (FBT), to those of a newly established modality, Family-Centered Intensive Case Management (FCICM), in three rural counties. The goal of this study was to determine if children who remain at home within a family receiving intensive supports experience outcomes the same as or better than those of children who are placed in the homes of professional parents. Rural areas were selected as the site for the research demonstration because of the paucity of resources available to support families in caring for children with SED. The grant's resources would allow for the development of a program model that would enhance local resources and a research plan to test whether relatively inexpensive supportive services could be effective in keeping children with SED in their own homes.

Established in 1988, FBT was one of the first community-based programs to be implemented by the New York State Office of Mental Health. The goal of FBT is to provide training, support, and respite to treatment (foster) families to care for a child with SED in the community (Armstrong & Evans, 1992). A family specialist provides training and support to a cluster of five treatment families and one respite family. The family specialist also works with the child's family to promote reunification, whenever possible, as treatment goals are met. FCICM, however, was designed to support families with services that paralleled and supplemented those available to treatment families in FBT.[1] The development of FCICM was influenced, in part, by the demand of families attending state planning and informational meetings for the same level of intensive support and services offered to treatment parents. These demands reflected the growing strength and influence of parents of children with SED on both national and state levels. State policymakers were told by parents that this type of support would increase the likelihood that they would be able to keep their children at home.

Even though the concept of tailoring services to the individual needs of each child and family was one of the original CASSP values (Stroul & Friedman, 1986), it has taken several years for professionals to translate the values of individualized care into services (Evans, Armstrong, & Kuppinger, 1996). The development of FCICM is an early application of an expanding knowledge base on individualized care, which is characterized by four key service elements: case management/case coordination, wraparound services, flexibility of funding and services, and interagency collaboration (Katz-Leavy, Lourie, Stroul, & Zeigler-Dendy, 1992). FCICM uses an individualized care framework that incorporates these elements and is implemented through a team composed of a case manager and a parent advocate who has raised a child with SED. The team is committed to doing "whatever it takes" (Katz-Leavy et al., 1992) to support a group of eight families in caring for their children. Although varying by site, the resources and services the team offers to families might include behavior management skills development, support groups, in-home and out-of-home respite care, sibling recreational groups, and expenditure of flexible service dollars. In addition, case managers access concrete services needed by families.

The purpose of this chapter is to (a) describe both program models as developed and implemented in New York, (b) report on the characteristics of children and families served through July 1995, (c) describe the evaluation being used to assess the outcomes of these two models, (d) present preliminary data comparing the outcomes between enrollment and 12 months for children and families served in these two programs, and (e) share some initial thoughts about what has been learned in conducting this research demonstration.

Description of the Two Program Models

Family-Based Treatment

FBT is New York's version of treatment foster care (see Table 19.1). The program implemented in New York was developed at People Places in Staunton, Virginia (Bryant, 1981; Snodgrass & Bryant, 1991). The goal of the program is to provide care and treatment for children with SED within a therapeutic family setting and to prepare them for placement in a permanent family setting, which could mean a return to the family of origin or placement with an adoptive family, or to improve relationships between the youth and the youth's family.

As implemented in New York, the FBT program is premised on two principles. The first is that the professional or treatment parents are the most

Table 19.1

Comparison of FBT and FCICM Program Components

Attribute	FBT	FCICM
Target population	Children with SED currently out of home or at risk of restrictive placement	Children with SED currently out of home or at risk of restrictive placement
Program focus	Child	Child and family
Program goals	To provide familylike treatment foster home and to prepare child for return to family	To support family in caring for child at home
Intake	Interagency committee	Interagency committee
Staff	Family specialist	Case manager–parent advocate team
Staff availability	24 hours a day/7 days a week to professional families	24 hours a day/7 days a week to families
Cluster	Five professional families and one respite family	Eight families and two respite families
Planned and emergency respite	For professional families	For families
Behavior management skills training	For professional families	For families
Needs assessment	For identified child	For families
Linkage to needed services	For identified child	For families
Monetary resources	Support identified child	Support child and family
Home visit frequency	Regularly to professional families, occasionally to families	Regularly to families
Advocacy focus	Child	Child, family, and service system
Parent support	To professional and respite families in group setting	To families on group and parent-to-parent level

important component of the foster care intervention because they teach coping skills, create an atmosphere of social and emotional support within the home, and provide a model of positive family functioning. Professional parents are integral members of the professional staff. The second principle is that professional families can offer support and assistance to each other in the development of problem-solving skills necessary to provide care and treatment to children with SED. To be maximally effective, professional families require the assistance and support of a respite family and a family specialist—a child mental health professional who assists in the development of individualized service plans, coordinates service plans, and supports the treatment families.

The FBT model uses a cluster approach with each cluster, each consisting of five professional families caring for one child each and a respite family providing planned and emergency respite to other families in the cluster. The cluster meets together on a regular basis, ranging from weekly to monthly, and functions as a support base, forum for the exchange of problems and interventions, and a structure in which to provide training (Armstrong & Evans, 1992; Evans et al., 1994).

Professional parents are specifically recruited to work with children and youth with SED and receive an additional stipend, beyond that paid to regular foster parents, for their participation in the program. These parents are required to attend 18 hours of training based upon the Parent Skills Training developed by Snodgrass (1986). Once it has been completed, a careful matching process between the child and professional parents occurs to ensure the compatibility of the child and treatment family as well as positive outcomes. Only one child or adolescent is placed with each professional family, although waivers are permitted for special situations, such as sibling placement. A mental health professional—the family specialist—carries a small caseload and works closely with the child, the professional parents, and the child's family or persons in the goal environment.

There is no predetermined length of service. An evaluation of New York State's FBT program indicated that the mean length of stay of those discharged from the program was 17 months (Huz, McNulty, & Evans, 1994). While family specialists and professional families work closely with the child's family to prepare for reunification, whenever possible, the emphasis is on the child receiving treatment and less on the family of origin.

Target Population

The target population is children and adolescents 5–18 years of age who have SED (New York State Office of Mental Health, 1992), score within the clinical range on the Child Behavior Checklist (CBCL; Achenbach, 1991), have a DSM III-R/DSM IV diagnosis, and have experienced functional limitations caused by emotional disturbance over the past 12 months. These children require individualized, intensive treatment and rehabilitation services and usually exhibit a range of mental health diagnoses and problem behaviors. Typically, these children have been referred for out-of-home placement because their current caregivers have been unable to provide the intensity of support necessary to manage their behavior, keep them in school and out of jail, and maintain their functioning in the community. Typically, these children have a history of poor educational performance, difficulties in relating to their family, low self-esteem, poor social adaptation, and aggressive, acting-out behaviors. Some have experienced physical or sexual abuse. Most often these children have had multiple placements in psychiatric inpatient programs, residential care settings, generic foster care, or juvenile justice settings.

Data from an evaluation of the first 255 children served in FBT in New York (Huz et al., 1994) show that on average, a child enrolled in the program was about 10 years old, white and non-Hispanic (58%), and male (69%). Most likely he was in the custody of a local department of social services (57%) and receiving special education services (68%). On admission to FBT, these children displayed an average of 6.2 problem behaviors and symptoms (from a list of 26 adapted from the CBCL) and were functionally impaired because of SED in an average of nearly three out of five possible areas. Disruptive behaviors were identified as the most common diagnostic category (55%). These children had been hospitalized or placed out of home an average of 3.4 times, because of their mental health problem prior to enrollment in FBT. More than half of them (56%) had been in foster care placement at least once prior to FBT and one third had experienced more than one placement.

Intake and Assignment

Referrals for FBT placement are reviewed by an interagency intake committee comprising representatives from the local child-serving agencies. Once accepted for placement, the child and professional family are matched. They view videotapes of each other and begin a series of meetings, culminating in an overnight stay at the treatment home. A typical matching process takes 3–4 months and is concluded only when the child, professional family, and family specialist are convinced that placement should occur.

Staffing Patterns, Training, Responsibilities, and Ongoing Support

FBT staff includes a family specialist, a cluster of five treatment families, and one respite family. The family specialist, typically an experienced mental health professional, works with the cluster, helping to identify service needs and advocate for each child and the child's natural or foster parents.

Each family specialist provides support and training to the treatment and respite parents and works with families to prepare them for reunification. Each family specialist receives 8 days of orientation and training focused on the FBT philosophy, recruitment and training of treatment families, opportunities to practice techniques they will teach treatment and respite parents, and strategies for working with families. An integral part of these sessions is training in the Parent Skills Training curriculum, which is also taught to all FBT professional parents. The curriculum includes modules on setting expectations and goals, identifying and providing reinforcers and consequences, recognizing and acknowledging positive behaviors, and facilitating a child's adjustment. The training, which is delivered over the course of 6 weeks with treatment and respite parent groups, is completed before placement of the child with special needs in the home. Respite parents may also receive additional training tailored to respite providers. The skills emphasized during training are selected for their ability to teach alternative prosocial behavior, their generalizability to all family situations, and their ability to be rehearsed and practiced in real-life situations. Such skills include easy listening, positive scan, positive time, pure descriptive praise, and explaining/negotiating a program. At the heart of the training is the use of the ABC Model for behavior analysis and planning—Antecedents to problem behaviors, Behaviors, and Reinforcing/Consequences. Everyone on the team uses this approach in thinking and communicating about problems and solutions.

Treatment and respite families are responsible for meeting the physical and emotional needs of the children as well as providing structure, implementing behavior-management plans, and working with the children toward the attainment of clinical goals. The treatment families are involved in all aspects of treatment planning, implementation, and the monitoring of children's progress. Respite families provide planned and emergency out-of-home respite care. They have ongoing involvement and familiarity with the children in their clusters and promote continuity of treatment procedures and goals through the behavior-management plans. Treatment and respite family training and ongoing support are provided through monthly group meetings of treatment and respite parents. Some sites also hold recreational events for children in conjunction with group meetings to alleviate child-care problems. Sites also hold several social events each year, such as holiday parties and picnics.

The FBT program budget includes a line item for purchase of psychiatric consultation. In addition, each FBT program has a formal relationship with a local clinic treatment program for access to individual, group, and family treatment, and with a local acute inpatient program if psychiatric inpatient care is required.

Four family specialists provided services across the three study sites through July 1995. All were white, non-Hispanic; two of the four were female and, on average, they were hired at the age of 34.5 years (range 31–39). Three of four family specialists had bachelor's degrees, most in nonclinical psychology, and the fourth had a post-baccalaureate degree. All family specialists had prior experience in children's mental health, with an average of 5.5 years of experience in community-based children's mental health services, including case management. Over the course of 5 years, only one staff change occurred among the family specialists across the three sites.

Role of the Family

Family specialists maintain contact with the child's family of origin and include them in some training sessions. The family are involved in many decisions that affect the child but are not the child's primary caretaker. Through a child's stay in FBT, family specialists work with the child's family to develop the skills and resources needed to facilitate their child's return home. As discharge approaches, the child spends more time with his or her family and typically makes visits of increasing duration. Family specialists support the family and child as they work toward the goal of reunification.

Funding

FBT treatment parents receive monthly retainers and per diem payments in compensation for their work and to cover the expenses of additional family members. Additional funding, currently $1,000/child/year, is also provided on a child-specific basis to meet important personal needs of the child, including clinical supports (e.g., behavior plan rewards), social/recreation supports, or economic costs (e.g., winter clothing and birthday celebrations). Management of these funds varies by site. In some cases, treatment parents buy items for the children and are reimbursed and, in others, monthly or quarterly disbursements are paid in advance with reconciliations made afterwards. In the first year of the study, the greatest proportion of child-specific funds used in FBT were for economic costs (41%), clinical supports (16%), and social/recreational supports (5%). Crisis supports (5%), other expenses (predominantly holiday and birthday; 27%), medical/dental (2%), and school supports (4%) accounted for the remaining expenditures.

Family-Centered Intensive Case Management

The FCICM program model acknowledges that families need a comprehensive array of services and supports to help them keep their children at home. FCICM's development is based on ICM principles (Armstrong & Evans, 1992; Evans, Banks, Huz, & McNulty, 1994; Surles & Blanch, 1989), individualized care philosophy (Burchard & Clarke, 1990), and FBT cluster features (see Table 19.1), and the program is enriched with the additional resources of advocacy and parent-to-parent support from a parent advocate who is the parent of a child with SED.

FCICM is distinguished from both FBT and New York's ICM program (Armstrong & Evans, 1992) by its emphasis on the central role of the family in accomplishing treatment goals for children with SED. The generic ICM program in New York is an intensive, child-centered service provided to children with SED in home, school, and community settings. Through linkage to services and advocacy efforts, case managers carry small caseloads (10 children;

since October 1996, 12 children) and work to maintain children in their natural environments.

The decision to focus on families in this federally funded research demonstration grew out of an evaluation of New York's generic ICM program, which showed that although children experienced improvement in functioning, their families failed to show measurable improvement in areas of family functioning or ability to provide supportive care for the child (Huz, Evans, Rahn, & McNulty, 1993). FCICM builds on the core features of assessment, linkage, and advocacy that are part of New York's ICM program. Compared to ICM, FCICM involves more teaching, skills building, family support, and direct therapeutic intervention, all of which are made possible by lower caseloads and the addition of the parent advocate role. The behavior management skills training offered in FCICM also allies more closely with a therapeutic or personal strengths model, rather than the expanded broker model (Solomon, 1992) that characterizes New York's ICM model. While the expanded broker model focuses on assessment, linkage services and client advocacy, the personal strengths model emphasizes the provision of resources and supports to the client, enabling clients to maximize their potential. In FCICM, these resources are provided to the family, including the child, to support them in providing care and support for their child (Solomon, 1992). Families enrolled in FCICM have access to planned and emergency respite care, flexible service dollars to pay for such things as home repair and recreational opportunities for children, and parent-to-parent support from the parent advocate and family support groups.

Target Population

The FCICM target population is children who meet the eligibility requirements for FBT. To be eligible for enrollment in FCICM, however, a child must be able to be returned home, because the random assignment process could possibly send them either to FBT or FCICM.

Intake and Assignment

The same interagency intake committee that reviewed cases for placement of children in FBT also screened cases for enrollment of children in FCICM.

Staffing Patterns, Training, Responsibilities, and Ongoing Support

Families enrolled in FCICM receive intensive professional support from a case manager–parent advocate team whose maximum caseload does not exceed eight families. In working with families, the case manager–parent advocate team identifies each family's strengths, service needs and goals, and develops a comprehensive treatment plan with full participation of the child and the child's family, advocates for the family, links the family to services, and teaches behavior management and self-help skills based on the needs expressed by family members. The team also models advocacy skills and empowers families through the teaching of these skills to family members.

Case managers, parent advocates, and their supervisors each receive three days of orientation and training. This training includes an overview of relevant research, detailed training in the use of data collection instruments, discussions about parent-provider collaboration and family-centered service, and parenting training using the Parent Skills Training curriculum. Some parent advocates receive further training provided by their agencies. Additionally, case managers receive the standard 10-day ICM training, which typically focuses on assessment of needs and linkage to ongoing services and includes the following components: introduction to the state mental health system, systems assessment, advocacy and overcoming barriers to resources, typical child development and disorders of childhood and adolescence, concepts and interventions of ICM family practice, family and child needs assessment, treatment planning impact of trauma, crisis management theory and interventions, follow-up procedures, and administrative issues.

Through July 1995, four parent advocates and five case managers provided services at the three study sites. All but one member of the case manager—parent advocate teams were female and white non-Hispanic, reflecting the racial composition of the counties they served. The one exception to this was at one site at which a male parent of a child with SED was hired in the parent advocate role. Case managers began their employment with the project at the mean age of 30 (range 26–34) and parent advocates were slightly older, with a mean age of 39 (range 32–48). Case managers usually held master's degrees, although one held a bachelor's degree. As was true of family specialists, the case managers' most common field of study was psychology or a related discipline, such as community mental health. The educational experience of parent advocates ranged from less than high school to a bachelor's degree.

Both case managers and parent advocates were experienced in the field of children's mental health services from both provider and family member perspectives. All case managers had prior experience in children's mental health, with an average of 9 months of experience in inpatient mental health services and 4 years of outpatient experience. Parent advocates at each of our sites had at least one child with SED, ranging in age from 6–15 years. Parent advocates were selected by program directors for their experience, skills relating to families, and knowledge of and interest in learning about the service system and advocacy. Parent advocates were employed approximately 10–15 hours per week. All received support from a statewide parent advocate who has been a consultant to this project. During the 3 years of the project, three parent advocates and two case managers left their positions. These staff changes were apparently unrelated to the project or any particular agency problems.

The precise role played by each parent advocate evolved differently at the study sites, yet common features emerged. Parent advocates provided parent-to-parent support and case-specific and systems advocacy. They represented a "family perspective" in their encounters with professionals. Parent advocates also worked to create better communication between families and professional service providers. Much of their work involved providing informal support to parents through home visits and by telephone. Whereas case managers focused most of their attention on the children, parent advocates tended to have much less contact with children. Parent advocates modeled self-advocacy skills for parents in the project. They prepared parents for meetings—for example, they set up individual education plan meetings, attended the meetings with them, and over time helped the parents feel comfortable advocating for their own children.

Role of the Family

The goal of FCICM is to provide supports and services to keep the child at home and avoid out-of-home placement. Typically, the family enrolled in FCICM had at least one child who was referred for out-of-home placement at the time that the child was admitted to the study. The family in FCICM is the child's primary resource. FCICM views the family as an integral participant in planning, service delivery, advocacy, and decision making, and the services are tailored to facilitate accomplishment of the family's goals.

Parent Training

FCICM uses a modified version of the Parent Skills Training curriculum to disseminate behavior management skills to families. While the content taught remains the same, the delivery is tailored to the immediate needs and circumstances of the family. Unlike FBT, the training is delivered on an individual basis, with the sequence and pace of skills-building determined by the family. This represents a change from the original plan to conduct training in groups. Group training was made difficult by the prolonged period of enrollment, differing concerns of the families, and the distances between families in these rural counties.

Parent Support Groups

In general, group support included the group components that Grealish et al., (1989) identified as particularly important. These included transportation support, child care support, refreshments, and an approach of starting at the parents' level of functioning. Parent support groups evolved differently at each site, though typically support group meetings had a social aspect. Parents shared their experiences, brainstormed ideas, and listened to occasional outside speakers. In one county, parents were referred to existing support groups, and project staff focused their efforts on organizing "family fun" events and activities for siblings. The second county had success holding monthly meetings, and parents who chose to be involved found each other to be a tremendous source of support. In the third county, efforts to organize a support group were unsuccessful. Although individual parent-to-parent support was strong, staff cited distance, transportation problems, and socioeconomic differences among group members as obstacles to the development of groups.

Respite Care

Similar to FBT, trained respite families were available for planned and emergency respite. FCICM respite families received training in the Rest-A-Bit (Donner, 1988) curriculum. Unlike FBT, FCICM families used in-home as well as out-of-home respite care. FCICM parents expressed a preference for in-home respite and the program model was amended accordingly. In-home respite providers were recruited for their experience working with children and adolescents with special needs. When necessary or desired, respite care was also provided for siblings of enrolled children.

Funding

An important component of FCICM is flexible service dollars to support the achievement of treatment goals of individual children and families and to expand the array of services available to all children with SED and their families. From the inception of the project until July 1995, $2,000 per family per year was available. From that date onward between $1,000 and $1,750 was available. A portion of this money is earmarked for general service-system expansion (e.g., after-school programs, psychiatric emergency services), and the remainder (approximately 25%) is available to meet child and family-specific needs. Families play a major part in deciding how these expenditures are made. Unlike the funds expended in the FBT program, these monies may be used for all family members, insofar as expenditures relate to clinical goals, quality of life, and so forth. With oversight from their supervisors, case managers gain access to these funds through automatic teller machine accounts, vouchers, and contracts for services.

Expenditures during the first year of the FCICM program clearly reflect the multiple needs of children and families. Similar to FBT expenditures during the same period, economic expenses (33%) and clinical supports (13%) were among the most common FCICM flexible service dollar expenditure categories. Unlike FBT expenditures, however, in-home respite (16%), social/recreational supports (16%), and school costs (9%) accounted for a large share of disbursements. This pattern reflects the case manager–parent advocate team's charge to do "whatever it takes" to link the children and family to needed services and supports in ways that are consistent with the family's needs and values. The pattern of use is also markedly similar to individualized services provision in other rural areas (Dollard, Evans, Lubrecht, & Schaeffer, 1994).

Methods

Research Design

To test the assertion that a child's parents can provide care as effectively as treatment parents, a research demonstration composed of integrated program and evaluation components was developed. The research used a positive controlled randomized design, meaning that there are two treatment conditions rather than a treatment and no-treatment control condition, in which children 6–12 years of age who are referred to FBT for out-of-home placement are randomly assigned either to FBT or FCICM. A no-treatment group was not used, since treatment foster care has been shown to be superior to no treatment and to more restrictive residential treatment (Hawkins, 1989; Hawkins, Almeida, & Samet, 1989), and since our questions were focused on whether children in intensively supported natural families could experience the same outcomes as children placed in treatment foster care with professional parents. Repeated measures of functioning and problem behaviors were taken at 6-month intervals, including 6 months after discharge.

The demonstration is aimed at determining the child, family, and system outcomes of FCICM and FBT. As a result of random assignment, it was expected that families in both conditions would have similar characteristics and functioning on admission to the study, but that they would begin to evidence differences in status and functioning over the course of the intervention. It was hypothesized that the supports and intensive work with natural families in FCICM would result in building parenting skills and confidence, which in turn were expected to result in benefits to families, particularly in regard to the mental health and functioning of other children in the family. It was also hypothesized that on enrollment, family adaptability and cohesion would be similar in both treatment groups and that, during the treatment period, families of children in FCICM might experience greater strains; on reintroduction of the child in FBT into their natural family, however, the adaptability and cohesion of these families would reflect the strains associated with reintegration and resumption of caring for the child. The target children were expected to show improvement in functioning and a decrease in problem behavior equally across treatment conditions, since both conditions represent intensive treatment approaches. It was also expected that costs would be comparable under the two treatment conditions.

Briefly, the logic model guiding this research indicates that the characteristics of the service system, families, children, and providers of services interact and influence the behaviors of and services offered by case managers, family specialists, and parent advocates. The resulting behaviors and services are believed to affect system outcomes such as differential costs, expenditures of flexible service dollars, and hospitalization rates. Hypothesized family outcomes include improved adaptability and cohesion among families in FCICM, improved self-esteem among siblings in FCICM, and greater confidence in the use of behavior management skills by parents in FCICM than by parents with children enrolled in FBT. These family outcomes and the services directly provided to children are expected to result in symptom reduction and improved functioning of children. We hypothesize that the child outcomes from both interventions are likely to be quite similar during enrollment and at discharge, since both programs are intensive, community-based interventions focused on support and behavior management. However, because of the family supports provided in FCICM, it was expected that children enrolled in this intervention will maintain the level of functioning they had at discharge, while children enrolled in FBT will not necessarily maintain the level of functioning they had at discharge. Because of the intensive supports provided to the family of origin and because the target child in FCICM remains at home rather than being removed and later reintegrated, the siblings in FCICM families are expected to evidence fewer problems and greater self-esteem at the post-discharge follow up.

Instrumentation

The Client Description Form for Children and Adolescents (New York State Office of Mental Health, 1991) and the Baseline Supplemental Form (New York State Office of Mental Health, 1991) are two instruments that were used to elicit information on the demographic characteristics, behavioral and functional status, treatment history, strengths, and unmet needs of each child and family. The child's status in the areas of role performance, thinking, behavior toward others/self, moods and emotions, substance use, and family resources were measured using the Child and Adolescent Functional Assessment Scales (CAFAS; Hodges, 1990) and are completed by the case manager or family specialist.[2] The CAFAS levels range from 0 to 30 and are as follows: Average—no disruption of functioning (score of 0); Mild—significant problems or distress (score of 10); Moderate—major or persistent disruption (score of 20); Severe—severe disruption or incapacitation (score of 30). Higher CAFAS scores indicate greater levels of functional impairment. The CBCL, which is completed by parents, and the Teacher Report Form (TRF; Achenbach, 1991) have nearly identical formats that include 118 behavior problem items with three responses (not true, somewhat or sometimes true, and very true or often true). These items are summed to form a total problem score (T-score) and several subscales, (e.g., anxiety; Freeman, 1985). On both the CBCL and the TRF, T-scores in excess of 63 are considered to be in the clinical range. The Piers-Harris Children's Self-Concept Scale (Piers, 1984), a measure of a child's self-image and self-esteem, is composed of 80 items, administered to children 8 years of age and older. A total raw score is calculated by summing all of the items, with greater scores indicating higher levels of self-esteem. Finally, family adaptability and cohesion were measured by the Family Adaptability and Cohesion Scales III (FACES III; Olson, Portner, & Lavee, 1985). The instrument comprises two scales, with 10 adaptability items (e.g., "Children have a say in their discipline") and 10 cohesion items (e.g., "Family togetherness is very important"). It was administered to all family members over 12 years of age. Midrange family adaptability and cohesion scale scores are considered most positive. Scores at either high or low extremes are considered unfavorable.

Intake and Eligibility Criteria

FBT and FCICM staff and a local interagency referral committee screened families for inclusion in the study. Referral to FBT was usually based on a child's need either for the transition from more restrictive residential care to family living for a period of specialized care when remaining at home is not feasible, or to facilitate successful adoption. Local mental health providers, social services, and schools made the majority of referrals (54%), with an additional 41% from parents, either independently or in conjunction with other human service providers, and the remaining 5% came from other referral sources. The determination of eligibility for the study included a review of psychological, psychiatric, educational, general health and family/social histories and FBT intake criteria (New York State Office of Mental Health, 1990). FBT intake criteria incorporated the New York State Office of Mental Health criteria for SED of (a) a DSM-III-R or DSM IV diagnosis, exclusive of mental retardation, developmental disability, or organic disorder; (b) a history of psychiatric hospitalization, several crisis-related contacts with mental health services or out-of-home placements related to psychiatric impairment; and (c) the risk of imminent hospitalization or other restrictive placement. Two criteria were added for research purposes to ensure comparability between groups. First, children must be between the ages of 6 and 12. Second, the families must not be involved in active child protective cases, ensuring safe living environments for children assigned to FCICM or FBT. A child was not eligible for the project if there was no family with whom the child could live or to whom the child could return.

After examination of referral information, each family met with both the FCICM case manager and the FBT family specialist. If the family decided to participate, the child was screened by the intake committee for eligibility for community-based treatment. If the child was deemed eligible to participate, assignment to FCICM or FBT was made by the research team, witnessed parental consent and child assent were obtained, and the child was enrolled in the program (see Figure 19.1).

The rigorous process of informing families and children of the risks and opportunities that accompany participation in the research protocol made initial dropout from the study nonexistent. Although families can refuse to participate at any time after random assignment to FCICM or FBT, all families

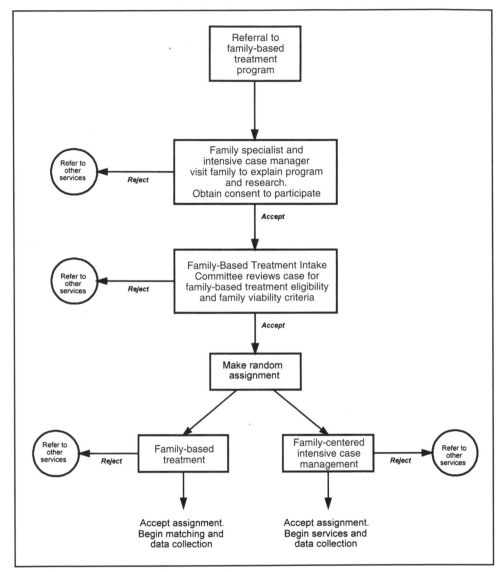

Figure 19.1. Flow chart for the referral process used to assign children to treatment conditions.

who agreed to participate in the research at the onset followed through on their commitment. Issues related to attrition from the study became more pronounced over time, as children and families left active enrollment in the study at various points in time. These issues arose more from natural program processes and were unrelated to refusal to participate in the research protocol.

Description of Children and Families

As of July 1995, 42 children had been randomly assigned and enrolled in either FCICM ($n = 27$) or FBT ($n = 15$). The differences in numbers are due to the use of the Efron's Coin (Efron, 1971) approach for random assignment. This approach facilitates randomization and a balanced design when an unequal number of slots are available in the conditions to which subjects are being randomized. Weights placed on probabilities of condition assignment reflect the relative availability of program slots. Use of this technique allows researchers to retain a random selection procedure while considering the reality of service availability for children and families in great need of service. Some children had enrolled only recently in the intervention and staggered return and analysis of data are reflected in the numbers given. Enrollment data available for the 42 children demonstrate a substantial level of need among the children and their families. At the time of enrollment, there were no significant differences between the characteristics of children in the two interventions (see Table 19.2).

Demographic, functioning, custody, and treatment history were collected with the Client Description Form for Children and Adolescents. As indicated in Table 19.2, children ranged in age from 5–13 years ($M = 9$ years). Ninety percent of enrolled children ($n = 38$) were male. Although this percentage of males was higher than anticipated, the percentage of males in the more restrictive interventions in New York State tends to be around 75% or higher, depending on the age distribution of children in the program. Racial and ethnic characteristics of the sample reflected the geographic areas where the interventions were made and continue to be delivered. Eighty-three percent ($n = 35$) were white, two children were Native American, two children were African American, one child was Hispanic, and two children were of mixed racial/ethnic background. Disruptive behavior disorders, such as attention deficit hyperactivity disorder, were the most common category of primary diagnosis (69%, $n = 29$). Fifty-seven percent ($n = 24$) of the children were educated in either special education or day-treatment classes. Children were found to be functionally impaired in an average of 2.4 ($SD = 1.00$) of 5 areas, with the greatest degree of impairment reported in social relationships (86%, $n = 36$), self-direction (71%, $n = 30$), and cognitive/communication functioning (52%, $n = 22$). In the areas of self-care and motor skills, 17% ($n = 7$) and 10% ($n = 4$), respectively, had difficulty.

Assessments of child functioning ($n = 40$) from the CAFAS are presented in Table 19.2. The majority of children were rated as having major/severe disruption in their behavior toward others (77%, $n = 30$), in their moods and emotions (72%, $n = 28$), and in age-appropriate role performance (74%, $n = 29$). The area of least disruption in functioning was in thinking, where only 31% ($n = 12$) of children were reported as experiencing major or persistent problems or distress. On average, ratings provided by parents completing the CBCL described the children as clinically needy. The mean total problem T-score for children ($n = 40$) was 71

Table 19.2

Characteristics of Children Enrolled in Family-Based Treatment (FBT)
and Family-Centered Intensive Case Management (FCICM)

	FBT			FCICM		
	M	*SD*	*N*	*M*	*SD*	*N*
Age at enrollment	9.24	—	15	9.04	—	27
Race (percentage non-Hispanic white)	87%	—	15	81%	—	27
Gender (percentage male)	87%	—	15	93%	—	27
Number problem behaviors/ symptoms	6.93	3.37	15	6.33	3.64	27
Functional impairment areas	2.73	0.88	15	2.15	1.03	27
Family disruptions	1.64	1.36	11	1.10	1.30	21
CAFAS						
Role performance	20.00	10.00	15	17.69	8.63	26
Cognition	8.67	9.90	15	10.38	8.71	26
Behavior toward self/others	18.00	9.41	15	21.15	7.11	26
Moods/emotions	17.33	5.94	15	18.46	6.75	26
CBCL						
Total problem scale	68.69	8.89	15	74.08	5.80	25
Total internalizing scale	64.90	10.16	15	68.11	9.47	25
Total externalizing scale	68.44	11.35	15	76.30	7.28	25
Selected CBCL subscales						
Somatic scale	60.19	12.31	15	60.97	9.37	25
Social problem scale	63.81	11.69	15	66.27	7.77	25
Thought problem scale	62.87	11.00	15	66.50	8.01	25
Delinquency scale	66.00	9.97	15	74.73	6.01	25
Teacher Report Form						
Total problem *T*-score[1]	70.21	8.75	14	63.30	10.37	20
Piers-Harris						
Total raw score	54.00	12.99	11	49.86	13.94	22

[1]Significantly different group means at enrollment.

(*SD* = 8.9), well within the clinical range. On the major CBCL subscales for internalizing and externalizing problems, mean *T*-scores of 66 (*SD* = 10.6) and 72 (*SD* = 11.5), respectively, were observed. Both of these scores fall in the clinical range (i.e., above *T*-score of 63). Mean raw scores (*M* = 52.6, *n* = 40) on the Piers-Harris Children's Self-Concept Scale showed that the children evidence self-esteem below the normative mean for young boys (Ward & Braun, 1972), and nearly the same as those of behaviorally disordered youth (Bloom, Shea, & Eun, 1979).

At enrollment, unmet service needs for children were reported to be greatest in the areas of recreation (78%, $n = 32$), mental health (51%, $n = 21$), education (41%, $n = 17$), dental (31%, $n = 13$), and medical (22%, $n = 9$). In the mental health area, the greatest need was reported for respite care (34%, $n = 14$). Clinic services (34%, $n = 14$), adjustment to daily living skills training (34%, $n = 14$), psychotropic medication management (7%, $n = 3$), and day treatment (2%, $n = 1$) were also identified as needed services.

In 56% ($n = 23$) of enrolled families, FCICM case managers or FBT family specialists identified poverty as interfering with the child's receipt of services and the ability to remain at home. The next most frequent family problem conditions reported were unstable relationships among parents (54%, $n = 22$), adults abused as children (37%, $n = 15$), and mental illness among parents (44%, $n = 18$). Chronic unemployment (34%, $n = 14$) and domestic violence (27%, $n = 11$) were also cited as substantial problems among families of enrolled children. Family strengths identified by service providers included parents' ability to call the treatment team when necessary (61%, $n = 25$) and to make the child feel loved (56%, $n = 23$). Data on family adaptability and cohesion from FACES III show that a minority of family members perceived their families as falling into the extreme category (16%, $n = 9$), while about equal numbers of family members rated themselves as falling into either the "balanced range" (40%, $n = 23$) or the "midrange" (44%, $n = 25$) family types. These data suggest that many family members shared a positive image of the strength of their families.

Project Management

To provide a broad perspective on both the program and the research, a state-based management team was formed to include the director of the New York State Office of Mental Health Bureau of Children and Families, the assistant director of the Bureau of Evaluation and Services Research, a program implementation specialist, two researchers, and a state-level parent advocate. The state team has convened an annual meeting of consultants who are experts in treatment foster care, health care finance, and research design and methodology. At the local level, provider agency directors or county mental health directors have been actively involved in program implementation and administration.

State team members met regularly with FBT and FCICM staff members and program coordinators from all sites. These meetings made possible a timely response to any issues that affected service delivery or research. Special focus group meetings were arranged to discuss topics such as the role of parent advocates, data collection concerns, behavior management skills training, and enrollment. Training for new staff was provided as needed.

Case Studies of FBT and FCICM

Prior to examining preliminary outcomes for the demonstration project, case studies from the FBT and FCICM interventions will be presented to foster an understanding of the manner in which both programs were operationalized and to portray the complexities of meeting the individualized needs of children and their families in community settings.

 ## FBT—"Ron"

Ron was referred to FBT in late 1993 at the age of 10. He had lived most of his life with tremendous uncertainty—spending more time out of home than with his birth family. He had not had many stable relationships in his life, had trouble in school, and had numerous challenging behaviors. Prior to his referral to FBT, he had been in a residential treatment center for 3 years, and prior to that he had lived with a foster family who eventually adopted two of his siblings but not him. During these years in foster care, Ron was hospitalized and placed in temporary shelter homes frequently.

At the time this case study was prepared in early 1996, Ron had been living with the M. family, an FBT professional family, for 2½ years. Mr. and Mrs. M. had raised six sons, the youngest of whom was 17 when Ron arrived. Ron came to the M. family as an isolated, very angry, and troubled child. He frequently had temper tantrums, experienced enuresis, would not get out of bed in the morning. For long periods of time, he refused to bathe or take care of himself in an age-appropriate way. He hit himself, set fires, had immediate negative responses to authority figures especially in group settings, and was very loud. He truly did not know how to interact with others and, according to his family specialist, he would have been happy to simply "melt into the TV" and do nothing else. Ron had a history of school-related difficulties and was initially described as being very limited academically. He had been in day treatment programs or self-contained special education placements for most of his schooling.

With the support of the M family and the FBT staff, Ron made significant progress. He gradually spent less time in special education and he eventually moved to a parochial school and a regular classroom. He now spends much more time outdoors. His FBT family got Ron involved in a youth soccer league and in the choir at church. Ron loves animals, riding his bike, building models, and he is an excellent cook who plans to become a chef some day. Much of the time, Ron is a fun kid to be around, and he and his FBT family clearly enjoy one another. He sees his siblings once a month. With his FBT family's encouragement, Ron has even started to think far enough into the future to make college and career plans.

Ron learned to interact appropriately with adults and gets along well enough with his classmates, but he still has no real friends. He brags a lot and doesn't know how to initiate activities with others his own age. The family specialist takes him out twice a month with another boy his age and coaches him on how to interact. This is still a significant focus for everyone.

The story of Ron's involvement in FBT is also the story of his professional family's adjustment to their role. Mr. and Mrs. M. missed having children at home and saw parenting Ron as a challenge. It has often been very stressful. This was not a home with a tremendous amount of structure—something Ron needed. The family specialist encouraged the M. family to adopt some basic routines, and Ron responded well. The M. family initially refused respite care and then, when they agreed to try it, they found that many respite providers could not handle Ron's behavior. Eventually a Saturday afternoon and evening respite arrangement was worked out. Ron's FBT mother has learned to react less to his behaviors and to avoid verbal sparring, while giving Ron clear expectations. He has responded well and over time he and his FBT mother have developed a good rapport. Ron's FBT father is devoted to Ron and is a driving force behind this successful relationship.

The family specialist met regularly with Ron, provided ideas for intervening on behavioral issues, linked the family up with a variety of services, advocated for Ron, and provided support to the M. family during stressful times. The family specialist also played a coordinating role among the many professionals in Ron's life: the clinic therapists (he has had three over time), his teachers, his professional parents, his physicians, respite workers, and the Department of Social Services. In one dramatic event, Ron was brought to the emergency room during a crisis with the idea of resuming his medication. The psychiatrist, who had never seen Ron before, reacted strongly and wanted to hospitalize him. The family specialist was able to provide some perspective and assemble an alternative plan to keep Ron at home. Ron's success in school has also been hard-won and requires a constant and knowledgeable facilitator. This responsibility is shared by Ron's FBT father and the family specialist.

Ron is described by everyone as a "new kid," even though he still has significant, long-term mental health treatment and support needs. Unlike many children enrolled in FBT, Ron does not have a family to which he can return. His siblings have experienced continued instability and his teenage sister now lives in a shelter and has a child. Adoption is not an option for the M. family right now, in part because they feel they need the support that FBT offers—both financial and otherwise—to be able to care for Ron. Nevertheless, Ron has made tremendous strides and continues to thrive as a member of the M. family.

 ## FCICM—"Karl"

Karl is a 7-year-old boy who was referred to the study by a staff member at the mental health clinic where he was receiving weekly outpatient therapy. Though his mother, Ms. S, found their current therapist to be helpful, she felt her family needed more comprehensive assistance. As Karl grew older, his aggressive behaviors were increasingly difficult to manage and residential placement had been discussed. Ms. S was adamant that "even with all of his problems, he belongs at home." On referral to the study, Karl was randomly assigned to FCICM.

Karl liked to bowl, fish, and play soccer. His mother described him as a very loving and generous child who could be helpful when he wanted to be. Karl liked school but had low-average school achievement and received additional help in reading and math. Karl's teacher reported that he had some behavioral problems in school and difficulty with peer relationships.

At home, Karl behaved aggressively toward his younger sister and mother. Ms. S reported that he had violent temper tantrums. He was found once putting a pillow over his sister's face, and he had harmed her in other ways. Ms. S. did not feel that she could leave the two children alone for even a few minutes. Karl had purposefully injured a pet hamster and animals he found in the yard and had also set several small fires. His mother was concerned about his increasing withdrawal and "not telling me how he was feeling." He had tried to hang himself with a belt, dashed into busy roads, and engaged in other risk-taking behaviors. He experienced sleep problems, was diagnosed as having depression, and was assessed as functionally impaired in social relationships and self-direction.

Karl's needs contributed to the tension between his mother and stepfather, and the relationship between Karl and his stepfather was difficult. Karl was confused and distressed by the lack of contact with his birth father and imagined his father to be coming for a visit or being able to live with him when there was virtually no contact between them. Karl had lived with his birth father for a period of time, and both Karl and his mother had made allegations of psychological abuse and neglect.

The FCICM team, in conjunction with Ms. S and Karl, made a commitment to keep Karl at home. Over the course of Karl's 2 years in FCICM, the team responded to the changing needs of Karl and his family members. Ms. S's primary concern was with his aggressive behavior at home. The case manager worked with her to assess what triggered Karl's angry outbursts and how she responded, and together they developed strategies for structuring his time and establishing a system of rewards and other consequences.

Ms. S was concerned that she had little time for Karl's younger sister, so respite care was provided for Karl, to permit his mother to spend some time with his sister. When Karl's mother expressed reservations about out-of-home respite, in-home respite care was arranged. When Karl's mother was about to lose her hard-won new job because no family member was willing to care for Karl, a respite worker was found and paid with flexible service funds.

The case manager met with Karl's teachers and arranged remedial help for Karl. Ms. S noted that at least one member of her FCICM team, either the case manager or the parent advocate, had been at every school meeting to "really stick up for me." The case manager also coordinated her work with that of Karl's therapist at the clinic.

Karl's family lived in a rural area and he had little opportunity for recreation, so the FCICM team arranged to have him attend a summer program and *offered support to the program staff. Fees for the summer program were paid with flexible service dollars.*

The case manager continued to work with the family when Karl was hospitalized for 2½ weeks because of a series of increasingly aggressive episodes, culminating in an attempt to suffocate his sister with a pillow. Toward the end of the family's involvement with FCICM, Karl's stepfather filed for divorce and there was a bitter custody fight over Karl's sister in which Karl's behavior was cited as one of the primary reasons maternal custody should be denied. An extended out-of-home respite placement was used during this time to prevent Karl's long-term residential placement. Respite placement was used 3 days a week so Ms. S could have time with Karl's sister, who visited him on weekends at his respite placement home.

The parent advocate provided support to help Ms. S express her feelings about painful past and present personal experiences. Karl's mother said that the parent advocate "is someone who can give me support. She believes me because she has been through this." Ms. S also added that the parent advocate could "make observations as an outsider [to the family] and that she [Ms. S] could see the truth in them." Perhaps most important, Ms. S found that the FCICM team members believed that Karl had special needs and was not simply being bad.

Karl has remained at home and continues to receive both remedial assistance and guidance counseling regularly at school. As a result of her involvement in the FCICM program, Ms. S feels that she has a better sense of "how to stand up for myself and that it can be okay to ask for help." Overall, she was very satisfied with FCICM, saying that it was "different than any service Karl had received before because it is really trying to help me keep him at home."

Preliminary Outcomes

Preliminary outcomes at 12 months after enrollment in FBT or FCICM are shown in Table 19.3. Sample sizes shown in Table 19.3 differ at enrollment from those in Table 19.2 on some measures because of discharges from FCICM and FBT that preceded the next scheduled administration of these measures. The data collection schedule was later adjusted so that a more complete assessment of each child was collected at discharge regardless of when children left either service. TRF data are omitted from Table 19.3 because of difficulties in collecting these data from teachers for some children participating in the study. Nonetheless, outcome measures indicate changes in behavioral, emotional, and functional status of children over time and by program type, assessed within a repeated measures analysis of variance design. Outcomes measured at 12 months or discharge show that children who remained home and received FCICM services were not disadvantaged by remaining in their homes and avoiding placement in treatment foster care homes.

Table 19.3

Changes Between Enrollment (T1) and 12 Months (T2) Among Children in FCICM and FBT (Mean Score Repeated Measures Analysis of Variance)

	FBT			FCICM			Group	Time	Group x Time
	T1	T2	N¹	T1	T2	N	Effect f p	Effect f p	Effect f p
Problem behaviors/symptoms	6.93	3.37	15	6.33	3.64	27	.09; NS²	35.13; .000	.67; ns
CAFAS									
Role performance	18.46	13.08	13	17.78	12.78	18	.03; ns	9.17; .005	.01; ns
Cognition	7.69	4.62	13	9.44	7.22	18	.80; ns	1.71; ns	.04; ns
Behavior	16.15	13.85	13	22.22	12.78	18	1.04; ns	17.52; .000	6.46; .017
Moods/emotions	16.15	14.62	13	20.00	11.67	18	.05; ns	13.17; .001	6.24; .018
CBCL (T-scores)									
Total problem scale	67.25	67.83	12	73.93	69.06	16	3.41; .076	1.62; ns	2.62; ns
Total internalizing scale	63.92	61.17	12	68.17	61.50	16	.74; ns	3.98; .057	.69; ns
Total externalizing scale	67.00	68.67	12	76.46	73.19	16	6.94; .014	.25; ns	2.36; ns
Selected CBCL subscales									
Somatic scale	57.58	54.92	12	61.52	55.38	16	.75; ns	5.18; .031	.81; ns

(continues)

Table 19.3 *Continued*

	FBT			FCICM			Group	Time	Group x Time
	T1	T2	N[1]	T1	T2	N	Effect f p	Effect f p	Effect f p
Social problem scale	62.25	66.50	12	66.29	62.50	16	.00; ns	.01; ns	3.76; .063
Thought problem scale	60.33	63.67	12	67.82	60.81	16	.58; ns	1.07; ns	8.46; .007
Delinquency scale	64.25	65.42	12	74.72	69.81	16	9.16; .006	1.36; ns	3.58; .070
Piers-Harris Total raw score	55.90	55.80	10	50.62	49.62	13	1.43; ns	.05; ns	.03; ns
FACES III Cohesion	36.79	36.93	14	37.18	36.62	21	.00; ns	.04; ns	.11; ns
Adaptability	21.50	22.57	14	23.86	24.86	21	1.85; ns	1.18; ns	.00; ns

[1]Sample sizes shown in Table 19.3 differ at enrollment from those in Table 19.2 on some measures because of discharges from FCICM and FBT that preceded the next scheduled administration of these measures.

[2]*ns* = not significant.

Group Effects

Analyses of measures for differences attributable to assignment to FBT or FCICM show significant difference among children solely from the perspective of the caregiver. Compared to ratings of children in FBT by their parents, children enrolled in FCICM were rated by their parents as being more impaired. Significant group effects were detected on the CBCL total problem scale ($f = 3.41$; $p < .10$), total externalizing scale ($f = 6.94$, $p < .05$), and the delinquency scale ($f = 9.16$; $p < .01$). On all other available measures of child family status, no significant differences were observed. No significant group effects were noted on the Piers-Harris Self-Concept Scale or on FACES III.

Time Effects

Both groups experienced significant reductions ($f = 35.1$; $p < .001$) in problem behaviors and symptomatology between baseline and 12 months. CAFAS measures, indicating changes in child functioning, also showed changes over time, with higher CAFAS scores indicating more severe disruption of functioning ability. Children in both programs experienced significant improvements ($f = 9.17$; $p < .01$) in role performance. Overall, children from both groups also experienced significant improvements in behavior toward self/others ($f = 17.52$; $p = .001$) and moods/emotions ($f = 13.17$; $p < .01$), with children enrolled in FCICM experiencing a much greater rate of improvement than those enrolled in FBT. For example, observed shifts for children enrolled in FCICM in the domains of behavior toward self/others and moods/emotions were from 22.22 to 12.78 and 20.00 to 11.67, respectively, compared to more modest shifts in the same functioning domains from 16.15 to 13.85 and 16.15 to 14.62 for children enrolled in FBT. No significant time effects were noted for the Piers-Harris Children's Self-Concept Scale and for cohesion and adaptability as measured by FACES III.

CBCL measures (expressed as standardized T-scores) provide data from the caregiver perspective. Overall significant improvement ($f = 3.98$; $p < .10$) was observed regarding internalizing behaviors, but neither children in FBT nor FCICM experienced improvement as measured by the total problem or externalizing CBCL scales. On the selected subscales, children showed improvement regarding somatic complaints ($f = 5.18$; $p < .05$).

Interaction Effects

The interaction between the impact of time and program assignment to either FBT or FCICM was found to be significant in two areas of functioning assessed by the CAFAS. In the domains of behavior toward self and others ($f = 6.46$; $p < .05$) and moods and emotions ($f = 6.24$; $p < .05$), significant change was observed due to the interaction between time and program assignment. CBCL data show these differences only in the social problem ($f = 3.76$; $p < .10$), thought problem ($f = 8.46$; $p < .01$) and delinquency subscales ($f = 3.58$; $p < .10$).

These findings are comparable to or better than those observed for children served in similar services in New York State. An evaluation of children served in generic ICM services in New York State detected significant change over time in only the CAFAS behavior toward self/others scale (Huz, Evans, and, McNulty, 1996). The lack of significant change on the CBCL total problem scale, total internalizing scale, and total externalizing scale are also consistent with research on emergency services for children with serious emotional and behavioral problems in New York State.

Discussion

Preliminary data from the project indicate that in both interventions, staff were working with the target group of children and families. Many of these families had been multistressed and had exhausted many of their personal resources and most, if not all, of the treatment options available in their communities. We have learned that once programs have been implemented, it takes time for family specialists and case manager–parent advocate teams to establish linkages and to design creative, individualized services for children and families, especially in resource-poor communities. With this in mind, this discussion focuses on what has been learned to date regarding the design and implementation of FCICM and the conduct of a research demonstration to test the efficacy of both program models.

We had hypothesized that because of the intensity of the interventions, children placed in both study conditions would show improvement over time. Preliminary results support this hypothesis, with both groups experiencing significant reductions in problem behaviors and symptomatology and improvement in role performance over time. Both groups also showed a significant decrease in internalizing behaviors. Children enrolled in FCICM experienced improvement in behavior toward self and others and in moods and emotions as measured by the CAFAS. Greater improvement of children in FCICM was also noted in thought problems, somatic complaints, and delinquency as measured by the CBCL. There were some areas in which no significant improvement occurred, including self-esteem and externalizing behaviors, nor did families in either study condition improve in their adaptability or cohesion.

Overall, based on the preliminary results, it appears that children kept at home with their families were not disadvantaged in terms of positive outcomes and, in some cases, they actually showed greater gains than children who had been placed out of home. These results are encouraging, although it is somewhat disappointing that families enrolled in FCICM failed to show the expected gain in adaptability and cohesion. The general approach to supporting families seems sound, however, and further data analyses are now being undertaken to examine parent satisfaction with services, parent skills, and parental self-efficacy in both study conditions. It is anticipated that caregivers in the FCICM condition should show satisfaction, skills, and self-efficacy superior to those in the FBT condition, because particular services were target to caregivers in FCICM.

Surprisingly, there has been little rigorous research on either therapeutic foster care or case management. A review of the outcomes of therapeutic foster care by Kutash and Rivera (1996) shows that the studies conducted in this area have focused on outcomes for children, particularly restrictiveness of subsequent placement. Additional research is needed to incorporate a range of child and family outcomes related to exposure to therapeutic foster care. Likewise, there have been few controlled studies of case management (Kutash and Rivera, 1996). Those that have been conducted have compared two models of case management (Burns, Farmer, Angold, Costello, & Behar, 1996; Cauce et al., 1994) or compared children under case management with eligible children not under case management (Evans et al., 1994). These studies have focused on child outcomes primarily. Additional study is needed to determine whether there are differential child and family outcomes associated with case management when the intervention is targeted to children or targeted to families.

In addition to the outcomes described above for the current study, there are a number of other lessons learned from this research demonstration. The section that follows identifies some of these lessons.

Local Conditions

Sites began to enroll families in services in the spring of 1991. From this point onward, the project's implementation was influenced by the strengths, experiences, biases, and creativity of service providers, parent advocates, children and their families, agency cultures, and local politics. Because of the different organizations providing services and the resources available in the counties, this project established itself differently in the three counties. The project sites are geographically disparate and each has its own political context and established patterns of delivering services. The study was designed as an effectiveness, rather than an efficacy, study, and the variation in sites and staff represent both a strength (strong external validity) and a challenge (maintaining internal validity) in this research. Such differences among the sites have often introduced a dynamic tension of tailoring the study and its interventions to make them sensitive to local conditions, while still ensuring sufficient similarities among staff, programs, and enrollees to allow for pooling of data. It has been particularly challenging to have program sites located from 60 to 230 miles from the central research office, thus limiting daily face-to-face interactions among key participating agencies. Site visits, periodic multisite meetings and training, and frequent telephone contact have been helpful in maintaining linkages with the sites.

Rural Nature of the Project

The research team was particularly interested in developing interventions that could be used successfully in rural areas, with their unique problems of considerable distances between families and programs, and the common reliance on hospitalization and clinic treatment because of the paucity of resources to support other service options. Even when additional resources became available to these communities, the difficulties of gaining access were barriers to their use. In this project, for example, in-home and out-of-home respite care were available for families in FCICM, and out-of-home respite was available for treatment families in FBT. We soon learned, however, that out-of-home respite was not being used as often as we anticipated, particularly by FCICM families, in part because of the difficulties inherent in transporting a child up to 2 hours to the nearest trained respite provider, and possibly because of the lack of sufficient meetings to help parents develop good relationships with respite providers. Distance, low population density, and service scarcity also played a role in the formation of support groups, the number of unmet service needs, and the nature of flexible service dollar expenditures.

Random Assignment and Enrollment

Several aspects of the random assignment process contributed to a slow rate of enrollment in the project. While both FBT and FCICM shared the goal of strengthening families and of maintaining children in, or returning children to, their families, the stark choice of in-home versus out-of-home placement made the random assignment process difficult. A minority of families were open to either option, but most expressed a strong preference for either FCICM or FBT. Families who declined to participate were referred to other services in the community. Although in some cases families expressed strong preferences for a particular assignment, it is our belief that the families who did agree to participate were those who had exhausted other options; they may, therefore, represent a strong test of both models of community-based services.

Some potential referral sources had difficulty with the lack of control they had in choosing services for their clients. Many providers had concerns that the research team was interfering with their clinical judgment, and some who did refer children were certain that only one of the interventions would result in positive outcomes for a particular child and family. Several clinicians later told us that they were very surprised that a child they had expected to remain in the community only with FBT was actually doing well in FCICM. Referral sources were also slow in processing referrals because of the time it took to complete the extensive paperwork requirements that accompanied all applications.

Our sense of the random assignment process is that the researchers need to maintain control of the process, since it is tempting for clinicians to circumvent the process, and select an option for the child. Moreover, it is occasionally also necessary for the research team to talk directly with clinicians who represent the pool of referrals for the interventions to ensure that they understand the nature of the interventions, the safeguards for the child that are built into the study, and the necessity for experimental studies on the effectiveness of the programs. After some early difficulties encountered with the random assignment process and the consent/assent process, our institutional review board allowed us to modify these processes. Initially, eligible families were informed about the research project and the potential service options, consented to participate (or did not), were then randomly assigned to either FBT or FCICM, and consented to participate (or did not). Under the revised protocol, eligible families were randomly assigned by the researchers to either FBT or FCICM, were informed about the research and their assignment, and then consented to participate (or did not). This one-step consent process seemed to induce less stress in families and appeared to enhance the likelihood of their participation in the research. Other factors that contributed to a slow enrollment were difficult intracounty service provider relationships that blocked likely referral channels, and fewer than anticipated referrals from inpatient settings.

Medicaid/Fiscal Management

Staggered enrollment, resulting in low census, had implications for program funding at each of the sites. This affected Medicaid revenues and produced budget shortfalls. In counties where nonresearch FBT clusters and ICM slots were not available, referring providers were frustrated that they could not use unfilled research slots with families not participating in the research. These same administrators, however, have voiced unequivocal support for the FCICM program model and have demonstrated their commitment by continuing aspects of the enhanced program model with local funding.

Parent Training

Changes were made in the way Parent Skills Training was presented to families in FCICM. Initial planning called for training parents during support group meetings and review of skills during home visits to families. Staggered enrollment, distance, differences in families' education levels, concerns and needs, and the slow start-up of support groups made it preferable to deliver this training to families on an individual basis rather than in group settings. Case managers adapted their use of the materials to individual families, beginning with the skills the parents indicated they most needed, rather than following the curriculum sequentially. In some cases skills were taught without using the written materials because some parents had limited reading ability. In interviews, families often made reference to their use of behavior management skills contained in the curriculum. Additionally, the name of the curriculum was changed because the original title was perceived as pejorative and condescending to parents and parent advocates, even though they embraced the content and objectives of most modules. The name was revised to Behavior Management Skills Training to more accurately capture the intent of the training.

An additional challenge was posed by staff changes. Initial training for new staff and periodic inservice training are necessary to ensure that staff are well trained and comfortable in working with families on behavior management skills. Ongoing training is also an important element in maintaining program fidelity.

Parent Support Groups

From the outset of this project, we incorporated program features that would be useful to parents and, based on their wishes and needs, strived to meet them in a flexible, responsive way. The need to be flexible within the framework of the research design was evidenced time and again. In particular, the challenge of starting and nurturing successful support groups in rural areas cannot be overestimated. For example, parent support groups did not serve as a vehicle for formal training and support as originally planned. Because of their staggered entry into service, geographic distance, and different interests, families did not really form clusters of support. Support group organizers at the three sites had to find ways to bring together diverse groups of parents and help them feel comfortable in meeting as groups. The support groups that were the most successful resolved transportation problems, provided child care and food, met at times that were convenient for families, and had a family-driven agenda. Successful groups also tended to consist of a few core families who developed personal friendships early in the study. Despite the challenges to organizers and parents, however, the goals of providing guidance in behavior management and parent-to-parent support were accomplished. Our experience would argue for a broad definition of support, using multiple strategies for providing support, including parent-to-parent support provided by parent advocates. The project staff also learned to value the importance of family fun nights, social events that engaged families enrolled in the study in social activities. Families expressed feelings of social isolation because of the rural nature of their community and their child's behavior, which often made them unwelcome at other social events. They also reminded staff that many of their contacts with others involved seeking services for their child or receiving training. They were concerned that they learn skills related to having fun as a family and have opportunities for engaging in enjoyable activities.

Another strategy of fostering support is one developed by parents. Telephone support on an informal basis occurred between several dyads of families in the project who met at support groups or social events. In one county, this unplanned and informal support by telephone was especially important to families during a period of staff transition.

Flexible Funding

Flexible funding is an important tool in the provision of individualized services, and staff at the program sites were creative in the use of flexible service dollars in responding to the needs of children and families, particularly in the area of recreational services. Other studies have shown that when asked, parents frequently cite the need for recreational activities in which children with special needs can participate (Palma, 1994; Trupin, Forsyth-Stephens, & Low, 1991). The rural nature of our study counties also contributed to the challenges of meeting the recreational needs of children and their families. Preliminary data show that the proportion of children in both interventions with unmet recreational needs decreased over time as flexible service money or subsistence allowance monies were spent on recreational activities. Recreation, nevertheless, continues to be an important unmet need for some children enrolled in the study.

Flexible funding was also used to purchase in-home respite. Although not used as extensively as anticipated when the research was designed, in-home respite was an important option for many families.

Role of the Parent Advocate and the Parent–Provider Relationship

While the process of defining the priorities and roles for parent advocates is ongoing, parent advocates have emerged as important players at each site. Parent advocates each formed a highly effective partnership with the case manager and achieved high levels of coordination and trust. Case managers, parents, and local program coordinators all expressed a strong belief that the parent advocate role provided important support to families in the project and had a much broader influence as well. Having regular contact with a colleague who is the parent of a child with SED increased awareness in the professional community about the multiple strengths and needs of families. This awareness was further heightened when a parent advocate needed flexibility and support during periods of her child's hospitalization or during a crisis.

Parents pointed out that parent advocates understand what they have experienced and do not blame them. They described a very different type of support that can come only from someone who has struggled to obtain services and shared the uncertainties of raising a child with SED. Parent advocates have a repertoire of strategies (e.g., coping with erratic behaviors, navigating the "system") that they share with parents.

Over the course of the project, a great deal has been learned about the roles that parents can play in service provision and research. The unique personal styles of the parent advocates who are working or have worked with families in FCICM have expanded our understanding of the multiple contributions that such parents can make in individualizing care. At the family level, they offer specific advice on topics ranging from accessing educational services to developing household budgets, an essential task for many of the families because of their limited incomes. At a program and policy level, they have contributed to the design and conduct of research demonstrations (e.g., a parent advocate was a member of our project management team).

In working with parents, parent advocates must maintain a distinct perspective. On one hand, parent advocates must act as allies of parents who are often at odds with the established system. At the same time, the advocates must understand and work with the complex service system without becoming co-opted by it. This has a number of practical implications and raises the questions of who should employ and supervise parent advocates and what activities should *not* be a part of the parent advocate's job description (e.g. serving as assistant case managers, spending more time with the children than the parents, etc.). Moreover, to be effective, parent advocates need a certain amount of flexibility to modify their role to fit their strengths and to meet the needs of communities, different cultural groups, and individual parents. Parent advocates also need a support system of other parents and committed liaisons in key places within the formal service system.

Other Lessons Learned

Finally, despite the multiple stressors to which the families in both interventions have been exposed, we have learned about the strengths that they bring to caring for their children. Although this project is not yet finished, we note support for the assertion that, given intensive and individualized supports, children with SED, including those referred for out-of-home placement, can be cared for effectively in their own homes. Preliminary data on functioning, symptoms, and behaviors show that children maintained in their own homes do not appear to be disadvantaged when compared to their peers who have been placed out of their homes. Overall, the families of children placed in FCICM, while still grappling with their children's special needs, were grateful to have the opportunity and the support to keep their child at home. Many parents expressed new confidence in their capacity to care for their children with support, and families appear to have gained skills that may be helpful in parenting children with special needs and their other children.

We learned through this study that the original FCICM model was too component driven. There was an implicit assumption that families would need and use all of the various services included in the model. Families receiving FCICM have taught us firsthand what "individualized" means and how to use a strengths-based assessment that begins with what each family says it needs. We have learned, for example, that many families do not initially want out-of-home respite care and are much more comfortable with and willing to use in-home respite care when it is tailored to their needs. We have also learned that families are unique in the kinds of support they need and want. Many families do not want or do not have the time to attend family support groups but welcome a telephone support system and other forms of informal support. Karl's mother, for example, lived over an hour away from where the support group met, a common occurrence in rural areas, and she did not especially want to be a member of the group.

To date, the lessons we have learned from this research demonstration project have helped us plan an agenda of additional research projects and new service initiatives. Meanwhile, we look forward to completing the data collection and analysis on this research demonstration and hope to provide a complete report of the study's findings within a year.

Endnotes

1. The terms "family," "family of origin," and "parents" include adoptive families, biological families, stepfamilies, and families composed of the child and other relatives. "Family" is used to describe the people with whom the child regularly makes his or her home, to distinguish them from the treatment families in FBT.

2. The psychometric properties of the Child and Adolescent Functional Assessment Scales, Child Behavior Checklist, Teacher Report Form, Piers-Harris Children's Self-Concept Scale, and Family Adaptation and Cohesion Scales III have been investigated and are reported elsewhere.

Authors' Note

The authors are indebted to Elizabeth Pease of the New York State Office of Mental Health's Bureau of Evaluation and Services Research for her critical reading and revision of this manuscript. The authors are also indebted to the staff of Franklin County Community Services and North Star Industries, Inc., in Franklin County; the Northern New York Center in Clinton County; the Mental

(continues)

Authors' Note *Continued*

Health Association in Ulster County, Inc.; Pathways, Inc.; Steuben County Mental Health in Steuben County; and the families who are enrolled in this study for their help in conducting this research demonstration project.

Mary E. Evans, RN, PhD, is a visiting research professor, College of Nursing, University of South Florida in Tampa. Until recently, Dr. Evans was principal research scientist at the New York State Office of Mental Health. Dr. Evans earned her doctorate in sociology from the University at Albany of the State University of New York. She has been working in services research for over 20 years and is currently the principal investigator of three federally funded research demonstration grants in children's mental health services in New York State.

Mary I. Armstrong, MBA, MSW, is the director of the division of State and Local Activities in the Department of Child and Family Studies, Florida Mental Health Institute, University of South Florida. She was previously the Director of the Bureau of Children and Families in the New York State Office of Mental Health. Ms. Armstrong earned her MBA degree from the University at Albany of the State University of New York and her MSW degree from Temple University. Ms. Armstrong worked in child and adolescent services for over 25 years in New York and Pennsylvania.

Anne D. Kuppinger, MEd, is a program development and implementation specialist in the Bureau of Children and Families in the New York State Office of Mental Health. Ms. Kuppinger earned her master's degree in education from the University of Maryland. She has diverse experience with children, including teaching, working for the Center

(*continues*)

Authors' Note *Continued*

for the Study of Social Policy, and serving as a consultant on family preservation services throughout the country.

Steven Huz, MPA, is a research scientist II with the Bureau of Evaluation and Services Research in the New York State Office of Mental Health. Mr. Huz earned his master's degree in public administration/policy analysis from the Nelson A. Rockefeller College of Public Affairs and Policy, University of Albany, State University of New York. His experience includes 15 years in needs assessment and services research.

Thomas L. McNulty, PhD, is an assistant professor in the Department of Sociology at the University of Georgia. He earned his doctoral degree in sociology from the University at Albany, State University of New York. Dr. McNulty, who has served as primary data analyst on this project, has had several years of experience working with Dr. Evans and Mr. Huz on the evaluation of intensive case management for children and youth.

References

Achenbach, T. M. (1991). *Manual for the child behavior checklist and 1991 profile.* Burlington: University of Vermont, Department of Psychiatry.

Armstrong, M. I., & Evans, M. E. (1992). Three intensive community-based programs for children with serious emotional disturbance. *Journal of Child and Family Studies, 1,* 61–74.

Bloom, R. B., Shea, R. J., & Eun, B. (1979). The Piers-Harris self-concept scale: Norms for behaviorally disordered children. *Psychology in the Schools, 16,* 483–487.

Bryant, B. (1981). Special foster care. *Journal of Clinical Child Psychology, 10,* 8–20.

Burchard, J. D., & Clarke, R. T. (1990). The role of individualized care in a service delivery system for children and adolescents with severely maladjusted behavior. *Journal of Mental Health Administration, 17,* 48–60.

Burns, B. J., Farmer, E. M. Z., Angold, A., Costello, E. J., & Behar, L. (1996). A randomized trial of case management for youths with serious emotional disturbances. *Journal of Clinical Child Psychology, 25,* 476–486.

Cauce, A. M., Morgan, C. J., Wagner, V., Moore, E., Sy, J., Wurzbacher, K., Weeden, K., Tomlin, S., & Blanchard, T. (1994). Effectiveness of intensive case management for homeless adolescents: Results of a three month follow-up. *Journal of Emotional and Behavioral Disorders, 2*(4), 219–227.

Cole, R. F., & Poe, S. L. (1993). *Partnerships for care: Interim report of the mental health services program for youth.* Washington, DC: Washington Business Group of Health.

Dollard, N., Evans, M. E., Lubrecht, J., & Schaeffer, G. (1994). The use of flexible service dollars in rural community-based programs for children with serious emotional disturbance and their families. *Journal of Emotional and Behavioral Disorders, 2,* 117–125.

Donner, R. (1988, June). *Rest-a-bit: Respite care training project.* Topeka, KS: Families Together.

Dougherty, D. M., Saxe, L. M., Cross, T., & Silverman, N. (1987). *Children's mental health: Problems and services.* [A report by the Office of Technology Assessment]. Durham, NC: Duke University Press.

Efron, B. (1971). Forcing a sequential experiment to be balanced. *Biometrika, 58,* 403–417.

Evans, M. E. (1990). *Outcomes of two intensive services for children.* Proposal submitted to the National Institute of Mental Health (1 R18 MH 48072/CMHS 5HD5 SM 48072). Albany: New York State Office of Mental Health, Bureau of Evaluation and Services Research.

Evans, M. E., Armstrong, M. I., Dollard, N., Kuppinger, A. D., Huz, S., & Wood, V. M. (1994). Development and evaluation of treatment foster care and family-centered intensive case management in New York. *Journal of Emotional and Behavioral Disorders, 2,* 228–239.

Evans, M. E., Armstrong, M. I., & Kuppinger, A. D. (1996). Family-centered intensive case management: A step toward understanding individualized care. *Journal of Child and Family Studies, 5,* 55–65.

Evans, M. E., Banks, S. M., Huz, S., & McNulty (1994). Initial hospitalization and community tenure outcomes of intensive case management for children and youth with serious emotional disturbance. *Journal of Child and Family Studies, 3,* 225–234.

Freeman, B. J. (1985). *Review of the child behavior checklist in the ninth mental measurement yearbook.* Lincoln: University of Nebraska Press.

Friedman, R. M., & Duchnowski, A. J. (1990). Children's mental health: Challenges for the nineties. *Journal of Mental Health Administration, 17,* 3–12.

Grealish, E. M., Hawkins, R. P., Meadowcroft, P., Weaver, P., Frost, S. S., & Lynch, P. L. (1989). A behavioral group procedure for parents of severely troubled and troubling youths in out-of-home care: Alternative to conventional training. *Child and Youth Care Quarterly, 18,* 49–61.

Hawkins, R. P. (1989). The nature and potential of therapeutic foster care programs. In R. P. Hawkins & J. Breiling (Eds.), *Therapeutic foster care: Critical issues* (pp. 5–36). Washington, DC: Child Welfare League of America.

Hawkins, R. P., Almeida, M. C., & Samet, M. (1989). *Comparative evaluation of foster family–based treatment and five other placement choices: A preliminary report.* Paper presented at the Conference on Children's Mental Health Services & Policy, Tampa, FL.

Hodges, K. (1990, October). *Child and adolescent functional assessment scales.* Nashville, TN: Vanderbilt Child Mental Health Services Evaluation Project.

Huz, S., Evans, M. E., & McNulty. T. L. (1996). *Outcomes of intensive case management for children and youth in New York state—Final evaluation report.* Albany: New York State Office of Mental Health, Bureau of Evaluation and Services Research.

Huz, S., Evans, M. E., Rahn, D. S., & McNulty, T. L. (1993). *Evaluation of intensive case management for children and youth: Year 3 final report.* Albany: New York State Office of Mental Health, Bureau of Evaluation and Services Research.

Huz, S., McNulty, T. L., & Evans, M. E. (1994, June). *Family based treatment in New York State: Evaluation report.* Albany: New York State Office of Mental Health, Bureau of Evaluation and Services Research.

Katz-Leavy, J. W., Lourie, I. S., Stroul, B. A., & Zeigler-Dendy, C. (1992, July). Individualized services in a system of care. In *Profiles of local systems of care for children and adolescents with severe emotional disturbances* (pp. 7–11). Washington, DC: Georgetown University, CASSP Technical Assistance Center.

Knitzer, J. (1982). *Unclaimed Children.* Washington, DC: Children's Defense Fund.

Kutash, K., & Rivera, V. R. (1996). *What works in children's mental health services? Uncovering answers to critical questions.* Baltimore: Brookes.

New York State Office of Mental Health. (1990). *Family-based treatment program description.* Albany: New York State Office of Mental Health, Bureau of Children and Families.

New York State Office of Mental Health. (1991). *Baseline supplemental form.* Albany: New York State Office of Mental Health, Bureau of Evaluation and Services Research.

New York State Office of Mental Health. (1991). *Client description form.* Albany: New York State Office of Mental Health, Bureau of Evaluation and Services Research.

New York State Office of Mental Health. (1992). *At the crossroads: Expanding community-based care for children and families: The New York State plan for children and families mental health services.* Albany: New York State Office of Mental Health, Bureau of Children and Families and the Bureau of Planning, Assistance and Coordination.

Olson, D. H., Portner, J., & Lavee, Y. (1985). *Family adaptability and cohesion scales III.* St. Paul: University of Minnesota, Family Social Science.

Palma, P. B. (1994). *Responding to the needs of families: Preliminary results of families of children receiving intensive case management services.* Poster presented at the 7th annual System of Care for Children's Mental Health: Expanding the Research Base. Tampa: University of South Florida, Florida Mental Health Institute, Research and Training Center for Children's Mental Health.

Piers, E. V. (1984). *Manual for the Piers-Harris children's self-concept scale.* Nashville, TN: Counselor Recordings and Tests.

Saxe, L., Cross, T., & Silverman, N. (1988). Children's mental health: The gap between what we know and what we do. *American Psychologist 41,* 800–807.

Snodgrass, R. (1986). *Parent skills training.* Staunton, VA: People Places.

Snodgrass, R., & Bryant, B. (1991). *New York family-based treatment program year-end report to the office of mental health.* Staunton, VA: People Places.

Solomon, P. (1992). The efficacy of case management services for severely mentally disabled clients. *Community Mental Health Journal, 28,* 163–180.

Surles, R. C., & Blanch, A. K. (1989). *Case management as a strategy for systems change.* Paper presented at the Innovation and Management in Public Mental Health Systems Conference, Philadelphia.

Stroul, B. A., & Friedman, R. M. (1986). *A system of care for severely emotionally disturbed children and youth.* Washington, DC: Georgetown University, CASSP Technical Assistance Center.

Trupin, E. W., Forsyth-Stephens, A., & Low, B. P. (1991). Service needs of severely disturbed children. *American Journal of Public Health, 81,* 975–980.

Ward, S. H., & Braun, J. R. (1972). Self-esteem and racial preference in black children. *American Journal of Orthopsychiatry, 42,* 644–647.

Improving Access to Children's Mental Health Services: The Family Associate Approach

20

Debra J. Elliott, Nancy M. Koroloff,
Paul E. Koren, and Barbara J. Friesen

Parents who face a new situation with their child often turn to a grandparent, aunt, friend, or neighbor for advice. However, when a child suffers from an emotional disorder and needs mental health treatment, support and advice are sometimes unavailable. Parents are often unclear about whom to call, unable to afford the costs associated with weekly appointments, and afraid of what lies ahead in treatment. This may be especially true for low-income families and for those who lack experience with the mental health system.

In this chapter, we describe an intervention designed to provide outreach to low-income families whose children have been identified as needing mental health services. The intervention was intended to encourage and enable families to enroll their children in mental health services and to continue the services as recommended. It involved the use of paraprofessionals, called family associates, who served as system guides, providing families with information, emotional support, and help with specific barriers such as lack of transportation or child care. To evaluate this intervention, we focused on how well families receiving it initiated and continued mental health services in comparison to a sample of families who did not receive it. In addition, since families' sense of mastery over various aspects of their lives might influence their ability to initiate and use services, we also examined the issue of empowerment. To begin, we present an overview of research about service initiation and dropout, the concept of empowerment, and the potential benefits of paraprofessional outreach.

Service Continuance

Depending on the definition of service dropout used and the phases of the intake and treatment process considered, estimates of dropout rates for children in mental health services range between 25 and 93% (Mannarino, Michelson, Beck, & Figueroa, 1982; Sirles, 1990; Wierzbicki & Pekarik, 1993). Definitions of dropout varied throughout the literature from failure to attend a scheduled session to idiosyncratic judgments by therapists of inappropriate termination. The findings from two meta-analyses (Garfield, 1986; Wierzbicki & Pekarik, 1993) suggest that dropout rates for both adults and children are related to such demographic variables as lower socioeconomic status, low level of education, and minority racial status. Other researchers note that demographic characteristics, especially income, are not consistently related to continuance (Day & Reznikoff, 1980; Sirles, 1990; Sledge, Moras, Hartley, & Levine, 1990) or are not as important as service-delivery-system issues (Goldin, 1990; Good, 1990; Sirles, 1990; Wise & Rinn, 1983). Additionally, the severity of problems may influence service continuance, with those children experiencing less severe problems being more likely to drop out of service, especially if the assessment process was prolonged (Sirles, 1990).

Furthermore, the research focus has shifted from demographic characteristics of service recipients to service-system barriers and pragmatic day-to-day problems. Researchers have increasingly addressed barriers related to affordability (Lorefice, Borus, & Keefe, 1982; Sharfstein & Taube, 1982; Takeuchi, Leaf, & Kuo, 1988), transportation and child care (Margolis & Meisels, 1987; Temkin-Greener, 1986), accessibility (Acosta, 1980; Cohen, 1972; Graziano & Fink, 1973; Stefl & Prosperi, 1985), and system characteristics such as the availability of services (Leaf, Bruce, Tischler, & Holzer, 1987; Scott, Balch, & Flynn, 1984; Stefl & Prosperi, 1985), hours of operation and configuration of services (Good, 1990; Margolis & Meisels, 1987; Sledge et al., 1990), and delays in scheduling appointments (Leigh, Ogborne, & Cleland, 1984; Sirles, 1990).

Low-income families are particularly challenged by the difficulties of meeting basic daily living needs, which can interfere with accessing and continuing services for their children. In a study of children with developmental disabilities who had been screened through the Early and Periodic Screening, Diagnosis, and Treatment program (EPSDT), Margolis and Meisels (1987) identified three sets of barriers to services: (a) content barriers, such as problems with the design and organization of the screening process, as well as the sensitivity of the screening process to the needs of children with disabilities; (b) facilities-personnel barriers, such as a lack of public awareness of EPSDT, lack of transportation, and lack of sensitivity and knowledge about developmental disabilities on the part of the health care professionals; and (c) referral barriers, such as lack of qualified providers and parents' inability to pay for additional services not reimbursed by Medicaid. Other research on barriers to services (Manela, Anderson, & Lauffer, 1977; Meisels & Margolis, 1988) suggests that efforts to address the problem of families ending services prematurely are best served by identifying practical solutions directly with the caregivers. The large number and wide variety of barriers that are being identified suggest that interventions must take a flexible approach that addresses the unique circumstances.

Empowerment

Although the concept of empowerment has been in use for some time, only recently have efforts been made to define and measure it as a construct that lends itself to outcome evaluation (Heflinger, 1995; Koren, DeChillo, & Friesen, 1992; Singh, Janes, & Schechtman, 1982). Empowerment may be defined as "the ongoing capacity of individuals or groups to act on their own behalf to achieve a greater measure of control over their lives and destinies" (Staples, 1990, p. 30). This general notion has broad applicability and can be used to describe a variety of circumstances. Historically, empowerment has been accepted as an explanatory mechanism for describing relationships among groups. Thus, for example, groups or communities who gain control over their own resources and who develop a sense of self-efficacy relative to the greater society are seen as achieving a degree of empowerment. While this perspective of empowerment based on groups is still very prevalent, the concept has been expanded to include the experiences of individuals as well (Gutierrez & Ortega, 1991; Solomon, 1976). Thus the literature supports thinking about empowerment in three distinct ways (a) the empowerment of individuals with respect to their own circumstances, (b) the empowerment of individuals with respect to others, and (c) the empowerment of groups in relation to the larger society.

For children's mental health, Koren et al. (1992) suggested three major domains in which parents and other caregivers can express and achieve empowerment: their immediate families, the service system as it directly affects their own children and families, and the community as it affects children and families in general. Family members may express empowerment in each of these separate areas. Empowerment within the family pertains to a sense of efficacy in handling difficulties at home and managing day-to-day circumstances. Empowerment with respect to the service system involves taking action to obtain appropriate services for one's child and generally functioning as an active, knowledgeable consumer. Community/political empowerment signifies efforts to improve services for families and children in general and includes activities ranging from public advocacy to forming parent support groups. Koren et al. (1992) developed an instrument for measuring these three types of empowerment and reported positive findings on its psychometric properties. These findings were subsequently and independently confirmed by Singh et al. (1995), although they suggested a somewhat different conceptual scheme for scoring item responses.

This three-pronged view of empowerment has substantial relevance to evaluating the effects of service interventions. To the extent that services are successful in helping families address difficulties with their children, parents' feelings of empowerment within their own families may be expected to grow. Also, the knowledge and understanding gained through experience with the service system may affect parents' sense of empowerment in either a positive or negative direction. The third type of empowerment, community/political empowerment, has less direct plausibility as an intervention outcome, as it is probably a reflection of many factors including altruism, opportunity, and the extent to which an individual has an outgoing nature. In this study, we viewed the process of helping families overcome barriers to service utilization as potentially leading to an increased sense of both family empowerment and system empowerment.

Paraprofessionals

Several fields of practice have traditionally employed paraprofessionals to assist with service delivery. These include health care (Dawson, Van Doorninck, & Robinson, 1989; Poland, Giblin, Waller, & Hankin, 1992; Sparer & Johnson, 1971), education (Frith & Lindsey, 1980; Jones & Bender, 1993) and mental health (Durlak, 1973; Gartner, 1981; Karlsruher, 1974). A number of studies have examined the functions that paraprofessionals have served. Sobey (1970) studied 10,000 paraprofessionals and found that they performed three major functions (therapeutic, special skill training, and community adjustment) and five less frequently mentioned functions (case finding, orientation to services, screening, caretaking, and community improvement). She concluded that paraprofessionals were employed "not simply because professional manpower is unavailable, but rather to provide new services in innovative ways" (p. 133). Frith and Armstrong (1984) identified a number of reasons for expanding the use of paraprofessionals, including versatility in working within different settings, the ability to work with highly diverse groups, an established track record in efficacy studies, cost effectiveness, and greater availability compared to professional staff, particularly in rural areas. They emphasized the utility of the paraprofessional as an intermediary between service providers and the community.

The family associate role was created to address the major problems associated with children's mental health service initiation and continuance, particularly those encountered by low-income families. These barriers include the cost of travel and child care associated with frequent appointments, limited information about the service system, problems accessing community resources, unmet caregiver needs, and the challenges of daily living in poverty. The intervention was intended to ultimately increase the number of families who receive mental health services for their children. This was accomplished by having the family associate work with the families to reduce the barriers to service involvement. The research focused on whether Family Associate services increased children's mental health service initiation, attendance, and continuance, and the empowerment of parents or other caregivers. Additionally, we were interested in describing the barriers to children's mental health services encountered by families and the extent to which the Family Associate Intervention addressed them.

Method

Participants

Families with a child 4–18 years old who had been referred for mental health services through EPSDT were included if: (a) the referred child was not in an institutional placement (e.g., residential treatment, correctional facility), (b) a caregiver was involved in the management of the child's mental health services and was available for the research interviews, and (c) the referred child had participated in no more than three mental health services appointments associated with this referral. Families were excluded from the study if (a) no follow-up interview was completed ($n = 14$), (b) the respondents were foster parents whose resources and mental health service system experiences were different from those of the other families ($n = 16$), (c) the family was identified as ineligible after performing the initial interview ($n = 12$), or (d) no contact with the family associate occurred beyond the initial interview ($n = 15$). This resulted in a final sample of 239 families, 96 of whom received the intervention and 143 of whom served as comparison families.

The respondents in the intervention group were primarily birth parents (91%), single parents (74%), and educated at the high school level or higher (78%). Over half of the children in the intervention group who were referred for mental health services were boys (61%), the majority between 4 and 12 years of age (88%). Eighty-two percent of the children were white, 7% were African American, 4% were American Indian, 3% were Hispanic, and 3% were Asian-Pacific Islander (percentages have been rounded). Over two thirds of the families had an annual household income of less than $10,000 (71%) and an annual household income per person of less than $3,000 (72%). Most of the families (74%) lived within 9 miles of the mental health center to which they were referred. No statistically significant differences were found between the comparison and intervention groups on any of these demographic characteristics (see Table 20.1).

Procedures

Design

For this research, a quasi-experimental design incorporating two conditions was used: an intervention condition in three Oregon counties using family associates (one in each county) to augment the usual mental health services, and a comparison condition in four other Oregon counties consisting of only

Table 20.1

Family Characteristics By Group

Characteristic	Intervention Group[a]		Comparison Group[b]	
	n	Percentage	*n*	Percentage
Respondent's relationship to child				
Birth parent	87	91	128	90
Other	9	9	15	10
Respondent's marital status				
Single parent[c]	71	74	93	56
Married	25	26	50	35
Respondent's educational level				
No high school diploma	21	22	30	21
High school diploma	36	37	42	29
Beyond high school	39	41	71	50
Child's gender				
Female	37	39	57	40
Male	59	61	86	60
Child's age				
4–7 years	42	44	71	50
8–12 years	42	44	54	38
13–18 years	12	12	18	12
Child's race				
White	79	82	114	80
Other	17	18	29	20
Annual household income				
< $10,000	68	71	96	67
$10,000–$19,999	21	22	38	27
$20,000+	7	7	9	6
Annual household income per person				
< $2,000	26	27	33	23
$2,000–$2,999	43	45	69	48
$3,000–$4,999	19	20	30	21
$5,000+	8	8	11	8
Distance to the mental health office				
≤1 mile	19	20	25	18
2–4 miles	29	30	36	26
5–9 miles	23	24	40	29
10–19 miles	13	13	20	15
20+ miles	12	13	16	12

[a]*n* = 96. [b]*n* = 143. [c]Includes respondents who were divorced, separated, widowed, or never married.

the usual mental health services. No condition involved the withholding of services; instead, the intervention condition supplemented the services families would have otherwise received under EPSDT. Counties were randomly assigned to either the intervention or comparison groups from three pairs of matched counties that were approximately equal in population density and proximity to metropolitan areas with extensive and specialized mental health services. After the project began, a seventh county was added to the comparison condition to augment referrals.

Intervention

The Family Associate intervention was developed to address the barriers to accessing mental health services that low income families might encounter, thus increasing the number of families who ultimately access and use mental health services for their children. The key components of the intervention were support and tangible service provided through parent-to-parent contact. As family associates modeled new skills and collaborated with the caregivers, they encouraged self-reliance and supported family strengths, served as system guides, and helped families maneuver within the mental health system. For example, many times family associates taught family members how to locate free resources in the community, as well as how to proactively get their voices heard within the service system.

The family associates received referrals through the EPSDT process within their respective counties. In order to intervene early in the service initiation process when dropout was most likely (Baekeland & Lundwall, 1975; Larsen, Attkisson, Hargreaves, & Nguyen, 1979; Sirles, 1990), the family associates contacted the parents or other caregivers soon after the referral for mental health services was made. Following the completion of a research interview, the family associates began providing services, the most common of which were (a) providing families with information (e.g., pamphlets on emotional disorders in children), (b) providing caregivers with social and emotional support through personal contact and telephone support, and (c) linking families to community resources and services.

An innovative feature of this intervention was the availability of a flexible cash fund. Each county was allocated approximately $250 in grant funds per family to spend throughout the duration of the project. The purpose of this fund was to help families obtain those services or items that were identified as instrumental in getting their children to mental health services or in easing their daily living burden. Expenses for which the flexible cash support fund were used included the following:

1. Child care, especially for the family's other children while the referred child attended appointments.

2. Transportation costs including public transportation, gasoline, car repairs, and automobile insurance.

3. Clothing and personal effects for family members.

4. Recreational activities to help the child, parent, or family reduce tension and interact with the community.

5. Respite care to temporarily relieve parents from the ongoing responsibility of taking care of children with an emotional or behavioral disorder.

The family associates were recruited and hired by the county mental health programs in which they worked. The three family associates were women, two of whom had previous experience accessing complex service systems for their own children. The third family associate was the parent of young children who had previous experience receiving public assistance. One of the family associates was African American. None of the three had prior training as a mental health service provider, although all three had worked in paraprofessional or support staff positions and were familiar with the internal workings of social services. The family associate in the largest county worked full-time with approximately 10 families at one time, whereas the family associates in the two smaller counties worked half-time, with approximately five families at one time.

Before data collection began, two multiple-day training sessions for the family associates and their supervisors were conducted. During the first training session, we provided an overview of the philosophy of the project and the family associate role, an orientation to family support concepts and services, and an introduction to available community resources. The training also included a discussion of ways to implement the role and to define boundaries. We emphasized working with the families to demonstrate how to get their needs met without creating a dependent relationship on the project. During the second training session, the family associates shared common strategies and experiences and helped us work through a number of critical issues that became evident during the 3-month trial period. An ongoing theme was the need to clarify the relationship between the family associate role and the traditional provision of mental health services.

Early in the process, supervision was recognized as a critical support to the family associates. Because the family associates made the initial contact with families, it was important that they have support and backup from a trained mental health professional. The project was designed such that the supervision was provided either by the person responsible for monitoring EPSDT procedures and services or by another qualified mental health professional. Over time, the family associates' supervision needs changed. Initially, supervisory discussion focused on finding local resources, learning county-specific procedures, and developing relationships with referral sources and mental health providers in the county. These last two issues were significant because the county mental health systems had not previously employed a paraprofessional working directly with families, nor had they used flexible funding to meet families' needs. Later in the project, the focus of supervision shifted to the needs of families who were involved in multiple services and whose circumstances were more difficult.

Data Collection

Procedures for obtaining the EPSDT referral information were established separately with each of the seven participating counties. Referrals were usually collected at medical facilities, schools, mental health agencies, the county mental health and health programs, or a combination of these sites, depending upon the primary referral source(s) for a given county. As soon as possible after receiving the referral, the initial contact was made by either letter or telephone by the family associates (in the case of intervention families) and research interviewers (in the case of comparison families). If the caregiver agreed to participate, an appointment for the initial research interview was made, with the option that the interview could take place at the caregiver's home for her or his convenience. After securing the caregiver's informed consent, the initial interview and associated questionnaires were completed (taking approximately 1½ hours). The caregiver was paid $25 for providing the information.

The family associates began their first contact with families by collecting research data; family associate services were discussed only after the research interview was completed. Initial interviews with comparison families, as well as the follow-up interviews with all families, were conducted by research interviewers. Extensive instruction about data collection and research interviewing was incorporated into the project orientation and training meetings for the family associates; the project manager provided this instruction separately for the research interviewers. Periodic meetings and telephone contacts with both the family associates and the research interviewers were done to monitor the integrity of the data-collection process.

Immediately following the initial research interview, the family associates began working with each family until the referred child had participated in three mental health appointments or for 3 months, whichever came first. The family associates compiled additional data in the form of a log documenting the details of their work with each family and a final rating of the barriers to mental health services experienced by the families while they were involved with the family associates. Approximately 4 months after the initial research interview, research interviewers contacted caregivers to schedule the follow-up interview. This interval allowed enough time for family associate services to be completed and the opportunity for mental health services to be initiated. At the follow-up interview, caregivers were asked about experiences in the intervening period and completed a second set of questionnaires. For doing this, each caregiver received another $25.

Measures

The data collection protocol included both widely used and newly developed measures. In order to meet the needs of the large Hispanic population in Oregon, all of the questionnaires were translated into Spanish, and Spanish-speaking interviewers were available to conduct the initial and follow-up interviews. Brief descriptions of each of the assessment tools used are presented below.

The initial interview addressed information about (a) child and family demographics; (b) previous mental health services received by the referred child and the respondent, as well as the respondent's satisfaction with those services; (c) barriers to mental health services previously experienced; and (d) the respondent's experiences throughout the current referral process. The follow-up interview measured (a) changes in child and family demographics; (b) the mental health services the child or the family had received, their satisfaction with those services, and barriers to the services experienced by the family; and (c) utilization and assessment of either the family associate services (intervention families) or assistance the family could have used to facilitate the process of initiating mental health services for their child (comparison families).

Based on the information gathered during the follow-up interview, families' involvement in mental health services was assessed. A family was defined as having initiated children's mental health services if at least one appointment was kept after the EPSDT referral was made. Continuance was defined as still receiving recommended treatment at the point of the follow-up interview. Conversely, dropout was defined as discontinuing treatment before the follow-up interview. Families were not considered dropouts if the therapist decided that treatment was completed or if the family decided to discontinue mental health services because the child had improved and no longer needed treatment.

The Family Empowerment Scale (FES; Koren et al., 1992) was used to measure the level of the respondent's sense of empowerment at both assessment points. This 34-item self-report scale presents the respondent with a 5-point Likert scale for each item (1 = not true at all, 5 = very true). Responses are grouped into three empowerment subscores: family (e.g., "I know what to do when problems arise in my family"), service system (e.g., "I know what services my child needs"), and community/political (e.g., "I feel I can have a part in improving services for children in my community"). The published alpha coefficients of internal consistency for the three scores are .88, .87, and .88, respectively (Koren et al., 1992). All meet conventional standards for internal consistency reliability (DeVellis, 1991; see Appendix 20.A).

The Family Barriers Checklist was developed for this project in order to assess the barriers to children's mental health services experienced by the respondent. This measure uses a 4-point Likert scale (1 = not important, 4 = very important) and asks the respondent to rate the degree to which each of 13 areas (e.g., transportation to mental health services, child care for other children during mental health appointments, and information about mental health services) poses a barrier to service involvement. Intervention families also were asked to identify "each area you worked on with your Family Associate" and to rate how much the Family Associate services, in general, were needed by their family (1 = not at all, 4 = very much). (See Appendix 20.B.)

The Ratings of Important Issues for Families (RIIFF) is a 16-item measure developed for this project to capture the family associate's assessment of barriers to service involvement, using the same format as the Family Barriers Checklist. It was completed by the family associates at the end of their involvement with each family. Like the Family Barriers Checklist, it asked the family associate to rate the importance of the areas for each family. It also asked the family associate to identify the areas worked on with each family and to rate the extent to which each family needed the family associate.

The Family Associate Activity Log was created to document the general types of services provided by a family associate over the course of her involvement with each family. The Activity Log included the date of the contact, the person contacted, and the type (telephone, in-person, or other), duration, and location (office, home, or other) of the contact; the type of activity; and comments about the activity. The types of activities that could be recorded were scheduling, data collection, flexible cash fund, providing information, finding resources, and providing support. Whenever the flexible cash fund was accessed, the dollar amount and the purpose of the expenditure was recorded.

Two additional instruments were included in the pretest to assess the comparability of the intervention and comparison groups. The Child Behavior Checklist/4-18 (CBCL; Achenbach, 1991) was used to measure the level of each child's behavior problems from the caregiver's perspective. The CBCL is a 118-item rating scale completed by an adult that assesses the emotional and behavioral adjustment of children. The scale provides a total problem score, two syndrome scores (externalizing and internalizing), and eight problem subscales. Of the CBCL scores available, those pertaining to total, internalizing, and externalizing behavior problems were included in this study. Family coping strategies were measured from the respondent's perspective with the Family Crisis Oriented Personal Evaluation Scales (F-COPES; McCubbin, Olson, & Larsen, 1991). The F-COPES is a 30-item rating scale that identifies problem-solving strategies used by families in difficult situations. It provides six sub-scores: acquiring social support, reframing, seeking spiritual support, mobilizing the family to acquire and accept help, passive appraisal, and support from neighbors. Published alpha coefficients of internal consistency range from .63 to .83 and test-retest reliability coefficients over a 4-week period range from .61 to .95 (McCubbin et al., 1991).

Results

Comparability of Groups

When the two groups were compared using T-test and chi square analyses, the families included in the intervention ($n = 96$) and comparison ($n = 143$) groups were not significantly different on any of the family characteristics measured (see Table 20.1). Additional group comparisons on the three CBCL scores, the six F-COPES scores, and the pretest FES service system and community/political empowerment scores also showed no significant differences (see Table 20.2). However, the initial means on the FES family subscale were significantly different for the two groups ($p < .05$), with the intervention group reporting a lower level of family empowerment than the comparison group.

Table 20.2

Group Comparisons on Initial Interview
CBCL, F-COPES, and FES Scores

Score	Intervention[a]		Comparison[b]		
	M	SD	M	SD	t
CBCL					
Internalizing T	63.0	12.9	62.7	11.1	0.24
Externalizing T	65.1	12.1	63.9	11.5	0.76
Total T	65.5	11.7	65.5	10.1	0.03
F-COPES					
Social Support	24.4	6.6	25.4	5.9	1.29
Reframing	29.7	5.1	30.1	5.0	0.59
Spiritual Support	13.0	4.1	12.9	4.7	0.06
Mobilization	12.4	2.5	13.0	1.8	1.79
Passive Appraisal	15.1	3.2	15.4	2.9	0.80
Support from Neighbors	7.4	3.2	7.3	2.7	0.15
FES					
Family	45.6	7.1	47.6	6.4	2.29*
Service System	49.6	5.8	49.4	6.0	0.16
Community/Political	27.8	7.3	28.9	7.7	1.08

[a]$n = 96$.

[b]$n = 143$.

*$p < .05$.

Impact of the Intervention

Service Participation

The impact of the Family Associate intervention on mental health service participation was examined using chi square analyses (see Table 20.3). The intervention group was significantly more likely to initiate children's mental health services, $\chi^2(1, N = 239) = 6.94, p < .01$. The associated Yule's Q statistic was .51, suggesting a moderately strong relationship between the intervention and initiation of services (Bohrnstedt & Knoke, 1994). Attendance at mental health appointments was treated as a dichotomous variable (missing no appointments was scored as 0, missing any appointments was scored as 1) because the time period was short and a variable based on proportion of appointments would be misleading (e.g., 50% attendance could reflect missing 5 of 10 scheduled appointments, or 1 of 2 scheduled appointments). The groups did not differ in attendance, $\chi^2(1, N = 204) = .63, p = .43$, with roughly one third of both groups missing no appointments. In addition, the two groups did not differ with respect to discontinuing mental health services prematurely, $\chi^2(1, 203) = .002, p = .96$; roughly one quarter of both groups dropped out of services.

Table 20.3

Impact of Family Associate Services on Mental Health Service Participation

Variable	Intervention Group[a]		Comparison Group[b]	
	n	Percentage	n	Percentage
Service Initiation[a,**]				
Initiated Services	89	93	115	80
Did Not Initiate Services	7	7	28	20
Attendance[b]				
Missed No Appointments	30	34	45	39
Missed Any Appointments	59	66	70	61
Service Continuance[c]				
Continued Services	64	73	84	73
Dropped Out of Services	24	27	31	27

[a]$n = 96$, intervention group; $n = 143$, comparison group.

[b]$n = 89$, intervention group; $n = 115$, comparison group (these sample sizes reflect the number of families who initiated services).

[c]$n = 88$, intervention group, $n = 115$, comparison group (these sample sizes also reflect the number of families who initiated services, but one of the intervention families did not know the status of the child's involvement in treatment at the follow-up interview).

**$p < .01$

Because it was possible that initial sample characteristics might have accounted for the significant difference in service initiation rather than the intervention, a hierarchical logistic regression was performed. Six variables representing sample characteristics were entered into the equation first, followed by a dichotomous variable representing the intervention/comparison distinction. The variables were respondent's years of education, child's race (white or other), annual household income, miles to mental health services, CBCL total problem behavior score, and FES family empowerment score. These six variables were chosen on the basis of their importance in previous studies or, in one instance (FES family empowerment score), on a significant difference between the intervention and comparison groups at the initial interview. Although the model chi-square for the combination of family characteristics was significant, $\chi^2(6, N = 239) = 12.74$, $p < .05$, the addition of the intervention/comparison variable improved the model, $\chi^2(1, N = 239) = 6.28$, $p < .05$. The R statistic associated with the intervention/comparison variable was .14 ($p < .05$), whereas only one other R statistic, that for respondent education, was significant ($R = .13$, $p < .05$). This pattern of findings suggested that receiving family associate services was significantly associated with service initiation after the effects of various sample characteristics had been taken into account, and that a higher level of respondent education was also associated with service initiation.

Levels of Empowerment

In order to explore levels of empowerment at follow up, analyses of covariance (ANCOVA) were conducted on each of the three empowerment scores, with pretest scores serving as covariates. The sample in these analyses was limited to those families who initiated services. Tests for heterogeneous regression slopes were nonsignificant, suggesting that the use of common slopes here was appropriate. Because ANCOVA procedures applied to quasi-experimental data potentially yield biased results due to covariate measurement error (Huitema, 1980; Pedhazur, 1982; Pedhazur & Schmelkin, 1991), parallel analyses were also performed with true-score corrected covariates (Huitema, 1980). Separate analyses were based on covariates corrected with alpha coefficients and with pooled within-group test-retest coefficients. The results from these analyses indicated modest but significant differences in both family and service-system empowerment between the intervention and comparison groups. For family empowerment, adjusted posttest means based on the standard ANCOVA were 47.6 and 46.4, $F(1, 200) = 7.99$, $p < .01$, $eta^2 = .03$, for intervention and comparison groups, respectively. For service system empowerment, adjusted posttest means based on the standard ANCOVA were 50.9 and 49.3, $F(1, 200) = 4.43$, $p < .05$, $eta^2 = .02$, for the intervention and comparison groups, respectively. No significant differences were found with respect to community/political empowerment.

Barriers to Children's Mental Health Services

Past research efforts have virtually ignored the barriers experienced by families as they enter the mental health service system. One of the research goals was to better describe these barriers and to identify those that can be addressed by a service such as Family Associate intervention. Here, barriers were examined even if they were reported by families as posing a minor level of difficulty. As illustrated in Table 20.4, the barriers most commonly experienced by the intervention families were: (a) lack of respite care (55%), (b) transportation problems (51%), (c) lack of recreational opportunities (48%), (d) lack of emotional support (48%), and (e) difficulty paying for utilities (41%). Of all the barriers, the family associates most frequently addressed problems such as the lack of information about mental health services, transportation problems, the lack of emotional support, and the lack of recreational opportunities. The family associates in this study were able to fully meet the needs of families in only one area: lack of information about mental health services.

Data regarding barriers to mental health services and the accompanying family associate services were also collected from the family associates using the Ratings of Important Issues for Families (RIIFF). These data were analyzed using the same approach as that described for the Family Barriers Checklist and are presented in Table 20.5. From the family associates' points of view, the barriers most frequently experienced by the intervention families were (a) lack of emotional support (86%), (b) lack of information about mental health services (68%), (c) transportation problems (53%), (d) lack of information about emotional and behavioral disorders (EBD) in children (51%), and (e) lack of recreational opportunities (46%). As can be seen by comparing the figures in Tables 20.4 and 20.5, the family associates and families tended to identify barriers with different frequencies.

Evaluation of the Family Associate Services

In general, Family Associate services were rated positively by the intervention families. The Family Barriers Checklist included a 4-point Likert scale (1 = None, 4 = High) on which families rated their need for family associate services. The majority of families (91%) reported a moderate to high need for the services. Results from a similar item on the Ratings of Important Issues for Families suggest that the family associates perceived only 71% of the families as having a moderate to high need for Family Associate services. A more detailed look at these data showed that although the two items are significantly correlated ($r = .24$, $p < .05$), the ratings from the two sources (respondents and family associates) are significantly different ($t = 4.68$, $p < .001$). This difference could be accounted for by respondents' appreciation for the attention to their needs and the family associates' avoidance of overvaluing their services.

The follow-up interview included additional items that measured the intervention families' assessment of the Family Associate services. The majority of

(text continues on page 598)

Table 20.4

Barriers Experienced and Barriers Addressed by Family Associate (FA)
Services: Respondent Report

	Percentage of Intervention Families			
	Experienced Barrier[a]		Received FA Services	
Barrier	n	Percentage	n	Percentage
Respite Care	53	55	10	10
Transportation Problems	49	51	40	42
Recreation Opportunities	46	48	29	30
Emotional Support[b]	45	48	36	38
Paying for Utilities	39	41	8	8
Childcare[b]	37	39	10	11
Daily Living Tasks[b]	35	37	4	4
Information About EBD	33	34	13	14
Information About MHS	33	34	37	39
Clothing	31	32	10	10
Food	25	26	1	1
Contact with Other Parents[b,c]	24	25	2	2
Obtaining Benefits	17	18	3	3

Note. n = 96 (except where noted differently). Data are based on Family Barriers Checklist ratings provided by the caregivers. Barriers have been abbreviated to fit into the table and should be interpreted as difficulty with the areas listed (e.g., lack of respite care). FA = family associate. EBD = emotional and behavioral disorders. MHS = mental health services.

[a]Based on combining the ratings of *slightly important, moderately important,* and *very important.*

[b]n = 95.

[c]Contact with other parents who have children in mental health services.

Table 20.5

Barriers Experienced and Barriers Addressed by Family Associate (FA)
Services: Family Associate Report

	Percentage of Intervention Families			
	Experienced Barrier[a]		Received FA Services	
Barrier	n	Percentage	n	Percentage
Emotional Support	82	86	78	82
Information About MHS	65	68	54	57
Transportation Problems	50	53	48	51
Information About EBD	48	51	35	37
Recreational Opportunities[b]	43	46	36	38
Clothing[b]	24	26	20	21
Child Care	24	25	15	16
Respite Care	22	23	13	14
Daily Living Tasks	13	14	6	6
Obtaining Benefits	12	13	5	5
Paying Utilities[b]	10	11	8	9
Contact With Other Parents[c]	9	10	8	8
Food[d]	1	1	1	0

Note. n = 95 (except where noted differently). Barriers were rank ordered by proportion of families experiencing each barrier. Barriers have been abbreviated to fit into the table and should be interpreted as difficulty with the areas listed (e.g., lack of respite care). FA = family associate. EBD = emotional and behavioral disorders. MHS = mental health services.

[a]Based on combining the ratings of *slightly important, moderately important,* and *very important.*

[b]n = 94.

[c]Contact with other parents who have children in mental health services.

[d]n = 93.

families were "very satisfied" with their relationship with the family associate (86%) and reported that the family associate was "very helpful" with initiating mental health services for their children (77%).

Furthermore, respondents were asked to identify the most helpful thing the family associate did for them. These responses fell into three general categories, although some respondents' comments fit into more than one category. The majority of families (63%) included at least one comment about "practical assistance," defined as paying for, finding, developing, or coordinating services (i.e., the concrete assistance provided to break down barriers). Nearly half of the families (45%) included at least one comment about "supportive understanding," which involved the family associate conveying a caring attitude, taking a parent's opinions and concerns seriously, treating the family as a key resource, recognizing a parent's limitations and competing responsibilities, and including the parent in the decision-making process. Roughly one quarter (23%) of the families included at least one comment about "information sharing," defined as informing the parent about service options, reasons for certain requirements within the service-delivery system, mechanisms for parents to be involved in service planning, and available community services and resources.

Flexible Fund Support

Data from the family associate Activity Log revealed that the majority of intervention families received flexible fund support (77%), with an average of $175 spent for each family. The majority of families reported that receiving the money made initiating mental health services easier (see Table 20.6). The family associates most frequently paid for private transportation (e.g., car repairs, gas, tires, and insurance) to reduce families' barriers to service participation. The highest average expenditure occurred in the daily living needs category (e.g., heating costs, telephone installation, laundromat expenses). The amount spent on recreation and entertainment was also notable. The family associates found that this resource provided parents, oftentimes exhausted from taking care of a child with special needs, a much-needed break by offering the children recreational opportunities (e.g., martial arts, scouting, swimming) outside of the home. This recreation and entertainment was often a substitute for more traditional child/respite care services, which were difficult to locate.

Discussion

The aim of this research was to test the effectiveness of using family associates who provided outreach, information, and support to families initiating children's mental health services following an EPSDT referral. The family associates were not mental health professionals, but rather parents who had

Table 20.6

Family Support Cash Fund Expenditures

Expenditure Category	Number of Families[a]	Number of Expen- ditures[b]	Average $ Per Expenditure	Total $ Per Category
Transportation-Private	38	57	$89	$5,054
Recreation/ Entertainment	29	37	$69	$3,318
Daily Living Needs	19	22	$97	$2,143
Transportation-Public	9	15	$33	$491
Personal Effects	9	13	$78	$1,568
Respite/Child Care	6	7	$56	$391

[a]$n = 74.$ [b]$n = 151.$

experience negotiating complex service systems on behalf of their own children. These qualities enabled them to provide services to parents of children referred to the mental health system in a parent-to-parent fashion.

Service Initiation

I tried to get [my child] help some time ago, but got frustrated with the system. This time, with the family associate, her help and support, I was able to understand and navigate the process and not give up in frustration.

The results of this study demonstrated that the intervention provided by the family associates was effective in helping families initiate mental health services. Families were more likely to make and keep a first appointment at the mental health clinic if they had received supportive services from the family associate. As would be expected with an intervention of relatively low intensity and short duration, the effect of the intervention was moderate; however, this effect held while controlling for demographic characteristics, providing support for the intervention's general effectiveness.

Empowerment

She boosted my self-esteem enormously. She was encouraging. It changed our family.

In addition to helping families get started in mental health services, Family Associate services helped families improve their sense of empowerment. As earlier described, empowerment is characterized by a greater sense of control over one's life and resources, and a greater sense of self-efficacy with respect to one's own circumstances, with respect to others, and with respect to the larger society. Families in the intervention group scored significantly higher than families in the comparison group on both family and service-system subscales of the Family Empowerment Scale, although the differences were modest. These findings suggest that outreach at the point of entry into the system may do more than just get families into services. It may also have a positive impact on a family's sense of mastery and ability to cope with difficult situations.

Reducing Barriers to Initiating Children's Mental Health Services

> She fixed my car! Yes, it helped me get [my child] to counseling. I probably wouldn't have gone without it!

The findings from this study illustrate the complexity of the barriers families face in initiating mental health services. Intervention families most often reported facing barriers with respect to finding respite care, transportation to services, appropriate recreational opportunities, and emotional support, which have also been reported in previous research (Manela et al., 1977; Meisels & Margolis, 1988). The family associates were most often able to provide help with transportation, information about emotional and behavioral disabilities, and emotional support. They were less successful in meeting needs for respite care and child care, often because these resources were not readily available in the community. In addition, approximately one third of the families reported difficulties with circumstances that are usually not associated with access to mental health services yet that can impede the family's ability to concentrate on supporting their child's treatment. These circumstances, such as not enough money to pay for utilities, not enough clothing, and not enough food, represented areas that the family associates were largely unable to address. Efforts to improve access to services should address a broad range of barriers for low-income families and develop mechanisms to increase the availability of family support resources within the community.

Barriers to Continuing Children's Mental Health Services

> The missed appointments occurred after [the family associate] had quit working with us.

The Family Associate intervention did not increase the likelihood that families would maintain uninterrupted attendance at clinic appointments. Both intervention and comparison families missed some appointments, and there was minimal difference between the two groups with regard to the pattern or frequency with which appointments were missed. While about one third of both groups missed no appointments, about 20% missed more than two clinic appointments. These families clearly faced barriers to regular attendance that the family associate was unable to address. The Family Associate intervention intentionally covered a short timespan at the beginning of treatment. A longer period of intervention may be necessary, however, to address the needs of families who continue to have difficulty regularly attending appointments.

Similarly, restricting the duration of the family associates' intervention through the point at which a family's third mental health appointment occurred may account, at least in part, for why the two groups did not differ regarding treatment continuance. Roughly one quarter of the families in both groups ended services prematurely. It is likely that issues such as transportation problems or lack of child care can pose difficulties at any time, not just at the point of service initiation. Additionally, barriers to service continuance may be different from barriers to service initiation. Families who were able to initiate services (with or without the help of a family associate), might not have been able to deal with the barriers to continuing services, such as not knowing how to deal with unsatisfactory services or not having the confidence to work with a clinician to make the services best fit one's family. If the family associates had been allowed to stay in contact with families for a longer period of time, they might have been able to address barriers to services that arose later in treatment.

Final Comment

This research demonstration project provided us with the opportunity to examine the effectiveness of an advocate that can provide consumer-friendly services. The family associates were accepted by the families because they had tackled public service systems before, they were members of the community in which the families lived, they conveyed a nonblaming attitude, and, perhaps, they were not professional mental health service providers fully aligned with "the system." They filled the role of a knowledgeable neighbor, friend, or relative whom most parents seek out when faced with an unfamiliar experience. Given that significant findings emerged with an intervention of relatively narrow focus, there is great potential for further development of this outreach strategy.

Appendix 20.A

Family Empowerment Scale Items by Subscore

Items (Item Number in Parentheses)	Alpha Coefficient
Family Empowerment	.86

When problems arise with my child, I handle them pretty well. (2)

I feel confident in my ability to help my child grow and develop. (4)

I know what to do when problems arise with my child. (7)

I feel my family life is under control. (9)

I am able to get information to help me better understand my child. (16)

I believe I can solve problems with my child when they happen. (21)

When I need help with problems in my family, I am able to ask for help from others. (26)

I make efforts to learn new ways to help my child grow and develop. (29)

When faced with a problem involving my child, I decide what to do and then do it. (31)

I have a good understanding of my child's disorder. (33)

I feel I am a good parent. (34)

Service System Empowerment	.80

I feel that I have a right to approve all services my child receives. (1)

I know the steps to take when I am concerned my child is receiving poor services. (5)

I make sure that professionals understand my opinion about what services my child needs. (6)

I am able to make good decisions about what services my child needs. (11)

I am able to work with agencies and professionals to decide what services my child needs. (12)

I make sure I stay in regular contact with professionals who are providing services to my child. (13)

(continues)

Appendix 20.A *Continued*

Items (Item Number in Parentheses)	Alpha Coefficient

My opinion is just as important as professionals' opinions in deciding what services my child needs. (18)

I tell professionals what I think about services being provided to my child. (19)

I know what services my child needs. (23)

When necessary, I take the initiative in looking for services for my child and family. (28)

I have a good understanding of the service-system that my child is involved in. (30)

Professionals should ask me what services I want for my child. (32)

Community/Political Empowerment .84

I feel I can have a part in improving services for children in my community. (3)

I get in touch with my legislators when important bills or issues concerning children are pending. (8)

I understand how the service-system for children is organized. (10)

I have ideas about the ideal service-system for children. (14)

I help other families get the services they need. (15)

I believe that other parents and I can have an influence on services for children. (17)

I tell people in agencies and government how services for children can be improved. (20)

I know how to get agency administrators or legislators to listen to me. (22)

I know what the rights of parents and children are under the special education laws. (24)

I feel that my knowledge and experience as a parent can be used to improve services for children and families. (25)

Appendix 20.B

Family Barriers Checklist (Intervention)

STEP 1: Listed below are some areas that can get in a parent's way of getting their child to mental health services. These things can be problems that keep a child from *getting started* in mental health services, cause *appointments to be missed,* or result in *ending services* before they are done. For each area listed, please check (✓) the box to show how much of a problem it was for you as you were getting your child to mental health services

	Not A Problem	Slight Problem	Moderate Problem	Major Problem
1. Transportation to mental health services	☐	☐	☐	☐
2. Child care for other children during mental health appointments	☐	☐	☐	☐
3. Emotional support	☐	☐	☐	☐
4. Information about mental health services	☐	☐	☐	☐
5. Respite care (getting relief from childcaring responsibilities for a short time)	☐	☐	☐	☐
6. Getting benefits (e.g., food stamps)	☐	☐	☐	☐
7. Help with daily living tasks	☐	☐	☐	☐
8. Contact with other parents who have children in mental health services	☐	☐	☐	☐
9. Information about emotional/behavioral disorders in children	☐	☐	☐	☐
10. Information about recreational opportunities for children	☐	☐	☐	☐
11. Not enough clothing	☐	☐	☐	☐
12. Not enough food	☐	☐	☐	☐
13. Paying for utilities	☐	☐	☐	☐

(continues)

Appendix 20.B *Continued*

STEP 2: Please circle the number of each area that you worked on with your family associate.

STEP 3: Overall, how much did you need the Family Associate services? (circle the best choice)

Not At All	Slightly	Moderately	Very Much
1	2	3	4

Family Barriers Checklist, developed for use with the Family Connections Research and Demonstration Project, funded by the Center for Mental Health Services, Substance Abuse and Mental Health Services Administration (Grant No. MH49072-02).

Authors' Note

This study was supported with funding from the Center for Mental Health Services, Substance Abuse and Mental Health Services Administration, Grant No. MH49072-02.

Debra J. Elliott, PhD, is a project manager at the Regional Research Institute for Human Services, Portland State University.

Nancy M. Koroloff, PhD, is a professor of social work at Portland State University and the interim director of the Regional Research Institute for Human Services. She served as principal investigator for the Family Connections Research and Demonstration Project.

Paul E. Koren, PhD, is a research associate at the Regional Research Institute for Human Services, Portland State University.

Barbara J. Friesen, P.D, is a professor of social work and the director of the Research and Training Center on Family Support and Children's Mental Health at Portland State University.

Address for Reprint Requests: Debra Elliott, Regional Research Institute, Portland State University, P.O. Box 751, Portland, OR 97207.

References

Achenbach, T. M. (1991). *Manual for the child behavior checklist/4-18 and 1991 profile*. Burlington: University of Vermont, Department of Psychiatry.

Acosta, F. X. (1980). Self-described reasons for premature termination of psychotherapy by Mexican American, Black American and Anglo-American patients. *Psychological Reports, 47,* 434–443.

Baekeland, F., & Lundwall, L. (1975). Dropping out of treatment: A critical review. *Psychological Bulletin, 82,* 738–783.

Bohrnstedt, G. W., & Knoke, D. (1994). *Statistics for social data analysis*(3rd ed.). Itasca, IL: F. E. Peacock.

Cohen, J. (1972). The effects of distance on use of outpatient services in a rural mental health center. *Hospital and Community Psychiatry, 23,* 27–28.

Dawson, P., Van Doorninck, W. J., & Robinson, J. L. (1989). Effects of home-based, informal social support on child health. *Journal of Developmental and Behavioral Pediatrics, 10*(2), 63–67.

Day, L., & Reznikoff, M. (1980). Social class, the treatment process, and parents' and children's expectations about child psychotherapy. *Journal of Clinical Child Psychology, 9,* 195–198.

DeVellis, R. F. (1991). *Scale development: Theory and applications.* Newbury Park, CA: Sage.

Durlak, J. A. (1973). Myths concerning the nonprofessional therapist. *Professional Psychology, 4,* 300–304.

Frith, G. H., & Armstrong, S. W. (1984). The versatility of paraprofessionals in programs for children with behavioral disorders. *Behavioral Disorders, 9*(2), 113–116.

Frith, G. H., & Lindsey, J. D. (1980). Paraprofessional roles in mainstreaming multihandicapped students. *Education Unlimited, 2,* 17–21.

Garfield, S. L. (1986). Research on client variables in psychotherapy. In S. L. Garfield & A. E. Bergin (Eds.), *Handbook of psychotherapy and behavior change* (3rd ed.). New York: John Wiley & Sons.

Gartner, A. (1981). Paraprofessionals in mental health. In S. S. Robin & M. O. Wagenfeld (Eds.), *Paraprofessionals in the human services* (pp. 127–142). New York: Human Science Press.

Goldin, M. (1990). Factors associated with the length of time in treatment at a mental health clinic. *Dissertation Abstracts International, 51*(4),1389-A.

Good, M. I. (1990). Treatment dropout rates. *Hospital and Community Psychiatry, 41,* 928–929.

Graziano, A. M., & Fink, R. S. (1973). Second-order effects in mental health treatment. *Journal of Consulting & Clinical Psychology, 40,* 356–364.

Gutierrez, L. M., & Ortega, R. (1991). Developing methods to empower Latinos: The importance of groups. *Social Work with Groups, 14*(2), 23–43.

Heflinger, C. A. (1995, Spring). Studying family empowerment and parental involvement in their child's mental health treatment. In M. McManus (Ed.), *Focal point* (pp. 6–9). (Available from the Research and Training Center on Family Support and Children's Mental Health, Regional Research Institute, Portland State University, P.O. Box 751, Portland, OR 97207-0751.)

Huitema, B. E. (1980). *The analysis of covariance and alternatives.* New York: John Wiley & Sons.

Jones, K. H., & Bender, W. N. (1993). Utilization of paraprofessionals in special education: A review of the literature. *Remedial and Special Education, 14*(1), 7–14.

Karlsruher, A. E. (1974). The non-professional as a psychotherapeutic agent: An empirical investigation of the influence of supervision, expectation and facilitative conditions on his therapeutic effectiveness. *Dissertation Abstracts International, 34*(12 B, Pt. 1), 6213.

Koren, P. E., DeChillo, N., & Friesen, B. J. (1992). Measuring empowerment in families whose children have emotional disabilities: A brief questionnaire. *Rehabilitation Psychology, 37,* 305–321.

Larsen, D. L., Attkisson, C. C., Hargreaves, W. A., & Nguyen, T. D. (1979). Assessment of client/patient satisfaction: Development of a general scale. *Evaluation and Program Planning, 2,* 197–207.

Leaf, P. J., Bruce, M. L., Tischler, G. L., & Holzer, C. E. (1987). The relationship between demographic factors and attitudes toward mental health services. *Journal of Community Psychology, 15,* 275–284.

Leigh, G., Ogborne, A. C., & Cleland, P. (1984). Factors associated with patient dropout from an outpatient alcoholism treatment service. *Journal of Studies on Alcohol, 45,* 359–362.

Lorefice, L. S., Borus, J. F., & Keefe, C. (1982). Consumer evaluation of a community mental health service, I: Care delivery patterns. *American Journal of Psychiatry, 139,* 1331–1334.

Manela, R., Anderson, R., & Lauffer, A. (1977). *Delivering EPSDT services: Outreach and follow-up in Medicaid's program of Early and Periodic Screening, Diagnosis and Treatment* (Report No. PS-011-211). Washington, DC: U.S. Department of Health, Education and Welfare, Health Care Financing Administration (ERIC Document Reproduction Service No. ED 182 053).

Mannarino, A. P., Michelson, L., Beck, S., & Figueroa, J. (1982). Treatment research in a child psychiatric clinic: Implementation and evaluation issues. *Journal of Clinical Child Psychology, 11,* 50–55.

Margolis, L. H., & Meisels, S. J. (1987). Barriers to the effectiveness of EPSDT for children with moderate and severe developmental disabilities. *American Journal of Orthopsychiatry, 57,* 424–430.

McCubbin, H. I., Olson, D. H., & Larsen, A. S. (1991). F-COPES Family Crisis Oriented Personal Evaluation Scales. In H. I. McCubbin & A. I. Thompson (Eds.), *Family assessment inventories for research and practice* (pp. 203–216). Madison: University of Wisconsin.

Meisels, S. J., & Margolis, L. H. (1988). Is the early and periodic screening, diagnosis, and treatment program effective with developmentally disabled children? *Pediatrics, 81,* 262–271.

Pedhazur, E. J. (1982). *Multiple regression in behavioral research: Explanation and prediction* (2nd ed.). Fort Worth, TX: Harcourt Brace College.

Pedhazur, E. J., & Schmelkin, L. P. (1991). *Measurement, design, and analysis: An integrated approach.* Hillsdale, NJ: Lawrence Erlbaum.

Poland, M. L., Giblin, P. T., Waller, J. B., & Hankin, J. (1992). Effects of a home visiting program on prenatal care and birthweight: A case comparison study. *Journal of Community Health, 17,* 221–229.

Scott, R. R., Balch, P., & Flynn, T. C. (1984). Assessing a CMHC's impact: Resident and gatekeeper awareness of center services. *Journal of Community Psychology, 12*(1), 61–66.

Sharfstein, S. S., & Taube, C. A. (1982). Reductions in insurance for mental health disorders: Adverse selection, moral hazard, and consumer demand. *American Journal of Psychiatry, 139,* 1425–1430.

Singh, H., Janes, C. L., & Schechtman, J. M. (1982). Problem children's treatment attrition and parents' perception of the diagnostic evaluation. *Journal of Psychiatric Treatment Evaluation, 4,* 257–263.

Singh, N. N., Curtis, W. J., Ellis, C. R., Nicholson, M. W., Villani, T. M., & Wechsler, H. A. (1995). Psychometric analysis of the Family Empowerment Scale. *Journal of Emotional and Behavioral Disorders, 3,* 85–91.

Sirles, E. A. (1990). Dropout from intake, diagnostics, and treatment. *Community Mental Health Journal, 26,* 345–360.

Sledge, W. H., Moras, K., Hartley, D., & Levine, M. (1990). Effect of time-limited psychotherapy on patient dropout rates. *American Journal of Psychiatry, 147,* 1341–1347.

Sobey, F. (1970). *The nonprofessional revolution in mental health.* New York: Columbia University Press.

Solomon, B. B. (1976). *Black empowerment: Social work in oppressed communities.* New York: Columbia University.

Sparer, G., & Johnson, J. (1971). Evaluation of OEO neighborhood health centers. *American Journal of Public Health, 61,* 931–942.

Staples, L. H. (1990). Powerful ideas about empowerment. *Administration in Social Work, 14*(2), 29–42.

Stefl, M. E., & Prosperi, D. C. (1985). Barriers to mental health service utilization. *Community Mental Health Journal, 21,* 167–178.

Takeuchi, D. T., Leaf, P. J., & Kuo, H. (1988). Ethnic differences in the perception of barriers to help-seeking. *Social Psychiatry and Psychiatric Epidemiology, 23,* 273–280.

Temkin-Greener, H. (1986). Medicaid families under managed care: Anticipated behavior. *Medical Care, 24,* 721–732.

Wierzbicki, M., & Pekarik, G. (1993). A meta-analysis of psychotherapy dropout. *Professional Psychology: Research and Practice, 24,* 190–195.

Wise, M. J., & Rinn, R. C. (1983). Premature client termination from psychotherapy as a function of continuity of care. *Journal of Psychiatric Treatment and Evaluation, 5*(1), 63–65.

Homeless Youth in Seattle: Youth Characteristics, Mental Health Needs, and Intensive Case Management

21

Ana Mari Cauce, Matthew Paradise, Lara Embry, Charles J. Morgan,
Yvette Lohr, James Theofelis, Jennifer Heger, and Victoria Wagner

· ·

Homelessness in the United States has become one of the most intractable social problems of the last decade. While estimates of the size of the homeless population vary, there is broad consensus that the numbers are growing, with no abatement in sight. The adolescent homeless population remains the most understudied group among the homeless, barely present in the current portrait of homelessness. They are, however, significant in number, with estimates of up to 2 million youth utilizing overnight shelters each year (National Network, 1985). This number represents only those youth who are willing or able to use shelter services. Many other youths "squat" in abandoned buildings, live in makeshift housing, sleep on the streets, exchange sex for housing, or move from relative to relative, friend to friend, piecing together an existence migrating from one unstable situation to the next.

Variously referred to as "runaways," "throwaways," or "street kids," adolescents who are homeless on their own (e.g., not as part of a homeless family) often come from conflict-laden, violent, and dysfunctional families (National Network, 1985; Rothman & David, 1985). Many, and perhaps most, have experienced neglect, physical abuse, or sexual abuse (U.S. Department of Health and Human Services, 1986). Accordingly, a substantial proportion of these youth have had lengthy unsuccessful histories of contact with social service systems, including multiple placements in foster care and residential treatment programs (Greater Boston Emergency Network, 1985; New York State Council on Children and Families, 1984; Rothman & David, 1985).

The scant research examining homeless adolescents strongly suggests that this is a population at risk for a myriad of emotional problems. Many of these problems have been attributed to the high rates of abuse and neglect they have experienced in the past (Boyer, 1986) as well as their current unstable living situation, which places them at risk for victimization on the streets (Whitbeck & Simons, 1990). The most commonly reported effects of such experiences are fear and anxiety, depression, posttraumatic reactions, sexual problems, drug and alcohol abuse, poor school adjustment, and delinquent acting-out and aggressive behaviors (Browne & Finkelhor, 1986; Conte, 1985). A New York City sample was found to have psychiatric profiles comparable to those of adolescents attending a psychiatric clinic (Shaffer & Caton, 1984). This is not surprising given that a Los Angeles study found that almost a quarter of homeless youth had received inpatient mental health treatment at some time (Robertson, Koegel, & Fergusen, 1990).

Nonetheless, much of the existing research on the mental health needs of homeless youth is limited by the fact that they are seldom assessed with standardized measures with sound psychometric properties. For example, in a recent study the mental health of homeless youth was assessed by asking youth to rate, on a 5-point scale, how often they had felt "angry," "sad or depressed," "nervous or worried," or as if they "did not want to go on living" (Van Houten & Macro International, 1993). While this type of research suggests that many homeless youth are troubled, it sheds little light on how many such youth could be considered mentally ill according to standardized criteria, as represented by the diagnostic manual of the American Psychiatric Association (American Psychiatric Association, 1987) or other commonly used and psychometrically sound measures of behavioral problems (Achenbach, 1991; Farrow, Deisher, Brown, Kulig, & Kipke, 1992; Kurtz, Jarvis, & Kurtz, 1991; Rotheram-Borus, Koopman, & Ehrhardt, 1991; Van Houten & Golembiewski, 1978; Yates, Mackenzie, Pennbridge, & Cohen, 1988). Thus far, only two published studies of homeless youth have reported DSM diagnoses for selected disorders based on standardized instruments (Feitel et al., 1992; Robertson et al., 1990). Similarly, only one study has published data from the youth self-report (Schweitzer & Heir, 1993). Thus, an accurate picture of the mental health profiles of homeless youth is only now emerging.

In this chapter we highlight our own recent findings about the background characteristics and mental health status of homeless youth, and examine the relative efficacy of two case-management programs developed to serve these youth. Findings highlighted are drawn from the Seattle Homeless Adolescent Research Project (SHARP). SHARP was a joint project conducted by the University of Washington, YouthCare, Inc., Seattle Mental Health Institute, and the State of Washington, Department of Mental Health.

Methods

Data-Collection Procedures

Data presented here were collected during face-to-face interviews with study participants. Over the course of the study, the interview team consisted of 2 males and 6 females. All interviewers had previous youthwork or interview experience. Additional training and supervision was provided by PhD-level staff. Interviews were conducted in private areas, generally within Youth-Care's Orion Center, a multipurpose drop-in center for homeless youth operated under the auspices of YouthCare, Inc. However, some took place in local restaurants or in parked cars.

In order to assess the effectiveness of two approaches to case management, we attempted to follow all youths for a 1-year period. Interviews were administered every 3 months for a total of five assessments, one at baseline and four follow-ups. The baseline assessment took between 2 and 4 hours to complete, and it was usually conducted over two sessions in the same week. Quarterly follow-up interviews took about an hour to complete. Youths were compensated for their participation. Payment for the two-part first assessment was $25, and payment for the first quarterly interview was $15.

Interviews included open- and closed-ended questions addressing youths' reasons for leaving home, residential history, and emotional and social functioning. Youths also were asked to complete a self-report booklet consisting of a series of questions using forced-choice formats.

Participants

Three hundred and fifty-four Seattle-area adolescents were originally recruited into a study of case management conducted through YouthCare's Orion Center. Of these, 304 (87%) completed the first assessment. The 14% attrition rate ($n = 50$) between recruitment and the first assessment represents both youth who failed to return for the second part of the first assessment (5%), and those who were deemed not eligible for the study (8%). The most common reason for ineligibility was inappropriate age.

Youths enrolled in the study were between the ages of 13 and 21, and had no stable residence. Qualifications for taking part in the study also included an interest in receiving services and a willingness to participate in the research. The 304 youths were 61% male, with a mean age of 17 years. The sample composition was 60% white, 16% African American, 6% Latino, 5% Native American, and 3% Asian or Pacific Islanders. Ten percent of all youths were best identified as of mixed or other ethnicity.

Measures

Basic demographic information, such as age and ethnicity, was obtained during an initial life history interview. At this time, interviewers also administered the Diagnostic Interview Schedule for Children (DISC-R 2.1). All other measures examined here were contained in a self-report booklet that is completed by the youth in the presence of the interviewer, though some of the youths requested that the booklet be administered orally as well. The measures were chosen to be age-appropriate for a typical adolescent sample and relatively easy to read and complete. All measures had demonstrated reliability and validity.

The Diagnostic Interview Schedule for Children-Revised (DISC-R 2.1) is a highly structured diagnostic instrument intended for use by lay interviewers. The DISC was originally developed by the National Institute of Mental Health to assess the prevalence of mental disorders in children and adolescents, and this version is consistent with the diagnostic criteria contained in DSM-IIIR. Modules of the DISC-IIIR related to Axis II disorders were not administered in the present interview in the interest of saving time.

The Youth Self-Report form (YSR; Achenbach, 1991) is one of the most widely used self-report behavior problem inventories; it consists of a list of 113 items such as "I argue a lot" and "I feel that no one loves me." Youths respond by circling 0 if the item is "not true," 1 if the item is "somewhat or sometimes true," and 2 if the item is "very true or often true." In this study, we report on the results of the two broad-band syndrome scales identified: internalizing (e.g., "I am too fearful or anxious") and externalizing (e.g., "I get in many fights").

Depression was assessed separately using the Reynolds Adolescent Depression Scale (RADS; Davis, 1990; Reynolds, 1987). The RADS is a frequently used measure, containing 30 items (e.g., "I feel happy," "I feel worried") to which youths respond on a 4-point scale ranging from "almost never" to "most of the time." Items on the RADS were developed on the basis of their congruence with specified clinical symptomatology for depression.

Anxiety was assessed with the Children's Manifest Anxiety Scale-Revised (RCMAS; Reynolds & Richmond, 1990). The RCMAS is a 37-item self-report questionnaire designed to assess the nature and level of anxiety in children. The revised version contains 28 anxiety and 9 "lie scale" items. Sample items include "I have bad dreams" and "I worry a lot of the time."

The Problem Behavior Scale (PBS; Mason, Cauce, Gonzales, Hiraga, & Grove, 1994) is a 14-item questionnaire that measures the degree to which a youth displays an antisocial problem behavior syndrome (Jessor & Jessor, 1977). In completing the questionnaire, adolescents answer on a 1 (never) to 7 (very often) scale how frequently they engage in behaviors like "vandalize/trash property" or "sell drugs." The PBS was adapted to include two additional items (e.g., "trade sex for food or money") considered of significance for this population. Conversely, 2 items (e.g., "missed school without parent's permission") were dropped because they were perceived to be inappropriate for homeless youth.

The Personal Experience Screening Questionnaire (PESQ) was used to assess alcohol and drug use (Winters, 1991). In this study, we report on items in the problem severity scale. This scale assesses the frequency of substance use in various situations (e.g., "How often have you used alcohol or other drugs with older friends?") and symptoms of alcohol and drug abuse (e.g., "How often have you used alcohol or drugs secretly so nobody would know you used?"). The problem severity scale is formatted with a 4-point response option scheme (never/once or twice/sometimes/often). The time framework for responses is the previous 3 months.

The Rosenberg Self-Esteem Scale (RSES; Rosenberg, 1965, 1979) is a widely used scale that consists of 10 items such as "I take a positive attitude toward myself" and "At times I feel I am no good at all" and asks the respondents for their endorsement (1 = "strongly agree" to 4 = "strongly disagree").

The Satisfaction with Life Domains Scale (SLDS; Baker & Intagliata, 1982) provides an assessment of satisfaction with the quality of life in 15 domains. Youths are asked to rate (on a scale from 1 = very unhappy or very dissatisfied to 5 = very happy or very satisfied) how they feel about "the place you're staying at overnight," "the clothing you wear," "your friends," "how you spend your day," "the food you eat," "your health," "the people you live with," and so forth.

Youth Characteristics and Mental Health Needs: Results

Mental health needs are reported in two ways. First, rates of disorder according to DSM-III-R criteria are provided. Second, emotional and behavioral problems according to the YSR are examined.

Youth Characteristics

For the purposes of this study, we were interested both in youth who were homeless and those who were precariously housed and at risk for homelessness. Nonetheless, nearly all (95%) youths had experienced an episode of actual homelessness. Youths were considered homeless if they were not living with family members, in a recognized institutional setting (e.g., detention), or by themselves in a situation that included paying rent. Living situations classified as homeless included living in an emergency shelter, on the street or in abandoned housing, with friends (without an adult present and not paying rent), in hotels or motels, or with an adult friend.

At the time of their first interview, most youths (53%) were living in an emergency shelter. Another 12% were living in abandoned buildings or on the street, and 11% were living with friends, without any parental supervision or contribution to the rent. The remainder were living in a variety of other arrangements, (e.g., receiving homes, emergency foster home placements, or with adult "friends"). However, it is important to note that these arrangements were generally temporary and unstable. During the 6 months prior to their first interview, youths reported that they had moved an average of 4 times, or one move about every 45 days. Over a quarter (27%) of the youths indicated that they did not have a place to keep belongings.

The average age of the first homeless episode for youths was 14.7 years, about the time that most adolescents are entering high school. Females tended to become homeless at an earlier age (14.0 years) than males (15.1 years), $t = 2.08, p < .05$. The most frequent reason given for leaving home was physical abuse (21%), followed by violence at home (19%), drug use by a family member (12%), neglect (12%), simply not getting along with family members (12%), conflict with a "stepparent" (9%), sexual abuse (7%), and family poverty (7%). A fair number of youths (9%) also acknowledged that their own behavioral problems led to their leaving home. Although it was not always reported as a reason for leaving home, entry onto the streets was often preceded by physical or sexual abuse. Among males, 45% reported that they had been physically abused and 19% reported that they had been sexually abused. Among females, 41% reported that they had been physically abused and 47% reported that they had been sexually abused.

Among all study participants, 35% indicated that the decision to leave home was made by their parents or equivalents. One third (33%) said that the decision to leave was their own. Another 19% of the youths had been removed from their family of origin and placed in a protective placement. This figure is not surprising given the high rates of abuse and the fact that 85% of our sample reported that at least one family member had an alcohol or drug problem. In addition, 65% indicated that at least one person in their family had a history in the criminal justice system.

Consistent with these indicators of family dysfunction, almost a third (31%) of all youth reported at least one foster placement, beginning at a median age of 12 years. Ten percent of the youths reported more than four placements.

In contrast to this consistent picture of troubled and chaotic family backgrounds and histories, the socioeconomic status of adolescents' families, as indicated by parents' education, was quite varied. About a quarter (23%) of the sample reported that their parents had not graduated from high school, with another quarter (24%) reporting that their parents were high school graduates. Almost a third reported that their parents (29%) had some college or technical school, with 17% reporting college or technical school graduates. An additional 6% reported that their parents had attended some graduate or professional school.

Mental Health

DSM-III-R Disorders

The percentage of youth who met criteria for a diagnosis based on DSM-III-R criteria as indicated by the DISC-R was substantial. About two thirds (67.9%) of all youth interviewed met criteria for at least one diagnosis. About half (48.2%) met the criteria for conduct disorder, slightly less than one third (28.4%) showed attention deficit/hyperactivity, a fifth were depressed (18.7%) or dysthymic (14.3%), about a tenth manic (12.6%) or hypomanic (8.8%), and about a tenth (9.1%) met criteria for schizophrenia. An additional 12–19% met criteria for posttraumatic stress disorder.[1]

Some types of disorder, like conduct disorder or oppositional defiant disorder, might be considered central to life on the streets. For example, running away from home is considered a symptom of conduct disorder. However, other rates of disorder were also remarkably high. Indeed, 44.5% of the youths demonstrated a diagnosable mental illness other than oppositional disorder and conduct disorder. That is, almost one half of all the homeless youth interviewed could be described as mentally ill, without including conduct disorder or oppositional defiant disorder as mental illness. Obviously, these are more than simply "bad," "incorrigible," or "disobedient" adolescents.

As part of the DISC-R interviews, youths were asked if they had ever attempted suicide, another indicator of the amount of distress that they are experiencing. In total, 43% of the adolescents reported that they had attempted suicide. Of those who had attempted suicide, 46% had made more than two previous attempts. Furthermore, a third (33%) of the youth who had ever attempted suicide reported an attempt within the past six months. This suggests that the suicide potential among homeless youth is extremely high.

Emotional and Behavioral Disorders

The percentage of youths in the sample who score in either the "borderline" or "clinical" range as established by the YSR are presented in Table 21.1 (Achenbach, 1991). These results reinforce what the percentages of diagnosable disorder had already suggested. There is much reason to be concerned about the mental and emotional health of homeless adolescents. Specifically, between 20 and 60% of these youths were scoring in a range that is equivalent to the top 5% of a normative sample on each subscale of the YSR. These high rates of behavioral problems are most striking in terms of externalizing problems, a construct very similar to that of conduct disorder. However, the problems that youths were experiencing go well beyond externalizing behaviors, which they may engage in

Table 21.1

Percentage of Youths Exhibiting
Behavioral Problems in the
"Borderline" or "Clinical" Range

Scale	Total Sample
Withdrawal	22.0%
Somatic Complaint	29.8%
Anxiety/Depression	20.3%
Social Problems	15.6%
Thought Problems	26.1%
Attention Problems	27.1%
Delinquency	51.9%
Aggression	26.1%
Internalizing	46.8%
Externalizing	58.9%
Total	62.2%

Note. *N*s vary from 295 to 302.

as part of subsistence on the street. They were also experiencing disturbingly high levels of distress as represented by depression/anxiety (20.3%), attention problems (27.1%), and social withdrawal (22%).

Discussion

This emerging portrait of homeless youth is an extremely disturbing one. Results of this study suggest that these young people often come from unstable family backgrounds, as indicated by the relatively large number who have been in foster care placements. In addition, most youths report that family members had substance abuse and legal problems. Quite often, abuse, both physical and sexual, is also a part of these youths' experiences prior to leaving their home. In light of these troubling backgrounds, it is not too surprising that these youths were so often troubled. As a group, the homeless youth in our sample experienced very high levels of emotional distress and diagnosable mental illness, even if delinquency or conduct disorder is not included as mental illness. In addition, almost half had attempted suicide. However, contrary to the popular stereotype of homeless youth as "crazy," only a small minority of youths evidenced obvious psychotic symptoms.

The high percentage of youths with emotional and behavioral problems found in this study was not unique to our sample. Indeed, fewer youths in our study met criteria for mental health disorders than was the case in previous studies with homeless youth. For example, Feitel et al. (1992) reported that 59.3% of their sample of homeless youth were conduct disordered, and 49.3% suffered from major depression, based on diagnostic interviewing. Furthermore, Schweitzer & Heir (1993) found that 33% of the youth in their sample could be classified as "clinically" depressed based on YSR scores. Nonetheless, our general finding was consistent with the previous literature; homeless youth suffer high levels of emotional distress and behavioral problems. If society seriously plans to curb the problems of homeless youth, services need to be targeted to reduce the very high rates of mental and emotional distress among those youths.

Efficacy of Case Management: Results

In this part of the chapter we present results relevant to the outcomes of two case-management programs that were implemented to help homeless youth deal with their problems, obtain more stable placements, and acquire the skills necessary to lead independent lives. First an overview and description of both case-management approaches are presented. This is followed by a presentation of outcomes about a year after youths were first enrolled in case-management services.

Program Setting and Description

The case-management treatment site was YouthCare's Orion Multi-Service Center in downtown Seattle. YouthCare's Orion Center's drop-in program serves homeless, runaway, and street-involved youths between the ages of 11 and 20. YouthCare's Orion offers a drop-in room, free meals, food and clothing banks, health services, a school program, and recreation programs. A drug and alcohol counselor is available, and group sessions on topics such as self-esteem, sexuality, parenting, and job skills are offered. Through Youth-Care's Orion, homeless adolescents are also eligible for case management (later referred to as regular case management or services-as-usual). Youth-Care's Orion case managers provide a range of services that may include assessment, treatment planning, linkage and advocacy, and case monitoring. They have a variety of skills in working with homeless youths, but few have advanced degrees or formal mental health training. As such, the extent of formal assessment and treatment planning available through regular services is limited. YouthCare's Orion regular case managers may have as many as 20 to 30 active cases at one time.

Youths who participated in this study of case management were randomly assigned either to YouthCare's Orion regular case management, which was the "treatment-as-usual" condition, or to Project Passage, an intensive case-management program developed specifically for this study. Random assignment was to the group, not to an individual therapist.

Project Passage: Goals and Philosophy

Project Passage had four interrelated goals: (a) to increase youths' daily living and coping skills and abilities; (b) to increase their self-esteem and reduce their level of risk-taking behavior; (c) to provide youths with support and advocacy in their environment; and (d) to change the environment by increasing youths' access to needed resources, including, but not limited to, appropriate housing, health services, and educational/vocational training. Youths in Project Passage were assigned to an intensive mental health case manager who was responsible for providing them with individualized services continuously from admission to termination. The case load for each intensive case manager did not exceed 12 active youths.

Intensive case management, as implemented by Project Passage, was not time limited, and contacts were over an extended period. All intensive case managers had a master's degree or equivalent mental health training so that they could offer assessment, treatment planning, and mental health counseling at professional levels. Given the resistance of homeless youth to mental health services in traditional settings, the ability to provide these mental health services in-house was an important component of the intervention. The Project Passage model included nine key components:

Assessment

Youth were assessed both formally, utilizing information from hospitals, courts, or prior treatment facilities, and informally by case managers during daily activities (e.g., at the dinner table).

Treatment Teams

Composed of service providers or representatives from service systems (e.g., juvenile justice) who are involved with the adolescent, these teams work to ensure continuity of services.

Treatment Planning

Treatment plans were individualized and structured around the youths' life domains (i.e., housing, social, cultural, educational/vocational, psychological, legal, health, and family). For example, most early-treatment plans focused on securing basic needs (e.g., shelter, food, clothing) for youths.

Linkage

Project Passage case managers developed an extensive network of contacts with agencies in the greater Seattle area that provide services to youth (e.g., vocational training, alcohol and drug abuse counseling).

Monitoring and Tracking

Case managers often used their relationship with the informal network of homeless youths to monitor and track these transient youths, some of whom moved 15 to 30 times in the course of treatment.

Advocacy

Case managers spent a significant amount of time advocating for youths' basic entitlements (e.g., housing, medication for mental illness, prenatal care for pregnant adolescents).

Crisis Service

Project passage provided youth a 24-hour crisis service.

Flexible Funds

Project passage managers had access to unrestricted funds for client needs (e.g., bus passes, school books, shoes, birth certificates) as well as for individual and group recreational activities (e.g., movies, camping trips).

The Therapeutic Relationship

This relationship was developed between each youth and case manager according to the youth's needs and readiness to engage in the relationship. Case managers communicated to youth that the youth's safety was of paramount importance by requiring that they be unarmed, reasonably drug and alcohol free, and that they wear a seat belt when in YouthCare cars.

The following case study of Natasha illustrates how the nine key components come together:

A Case Study: Natasha

Individualized treatment approaches are, by definition, difficult to describe generically. The case study presented here illustrates the integration of the various service components. This case study is not meant to provide evidence of the success or lack thereof for the intensive intervention, but rather to suggest the complexities involved in treating and assessing the outcome of intensive services to homeless youths.

Natasha's treatment history and course of treatment in this case are extensive and complex. As in any case study, it is not possible to present all the intricacies of either. Natasha, an African American woman, was 18 years old at the time of referral. She came to YouthCare's Orion Center to get a referral to the YWCA shelter after being asked to leave her family home. Over time, Natasha disclosed a long history of family chaos, sadistic abuse, and abandonment. Her mother had died while giving birth to her, and she was raised by her father and a series of stepmothers. While under their care, her punishments included having food withheld, being locked in a bedroom without bathroom privileges, and being beaten with a belt. She rarely received medical treatment for injuries sustained from abuse, which resulted in permanent deformation and scarring. She was also given alcohol as an infant, resulting in permanent brain damage. Natasha was sexually abused by an older half-brother. She was blamed and made the scapegoat for this abuse. In addition, she was denied normal socialization opportunities by being "home schooled" for several years. She returned to school in the 8th grade and for the first time spoke to persons outside the home, although she did not disclose the abuse. At the onset of high school, Natasha began acting out by shoplifting and fighting.

The first time Natasha met with her case manager, she was referred to a shelter. At the next visit, her case manager drove her to the hospital after she revealed that she had ingested 25 Ibuprofen tablets prior to the meeting. Relationship-building thus, quite typically, commenced during a crisis.

Her case manager helped Natasha obtain a placement at YouthCare's Shelter, an independent living program for 18–21-year-old homeless youths. The placement came through a week after the referral, and Natasha returned to the 12th grade and began a job search. With her custodial and immediate needs resolved, Natasha began to experience night terrors, depression, suicidal ideation, flashbacks, and tactile hallucinations. She again took an overdose of drugs. The next 10 days of service provision reflected the complex blend of creative services Project Passage was able to provide.

YouthCare's Shelter notified Project Passage's on-call service as soon as they realized Natasha had made a suicide attempt. Project Passage staff helped get her hospitalized and, after her medical needs had been taken care of, she was transferred to an inpatient mental health unit. During this time, her case manager maintained close contact with both hospital and YouthCare's Shelter staff, and visited Natasha to assess her readiness for discharge.

Before discharge, Natasha, with the help of her case manager, created a nontraditional treatment team, which included hospital staff, staff from Youth-Care's Shelter, and Natasha's godmother, who had been a high school teacher. The team's overall treatment plan included a crisis plan, twice weekly meetings with her Project Passage case manager, and a safety contract. Many young people in Natasha's situation would find themselves released to adult shelters or the street, because YouthCare's Shelter does not typically accept youths at such high risk for further suicide attempts. However, Natasha was able to return to YouthCare's Shelter. Two factors appeared especially important in bringing this about: (a) all interested parties, including Natasha and the staff from YouthCare's Shelter, were invited to come together in developing the treatment plan; and (b) the Project Passage case manager made herself available to provide supportive services to both Natasha and staff from YouthCare's Shelter.

The treatment team used flexible funds to buy Natasha a "therapy box" (i.e., a locked box) for her writings, artwork, family tree, and other items she created in her sessions with her case manager. This helped her contain the overwhelming emotions she experienced. As Natasha made the transition back to Youth-Care's Shelter, her treatment team expanded to include the school nurse. Natasha was so frequently overwhelmed by flashbacks and tactile hallucinations that sitting in class was difficult and daily coping was exhausting. The treatment team asked the nurse to allow Natasha to nap in the nurse's office daily, if needed. Once linked with the team, the nurse became a critical player in ongoing assessment and monitoring of Natasha's functioning.

After this rocky start, Natasha was able to graduate from high school, enjoy semiformal school functions, maintain employment, and have her first boyfriend. She also had an abortion, moved into her own apartment, struggled with her past, and at the time of this writing she is the parent of a baby girl.

Her case manager attended her graduation ceremony and baby shower and assisted Natasha in completing applications for financial assistance and for vocational school. She also supported this young parent whose mother had died giving birth to her to begin to process the entwined meanings of birth and death. Natasha's case manager continued to see her twice a week. She continued to assess and reassess Natasha's needs and develop treatment plans accordingly. Although the core treatment team remained unchanged (i.e., Natasha, her Project Passage case manager, her case worker from YouthCare's Shelter, and her godmother), some members, like the school nurse, dropped out, and others were added as Natasha became connected to new services. Thus, she continued to receive more intensive and comprehensive services than are typically available through the traditional mental health system.

The theoretical underpinnings guiding Project Passage and "regular" case management are not appreciably different, since the former evolved from the latter. However, the programs do differ in various fundamental respects. The most salient are the case load sizes per case manager, the amount of supervision and resources available to case managers, and the educational backgrounds of case managers. These differences are summarized in Table 21.2.

Evaluating the Effectiveness of Project Passage

Assessment Intervals

Baseline assessments of youths were completed in the week following intake and group assignment. Assessments were conducted every 3 months throughout the next year. Therefore, most youths are assessed at least once while in treatment and at multiple follow-up points. Frequency of assessment was a compromise between the methodological desirability for repeated assessments and the practical constraints related to the cost of each assessment.

Table 21.2

Key Differences Between Project Passage "Intensive" Case Management and "Regular" Case Management

	Project Passage Intensive Case Management	**Regular Case Management**
Caseload Size:	Maximum = 12	Minimum = 18 Maximum = 30
Supervision:	Individual: 1 hour/week Group: 1½ hours/week (minimums)	Individual: as needed Group: sporadic
Consultation:	Psychologist Group: 1 hour/week Psychiatrist Group: 1½ hour/week	Group: 1¾ hours/month Not Available
Drop-in Coverage:[2]	10% time	40% time
Flexible Funds:	Available	Not Available
Educational Qualifications:	Master's degree in social services	Bachelor's degree plus four years' experience

Note. From "Effectiveness of Intensive Case Management for Homeless Adolescents: Results of a 3-Month Follow-up," by A. M. Cauce et al., 1994, *Journal of Emotional and Behavioral Disorders,* 2(4), pp. 219–227. Copyright 1994 by A. M. Cauce et al. Reprinted with permission.

Evaluation Results

Evaluation results presented here are based on data collected from 150 adolescents (78 in the intensive condition, 72 in the regular condition) who completed at least two follow-up assessments, one at midpoint and one at endpoint. Midpoint assessment information was derived from the 6-month follow-up interview, if available. When not available, information from the 3-month follow-up was used for the midpoint assessment. Endpoint assessment information was derived from the year-end interview, unless this was not available. When not available, information for the 9-month interview was used to represent the endpoint.

Group Comparisons

A 2 (Group) X 3 (Time) repeated measures Analysis of Variance (ANOVA) was conducted on YSR syndrome scores in order to assess changes in behavioral problems over time and differential patterns of change between treatment groups. These analyses revealed an overall reduction in behavioral problems over time on both the internalizing, $F(1, 137) = 11.4, p < .001$, and externalizing, $F(1, 137) = 8.6, p < .001$ domains. In both cases, these effects were due to the significance of the linear trend over time. That is, the pattern of change across time was linear, with a downward trend between baseline and midpoint, which continues in the downward direction from the midpoint to the endpoint (see Table 21.3). No group effect was noted.

Table 21.3

Means for Psychological Functioning at Baseline, Midpoint, and Endpoint on Key Outcome Measures

	Intensive			Regular		
Time Point	Baseline	Mid	End	Baseline	Mid	End
YSR Internalizing	19.3	15.5	15.0	19.7	17.7	16.0
YSR Externalizing	19.4	17.6	17.2	21.4	20.5	18.0
Depression (RADS)	65.9	61.0	62.1	70.2	63.6	61.8
Anxiety (RCMAS)	11.0	10.0	10.1	13.3	10.9	11.0
Life Domains Scale	3.5	3.6	3.7	3.5	3.4	3.6
Self-Esteem (Rosenberg)	1.9	1.5	1.3	2.3	2.0	1.8
Problem Behavior Scale	2.1	1.8	1.6	2.3	2.0	1.8
PESQ	27.8	25.1	24.8	32.7	29.5	28.9
Days Homeless	36.9	23.6	19.1	45.2	25.9	19.0

Note. Ns for intensive case management range from 73 to76. Ns for regular case management range from 64 to 69.

This table also reports mean scores and standard deviations by group on the other five indices of psychological and social adjustment administered. Repeated-measures ANOVAs indicated that there were significant overall differences between the baseline and the follow-up assessments across group on measures of depression F (1, 143) = 11.8, $p < .001$, anxiety F (1, 142) = 6.2, $p < .005$, problem behavior F (1, 143) = 14.3, $p < .001$, substance use F (1, 141) = 5.7, $p < .005$, self-esteem F (1, 136) = 9.2, $p < .001$, and life domains scale, F (1, 143) = 4.2, $p < .05$. For all scales examined, results supported a linear change indicative of less severe or fewer problems and better adjustment from baseline to midpoint, and midpoint to endpoint. Quadratic effects were also detected on measures of depression, F (1, 143) = 8.1, $p < .01$, and anxiety, F (1,143) = 5.3, $p < .05$. These findings indicate that for depression and anxiety the magnitude of change over time was not uniform across the three assessment points. It both cases, improvement was more pronounced between baseline and midpoint than it was from midpoint to endpoint.

When youths' reports of the amount of time they spent homeless in the last 3 months were examined, a significant time effect also emerged, omnibus F (1, 141) = 20.8, $p < .001$. As with the other analyses, this was due to a linear effect, suggesting that the number of days homeless decreased between baseline and midpoint, then again from midpoint to endpoint.

Discussion

The results of the analysis examining the effectiveness of two case-management approaches were exceedingly consistent. The mental health and social adjustment of youths receiving case management services through YouthCare's Orion Center improved over time, and the number of days they spent homeless decreased. These uniformly positive results provide support for the benefits of case-management services for these hard-to-serve and difficult-to-reach youths. Not only was there a noticeable change from baseline to midpoint, but these positive improvements were also maintained over the course of 9 months to a year. However, given the limitations of our design (i.e., no nontreatment control group), it is not possible to rule out the possibility that these youths would have improved without any treatment whatsoever.

Nonetheless, there was no indication that youth in Project Passage improved more than those in regular case management. While some trends suggested that increased benefits were accrued by homeless youth in Project Passage at the end of 3 months (Cauce et al., 1994), these were not maintained through the mid- or endpoint assessment period. There are multiple reasons that may account for the fact that we did not find greater benefits for youths in the intensive program, as was expected. This program was developed expressly for this project and suffered from the types of problems typical in the initial implementation of a new program. For example, the staff in the experimental, intensive condition was generally inexperienced with the new treatment approach, and continual fine-tuning of the treatment protocol continued throughout the project. In addition, intensive case managers were relatively inexperienced working with street youth. In contrast, regular case managers had typically been working with street youth using a case-management approach for many years. There was also a fair amount of turnover of intensive case managers, which may have led to a less intensive experience than desirable. It is quite possible that the strengths of an intensive case-management approach might have been more evident given more time to establish a treatment protocol and develop a team of more experienced case managers.

Observations from participants, treatment staff, and the research team also suggest that the strengths of the regular case-management approach may have been underestimated. The regular team not only included individuals with more experience with homeless youth, but also individuals with more varied life experiences than is typical of new master's level mental health providers. It is also worth noting that when two interventions are housed in the same site, compensatory equalization of treatment and treatment diffusion or imitation can introduce threats to the internal validity of evaluation studies (Cook & Campbell, 1979). In other words, any benefits that result from the experimental intensive intervention may extend over into the regular control intervention. For example, if an intensive mental health case manager develops a special arrangement with a community agency for one of her youths, it is quite likely that a regular case manager will know about this and build upon that new link if appropriate for one of his youths. In this way, the regular case-management group also benefited from the presence of intensive mental health case managers at YouthCare's Orion. In retrospect, it would have been valuable to have taken baseline assessments of services provided to youth in YouthCare's Orion regular case management prior to the introduction of Project Passage.

In addition to these issues in the implementation of this study of case management, we have come to question one of the key assumptions of the intensive case-management approach. This approach assumes that providing youths with more intensive contact and more services is always more beneficial. However, over the course of this study it became clear that many youths are so skeptical of social services providers, and adults more generally, that they are put off by case managers' attempts to become more involved with them. This was especially the case for the boys with problems of an externalizing nature. The regular approach, which may at first glance appear more superficial, may be much better suited to youths such as these. Further analyses are presently underway to examine whether there was a specific subgroup among the youth that may have benefited from one case management approach more than the other. The working hypothesis is that girls, particularly those who are depressed or have experienced abuse, may benefit more from intensive case management than boys. This may not be the final chapter on the effects of intensive case management for homeless youth.

General Discussion

Results of this research clearly suggest that homeless adolescents are not only a sample at risk, but that many and perhaps most are already displaying serious emotional disorders. Whether these problems predated homelessness or are a result of homelessness is not certain. Regardless, their needs are great. These needs include safe places to stay, such as shelter facilities, as well as interventions focusing on their emotional and behavioral problems.

While the results of this study suggest that the emotional and behavioral functioning of these youths improved across time, without aid they may have worsened. High rates of victimization on the streets, substance abuse, and participation in delinquent subsistence strategies may increase feelings of alienation from mainstream society and decrease opportunities for future reintegration. Indeed, it has been suggested that prolonged homelessness during adolescence may increase a person's risk for homelessness as an adult (Simons & Whitbeck, 1991).

The uniformly positive results of the two case-management programs provide limited support for the efficacy of case management for these hard-to-serve and difficult-to-reach youths. However, without a no-intervention control group, one cannot be certain of the effects found. This is one of the greatest difficulties involved in conducting evaluations of mental health intervention in community settings. Although the comparison of two approaches, both assumed to be efficacious, makes it less likely to find differences in outcome, it is considered the best way to determine the most effective strategy for serving youths and family (Burns & Friedman, 1990). It also bypasses many of the ethical issues raised by having a no-intervention control group of disturbed youth. Indeed, we had originally planned to have such a group, consisting of homeless youth from surrounding communities. However, they were demographically quite different from the Seattle sample and we found it very difficult not to help such youths obtain the services they needed. So we ended up providing them with referrals to local services and dropping them from further comparative study.

The challenge of evaluating interventions carried out in the community is great. When conducting intervention research in the laboratory, the intervention is constructed to fit around the research protocol, but when intervention research is conducted in the community (or in a clinic setting) the research is constructed to fit around the treatment. Our analytic strategies are designed for the former situation rather than the latter. For example, case managers did their best to individually tailor their interventions to specific youths, regardless of the specific intervention condition they were in. Thus, in reality, rather that two broad intervention programs, we had several hundred interventions developed around the specific needs of each client. The case study of Natasha illustrates this. The treatment package she received was very different from what would be given to someone heavily involved in substance abuse or street violence. Our present statistical techniques are not yet sufficiently sophisticated to effectively model the host of specific interventions that are nested within each broad-based case-management approach.

A further challenge both in the implementation and evaluation of programs in the community is keeping personnel committed to the project as the intervention winds down and comes close to termination. When interventions are carried out by researchers or their assistants, some of the most exciting work takes place after the intervention is over, when it comes time to evaluate the study and write up the results. The interest for researchers is as much the knowledge to be gained from an intervention as the intervention itself. But for practitioners hired exclusively to carry out a treatment program, the end of the intervention is equivalent to the end of the job. Thus, as the project nears its end it becomes especially hard to keep the best practitioners, or in this case, the best case managers.

In a similar vein, it was extremely difficult to retain study participants over a year-long period. Homeless youth are extremely mobile. As previously noted, these youth were changing residences about once every month and half. In view of this, our retention rate of about 50% across three time points was quite good. And, there was no evidence that the attrition was differential, at least in terms of initial level of psychological or behavioral functioning (Whitbeck, Hoyt, & Cauce, 1996). Still, the relatively high attrition rate in this study suggests that in order to evaluate programs for homeless youth one needs to begin with a fairly large number of youth at the outset to retain sufficient power for analyses at the end. This makes the evaluation of programs like this extremely involved and expensive. It is precisely for this reason that it might make more sense if agencies could fund the intervention for several years before mandating evaluation. The cost of the evaluation might be more wisely used for programs that are mature.

One lesson that can be drawn from the fact that intensive mental health focused treatment was not more effective than regular case management is that we have not yet grasped the diversity and specificity of the needs of this population. As descriptive analyses have illustrated, homeless youth are quite heterogeneous. While their backgrounds and histories are generally marked by instability and disorganization, some have mental health problems, some do not. Some have been sexually abused, others have not. Some come from poor backgrounds, some are products of affluence. Future research, including further analysis of these data, may enrich our understanding of who among these youth may benefit from more intensive mental health focused contacts, and what forms this contact need take. Intensive treatment may be best when focused on youth with certain clusters of symptoms, and those who express a desire for closer contact with a case manager or mental health provider. Given the extreme needs of some homeless youth, we believe that the option for more intensive services should be available as part of a continuum of care.

Early intervention should also be part of this continuum. Such efforts could include school-based interventions to make early identifications of youth who run away, before they become chronic runaways and then homeless youth (Simons & Whitbeck, 1991). These youth may need extra help, and individualized attention, to gain the vocational and educational training that will aid their transition to stability as an adult (Kurtz, Jarvis, & Kurtz, 1991).

Family-based preventive interventions could also benefit youth at risk for homelessness. The existing research suggests that those at greatest risk are from low socioeconomic status homes and dysfunctional family environments that are often violent, and that many have experienced out-of-home placements such as foster care (Toro & Bukowski, 1995). Targeted interventions for these adolescents and their families aimed at conflict resolution, and prevention of family violence, may slow the increasing flow of adolescents onto our streets (Smart, 1991).

The increasing number of homeless youth should serve as a call for the coordination of efforts by various community services to provide them with a continuum of care, including prevention efforts, crisis management, and long-term services. These youth are a part of the fabric and future of our society, and the problems they face, and contribute to, are the problems of our society as a whole.

Endnotes

1. Approximately 7% of youths were not administered the PTSD subsection of the DISC because administration of earlier versions of the DISC had already exhausted our time limit. Since those who had taken a long time to complete the DISC are precisely those most likely to suffer from PTSD, these rates are probably an underestimate. The true rate of PTSD in this sample, according to DSM III-R criteria, is more likely about 19%.

2 This indicates how much time case managers are required to provide coverage for drop-in youths at YouthCare's Orion Center.

Authors' Note

This study was supported by grants from NIMH/SAMSHA (HD5 SM48087). The authors wish to thank John Whitbeck, Elizabeth Moore, Trish Blanchard, and Sandi Tomlin for their help throughout the project.

References

Achenbach, T. M. (1991). *Manual for the Youth Self-Report and 1991 Profile.* Burlington: University of Vermont, Department of Psychiatry.

American Psychiatric Association. (1987). *Diagnostic and Statistical Manual of Mental Disorders* (3rd ed., rev.). Washington, DC: American Psychiatric Association.

Baker, R., & Intagliata, J. (1982). Quality of life in the evaluation of community support programs. *Evaluation and Program Planning, 5,* 69–79.

Boyer, D. (1986). *Street Exit Project.* Report for the Department of Health and Human Services, Office of Human Development Services (Grant 90-CY-0360).

Browne, A., & Finkelhor, D. (1986). Impact of child sexual abuse: A review of the research. *Psychological Bulletin, 1,* 66–77.

Burns, B. M., & Friedman, R. M. (1990). Examining the research base for child mental health services and policy. *Journal of Mental Health Administration, 17,* 3–12.

Cauce, A. M., Morgan, C. J., Wagner, V., Moore, E., Sy, J., Wurzbacher, K., Weeden, K., Tomlin, S., & Blanchard, T. (1994). Effectiveness of intensive case management for homeless adolescents: Results of a 3-month follow-up. *Journal of Emotional and Behavioral Disorders, 2*(4), 219–227.

Cook, T. D., & Campbell, D. T. (1979). *Quasi-experimentation: Design and analysis issues for field settings.* Chicago, IL: Rand McNally.

Davis, N. L. (1990). The Reynolds Adolescent Depression Scale. *Measurement and Evaluation, 23,* 88–91.

Farrow, J. A., Deisher, R. W., Brown, R., Kulig, J. W., & Kipke, M. D. (1992). Health and health needs of homeless and runaway youth. *Journal of Adolescent Health, 13,* 717–726.

Feitel, B., Margetson, N., Chamas, J., & Lipman, C. (1992). Psychosocial background and behavioral and emotional disorders of homeless and runaway youth. *Hospital and Community Psychiatry, 43*(2), 155–159.

Greater Boston Emergency Network. (1985). *Ride a painted pony on a spinning wheel ride.* Boston: Massachusetts Committee for Children and Youth.

Jessor, R., & Jessor, S. (1977). *Problem behavior and psychosocial development: A longitudinal study of youth.* New York: Academic Press.

Kurtz, P. D., Jarvis, S. V., & Kurtz, G. L. (1991). Problems of homeless youths: Empirical findings and human services issues. *Journal of the National Association of Social Work, 36,* 273–368.

Mason, C., Cauce, A. M., Gonzales, N., Hiraga, Y., & Grove, K. (1994). An ecological model of externalizing in African American Adolescents: No family is an island. *Journal of Research on Adolescence, 4,* 639–655.

National Network of Runaway and Youth Services, Inc. (1985). *To whom do they belong? A profile of America's runaway and homeless youth and the programs that help them.* Washington, DC: Author.

New York State Council on Children and Families. (1984). *Meeting the needs of homeless youth.* Albany, NY: Author.

Reynolds, C., & Richmond, B. (1990). *Revised Children's Manifest Anxiety Scale (RCMAS).* Los Angeles: Western Psychological Services.

Reynolds, W. M. (1987). *Reynolds Adolescent Depression Scale: Professional manual.* Odessa, FL: Psychological Assessment Research.

Robertson, M., Koegel, P., & Fergusen, L. (1990). Alcohol use and abuse among homeless adolescents in Hollywood. *Contemporary Drug Problems, 45,* 1011–1018.

Rosenberg, M. (1965). *Society and the adolescent self image.* Princeton, NJ: Princeton University Press.

Rosenberg, M. (1979). *Conceiving the self.* New York: Basic Books.

Rotheram-Borus, M. J., Koopman, C., & Ehrhardt, A. A. (1991). Homeless youth and HIV infection. *American Psychologist, 44,* 1188–1197.

Rothman, J., & David, T. (1985). *Status offenders in Los Angeles County: Focus on runaway and homeless youth.* Los Angeles: School of Social Welfare, University of California, Los Angeles.

Schweitzer, R. D., & Heir, S. J. (1993). Psychological maladjustment among homeless adolescents. *Australian and New Zealand Journal of Psychiatry, 27,* 275–280.

Shaffer, D., & Caton, D. (1984). *Runaway and homeless youth in New York City: A report to the Ittleson Foundation.* New York: Ittleson Foundation.

Simons, R., & Whitbeck, L. B. (1991, June). Running away during adolescence as a precursor to adult homelessness. *Social Service Review, 12,* 225–247.

Smart, D. (1991). Homeless youth in Seattle: Planning and policy-making at the local government level. *Journal of Adolescent Health, 12,* 519–527.

Toro, P., & Bukowski, P. (1995). Homeless adolescents: What we know and what can be done. Unpublished manuscript, Wayne State University, Detroit, MI.

U.S. Department of Health and Human Services. (1986). *Runaway and homeless youth: FY 1986 report to the Congress.* Washington, DC: Office of Human Development Services, Administration for Children, Youth, and Families.

Van Houten, T., & Golembiewski, G. (1978). *Life stress as a predictor of alcohol abuse and runaway behavior.* Washington, DC: American Youth Work Center.

Van Houten, T., & Macro International (1993). Study of the underlying causes of youth homelessness. Final Report submitted to the Department of Health and Human Services, Administration on Children, Youth, and Families.

Whitbeck, L. B., & Simons, R. (1990). Life on the streets: Victimization of homeless and runaway adolescents. *Youth and Adolescence, 22,* 108–125.

Whitbeck, L. B., Hoyt, D., & Cauce, A. M. (1996). *Psychosocial risk in runaway and homeless youth.* Grant proposal submitted to the National Institutes of Mental Health.

Winters, K. C. (1991). *The Personal Experience Screening Questionnaire (PESQ): Manual.* Los Angeles: Western Psychological Services.

Yates, G., MacKenzie, R., Pennbridge, J., & Cohen, E. (1988). A risk profile comparison of runaway and non-runaway youth. *American Journal of Public Health, 78,* 820–821.

Posttreatment Results After 2 Years of Services in the Vanderbilt School-Based Counseling Project

22

Thomas Catron, Vicki S. Harris,
and Bahr Weiss

The Vanderbilt School-Based Counseling (SBC)[1] program originally was developed in the Nashville-Davidson County Schools largely in response to an increased need for mental health services following budgetary cuts in school counselor positions. With school guidance counselor and school psychologist positions being eliminated or severely reduced in most cases, one part-time social worker was often responsible for intervening in the lives of over 400 students. Faculty and administrators from these schools expressed concerns about the ever-increasing numbers of students who were exhibiting mental health–related problems, in conjunction with a lack of appropriately trained school personnel available to serve these children.

These cutbacks were particularly problematic for children from socio-economically disadvantaged backgrounds, who are at higher risk for mental health problems. The estimate of the prevalence of mental health disorders among the general population under 18 in the United States is approximately 12%, whereas the estimate for these children and families is 20% or higher (Gould, Wunsch-Hitzig, & Dohrenwend, 1981; Institute of Medicine, 1989). This increased risk is not surprising, given that these children often are exposed to high levels of violence, crime, substance abuse, marital discord, and poor adult supervision (e.g., Schorr, 1988; Wilson, 1987).

Exacerbating the problems caused by the reduction in school personnel was the fact that families from disadvantaged neighborhoods typically do not access traditional community-based mental health services, at least not until their problems reach such proportions that restrictive and costly measures such as hospitalization become necessary. One reason for this may be a lack of appropriate, accessible mental health services; other reasons include a lack of motivation or recognition of mental health problems, limited transportation or financial resources, parental psychopathology, or a general distrust of professionals (Dryfoos, 1990; Kendall & Morris, 1991). Further, even when children and families make initial appointments, it is unlikely that they will continue in treatment (Weisz, Weiss, & Langmeyer, 1987); in fact, statistics indicate that few of these youngsters and their families receive needed mental health services (Shuchman, 1991). Thus referrals to local community mental health centers were not a solution for concerned educators. However, without services, such at-risk children may grow up to be adults with mental health disturbances, perpetuating a cycle of poverty and psychological problems (Tolmach, 1985). Given these factors, the first goal of the SBC program was to make treatment accessible to this high-risk population.

As part of this first goal, it was important to make available in a coordinated fashion the multiple services required by this population. Traditional clinic-based services tend to be specialized and fragmented, with multiple services typically requiring multiple providers (e.g., case managers, therapists, and psychiatrists) and multiple appointments. Consequently, it was decided that the new system should be structured to minimize such fragmentation.

Toward these ends, two nontraditional service-delivery systems were considered: home-based and school-based mental health services. However, it was readily apparent that home-based services were not feasible, because of a lack of payor sources (Medicaid reimbursement for home-based services was not permissible at the time of the program's inception). School-based services, in contrast, were reimbursable, and at the same time a more workable alternative to traditional clinic-based services. School sites could be licensed as satellite offices of the community mental health center for the purpose of Medicaid reimbursement. Services provided during school hours are easily accessible to students because children are required to attend school, and transportation, if necessary, is provided by the school system. In addition, the school is a familiar institution and thus potentially less intimidating than clinics, which might foster parent involvement in treatment. Finally, school-based services provide opportunities to work directly in one of the child's important natural settings, to assist teachers in addressing students' mental health issues, and to promote the education mission of the host schools.

Because neighborhood schools often serve a large number of children from low-income populations, it thus was logical to consider delivering mental health services at these neighborhood schools. In fact, in preliminary discussions with the school system, the greatest need for mental health services was expressed by principals and faculty from schools in which a large number of children from economically disadvantaged neighborhoods were enrolled. Consequently, schools were selected for the program on the basis of the percentage (70% or greater) of children enrolled in the federally subsidized free lunch program (a general indicator of the number of urban poor children attending a given school).

The pilot SBC program focused on children in kindergarten through 6th grade. A primary care model, with a single clinician providing a range of services to each child within the school setting, was used. Ancillary services were brought to the school as necessary (e.g., psychiatry) or coordinated with other agencies (e.g., social welfare). Trained and licensed mental health clinicians (master's level social workers, psychiatric nurses, psychologists, or master's-level graduates from related disciplines) were located full-time in the school to provide services to each referred student (for a complete program description, see Catron & Weiss, 1994). Initially, referrals were limited to children who could not access more traditional services.

The unique features of the pilot SBC program were its location in the school and the coordinated fashion in which services were provided. The location of the pilot SBC programs readily permitted the identification of children at risk or in need of services prior to the time that they might require restrictive placements, and greatly improved the children's access to mental health services. The student and family or parent could receive services conveniently provided in the neighborhood school, without the problems associated with attending traditional, clinic-based centers. Because the program was located in schools rather than in a community clinic, clinicians had easy direct access (via teachers, principals, other school staff, or by classroom observation) to information regarding the children's behavioral and emotional functioning. In addition, clinicians were readily available to provide teachers with consultation relating to matters such as classroom and behavior management. Reports from teachers, principals, and parents, together with clinical observation, suggested that this pilot program was successful in increasing service utilization and improving children's mental health functioning.

However, a nonsystematic assessment of treatment effectiveness may be influenced by factors other than treatment effectiveness (e.g., natural improvement of children's mental health problems; Weiss & Weisz, 1990), leading to inappropriate conclusions. Consequently, a more precise, empirical assessment of the SBC program was necessary. In this chapter, we describe the evaluation project designed to assess the effectiveness of the SBC program, and findings at the end of treatment, after 2 years of intervention.

Method

Design

Nine metropolitan Nashville schools were selected based on the percentage (≥70%) of children enrolled in the federally subsidized free lunch program; after hearing a description of the project, all nine schools agreed to participate. Six of the nine schools were assigned randomly to serve as school-based treatment sites; within each of these six schools approximately 30 children were assigned randomly to receive either school-based counseling or academic tutoring. The other three schools served as community comparison sites; within each of these schools approximately 30 youngsters were referred to one of three community mental health centers (CMHC) for traditional outpatient treatment. These participants were assigned to a particular CMHC according to the catchment area within which the participant was living, unless the participant requested a different clinic. Randomization across all three conditions was not possible because it was necessary to ensure that the SBC program in each of the SBC schools was large enough to provide a reasonably sized caseload for the therapists. This would not have been possible if participants had been randomly assigned across the three groups rather than placed only in two because of anticipated attrition rates in the community-based condition.

Thus, there were three experimental groups in the SBC evaluation project. The community-based counseling (CBC) versus school-based counseling (SBC) comparison allowed us to determine whether basing services in the school setting increased accessibility and utilization. The comparison of the SBC condition with the academic tutoring (AT) condition assessed the effectiveness of SBC services, relative to the effects obtained by having the consistent attention of a caring adult working toward positive goals (i.e., academics).

Participants and Participant Selection

The SBC and AT participants reported on in this chapter totaled 106 children and their families; CBC participants consisted of 80 children and their families. Forty-nine percent of the children were male, and at the time of participant selection, the average age of the children was 10.3 (SD = 1.3), with a range of 8–13 years. Fifty-four percent were African American, and 42% were Caucasian. Table 22.1 contains family demographic information.

Rather than serving children with a specific subset of problems (e.g., conduct problems), the goal of the SBC program is to serve children with a wide array of mental health problems. Because there is some evidence suggesting that teacher referrals may overemphasize certain problems and underemphasize others (e.g., Pearcy, Clopton, & Pope, 1993), children were selected for participation in the project based on a set of multi-informant mental health screening assessments. These screenings consisted of teacher, peer, and self-report mental health measures covering six domains of psychopathology: delinquency, aggression, hyperactivity, depression, anxiety, and somatization (specific measures are described below).

Because most measures of child mental health have been developed for use with non–at risk, nondisadvantaged populations, rather than using established clinical cutoffs a weighting system was developed for this project. Within each of the six psychopathology domains, the three informant's reports were combined by first weighting each informant's report and then summing across the

Table 22.1

Family Demographic Information

Caretaker Age	35.1(8.1)
Average Age Range	23–75
Caretaker Education	
Did not graduate high school:	35%
High school graduate but no college:	36%
Some college but no degree:	25%
College graduate or beyond:	4%
Family Income	
less than $5,000:	24%
$5,000 to $10,000:	15%
$10,000 to $15,000:	11%
$15,000 to $20,000:	15%
$20,000 to $30,000:	22%
$30,000 to $40,000:	7%
$40,000 to $60,000:	4%
over $60,000:	2%
Family Structure	
Two-parent biological:	36%
One biological/one foster parent:	11%
Single parent w/nonmarital partner:	7%
Single mother:	35%
Single father:	1%
Living w/relative	9%
Living w/nonrelative	1%
Number of Children in Home	2.96 (1.29) 1–8

three informants. The weightings were based on the relative discriminative validity of each informant for that particular domain of psychopathology (e.g., Hart, Lahey, Loeber, & Hanson, 1994; Kazdin, Esveldt-Dawson, Unis, & Rancurello, 1983; Weissman et al., 1987). For example, because teacher and peer reports appear to be less reliable in regard to internalizing symptoms than self-reports, teacher and peer scores on depression (as well as anxiety and somatization) received relatively low weights compared to self-reports of depression.

This procedure produced six problem domain scores for each child, which then were weighted by each problem domain's relative clinical seriousness (Catron & Weiss, 1994; Weisz & Weiss, 1991). After this weighting, the two highest scores (across the six domains) were summed to produce an "overall psychopathology score." The two top domains were summed, rather than using either the single top domain or three or more domains, in order that our selection would be a balance of breadth and severity of psychopathology. Students were rank-ordered according to this overall psychopathology score and recruited from this list to participate in the study. As a final check to make certain that children who were selected were in need of services, when children entered treatment their clinicians were asked to determine whether the children in fact did need services. Two children were judged not to need services, and treatment was discontinued after 6 weeks. Table 22.2 contains the proportion of participant children who were in the borderline clinic range based on the Teacher Report Form (Achenbach, 1991b). The borderline rather than clinical range was used because the borderline clinical range discriminates more accurately between referred and nonreferred children than the clinical range (Achenbach, 1991b).

For comparisons of the SBC and AT children reported on in this chapter, we focused on those children who had completed their program (i.e., those children who had either received 2 years of school-based services or tutoring, or who terminated treatment with the concurrence of the therapist and parent prior to 2 years of treatment).[2] We focused on this "2-year" group rather than all children assigned to the SBC or AT groups because although the use of this sample placed a limit on generalizability, we felt that it represented the best test of the SBC program, as these children received the full benefits of the program.

It is important to note that comparisons involving the community-based sample were restricted to those analyses targeting utilization of and access to services rather than outcome. As noted below, despite considerable efforts to enroll a sufficient number of students in community-based mental health treatment to secure an appropriate comparison sample, the large majority of families did not follow through on referrals for outpatient treatment. Although this was a very important finding, as a result, it was not possible to select SBC and CBC groups that received comparable levels of treatment. Thus, comparisons between the two groups with regard to improvement in mental health functioning were not meaningful.

Table 22.2

Demographic Characteristics
of Project Participants

Percent of Children in Borderline Clinical Range

Anxiety-Depression:	60.1%
Somatic Problems:	57.4%
Aggression:	73.7%
Delinquency:	69.8%
Attention Problems	77.6%
One or more domains:	94.2%

Services Provided to Participants

School-Based Services

In the six SBC clinics, services were provided by one of seven therapists.[3] These included two MA psychologists, three social workers with LCSW certification, one psychiatric MSN, and one PhD clinical psychologist. The number of years of experience ranged from 1 (for the PhD psychologist) to 13 (for one of the social workers), the average being around 6 years. These clinicians were hired via standard hiring procedures (e.g., "word of mouth" referrals; newspaper ads) for recruiting outpatient clinicians at the Vanderbilt Child and Adolescent Psychiatry Outpatient Clinic. The clinical coordinator and primary supervisor was an LCSW social worker housed within the Department of Psychiatry who had 15 years of experience. Clinicians received both individual and group supervision each week.

Because the purpose of the SBC condition was to evaluate the effectiveness of standard clinical services provided within the school, each clinician was free to decide which services and how services were provided. The range of interventions provided included psychotherapy (individual, group, family, and marital), parent skill training and education, behavioral and psychiatric consultation to staff and faculty, community liaison, and case management. The intensity (e.g., one to five sessions per week) and comprehensiveness of the services varied according to clinicians' perceptions of the client's need. Because home visits often were not practical (e.g., because of safety concerns and the consequent need to travel in pairs), most treatment sessions occurred in the school. Preventive services also were provided for such issues as divorce adjustment and substance abuse. Table 22.3 contains the number of sessions of different types of services that children in this experimental condition received.

Parent meetings, which occurred both individually and in groups, focused on helping parents improve behavior management skills (e.g., learning the importance of consistency). Parents also received individual counseling or referrals to other appropriate providers (e.g., substance abuse counselors) to address their own mental health problems. Parent support groups also were provided to allow parents to share ideas and support each other in coping with the many problems associated with the neighborhoods in which they lived.

Child psychiatry residents provided consultation to both clinicians and teachers. The psychiatrists provided direct medication management services to students as well as diagnostic and conceptual guidance to the clinicians and teachers (i.e., making treatment recommendations). Psychiatrists visited schools every 2 weeks for approximately 2–3 hours. These services were offered free of charge to participating children and families throughout the academic year. For the summer months, if clinically indicated, referrals were made for ongoing treatment at local community mental health centers. Services were resumed in the

Table 22.3

Service Utilization

Type of Service	Number of Sessions
1. School-Based Treatment Sessions	
Individual	60.05 (19.70)
Group	4.20 (5.76)
School personnel consult	12.64 (15.02)
Psychiatric consult	1.41 (3.10)
Parent	9.44 (8.69)
2. Tutoring Sessions	
Individual	52.94 (9.59)

	Total Sample	Treated Sample
3. Community-Based Sessions		
Individual	0.79 (2.82)	5.29 (5.50)
Group	0	0
Parent	0.49 (2.60)	5.75 (7.26)

child's school by project clinicians at the beginning of the next school year (i.e., the final year of the SBC intervention).

Academic Tutoring

Tutoring was provided in the schools by college students, graduate students in special education, and one former elementary teacher. Tutors received two sessions of training focusing on tutoring (e.g., use of games; planning) and how to avoid therapeutic interactions (e.g., how to steer conversations away from personal problems). Tutors met weekly for group supervision. Table 22.3 contains the number of sessions, which typically were 45 minutes in length, for children in the tutoring condition. Although project participants were selected based on evidence of social and emotional problems rather than academic difficulties, consultation with teachers and assessment by tutors indicated that remedial instruction in basic academics (e.g., reading skills) was an appropriate focus of tutoring for most children. In the few other instances, sessions focused on enhancement of academic skills.

In order to determine whether tutoring sessions involved overtly therapeutic interactions (e.g., discussing a child's nonacademic problems and providing advice or support), random tutoring sessions were audiotaped. These tapes were then coded by trained coders who recorded the different tutoring behaviors. Across the tapes for the 2 years, there were no instances that could be characterized as therapeutic in content. Conversations about day-to-day activities were documented but none that fit criteria for a therapeutic interchange. In each instance, when children raised personal issues, tutors responded as they had been trained, in a polite but noncommittal manner, leading the focus back to the tutoring. Most codings from the tape involved the academic games used by the tutors targeting areas of scholastic deficit (e.g., spelling contests), social praise for successful attempts and effort in academic pursuits, or silence while the child worked on a problem.

Community-Based Services

Because the purpose of the community-based condition was to evaluate community-based services as they are typically provided, the decision in regard to what services these children would receive was made by the community clinic with no influence from the project. Thus, children assigned to the CBC condition received the regular services provided in the community clinics. However, information in regard to services provided to the children was collected by the project. Table 22.3 contains the number of sessions of different types of services that these children received. In order that the school-based and community-based services be comparable, services were offered to participating children at no cost to parents (i.e., the project covered clinic-related out-of-pocket expenses for the families) and, if clinically indicated, were available to youngsters year-round for the 2-year period of the intervention program.

Assessment Instruments

Teacher Reports

For the screening, teachers completed the Teacher Behavior Questionnaire (Catron & Weiss, 1994). The TBQ was used rather than more established instruments such as the Teacher Report Form (TRF; Achenbach, 1991b) because these latter instruments were too long for use in a screening where one teacher was responsible for providing data for up to 30 children. The TBQ is a 28-item screening inventory designed to assess teachers' perceptions of children's behavioral and emotional problems. This inventory was developed for use with the SBC clinics by: (a) compiling the reasons that the teachers at the SBC pilot sites had listed as the cause of their referral(s) to the pilot clinics, (b) categorizing these items in regard to our six problem domains (e.g., anxiety; delinquency), and (c) selecting the items within each category with the highest frequency for inclusion in the TBQ. The TBQ produces six scales, matching the psychopathology domains of delinquency, aggression, hyperactivity, depression, anxiety, and somatization. The mean (across the genders and psychopathology domains) squared multiple correlation between comparable TBQ and TRF scales was .79; the validity of the TRF has been established in a number of studies (Achenbach, 1991b). For the outcome evaluation, because no teacher was responsible for providing data for more than five children, teachers completed the TRF. The TRF produces two broad-band scales, internalizing problems and externalizing problems, as well as eight narrow-band scales (e.g., somatic complaints).

Peer Report

Peer reports for the six domains were obtained by having children nominate up to three children within their classroom for each of 16 descriptors, which were derived from existing peer nomination inventories (e.g., Quiggle, Garber, Panak, & Dodge, 1992; Lefkowitz & Tesiny, 1980) as well as from DSM III-R (APA, 1987). For instance, items for the peer aggression scale included "who gets in fights a lot" and "who picks on other kids or teases them," and items for the peer depression scale included "who often looks sad" and "who doesn't seem to have much fun." Nominations for each item were summed for each child and then standardized within the classroom. These standardized nominations were then summed to create the peer report scales. The same peer nomination scales were used for both the screening and outcome assessments.

Self-Reports

Students completed three self-report questionnaires for both the screening and the outcome assessments. The State Trait Anxiety Inventory for Children (STAIC; Spielberger, 1973) was used to obtain self-reports of anxiety. This scale contains 20 items assessing various cognitive and physiological aspects of anxiety (e.g., worrying about making mistakes; sweaty hands) as well as more generalized distress (e.g., crying; feeling unhappy). Only those items assessing either the specific cognitive or physiological components of anxiety were included in the analyses reported here.

The Vanderbilt Depression Inventory (VDI; Weiss & Garber, 1993) was used to obtain self-reports of depression. This inventory was designed for making developmental comparisons involving specific depressive and depression-related symptoms. The VDI contains 26 items that are rated on a Likert 1–5 scale. Most symptoms are assessed with one item; however, key symptoms such as sadness have two items. The VDI contains two scales, a core DSM scale containing items from DSM III-R, and an associated features scale, containing items such as somatic complaints and anxiety. In a separate sample, it was found that: (a) children as young as those in the second grade can understand the items, as long as the items are read to them; (b) the VDI correlates .52 with the STAIC, which is significantly smaller than the correlation with the Children's Depression Inventory (.71), indicating discriminate validity; (c) the VDI has a 1-week test-retest reliability of 0.62; and (d) there is an internal consistency reliability of .88 (Weiss & Catron, 1993).

To obtain self-reports of aggression, delinquency, and somatization, the Student Behavior Questionnaire (Catron & Weiss, 1993) was used; because self-reports of hyperactivity and attentional problems are of questionable validity with children (e.g., Loeber, Green, Lahey, & Stouthamer-Loeber, 1990), this domain was not assessed via self-report. The SBQ contains 14 items adapted from the Teacher Behavior Questionnaire, and produces an aggressive behavior, a delinquent behavior, and a somatization scale.

Parent Report

Parents completed the Child Behavior Checklist (CBCL; Achenbach, 1991a), a broad-band measure of children's social competencies, and behavioral and emotional problems. The CBCL produces two broad-band scales, internalizing problems and externalizing problems, as well as eight narrow-band scales (e.g., somatic complaints). The validity of the CBCL has been established in a number of studies (Achenbach, 1991a).

Procedure

The screening occurred in the spring of 1993, when students were in the 2nd–5th grades, and the baseline assessment occurred in the fall of 1993. SBC and AT services ended 2 school years later, in the spring of 1995, when students completed the 4th–7th grades (excluding those retained in grade). The outcome assessment occurred during the spring and early summer of 1995. In all classroom assessments, peer nomination and self-report measures were read to the children by the investigators or graduate students who circulated through the room to ensure that children did not have difficulty completing the measures. Teachers completed their forms after school and received $50 for each assessment in which they participated. The CBCL was read to parents in their home; parents followed along on their own copy of the CBCL. Answers were recorded by a research assistant.

Results

This report focuses on two questions. The first is whether the provision of services within the public school increased service utilization. The second question is whether children who received SBC services had better mental health outcomes than children who received academic tutoring.

Service Utilization

Table 22.3 presents service utilization data. To determine whether basing services within the school increased utilization, we compared the proportion of families who began services to those offered services for the SBC vs. CBC groups. Of those to whom they were offered, 96% of the SBC children began services, whereas 13% of the CBC children did ($p < .0001$). Thus, basing services within the school was associated with significantly greater utilization.

We also sought to determine what factors might be related to parents' decision not to seek community-based services (we looked only at the CBC sample, since 96% of SBC children began services). Toward this end, we compared the children who began community-based treatment with those who were referred but failed to seek treatment on demographic and psychopathology variables. None of the demographic variables discriminated between clinic attenders and nonattenders. However, the mean total CBCL score was significantly higher ($p < .05$) for attenders than for nonattenders, although there were no significant differences between the two groups in regard to the peer, teacher, or self-reports of psychopathology.

Mental Health Outcomes

The basic statistical model used was a general mixed model with *Post = Pre-School Group,* where *Post* was the outcome measure taken at posttreatment (end of school year, spring of 1995), *Pre* was the outcome measure taken at pretreatment (beginning of school year, fall of 1993), *School* was a random factor representing the five experimental schools, and *Group* was a random factor representing the AT vs. SBC comparison. Two related variables served as our measures of outcome vis-à-vis psychopathology. The first was the primary problem area, which was the domain for which the child received the highest standardized score at baseline. Thus, for instance, a child whose highest standardized score at pretreatment was the delinquency score would have for pre- and posttreatment scores the delinquency score at pre- and posttreatment. This variable was selected because it represented each child's most problematic psychopathology domain. For the second variable, we included all domains for which the child was at least half a standard deviation above the mean at pretreatment. This variable was selected because it represented all domains with which a child was having some difficulty. For both variables, we analyzed school and home data separately, collapsing across informants for the school data (i.e., collapsing across teacher, peer, and self-report).

Primary Problem Domain

For the school data, the pretreatment group means on this standardized variable were 1.78 for the AT group and 1.71 for the SBC group (see Table 22.4;

higher scores indicate higher levels of psychopathology). The mean change effect size (i.e., the effect size representing within-group change; Cohen, 1983) was .56 for the AT group and .90 for the SBC group (higher scores indicate more improvement). These effect sizes both differed significantly from zero, $t(49) = 3.97$, $p < .0005$; $t(48) = 6.33$, $p < .0001$, respectively. Thus, both groups showed significant and substantial improvement. However, when we compared the two groups using the mixed model described above, the two groups did not differ significantly, $F(1,92) = 3.23$, ns, with posttreatment adjusted means of .93 for the AT and .49 for the SBC group (again, higher scores indicate higher levels of psychopathology).

For the home data, the mean change effect size for this variable was .45 for the AT group and .44 for the SBC group (with higher scores again indicating more improvement). These effect sizes both differed significantly from zero, $t(48) = 3.16$, $p < .005$; $t(49) = 3.10$, $p < .005$, respectively. Thus, both groups showed significant and substantial improvement. However, when we compared the two groups using the mixed model described above, the two groups did not differ significantly, $F(1,92) = .01$, ns.

Table 22.4

Primary Outcome Variables

| | Primary Problem Domain Score | |
	Academic Tutoring	School-Based Counseling
School		
Pretreatment	1.78 (0.98)	1.71 (1.11)
Posttreatment	1.09 (1.36)	0.69 (1.15)
Home		
Pretreatment	7.04 (4.10)	7.32 (5.23)
Posttreatment	5.21 (3.67)	5.07 (4.76)

| | "Domains > ½ SD Above Mean" Score | |
	Academic Tutoring	School-Based Counseling
School		
Pretreatment	1.49 (0.61)	1.44 (0.56)
Posttreatment	0.78 (1.03)	0.67 (0.85)
Home		
Pretreatment	8.05 (4.37)	9.34 (5.87)
Posttreatment	5.03 (4.08)	5.07 (4.61)

Domains > ½ *SD* Above Mean

For the school data, the pretreatment group means on this variable were 1.49 for the AT group and 1.44 for the SBC group. The mean change effect size was .79 for the AT group and 1.03 for the SBC group. These effect sizes both differed significantly from zero, $t(46) = 5.42$, $p < .0001$; $t(47) = 7.14$, $p < .0001$, respectively. Thus, both groups showed significant and substantial improvement. However, when we compared the two groups using the mixed model described above, the two groups again did not differ significantly, $F(1,88) = .90$, *ns*, with post-treatment adjusted means of .74 for the AT and .57 for the SBC group.

For the home data, the mean change effect size for this variable was .72 for the AT group and .83 for the SBC group. These effect sizes both differed significantly from zero, $t(44) = 4.82$, $p < .0001$; $t(46) = 5.67$, $p < .0001$, respectively. Thus, both groups showed significant and substantial improvement. However, when we compared the two groups using the mixed model described above, the two groups again did not differ significantly, $F(1,85) = .47$, *ns*.

Mental Health–Related Outcomes

Table 22.5 contains comparison between groups on several other measures related to mental health: (a) school attendance, (b) sociometric status (i.e., peer

Table 22.5

Mental Health-Related Outcomes

	Academic Tutoring	School-Based Counseling
Absenteeism Pre-tx	0.73 (0.93)	0.88 (1.21)
Absenteeism Post-tx	2.86 (4.69)	3.37 (13.30)
Grades Pre-tx	78.84 (9.82)	78.82 (8.76)
Grades Post-tx	79.57 (9.13)	76.96 (10.64)
+ Nominations Pre-tx	−0.15 (0.81)	−0.16 (1.05)
+ Nominations Post-tx	−0.29 (0.82)	−0.17 (0.84)
− Nominations Pre-tx	0.56 (1.09)	0.60 (1.28)
− Nominations Post-tx	0.76 (1.21)	0.49 (1.08)

Note. + Nominations = "Most liked" peer nomination; − Nominations = "Liked least" peer nominations.

nomination of liking minus peer nominations of disliking), and (c) grades (averaged across academic subjects). Unlike the SBC group, the AT group showed a significant increase in absenteeism, $t(33) = 2.10$, with a change effect size of .36. All other tests of within-group change for these variables were nonsignificant. The two groups did not differ in regard to improvement on any of these variables, although there was a marginal effect, $p < .10$, for peer nominations for disliking, with SBC children showing approximately one fifth of a standard deviation more improvement than AT children.

Discussion

The School-Based Counseling project had two primary objectives. The first was to increase accessibility and utilization of children's mental health services for families in need of, but not receiving, such services. The second objective was to improve the behavioral and emotional functioning of the children.

At the beginning of the project, a multidomain, multi-informant screening battery was used to identify children in need of but not receiving mental health services. Given estimates that up to 18% or more of children in the general population are in need of services (e.g., Bickman et al., 1995) but that only about 2% receive services (Burns, 1991), we anticipated relatively little difficulty in identifying such children. This was particularly true given that our sample was selected from a low-income population, and thus exposed to the increased physical and mental health risks associated with poverty (Epstein, Cullinan, Quinn, & Cumbald, 1995). The results of our screening suggest that approximately 30% of the children in our population were in need of services, which supports previous findings of increased need for child mental health services among low-income populations. Unfortunately, although over 90% of the children selected to participate in the SBC evaluation project were in the borderline clinical range or above (with only two judged by clinicians not to need services), fewer than 5% were actually receiving services.

Following the identification of this sample, the objective of the program was to increase accessibility and appropriate utilization of services. Our data suggest that placing services in the school setting does result in greatly increased accessibility and utilization of a range of intervention services. When compared to a group of youngsters exhibiting similar emotional and behavioral problems referred to comparable outpatient treatment at local community mental health centers, students referred for school-based services received approximately 10 times as much service.

The large majority of parents in our community treatment sample agreed to bring their children for outpatient services but failed to make or keep appointments; only 13% of families followed through with the initial referral from project personnel. Repeated efforts were made to facilitate the families' enrollment in outpatient therapy by removing whatever physical barriers to treatment may have kept families from getting involved (e.g., services were offered at no expense to families; follow-up telephone contact was made with the family; contact was set up with a therapist within 48 hours of the families' calls). Yet enrollment in this group remained low. These results suggest that the failure to obtain services was not strictly a function of lack of accessibility.

Follow-up interviews with parents of children referred for outpatient treatment who did not call the community clinic or follow through with therapy appointments suggested that parental beliefs about the severity of their child's problems were an important determinant in whether families followed through on a referral, and, in fact, the more severe were parents' reports of their child's adjustment difficulties, the more likely they were to bring their child for treatment in a community mental health center. The fact that teacher and peer reports as well as child self-report were unrelated to the likelihood of following through on the referral suggests that parental perceptions, in conjunction with or in contrast to actual behavior, may play an independent but important role in the referral process. Thus, helping parents understand the nature and significance of their children's behavioral and emotional problems may be an important component in increasing appropriate service utilization.

In comparison to our findings, in their continuum-of-care demonstration project, Fort Bragg investigators (Bickman, in press) successfully increased utilization of outpatient services by systematically removing the financial barriers to professional consultation, increasing the speed with which patients were seen, and enhancing community awareness about the availability of care. One important difference between their sample and ours was the manner in which families become involved with the mental health system: Our parents did not self-refer, but rather students were identified through our school-based assessment; parents were contacted by the school and then referred to community clinics. This different path of referral may be responsible for the differences in success in increasing outpatient-based services. It also is possible that sample differences (e.g., SES) may have been responsible for the difference.

However, for many children, the referral process actually begins outside the home, with teachers or other professionals making the initial referral for mental health services (Gould, Shaffer, & Kaplan, 1985), after a moderately lengthy period of discussion with the parents (e.g., after several months of parent meetings, teachers finally might suggest to the parents that they seek mental health treatment for their child). In our sample, in contrast, in many cases the parents did not appear to be aware of the seriousness of their children's difficulties when contacted by the project. It is possible, then, that the critical difference between our community sample and the Fort Bragg sample may have been the length of time for which parents had been aware of their child's difficulties.

As well as increasing accessibility of mental health services, part of the first goal of the SBC project was to provide students enrolled in the school-based treatment with a comprehensive set of mental health services including individual, group, and family therapy, and psychiatric and classroom consultation. Our data demonstrate that it is possible to provide a broad range of mental health services within the school setting. All students in our 2-year sample in fact were provided with regular, consistent individual therapy, and, in many cases, family therapy, child group therapy, psychiatric consultation, and teacher consultation. Further, discussions with our therapists indicated that in some instances our data probably are an underrepresentation of the frequency of service provision. For example, with respect to teacher consultation, our data were limited to formal contacts with teachers documented in clinical charts and did not include more casual contacts and consultation provided in a more informal context. Included among these informal but important meetings are discussions with the teacher when the therapist brought the child to the classroom following treatment, and brief conversations in the teachers' lounge. That is in fact an advantage of a school-based program: Clinicians, teachers, and other school personnel are presented with frequent opportunities for informal meetings to discuss their children.

The most important goal of the SBC project was to determine the impact of the SBC program on the psychosocial functioning of our population of underserved children. Toward this end, our participants were assessed using a variety of social, emotional, behavioral, and academic indicators, provided by several different informants. Students enrolled in the SBC program made significant as well as substantial gains in mental health. However, similar improvements in psychosocial functioning were evident in the scores of students enrolled in AT. Improvement did not differ significantly for the SBC and Tutoring children.

The simplest interpretation of this finding is that traditional mental health services may not be particularly effective in helping children living in low-income environments. This possibility is supported by findings that suggest that more structured, time-limited, focused treatments closely derived from empirical research may possess greater effectiveness than more traditional open-ended services (e.g., Weisz, Donenberg, Han, & Weiss, 1995; Weisz, Weiss, & Donenberg, 1992). This suggests that a useful combination might consist of providing the more structured and focused treatments, with their apparent greater effectiveness, in the school setting, demonstrated here to be associated with increased accessibility.

There are several alternative explanations for the lack of differential outcomes between treatment and control groups, however. First, it is possible that our results are an artifact or the result of some factor other than a true test of our group variable. For instance, some authors (e.g., Robinson, Berman, & Neimeyer, 1990) have suggested that the apparent superiority of certain forms of treatment may be due to investigator allegiance effects. That is, researchers' or clinicians' preferences for or differential expertise with one particular intervention may influence the apparent effectiveness of the treatments. More specifically, Shirk and Russell (1992) have suggested that estimates of the effectiveness of nonbehavioral child therapy may be inaccurately low, because of investigator allegiance effects manifested through such factors as inexperienced supervision of nonbehavioral treatments. Thus, our results potentially could be attributed to clinicians' or supervisors' lack of experience or investment in nonbehavioral treatments. However, in the present study our clinicians determined the treatments that they themselves provided, and they were supervised by experienced clinicians who themselves were primarily nonbehavioral. Thus it seems unlikely that "experimenter allegiance" effects influenced our results greatly.

For many children in the project, treatment was terminated because the research project was ending rather than because the clinician and parent decided that the child had improved significantly. Thus, another possible explanation for our null findings is that our children failed to receive sufficient services. However, in a study of child therapy involving nine different outpatient centers, Weisz and Weiss (1989) reported that the average child who completed treatment and terminated with the concurrence of the therapist had received 12.4 sessions; the 2-year sample in the current project received almost five times that number. Thus, our children received a much larger amount of services than is typical for outpatient services.

Another alternative interpretation for our results is that the SBC program was effective in treating the children, but academic tutoring was as well, producing a nonsignificant comparison—that is, both groups might have shown significantly more improvement than a no-treatment control group. Some researchers (e.g., Strupp, 1993) have suggested that the effects of treatment may at least in part be due to "non-specific" effects—that is, factors that most if not all interventions share, such as increasing the client's hope or generating experiences of success. Some, although certainly not all, students in our program were lacking relationships with supportive adults, and home and school too often provided contexts for punishment and failure. Thus, the tutoring experience of being involved with a caring adult in a relationship focused on positive goals, of achieving success in an important domain, of receiving contingent but frequent praise, may have served as a nonspecific treatment. Our null findings might represent two equally effective treatments, rather than an ineffective treatment and a control group.

If this is the case, however, the effectiveness of traditional mental health services such as provided by the SBC program remains problematic. The tutors were for the most part college students or graduate students in special education, all without clinical training. Thus, if the tutoring program did function as a successful treatment, the lengthy and expensive formal training associated with most clinical training programs appears unnecessary. In fact, there is evidence suggesting that formal clinical training may not be associated with significantly greater effectiveness (e.g., Berman, 1985; Weisz, Weiss, Alicke, & Klotz, 1987), which is consistent with the possibility that our tutors functioned as untrained, nonspecific therapists, despite the lack of overtly therapeutic content in the tutoring sessions.

It should be noted that there is evidence arguing against the hypothesis that academic tutoring functioned as a nonspecific treatment. In a meta-analysis of child therapy studies, Weiss and Weisz (1990) compared outcome effect sizes for studies using attention-placebo control groups to effect sizes for studies using other forms of control groups. If attention-placebo control groups such as our academic tutoring condition do function as nonspecific forms of treatment, then one would expect that studies using attention-placebo control groups would be associated with smaller effect sizes than studies using other forms of control groups, since in the former studies the nonspecific effects are, in essence, being removed from the effect size. However, the effect of control group in Weiss and Weisz (1990) was nonsignificant.

If academic tutoring did function as a nonspecific treatment, it is possible that its effects are less durable than those of the treatments provided by our clinicians. In general, when child treatments are effective, the effects do appear to be lasting (Weisz, Weiss, Alicke, & Klotz, 1987; Weisz, Weiss, Han, Granger, & Morton, 1995). However, it is possible that this durability is due to the specific components of treatment. The social support and other positive experiences provided by tutoring may have been sufficient to improve children's functioning while these experiences were occurring, but may not have been sufficient to produce lasting changes. Unlike the more developed treatments provided by the clinicians, the nonspecific effects of tutoring may not have impacted on coping styles, underlying cognitive styles, and so forth, sufficiently to produce lasting changes. This possibility will be tested when 1-year follow-up data are collected for the project.

It is also possible that the Tutoring versus SBC comparison was nonsignificant because our measures were insensitive to change, or because the nonclinically referred children whom we selected did not need treatment, and thus were unresponsive to treatment. However, arguing against both of these hypotheses is the fact that both the Tutoring and SBC groups showed substantial improvement.

A final alternative explanation is that the Tutoring and SBC children may have not differed in regard to outcome because the tutoring children derived indirect benefits from the SBC program. For instance, students were randomly assigned to the Tutoring or SBC condition, and students from both conditions sometimes were in the same classroom. Consequently, it is possible that Tutoring students may have indirectly benefited from interventions and consultations directed toward the students in the SBC condition. For example, teachers may have applied behavior management skills to the entire class even though the consultation was intended to target the students in the counseling condition. In this way, the SBC program may have created a therapeutic environment throughout the classroom or school. It is also possible that as the behavior and affect of SBC children improved in response to treatment, their changes positively influenced other children in the school.

In conclusion, the SBC evaluation project demonstrated that service systems can be successfully implemented to identify children in need of services but not receiving them, and access and utilization of services can be increased using a school-based model. The effectiveness of traditional mental health services delivered in this manner remains unclear, however, until the results of our 1-year follow up have been completed. If these results are similar to the present results, it may be important to implement more structured, time-limited treatments in the schools rather than traditional mental health services. Indeed, future research might focus on the adaptation of empirically derived treatment techniques in the school setting and perhaps look at stronger interventions with teachers and classrooms. Though some research-based treatment techniques currently exist for specific types of disorders, the applicability of these models with the target population we have described (particularly those students that have co-morbid conditions) is not clear. New treatment techniques specifically for this population may have to be devised and tested.

Lessons Learned

Conducting an experiment of this magnitude in a naturalistic setting posed many challenges, providing us with an opportunity to learn a number of lessons. Probably the foremost lesson was that when one is working in a naturalistic setting, despite the best planning, it is inevitable that an evaluation project will run into unexpected events requiring difficult yet rapid decision making. For instance, as noted above, one of the SBC clinicians developed a chronic illness during the course of the project, necessitating her caseload's being precipitously transferred to another clinician. This event was unanticipated and required a quick decision in order to minimize the impact on the research. The radical change in school busing patterns, and the potential reassignment of many of our participants to nonproject schools subsequent to the end of the federally mandated desegregation plan for the metro school district, provides another example of an unanticipated challenge to the integrity of our research design. (Fortunately, for the project at least, the end of the desegregation plan was delayed until after the completion of our project).

Implications for Policy and Practice

Our experiences and the results of our data analyses suggest some important implications for policy and practice. To begin, the organization and delivery of mental health services to students from socioeconomically disadvantaged backgrounds can be enhanced through an ongoing collaboration of school officials and mental health professionals. The school setting, with its mandatory attendance policy for children, provides an excellent setting for the delivery of mental health interventions; services become accessible to a population of youngsters whose mental health needs typically go unmet. It follows that satellite clinics based in schools should be considered a legitimate service-delivery platform by federal, state and commercial payers.

However, one apparent drawback to the use of a school-based setting for provision of services to children may be reduced parental involvement, relative to parental involvement for clinic-based services. One of the most frequent complaints voiced by the SBC clinicians was the difficulty they often experienced in getting parents to attend meetings at the schools. This may have been due to the fact that to bring a child to a mental health clinic requires a certain level of motivation on the part of the parent, whereas child involvement in school-based services requires relatively little motivation on the part of the parent. Thus, school-based services may access a less motivated population than clinic-based services.

A corollary of this is that if providers are interested in using a school-based setting for service provision, an extra effort may be necessary to involve parents. This might take the form of providing transportation, use of group meetings where refreshments are served, providing child care during the group meetings, and so forth.

Another implication of our SBC experiences is that global policies that promote the application of untested mental health interventions should be questioned. The current findings provide support for basing services in the schools on an effort to meet the mental health needs of an underserved population. However, these data further demonstrate that more scientific inquiry is needed to determine what kinds of services will result in psychosocial improvements for students enrolled in counseling. Students enrolled in SBC made significant improvements in mental health functioning. Had this not been a controlled study of mental health outcome, these findings might have been misinterpreted. As consumers of mental health programs for children, it is important that we pay careful attention to whether or not programs that promise improvements in psychosocial outcomes have been subject to experimental evaluation. Policymakers and practitioners should be careful to distinguish between an innovative service-delivery model (i.e., school-based) and intervention techniques that are as yet untested, especially when limited financial resources are at stake. In light of these findings, local, state, and federal authorities would do well to secure data from systematic evaluations of prospective interventions and innovative models of service delivery prior to making determinations regarding resource allocation, thus avoiding the wholesale endorsement of potentially ineffective programs.

Endnotes

1. Experience with similar child populations indicated that the term "counseling" was less threatening to families than other terms such as "psychotherapy" or "mental health services," which might more accurately describe the treatment and services provided in the project. Consequently, the term "counseling" was used throughout the project.

2. In all except three instances, children failed to complete the tutoring or counseling programs because their families left the area. In one of these three instances (an SBC child), the family left the program because the family was reported for suspected child abuse. In the other two instances (one SBC child, one Tutoring child), the families left because they were "tired" of being involved in the program.

3. During the latter half of the first year of the intervention, one of the SBC therapists developed a chronic illness that resulted in her being absent a number of days over a period of several months. Toward the end of the school year, the therapist missed a 2-week period of work because of her illness. As a result, a new therapist was hired to continue working with students at that treatment site for the remainder of the intervention. Students at this school were not included in the 2-year outcome data presented in this chapter.

Authors' Notes

This research was supported in part by grants from the National Institute of Mental Health (NIMH 1-R18-MH50265) and Substance Abuse and Mental Health Services Administration (SAMHSA 5-HD5-SM50265). The authors wish to thank Patsi Bleecker for her assistance in managing the project; Terry Katzman-Rosenblum, Allyson Ross, and Susan Ratcliffe for their contributions to the program development and implementation; the Metropolitan Nashville Public Schools; Dr. James Zerface; Dr. Warren Thompson; Dede Wallace Health Care Systems; Elam Mental Health Center; Meharry Mental Health Center; the Vanderbilt Child and Adolescent Psychiatry Outpatient Clinic; the principals and teachers of participating schools for their organizational assistance in providing services; the therapists and supervisors who provided the services; and most important, the families and children who participated in the project.

Correspondence regarding this chapter should be sent to Thomas Catron, PhD, Vanderbilt University, 1500 21st Avenue South, Suite 2200, Nashville, TN 37212, or via email at catrontf@ctrvax.vanderbilt.edu.

References

Achenbach, T. M. (1991a). *Manual for the Child Behavior Checklist/4-18 and 1991 Profile.* Burlington: University of Vermont, Department of Psychiatry.

Achenbach, T. M. (1991b). *Manual for the Teacher's Report Form and 1991 Profile.* Burlington: University of Vermont, Department of Psychiatry.

American Psychiatric Association (APA). (1987). *Diagnostic and statistical manual of mental disorders* (3rd ed., rev.). Washington, DC: Author.

Berman, J. S. (1985). Does professional training make a therapist more effective? *Psychological Bulletin, 98,* 401–407.

Bickman, L. (in press). Implications of a children's mental health managed care demonstration evaluation. *Journal of the American Medical Association.*

Bickman, L., Guthrie, P., Foster, E. M., Lambert, E. W., Summerfelt, W. T., Breda, C., & Heflinger, C. A. (1995). *Evaluating managed mental health services: The Fort Bragg Experiment.* New York: Plenum Press.

Burns, B. J. (1991). Mental health service use by adolescents in the 1970's and 1980's. *Journal of the American Academy of Child and Adolescent Psychiatry, 30,* 144–150.

Catron, T., & Weiss, B. (1994). The Vanderbilt School-Based Counseling Program. *Journal of Emotional and Behavioral Disorders, 2,* 247–253.

Cohen, J. (1988). *Statistical power analysis for the behavioral sciences* (2nd. ed.). Hillsdale, NJ: Erlbaum.

Cohen, J. (1990). Things I have learned (so far). *American Psychologist, 45,* 1304–1312.

Dryfoos, J. (1990). *Adolescents at risk: Prevalence and prevention.* New York: Oxford University Press.

Epstein, M., Cullinan, D., Quinn, K., & Cumbald, C. (1995). Personal, family, and service use characteristics of young people served by an interagency community-based system of care. *Journal of Emotional and Behavioral Disorders, 3,* 55–64.

Gould, M. S., Shaffer, D., & Kaplan, D. (1985). The characteristics of dropouts from a child psychiatry clinic. *Journal of the American Academy of Child Psychiatry, 24,* 316–328.

Gould, M. S., Wunsch-Hitzig, R., & Dohrenwend, B. (1981). Estimating the prevalence of childhood psychopathology. *Journal of the American Academy of Child Psychiatry, 20,* 462–476.

Hart, E. L., Lahey, B. B., Loeber, R., & Hanson, K. S. (1994). Criterion validity of informants in the diagnosis of disruptive behavior disorders in children: A preliminary study. *Journal of Consulting & Clinical Psychology, 62,* 410–414.

Institute of Medicine. (1989). *Research on children and adolescents with mental behavioral and developmental disorders.* Washington, DC: National Academy Press.

Kazdin, A. E., Esveldt-Dawson, K., Unis, A. S., & Rancurello, M. D. (1983). Child and parent evaluations of depression and aggression in psychiatric inpatient children. *Journal of Abnormal Child Psychology, 3,* 401–413.

Kendall, P. C., & Morris, R. J. (1991). Child therapy: Issues and recommendations. *Journal of Consulting and Clinical Psychology, 59,* 777–784.

Lefkowitz, M. M., & Tesiny, E. P. (1980). Assessment of childhood depression. *Journal of Consulting and Clinical Psychology, 48,* 433–450.

Loeber, R., Green, S. M., Lahey, B. B., & Stouthamer-Loeber, M. (1990). Optimal informants on childhood disruptive behaviors. *Development and Psychopathology, 1,* 317–337.

Pearcy, M. T., Clopton, J. R., & Pope, A. W. (1993). Influences on teacher referral of children to mental health services: Gender, severity, and internalizing versus externalizing problems. *Journal of Emotional & Behavioral Disorders, 1,* 165–169.

Quiggle, N. L., Garber, J., Panak, W. F., & Dodge, K. A. (1992). Social information processing patterns in depressed and aggressive children. *Child Development, 63,* 1305–1320.

Robinson, L. A., Berman, J. S., & Neimeyer, R. A. (1990). Psychotherapy for the treatment of depression: A comprehensive review of controlled outcome research. *Psychological Bulletin, 108,* 30–49.

Schorr, L. B. (1988). *Within our reach: Breaking the cycle of disadvantage.* New York: Doubleday.

Shirk, S. R., & Russell, R. L. (1992). A reevaluation of estimates of child therapy effectiveness. *Journal of the American Academy of Child and Adolescent Psychiatry, 31,* 703–709.

Shuchman, M. (1991, February 21). How urban children suffer from witnessing violence. *New York Times,* pp. B6-B7.

Spielberger, C. D. (1973). *Manual for the State-Trait Anxiety Inventory for Children.* Palo Alto: Consulting Psychologists Press.

Strupp, H. H. (1993). The Vanderbilt psychotherapy studies: Synopsis. *Journal of Consulting & Clinical Psychology, 61,* 431–433.

Tolmach, J. (1985). There ain't nobody on my side: A new day treatment program for black urban youth. *Journal of Clinical Psychology, 14*(3), 214–219.

Weiss, B., & Garber, J. (1993). The Vanderbilt Depression Inventory. Unpublished manuscript, Vanderbilt University, Nashville, TN.

Weiss, B., & Weisz, J. R. (1990). The impact of methodological factors on child psychotherapy outcome research: A meta-analysis for researchers. *Journal of Abnormal Child Psychology, 18,* 639–670.

Weiss, B., & Weisz, J. R. (1995). Relative effectiveness of behavioral versus nonbehavioral child psychotherapy. *Journal of Consulting and Clinical Psychology,* 317–320.

Weissman, M. M., Wickramaratne, P., Warner, V., John, K., Prusoff, B. A., Merikangas, K. R., & Gammon, D. (1987). Assessing psychiatric disorders in children: Discrepancies between mother's and children's report. *Archives of General Psychiatry, 44,* 747–753.

Weisz, J. R., Donenberg, G. R., Han, S. S., & Weiss, B. (1995). Bridging the gap between lab and clinic in child and adolescent psychotherapy. *Journal of Consulting and Clinical Psychology, 63,*(5), 688–701.

Weisz, J. R., & Weiss, B. (1989). Assessing the effects of clinic-based psychotherapy with children and adolescents. *Journal of Consulting and Clinical Psychology, 57,* 741–746.

Weisz, J. R., & Weiss, B. (1991). Studying the "referability" of child clinical problems. *Journal of Consulting and Clinical Psychology, 59,* 266–273.

Weisz, J. R., Weiss, B., Alicke, M. D., & Klotz, M. L. (1987). Effectiveness of psychotherapy with children and adolescents: A meta-analysis for clinicians. *Journal of Consulting and Clinical Psychology, 55,* 542–549.

Weisz, J. R., Weiss, B., & Donenberg, G. R. (1992). The lab versus the clinic: Effects of child and adolescent psychotherapy. *American Psychologist, 47,* 1578–1585.

Weisz, J. R., Weiss, B., & Langmeyer, D. (1987). Giving up on child psychotherapy: Who drops out? *Journal of Consulting and Clinical Psychology, 55,* 916–918.

Wilson, W. J. (1987). *The truly disadvantaged: The inner city, the underclass and public policy.* Chicago: University of Chicago Press.

Conclusion

V

Managed Care: Opportunities and Threats for Children with Serious Emotional Disturbance and Their Families

23

Sarah Hudson Scholle,
and Kelly J. Kelleher

Despite the failure of national health reform efforts, the U.S. health system is undergoing dramatic change because of the widespread growth of managed care. In this chapter, we use the term "managed care" to refer to insurance arrangements that link the financing of health care to service delivery with the goals of improving health care and reducing costs.[1] The most common techniques used by managed care organizations (MCOs) include the definition of a preferred provider network, the employment of utilization review methods, and the monitoring of high-cost cases. In addition to MCOs that sponsor full health insurance coverage, there is a growing market of companies that specialize in managing behavioral health (including mental health and substance abuse) services.

The growth of managed care has profound implications for children with serious emotional disturbance (SED). MCOs generally espouse a commitment to improving coordination, continuity, and access to health services through clearly delineated care-seeking pathways, improved management information systems, and enhanced linkages among various levels of care. These mechanisms offer opportunities for reducing the fragmentation of mental health services frequently experienced by children with SED. The goals often cited by MCOs are similar to the defining principles of public agency systems caring for children and adolescents with SED derived from the National Institute of Mental Health (NIMH) Child and Adolescent Service System Program (CASSP) program (Stroul & Friedman, 1986).

Some goals of managed care organizations (MCOs) are closely tied to the ideal "system of care" espoused as the cornerstone of CASSP (Stroul & Friedman,

1986). In fact, both philosophies were a reaction to fragmented fee-for-service (FFS) systems that had evolved over time in a piecemeal fashion. Child and family advocates have pushed for a system of care that promotes a particular set of core principles. These include the child as the center of care so that individual treatment plans are developed, rather than building services and then requiring children to "fit in." In addition, services should be family focused and community based. In other words, the strengths and needs of the family should be a core element of service design, and service delivery should occur locally and in the community whenever possible. Mental health services should be coordinated and culturally competent. Thus, information is required to flow across various service settings and provider groups for improving coordination, while cultural competency is enhanced through training and the local provision of care. Finally, services should be delivered in the least restrictive setting to avoid hospitalizations and out-of-home placements whenever possible.

Although there was and continues to be considerable consensus around these core CASSP or system-of-care principles among advocates and academics, limited gains in establishing such systems were made outside of demonstration projects prior to the early 1990s. However, the expansion of managed care has provided many of the key elements necessary to achieve these principles (Center for Vulnerable Populations, 1996). First, MCOs employ coordinated service-delivery networks that discourage the use of restrictive settings. In addition, their sophisticated information systems allow much greater coordination of care. Finally, MCOs have expanded alternative service-delivery mechanisms in order to limit the use of inpatient settings. Unfortunately, given the financial incentives MCOs have to restrict overall utilization, it is not clear whether MCO members, especially children with the greatest services needs, will benefit from these advances in coordination and community orientation.

The attractiveness of managed care for children with SED is also evident for those concerned about costs. Mental health care utilization and costs for children have increased dramatically in the last decade, outpacing the rate of increase among adults (Hoagwood, 1994). The growth in services utilization, especially of inpatient and other restrictive types of care, is thought to be related to the development and marketing of psychiatric facilities to serve the privately insured population. To control these costs, both fee-for-service and managed care insurance plans are contracting with behavioral health care firms that specialize in the management of mental health and substance use services. In 1994, over half of the persons with private insurance (106.6 million out of 185.7 million persons) were enrolled in plans that used some type of behavioral health care management program (Iglehart, 1996).

The promise of reduced health care costs has been particularly enticing for state Medicaid programs, given their increasing costs and decreasing federal payments. The number of Medicaid enrollees in MCOs tripled in 1994 and now include 25% of the Medicaid enrollees in the country (Frank & McGuire, 1994). Because Medicaid accounts for at least 20% of U.S. expenditures for mental health services, the impact of this shift on persons with psychiatric disorders is likely to be dramatic. In addition, many states have plans to institute MCOs for general medical and behavioral services in the near future (Essock & Goldman, 1995).

The rapid growth of managed care and its potential for changing the care of children with SED make it important to understand how MCOs function, their historical record of impact on other populations, and potential implications for children with SED. The purposes of this chapter are (a) to describe the mechanisms for controlling costs and improving efficiency employed by MCOs and increasingly adopted by other health insurers, (b) to review the limited data available about the effects of managed care on utilization and outcomes of care, (c) to suggest potential implications for developing a system of care for children with SED and their families, and (d) to examine future research opportunities.

Mechanisms Used by Managed Care Organizations

Under the broad goals of discouraging utilization, lowering costs, and improving the quality of care, MCOs have adopted a variety of structures and mechanisms. In this section, mechanisms relating to the financing, organization, and content of health care will be described, along with the common organizational structures, such as health maintenance organizations, primary care case management plans, preferred provider organizations, and mental health "carve-out" plans.

Financing

In contrast to traditional FFS insurance that rewards providers for increased use of services, MCOs give providers and patients financial incentives to discourage utilization. MCOs often reduce the amount paid for particular services or place providers at financial risk for utilization above a predicted amount. Many early managed care arrangements relied on FFS financing at discounted rates through the use of preferred provider networks. Individual providers or groups of providers were guaranteed a particular volume of patients in exchange for reducing their fees for specific services. However, this payment option still encouraged increased use because the payment was for services rendered. Thus, plans have also tied physician income to the utilization experience of their patients by withholding a portion of physicians' fees or by giving bonuses based on utilization reports at the end of the year. Increasingly, plans are using capitation arrangements, whereby providers assume responsibility for the care of a particular population at a certain amount per person, per month. Capitation arrangements may cover all health care or be limited to specialty services (e.g., mental health care.)

Cost-sharing can also extend to the patient side through the use of financial incentives and benefit limitations. The amount of consumer cost-sharing is often tied to whether patients use network or out-of-network services and to whether the patients obtain authorization in advance for services. MCOs frequently encourage primary care use by charging minimal or no co-payments for preventive services or primary care visits, while steep fees are incurred for unauthorized use of specialty providers, use of out-of-plan providers, or use of brand name drugs.

Organization

MCOs exercise more control over the organization of health care services than do traditional FFS plans. They often rely on primary care clinicians to act as gatekeepers to more expensive forms of care. Plans frequently require that referrals be made to selected networks of specialty providers and offer significant financial incentives for patients and physicians to use network providers. All of these events are monitored through the extensive use of computerized management information systems that allow feedback about particular patterns of use by specific patients or by the patient population of specific providers.

Content

Managed care systems increase administrative oversight of the content of care through utilization review practices and mandated use of guidelines and protocols. Utilization review techniques are usually focused on particular events (e.g., inpatient admissions) and include precertification, concurrent review, and case management practices. The purpose of precertification is to determine whether hospitalization or other placement is warranted, given a patient's psychiatric symptoms and circumstances. Concurrent review and case management techniques include review of the treatment plans, required compliance with standards of care, and discharge planning. In contrast to these routine utilization review mechanisms, which focus on particular events, some plans have developed case management services of a broader scope that target persons who meet a threshold level of expenditures. For these high-cost users, the assigned case manager reviews care over the duration of the illness and often has the ability to create individual treatment plans that substitute services not usually covered for more expensive treatments (e.g., respite care or a home health aide).

In addition to utilization review, growing numbers of MCOs are instituting practice guidelines and outcomes management systems to reduce the variations in diagnostic and treatment services, to control costs, and to enhance quality.

The increasing availability of nationally recognized practice guidelines for common conditions has made these efforts feasible. Less common is the use of outcomes management to improve practice and to document quality.

Types of Managed Care Organizations

Various forms of MCOs use the tools just described in controlling utilization and improving efficiency to different degrees. Today, virtually all traditional FFS or indemnity plans have instituted activities associated with managed care, such as utilization review (Mechanic, Schlesinger, & McAlpine, 1995). The MCOs that use the mechanisms described above include several basic models. Health maintenance organizations (HMOs) provide specified health services for a fixed fee per member, per month. Primary care case-management programs (PCCMs), often used by Medicaid programs, pay physicians a monthly fee to accept responsibility for coordinating a patient's care, but pay physicians on a FFS basis for care rendered (Hurley, Freund, & Paul, 1993). Preferred provider organizations (PPOs) are networks of providers who offer discounted fees to patients and utilization management to employers and insurers. Newer variants such as triple-option plans and point-of-service plans allow for more patient choice by offering consumers the ability to obtain services through HMO-type plans with lower out-of-pocket costs, or the option of seeing providers outside of a specified provider network at higher out-of-pocket costs.

Many MCOs also make special arrangements for management and delivery of specialty services such as mental health care. In particular, a large number of MCOs "carve out" mental health and substance abuse benefits to firms specializing in the management of these services. MCOs (and many FFS plans and self-insured employers) pay behavioral managed care organizations (BMCOs) an administrative fee for managing behavioral health services. However, increasingly employers and insurers are contracting with BMCOs on a risk basis; that is, the BMCOs receive a fixed sum per capita annually to provide mental health and substance abuse services and, thus, have financial incentives to restrict utilization of services. The methods used by behavioral MCOs to manage care are familiar: Patients are required to obtain prior authorization for services, often by calling a toll-free phone number and reviewing their circumstances with a staff member who assesses their needs according to a standardized protocol. The protocols used to determine level of need, which may be proprietary and unavailable to providers or patients, emphasize the use of least expensive services and favor outpatient services over more restrictive settings. Patients are usually referred to a selected provider network.

Several states have experimented with carve-outs for behavioral health care in the public sectors. The managed care program for mental health services among Massachusetts Medicaid recipients (Callahan, Shepard, Beinecke, Larson, & Cavanaugh, 1995; Dickey et al., 1995) exemplifies the types of mechanisms used by BMCOs to reduce expenditures. Massachusetts contracted on a capitated basis with a private behavioral MCO. The BMCO negotiated reimbursement rates with a network of providers who were paid on a FFS basis, conducted aggressive utilization review, encouraged community-based alternatives to hospitalization, and worked with the Department of Mental Health to establish emergency service teams to reduce hospitalizations. Other states (e.g., Pennsylvania and Oregon) have contracted with public sector agencies to provide care with a limited level of financial risk.

Effects of Managed Care on Mental Health Care

Although the growth of managed care systems has been explosive, little knowledge exists to inform professionals about their impact of managed care systems on patient services or outcomes, especially among the most vulnerable population of children and adolescents with SED. Very few researchers have examined the effects of managed care on children and adolescents in general (Freund & Hurley, 1995; Kelleher & Scholle, 1995), and only in one study was the focus on the effects of managed care on children with emotional problems (Burns, Thompson, & Goldman, 1993). Thus, in this review, we will draw primarily on studies of mental health care for adult populations. The studies conducted to date are primarily of two types: (a) detailed studies comparing mental health care among general populations of persons in FFS and MCO, and (b) studies of government efforts designed specifically to manage mental health services.

The first group, managed care research studies, are described in Table 23.1. The RAND Health Insurance Experiment, a large multisite study conducted during the early 1980s, is the only U.S. study that randomly assigned individuals to FFS versus prepaid care. Data on mental health services use and outcomes were analyzed only for the Seattle site. While the RAND experiment has the most rigorous design of studies to date, the comparison of an established prepaid health maintenance organization to traditional FFS may not be as relevant in today's complex managed care market.

The other two studies used observational designs to examine services use and outcomes under different forms of managed care. The RAND Preferred Provider Organization study compared mental health services use among persons receiving coverage through three large employers in Florida and California. Services use and costs were compared between individuals who primarily used PPO providers and those who primarily used non-PPO providers. In the third study, the Medical Outcomes Study, adults with chronic conditions (including diabetes, hypertension, and depression) were recruited from primary care and specialty physicians' offices and HMOs in Boston, Chicago, and Los Angeles. Persons were stratified by type of plan (HMO, Independent Practice Association [IPA], and FFS), and services and outcomes were compared among

Table 23.1

Managed Care Research Studies

Study Title and Location (Reference)	Methods	Results
RAND Health Insurance Study, Seattle (Wells et al, 1986a; Manning et al, 1987; Wells et al., 1989).	Design: Random assignment of general population to fee-for-service or prepaid HMO care. Sample size: Services: 3,773 in prepaid; 2,687 in FFS. Outcomes: 3,040 person-years in prepaid; 2,687 person-years in FFS. Dependent variables: Any mental health use, number of mental health visits, use of mental health specialty care, costs, mental health status.	Access: Percent of HMO participants using mental health care was similar to or higher than that among FFS participants. Use: Average number of specialty mental health visits was three times higher in FFS than HMO (17.2 in free FFS care vs. 4.7 in HMO). Intensity of treatment was lower in HMO group: Psychiatric social workers were substituted for psychiatrists and psychologists, and group therapy for individual therapy. Costs: Costs of mental health care for patients in FFS with no cost-sharing were 2.8 times the costs of those in prepaid plan. Outcomes: No differences in mental health outcomes were noted, although low-income persons with initially poor mental health status fared less well in prepaid plan.
RAND Preferred Provider Organization Study, Florida and California. (Wells et al., 1992).	Design: Quasi-experimental study comparing mental health services before and after implementation of PPO option in FFS plan. Sample size: Three employer groups totaling 58,000 enrollees. Dependent variables: Probability of mental health use, number of outpatient mental health visits, outpatient charges.	Access: Decrease in access among those with no regular provider intending to use PPO in first PPO year. Use: Lower levels of use were found among patients who regularly used PPO providers than patients who used non-PPO providers. Costs: Lower costs were observed among patients who regularly used PPO providers than patients who used non-PPO providers.

(continues)

Table 23.1 *Continued*

Study Title and Location (Reference)	Methods	Results
Medical Outcomes Study, Boston, Chicago, and Los Angeles. (Rogers et al., 1993; Sturm et al., 1994; Wells et al., 1994; Sturm et al., 1995; Wells et al., 1995).	Design: Observational study of care for adults with chronic conditions in fee-for-service or prepaid (HMO and IPA). Sample size: Services: 389 prepaid, 384 FFS. Outcomes: 288 prepaid, 329 FFS. Dependent variables: Any mental health use, number of mental health visits, depressive symptoms, functional limitations.	Access: Six percent decrease in access among managed care enrollees vs. FFS. Use: 35–40% fewer mental health visits among managed care than FFS enrollees. MC enrollees had a more rapid decline in antidepressant use. Outcomes: No differences in outcomes were noted among patients of general medical clinicians, psychologists, or other therapists; however, patients initially enrolled in prepaid plan were more likely than FFS enrollees to develop a functional limitation.

groups both cross-sectionally and in longitudinal follow-ups. Together, these three studies, which have followed individuals over time, provide valuable, detailed information on mental health services and outcomes for the general population. However, even the Medical Outcomes Study, which was begun in the mid-1980s and has generated a large body of evidence comparing services use and outcomes for adults with chronic illnesses in prepaid versus fee-for-service care, may not capture the diversity of managed care plans active today.

Capitation studies (listed in Table 23.2) have largely been conducted to evaluate policy changes in the organization and delivery of care. Three studies focusing on Medicaid populations illustrate the different methods of managed care contracting used by state Medicaid programs. These include (a) contracts with MCOs for all services (including mental health services), (b) capitation contracts with community-based providers, and (c) capitation contracts with behavioral MCOs. The Hennepin County program randomly assigned chronically mentally ill patients to a prepaid HMO plan as part of a demonstration of managed care for all Medicaid recipients. Services costs and outcomes were compared for participants in the prepaid plans versus FFS participants. However, the period of follow up was brief because the demonstration was discontinued after only 1 year. In Utah, the state Medicaid program contracted with community mental health centers to provide MH/SA services for Medicaid recipients in specific catchment areas. The evaluation includes pre-post comparison of services and outcomes as well as comparisons with Medicaid recipients in other catchment areas where FFS reimbursement continued. The Massachusetts plan, with all mental health services carved out to a behavioral MCO, has been evaluated using pre-post data.

Several of the other studies addressing capitation arrangements focused specifically on persons with severe mental illness (SMI). In both the Monroe-Livingston Project and the Arizona study, persons with SMI were randomly assigned to either FFS or capitated services. The Monroe-Livingston project provides the greatest detail on services use and outcomes, comparing capitated and FFS participants.

The only published study to focus on children with SED in managed care is the Tidewater Study (Burns et al., 1993). In this demonstration project, the federal health insurance program for dependents of military personnel (CHAMPUS) contracted on a capitated basis with independent firms to manage mental health services for all children. This study used administratively collected data to report observational findings for children in the capitated program. For this reason, limited information on the processes and outcomes of care were available, and no comparison group was used.

The results from the managed care research studies described above with regard to selective enrollment, utilization, quality, outcomes, and satisfaction will be reviewed. Also, findings from capitation programs will be discussed and compared with the findings from research studies.

Table 23.2

Evaluation of Capitation Programs

Study Title and Location (Reference)	Methods	Results
Arizona. (Leff et al., 1994).	Design: State contracted on capitated basis with providers to provide services for severely mentally ill. Patients randomly assigned to capitated plans (with replacement for refusals) compared to FFS participants. Sample size: 7,539 client-months of observation. Dependent variables: Probability of use, intensity of use, total utilization, access, adequacy, appropriateness.	Access: Compared to standard recommended by expert panel, persons in capitated programs were more likely to have any use than FFS clients. Use: Compared to standard recommended by expert panel, persons in capitated programs were more likely to have recommended amount of services than FFS clients.
CHAMPUS Tidewater Demonstration, Virginia. (Burns et al., 1993).	Design: Contractor Provider Arrangement where federal CHAMPUS program pays independent health care contractors on capitated basis to manage care with emphasis on use of partial hospitalization services. Three-year follow-up of children age 0–17. Sample size: The number of service users was 1,552 in year 1, 2,033 in year 2, and 3,648 in year 3. The number of eligible beneficiaries was approximately 105,000 in each year. Dependent variables: Services use by level of care (outpatient, partial hospitalization, residential treatment center, and inpatient).	Use: Admissions to inpatient (IP) and residential treatment centers (RTC) decreased over the 3-year period from 17.0 to 3.7 for IP and from 3.5 to 0.2 for RTC. Quality: Some youths with very low functioning and exhibiting suicidal behavior were admitted to outpatient treatment.

Table 23.2 Continued

Study Title and Location (Reference)	Methods	Results
Massachusetts Medicaid Managed Mental Health. (Dickey et al., 1995; Callahan et al., 1995).	Description: Medicaid program contracted with single, private for-profit company to manage mental health under capitated plan. All disabled and AFDC recipients were included in plan. Evaluation design: Pre-post comparison with 1-year follow-up. Sample size: 375,000 Medicaid recipients in 1992. Dependent variables: Predicted vs. actual costs, expenditures, rate of use per 1,000 enrollees by type of service.	Access: Increase in rate of medicaid recipients using mental health and substance abuse services. Use: Decrease in rate of inpatient admissions. Quality: Readmission rates were slightly lower overall, but increased for the nondisabled and for children (from 7.5–10.1%). Proportion of patients with no outpatient follow-up after inpatient event increased during the study period from 26 to 37%. Costs: State expenditures for mental health and substance abuse were 22% lower than predicted.
Monroe-Livingston Demonstration Project, New York. (Babigian et al., 1991; Reed et al., 1994; Cole et al., 1994).	Description: State Office of Mental Health paid capitation rate to local CMHCs to coordinate and provide care for SMI adults with prior admission to state psychiatric hospitals. Evaluation design: Random assignment with 2-year follow-up. Sample size: Use and costs: 138 experimental, 63 control patients. Outcomes: 153 experimental, 74 control continuous patients. Dependent variables: Number of hospital days, number of psychiatric symptoms, level of functioning, costs, time to rehospitalization.	Use: Patients in capitated program had fewer hospital days (after controlling for initial functioning and symptoms): Mean hospital days for year 1 were 182 in capitated program vs. 230 in the control group; in year 2, mean days were 126 vs. 165. Quality: Time to first rehospitalization was shorter in capitated plan. Outcomes: Functioning and symptoms were similar in the two groups. Costs: In year 1, average costs per person were $91,183 in the capitated program vs. $105,773 in the control group; in year 2, $73,655 vs. $86,190.

(continues)

Table 23.2 *Continued*

Study Title and Location (Reference)	Methods	Results
Hennepin County Medicaid Demonstration Program, Minnesota. (Lurie et al., 1992; Christianson et al., 1992).	Description: Medicaid contracted with four prepaid IPA plans, including one sponsored by the county. Medicaid recipients including chronically mentally ill adults were randomly assigned to prepaid HMO plan. Evaluation design: Follow-up interviews were conducted between 7 and 12 months after implementation. Patients with schizophrenia were followed an additional 9–11 months. Sample size: 354 prepaid, 355 FFS Dependent variables: use of community-based mental health services, health status, functioning, psychiatric symptoms.	Cost: No difference in use of community-based mental health treatment programs in prepaid vs. FFS, but prepaid clients had larger write-offs. Outcomes: No differences in psychiatric symptoms and general health in FFS vs. prepaid, although functioning worsened among persons with schizophrenia in prepaid care.
Utah-Prepaid Mental Health Plan. (Christianson et al., 1995).	Description: Capitated payments to CMHCs for provision of services to all Medicaid beneficiaries in catchment area. Evaluation design: Pre-post comparison and contemporaneous control group with 1-year follow-up. Sample size: Not stated. Dependent variables: Inpatient, outpatient, and emergency department mental health use; inpatient and overall mental health costs.	Use: Decrease in inpatient admissions under capitated program but not in outpatient or emergency department use for mental health. Costs: Decreases in inpatient expenditures were found under capitated program. Payments per beneficiary per month were $6.72 under the prepaid plan, compared to the $12.02 expected without the plan (from regression estimates). Savings of $2.3 million were estimated by comparing amount paid under capitation to predicted amount of reimbursements.

Findings from Managed Care Studies

Enrollment

The potential for selective enrollment in MCOs has been a key concern for policymakers and researchers. There is strong evidence of favorable selection bias to managed care; persons who join HMOs or PPOs have lower baseline use and costs, better self-reported health status and functional status, and fewer medical conditions and functional impairments (Eggers & Prihoda, 1982; Harrington, Newcomer, & Preston, 1993; Hill & Brown, 1990; Lichtenstein, Thomas, Adams-Watson, Lepkowski, & Simone, 1991; Strumwasser et al., 1989; Wouters & Hester, 1988). Favorable selection is likely, because of the unwillingness of persons with ongoing health problems to change health providers (Hellinger, 1995)

There is conflicting evidence as to whether previous mental health care use, costs, and status affect enrollment in managed care. Several investigators have reported similar levels of psychiatric conditions among FFS and prepaid enrollees (Norquist & Wells, 1991) while Wells et al. (1986a) found no evidence of selective enrollment in managed care based on outpatient mental health services use. A recent study in Switzerland compared persons who joined a new managed care plan that controlled access to specialty and restricted psychiatric benefits to persons who remained with a FFS health plan (Perneger, Allaz, Etter, & Rougemont, 1995). Persons who stayed with the FFS plan had on average 2.3 more prior visits to psychiatrists than those who joined the managed care plan; however, joiners reported significantly lower mental health status, suggesting that persons receiving ongoing care for mental disorders are reluctant to change plans. McFarland et al. (1996) reported no evidence for early termination of HMO enrollment among persons with severe mental illness.

Several researchers have suggested that MCOs may experience favorable selection over time as persons with more severe conditions disenroll at higher rates. In the Medical Outcomes Study, the annualized rate of enrollment change was 8.1% among FFS patients using mental health specialists versus 11.7% among specialty patients in prepaid plans (Sturm et al., 1994). The rate of enrollment changes observed in this study of chronically ill patients was surprisingly high. Switching rates of 3–10% have commonly been reported in the general population, and persons under care for chronic illness were expected to switch plans less frequently. A recent survey by the Commonwealth Fund (1995) supports these findings, in that managed care enrollees were more likely to have switched plans recently and not to have an ongoing relationship with a particular provider. Thus studies conducted to date suggest that enrolled populations in managed care and FFS plans may not be significantly different with regard to mental health problems or use at enrollment, but may tend to diverge over time so that MCOs have fewer patients with significant mental health needs.

Utilization and Expenditures

Managed care research studies have focused on access to and use of specialty mental health services and have examined the types of services used, in terms of specialty care versus primary care, group versus individual therapy, and psychiatrists versus nonphysician providers.

Access

Most general studies have shown no differences in access to mental health services in FFS versus MCO (Norquist & Wells, 1991; Wells, Hosek, & Marquis, 1992; Wells et al., 1986a). A few investigations comparing enrollees in a Seattle group-practice style HMO to FFS enrollees found that HMO enrollees were more likely to receive mental health care than their FFS counterparts (Manning, Wells, & Benjamin, 1987; Williams, Diehr, Drucker, & Richardson, 1979), while several more recent studies found small decreases in access among managed care enrollees (Sturm et al., 1994; Zwanziger & Auerbach, 1991).

Use of Specialty Services

While managed care does not appear to have a negative effect on whether or not individuals use any mental health services, persons enrolled in these plans have significantly lower utilization of mental health specialty and inpatient services over time. In the RAND Health Insurance Experiment, the average number of outpatient visits to a mental health specialist (among those with any use) was three times higher among FFS participants than among HMO participants (for example, a mean of 17.2 visits among participants in free FFS care versus 4.7 in HMO; Wells et al., 1986a). Other investigators have reported 35–40% fewer mental health visits among managed care versus FFS enrollees (Norquist & Wells, 1991; Sturm et al., 1994). Significantly lower levels of use have also been found among persons using selected network providers in PPO arrangements (Wells et al., 1992). Overall, managed care appears to reduce the volume of services that patients receive from specialists.

Intensity of Services

Other differences in treatment documented between managed care and fee-for-service plans relate to the type of therapists and modality (i.e., group versus individual therapy) of care used. The RAND study showed that group practice style HMOs had greater use of primary care providers for mental health services (Wells et al., 1986a; Manning et al., 1987). Researchers also have documented the increased use of less expensive modalities of treatments in MCOs (Wells et al., 1986a; Williams et al., 1979). Among people who used specialty mental health services, FFS patients were 50% more likely to see a psychiatrist or psychologist than were HMO patients (79.5% versus 55.3%); HMO patients were three times as likely to see nonphysician therapists, usually psychiatric social workers (56.5% among HMO patients versus 18.1% among FFS users). Patients in group-practice-style HMOs were more likely to have group and family therapy than individual psychotherapy in both observational and randomized studies (Wells, Manning, Duan, Newhouse, & Ware, 1986b; Wells et al., 1992). Across the board, managed care arrangements substitute less expensive providers and group therapy where possible to reduce costs and improve efficiency.

Quality of Care

Evidence regarding the quality of care in MCOs is not conclusive. In general, investigators have not shown differences in the quality of care for acute conditions (e.g., Braveman, Schaaf, Egerter, Bennett, & Schecter, 1994). For patients with chronic conditions, the evidence is less clear. Patients with hypertension and arthritis received better care in some prepaid plans (Udvarhelyi, Jennison, Phillips, & Epstein, 1991; Yelin, Shearn, & Epstein, 1986), while patients with depression fared better in FFS care (Rogers, Wells, Meredith, Sturn, & Burnam, 1993). In the Medical Outcomes Study, patterns of medication use among prepaid enrollees suggested possible problems in the quality of care. Depressed patients in prepaid plans were more likely to use minor tranquilizers, despite their questionable effectiveness for this disorder (Wells, Katon, Rogers, & Camp, 1994). Further, among patients of psychiatrists, those in prepaid plans tend to stop antidepressants over time (Rogers et al., 1993). It is unclear whether the cessation in medications was related to improved symptoms and functioning or to some other factors (e.g., difficulty in obtaining or filling prescriptions). Furthermore, it is uncertain how these studies of primary care mental health services in the mid-1980s are related to current practices. The quality of managed mental health care has not been adequately documented.

Outcomes

Although it appears that managed care arrangements, especially in their more restrictive forms, reduce utilization and change treatment styles, there is little evidence to suggest that significant differences in health outcomes occur in managed care for most patients. However, specific subgroups may be more vulnerable in MCOs. For example, the Medical Outcomes Study on average found few differences in health outcomes in managed care versus FFS participants. Yet, within the subgroups of the elderly and poor with chronic illness, managed care participants had poorer physical health outcomes compared to FFS enrollees (Ware, Bayliss, Rogers, Kosinski, & Tarlov, 1996). It is not clear whether these findings extend to subgroups with chronic mental health problems.

For children with SED, no data exist to inform this discussion, and the limited number of studies that have been conducted among mentally ill adults are equivocal. In the RAND Health Insurance Experiment, no differences in clinical outcomes could be demonstrated between FFS and prepaid or HMO plans (Wells, Stewart, et al., 1989). In the Medical Outcomes Study, no differences in outcomes were found among patients using general medical clinicians or psychologists and other therapists. However, among patients who used psychiatrists (and tended to have more severe depression), patients initially enrolled in prepaid plans were more likely than FFS enrollees to develop a functional limitation of a magnitude that would prevent them from working around the house or at a paying job (Rogers et al., 1993).

Patient Perceptions

In studies conducted among adults, most respondents indicate high levels of satisfaction with their care (Commonwealth Fund, 1995; Rubin et al., 1993; Safran, Tarlov, & Rogers, 1994). However, FFS and managed care enrollees reported different concerns. FFS patients report fewer administrative barriers to care and better perceived quality. While managed care enrollees reported fewer financial barriers to care and greater access to primary care services, they were also more likely to regard access to specialty care, the quality of the services, and the choice of providers as problems (Commonwealth Fund, 1995; Safran et al., 1994). In addition, low-income groups were especially dissatisfied with managed care, as compared to FFS (Commonwealth Fund, 1995). In summary, studies of newer MCOs suggest that particular segments of the population may be especially vulnerable to the restrictions placed on patients and providers in managed care.

Findings from State Capitation Studies

Evaluations of state programs have documented reductions in expenditures under managed care, yet the impact of these programs on quality and outcomes is not clear. Evaluations in Massachusetts, Utah, and other states report significant reductions in expenditures on mental health and substance abuse services (Arons, Frank, Goldman, McGuire, & Stephens, 1994; Christianson et al., 1995; Dickey et al., 1995) primarily because of discounted per-diem rates negotiated by behavioral MCOs as well as reductions in inpatient days. In Utah, state expenditures per beneficiary per month were $6.72 under the prepaid plan, compared to the $12.02 expected without the plan, yielding an estimated savings of $2.3 million. In the CHAMPUS Tidewater Demonstration Project, residential treatment for children with SED was virtually eliminated, and inpatient admissions dropped 78%.

Evidence from state demonstration programs about the effects of managed care on quality is mixed, but it suggests potential problems for children and the chronically ill. In Massachusetts, readmission rates were slightly lower overall, but they increased for the nondisabled and for children (from 7.5% to

10.1%). Patients were more likely to use the same hospital for multiple psychiatric admissions and less likely to have rapid repeat admissions. However, the proportion of patients with no outpatient follow-up after discharges from psychiatric beds increased during the study period from 26% to 37% (Callahan et al., 1995). In the Tidewater Demonstration evaluation, the use of outpatient care for some youth exhibiting suicidal behavior and the placement of very low functioning youth in outpatient care was questioned (Burns et al., 1993).

The Hennepin County, Minnesota, Medicaid demonstration found no statistically significant differences in clinical outcomes among adults with severe mental illness in prepaid plans versus FFS plans (Lurie, Moscovice, Finch, Christianson, & Popkin, 1992). However persons with schizophrenia in managed care developed more problems in functioning than their counterparts in FFS.

The failure to detect differences between managed care and FFS systems may, in part, be related to methodological issues. The first issue is the variety in MCOs. Managed care is not a single entity; as described above, it represents a variety of organizational structures. So far, the most positive studies have largely examined HMOs with comprehensive benefit packages, carefully coordinated care, and extensive information systems. The advantages of managed care may be less consistent in more loosely structured MCOs such as IPAs and related organizations. Some data exist to support such concerns. In research from the Medical Outcomes Study, the poorest outcomes occurred among patients with depression enrolled in IPAs (Rogers et al., 1993).

A second methodologic problem is selection bias. In an ongoing study of voluntary Medicaid managed care participants in Pennsylvania, it was reported that children with prior psychiatric admissions were significantly less likely to join managed care, and when they did join, they were much less likely to remain in managed care (Scholle, Kelleher, Childs, Mendeloff, & Gardner, 1997). Comparisons of managed care and FFS plans are difficult to conduct and to interpret when patients are able to disenroll without penalty in as little as 30 days. Research demonstrating the clear superiority of one system or another for patients with mental disorders has not been conducted.

Implications of Managed Care for Children with SED

Some conclusions about the likely impact of managed care on a system of care for children with SED can be drawn. First, families enrolled in MCOs will have fewer options for choosing providers, since MCOs limit provider networks. This is particularly true with regard to specialty care, where exclusive contracts and required referral patterns are the rule rather than the exception. In the Commonwealth Fund (1995) study, 4 out of 10 persons enrolling in managed care were required to change their primary care provider. It is not clear how many patients are required to change specialty providers upon entering MCOs. Access to primary care and general medical services is likely to be improved, since MCOs more often cover preventive services. However, specialty visits are more often restricted, and children with SED may be particularly vulnerable in this regard. With respect to comprehensiveness, MCOs have tended to offer a wider range of benefits than FFS plans. Therefore, finding alternative types of services may be easier in MCOs. However, the strict limits on the number of visits and total use of services is likely to affect children with SED disproportionately. In total, families with children with SED are likely to receive a wider array of services from MCOs, with potentially more flexible benefits. However, long-term placements and extended psychotherapy are not likely to be options in most plans. For example, 64% of MCOs in one study did not offer long-term psychotherapy (Fox, Wicks, Newacheck, 1993).

Coordination of care for children with SED may either improve or deteriorate in MCOs. Most MCOs rely extensively on case-management services for coordinating utilization and services. Because of the flexibility inherent in the capitation payments for many such plans, better coordination for the child or adolescent with SED may be possible. Moreover, the extensive management-information systems employed by most MCOs allow for careful monitoring of patient utilization and coordination of medical information across different inpatient and outpatient settings. Finally, the fixed capitation fee paid to MCOs should encourage plan administrators to improve coordination with other human services resources, avoiding unnecessary duplication and expenditures. However, two factors that may discourage coordination of services by MCOs are the relatively high rates of clinician turnover in MCOs (Kerstein, Pauly, & Hillman, 1994) and changes in health plan enrollment by patients (both voluntary and involuntary). This lack of continuity may make coordination of services more difficult for families with children with SED, who have complicated histories and long-standing relationships with particular providers.

Ideally, MCOs should provide more community-based and less restrictive services to children and adolescents with SED and their families than traditional FFS plans. Clearly, they limit the use of the most restrictive settings and may increase the use of ambulatory care. Case managers often have flexibility in arranging coverage for services not formally listed in benefits packages. Moreover, they have strong incentives to coordinate resources with other public sector services to maximize services. However, the use of national MCOs for managing mental health and substance abuse care may complicate the help-seeking process for families. This may be particularly likely in instances where cases are reviewed and treatment determined through telephone contact with a manager at a national referral center using standardized referral processes and having limited knowledge of local resources. Some professionals are convinced that MCOs will increasingly strive to integrate their mental health services with primary health care services in an effort to improve coordination between medical and mental health services. This would eliminate the need for an additional contract with its associated overhead, as would developing early prevention and intervention services in the general medical setting (Ludden, 1996). However, the incentives for MCOs to seek services for their patients from other public payers may result in cost-shifting. For example, in the Hennepin County Medicaid Demonstration, public mental health clinics had higher write-offs for severely mentally ill adults enrolled in managed care than in FFS plans (Christianson, Lurie, Finch, Moscovice, & Hartley, 1992). In addition, MCOs may not provide a broad array of social services incorporated in care for persons with serious mental problems. This problem could be particularly difficult for children with SED, who often receive service in multiple sectors, including education, vocational training, welfare, and corrections services (Burns et al., 1995). MCOs tend to have a larger number of mental health services provided in the primary care setting than FFS plans. It is unclear whether these efforts will take place for children with persistent and chronic mental disorders.

No specific characteristics of managed care make it inherently more or less culturally competent than traditional mental health systems, which have been indicted for their lack of cultural sensitivity at best, and for racism at worst. For example, after controlling for severity, African Americans are less likely to use specialty mental health services, less likely to receive antidepressant medication for depression, and more likely to be referred to correctional facilities and restrictive services than comparable non-Hispanic whites (Cooper-Patrick, Crum, & Ford, 1994; Frank & Kamlet, 1989; Wells et al., 1989; Wells et al., 1994). These researchers have confirmed criticisms of current mental health services. Nevertheless, there is room for concern about how MCOs will address the unique needs of diverse populations as well. For example, outcomes for minority groups and low-income patients in the Medical Outcomes Study were worse for managed care patients than for FFS patients (Rogers et al., 1993). It is possible that the additional administrative barriers that must be overcome to obtain specialty services in MCOs add one more set of hurdles for persons who already feel distant or foreign in the medical or mental health setting.

Research Needs Related to Managed Care and Children with SED

The research literature on the impact of managed care on outcomes and effectiveness of health services is obviously inadequate. A tremendous amount of investigative work will be required to inform efforts to realize the core principles of a system of care for children with SED within the context of MCOs. To understand how managed care affects the outcomes and effectiveness of care for children with SED, researchers should focus on several key questions.

How Will Access to Care Be Determined in MCOs?

Overall access to mental health services is likely to increase in MCOs. However, utilization of speciality services are sharply curtailed in most plans. Research on which types of services will be most restricted and whether these restrictions have an impact on child outcomes is needed. This is particularly important in developing child-centered and family-focused treatment plans. Because of their flexible funding, MCOs are uniquely positioned to engage the family in a therapeutic intervention and to design individual treatment plans. How often this will happen and for whom is unclear.

Which Administrative and Financial Mechanisms Employed by MCOs Will Encourage Culturally Competent and Coordinated Services?

Researchers to date have not examined how minority populations enrolled in MCOs perceive access, quality, and cultural competence of care. It is likely that particular aspects of MCOs, such as the gatekeeper requirements for preauthorization or the limited provider networks, may be particularly challenging or distasteful to minority families. Research should focus on the experiences of minority populations in managed care and how the process of care affects outcomes.

How Do Contractual Arrangements Between Providers and MCOs Alter the Appropriateness of Treatment Services and the Community Nature of Services?

Increasingly, MCO contracts contain financial incentives to alter provider behavior. These contracts may encourage provider groups to employ less highly trained individuals and encourage group therapy rather than individual therapy. Similarly, medication therapy rather than psychotherapy may be encouraged. How contract incentives affect therapeutic choices is a critical area for research. Provider contracts may also limit the development or inclusion of some community-based services in mental health plans because requirements for utilization management and outcomes assessment pose significant administrative challenges for small provider agencies. These trends will accelerate as service systems consolidate both vertically (through integrated delivery networks composed of inpatient and outpatient providers) and horizontally (through hospital mergers and consolidation of outpatient facilities).

What Role Will Families and Advocacy Groups Play in MCOs?

In the past, research on families receiving mental health services was largely focused on the role of the family in care-seeking and participation in therapy. However, MCOs, especially those in the public sector, will have incentives to offer families and advocates some opportunities for input on the enrollment of members, the design of services, and the provision of care. In particular, current proposals for accountability standards for Medicaid HMOs at both the national and state level reward MCOs for the inclusion of families and consumers in governance structures. To what extent the inclusion of a family perspective in an MCO alters or enhances mental health care is not clear.

Even more important, families and advocates have a cornerstone role in the development and monitoring of accountability standards for MCOs. A tremendous amount of research will be required to identify multi-informant, multisource methods for evaluating the performance of MCOs from a financial, clinical, and family perspective. The outcomes and clinical performance indicators of relevance to families should be identified, standardized, and collected to assess MCOs.

The Future of Managed Care Plans in a System of Care for Children with SED

There is little doubt that MCOs will continue to expand rapidly and have a profound impact on the delivery of health care services in the United States, barring any surprising legislative efforts at the federal level. These changes are being fueled by employers and state Medicaid programs that seek to decrease expenditures for behavioral health care. Medicaid budget cuts will play an important role in moving individuals with disabilities into MCOs. To date, 17 states have Medicaid managed care programs that include the disabled, and 13 more have submitted proposals to enroll disabled beneficiaries in MCOs (U.S. General Accounting Office, 1996). How these transitions will affect the development of an ideal system of care for children and adolescents with SED is unclear. Some rationale for speculation exists, as noted above; however, it is unclear whether managed care's continued evolution will shape it to a system that is more comprehensive, coordinated, child centered, and community-based, or less so.

The specific direction of this evolution will be dependent on a variety of factors. First, the role of legislative action in establishing ground rules and favoring particular types of plans or services will be critical. In Minnesota, the passage of legislation encouraging integrated-service delivery networks precipitated multiple mergers among insurers, physicians, and hospitals in the Twin City area. Similarly, new laws in Maryland requiring a point-of-service option for all HMOs will expand patient choice of providers but also increase premiums. It is unclear how current national legislative initiatives to require parity in mental health and physical health benefits will affect access to services. Legislative efforts are likely to be limited, since they are generally inflexible, slow, and imprecise tools for dealing with the complexity of health care benefits.

In addition to legislative influences, the evolution of MCOs will be shaped considerably by the organization of purchasing groups. In particular, the banding together of businesses and other employers, state workers, and even state and federal health programs into effective purchasing groups will decrease health care premiums and generally improve the responsiveness of MCOs. California, Rochester, the Twin Cities, and parts of Arizona all experienced such changes after the development of purchasing coalitions.

While legislative and purchasing coalitions will have profound influence on the shape of managed care and systems for children and adolescents with SED, much of the information used to make decisions in these various bodies will be derived from the growing accountability movement in managed care. Because employers are showing growing interest in the value they receive for their health care dollar, MCOs are beginning to monitor the effectiveness of services for their members. Initially, these efforts have largely relied on measures of process and access, such as number of patients served, total visits, admission rates, and readmission rates. While informative, these efforts have not provided sufficient information for examining the quality of medical or mental health care offered by MCOs. Thus, purchasing groups, academic investigators, and some patient advocates have called for a greater focus on actual patient outcomes measured over time (Ellwood & Enthoven, 1995). Currently, most of the outcome measures used are largely measure of patient satisfaction; however, an increasing number of plans are using some form of standardized measure of patient outcomes across multiple domains.

The rapid evolution of managed care under these and other unforeseen influences will require constant vigilance and participation by advocates for and families of children and adolescents with SED as MCOs grow to play the dominant role in the health and mental health care market in the United States. The variety of plans constituting managed care will increasingly require an educated consumer to overcome administrative and financial barriers often imposed by such plans. In addition, consumer advocacy may also help patients "grandfather" in their longstanding relationships with particular clinicians who may not be in certain networks and acquire unique services that may be necessary for the child or adolescent with severe emotional or behavioral disorders. The achievement of a system of care for children with SED that is comprehensive, coordinated, community-based, culturally competent, child centered and family focused is potentially closer with the growth of managed care, but only when appropriate incentives and accountability are included and when patients, families, and advocates are active and informed participants.

Endnote

1. This is distinct from programs that emphasize the coordination and delivery of comprehensive services through the use of assigned case managers but that do not have the fiscal restrictions and financial incentives associated with managed care insurance plans. The Fort Bragg experiment (Bickman, 1996) is an example of such a program and will not be considered in this chapter.

Authors' Note

This paper is supported in part by the Staunton Farm Foundation of Pittsburgh, Pennsylvania.

Correspondence may be addressd to Dr. Scholle, University of Pittsburgh, 3510 Fifth Avenue, Ste. 1, Pittsburgh, PA 15213; (412) 692-7840; fax (412) 692-7844; e-mail, scholles@pitt.edu.

References

Arons, B. S., Frank, R. G., Goldman, H. H., McGuire, T. G., & Stephens, S. (1994). Mental health and substance abuse coverage under health reform. *Health Affairs, 1*, 192–205.

Babigian, H. M., Cole, R. E., Reed, S. K., Brown, S. W., & Lehman, A. F. (1991). Methodology for evaluating the Monroe-Livingston capitation system. *Hospital and Community Psychiatry, 42*, 913–919.

Bickman, L., (1996). The evaluation of a children's mental health managed care demonstration. *Journal of Mental Health Administration, 23*, 7–15.

Braveman, P., Schaaf, V. M., Egerter, S., Bennett, T., & Schecter, W. (1994). Insurance-related differences in the risk of ruptured appendix. *New England Journal of Medicine, 33*, 444–449.

Burns, B. J., Costello, E. J., Angold, A., Twees, D., Stangl, D., Farmer, E. M. Z., & Erkanli, A. (1995). Children's mental health service use across service sectors. *Health Affairs, 14*, 148–159.

Burns, B. J., Thompson, J. W., & Goldman, H. H. (1993). Initial treatment decisions by level of care for youth in the CHAMPUS Tidewater demonstration. *Administration and Policy in Mental Health, 20*, 231–246.

Callahan, J. J., Shepard, D. S., Beinecke, R. H., Larson, M. J., & Cavanaugh, D. (1995). Mental health/substance abuse treatment in managed care: The Massachusetts Medicaid experience. *Health Affairs, 14*, 173–184.

Center for Vulnerable Populations. (1996). People with disabilities and the 3rd wave of Medicaid managed care. *Spotlight, 3*.

Commonwealth Fund. (1995). Patient experiences with managed care: A survey.

Christianson, J. B., Lurie, N., Finch, M., Moscovice, I. S., & Hartley, D. (1992). Use of community-based mental health programs by HMOs: Evidence from a Medicaid demonstration. *American Journal of Public Health, 82,* 790–798.

Christianson, J. B., Manning, W., Lurie, N., Stoner, T. J., Gray, D. Z., Popkin, M., & Marriott, S. (1995). Utah's prepaid mental health plan: The first year. *Health Affairs, 14,* 161–172.

Cole, R. E., Reed, S. K., Babigian, H. M., Brown, S. W., & Fray, J. (1994). A mental health capitation program: I. Patient outcomes. *Hospital and Community Psychiatry, 45*(11), 1090–1096.

Cooper-Patrick, L., Crum, R. M., & Ford, D. E. (1994). Characteristics of patients with major depression who received care in general medical and specialty mental health settings. *Medical Care, 32,* 15–24.

Dickey, B., Norton, E. C., Normand, S. L., Azeni, H., Fisher, W., & Altaffer, F. (1995). Massachusetts Medicaid managed health care reform: Treatment for the psychiatrically disabled. *Advances in Health Economics and Health Services Research: Health Policy Reform and the States, 15,* 99–116.

Eggers, P., & Prihoda, R. (1982). Pre-enrollment reimbursement patterns of Medicare beneficiaries enrolled in "at risk" HMOs. *Health Care Financing Review, 4,* 5–73.

Ellwood, P. M., & Enthoven, A. C. (1995). "Responsible choices": The Jackson Hole Group plan for health reform. *Health Affairs, 14,* 24–39.

Essock, S. M., & Goldman, H. H. (1995). States' embrace of managed mental health care. *Health Affairs, 14,* 34–49.

Fox, H. B., Wicks, L. N., & Newacheck, P. W. (1993). Health maintenance organizations and children with special health needs. A suitable match? *American Journal of Diseases of Children 147,* 546–552.

Frank, R. G., & Kamlet, M. S. (1989). Determining provider choice for the treatment of mental disorder: The role of health and mental health status. *Health Services Research, 24,* 83–103.

Frank, R. G., & McGuire, T. G. (1994). Health care reform and financing of mental health services: Distributional consequences. In R. W. Manderscheid & M. A. Sonnenschein (Eds.), *Mental Health, United States* (pp. 8–21). Washington, DC: U.S. Government Printing Office.

Freund, D. A., & Hurley, R. E. (1995). Medicaid managed care: Contribution to issues of health reform. *Annual Review of Public Health, 16,* 473–495.

Harrington, C., Newcomer, R. J., & Preston, S. (1993). A comparison of S/HMO disenrollees and continuing members. *Inquiry, 30,* 429–440.

Hellinger, F. J. (1995). Selection bias in HMOs and PPOs: A review of the evidence. *Inquiry, 32,* 135–142.

Hill, J., & Brown, R. S. (1990). Biased selection in the TEFRA HMO/CMP program. Mathematica Policy Research. HCFA-500-88-006.

Hoagwood, K. (1994). Child mental health services. In R. W. Manderscheid & M. A. Sonnenschein (Eds.), *Mental Health, United States.* Washington, DC: U.S. Government Printing Office.

Hurley, R. E., Freund, D. A., & Paul, J. E. (1993). Describing and classifying programs: Discussion and implications of the evidence. In R. E. Hurley & D. A. Freund (Eds.), *Managed care in Medicaid: Lessons for policy and program design* (pp. 37–60; 97–116). Ann Arbor, MI: Health Administration Press.

Iglehart, J. K. (1996). Health policy report: Managed care and mental health. *New England Journal of Medicine, 334,* 131–135.

Kelleher, K. J., & Scholle, S. H. (1995). Children with chronic medical conditions: II. Managed care opportunities and threats. *Ambulatory Child Health, 1,* 139–146.

Kerstein, J., Pauly, M. V., & Hillman, A. (1994). Primary care physician turnover in HMOs. *Health Services Research, 29,* 18–37.

Leff, H. S., Mulkern, V., Liberman, M., & Raab, B. (1994). The effects of capitation on service access, adequacy, and appropriateness. *Administration and Policy in Mental Health, 21,* 141–160.

Lichtenstein, R., Thomas, J. W., Adams-Watson, J., Lepkowski, J., & Simone, B. (1991). Selection bias in TEFRA at-risk HMOs. *Medical Care, 29,* 318–331.

Ludden, J. M. (1996). Can the patient be the focus of managed care? *Physician Executive, 22,* 9–12.

Lurie, N., Moscovice, I. S., Finch, M., Christianson, J. B., & Popkin, M. K. (1992). Does capitation affect the health of the chronically mentally ill? Results from a randomized trial. *Journal of the American Medical Association, 267,* 3300–3304.

Manning, W. G., Jr., Wells, K. B., & Benjamin, B. (1987). Use of outpatient mental health services over time in a health maintenance organization and fee-for-service plans. *American Journal of Psychiatry, 144,* 283–287.

Mechanic, D., Schlesinger, M., & McAlpine, D. D. (1995). Management of mental health and substance abuse services: State of the art and early results. *Milbank Quarterly, 73,* 19–55.

Norquist, G. S., & Wells, K. B. (1991). How do HMOs reduce outpatient mental health care costs? *American Journal of Psychiatry, 148,* 96–101.

Perneger, T. V., Allaz, A. F., Etter, J. F., & Rougemont, A. (1995). Mental health and choice between managed care and indemnity health insurance. *American Journal of Psychiatry, 152,* 1020–1025.

Reed, S. K., Hennessy, K. D., Mitchell, O. S., & Babigian, H. M. (1994). A mental health capitation program: II. Cost-benefit analysis. *Hospital and Community Psychiatry, 45*(11), 1097–1103.

Rogers, W. H., Wells, K. B., Meredith, L. S., Sturn, R., & Burnam, A. (1993). Outcomes for adult outpatients with depression under prepaid or fee-for-service financing. *Archives of General Psychiatry, 50,* 517–525.

Rubin, H. R., Gandek, B., Rogers, W. H., Kosinski, M., McHorney, C. A., & Ware, J. E., Jr. (1993). Patients' ratings of outpatient visits in different practice settings. *Journal of the American Medical Association, 270,* 835–840.

Safran, D. G., Tarlov, A. R., & Rogers, W. H. (1994). Primary care performance in fee-for-service and prepaid health care systems. Results from the Medical Outcomes Study. *Journal of the American Medical Association, 271*(20), 1579–1586.

Scholle, S. H., Kelleher, K. J., Childs, G., Mendeloff, J., & Gardner, W. P. Changes in Medicaid managed care enrollment among children. Manuscript submitted for publication.

Stroul, B., & Friedman, R. M. (1986). A system of care for children and youth with severe emotional disturbances (Rev. ed.). Washington, DC: Georgetown University Child Development Center, CASSP Technical Assistance Center.

Strumwasser, I., Paranjpe, N. V., Ronis, D. L., McGinnis, J., Kee, D. W., & Hall, H. L. (1989). The triple option choice: Self-selection bias in traditional coverage, HMOs, and PPOs. *Inquiry, 26,* 432–441.

Sturm, R., Jackson, C. A., Meredith, L. S., Yip, W., Manning, W. G., Rugers, W. H., & Wells, K. B. (1995). Mental health care utilization in prepaid and fee-for-service plans among depressed patients in the Medical Outcomes Study. *Health Services Research, 30*(2), 319–340.

Sturm, R., McGlynn, E. A., Meredith, L. S., Wells, K. B., Manning, W. G., & Rogers, W. H. (1994). Switches between prepaid and fee-for-service health systems among depressed outpatients: Results from the Medical Outcomes Study. *Medical Care, 32,* 917–929.

Udvarhelyi, I. S., Jennison, K., Phillips, R., & Epstein, A. M. (1991). Comparison of the quality of ambulatory care for fee-for-service and prepaid patients. *Annals of Internal Medicine, 115,* 394–400.

U.S. General Accounting Office. (1996). Medicaid managed care: Serving the disabled challenges state programs. Washington, DC.

Ware, J. E., Bayliss, M. S., Rogers, W. H., Kosinski, M., & Tarlov, A. R. (1996). Differences in 4-year health outcomes for elderly and poor, chronically ill patients treated in HMO and fee-for-service systems: Results from the Medical Outcomes Study. *Journal of the American Medical Association, 276*, 1039–1047.

Wells, K. B., Burnam, M. A., & Camp, P. (1995). Severity of depression in prepaid and fee-for-service general medical and mental health specialty practices. *Medical Care, 33*(4), 350–364.

Wells, K. B., Hays, R. D., Burnam, M. A., Rogers, W., Greenfield, S., & Ware, J. E., Jr. (1989). Detection of depressive disorder for patients receiving prepaid or fee-for-service care: Results from the Medical Outcomes Study. *Journal of the American Medical Association, 262*, 3298–3302.

Wells, K. B., Hosek, S. D., & Marquis, M. S. (1992). The effects of preferred provider options in fee-for-service plans on use of outpatient mental health services by three employee groups. *Medical Care, 30*, 412–427.

Wells, K. B., Katon, W., Rogers, B., & Camp, P. (1994). Use of minor tranquilizers and antidepressant medications by depressed outpatients: Results from the Medical Outcomes Study. *American Journal of Psychiatry, 151*, 694–700.

Wells, K. B., Manning, W. G., Jr., & Benjamin, B. (1986a). Use of outpatient mental health services in HMO and fee-for-service plans: Results from a randomized controlled trial. *HSR: Health Services Research, 21*, 453–474.

Wells, K. B., Manning, W. G., Jr., Duan, N., Newhouse, J., & Ware, J. E., Jr. (1986b). Use of outpatient mental health services by a general population with health insurance coverage. *Hospital and Community Psychiatry, 37*(11), 1119–1125.

Wells, K. B., Stewart, A. S., Hays, R. D., Burnam, A., Rogers, W., Daniels, M., Berry, S., Greenfield, S., & Ware, J. (1989). The functioning and well-being of depressed patients. *Journal of the American Medical Association, 262*, 914–919.

Williams, S., Diehr, P., Drucker, W., & Richardson, W. C. (1979). Mental health services: Utilization by low income enrollees in a prepaid group practice and in an independent practice plan. *Medical Care, 17*, 139–151.

Wouters, A. V., & Hester, J. (1988). Patient choice of providers in a preferred provider organization. *Medical Care, 26*, 240–255.

Yelin, E. H., Shearn, M. A., & Epstein, W. V. (1986). Health outcomes for a chronic disease in prepaid group practice and fee-for-service settings. *Medical Care, 24*, 236–247.

Zwanziger, J., & Auerbach, R. (1991). Evaluating PPO performance using prior expenditure data. *Medical Care, 29*, 142–151.

Improving Outcomes for Children and Adolescents with Serious Emotional and Behavioral Disorders: Current and Future Directions

24

Barbara J. Burns,
Kimberly Hoagwood,
and Linda T. Maultsby

Consensus about the critical outcomes for children with serious emotional and behavioral disorders—at home, in school, and out of trouble—is not difficult to obtain (Rosenblatt 1993). Achieving such outcomes *and more* is the challenge! In this era of managed care, the emphasis on outcomes, including language about paying for services based on outcomes, may be precarious. Until all of the requisite steps to achieve good outcomes are in place, consistent positive results may be slow in coming. In the recent deliberations about outcomes and the haste to measure them, what has been missing is a full-fledged strategy to get there.

The aims of this chapter are three: (a) to lay out a comprehensive strategy for improving outcomes for children and families; (b) to assess what is in place, which if enhanced, could result in better outcomes in the near future; and (c) to propose a plan for the future, largely research-based, which will facilitate much improved outcomes over the long term.

Several assumptions underlie all three aims. The first is that outcomes are multidetermined—that is, many factors (e.g., policy, service-system characteristics, and adequacy of treatment) influence whether gains will occur for children and adolescents. And second, that improving outcomes is an iterative process, involving successive approximations toward the goal. Small gains at each stage will effect change in subsequent stages. What is presented is a process in which critical determinants of outcomes must move ahead in harmony to achieve the final goal of improved outcomes for children and adolescents.

A Strategy for Improving Outcomes

Designing a strategy to improve child outcomes first involves identification of the elements that either directly or indirectly are likely to affect child outcomes. A way to begin thinking about this at the child level is to inquire about the following determinants: that the child will have access to services, that the child will receive the appropriate services, and that the services will be provided in a way that is likely to result in benefit. While a number of child and family characteristics (including severity of the illness, family stresses and strengths, treatment compliance, and family preferences for treatment and outcomes) will influence the preceding, they have been reviewed elsewhere (Burns, 1996) and are not dealt with here. The focus of this chapter is the service system and the service-related factors that influence each of the preceding child-level events. Five elements are proposed:

1. Policy, which influences the potential to provide any services and pay for appropriate services;

2. The services research base, which establishes the limits of effective treatment;

3. Service-system capability, which determines accessibility to care and provides the laboratory for applying the services knowledge base;

4. Clinical capability, which defines the extent to which clinicians have the skills to apply specific interventions as intended; and

5. Quality of care, which ensures that the provision of services is appropriate in dose and duration and that the implementation of interventions can be monitored.

The preceding elements offer a logical sequence for the provision of effective interventions and all must be present to achieve desirable outcomes. Although there are flaws in each at the present time, there are steps that can be taken now (indicated on the right side of the model shown in Figure 24.1) and others in the future (left side of the model). For the immediate future, there is a sufficient knowledge base that can be applied to policy, to applying the services research base to service systems, to clinicians, and to the process of care (quality) to make possible incremental gains. For the future, the investment in the research base is critical and the major focus of this chapter. Future research developments can in turn influence the nature of subsequent changes in policy, clinical training, and standards of care. Although this appears simple, the complexity of achieving the above steps is apparent in the text that follows.

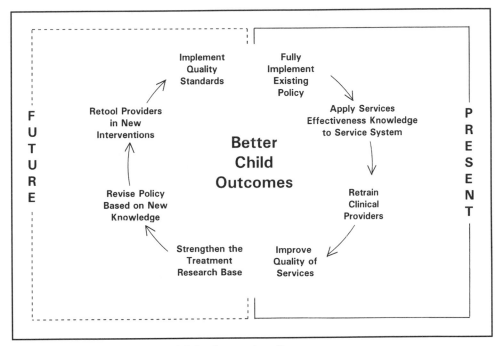

Figure 24.1. A Strategic Model for Improving Outcomes.

Initial Steps to Improving Child Outcomes

Based on the preceding model for improving outcomes for children, the first step is implementation of existing policy, described largely as further application of CASSP values and principles; major obstacles are also acknowledged. The second step, application of the services knowledge base to service systems, includes tentative recommendations for adding interventions that appear promising, and are consistent with CASSP, to service systems; widespread gaps in service provision are also recognized. The third step, retaining clinical providers, is addressed briefly. Finally, major quality problems are identified, implying an immediate agenda for administrator- and clinician-initiated changes.

Implement Existing Policy

The first step toward improving outcomes—implementing existing policy—began as the Child and Adolescent Service System Program (CASSP) philosophy, published 10 years ago by Stroul & Friedman (1986). It has now been adopted as policy for developing systems of care in all 50 states, and there is consensus about these values, which are supported by the following set of principles:

Services will be individualized, based on the specific needs of an individual child and family, not on the availability of a particular categorical service;

Services will be family centered. Families will participate in planning and treatment and will be perceived as a partner in the treatment process;

Services will be community based. A continuum of services in the community will provide the care necessary to prevent institutional placement;

Services will be provided in the least restrictive setting. The aim is to normalize the life experience through mainstreaming the child as much as is feasible;

Services will be culturally competent, sensitive to cultural and ethnic values and preferences, and offering language capability.

Incentives and Obstacles

Given the widespread acceptance of these CASSP values and principals, what are the obstacles to implementation? Probably the major one is that child mental health dollars are still locked up in the most restrictive forms of care—hospitals and residential treatment centers. To a great extent, CASSP values (e.g., least restrictive care) have been in conflict with fiscal incentives which are more likely to drive decisions about service provision. According to the slightly dated but probably unchanged, estimate of the distribution of costs shown in Figure 24.2, three fourths of the child mental health dollar has been tied up in institutional care; and this emphasis has been fully supported by the insurance industry, the public mental health sector, child welfare, juvenile justice, and schools (Burns, 1991). Historically, the incentives have been on the side of institutional use.

Shifts are beginning to be observed in the allocation of mental health service dollars under managed care. Several managed care companies have reported a major reversal, such that 80% of the resources go into outpatient care and only 20% to inpatient care (W. Goldman, personal communication, March 17, 1993; H. G. Whittington, personal communication, March 11, 1993). Similar evidence from a recent public sector run initiative to manage child mental health services under a Medicaid waiver in North Carolina revealed a dramatic reduction in inpatient dollars (50%) in the first year, when there was an incentive to apply saved inpatient dollars to community services. Outpatient dollars doubled, demonstrating some potential to make this shift to noninstitutional services, but the dollars for community residential services

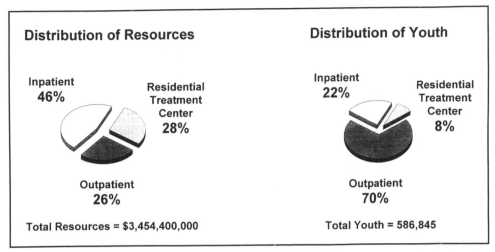

Figure 24.2. The distribution of resources and mental health service admissions by setting for youth (10–18 years), 1986.

(not included in the cap) increased dramatically (Stangl et al., 1997). As some of the residential services are less institutional in nature (e.g., small group homes, therapeutic foster care in the community) and are located in the community, this may represent a gain. More likely, however, local mental health programs were not sufficiently confident that future financial arrangements would allow them to truly invest in a full continuum of community-based services (e.g., in-home services, respite care), which potentially could have reduced the amount of community residential (nonhospital) use.

The extent to which the preceding findings will generalize to managed care organizations may be influenced by whether managed care companies will be burdened with the capital cots of maintaining institutions. Also, evidence of quality care and sufficient intensity of services under managed care is not yet available. Since future increases in fiscal resources are not expected, the critical issues here are how to shift institutional funds into community services before they disappear in Medicaid block grants or managed care profits, and how to enhance the mental health and Medicaid dollars by blending funds with other child agencies, as suggested by England and Cole (1992).

Apply Existing Services Research Base to Service Systems

The availability of evidence-based comprehensive community interve for children with serious emotional and behavioral disorders lags behi for adults with severe mental disorders. For example, Assertive Co

Treatment (ACT), a program for adults with severe mental disorders, has recently been endorsed by the National Alliance for the Mentally Ill because of the extensive research base supporting the benefits (Burns & Santos, 1995). The problem for children is not that candidates for comprehensive interventions are lacking, but that the research on them is either nonexistent or partially flawed (e.g., either in the specification of the intervention, the adequacy of the design, or the measurement of the outcomes). On the assumption that child outcomes under conditions of usual care are not likely to exceed the research base, we next look to research on effectiveness of specific interventions services to consider implications for child outcomes. The authors' summary of research reviews (Burns & Friedman, 1990; Jensen, Hoagwood, & Petti, 1996; Kutash & Rivera, 1996) by intervention follows:

Inpatient/Residential: very limited evidence; shorter stays are associated with more positive outcomes;

Psychotherapy: Stronger findings for highly controlled laboratory studies than clinic-based ones;

Day Treatment: Useful for a limited population; family involvement is critical;

Psychotropic Medication: A mixed picture; very few of the efficacy studies were conducted on children or adolescents; there is a body of evidence for some disorders (e.g., attention deficit hyperactivity disorder);

Family Preservation: 70–96% of youth remain with the family; effects are short-term only;

Crisis and Emergency: Out-of-home placement is prevented in 60–90% of cases;

Case Management: Initial studies point to positive outcomes for "high risk" groups, at least for service-system level outcomes;

Wraparound: Evidence of improved child/family functioning and less restrictive placements is emerging;

Family Education/Support: Family satisfaction, reduced stress, and increased parenting skills are observed;

Therapeutic Foster Care: 62–89% are discharged to a less restrictive setting.

A dominant observation is that the least evidence of effectiveness exists for ·sidential services, where the vast majority of dollars are spent. The last ran- nized trial of inpatient care for children occurred in 1978 (Winsberg, Bialer, ietz, Botti, & Balka, 1980). A new trial, supported by the National Institute ·ntal Health and underway in South Caroline, will compare multisystemic ·y (MST)—a home and community-based team intervention (Henggeler & ·, 1990; Santos, Henggeler, Burns, Arana, & Meisler, 1995)—with inpa- ·.

The more innovative services (those listed above from family preservation on) were developed recently, and thus the evidence is just beginning to emerge. Nonetheless, the outcomes look more positive than outcomes for the interventions traditionally utilized by "deep end" youth. The March 1996 issue of the *Journal of Child and Family Studies* expands the evidence for wraparound. Family education/support is emerging as both inexpensive and potentially effective, at least based on adult research showing reduced relapse rates and higher employment (MacFarlane et al., 1993). For example, it is possible that dropping into a family resource center may be more relevant for a young mother with a disturbed son than a visit with a social worker once a week. Case management has already undergone widespread dissemination as a result of Medicaid funding, despite a paltry research base. Two controlled trials, one in New York (Evans, Armstrong, Dollard, & Kuppinger, 1994) and one in North Carolina (Burns, Farmer, Angold, Costello, & Behar, 1996), have documented service-system outcomes but not clinical or functional outcomes. At a minimum, these newer types of services are beginning to document decreased use of institutional care and some cost reductions.

More extensive implementation of some of these newer services, in place of high-end institutional care, is merited. Candidates, suggested in priority order based upon research evidence, include multisystemic therapy, therapeutic foster care, wraparound and family education/support. Despite limitations in the research base, the next steps are to translate and embed clinical treatments (e.g., psychotherapy and pharmacotherapy) with demonstrable efficacy into services and to apply the findings of studies on selected intensive community-based services to service systems.

Access to Services

In conjunction with introducing promising interventions into the service system, the prior issue of access to services continues to need attention. Very high rates of unmet need are consistent with earlier studies (Burns, 1991; Burns et al., 1995). Without any care, much less appropriate care, achieving positive outcomes for children is obviously not possible. The use of professional mental health care, however, does seem to be increasing. Nearly 8% of children and adolescents in the Great Smoky Mountains Study in North Carolina receive such professional mental health care in a year (Farmer, Stangl, Burns, Coste⌐ & Angold, 1997), in contrast to earlier estimates of 1–5% of the child popula (Burns, 1991). However, even with the recent gains, only one third of youth serious emotional and behavioral disorders received professional mental services and only one third of them received special education service et al., 1995). Less is known about the capacity to provide intensive (e.g., wraparound, MST) for youth with serious emotional and beha orders across service systems in the United States.

The availability of alternatives to institutional care remain limited, partially because it is not feasible to shift institutional dollars into community-based resources or to blend funds across child agencies. Exceptions that will be instructive are models like the Robert Wood Johnson Mental Health Services Program for Youth (England & Cole, 1992), or the Comprehensive Community Mental Health Services Program for Children with Serious Emotional Disturbances supported by the Center for Mental Health Services.

Retrain Clinical Providers

In the interim, to increase service-system capacity for youth with serious emotional and behavioral disorders, attention needs to be directed toward training clinicians and providers. As discussed above, evidence is beginning to accumulate on the effectiveness of the more recent and innovative interventions. These community-based and family-oriented interventions tend to be conceptually grounded in ecological and behavioral models. The relevant conceptual/theoretical models need to be introduced into graduate education curricula and into in-service training for practicing providers. Clinicians need to be educated regarding the most effective interventions based on research, in contrast to the limited evidence for institutional care. This involves replacing an emphasis on traditional outpatient and residential treatment with community-based care that is not office-based. The infusion of relevant theory and treatment models into graduate programs that train child clinicians is a step calling for action.

In addition, manualized treatments for specific childhood disorders (e.g., attention deficit hyperactivity disorder, anxiety, depression) have been developed and refined but not yet tested in community settings or with community providers. One of the next steps in translating the findings from clinical efficacy studies into service effectiveness will be to develop and reengineer these treatments by creating integrated treatment manuals that combine state-of-the-art interventions that involve families in the delivery of the intervention and that have practical clinical significance for community providers.

Improve the Quality of Services

Quality care, the provision of accessible and appropriate care, has been part of the professional lingo for decades. While there is no research on child mental health services that links the quality of care to outcomes, problems with the provision of care are so obvious that improvements are required even before it is necessary to conduct research connecting quality to outcomes. For example, in the very best clinics, dropout rates run 30–50% after a visit or two (1992), suggesting a need for aggressive outreach to families who do follow-up appointments. Services must first be accessible: timely, affordable, and nearby. Cultural sensitivity is also key to the enhancement of quality of care. The proceeding generic quality indicators provide the starting point for quality improvement; they are primarily administrator and clinician-driven, and are potentially ready for concerted attention.

The issue of affordability may be more difficult to alter, as this most often is not controlled by administrators or clinicians but is directly determined by benefits established by third-party payers or the availability of public sector resources. In a recent analysis of the Great Smoky Mountains Study (GSMS), youths with public insurance (Medicaid) coverage were four times more likely to access mental health services than youth without insurance (Burns et al., 1997). The preceding finding was not unexpected. The surprising finding was that youth with private insurance were as likely to receive mental health services as those with no insurance, and at the same low rate. For the GSMS population, private insurance, with its deductibles, co-payments, and historical caps, functioned as a barrier to service use even for very high need youth. This relationship between income, private insurance, and service use was also found in a national survey of ambulatory mental health service use by children and adolescents (Cunningham & Freiman, 1996).

A second level of definition of quality is child specific and relates to the appropriateness of treatment. This begins with matching clinical needs to a treatment plan. Since research-based clinical practice guidelines are available to date for just a few disorders (AACAP, 1992; AACAP, 1993; McClellan and Werry, 1994), clinical judgment remains the current basis for decision making. In addition to the appropriate type of treatment, intensity of services (frequency of service provision) and keeping services going long enough (duration) to achieve therapeutic benefit are the next challenge—both issues of dose.

A third-level definition of quality relates to the adequacy of technical capability to provide a given intervention. Ensuring the fidelity of specific interventions is a related further requirement—that is, that clinicians have the requisite skill to provide the planned treatment. The lack of adequate clinician skills is a likely cause of no findings for psychotherapy in usual care settings studied by Weisz, Weiss, & Donenberg (1992), in contrast to the positive meta-analysis findings from studies conducted in university-based setting (Weisz & Weiss, 1989). Without a doubt, research on quality at the level of fidelity is not very advanced at the present time. Until interventions are better specified in guidelines, treatment protocols, manuals, and other training materials, quality improvements related to fidelity will be slower in occurring.

Strengthening the Services Effectiveness Research Base

Moving into the future, the next major step is to strengthen the research The expected achievement of this long-term endeavor is to produce evide effective services for children and adolescents with serious emotional and behavioral disorders. To be considered effective, services for "real world" patients provided in "real world settings" will need to manifest expected outcomes. Research findings will ultimately fit into the larger outcomes strategy (see Figure 24.1) when they are strong enough to inform policy and clinical practice. To move ahead, general considerations and challenges faced in effectiveness research are described and a research plan is delineated.

General Research Considerations

Conducting research on children with serious emotional and behavioral disorders, whether efficacy or effectiveness, begins with some general considerations. First, children with chronic conditions are likely to require a range of interventions over an extended period. From the perspective of examining the usefulness of a given intervention (even a comprehensive one), the type of treatment history may influence a child's response to a new intervention. At any given time, in addition to assignment to an experimental intervention, these youths most often also receive a mix of other clinical interventions (e.g., medications) that are outside of the control of a study. Thus, it will be necessary to examine the mix of treatment components and the sequence of services over time, suggesting attention to episodes of care and patterns of care.

A second and related point is that outcomes are affected by a larger world than formal mental health treatment. The point is that it is not sufficient to assess mental health specialist services only, but that inclusion of other sectors and informal services is also essential. Probably the sector serving the largest proportion of youth with emotional and behavioral disorders is schools (Burns et al., 1995). Little is known about the extent to which schools or other sectors, such as child welfare or juvenile justice, engage in the provision of mental health services versus the extent to which they serve as gatekeepers and refer to specialty mental health services, or fail to do so (Borduin, 1994; Duchnowski, 1994; Nelson, 1994).

A third consideration is that outcomes will vary with the type and stage of treatment and the developmental status of the child. For example, respite care may be very appropriate for a family that is stressed by the intensity of the care they are giving their 1-year-old foster child, but it may be very traumatic for the child to be separated from a caring adult at this period. Attention to the interaction between type of service and developmental capacities is thus warranted. The implication here is to assess outcomes, both short term and long term, and to asses utcomes at multiple levels (child, family, system). Despite insurance carrier or en public sector orientations to very brief budget periods (typically 1 year), ognition that the benefits of treatment may not emerge for several years, or longer, requires a longitudinal focus to determine the usefulness of services. fourth consideration relates to the measurement of outcomes. These individobviously need to be selected carefully. For youths with serious and chronic rs, deterioration is not unusual despite quality treatment, and maintenance of functioning may even be a good outcome for some (Greenbaum et al., 1996). Also, the outcomes targeted should consider the preferences of families, children, clinicians, and payers—something we know little about, except that the safety of the child and the community is primary (Rugs & Kutash, 1994). And there may not be full agreement among stakeholder groups regarding the primary outcomes. Nonetheless, if the preferences of relevant stakeholders are not attended to, compliance with treatment or payment for services may not occur.

A classification of outcomes by Hoagwood, Jensen, Petti, & Burns (1996) can be utilized to assess the relative value assigned to given outcome domains and to offer an array of outcomes for research. These categories, adapted from a classification for adults developed by Rosenblatt and Attkisson (1993) include the following:

Symptomatic/diagnostic: Impact of services on clinical status (diagnosis, symptoms, disability);

Functional: Impact of services on child's behavior at home, in school, and in the community;

Consumer perspectives: Impact of services on child and family quality of life, family burden (stress), and child and family satisfaction with care;

Environmental: Impact of services on the child's environment—family, school, peers, neighborhood;

Service system: Changes in restrictiveness of living situations, in access, or costs of care.

This classification system begins with the familiar indicators of clinical status, which seem to be somewhat less difficult to change than the second category of functional status (Greenbaum et al., 1996). More recently, consumer outcomes (measures of quality of life, family stress, and satisfaction with care) have appropriately been added to the battery of outcomes for children and families. The environmental outcomes apply clearly to community-based preventive interventions such as school-based prevention programs. Service system–level outcomes, often measured as reduced hospital admissions, days, and costs, appear quite responsive to the provision of better services. Multiple tasks remain relevant to the selection of outcome measures which (a) have adequate psychometric properties, (b) are sensitive to change, and (c) are responsive to stakeholder preferences.

The Challenges of Effectiveness Research

Moving the effectiveness research agenda forward, particularly for inno services showing promise, is not easy because it involves "real world p and providers" necessary to ensure external validity. Much is beyond trol of investigators (e.g., history—where case manager caseloads do change in state policy in the middle of a study). The risk in research terms of a type II error—failure to find results when they are there—can prematurely discredit an intervention that might be effective if the research had been conducted correctly. A range of factors both internal and external to studies, discussed in this section of the chapter, contribute to type II errors. If such problems are unavoidable, then practicing on the basis of clinical lore will be better than doing so on the basis of poor-quality research. Even though effectiveness research on child interventions is a recent phenomenon, the learning curve must be short or the opportunity to introduce effective interventions into rapidly changing systems of care will be lost.

To begin to delineate why effectiveness research is challenging, efficacy and effectiveness research are contrasted in the following definitions: "Efficacy" refers to the probability of benefit to individuals in a defined population from a medical technology applied for a given medical problem under ideal conditions of use (OTA, 1978). "Effectiveness" has all the attributes of efficacy except one: It reflects performance under ordinary conditions by the average practitioner for the typical patient (Brook & Long, 1985).

Effectiveness studies thus, further assume the role of testing the transferability of interventions from highly controlled conditions to usual care patients, providers, and settings. A serious problem has been that there is no corollary in services research for the earlier, more protected phases of clinical efficacy research (small Ns, laboratory setting), as revealed in the subsequent discussion of phases of clinical trials. For example, multisystemic therapy, which has an established efficacy base with juvenile delinquents, is now being extended to youths with serious emotional and behavioral disorders in the mental health system in South Carolina. Henggeler and colleagues have discovered that their well-specified brief intervention required adaptation before transferring MST to this more difficult and dangerous-to-self group of young patients (S. W. Henggeler, personal communication, May 5, 1996).

The set of comparisons shown in Table 24.1 contrast what investigators face in moving from clinical efficacy to clinical services effectiveness research.

Sample: Despite ample estimates of study subjects, such clients disappear miraculously when there is a study (Sechrest, 1979). Without a sufficient sample, statistical power is threatened. The ability to recruit large enough samples needs to be adequately demonstrated before a study is conducted and consideration given to more multisite studies to reduce the pressure on single sites for large Ns. Differential attrition, usually associated with the less desirable arm of the experiment, risks introducing bias—the prime reason for investing in a controlled design. Because of the heterogeneous nature of samples, consisting of real world clients and the comprehensive interventions being tested, a large sample size is required. In addition, for generalizability, the same needs to be representative of an identifiable treated population (e.g., children at risk of out-of-home placement).

Table 24.1

From Efficacy to Effectiveness Research: Differences
in Requirements and Conditions

Characteristic	Clinical Efficacy (Internal Validity)	Services Effectiveness (External Validity)
Research Question	**Does intervention work under ideal conditions?**	**Does intervention work with "real world" patients, providers, and settings?**
Sample		
Recruitment (inclusion criteria, exclusion criteria)	homogeneous (restricted by age, diagnosis, comorbidity)	heterogeneous
Attrition	usually low	may be high and differential
Size	small	large
Source	often volunteers	representative of a definable universe
Providers	employed by researcher	employed by clinical settings
	neutral regarding intervention	may be biased
	decision-making not expected	loss of decision-making
	part of job	research a burden
Experimental Intervention	discrete	usually multiple components
	fidelity controlled; protocol driven	fidelity monitored; drift a risk
	dose controlled	dose variable
	blind to condition	assignment usually known
Comparison Condition	usual care	state-of-the-art care
Site of Intervention	academic center	public sector with limited resources
	single setting	multiple settings and geographically dispersed

(conti

Table 24.1 *Continued*

Characteristic	Clinical Efficacy (Internal Validity)	Services Effectiveness (External Validity)
Duration of Intervention and Follow-up	usually brief	long-term
Measurement	under standardized conditions in laboratory	in natural environment
	clinical outcomes	wide range of outcomes
Incentives		
To patients	yes	yes
To providers	yes	no
Community Resources	not relevant	variable across sites
Policy Context	not relevant	changing, not controlled by investigators

Providers: Providers employed in clinical settings, rather than research ones, are likely to have their own preferences for interventions and ideas about what is likely to work for a given patient. They often function under so many constraints that clinical decision making may be one of the few activities under their control. Further, research is usually seen as another burden. Approaches for increasing clinician cooperation have been articulated by Dennis (1994).

Experimental intervention: Comprehensive interventions conducted in the community are not as easily monitored as more discrete interventions conducted in a laboratory. Controlling the dose of the intervention, although monitored retrospectively, can be problematic. Achieving blindness to community-based interventions is not any more possible than for surgical interventions where concern about blindness to the intervention has vanished as an issue, although it continues to be raised as a concern in services research.

Comparison condition: The tendency in effectiveness studies has been to test two state-of-the-art interventions against each other. This results in very conservative tests of new interventions, leaving little room for differential outcomes. In the early phases of clinical trials, usual care is more likely to serve as the comparison condition. Ethical considerations seem to have dictated the toughest comparisons in services research with clinical populations, even without prior research evidence. For example, a randomized trial of case management in North Carolina provides a case in point. To test case management, treatment by clinical teams with and without case managers was compared—both state-of-the-art interventions. Such a comparison was probably premature because case management had not been subject to any controlled research at the time this study was conducted (Burns et al., 1996).

Site of intervention: Research is usually more difficult to conduct in public settings, where research requirements are not familiar and may not be as highly valued as in academic centers. Further, such settings are likely to have a small number of clients eligible for a given study, creating a need for multiple settings. Geographically dispersed settings demand additional relationship building and travel.

Duration of intervention and follow-up: Comprehensive interventions usually require long-term treatment and follow up to find an effect—both a subject retention and a cost issue.

Measurement: Clinic and community-based measurement is confined to a large extent to self-report and unstandardized observation. Effectiveness studies of community-based interventions require attention to both internal and external validity. Effectiveness researchers must develop methods for preserving the internal validity of an efficacious intervention as it is deployed into natural settings with heterogeneous and often co-morbid populations of children (Hoagwood, Hibbs, Brent, & Jensen, 1995).

Incentives: While effectiveness studies generally provide some reimbursement to patients, this occurs less often and seems to be more difficult to achieve in a meaningful way for providers.

Community resources: Youth with serious emotional and behavioral disorders need, and are likely to utilize, a wide range of community resources beyond the confines of even quite comprehensive research interventions; such resource use is likely to vary across patient groups and areas. This requires collection of data about service use (beyond the experimental or control services) and dealing with it in the analysis.

Policy context: With the requirements for longitudinal studies for children with serious emotional and behavioral disorders and the need for investigation in public settings, such studies are subject to changes in public policy (e.g., change in caseload size in a study of intensive case management). Such an event actually alters the research plan or can create a situation in which abandoning the study is the route to take.

Research Models That Bridge Efficacy and Effectiveness: Problems and Suggested Approaches

Traditional models of the sequence of research phases have guided recent cumulative scientific programs (Friedman, Furberg, & DeMets, 1995; Pocock, 1983).

Several federal agencies and research programs within them (e.g., Agency for Health Care Policy [AHCPR], the National Health Services Center [NHS], the Food and Drug Administration [FDA], the National Cancer Institute [NCI], and the National Institute on Drug Abuse [NIDA]) have guided scientific program development with phase models that prescribe an orderly sequence of research states. The models usually include several phases, the first of which involves hypothesis development and refinement, based upon reviews of the scientific literature. This phase is followed by methods development, wherein tools for testing the hypotheses are developed, piloted, and improved. The hypotheses and tools are then applied in controlled-intervention trials that test the efficacy of the intervention with carefully defined populations. These trials are usually replicated with other defined populations. After replication, the intervention moves to phase IV, which is testing of the transportability of the intervention with defined populations in community settings (i.e., effectiveness studies). In phase V, if the intervention is found to be effective, it is implemented through widescale dissemination and training efforts. The Prevention Research Program at the National Institute of Mental Health has used this model to guide its program development (D. Koretz, personal communication, December 5, 1994).

Applying this model to the development of manualized behavioral therapies for drug-abusing populations, Onken, Blaine, and Battjes (1997) describe three major phases: phase I, therapy development, which includes the identification of promising interventions and operationalization of them into manuals; phase II, small-scale clinical trials, including replication studies; and phase III, transferability studies, which take a therapy that has been replicated in controlled clinical trials and package it such that it can be piloted and tested in community settings.

The applicability of this model to the research base on service effectiveness for children, however, is problematic, because studies of services provided in the naturalistic settings may not fit this orderly model. For example, some services are not reducible to discrete units capable of being tested through clinical trials. Case management, wraparound, and respite care are not conducive to phase III trials because they cannot be broken apart into discrete, isolatable units that can be tested in laboratory settings or with carefully defined populations. Further complicating the problem is the fact that specification of a carefully honed and homogeneously defined population (such as only children with school phobia) is generally not feasible in community settings.

However, the greatest problem with studies of service effectiveness is specification of the plethora of auxiliary or contextual variables that are often not anticipated nor built into the theoretical model under investigation. For example, a study of the effectiveness of an intensive case-management model may find no effect between the standard model and an intensively augmented one, because the influential contextual variable is whether the model was designed or delivered by consumers or by professionals. Until the context of production and delivery of the service is manipulated as an independent variable, no effects may be found. The next phase of research, then, would be comparison of parent-driven models with professionally driven ones. Developing clinically sensitive and relevant decision algorithms that incorporate contextual models of delivery into studies of service effectiveness is an important next step for advancing this field (Arnold, Hoagwood, Jensen, & Vitiello, 1997).

In addition, concerted efforts should be made to specify more clearly in advance the hypothetical relationship of auxiliary variables to the intervention or service under investigation. Without this, the theoretical underpinnings of the intervention will be seriously weakened (Meehl, 1978).

The reasons what the gap between efficacy and effectiveness is so wide are traceable, therefore, to the nature of services themselves: in flux, contextualized by their natural and organizational world, and not transportable into laboratories. These features of community-based services do not mean, however, that they cannot be rigorously tested. It does mean that tools have to be developed, that contextual variables have to be identified and assessed, and that designs have to be staged and timed to build toward the strongest field trials possible.

One approach to sequencing the phases of research would be to model increasingly strenuous designs that eliminate specificable threats to validity and to map these against the types of services that are being studied. For example, some services, such as wraparound, might best be first studied with a single case design that could then be replicated and extended into a naturalistic observation study. Other services, such as system-level or countywide interventions, might best be investigated first through quasi-experimental designs; results from these studies might suggest specific interventions for specific subpopulations within the systems that could be studied through randomized clinical trials. These could be further expanded through randomized field trials to extend the intervention into different or more heterogeneous samples. Finally, meta-analyses of as few as six studies can be conducted to look for effect sizes across samples. A sequencing of designs from single case studies to meta-analyses then might serve as a framework for orchestrating the types of research needed at different times for specific services.

In a workshop convened by the National Institute of Mental Health, the Center for Mental Health Services, and the Florida Mental Health Institute in June 1996, a group of services researchers, methodologists, policymakers and family advocates addressed these issues. Several focused efforts were agreed upon as necessary to advance the field of service effectiveness. First, more attention to outcome measurement and to identifying a range of outcomes that represented clinical and consumer significance were needed. For example, outcomes should include stress on families and impact on families of caring for their children, not only family adaptability or functioning.

Second, consensus emerged that translation of effectiveness studies ne to be ensured from the outset. This is best accomplished by folding consur families, or policymakers into the research process. It is too late to begin to think about the translation after a body of research has been accumulated, if it has not already taken into account a range of practical outcomes and implications for policy change.

Third, while randomized clinical trials are considered to be the strongest design for eliminating threats to validity, they should be done selectively. They are especially useful for specific purposes—ruling out variables that may be presumed to exert influences on the dependent variable—but they pose ethical dilemmas, are expensive, and, if used prematurely, confuse rather than clarify results. Randomized clinical trials are very appropriate for answering certain kinds of questions, but they are best used after feasibility studies have first been conducted and after findings have been replicated.

Developing a Research Plan

Developing a research plan will require taking into account general considerations for research on interventions for children with serious emotional and behavioral disorders, the challenges encountered in services effectiveness studies, and the current effectiveness research base. The preceding section on paradigms for effectiveness research lead directly into the initial steps here.

A first step is to further examine existing models of efficacy/effectiveness research for potential adaptation to comprehensive child mental health interventions. The aim is to develop a logical and efficient classification of phases of services effectiveness research. A major advantage of clearly defined research phases is that less costly research designs would be utilized in early treatment development research, avoiding costly randomized clinical trials early on. Possible misuse of limited public research dollars as well as premature exclusion of interventions based on false negative findings are hazards that might be avoided if the research agenda is developed methodically through the research phases proposed previously. This might be achieved by convening a consensus panel with expertise in research methodology and child mental health interventions to review existing research paradigms and to devise a classification system with specific criteria for each phase.

Once consensus has been achieved on a classification system for each existing intervention that is sufficiently promising to merit further research, a second step is to assess readiness for each intervention for the next logical research phase. The level of sophistication of the research design utilized in prior research would guide phase selection, in addition to empirical evidence and other criteria. For some interventions, a more advanced design that appropriate may have been previously utilized (e.g., interventions exposed to a randomized clinical trial when the intervention was not properly specified, implying a need an earlier research phase). Assignment of interventions to a research phase be accomplished by convening a consensus panel of investigators about specific interventions. The phase identified for each intervention could guide the next type of research. The report of this panel would begin to constitute a research agenda. Acceptance by the field would be crucial as more stringent requirements for effectiveness research could emerge, as well as a mandate for research support for feasibility and later-phase, uncontrolled, large-scale studies that traditionally have not been supported by NIMH research funds.

A third set of activities involves the development of research and clinical tools to support the effectiveness research proposed. As indicated, some types of research measures are either underdeveloped or lacking (e.g., quality, functional assessment). Such work does not need to await steps one and two above. Investment in tools to specify intervention—guidelines/protocols, training modules and manuals, measures of intervention fidelity—could be initiated for interventions likely to be included in the research agenda.

Fourth, for interventions with a minimal research base, conducting small feasibility studies across multiple sites could facilitate treatment development and not tax clinical settings for large sample size. Such work might be achieved by organizing investigators interested in similar interventions, who offer client populations with different characteristics, to conduct preliminary studies.

Finally, the potential to utilize the strengths of sites with expertise in given interventions needs to be considered. For example, Vermont is known for its expertise in wraparound services, Oregon for therapeutic foster care, and California for group homes. Given the risks and challenges with randomized trials, the potential for cross-site studies with matched comparisons could be achieved. This would require a case mix measure that would allow subjects to be matched on factors related to severity (on prognosis for improvement given treatment).

Development of a research plan for comprehensive community-based interventions for the treatment of serious emotional and behavioral disorders in children and adolescents needs to be multifaceted and long term. Since such a plan could result in recommendations for using research support in new ways, the sanction or review by a group such as the NIMH National Advisory Mental Health Council or the Institute of Medicine would be beneficial. This could be analogous to the impact of the NIMH Counsel plan, "Caring for People with Severe Mental Disorders: A National Plan of Research to Improve Services for Severe Mental Disorders" (1991), which has moved the research on adult services forward.

Conclusions

This chapter has suggested interim actions to improve outcomes for children with serious emotional and behavioral disorders based on the application of existing knowledge. The authors recommend further implementation of policy based on CASSP, the introduction of comprehensive interventions with least a promising research base to service systems, training clinicians to provide such interventions, and attention to generic quality indicators.

Strengthening the services effectiveness research base was the primary focus for the future. The challenges of effectiveness research were explicated and options for adopting a research paradigm presented that could ensure a logical and more efficient research investment through carefully ordered phases of research. To move the research ahead, recommendations called for (a) expert panels to reach consensus about a research paradigm and the readiness of specific interventions for the next phase of research, (b) a national plan for effectiveness research on child interventions, and (c) child effectiveness laboratories that would operate as a consortium participating in treatment and methods of development efforts.

Assuming that gains in the research occur, the next step in the cycle is to translate research findings into policy. If clinical training shifts toward the more innovative interventions in the near future, adjustments to training following the next wave of research results may not have to be as drastic as it would appear now. Finally, given the research emphasis on fidelity, quality improvement will progress with treatment development, leaving the implementation of quality standards to occur in tandem with policy revision.

Authors' Note

This work was supported by grants MH51410 and MH48085 from the National Institute of Mental Health. The views expressed in this chapter are not to be construed as official or as reflecting the view of the National Institute of Health or of the National Institute of Mental Health.

Correspondence should be addressed to Barbara J. Burns, Box 3454, Duke University Medical Center, Durham, NC 27710.

References

American Academy of Child and Adolescent Psychiatry (AACAP). (1992). Practice parameters for the assessment and treatment of conduct disorders. *Journal of the American Academy of Child and Adolescent Psychiatry, 31,* IV–VII.

American Academy of Child and Adolescent Psychiatry (AACAP). (1993). Practice parameters for the assessment and treatment of anxiety disorders. *Journal of the American Academy of Child and Adolescent Psychiatry, 32,* 1089–1098.

Arnold, L. E., Hoagwood, K., Jensen, P. S., & Vitiello, B. (1997). Towards clinically relevant clinical trials. *Psychopharmacology Bulletin.*

Bordiun, C. M. (1994). Innovative models of treatment and service delivery in the juvenile justice system. *Journal of Clinical Child Psychology, 23,* 19–25.

Brook, R. H., & Long, K. N. (1985). Efficacy, effectiveness, variations, and quality: Boundary—crossing research. *Medical Care, 23,* 710–722.

Burns, B. J. (1991). Mental health service use by adolescents in the 1970s and 1980s. *Journal of the American Academy of Child and Adolescent Psychiatry, 30,* 144–150.

Burns, B. J. (1996). What drives outcomes for emotional and behavioral disorders in children and adolescents? In D. M. Steinwachs, L. M. Flynn, G. S. Norquist, & E. A. Skinner (Eds.), *Using client outcomes information to improve mental health and substance abuse treatment: New directions in mental health services, 71,* 89–102. San Francisco: Jossey-Bass.

Burns, B. J., Costello, E. J., Angold, A., Tweed, D., Stangl, D., Farmer, E. M. Z., & Erkanli, A. (1995). The Great Smoky Mountains study of youth: Mental health service use across the child service system. *Health Affairs, 14,* 147–159.

Burns, B. J., Costello, E. J., Erkanli, A., Tweed, D. L., Farmer, E. M. Z., & Angold, A. (1997). Insurance coverage and mental health service use by adolescents with serious emotional disturbance. *Journal of Child and Family Studies, 6,* 89–111.

Burns, B. J., Farmer, E. M. Z., Angold, A., Costello, E. J., & Behar, L. (1996). A randomized trial of case management for youths with serious emotional disturbance. *Journal of Clinical Child Psychology, 25,* 476–486.

Burns, B. J., & Friedman, R. M. (1990). Examining the research base for child mental health services and policy. *Journal of Mental Health Administration, 17,* 87–98.

Burns, B. J., & Santos, A. B. (1995). Assertive community treatment: An update of randomized trials. *Psychiatric Services, 46,* 669–675.

Cunningham, P. J., & Freiman, M. P. (1996). Determinants of ambulatory mental health services use for school-age children and adolescents. *Health Services Research, 31,* 409–427.

Dennis, M. L. (1994). Ethical and practical randomized field experiments. In J. S. Wholey, H. P. Hatry, & K. E. Newcomer (Eds.), *Handbook of practical program evaluation* (pp. 155–197). San Francisco: Jossey-Bass.

Duchnowski, A. J. (1994). Innovative service models: Education. *Journal of Clinical Child Psychology, 23,* 13–18.

England, M. J., & Cole, R. F. (1992). Building systems of care for youth with serious mental illness. *Hospital and Community Psychiatry, 43,* 630–633.

Evans, M. E., Armstrong, M. I., Dollard, N., & Kuppinger, A. D. (1994). Development and evaluation of treatment foster care and family-centered intensive case management in New York. *Journal of Emotional and Behavioral Disorders, 2,* 228–239.

Farmer, E. M. Z., Stangl, D. K., Burns, B. J., Costello, E. J., & Angold, A. (1997). Service use for children's mental health across one year: Patterns and predictors of use. Manuscript submitted for publication.

Friedman, L. M., Furberg, C. D., & DeMets, D. L. (1995). *Fundamentals of clinical trials.* St. Louis, MO: Mosby-Year Book.

Greenbaum, P. E., Dedrick, R. F., Friedman, R. F., Kutash, K., Brown, E. C., Lardieri, S. P., & Pugh, A. M. (1996). National Adolescent and Child Treatment Study (NACTS): Outcomes for children with serious emotional and behavioral disturbance. *Journal of Emotional and Behavioral Disorders, 4,* 130–146.

Hennegeler, S. W., & Borduin, C. M. (1990). *Family therapy and beyond, a multisystemic approach to treating the behavior problems of children and adolescents.* Pacific Grove, CA: Brooks/Cole.

Hoagwood, K., Hibbs, E., Brent, D., & Jensen, P. S. (1995). Efficacy and effectiveness in studies of child and adolescent psychotherapy. *Journal of Consulting and Clinical Psychology, 63,* 683–687.

Hoagwood, K., Jensen, P. S., Petti, T., & Burns, B. J. (1996). Outcomes of mental health care for children and adolescents: I. A comprehensive conceptual model. *Journal of the American Academy of Child and Adolescent Psychiatry, 35,* 1055–1062.

Jensen, P. S., Hoagwood, K., & Petti, T. (1996). Outcomes of mental health care for children and adolescents: II. Literature review and application of a comprehensive model. *Journal of the American Academy of Child and Adolescent Psychiatry, 35,* 1064–1077.

Kazdin, A. E. *Research design in clinical psychology.* (1992). Needham Heights, MA: Allyn and Bacon.

Kutash, K., & Rivera, V. R. (1996). *What works in children's mental health services: Uncovering answers to critical questions.* Baltimore: Brookes.

McClellan, J., & Werry J. (1994). Practice parameters for the assessment and treatment of children and adolescents with schizophrenia. *Journal of the American Academy of Child and Adolescent Psychiatry, 33,* 616–635.

McFarlane, W. R., Dunne, E., Lukens, E., Newmark, M., McLaughlin-Toran, J., Deakins, S., & Horen, B. (1993). From research to clinical practice: Dissemination of New York State's Family Psychoeducation Project. *Hospital and Community Psychiatry, 44,* 265–270.

Meehl, P. E. (1978). Theoretical risks and tabular asterisks: Sir Karl, Sir Ronald, and the slow progress of soft psychology. *Journal of Consulting and Clinical Psychology, 46,* 806–834.

National Institute of Mental Health. (1991). *Caring for people with severe mental disorders: A national plan of research to improve services.* DHHS Pub. No. (ADM)91-1762. Washington, DC: Superintendent of Documents, U.S. Government Printing Office.

Nelson, K.E. (1994). Innovative delivery models in social services. *Journal of Clinical Child Psychology, 23,* 26–31.

Office of Technology Assessment (OTA). (1978). Assessing the efficacy and safety of medical technologies. Washington, DC: Congress of the United States , OTA-H-75, p. 16.

Onken, L. S., Blaine, J. D., & Battjes, R. (1997). Behavioral and psychosocial therapy research: A conceptualization of a process. In S. W. Henggeler & A. B. Santos (Eds.), *Innovative approaches for difficult-to-treat populations* (pp. 477–485). American Psychiatric Press.

Pocock, S. J. (1983). *Clinical trials: A practical approach.* John Wiley & Sons.

Rosenblatt, A. (1993). In home, in school, and out of trouble. *Journal of Child and Family Studies, 2,* 275–282.

Rosenblatt, A., & Attkisson, C. C. (1993). Assessing outcomes for sufferers of severe mental disorder: A conceptual framework and review. *Evaluation and Program Planning, 16,* 347–363.

Rugs, D., & Kutash, K. (1994). Evaluating children's mental health service systems: An analysis of critical behaviors and events. *Journal of Child and Family Studies, 3,* 249–262.

Santos, A. B., Henggeler, S. W., Burns, B. J., Arana, G. W., & Meisler, N. (1995). Research on field-based services: Models for reform in the delivery of mental health care to difficult clinical populations. *American Journal of Psychiatry, 152,* 1111–1123.

Sechrest, L. (1979). Some neglected problems in evaluation research: Strength and integrity of treatments. In L. Sechrest, S. G. West, M. A. Phillips, R. Redner, and W. Yeaton (Eds.), *Evaluation Studies Review Annual, 4,* 15–35.

Stangl, D. K., Tweed, D. L., Farmer, E. M. Z., Langmeyer, D., Stelle, L., Behar, L., Gagliardi, J., & Burns, B. J. (1997). Symposium: Public-sector managed care for children's mental health services: Stakeholder's perspectives. In *Proceedings of the 9th Annual Research Conference, A Sys-*

tem of Care for Children's Mental Health: Expanding the Research Base, Tampa, Florida, February 26–28, 1996 (pp. 67–77). University of South Florida, Florida Mental Health Institute.

Stroul, B. A., & Friedman, R. M. (1986). A system of care for severely emotionally disturbed children and youth. Washington, DC: CASSP Technical Assistance Center.

Weisz, J. R., & Weiss, B. (1989). Assessing the effects of clinic-based psychotherapy with children and adolescents. *Journal of Consulting and Clinical Psychology, 57,* 741–746.

Weisz, J. R., Weiss, B., & Donenberg, G. R. (1992). The lab versus the clinic: Effects of child and adolescent psychotherapy. *American Psychologist, 47,* 1578–1585.

Winsberg, B. G., Bialer, I., Kupietz, S., Botti, E., & Balka, E B. (1980). Home versus hospital care of children with behavioral disorders. *Archives of General Psychiatry, 37,* 413–418.

Author Index

Subject Index